P9-CSW-554

BEYOND BORDERS

Thinking Critically About Global Issues

BEYOND BORDERS

Thinking Critically About Global Issues

PAULA S. ROTHENBERG

William Paterson University of New Jersey

WORTH PUBLISHERS

Sponsoring Editor: Erik Gilg
Marketing Director: John Britch
Production Editor: Margaret Comaskey
Art Director: Barbara Reingold
Text and Cover Design: Lee Ann Mahler
Photo Editor: Patricia Marx
Photo Researcher: Elyse Rieder
Production Manager: Barbara Anne Seixas
Composition: Matrix Publishing Services
Printing and Binding: RR Donnelley

Library of Congress Control Number: 2005928128

ISBN-13: 978-0-7167-7389-4
ISBN-10: 0-7167-7389-9

© 2006 by Worth Publishers

All rights reserved

Manufactured in the United States of America

Second printing

Worth Publishers
41 Madison Avenue
New York, NY 10010
www.worthpublishers.com

About the Author

Paula S. Rothenberg is Director of the New Jersey Project on Inclusive Scholarship, Curriculum, and Teaching and a professor at the William Paterson University of New Jersey. She attended the University of Chicago and received her undergraduate degree from New York University, where she also did her graduate work. Rothenberg has lectured and consulted on multicultural and gender issues and curriculum transformation at hundreds of colleges and universities throughout the country. Her articles and essays appear in journals and anthologies across the disciplines, and many have been widely reprinted. Rothenberg is the author of the autobiographical *Invisible Privilege: A Memoir About Race, Class, and Gender* and the best-selling anthologies *Race, Class, and Gender in the United States: An Integrated Study,* and *White Privilege: Essential Readings on the Other Side of Racism.* Among her other books are *Creating an Inclusive College Curriculum: A Teaching Sourcebook from the New Jersey Project* and *Feminist Frameworks,* both of which she co-edited.

Contents

part one *Putting Things in Perspective* **1**

> The Anglo West is the Mexican North, the Native American Homeland and the Asian East.
> *Ellen DuBois and Vicki Ruiz*

part two   *Colonialism and Its Legacy*   **75**

> The only thing worse than being occupied is being
> an occupier.
>   L. Paul Bremer III, *Chief Administrator of Occupied Iraq*

part three   *Constructing Difference: Creating "Other"*
Identities   **167**

> Power consists in the ability to make others inhabit
> your story of their reality—even as is so often the
> case, when that story is written in their blood.
>   *Philip Gourevitch*

part four *Patriarchy and Domination* **247**

> Patriarchy itself is an expression of
> socioeconomic oppression.
>
> *Nawal El Saadawi*

part five   *Poverty, Inequality, and Structural Violence*   317

20% of the population in the developed nations,
consume 86% of the worlds' goods.
1998 Human Development Report, United Nations
Development Programme

A mere 12% of the world's population uses 85% of
its water, and these 12% do not live in the Third
World.
Maude Barlow, National Chairperson,
Council of Canadians

part six *Transnational Institutions and the Global Economy* **411**

> What is called globalization is really another name for the dominant role of the United States.
>
> *Henry Kissinger, former U.S. Secretary of State.*

part seven *Globalization in Everyday Life* **471**

> The market is being made the organizing principle for the provisioning of food, water, health, education and other basic needs, it is being made the organizing principle of governance, it is being made the measure of our humanity.
>
> *Vandana Shiva*

part eight *Toward a More Equitable Future: Grassroots Movements for Social Change* **573**

> It is not that we should simply seek new and better ways for managing society, the economy, and the world. The point is that we should fundamentally change how we behave.
>
> *Vaclav Havel, 1992*

Preface

A not so funny, but perhaps sadly true, joke going around claims that people in the United States learn geography by going to war. This book proceeds on the assumption that there must be a better way to learn about the world and our place in it. As Michael Schwalbe suggests in the final article in this volume, in contrast to students born elsewhere, people born in the United States are often woefully ignorant about their own government and even more ignorant about the rest of the world. He calls this "American privilege" and suggests that, like other forms of privilege, it comes from membership in a dominant group, or more specifically in this case, it comes from identifying with the dominant role the United States plays in the world. But our ignorance comes at a heavy cost. This book is designed to help its readers learn to think critically about global issues so that each of us can make meaningful decisions about the kinds of policies we want our government to adopt and the values we want those policies to foster. In the end, democracy is no more than an empty promise unless citizens are educated and informed enough to make intelligent choices about the kind of society in which they wish to live and the kind of role they wish their country to play in the global community. In a world in which decisions made in Buenas Aires, New York, Beijing, Quebec, Dehli, Washington, or Accra can travel the globe in a matter of minutes and impact on the lives of billions of people in that same amount of time, ignorance of global realities is a luxury none of us can afford.

This text begins with an opening section that asks us to think about *how* we think about the world. It asks us to reflect on the assumptions, implicit and explicit, that we bring with us when we listen to TV or radio news, read a newspaper or magazine, or talk with friends and family about current events. Studies in a number of fields show that expectations shape both perceptions and outcomes, so why should it be any different when it comes to thinking about the world? For this reason, before this book turns its attention to past and present global realities, it asks its readers to spend a little time thinking about how we have come to think about the world and how what we have been taught to accept as objective knowledge and straightforward information has been framed. You can think of it as a kind of warm-up session.

In the remainder of this book we will be visiting many different countries and looking at the world through the eyes of women and men who are both rich and poor, privileged and powerless, young and old, well-educated and barely schooled, living in rural villages and major world cities, who identify with a broad array of ethnic/racial groups and traditions, and who embrace a variety of religious teachings and practices. If, as I believe, education is ultimately about learning to see the world through the eyes of many different people, then this book can truly promise you a broad education.

Overview

Part One of this text, "Putting Things in Perspective," encourages readers to think about the ways in which knowledge is presented. Critical thinking involves the ability to identify the assumptions or perspectives implicit in the way "facts" are presented and "reality" is described and circumscribed. By helping readers to identify the hidden interests and assumptions that are reflected in how maps, history, and statistics portray their subjects and by focusing on how both the language and the categories we use to analyze and describe often affect what we actually *see*, Part One is designed to help us develop the critical thinking skills we need to evaluate information rather than simply ingest it.

Part Two, "Colonialism and Its Legacy," encourages the reader to look at contemporary world issues in the context of their colonial past. Here we are introduced not merely to the history that shaped the current world, for example, a map of colonialism in Africa in 1914 showing the continent virtually divided among seven European nations, but also to the idea that policies and politics often flow from competing world views. My belief that it is impossible to do justice to the study of contemporary global issues without understanding how history and perspective shape what count as contemporary "realities" is reflected in this chapter and throughout the book.

Part Three, "Constructing Difference: Creating 'Other' Identities," looks at the crucial role played by the construction of "difference" and the process of "othering" certain groups within, between, and among nations. This theme, which was alluded to in Part Two, is now powerfully illustrated in Zillah Eisenstein's article describing the multiple ways hatred is written on the body and Philip Gourevitch's account of how the colonial powers in Rwanda set about radically re-engineering Rwandan society along ethnic lines. This section of the book examines the ways in which race, class, gender, and sexual difference get constructed in the interest of domination and serves as a bridge to Part Four, "Patriarchy and Domination."

In Part Four, the general subordination of women and the particular forms that violence against women have assumed are examined within the context of both the legacy of colonialism and the enormous force of patriarchal tradition. In this way, honor killings, battery, rape, and other forms of violence are properly understood in their historical context, and the general role that patriarchal values play in subordinating women in the workplace and society at large is explored.

Part Five, "Poverty, Inequality, and Structural Violence," presents a powerful picture of the extent and nature of poverty and inequality in the global village and introduces the concept of structural violence to help us understand some of the ways in which misery and suffering for some are seamlessly woven into the fabric of ordinary life. Paul Farmer's article, which is a chapter taken from his widely acclaimed book, *Pathologies of Power: Health, Human Rights and the New War on the Poor*, is unforgettable.

Taken together, Part Six, "Transnational Institutions and the Global Economy," and Part Seven, "Globalization in Everyday Life," offer a comprehensive account of how the global economy works and how globalization is altering the lives of people and communities all around the world. Part Six provides readers with an account of the origins and operation of the International Monetary Fund (IMF), the World Bank, and the World Trade Organization (WTO) and paints a broad picture of globalization—the process whereby goods and services, including capital, move more freely within and among nations. In Part Seven, the reader is offered concrete examples of how globalization as carried out by the current policies of transnational institutions and multinational corporations is impacting every aspect of life in the global village and wrecking havoc on the environment of this planet.

Part Eight, "Toward a More Equitable Future: Grassroots Movements for Social Change," offers readers accounts of how grassroots activists and NGOs (nongovernmental organizations) around the globe are responding to globalization. In addition to highlighting the successful efforts of women in Nigeria to shut down a ChevronTexaco oil plant, a people's victory against Coca-Cola in Plachimada, India, and a Mexican community's successful efforts to block an airport, this section also provides descriptions and contact information for a variety of NGOs working in the areas of human rights, development, violence against women, health, and the environment. Designed to empower the reader by showing the difference that people can make when working together, Part Eight will, I hope, leave us all with the understanding that history is made by the conscious choices of human beings; it is not something that simply happens to us. This section will introduce the reader to communities of people all over the world who are taking responsibility for the future.

The book concludes with an Afterword, the article by Michael Schwalbe mentioned earlier, that encourages U.S. readers to reflect on how this country is viewed by people in other parts of the world and to reflect on the "American privilege" that appears to allow people in the United States the "luxury" of not having to think or know very much about other people and other countries. You can take comfort that by the time you get to that final article, it will not apply to you!

What's Current

Many of the articles in this volume include statistics. Some of the statistics are very current and others are relatively dated. What does it mean to consider a statistic current? Well, with respect to data about living conditions around the world, or even within a single country, think for a moment about how long it takes to collect the data, how big a job it is to put it in some useful form, how long it takes to make it public, and how large and expensive the whole project is, and you will see why many major studies are only published or circulated every ten years or so. When you realize that, at best, data of that sort can provide only a general idea of what conditions are like and allow us to make general comparisons between and among countries, it should be clear that expecting data to be no more than a year or two old is both unrealistic and unnecessary. With reference to articles in this book that include data that appears to be out of date, they are included because their analysis is so cogent and so useful that it transcends the accuracy of the figures they provide. With respect to the desire for current data, students today are in an enviable position. The most current data available is only a computer screen away, so by all means, take it upon yourself to search for the data you need and to seek out data that confirm or call into question information presented in this book. That is part of what it means to think critically. You will find information about interesting and useful Websites to visit throughout this book.

Meet the Players

Articles in this book refer to many national, international, and transnational institutions and organizations, as well as trade agreements and treaties. Most of them have acronyms. You are probably familiar with some of these, such as NATO (the North Atlantic Treaty Organization, UNICEF (the United Nations Children's Fund), and OPEC (the Organization of Petroleum Exporting Countries), but many will be new to you. By the time you finish this book, you will be able to make alphabet soup as well as anyone else. In the short run however, you may find it useful to consult the list of such names and acronyms on page xxi to help you keep track of the players.

Questions for Thinking, Writing, and Discussion

Each section of this text includes some questions that are designed to help you think about the articles you have read and to make connections between them. You may find it useful to look at these questions when you begin the section or while you are reading the articles, because they may help you read more actively and more critically.

Feedback

I always appreciate reader feedback and will be happy to receive questions, comments, and suggestions. I can be reached at rothenbergp@wpunj.edu

Acknowledgments

Many people have contributed to this book in a variety of ways. I thank Steve Shalom for his early feedback on the table of contents, for sharing his expertise and his library with me, and for allowing me to impose on his time and patience in more ways than I can or care to enumerate. Erika Polokoff provided detailed and thoughtful comments on an early version of the table of contents and helped identify some of the pieces that ultimately found their way into this book. I thank her for sharing her knowledge and for her generosity of spirit. My friends Lois Tigay and Naomi Miller were also good enough to review the project with me, providing both intelligent feedback and friendly enthusiasm—and I am grateful for both. Cynthia Enloe responded to each of my e-mail queries with speed and generosity and enthusiasm. I thank her for this and for her work, which provides so many of us with a wonderful model of scholarship. Jan Monk was tremendously helpful as I worked on Part One and wonderfully flexible as she worked on her article for that part. A number of other friends and colleagues responded to my cries for help by aiding me in tracking down articles and information and I am very grateful to them. I thank Esther Kingston-Mann, Jack Spence, Pem Davidson-Buck, Stephanie Luce, Ellen Mutari, Isa Tavares-Mack, Lucinda Marshall, Beth Myers, Mary Bellman, Bill Fletcher, Jr., Paula Finn, the wonderful library staff at William Paterson University, and others whose names should be here as well. I also want to thank Ann Lutterman-Aguliar and Judy Shevelev and others at Casa Cemal in Cuernavaca for an amazing education over a period of years.

As always, I could not have done this book without the help and support that Judy Baker and Helena Farrell graciously provided for my work. I am in their debt. Thanks, too, to Tammy Voorhees, Tyria Stokes, and Rochelle Wilson for all those trips to the library and more.

For some time now I have been fortunate to work with a terrific publisher and an extraordinary editorial team. I want to thank Catherine Woods for her ongoing support for my work and for her vision. My thanks to Valerie Raymond for solid presence and good judgment, her integrity and values, her enthusiasm, and her commitment. She has been a wonderful editor. As for thanking editor number two, Erik Gilg, I'd run out of paper if I tried to enumerate all the ways in which he contributed to this volume and I sincerely hope that by the time you are reading this, I have made good on the lunch I owe him. Art Director Babs Reingold and Designer Lee Ann Mahler have as usual given 200% to this project. I feel very lucky to be able to continue to draw on their creativity and energy. Production Editor Margaret Comaskey doesn't miss a thing—which is why I am always grateful to have her serve as production editor on my books. She is every author/editor's dream! Countless others at Worth have contributed to this book. It would be impossible to mention them all individually but I would be remiss if I did not offer my thanks to John Britch, Barbara Anne Seixas, and Nancy Walker in particular.

Thanks to my family for years of travel and conversation that have enriched my perspective and challenged and educated me as well. Thanks to my son Alexi Mantsios for his measured and thoughtful approach to difficult issues and his willingness to listen. Thanks to my daughter Andrea Mantsios who provided feedback on the table of contents over coffee at Bluestone and helped me identify some topics that needed to be included. I always learn a lot by tagging along on Andrea's intellectual and activist journeys and I am grateful to her for introducing me to the world of public health. Finally, thanks to my partner Greg Mantsios—for everything.

Meet the Players

IMF (International Monetary Fund)—created at the Bretton Woods Conference in 1944. Along with the World Bank, charged with insuring the stability of the international monetary system after World War II. Does so by lending money to countries in serious economic trouble.

World Bank (International Bank for Reconstruction and Development)—created at Bretton Woods, 1944, along with the IMF. Charged with investing in programs to promote development of troubled economies.

WTO (World Trade Organization)—created in 1995 to replace GATT and incorporate its trade agreements; its rules apply to 90% of international trade.

GATT (General Agreement on Tariffs and Trade)—first signed in 1947, designed to encourage "free trade" among member nations. Replaced by and subsumed under the WTO in 1995.

WHO (World Health Organization)—the United Nations specialized agency for health.

ILO (International Labour Organization)—the United Nations specialized agency that seeks the promotion of social justice and internationally recognized human and labor rights.

NAFTA (North American Free Trade Agreement)—since 1994, governs trade and investment among the United States, Mexico, and Canada.

PPP (Plan Puebla Panama)—a megadevelopment plan proposed for Southern Mexico and Central America.

CAFTA (Central American Free Trade Agreement)—proposed agreement between the United States and Guatemala, El Salvador, Honduras, Costa Rica, and Nicaragua.

FTAA (Free Trade of the Americas)—a planned collaboration among 34 governments in the Americas, including Canada, to promote "free trade" in the hemisphere.

OPEC (Organization of Petroleum Exporting Countries)—comprised of Algeria, Indonesia, Iran, Kuwait, Libya, Nigeria, Qatar, Saudi Arabia, United Arab Emirates, and Venezuela.

ASEAN (Association of South East Asian Nations)—established in 1967; current membership: Indonesia, Malaysia, Philippines, Singapore, Thailand, Brunei Darussalam, Vietnam, Laos, Myanmar, and Cambodia.

EU (European Union)—established in 1992; current membership: Austria, Belgium, Cyprus, Czech Republic, Denmark, Estonia, Finland, France, Germany, Greece, Hungary, Ireland, Italy, Latvia, Lithuania, Luxembourg, Malta, Poland, Portugal, Slovakia, Slovenia, Spain, Sweden, The Netherlands, and the United Kingdom.

part

Putting Things in Perspective

The Anglo West is the Mexican North, the Native American Homeland
and the Asian East
–*Ellen DuBois and Vicky Ruiz*

In her fascinating book about the lives of women in India,* Elizabeth Bumiller recounts her arrival by plane at the old international airport in Delhi many hours after flying out of Washington, DC. She writes, "we had flown over Saudi Arabia on our way, and it took me a moment to readjust to 'my new place in the world'; the Middle East was now West." This section asks its readers to do the same thing, to rethink their place in the world by becoming aware of how much our location or position alters our perspective and shapes our vision.

Each of us sees the world differently, but few of us realize the extent to which what we notice is a function of who we are, how we are positioned in the world, and how the world has been presented to us. This section asks you to consider how your place in the world affects what you see and how you "see" it and to critically examine what factors and experiences have shaped your perspective on the world. More specifically, this section asks you to adopt a critical perspective toward the unarticulated assumptions you have internalized about relations between and among nations around the globe.

From the moment we begin to experience the world, that experience comes from a particular perspective both literally and figuratively. It is literally the case that where you stand places some things in your immediate range of vision and other things beyond it. In this sense, your position in the world literally determines what you see. It is also the case that how the world is presented to you through education and other social institutions shapes your perspective as well. Maps, statistics, language, history, and the media all play important roles in shaping our worldview. They help to determine what we see and hear and the importance we place on it. They define the center and the periphery for us and shape our sense of who the real stakeholders are in the global village. But, as this section makes clear, maps, statistics, history, language, and the media themselves always emanate from a particular perspective and often smuggle in value judgments about the world they purport to describe. Depending on the perspective from which the world is presented, freedom fighters will become terrorists and terrorists freedom fighters. Depending upon perspective, colonizers will be considered alternately traders, liberators, missionaries, invaders, and conquerors. The point of this section is to ask you to think about how an individual's place in the world affects what he or she takes to be real and true and to think critically about the ways in which we have been taught to see ourselves, our country, and other peoples and nations in the world. In this sense, it is all about learning to recognize and then cultivate the ability to change our perspective.

We begin by looking at some of the ways in which reality has been represented by maps and the power of the images they present to shape our view of the world. Which countries and continents are positioned at the center of our focus? How do particular maps choose to portray the relative size of different countries and what implications flow from this? What hidden messages and whose history are reflected in

---

*Elizabeth Bumiller. *May You Be the Mother of a Hundred Sons: A Journey Among the Women of India*. Westminster, Maryland: Fawcett Books, 1991.

the seemingly innocent use of color on maps? As David Turnbull says at the beginning of Article 1, "The Function of Maps," a map is always selective. The mapmaker decides what to include and what to leave out and his or her choices tend to reflect their own place in the world and the perspective and interests that come with it. The map offered to the viewer already presents a particular way of seeing the world but is rarely understood in these terms. For example, generation after generation of children in the United States have been taught to see the world using Mercator projection maps without ever being made aware of the particular distortions in that map and the interests and perspective those distortions embody and privilege.

At the most basic level, orientation itself, as Turnbull points out, is a matter of arbitrary convention. Though many of us take for granted that North is "up" and South is "down," he reminds us that space has no "up" or "down," in fact he tells us that at one time it was a common practice to place "East," the direction of the rising sun, at the top of the map. How then did it come about that "North" became up? According to Turnbull this new convention emerged as "the result of a historical process, closely connected with the global rise and economic dominance of northern Europe." In other words, economics and politics played a significant role in determining which convention would become the new "reality."

Like Turnbull, Janice Monk, in Article 2, "Are Things What They Seem to Be? Reading Maps and Statistics," asks us to think about the kinds of messages conveyed in the way maps portray the world. She believes that maps are powerful tools that not only influence how our voices are heard or not heard, but also play a role in determining who and what is important and powerful. In her essay, she draws important connections between the ways in which maps represent reality and the kinds of policy decisions we are likely to make based upon them. Like Turnbull, Monk argues that the way maps represent the world always portrays a particular set of power relations, and so she urges us to think critically about the strengths and weaknesses of particular representations and cautions us not to take the information that maps present simply as "objective."

Does all of this mean that no map is ever correct? Yes and no. Every map will have its strengths and weaknesses, and the task of an educated person and critical thinker is to understand the purpose for which a map was made and the implications that flow from it, as well as the implicit and explicit assumptions on which it rests. Ultimately, both the accuracy and usefulness of any map will depend at least as much on our purpose in referring to it as on the interests and perspective of the mapmaker. The bottom line is that both maps and statistics offer us a particular slice of "reality" and it is our job to determine which aspects of "reality" they include, exclude, distort, and privilege, and to decide whether they are useful to us based upon our needs and objectives.

Mark Twain is purported to have said that "there are three kinds of lies: lies, damned lies, and statistics." Because statistics can be so easily manipulated to support or undermine almost any conclusions, many people are inclined to dismiss them entirely. Unfortunately, this is a luxury we cannot afford. Statistics play a critical role in helping us define and track the social and economic needs of a population. Shall we spend our money on health care or education? Shall we focus our attention on decreasing infant mortality or on immunization programs for toddlers? Which programs appear to be most effective in decreasing deaths from malaria, halting the spread of HIV/AIDS, improving school attendance and literacy rates? It would be impossible to answer any of these questions without reference to statistics. We cannot do away with our dependency on them but we can think about how to ensure that the statistics we use to formulate policy are as accurate as possible.

In their articles in this section, both Janice Monk and Adriana Mata Greenwood take a critical look at the ways in which statistics are collected and presented and suggest that doing so raises some important questions about the visibility and invisibility of women's work and women's lives. In Article 3, "Gender Issues in Labour Statistics," Greenwood offers a detailed critique of the ways in which current approaches to categorizing work and collecting statistics often fail to adequately represent women's roles in the economy. Because statistics play a significant role in how we design, monitor, and evaluate the effectiveness of economic policies, it is essential that we learn to critically evaluate the information they present and to identify the perspective they adopt.

Another way in which specific constructions of reality are privileged without being acknowledged is through our use of language. Words like "democracy" and "freedom" are highly charged and it is always interesting to look carefully at how they are applied. Which countries are considered to have democratic governments by U.S. politicians and office holders and what criteria do they appear to use in bestowing that designation? Even a cursory look at recent history tells us that the same world leader may be considered a dictator one year and a democrat another. What considerations come into play? Does holding elections in itself qualify a nation as a democracy, regardless of the conditions under which the election is carried out or the nature of daily restrictions on the life of the population? To what extent is the decision to refer to a country as a democracy based on economic and political interests? The words we choose to describe what we take to be "reality" often carry with them a series of hidden messages and judgments. For example, most people who live in the United States refer to themselves as "Americans" but some would be less likely to apply that term to people who were born and live in Ecuador, Uruguay, Brazil, and other Central and South American nations although, strictly speaking, all of us are "American" and, in fact, the people in that part of the world had a prior claim to the title. What are the implications and consequences of limiting the use of the designation in this way? Whose reality is privileged? What does this tell us about the power of language? Finally, how does the way we characterize different parts of the world reflect and privilege particular values and economic choices? For example, what differences are implicit in choosing to refer to certain countries or certain parts of the world as "developed," "developing," "underdeveloped," or "overdeveloped"? Whose priorities do these designations reflect? What values do they reflect and promote? What kind of hierarchy is created by their use? What picture of the world and the relation between and among nations is implicit in our choice among these terms?

In Articles 4 and 5, Chilla Bulbeck and Chandra Mohanty ask us to turn a critical eye toward the ways in which the language we use to describe parts of the world reflect and bestow attention and power differently. Bulbeck is particularly concerned about the tendency in the West to think in terms of dualisms like "Third World" and "First World" or backward and modern. In an effort to "fracture binarisms," she offers a survey of the evolution of these terms while teasing out the politics and economics of the ways in which they have been applied. For example, originally, "Third World" "signified a 'third force' of non-aligned nations which would wedge themselves between the Cold War opposition of First World 'democracy' and second world 'communism.'" Now it carries with it the connotation of being underdeveloped, backward, and poor. Bulbeck's concern is to have us understand the political and economic power relations that are simultaneously reflected in and rendered invisible by the language we use to describe and differentiate regions of the world, as well as the inadequacy of a simplistic approach that posits a dualistic worldview in which countries are either good or bad, backward or modern, developed or underdeveloped.

Reflecting on her own use of the terms "Western" and "Third World" in a earlier essay, Mohanty continues Bulbeck's project by exploring the implications of a variety of linguistic alternatives that can be used to refer to different areas of the world, including "One-Third World" and "Two-Thirds World" and "North" and "South." The point of both articles is not so much that we need to adopt any particular terminology as it is about the need to think and recognize the implications that often flow from seemingly innocent language choices we make and the need to think carefully about the hidden meanings attached to our choices.

In Article 6, Dana Lindaman and Kyle Ward offer some interesting comments on the ways in which textbooks around the world portray U.S. history and then provide us with excerpts from a variety of such texts so that we can see the extent to which position and perspective shape how we view the world. The excerpts that are taken from history textbooks in Canada, Mexico, England, France, and Brazil describe the Monroe Doctrine and Manifest Destiny and offer a perspective on this period in U.S. history that differs markedly from that offered in standard U.S. history texts. In fact, you might find it interesting to compare these accounts with high school history books available in your library. If you do, you are likely to come away with a clearer idea of how position, perspectives, and interests alter the ways in which history is constructed, reported, and written.

Perhaps nothing in this first section provides a more dramatic or more straightforward illustration of the difference perspective makes than the two plaques reproduced in Article 7, "Lapulapu and Magellan," and described by Steve Shalom. "Commemorating" the same historical event, these plaques offer vastly different ways of looking at the arrival and subsequent death of Ferdinand Magellan on the small Island of Mactan in the Philippines in 1521. The fact that history, certainly in the past, was written almost entirely from the point of view of the victors rather than the vanquished, reminds us that there can be a very fine line between liberation and conquest—and history may not always get it right.

In the months before the war in Iraq, U.S. President George W. Bush and other members of his administration suggested that there was a link between Saddam Hussein and the September 11th attacks on the United States. In spite of the fact that no link had ever been found, in 2003, nearly two years later, almost 70 percent of the U.S. population continued to believe that Saddam Hussein was personally involved in the attacks. And a large number of people cited this belief as one of the reasons they supported the U.S. decision to go to war in Iraq. Where do these people get their information? What does the persistence of this utterly unfounded belief say about the U.S. news media? How is it possible for so many people to be so mistaken about such an important "fact"? In the final Article in Part One, "Mass Media: For the Many by the Few," Michael Parenti encourages us to take a critical look at the U.S. mass media and how it reports on domestic and global events and issues. Arguing that the media has become dominated by a small group of transnational corporate conglomerates that offer a largely conservative and probusiness perspective, Parenti suggests that there is good reason to be concerned about what gets reported, what information never reaches us, and the perspective and interests that shape what counts as "the news." Because our ability to think both critically and intelligently about U.S. policy and global issues clearly depends upon our access to accurate and comprehensive information, Parenti's article raises serious and important questions about the information we receive and the perspective we are offered.

The Function of Maps

–David Turnbull

David Turnbull is an itinerant scholar and a research associate at Deakin, Melbourne, Monash, and Lancaster Universities. His current work is predominantly concerned with knowledge and space, and comparative knowledge traditions. The article that follows is taken from his book Maps Are Territories: Science Is an Atlas, *which was published in 1989 by Deakin University, Victoria, Australia.*

A map is always selective. In other words, the mapmaker determines what *is*, and equally importantly, what *is not* included in the representation. This is the first important sense in which maps are *conventional*. What is on the map is determined not simply by what is in the environment but also by the human agent that produced it. Furthermore, maps employ non-iconic signs and symbols. These are as arbitrary as the letters of the alphabet and are therefore largely conventional. Of course, many elements of maps are at least partly iconic, portraying certain visual features of the landscape represented, but even these images partake to a significant degree of the conventions of the artist.

The historian of geology Martin Rudwick has discussed the inherent conventionality of maps in the context of his argument that geology could not become a fully developed science before the development of visual diagrams:

> . . . a geological map . . . is a document presented in a visual language; and like any ordinary verbal language this embodies a complex set of tacit rules and conventions that have to be learned by practice . . . [Therefore there also has to be] a social community which tacitly accepts these rules and shares an understanding of these conventions.
> *Martin Rudwick, 'The emergence of a visual language for geological science, 1760–1840', 1976, p. 151*

Another obvious way in which maps are conventional is in their use of 'projection'. No curved surface like that of the Earth can be projected in two dimensions without some distortion. Over the years many different modes of projection have been developed: some are better for conveying such elements as shape or size; some, for compass direction or relative position; some are more distorted toward the poles;

From *Maps Are Territories* by David Turnbull. Copyright 1993. Reprinted by permission of the University of Chicago Press and the author.

some, towards the equator. No one projection is the best or the most accurate. A particular projection is selected by the mapmaker on the basis of functional and perhaps aesthetic criteria, or because of a specification or convention.

The projection developed by Gerhard Mercator, a Flemish cartographer, in 1569 became the most commonly used projection because it portrayed compass directions as straight lines. However, this was achieved at the expense of distortion of relative size, especially towards the poles. Mercator's Greenland appears much larger than Australia, which is in reality more than three times the size of that North Atlantic island. But other more subtle effects result from Mercator's view of the world. If you compare the Mercator projection (Figure 1) with the Peters projection (Figure 2), a map which endeavours to preserve relative size, what differences do you discover which might have cultural or political significance? You may wish to ask yourself what interests are served in a Mercator projection. Is it a coincidence that a map which preserves compass direction, a boon for ocean navigation) shows Britain and Europe (the major sea-going and colonising powers of the past 400 years) as relatively large with respect to most of the colonised nations? (See Figure 1.) What if we turn the Peters projection upside down and centre on the Pacific? (See Figure 3, page 10.) A profoundly altered view of the world is obtained.

Of course, orientation is an arbitrary convention. Indeed, the very word *orientation* comes from 'East' being the direction of the rising sun and hence it was once common practice to put it at the top of the map. North, whilst being one end of

FIGURE 1

The distorted area effect of Mercator's projection. The area of Greenland is 2 176 000 square kilometres; the area of Australia is 7 690 000 square kilometres.

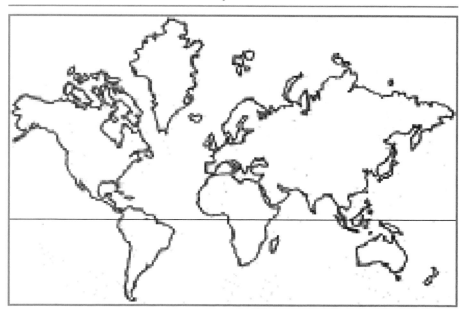

FIGURE 2

The Peters projection maintains north-south and east-west directions and preserves the relative size of countries at the expense of shape.

FIGURE 3
The Peters projection inverted and recentred.

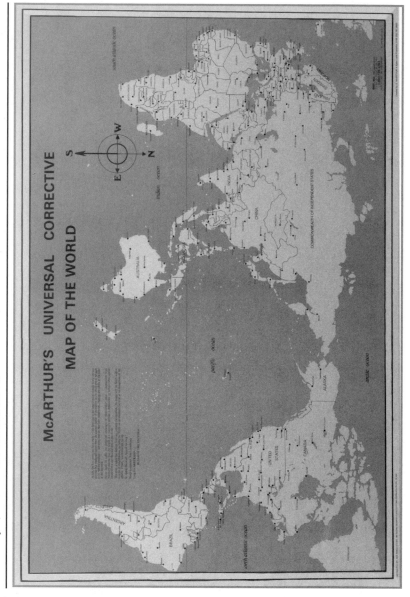

© 2002 Akademische Verlagsanstalt.

10

the Earth's axis of rotation, is not a privileged direction in space, which after all has no 'up' or 'down'. That North is traditionally 'up' on maps is the result of a historical process, closely connected with the global rise and economic dominance of northern Europe.

Another early example of map orientation reveals several interesting points (see Figure 4, page 12). This map, produced less than 100 years after the Spanish conquest of the Inca, was drawn by the Quechua writer Hawk Puma (Guaman Poma) to illustrate his moving account of Spanish misrule of Peru. Because his manuscript was part of a petition to the Spanish monarch, Hawk Puma employed a number of *European* conventions: he called it *Mappamundi*; he put 'North' at the top; he added pictorial elements such as the sun, ships, mountains, buildings in the towns and cartographically familiar sea creatures. The map shows little connection with the sophisticated relief maps which the 17th-century historian Garcilaso de la Vega attributes to the Inca, and it thus appears to avoid Incan cartographic conventions in favour of the European.

To modern eyes, the Hawk Puma map may at first seem fairly 'primitive', bearing, as commentators have suggested, only limited relation to the actual landscape depicted. For example, neighbouring countries seem to be wrongly placed, with the Pacific to the south instead of the west. But what happens if we rotate the map? Suddenly all the geographical relations fall into place. Even the rivers, the Maranon, Amazon and Pilcomayo begin to flow in the right directions again.

The significance of this rotation is much more interesting than a simple factual error. We now see that Hawk Puma's map follows long-standing *Incan* conventions after all. The explanation is historical. When the Inca expanded into Chile, a mountain pass had taken them by way of the great 'Eastern' society of the Collasuyu. Thus, Chile, to the south, came to be considered by the Inca as an *eastern* extension of their empire. Colombia, to the north, for similar reasons was considered a *western* extension. Furthermore, the map centres on Cuzco, the Inca capital, rather than on Lima, the Spanish capital; and its extent approximates the geographical limits of the Incan empire in South America, not the limits of the Spanish Indies, which the map purports to depict.

Thus, the story of the Hawk Puma map teaches us that conventions often follow cultural, political and even ideological interests, but that if conventions are to function properly they must be so well accepted as to be almost invisible. The map, if it is to have authority in Western society, must have the appearance of 'artless-ness'; that is, it must appear simply to exhibit the landscape, rather than to describe it with artifice or in accordance with the perceived interests of the mapmaker. For a map to be useful, it must of course offer information about the real world, but if this 'real world information' is to be credible, it must be transmitted in a code that by Western standards appears neutral, objective and impersonal, unadorned by stylistic device and unmediated by the arbitrary interests of individuals or social groups. (We frequently use maps that are highly stylised though: for example, guide maps to places and institutions.) Hawk Puma's map was almost certainly never seen by the King of Spain, and his petition never read. It may be

FIGURE 4
Hawk Puma's map (1613)

Sketch map of the west coast of South America showing the extent of the Inca empire before the arrival of the Spanish (top). Also shown are the approximate relations to Cuzco of the four neighbouring cultural groups which are identified on the four sides of Hawk Puma's map (bottom). Note that when rotated counterclockwise until the Condesuyu are south of Cuzco, this map approximates Hawk Puma's orientation.

The Royal Library, Copenhagen.

that this failure resulted at least in part from the visibility of the Incan conventions, which would have been read by the Spanish eye as inaccuracies, thus calling the map's credibility into doubt.

* * *

We have found that Western maps and aboriginal maps are more fruitfully compared in terms of their range and degree of workability or usability, rather than their accuracy. However, this leaves unexamined the dimension of power. Documents, texts, diagrams, lists, maps ('discourses' in general) embody power in a variety of ways. Discourses set the agenda of what kind of questions can be asked, what kind of answers are 'possible', and equally what kind of questions and answers are 'impossible' within that particular discourse or text. In terms of maps, for example, looking at a Mercator projection you can read off the relative direction of Anchorage from London as straight line, but you cannot read off the shortest route, it being a segment of a great circle. Maps, like theories, have power in virtue of introducing modes of manipulation and control that are not possible without them. They become evidence of reality in themselves and can only be challenged through the production of other maps or theories.

Joseph Rouse argues that

> all interpretation (which includes all intentional behavior, not just discourse) presupposes a configuration or field of practices, equipment, social roles, and purposes that sustains the intelligibility both of our interpretive possibilities and of the various other things that show up within that field. . . . Power has to do with the ways interpretations within the field reshape the field itself and thus reshape and constrain agents and their possible actions. Thus to say that a practice involves power relations, has effects of power, or deploys power is to say that in a significant way it shapes and constrains the field of possible actions of persons within some specific social context.
>
> *J. Rouse,* Knowledge and power: toward a political philosophy of science, *1987,*
> *pp. 210–11*

Bruno Latour, an anthropologist of science, has considered the question of power in a way that is of particular relevance to our analysis of maps and theories. Power is not, as many believe, the cause of society. It is not the glue that bonds classes or groups together. Rather, according to Latour, it is the consequence of association, and it is the varying techniques of association that should be the focus of study, in looking at power. John Law, a sociologist of science who takes a similar approach to Latour's, has looked at the methods of long-distance control that were necessary for the Portuguese to sustain a trading route to India. Law concludes that the power of the Portuguese trading empire derived from the forms of association embodied in three essential ingredients: documents, devices and drilled personnel (John Law, 'On the methods of long-distance control', 1986, p. 234ff).

Latour has discussed the difference between what he calls 'savage' and 'civilised' geography in the context of searching for an explanation of the difference between

Box 1

La Pérouse travels through the Pacific for Louis XVI with the explicit mission of bringing *back* a better map. One day, landing on what he calls Sakhalin he meets with the Chinese and tries to learn from them whether Sakhalin is an island or a peninsular. To his great surprise the Chinese understand geography quite well. An older man stands up and draws a map of his island on the sand with the scale and the details needed by La Pérouse. Another, who is younger, sees that the rising tide will soon erase the map and picks up one of La Pérouse's notebooks to draw the map again with a pencil. . . .

What are the differences between the savage geography and the civilized one? There is no need to bring a prescientific mind into the picture, nor any distinction between the close and open predicaments . . . nor primary and secondary theories . . . nor divisions between implicit and explicit, or concrete and abstract geography. The Chinese are quite able to think in terms of a map but also to talk about navigation on an equal footing with La Pérouse. Strictly speaking, the ability to draw and to visualize does not really make a difference either, since they all draw maps more or less based on the same principle of projection, first on sand, then on paper. So perhaps there is no difference after all and, geographies being equal, relativism is right? This, however, cannot be, because La Pérouse does something that is going to create an enormous difference between the Chinese and the European. What is, for the former, a drawing of no importance that the tide may erase, is for the latter the *single object* of his mission. What should be brought into the picture is how the picture is brought

back. The Chinese does not have to keep track, since he can generate many maps at will, being born on this island and fated to die on it. La Pérouse is not going to stay for more than a night; he is not born here and will die far away. What is he doing, then? He is passing through all these places, in order to take something *back* to Versailles where many people expect his map to determine who was right and wrong about whether Sakhalin was an island, who will own this and that part of the world, and along which routes the next ships should sail. Without this peculiar trajectory, La Pérouse's exclusive interest in traces and inscriptions will be impossible to understand—this is the first aspect; but without dozens of innovations in inscription, in projection, in writing, archiving and computing, his displacement through the Pacific would be totally wasted—and this is the second aspect, as crucial as the first. We have to hold the two together. Commercial interests, capitalist spirit, imperialism, thirst for knowledge, are empty terms as long as one does not take into account Mercator's projection, marine clocks and their markers, copper engraving of maps, rutters, the keeping of 'log books,' and the many printed editions of Cook's voyages that La Pérouse carries with him. This is where the deflating strategy I outlined above is so powerful. But, on the other hand, no innovation in the way longitude and latitudes are calculated, clocks are built, log books are compiled, copper plates are printed, would make any difference whatsoever if they did not help to muster, align, and win over new and unexpected allies, far away, in Versailles.

Bruno Latour, 'Visualisation and cognition', 1986, pp. 5–6.

what are often referred to as 'scientific' and 'primitive' cultures. This, he argues, must not be looked for in terms of some 'great divide' based on the postulation of radically different intellects, cultures or societies. Instead we have to look for small mundane differences. The answer, he claims, lies in the power of techniques of writing and imaging. They do not achieve this power in and of themselves but as a result of their capacity to muster allies on the spot—allies, that is, in the struggle over what is to count as fact. To illustrate his argument he tells the story of La Pérouse's encounter with the Chinese on Sakhalin Island (Read Box 1). This story has parallels with that of the Inuit and the Belcher Islands. Clearly the Hudson Bay Company acquired greater power than the Inuit through the production of a more powerful map.

Thus we can now see that the real distinguishing characteristic of Western maps is that they are more powerful than aboriginal maps, because they enable forms of association that make possible the building of empires, disciplines like cartography and the concept of land ownership that can be subject to juridical processes. Western and non-Western societies alike are based on knowledge networks, the important difference being in the mobility of the network. The Western one can be mobilised to cover the whole earth, if not the universe, whereas aboriginal ones are usually dependent on interpersonal oral modes of transmission. One of the most effective devices that Western maps employ in creating power is the grid, but the grid does not provide power of itself.

REFERENCES

B. Latour, 'Visualisation and cognition: thinking with eyes and hands', in H. Kuklick & E. Long (eds), *Knowledge and society: studies in the sociology of culture past and present*, vol. 6, JAI Press, Greenwich, Conn., 1986

J. Law, 'On the methods of long-distance control: vessels, navigation and the Portugese route to India', in J. Law (ed.), *Power, action and belief: a new sociology of knowledge?*, Routledge & Kegan Paul, London, 1986

J. Rouse, *Knowledge and power: toward a political philosophy of science*, Cornell University Press, Ithaca, NY, 1987

M. Rudwick, 'The emergence of a visual language for geological science', *History of science*, vol. 14, 1976, pp. 149–95

Are Things What They Seem to Be? Reading Maps and Statistics

–Janice Monk

Janice Monk is Professor of Geography and Regional Development and Research Professor in the Southwest Institute for Research on Women (SIROW) at the University of Arizona, of which she was Executive Director for more than 20 years. She has been president of the Association of American Geographers, from which she received Lifetime Careers Honors. The article that follows was written specially for this volume.

> As powerful tools of persuasion in science and public affairs, maps have had a remarkable effect on our view of the world, our health, and the impact of our votes. At the root of their power is our frequently unquestioning acceptance of cartographic messages.
>
> Monmonier, 1995, p. 1

> Lies, damned lies, and statistics.
>
> Courtney, 1895, p. 25

The "Truth" of Maps

David Turnbull's essay in this volume highlights some historical examples of how maps of the world have been made and used. He rightly notes that no map of the world can be "true"—it is not possible to represent a globe on a flat paper surface or to include all details. His essay reminds us that the widely known Mercator projection was created in an age of sea power and European colonial expansion, and that its strength is in being able to represent directions between places as straight lines, an advantage to navigators. Though the Mercator projection is rarely used today in professional atlases, it holds sway in a number of popular media, classroom maps, and cheaper atlases (Monmonier, 1995). My local newspaper, the *Arizona Daily Star*, for instance, uses the Mercator world map in a weekly feature "Mapping the News," which has the goal of educating the public (especially children) about current affairs. Yet this representation conveys serious areal distortions,

Reprinted by permission of Janice Monk.

making the "northern" countries and continents appear much larger (more signifi-cant) than the "southern." Greenland, for example, appears almost as large as South America, though if you look at a globe, you will quickly see that this is a misleading view.[1] Representing true directions between places as straight lines, the strong point of this map, is really not helpful; in fact, it is downright misleading when it comes to gaining perspectives on political, economic, or environmental issues.

In other, perhaps subtler ways, what and who are important and powerful have been embodied in maps and atlases. At the height of the British Empire it became conventional on maps to color Britain and its territories in pink—visually showing the extensive imperial reach. In the school atlases I used as a child in Australia, the first pages were given over to maps of Australia and its states, but then Britain (the imperial heartland and referred to then by many Australian-born people as "home") and Europe followed, and in some detail, well before the maps of neigh-boring Asia. You might find it interesting to reflect on the world maps and atlases to which you have been exposed. What role have they played in shaping your sense of what is significant? What message was conveyed to school children in Australia by the order in which maps were presented in their school atlases?

In presenting these questions I do not want to imply that there is one "best" way of making a map. It depends on the maker's purpose. Further, the map's im-pact reflects how it is distributed and promoted. What we need to be able to do is to identify the purpose, how it relates to the map we are reading, and how the rep-resentation can shape our views. The story of the Peters projection is an interesting one that reveals both sensitivity to issues of "fairness" in representing the world on a map and of the ways in which interest groups can promote a particular vision (Monmonier, 1995). Arno Peters, a German historian, introduced his equal area projection in the 1970s (see Figure 1, page 18). It was widely taken up in the 1980s by groups interested in development, equity, and justice, among them the (U.S.) National Council of Churches, the World Council of Churches, Christian Aid, UNESCO, and UNICEF. The importance of the Peters map, centering on Africa and enlarging Africa and South America so that their true size is presented relative to other continents, is that it challenges the impressions of the Mercator view. Peters's map was widely distributed by these groups. It does, however, dramatically distort the shapes of continents. Proponents of Peters argued that the Mercator's map enlargement of the Northern Hemisphere land masses was ethnocentric, colonialist, and racist.

The promotional campaign for Peters raised valuable questions, but obscured others. Peters's map was promoted as revolutionary and new, though equal area maps had been published for 400 years and there are many alternatives that give a "better" balance between shape and area. Why *area* should be the key way to

---

1. Areas in the high latitudes in the Southern Hemisphere are also enlarged by this projection, but since most of the area in question lies in oceans, impressions of relative size do not have the same impact on the reader as enlargement of the northern lands.

FIGURE 1
The Peters Projection.

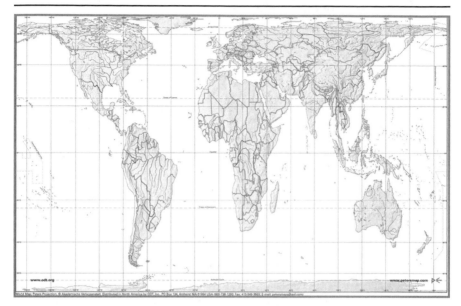

Courtesy ODT, Inc.

represent fairness did not seem to be part of the discussion. If we think about *numbers* of people, for example, as critical in representations of interest to concerns about development and human well-being, a cartogram (a map-like diagram that distorts space to portray a particular attribute of a place) showing nations in relation to the size of their populations might be more useful and relevant. In such a cartogram (Figure 2), India, for example, because of its large population, appears much more significant than it does in the Peters map. Cartograms have not had the same publicity or sponsors as Peters, however, mainly being used in technical reports and college geography texts. This situation helps us to question assumptions about what is important to whom and why. When do we think area should be prioritized? When do we think the number of people should be the key theme? And why? What is "fair"? Does it matter who adopts a particular map?

Focusing on processes of globalization, other representations may supplement more conventional world maps and challenge you to think about the importance of connections in world relations, not only area or population size. Figure 3, page 20, addresses this theme. It distorts conventional measures of distance, replacing them by the cost of communicating, in this case showing the cost per minute of phone calls made from the United States in 1998 to other parts of the world. Close inspection will demonstrate, for example, that Johannesburg, an important

FIGURE 2

Cartogram portraying countries according to the size of their populations.

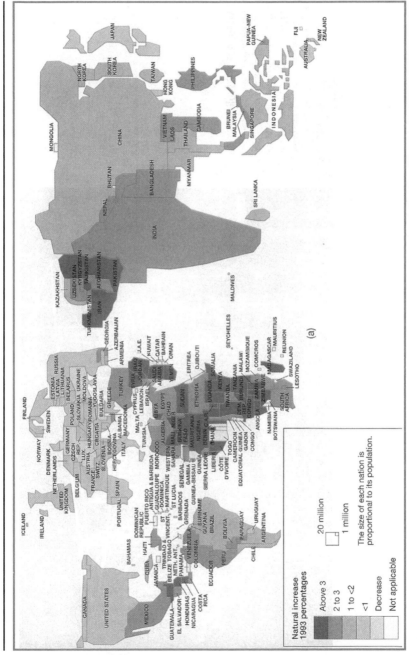

(a)

**Natural increase
1993 percentages**

- Above 3
- 2 to 3
- 1 to <2
- <1
- Decrease
- Not applicable

☐ 20 million
☐ 1 million

The size of each nation is
proportional to its population.

Reproduced with permission of Penguin Reference from M. Kidron and R. Segal (eds.) *The State of the World Atlas*, rev. 5th ed., London, Penguin Reference, 1995, pp. 28–29.

FIGURE 3

Cartogram portraying locations according to the cost of telephone calls per minute
from the United States.

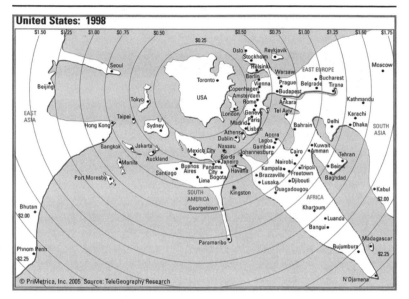

Reproduced with permission of Telegeography from G.C. Staple (ed.) *Telegeography*
1999. Washington DC: p. 82.

mining and economic center in South Africa (where English is the principal language of business and of much of the population), appears as markedly "closer" to
the United States than does N'Djamena, which is substantially nearer to the
United States in terms of miles but far removed from it in other ways as the capital
of economically poor and arid Chad where French and Arabic are the official languages but many other languages are spoken.

That the maps we have been exposed to and the place we are "coming from"
affect how we represent the world is well illustrated by sketch maps collected
by Tom Saarinen (1988) from almost 4,000 college students in 49 countries.
Regardless of where the students came from, the majority of their maps (almost
80 percent) were centered on Europe, reflecting the Eurocentric perspective that
many have been exposed to, but there are some interesting variations. Some students from the Americas center their home regions and provide much more detail
about places in them. Figure 4 offers one such map by a Peruvian student. One
Australian student who centered Europe in the traditional manner had to divide
the home country into two (unnamed) parts on each edge of the map. In contrast,
another who was clearly familiar with the Australian "upside down" map which is

FIGURE 4
Sketch map of the world by a Peruvian college student.

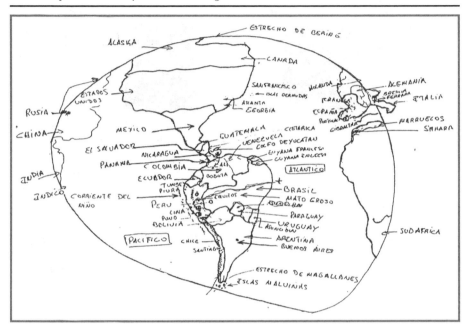

Reproduced with permission from the National Geographic Society from Thomas F. Saarinen,
"Centering of Mental Maps of the World," *National Geographic Research*, 4, 1988, p. 124.

sold there, placed south rather than north at the top and offered the heading
"Australia *IS* on top of the world, and not the USA!!!! and especially NOT Russia."
Politics and familiarity clearly shaped this student's map.

What Counts? Collecting and Presenting Statistics

Scholars and development practitioners concerned with women's lives have raised
many important questions about the hidden worlds of women. Widely used indicators such as gross national product, gross domestic product, and the United
National System of National Accounts have been criticized (see, for example,
Benería, 1982; Waring, 1988) for their lack of inclusion of what women do, the
significance of their activities to sustaining life, and the rendering invisible of
many social, economic, and political inequities, not only in relation to women but
because they conceal other distributional inequalities such as those of class.
Censuses of population, censuses of agriculture, and labor force statistics use concepts of employment and unemployment and of part-time and full-time work that
overlook women's unpaid and informal work; surveys that collect data based on

notions of household income and (male) head of household can hide unequal division of resources and power in the household. Work such as care for children, ill, and elderly, transportation of family members, or collecting of fuel and water, frequently go unrecorded. Yet such statistics are critical in formulating policies and development programs such as those of the World Bank, the International Monetary Fund, and various international and national aid organizations, particularly those relating to women in the global "south."

Among the techniques development specialists interested in improving recognition of what women do have adopted has been to record expenditures of time on work of particular types (see, for example, Mwaka, 1993; Oughton, 1993; Samarasinghe, 1997). They may compare hours spent by women and men on specific tasks, and separate the work of caring for the household from work that yields money but for which the individual may not be paid personally. Or they may look at seasonal variations in engagement with "work." Such data can be very time consuming to collect and may not be readily comparable from one setting to another. Yet they are important if planning for local programs is to be realistic and effective.

Another issue is whose practices are used as the standard by which concepts are defined in international comparative statistics. Data on the countries of the European Union (EU) offer an interesting example when we look at practices reporting "economically active" populations, deal with "full-time" versus "part-time" work, and consider what is labeled "typical" and "atypical" work (Vaiou, 1996). Women in Spain, Greece, and Italy are recorded as having much lower "economic activity rates" than the women in the EU in general. But is this accurate? Whereas many of the women working part-time in service sector jobs in the northern European countries are counted, those in southern European countries more often carry out work that is not counted—on family farms, in small family businesses, in industrial homeworking, or domestic services. These women also more often fall within the EU definition of "atypical work," that is, work that is seasonal, casual, home-based, or fixed term, whereas "typical" is conceptualized on a model of the (male) full-time worker with a permanent contract, more characteristic of the historical pattern of industrial eras in northern European countries. Comparing educational attainments and opportunities internationally provides another example of the hazards of making comparisons using statistics, given the different structures of national systems. It is hard to equate statistics that reflect different national laws that regulate age of leaving school, varying kinds of transitions between levels in educational systems, differing emphases on "school" versus vocational education (such as apprenticeship systems), and so on.

A number of years ago, interested in the effects of recent tourism on local livelihoods and migration, a colleague and I interviewed households in small communities on the Caribbean island of Margarita, paying particular attention to questions of gender and class differences (Monk and Alexander, 1986). The types of work the women reported are listed in Table 1.

We then looked at the way the Venezuelan census most recently available to us tabulated work (Table 2).

Table 1   Village Women's Work, Margarita Island, Venezuela, 1982

Housework	Shoemaker (at home)
Housework/seamstress	Housework/sells rabbits
Cleaner (in offices)	Chambermaid
Street seller of clothing	Raises chickens for direct sale to
Sells clothing in store	consumers
Laundress (home business)	Local government official
Weaves hammocks; repairs clothes	Housework/baby sitter
Operates drink stand in street	Housework/operate fruit & vegetable
Housework/sells corn	stand
School cook	Maid
Housework/small home grocery store	Teacher
Housework/rents out space for small store	Travelling saleswoman (clothes)
Housework/sells soft drinks from home	Sells shoes
Housework/takes in male boarder	Housework/makes and sells corn bread
Housework/weaves hammocks	Housework/works in family store/makes
Operates clothing store	parts of shoes.

As you compare these two tables, you will soon recognize how hard it is to place the women's work in the census classification system, since each person can only be counted once. To what category would you allocate a woman who is both producing goods (an artisan) and selling them (salespersons and kindred workers)? What about the women who combine housework with other economic activities? Does housework count? Is it categorized as "unemployed"? Will many of the women fall in the category "Other, not identifiable"? It becomes apparent that the classification is not especially useful for describing what and how these women contribute to sustaining themselves, their households, and the economy. Systems of accounting require that a person be identified in one category only, yet many people, across countries, hold more than one job, not necessarily in the same category. And especially in "Third World" countries, work in the "informal" sector or in family production goes unrecorded in national and international reporting.

Table 2   Occupational Classification in the 1970 Census of Venezuela

Professional, technical workers	Transport and communication workers
Agents, administrators, directors	Artisans and factory workers
Office employees and kindred workers	Service workers
Salespersons and kindred workers	Others, not identifiable
Agricultural, livestock, fisheries, hunting,	Unemployed
forestry, etc. workers	

The Devil Is in the Details

The saying "the devil is in the details" implies that if attention is not paid to details, a project is likely to go wrong. The variation, "God is in the details" highlights that getting it "right" is possible if we attend to details.[2] In the discussion above, I have focused on examples of definitions and categories established in statistical data and what criteria are given priority in map making. In a sense, I have been dealing with the big picture and the importance of thinking about the assumptions and power relations involved in the construction and dissemination of knowledge. Now I want to address the detail in which information is presented and how that affects the questions we might ask and the answers we might give. I offer just two examples.

The first relates to a series of maps produced in a project *Mapping the Census: The Geography of U.S. Diversity*, created by the U.S. Bureau of the Census using data from the 2000 Census (http://www.census.gov/population/cen2000/atlas/censr01-108.pdf). These maps are of considerable political interest, given the increasing international migration into the United States and issues about the implications of changing diversity in the U.S. population. A host of questions can be raised about the categories used in these maps, but my focus here is on the *scale* or detail used in presenting them. The page portraying "Number of People, 2000/One Race: Asian" for example, has two maps. The smaller map shows the data at the state scale (i.e., level of detail). The larger uses county units. Looking only at the state map, a person would conclude that the Asian "race" population is especially significant in California and New York, with secondary emphases in Texas, Florida, and selected midwestern and eastern/southeastern states. But the county map tells a more nuanced story. Large areas of the states that report the highest number of people of "exactly one race—Asian" have many counties where few Asians live. The major clustering in Texas is in the counties that include metropolitan Dallas and Houston, in Illinois it is in the Chicago area, in Minnesota in Minneapolis-St. Paul, in Washington in the Seattle area. In other words, if we want to research issues of importance to Asians in the United States, or relations between Asians and others, we would recognize the need to think first about selected counties not simply states. Researchers who are currently trying to understand changing trends in the social relations of Asian populations are, however, focusing on new expressions of *suburbanization* by immigrants. For their studies they use finer scales than the county level such as zip code areas, census tracts, and information from the Public Use Microdata Samples of the Census (e.g., Li, 1998; Li *et al.*, 2002; Singer *et al.*, 2001). Their findings take us away from old models of inner city Chinatowns or ethnic "ghettos" and raise a host of new questions and interpretations about inter- and intra-group relations, "racial" and ethnic stereotyping, the development of minority businesses, and the provision of culturally appropriate services. These themes would not be well researched if we relied solely on the maps at state or county scales. Still, those maps do provide some of the big

2. Background on this saying is offered in Titelman, 1986.

picture context to help select areas for detailed study. And if we neglected to use maps and what they can convey about spatial patterns, we might well continue to retain the old impressions of immigrants clustered in enclaves in inner cities and not understand emerging patterns related to contemporary globalization and international migration.

The second example I will offer deals with the detail in the presentation of national statistical indicators, particularly with how they are *disaggregated*, or separated into component parts. Beginning in 1990, the United Nations Development Program (UNDP) introduced the Human Development Index (HDI), a measure designed to make people and their well-being more central than measures of national income in assessing development across countries. The HDI brings together information on life expectancy at birth, adult literacy rates, enrollments in combined primary, secondary, and tertiary education, and estimated earned income. Countries are ranked on the basis of their HDI. The HDI, however, is a single number that is an average for all people in the country. In subsequent years, UNDP created a new indicator, the Gender Development Index (GDI), in recognition that circumstances for women and men differ (i.e., that the data need to be disaggregated by sex). The GDI uses the same variables as the HDI but calculates the values for men and women separately and then examines the discrepancies in values for each. When countries are ranked on the GDI index, their rankings often shift from those on the HDI, though to varying extents. Some countries show higher GDI rankings than their HDI rankings, implying that women in those countries are more "equal" to men than in those countries where the HDI ranking is higher than the GDI (http://hdr.undp.org/reports/global/2003). When the GDI ranking is lower than the HDI ranking, women are shown to be more disadvantaged. Though some statisticians have expressed dissatisfaction with the ways in which the indicators are calculated (e.g., Bardhan and Klasen, 1999), the point I wish to make is that disaggregation can reveal issues that are different from those when data are aggregated. Decisions about what level of disaggregation to use in publishing statistics are usually highly political, since they reveal inequalities by, for example, gender, ethnicity, age, and income, in well-being. Indeed, while it was possible for the 2003 UNDP report to publish HDI rankings for 175 countries, it could only rank 144 countries on the GDI because of lack of access to gender-disaggregated data in some countries.

Summary Comments

In presenting examples, I have tried to draw your attention to some attributes of maps and statistics that will help you be more sensitive to both their strengths and weaknesses and not to take their information simply as objective. I urge you to ask who is presenting the data, what are their goals, and how does the representation express power relationships. Maps and statistics, as presentations of "facts" shape the ways we understand and act in the world. We need to be critical and informed readers.

REFERENCES

Benería, Lourdes. 1982. "Accounting for Women's Work" in Lourdes Benería (ed.), *Women and Development: The Sexual Division of Labor in Rural Societies*. New York: Praeger.

Bardhan, Kalpana and Stephan Klasen. 1999. "UNDP's Gender-Related Indices: A Critical Review." *World Development* 27(6): 985–1010.

Courtney, Leonard Henry. 1895. "To My Fellow-Disciples at Saratoga Springs." *The National Review* (London) 26: 21–26 (http://www.york.ac.uk/depts/maths/histstat/lies.htm).

Li, Wei. 1998. "Ethnoburb vs. Chinatown: Two Types of Urban Ethnic Communities in Los Angeles." *Cybergeo* 10: 1–12 (http://www.cybergeo.presse.fr).

Li, Wei, Greg Dymski, Yu Zhou, Maria Chee, and Carolyn Aldana. 2002. "Chinese-American Banking and Community Development in Los Angeles County." *Annals of the Association of American Geographers* 92(4): 777–96.

Monmonier, Mark. 1995. *Drawing the Line: Tales of Maps and Cartocontroversy*. New York: Henry Holt and Company.

Mwaka, Victoria M. 1993. "Agricultural Production and Women's Time Budgets in Uganda" in Janet H. Momsen and Vivian Kinnaird, *Different Places, Different Voices: Gender and Development in Africa, Asia, and Latin America*. London: Routledge.

Oughton, Elizabeth. 1993. "Seasonality, Wage Labour and Women's Contribution to Household Income in Western India" in Janet H. Momsen and Vivian Kinnaird, *Different Places, Different Voices: Gender and Development in Africa, Asia, and Latin America*. London: Routledge.

Saarinen, Thomas F. 1988. "Centering of Mental Maps of the World." *National Geographic Research* 4: 112–127.

Samarasinghe, Vidyamali. 1997. "Counting Women's Work: Intersections of Time and Space" in John Paul Jones III, Heidi Nast, and Susan M. Roberts (eds), *Thresholds in Feminist Geography*. Lanham, MD: Rowman and Littlefield.

Singer, Audrey, Samantha Friedman, Ivan Cheung, and Marie Price. 2001. "The World in a Zip Code: Greater Washington D.C. as a New Region of Immigration." *The Brookings Institution Survey Series*. April.

Titelman, Gregory. 1996. *Random House Dictionary of Popular Proverbs and Sayings*. New York: Random House.

United Nations Development Program. 2003. *Human Development Reports*. http://hdr.undp.org/reports/global/2003 (accessed January 15, 2005).

Vaiou, Dina. 1996. "Women's Work and Everyday Life in Southern Europe in the Context of European Integration" in Maria Dolors García-Ramon and Janice Monk (eds.), *Women of the European Union: The Politics of Work and Daily Life*. London: Routledge.

Waring, Marilyn. 1988. *If Women Counted: A New Feminist Economics*. San Francisco: Harper and Row.

Gender Issues in Labour Statistics

–Adriana Mata Greenwood

The article that follows is by Adriana Mata Greenwood of the Bureau of Statistics at the International Labor Organization in Geneva, Switzerland. It appeared originally in the International Labour Review *in 1999.*

Labour statistics describe the numbers, structure, characteristics and contributions of the participants in the labour market and how these change over time. Conventionally, they cover many topics concerning the size and structure of the labour force and the characteristics of workers and employers. From an economic perspective, these statistics are necessary for analysing, evaluating and monitoring the way the economy is performing and the effectiveness of current and longer-term economic policies. From a social perspective, they are also necessary for designing policies and programmes for job creation, training and retraining schemes, and for assisting vulnerable groups, including the young, the old, women, etc., in finding and securing employment. To serve users, labour statistics need to reflect reality as closely as possible. This means that they should comprehensively cover all persons who actually participate in the labour market, and should describe their various work situations in equal detail and depth.

However, the production of statistics requires that reality be simplified—codified—into synthetic categories which highlight certain aspects of this reality while ignoring others. Whether these aspects are highlighted or ignored depends mainly on the *available methods of data collection* and on the *priorities and objectives* of the data collection process. The various methods of data collection all have their limitations, and measurement priorities depend to a large extent on the perceptions society has of how the labour market functions—perceptions which are not immutable. As a result, national labour statistics have generally been successful at identifying and characterizing "core" employment and unemployment situations, which reflect the conventional view of what "work" and "joblessness" are all about: i.e. workers in full-time regular employment in formal sector enterprises and persons who are looking for such jobs. They have been less successful at identifying and describing other work situations.

"Gender Issues in Labour Statistics" by Adriana Mata Greenwood ILO Bureau of Statistics, Geneva. Copyright 1999 International Labour Organization. Reprinted by permission.

Women are often to be found in these other work situations, which may go unnoticed or be inadequately described in labour statistics (United Nations, 1991). The validity of labour statistics would therefore be enhanced by a better understanding of what women do and how they behave in the labour market. Attempts to reflect as fully as possible women's work as compared with men's would reveal the statistics' strengths and shortcomings and would provide indications of how and where they can be improved. There are other reasons justifying such an endeavour. First, it would provide more complete information to users of the statistics, such as market analysts and policy decision-makers, which is important because men and women often do very different types of work and labour market changes tend to affect them differently. Second, it would enable users to understand and analyse female workers' particular position and constraints as compared with those of male workers, and would provide a more solid basis for promoting equality between the sexes in the labour market. For the systematic under-reporting and misrepresentation of women's contribution to the economy help maintain a distorted perception of the nature of a country's economy and its human resources, and thus perpetuate a vicious circle of inequality between men and women, and inappropriate policies and programmes.

So, it is important to establish the characteristics labour statistics need to acquire before they can fully reflect the similarities and differences in the respective situations of men and women in the labour market. This article seeks to establish the most important of these characteristics.

Gender Issues in Labour Statistics

It is generally accepted that inequality between men and women stems from attitudes, prejudices and assumptions concerning the different roles assigned to men and women in society (Overholt et al., 1984). These roles, which are learned, e.g., those of parent, housekeeper, provider of basic needs, etc., largely determine the type of work men and women do. For example, given their traditional role as homemakers, more female than male workers tend to combine economic activities with household (non-economic) activities, to work intermittently over the year and to work closer to home, often even at home for pay or in a family enterprise for family profit. Furthermore, because of their assigned role as dependent members of the household, women tend to be relatively more active than men in non-market activities and in the informal sector; to be considered by others and even by themselves as economically inactive; to receive less education, and thus to be more confined in occupations requiring lower skills and paying less well; to be considered as secondary workers in their family enterprise even when they have equal responsibility; and, in times of economic downturn or structural adjustment, to be amongst the first dismissed from their paid jobs. In addition, women find it hard to break through the "glass ceiling", which blocks their access to managerial or decision-making positions. Given structural constraints due to family responsibilities, women who are available and willing to work tend actively to seek work much less than men in the same situation, and employers tend to be reluctant to employ women outside typically female occupations.

Another area of gender differentiation is the allocation of resources and benefits among the members of a household. It has been observed, for example, that women who are self-employed have more limited access to production resources than men, which lowers their income (Dixon-Mueller and Anker, 1990). Furthermore, women do not necessarily have control over their use of the resources available to them, nor do they necessarily reap the full benefits accruing from their efforts. Women's and men's gender roles also determine their different needs and constraints. For example, the degree to which women actually participate in and contribute to the production process is highly dependent on their marital status, on whether they have small children, and on whether they have to care for other persons in their households. Men's participation in and contribution to the production process are also affected by these factors, but not in a constraining way.

In order to improve the description of the labour market and to provide a solid basis for promoting equality between women and men, gender differences such as those described above need to be considered when labour statistics are produced. Consequently, when determining which topics to include and how to define, measure and present them, one must consider how to reflect the distinct contributions, constraints and needs of women and of men in the resulting statistics.

Topics to Cover

Statistics are needed on the numbers of men and women producing the goods and services in a country (the employed population) and on the numbers of men and women exerting pressure on the labour market for jobs (the unemployed population). Various subgroups of the employed population are especially important for such an analysis:

- persons who, though working, are in jobs with insufficient hours of work (the population in time-related, or visible, underemployment);
- persons whose jobs are ill suited to them for other, labour-market related reasons (the population in inadequate employment situations);
- persons who work in small, unregistered economic units (those employed in the informal sector);
- and children who are in inappropriate work situations (child labour).

These population groups need to be further subdivided into more homogeneous categories, according to other work-related characteristics, for instance:

- occupation, given that men and women generally do very different jobs;
- employment status, in view of the steady decline of regular wage employment and the increase in other employment situations, such as casual and temporary/seasonal employment and self-employment, where men and women are present in different degrees;

- income from employment, given the pervasive difference between men's and women's income levels in all countries even after correcting for hours worked and level of education;
- working time, in order to provide a more accurate measure of their participation in the labour market;[1]
- participation in industrial disputes, as women are said to be more passive and less unionized than men, and may tend to be indirectly rather than directly implicated in industrial action and to work in industries less prone to industrial disputes;
- statistics of occupational injuries, given that men and women do very different jobs and thus face very different hazards.

All these topics are conventionally covered in national labour statistical programmes, as established by the ILO's Labour Statistics Convention, 1985 (No. 160), and therefore international guidelines on their measurement exist.[2]

However, it is clear that the topics likely to increase understanding of men's and women's position and interrelation in the labour market go well beyond those covered by conventional labour statistics. For example, information is needed on:

- the numbers of persons who "work" in the wider sense of the term, i.e. including workers producing goods and services for own consumption, given women's significant participation in these types of activity;
- workers' working-time arrangements, to indicate the degree to which men and women work in what is known as "regular full-time" working schedules or in more irregular schedules, such as intermittent or part-time employment, annualized working hours and other variable time schedules;
- overtime work, to evaluate whether establishments' responses to changing market demand affect men and women in different ways;
- absence from work, to indicate any differences in the types of absence taken by men and women, in particular in view of family responsibilities;
- occupational diseases, given men's tendency to be more exposed to injuries and women's tendency to be more exposed to diseases (Messing, 1998).

More information is also required on home-based work; contingent (or non-permanent) employment; levels of poverty; union participation; the duration of employment, unemployment and underemployment; access to productive resources;

---

1. The "number of persons employed" counts persons who work full time equally with those who work only a few hours during the week. Women work on average fewer hours than men (on economic activities) and as a consequence a measure of volume of employment based on the hours worked will reduce their relative participation in the labour market as compared to a measure based on head counts. Still, much of women's work remains unrecognized given that it excludes many unpaid activities carried out for the benefit of their households. If these activities were included in the scope of employment, and the hours spent in them were included in the measure of hours of work, then women's share of working hours would typically be greater than men's.

2. Current international guidelines can be consulted at http://www.ilo.org/stat/public/english/120stat/res/index.htm.

and the allocation of benefits among household members, etc. It may also be useful to calculate composite indexes or measures to reflect the respective occupational segregation, wage differentials, annual hours of work, etc., of men and women.

Defining the Topics

The crucial role played by definitions and classifications[3] in the production of relevant statistics is often underestimated. Definitions and classifications determine what is to be covered and in how much detail, and are the basis for the whole data production process. Thus, the quality of the resulting figures depends on how well these definitions and classifications mirror the actual situation of the different participants in the labour market. A change in definition can cause a change in the resulting statistics which may not reflect any change in reality. Therefore, when analysing time series or cross-country data, it is important to assess first whether observed changes are actually due to difference in definition.

In order to be useful in making gender distinctions, definitions should recognize that women and men do not necessarily perform the same tasks, that they do not always behave in the same way, and that they are not subject to the same constraints. In this connection, coverage and detail are essential. Definitions need both to cover all qualifying work situations, regardless of whether they are performed by a man or a woman; and to describe the different work situations in sufficient detail to bring out any gender distinctions.

Coverage

The range of activities constituting what is understood as "work" affects the scope of all topics in labour statistics. Employment, unemployment and income statistics are concerned only with persons carrying out or seeking to carry out "work". Occupational injury statistics include persons experiencing an injury only if it was sustained while performing such activities. And so on.

But, to be useful in making gender distinctions, "work" needs to cover *all* the activities carried out to produce the goods and services in society, regardless of whether they are remunerated, declared to the tax authorities, carried out intermittently, casually, simultaneously or seasonally, etc.; and regardless of whether the goods or services produced are intended for sale, for barter or for own household consumption. At present, however, the definition of "work" is limited to "economic" activities, i.e., those which contribute to the production of goods and services[4] according to a country's System of National Accounts (SNA). Such activities

3. A classification groups together units of a "similar" kind—"similarity" being determined in relation to specific criteria related to a characteristic of the units—often hierarchically, in order to describe the characteristic in a systematic and simplified way. In labour statistics, the three major classifications concern occupations, industries and employment status.
4. Activities of this type may include: growing or gathering field crops, cutting firewood, carrying water, weaving baskets and mats, making clay pots and plates, weaving textiles, and other handicrafts.

include those carried out to produce goods or render services for sale or barter in the market; and activities to produce goods for own consumption if they represent a significant proportion of those goods produced in the country. Domestic or personal services provided by unpaid household members[5] are excluded. In practice, few countries include the production of goods for own consumption within the scope of measured employment and none includes services for own consumption. Most work excluded from the scope of "economic" activities is done by women (UNDP, 1995), and this is an important cause of the underestimation of women's participation in production and of their contribution to the well-being of society. Thus, from the outset, labour statistics reflect at best a partial reality.

Child labour is one area in which such restricted coverage of "economic" activities dramatically affects the capacity of labour statistics to reflect reality. Statistics on child labour commonly show that more boys than girls work. This, however, conceals the fact that there are many children engaged in unpaid household activities who are prevented from going to school, just as if they were working for pay. As is to be expected, when these unpaid activities are included under child labour, it then emerges that more girls than boys work (Ashagrie, 1998). In view of the impact of such exclusions on policy decisions, the ILO systematically recommends that all countries include all (or a subset of) unpaid household activities in their national statistics on child labour.

Coverage of workers and work situations may also be affected by the criteria used to define a topic, and these often exclude particular groups of workers. Because the sex composition of these groups is generally uneven, the usefulness of resulting statistics for reflecting gender differences is hampered. Most of the time such exclusions affect more women than men, but not always. For example, some national definitions of employment exclude contributing (unpaid) family workers who work fewer than a fixed number of hours. The effect is probably greater on the number of women identified as employed, since unpaid family work is more prevalent among women than among men. Conversely, many countries exclude the armed forces from employment statistics, which affects more men than women. In many countries (e.g. in Scandinavia), a large proportion of paid workers are entitled to take relatively extended leave without losing their jobs, and national estimates of employment show a larger proportion of workers on extended forms of leave than those of other countries. Because of the likely family-related nature of such leave, e.g. for maternity reasons, most of these workers are women. The high levels of female employment reported in such countries may therefore partly reflect a definitional effect of generous leave entitlement, as in other countries an important proportion of these workers would not be classified as employed.

National definitions of employment in the informal sector may exclude persons whose main job is in the public service or agriculture, for example, but who

---

5. Activities of this type include: cleaning dwelling and household goods; preparing and serving meals; caring for, training and instructing children; caring for the sick, invalid or old people; transporting household members or their goods, etc.

have a second job in the informal sector; most of them are men. The definitions may also exclude certain activities in which women predominate, regardless of whether these activities otherwise satisfy the criteria for inclusion in the informal sector. Examples include: agricultural activities, activities by enterprises exclusively engaged in the production for own final use, activities of paid domestic workers and of outworkers.

Conversely, national definitions of time-related (or visible) underemployment, in line with international guidelines, generally exclude employed persons who work for more hours than a certain fixed threshold, which is considered to represent the level of "full-time employment" in legislation, collective agreements or usual practice in establishments. Those working at or above this threshold are considered to be fully employed even if they are willing and available to work additional hours. Unfortunately, in many countries the chosen threshold does not truly reflect "full" employment, because many workers are in fact compelled to work beyond those hours in order just to make a decent living. Most such workers are men.

National definitions of unemployment generally include unemployed persons who are "actively seeking work". But not everyone who wants to work actively seeks it, nor does everyone consider that their attempts to find it constitute "actively seeking work". Consequently, they do not report themselves as doing so. Thus, in countries where "formal" ways of finding work, e.g., through labour exchanges, are limited to the cities, or where more "informal" channels are commonly used, national definitions may exclude persons who are in fact looking for self-employment or for paid employment but who do not consider that their activities amount to "actively seeking work". Furthermore, in line with the standard international definition of unemployment, most national definitions exclude persons who want to work but do not "seek" work at all, either because work opportunities are so limited that they know there are none in practice, or because they have restricted labour mobility, or because they face discrimination or structural, social and cultural barriers in their search for work. Many of these workers, most of whom are women, tend to react positively to an actual chance of employment.

Statistics on income from employment also tend to be partial, for several reasons. They usually exclude wage and non-wage benefits such as social security benefits, profit-related pay and irregular payments, which may be significant in many cases and where differences between men and women may be important. Most important of all, national statistics usually exclude the remuneration of the self-employed where, again, there may be considerable differences between men and women.

Coverage may also be affected by the use of short reference periods. Definitions which aim at complete coverage of work situations should cover seasonal and occasional activities. However, international and national definitions of employment and unemployment generally provide an image of the labour force situation during a particular reference week. Statistics based on these definitions are useful for monitoring changes over time when the dominant form of employment is regular, full-time, non-agricultural, paid employment, but are less useful for monitoring other forms of employment. Since more women than men tend to work in seasonal and casual activities and/or on an intermittent basis throughout the year alternating household non-market activities with economic activities, measures of employment and unemployment based on a short reference period can only partially reflect this more complex reality. In order to capture this fully, it is necessary to identify persons who experienced employment or unemployment at any time within a longer period, for example, 12 months. Statistics on the experience of employment or unemployment within a 12-month period exist in a number of countries, but they tend to identify the predominant activity over that period, in line with international guidelines. However, this measure conceals seasonal patterns of work and excludes persons who, though working part of the year, are inactive for most of it. Many of these workers are women.

Detail

For definitions to be useful for gender concerns they need to ensure that men's and women's characteristics are described in sufficient detail to allow significant distinctions to emerge. The classification of occupations, for example, needs to be refined at a detailed level (Anker, 1998). If only broad occupational groups are used, the occupational segregation between men and women remains hidden: an analysis of the managerial group as a whole, for example, will not reveal that women managers tend to be concentrated in small enterprises, while managers in larger companies are men.

Similarly, to detect gender differences in workers' employment status, it is not enough merely to distinguish between "employees", "employers" and "own account workers", as most countries do. These are very heterogeneous categories, each comprising a diversity of employment situations. For example, the category "employees" includes not only regular employees but also outworkers (home-based workers), casual employees, work-gang members, etc. Women tend to predominate in the latter situations. In addition to employers and core own-account workers, the category of "self-employed workers" includes subsistence workers, share croppers, members of producer cooperatives, etc., amongst whom women are particularly numerous.

In income statistics, the various components of income must be identified separately, as they may not accrue to women and men to the same degree. For example, in systems where income statistics include social security benefits received by virtue of workers' employment status (as recommended in international guidelines), a worker's income includes all such benefits relating to his or her dependants. Similarly, the income of self-employed workers includes the income generated by the economic activities of the worker's contributing (unpaid) family members, as well as dependants' social security benefits. As men tend to be the primary earners in households, these income components can be expected to be more important for them than for women. Therefore, income statistics that include such components probably show a greater disparity between men and women in employment than statistics which do not include them. Estimates of the value of unpaid work are also important for gender distinctions. If such estimates attribute an economic value to unpaid work (most of it by women), this tends to reduce the differences between the measured contributions of men and women to the economy or their households.

Similarly, to enable valid gender comparisons as regards working time, it is important to separate out its various components (e.g., overtime, absence from work, work at home, travelling time, etc.), as they may affect women and men to different degrees.

Another relevant issue here is the need for female and male workers' characteristics to be described equally in substance and in detail. For example, all occupational groups at each level of a national classification of occupations should be identified separately to the same extent according to specified criteria. Thus, it is important to evaluate whether the distinctions made in occupational groups in which women predominate (e.g., clerical, agricultural and elementary occupations) are as detailed as those made in occupational groups where men predominate (e.g., in crafts and machine operators). Most national classifications tend to bulk in a few occupational groups the jobs in which women predominate, whereas jobs where men are numerous tend to be distinguished in greater detail.

In practice, women's situation may not be described equally as regards employment status. According to international guidelines, women who work in association, and on an equal footing, with their husbands in a family enterprise, are in partnership with them and should therefore be classified in the same employment status category as they are, i.e. as "core own-account workers" or "employers". However, there is a tendency in national statistics to classify women in such situations as contributing (or unpaid) family workers.

* * *

Presentation of Data

The way statistics are presented is central to the reflection of gender concerns. Tables and figures should portray differences in men's and women's contributions, conditions and constraints. This implies disaggregation by variables which describe the demographic, economic, social and family context of workers. All statistics on the numbers of employed and unemployed persons and their characteristics should make it possible to compare women with men. This means that, as a minimum, establishments' records and other administrative records should include information on persons' sex and that the statistical system should always publish statistics disaggregated by sex.

But statistics on the characteristics of workers should also be disaggregated by other variables which help describe the differences or similarities between men and women. For example, statistics on income should distinguish workers' hours of work and level of education, two factors which affect the level of total income earned. Similarly, for a more comprehensive picture of men's and women's occupational injuries, statistics should be presented for hours of work and seniority, and be shown by occupational groups.

Most important of all, statistics on the structure and characteristics of the labour force should be disaggregated by variables which reflect workers' personal and family situation, in order to provide a more complete picture of women's labour force participation and behaviour compared to men's. Such variables include age, level of education, whether the household includes children needing care, or other adults requiring assistance (e.g., handicapped persons, older family members), etc. All these factors variously constrain the time and energy which women and men can devote to their "economic" work. In many societies, a person's marital status also strongly affects participation in the labour force, and in polygamous societies an important variable is rank within marriage (ACOPAM, 1996). Another relevant descriptive variable is the type of household (e.g., single parent, female headed, etc.).

Though these variables are essential to the description of gender-based differences and similarities in the labour market, few countries actually present their statistics in this way. One reason may be that only household-based surveys are sufficiently flexible to produce such statistics, but the fact that international guidelines have never addressed the importance of linking labour market topics with workers' family context is certainly also important.

REFERENCES

ACOPAM (Appui associatif et cooperatif aux initiatives de développement à la base). 1996. *Genre et développement: Analyse de la place des femmes. Une experience au Sahel.* Geneva, ILO.

Anker, Richard. 1998. *Gender and jobs: Sex segregation of occupations in the world.* Geneva, ILO.

Ashagrie, Kebebew. 1998. *Statistics on working children and hazardous labour in brief.* Mimeo. Geneva, ILO. April.

Dixon-Mueller, Ruth; Anker, Richard. 1990. *Assessing women's economic contributions to development.* Training in Population, Human Resources and Development Planning Paper No. 6. Geneva, ILO.

Mata Greenwood, Adriana. Forthcoming. *Incorporating gender issues in labour statistics.* Working Paper No. 99-1. Geneva, ILO.

Messing, Karen. 1998. *One-eyed science: Occupational health and women workers.* Philadelphia, PA, Temple University Press.

Overholt, Catherine, et al. 1984. "Women in development: A framework for project analysis", in Catherine Overholt, Mary B. Anderson, Kathleen Cloud, and James E. Austin (eds.): *Gender roles in development projects: A case book.* West Hartford, CT, Kumarian Press, pp. 3–15.

United Nations. 1991. *The world's women 1970–1990: Trends and statistics.* Social Statistics and Indicators, Series K, No. 8. New York, NY.

UNDP. 1995. *Human Development Report 1995.* New York, NY.

Fracturing Binarisms:
First and Third Worlds

–Chilla Bulbeck

Historian Chilla Bulbeck is the Foundation Chair in Women's Studies at the University of Adelaide, to which she was appointed in 1997. She holds the only named chair of women's studies in Australia. The following excerpt was taken from her book Re-Orienting Western Feminism: Women's Diversity in a Post Colonial World, *which was published by Cambridge University Press in 1997.*

> Not so very long ago, the Earth numbered two thousand million inhabitants: five hundred million *men* and one thousand five hundred million *natives*. The former had the Word; the others merely had the use of it.
>
> Sartre 1967:7

What is the first and third world (and second, fourth and fifth worlds for that matter)? Can we neatly classify all the countries of the world into these pigeonholes? If not, why do these terms continue to have salience? Given the western tendency to think in dualisms like third world and first world or backward and modern, this section explores strategies for disrupting such black and white oppositions. Some writers have merely reversed the evaluative connotations of the former dualisms, so that west = bad and east = good. Such postcolonial desire does not overcome the dualism of east and west. We will explore the limitations of a dualist approach through notions of hybridisation, the ways in which east and west are constructed not only in opposition to each other but in an intermingling of one with the other.

***

The term 'third world' originally signified a 'third force' of non-aligned nations which would wedge themselves between the Cold War opposition of first world 'democracy' and second world 'communism' (Longley 1992:20). The second world has been variously defined as the Soviet Union, in which case it has now disappeared, or the communist countries, in which case it is reduced to a clutch of

From *Re-orienting Western Feminism: Women's Diversity in a Post Colonial World* by Chilla Bulbeck. Copyright 1998. Reprinted with permission of Cambridge University Press.

countries like Cuba, China, Burma, Vietnam and North Korea, countries which are often assimilated into the third world. . . .

Trinh Minh-ha (1987:17), quoting commentators like Julia Kristeva on communist China, suggests that the third world still has the positive resonance of a subversive, immense repressed voice about to burst into centre stage of the globe, supported perhaps by the increasing presence of the Southeast Asian economies, now the fastest growing in the world. 'Third world', however, generally signifies 'backward', 'poor' or 'developing' nations, which Trinh Minh-ha (1993:168) contests with her notion of the 'overdeveloping' nations of the west (instead of the 'underdeveloped' nations of the third world). Extending this definition based on deprivation, some commentators describe a 'fourth' and 'fifth' world of women, disadvantaged women who live in the nations of the west. The fourth world consists of indigenous peoples in settler societies in North America and Australia, while the fifth world consists of migrants dispossessed of their heritage (Longley, 1992:20). However, the colonisation of South America was also based on the dispossession of the indigenous populations, creating fourth world peoples in these 'third world' countries. Expulsion and genocide was greatest in southern countries like Argentina; in northern countries like Peru, the mestizo, or mixed-race Spanish and Indian people, control politics and the economy to the detriment of indigenous people like the Quechua. In contemporary Latin America, Indian women are sterilised without consent, beg for food in marketplaces, work as maids and have low literacy levels. In fact there are fourth world peoples in almost every corner of the globe, for example in Hokkaido in northern Japan, the minorities around the fringes of China, and the tribal people of India.

The third world has also been described as the 'two-thirds' world, a reference possibly both to the collapse of the second (communist) world and to the fact that at least two-thirds of the world's population live in countries with low average per capita incomes (for example United Nations 1991:12, xiii suggests that more than three-quarters of the world's women live in 'developing' regions). The term 'two-thirds' world focuses on the fact that a majority of women live 'beyond the west' and seeks to displace the pejorative connotations of 'third world'.

The third world is a category produced and reproduced by capitalist imperialism, referred to in the oppositions between industrialised north and developing south, or core and periphery. Powerful global agencies like the United Nations, the World Bank and the International Monetary Fund make distinctions between the first and third worlds which determine global economic policies. The political projects of institutions such as the Central Intelligence Agency and alliances between governments are also shaped by the identification of third world nations. However, and even for these powerful agencies, the third world contains anomalies which are quietly excluded from the all-embracing classification. The IMF does not tell the Japanese government how to spend its budget. The World Bank is not offering loans to the OPEC Gulf States, Kuwait's per capita income being the highest in the world in 1982 (Fakhro 1990:38). Even though their per capita income is now lower (Bello and Rosenfeld 1990:301), New Zealanders and

Australians have not yet become the recipients of aid from the generous citizens of Singapore. And not only western countries have been imperialist aggressors. In its long history of foreign influence and occupation, Korea adopted Confucianism from China during the Chosun Dynasty (1393–1910) and was forcibly occupied by Japan in 1910. Similarly, East Timor was occupied by the Portuguese, the Japanese and the Dutch before its present occupation by Indonesia, which includes systematic bombings and transmigration aimed at matching the numbers of East Timorese with Javanese (Franks 1996:161–3).

Perhaps the greatest challenge to the contrast between first and third world is provided by the no longer Newly Industrialising Countries of Asia: South Korea, Taiwan, Singapore and Hong Kong (at least before 1997 when it returned to mainland China). As a result of high per capita incomes, Hong Kong, Taiwan and Singapore (and the Gulf States) participate in guest worker schemes characteristic of European countries. Japanese feminists identify the benefits they gain from 'the exploitation of other Asian women', 'as do the women of the United States' (Yayori Matsui in Rowbotham 1992:267). Economic superiority is expressed in a racist register by non-white as well as white nations. Indigenous people in Guam accuse the Japanese corporations of being no less racist than white imperialists, bulldozing ancestral bones for a hotel (Ishtar 1994:75). Ilikano male migrant workers from the Philippines were surprised by whippings, amputations and beheadings as punishments in the Middle East. For their part the Arabs said that 'Filipinos are like dogs', loathsome, homeless and scavenging (Margold 1995:276, 288). However, a note on definitions is warranted here. Racial prejudice, when expressed by subordinate groups, should be distinguished from racism, which is prejudice backed by power. Thus while ethnocentrism or racial prejudice is quite possibly endemic to all communities, in white imperialist nations, economic, military and political control stands alongside ideological presumptions, reinforcing the ability to impose one's stereotype or definition of the 'other' on the other. Migrants of colour to the white west experience racial prejudice undergirded by racism (see Friedman 1995:23–4, 26 generally; Hitchcox 1993:149 for Vietnam; Peletz 1995:90 for the Malays; hooks 1992:170 and Zack 1993:37 for African Americans).

In some analyses, the third world is not treated all of a piece, even after the removal of anomalous instances such as those noted above. In their textbook survey of *Women in the Third World*, Lynne Brydon and Sylvia Chant (1989:14) reject from their analysis 'atypical' third world countries like China and South Africa. They also use different criteria for grouping countries. A history of British colonial rule conflates South Asia (India, Pakistan, Nepal, Sri Lanka and Bangladesh), while Spanish colonial rule produces South America. The shared religion of Islam unifies Sub-Saharan Africa and North Africa. Southeast Asia is a single region on the basis of high levels of workforce participation by women. The Caribbean has the 'shared history of slavery', along with the 'arguably' greater economic autonomy of Caribbean women (Brydon and Chant 1989:14, 21, 33, 38, 42; see also Momsen 1993:1–3, 6, who relates high levels of workforce participation and education to Caribbean women's historical roles as field labouring slaves). This classification is actually neatly geographical. But the justifications, produced by university teachers for a British audience, are the product of British colonial histories and contemporary international relations. Thus South Asia is known through British colonisation, the Caribbean through British participation in the slave trade. Africa and Southeast Asia are known through contemporary phenomena, in the former case Islam and in the second the high participation of women in the paid workforce.

Brydon and Chant's academic division of the world bears some resemblance to that imagined by the producers and readers of *National Geographic*. The Middle East tends to be conceived as the origin of western religions, a region of nomads and the veil. Africa is a place of poverty and underdevelopment. Micronesia is seen as a child maturing into adulthood, while Polynesia is the place of beautiful women and vagabond men, a paradise more recently turned to pollution (Lutz and Collins 1993:127, 256, 138, 144). Thus, compared with Brydon and Chant (1989:14), who ignore the Pacific completely because 'we have found little material' on this area, Lutz and Collins divide Oceania into two sub-regions. This reflects both their own research interests in Oceania and the undue attention *National Geographic* pays to this region; both of these may reflect, compared with Britain, a greater US preoccupation with the Pacific, given American involvement in the region, especially since World War II.

BIBLIOGRAPHY

Bello, Walden and Stephanie Rosenfeld (1990) *Dragons in Distress: Asia's Miracle Economies in Crisis*. San Francisco: Institute for Food and Development Policy

Brydon, Lynne and Sylvia Chant (1989) *Women in the Third World: Gender Issues in Rural and Urban Areas*. Aldershot, UK: Edward Elgar

Fakhro, Munira A. (1990) *Women at Work in the Gulf: A Case Study of Bahrain*. London: Kegan Paul

Franks, Emma (1996) 'Women and resistance in East Timor: "the centre, as they say, knows itself by the margins"', *Women's Studies International Forum* 19(1/2):155–68

Friedman, Susan Stanford (1995) 'Beyond White and Other: Relationality and Narratives of Race in Feminist Discourse', *Signs* 21(1):1–49

Hitchcox, Linda (1993) 'Vietnamese Refugees in Hong Kong: Behaviour and Control' in Buijs, *Migrant Women*

hooks, bell (1992) *Black Looks: Race and Representation*. Boston, MA: South End Press

Ishtar, Zoel dé (1994) *Daughters of the Pacific*. Melbourne: Spinifex Press

Longley, Kateryna O. (1992) 'Fifth World' in Sneja Gunew and Kateryna O. Longley, eds, *Striking Chords: Multicultural Literary Interpretations*. Sydney: Allen & Unwin

Lutz, Catherine A. and Jane L. Collins (1993) *Reading National Geographic*. Chicago: University of Chicago Press

Margold, Jane A. (1995) 'Narratives of masculinity and transnational migration: Filipino workers in the Middle East' in Ong and Peletz, *Bewitching Women, Pious Men*

Momsen, Janet Henshall (1991) *Women and Development in the Third World*. London and New York: Routledge

Peletz, Michael G. (1995) 'Neither Reasonable Nor Responsible: Contrasting Representations of Masculinity in a Malay Society' in Ong and Peletz, eds, *Bewitching Women, Pious Men*

Rowbotham, Sheila (1992) *Women in Movement: Feminism and Social Action.* London: Routledge

Trinh, Minh-ha T. (1987) 'Difference: "A Special Third World Women Issue"', *Feminist Review* 25:5–22

Trinh, Minh-ha T. (1993) 'All-owning Spectatorship' in Gunew and Yeatman. *Feminism and Politics of Difference*

United Nations (1991) *The World's Women 1970–1990: Trends and Statistics.* New York: United Nations

Zack, Naomi (1993) *Race and Mixed Race.* Philadelphia: Temple University Press

One-Third/Two-Thirds Worlds
–Chandra Talpade Mohanty

Chandra Talpade Mohanty is professor of Women's Studies and Dean's Professor of the Humanities at Syracuse University. Born in India, Mohanty holds a Ph.D. and master's degree from the University of Illinois at Urbana-Champaign and a master's degree and bachelor's degree from the University of Delhi, India. The selection that follows is an excerpt from her book Feminism without Borders, *which was published by Duke University Press in 2003.*

What are the urgent intellectual and political questions for feminist scholarship and organizing at this time in history? First, let me say that the terms "Western" and "Third World" retain a political and explanatory value in a world that appropriates and assimilates multiculturalism and "difference" through commodification and consumption. However, these are not the only terms I would choose to use now. With the United States, the European Community, and Japan as the

From *Feminism without Borders* by Chandra Talpade Mohanty. Copyright © 2003. Reprinted by permission of Duke University Press.

nodes of capitalist power in the early twenty-first century, the increasing proliferation of Third and Fourth Worlds within the national borders of these very countries, as well as the rising visibility and struggles for sovereignty by First Nations/indigenous peoples around the world, "Western" and "Third World" explain much less than the categorizations "North/South" or "One-Third/Two-Thirds Worlds."

"North/South" is used to distinguish between affluent, privileged nations and communities, and economically and politically marginalized nations and communities, as is "Western/non-Western." While these terms are meant to loosely distinguish the northern and southern hemispheres, affluent and marginal nations and communities obviously do not line up neatly within this geographical frame. And yet, as a political designation that attempts to distinguish between the "haves" and the "have-nots," it does have a certain political value. An example of this is Arif Dirlik's formulation of North/South as a metaphorical rather than geographical distinction, where "North" refers to the pathways of transnational capital and "South" to the marginalized poor of the world regardless of geographical distinction.

I find the language of "One-Third World" versus "Two-Thirds World" as elaborated by Gustavo Esteva and Madhu Suri Prakash (1998) particularly useful, especially in conjunction with "Third World/South" and "First World/North." These terms represent what Esteva and Prakash call social minorities and social majorities—categories based on the quality of life led by peoples and communities in both the North and the South.[1] The advantage of one-third/two-thirds world in relation to terms like "Western/Third World" and "North/South" is that they move away from misleading geographical and ideological binarisms.

By focusing on quality of life as the criteria for distinguishing between social minorities and majorities, "One-Third/Two-Thirds Worlds" draws attention to the continuities as well as the discontinuities between the haves and have-nots within the boundaries of nations and between nations and indigenous communities. This designation also highlights the fluidity and power of global forces that situate communities of people as social majorities/minorities in disparate form. "One-Third/Two-Thirds" is a nonessentialist categorization, but it incorporates an analysis of power and agency that is crucial. Yet what it misses is a history of colonization that the terms Western/Third World draw attention to.

* * *

Native or indigenous women's struggles, which do not follow a postcolonial trajectory based on the inclusions and exclusions of processes of capitalist, racist, heterosexist, and nationalist domination, cannot be addressed easily under the purview of categories such as "Western" and "Third World."[2] But they become visible and even central to the definition of One-Third/Two-Thirds Worlds because indigenous claims for sovereignty, their lifeways and environmental and spiritual practices, situate them as central to the definition of "social majority" (Two-Thirds World).

NOTES

1.   Esteva and Prakash (1998, 16–17) define these categorizations thus: The "social minorities" are those groups in both the North and the South that share homogeneous ways of modern (Western) life all over the world. Usually, they adopt as their own the basic paradigms of modernity. They are also usually classified as the upper classes of every society and are immersed in economic society: the so-called formal sector. The "social majorities" have no regular access to most of the goods and services defining the average "standard of living" in the industrial countries. Their definitions of "a good life," shaped by their local traditions, reflect their capacities to flourish outside the "help" offered by "global forces." Implicitly or explicitly they neither "need" nor are dependent on the bundle of "goods" promised by these forces. They, therefore, share a common freedom in their rejection of "global forces."

2.   I am not saying that native feminists consider capitalism irrelevant to their struggles (nor would Mohanram say this). The work of Winona La Duke, Haunani-Kay Trask, and Anna Marie James Guerrero offers very powerful critiques of capitalism and the effects of its structural violence in the lives of native communities. See Guerrero 1997; La Duke 1999; and Trask 1999.

BIBLIOGRAPHY

Esteva, Gustavo, and Madhu Suri Prakash. 1998. *Grassroots Post-Modernism: Remaking the Soil of Cultures.* London: Zed Press.

Guerrero, Marie Anne Jaimes. 1997. "Civil Rights versus Sovereignty: Native American Women in Life and Land Struggles." In *Feminist Genealogies, Colonial Legacies, Democratic Futures,* edited by M. Jacqui Alexander and Chandra Talpade Mohanty. New York: Routledge.

La Duke, Winona. 1999. *All Our Relations: Native Struggles for Land and Life.* Boston: South End Press.

Trask, Haunani-Kay. 1999. *From a Native Daughter: Colonialism and Sovereignty in Hawaii.* Honolulu: University of Hawaii Press.

6
six

How Textbooks Around the World Portray U.S. History
The Monroe Doctrine and Manifest Destiny

–Dana Lindaman and Kyle Ward

In their 2004 book, History Lessons: How Textbooks Around the World Portray U.S. History *(New Press, 2004) philologist Dana Lindaman and historian Kyle Ward gather accounts of U.S. history that have appeared in textbooks from around the world. In the section that follows we get a glimpse of how history texts used in various countries discuss The Monroe Doctrine and Manifest Destiny.*

We live in extraordinary times. Through our televisions, computers, radios, and newsprint we have access to what seems like the entire world. At almost any moment we can turn on the television and instantly see news dealing with hunger in developing nations, terrorism in the Middle East, and the economic situation in Japan and Western Europe. We can view documentaries that show us the daily routine for Aborigines in the Australian outback, life in a small Norwegian village, and work for people in the mountains of Peru. And as if these were not enough, we can search the Internet to research nearly any group, country, or society, past or present, in the world. One can check the daily news coming out of the Philippines, learn about the trials of the Tiv people in Nigeria, or simply get an update on the British Parliament and its next appearance on C-Span. What this instant access reveals to us is that people and groups around the world are very unique. The great variety of languages, dress, customs, diets, and beliefs all demonstrate the singularity of these different and distinctive societies throughout the world. One way to begin to understand these societies and their diversity is to look at their history, how time has formed them and made them who they are. History, then, is one possible avenue toward better understanding.

What makes this day and age so extraordinary, though, is the irony that, while we marvel at the exotic customs of distant peoples, the very media that provide this information also brings us closer to these distant cultures than we have been at any

Excerpts from *History Lessons* by Dana Lindaman and Kyle Ward. Copyright © 2004 by New Press.

other time in our collective history. The Internet, e-mail, satellite and cellular telephones, advances in the speed of travel, and a global economy have brought all these unique cultures into almost constant contact with one another. Certain societies that could have more easily ignored the United States fifty years ago find themselves today dealing with U.S. corporations, fashion, food, entertainment, and U.S. foreign policy on a daily basis. And this is hardly a one-way street. However, there is one distinct advantage that these other countries have over the United States in this relationship: They are constantly exposed to the U.S., receiving a daily dose of information on the U.S. and Americans, studying English at school, and in some cases continuing their studies in this country. Americans, in sharp contrast, seem to know relatively little about other countries and cultures. This isolationist tendency is nowhere more apparent than within our own educational system.

One of the few constants in history courses both in the U.S. and abroad is the use of textbooks to teach national history. These national histories are typically written by national authors with a national audience in mind, leading to a sort of insularity on any given historical topic. While this is an understandable initial approach to learning about history, in a diverse, global society, people must move past the bias of national history. One practical way to begin this approach is to examine the way our national texts approach the study of other nations.

History textbooks are an especially useful resource, because they typically represent the most widely read historical account in any country, and one encountered during the formative adolescent years. Unlike independently authored historical accounts, textbooks are a quasi-official story, a sort of state-sanctioned version of history. In nearly all countries the government takes some role in setting the standards for an acceptable cultural, political, and social history—i.e., what the authorities want the next generation to learn about its own national heritage—enfolding them, as it were, into a collective national identity. The fundamental contribution of any textbook is, of course, the story, an account that reveals much about a nation's priorities and values. Because history textbooks contain national narratives written by national authors for a national audience, they model the national identity in a very profound and unique way.

There are important cultural elements that surface when working with textbooks. U.S. history textbooks, for example, typically deal with national history from a political perspective, explaining events according to a chronology governed by presidential terms or political eras (i.e., Reconstruction, Progressive Era, Cold War, etc.). The French, *au contraire*, avoid this political history in favor of a more social or economic history, one in which the history of ideas figures prominently (the American Revolution and the French Revolution are discussed more as the end of authoritarian regimes than as political events). Formats, too, vary: The British, for example, are more inclined to include citations from authors and important figures in the text itself, whereas other countries include their primary source materials separate from the text. Furthermore, one finds a single story thread more prevalent in the Anglophone countries, whereas French textbooks eschew a long written narrative in favor of short summaries and pages of primary source materials. These may seem like small differences, but they inculcate a way of seeing the world and of seeing history. The simple fact that U.S. history textbooks contain a master narrative of more than 1,000 pages encased in a cover often emblazoned with a patriotic title is significant. It means something. It also means something that American students study the Declaration of Independence, the Constitution and the names of the Founding Fathers. In order to more fully compare historical perspectives, we must be willing to reflect on these cultural and political elements that underlie any text.

Cultural misunderstandings are often the result of our inability to read these cultural elements or cues. If we wish to move beyond judgment and toward understanding, we must honestly consider other perspectives. It is useless to say that a country is ridiculous or backward simply because its version of an historical event does not agree with the U.S.'s account. It is important, however, to ask why, and then to consider what is included and/or excluded, the language employed, and the educational context in which the book is used. Do the authors use the first-person *we* and speak of *our* nation, or do they use an impersonal construction? Does the text pass judgment on other nations, including the United States? Is there more than one account available in any given country? Since our goal is to provide readers with foreign perspectives on U.S. history, we have included only foreign material. Of course, the project that follows on these pages is best read with a U.S. history textbook in mind, if not next to, the reader. A few notes on these U.S. textbooks may prove useful.

Despite the generally attractive layout of the text with its graphics, charts, and dazzling pictures, one quickly notices that the content of U.S. history textbooks is rather bland. Over the last 20 to 30 years, textbook publishers have become averse to bold historical narratives for fear of being labeled as too liberal, too conservative, too patriotic, or too sexist and rendering themselves unattractive to buyers on the textbook market. Instead, they have become encyclopedias of historical names, places, and timelines. In order to meet the market's demands, they are doing away with what is most interesting about history: perspective, interpretation, historiography, bias, debate, and controversy. By reducing history to a series of inoffensive facts and figures, no matter how attractively packaged, textbook publishers are effectively judging students incapable of discussing and debating important topics and issues.

Instead of avoiding these difficult issues, this work embraces them, with the intention of bringing back to the study of history those very things that make it so interesting and important. Instead of just reading about specific events, our readers have the opportunity to develop their own historical perspective and discover how individual biases, perspectives, and interpretations from around the world have shaped our understanding of specific historical events.

It is ironic that, today, many history classes in the United States are taught from an isolationist standpoint, where events in U.S. history are portrayed as if they occurred within a historical vacuum. If other nations are mentioned in American textbooks, it is often only within the context of the impact of the United States' foreign policy or from the viewpoint of U.S. interests.

The United States developed in a global context. The U.S. received the majority of its population through immigration; it participates in a global economy, and rose to world supremacy within the context of an interwoven global system. Why not, then, consider these historical intersections as essential elements of U.S. history and examine the impact these events have had on both the U.S. and the other nations involved?

Comparative history is relatively new in the United States and, certainly now, more than ever, is relevant in our current political climate. In the minds of many Americans, the rest of the world suddenly matters again. Of the many things September 11, 2001, taught Americans about ourselves, one of the most pressing is that, despite all the opportunities we're given to learn about other cultures and societies, we still understand relatively little about the rest of the world and how they view us.

* * *

The Monroe Doctrine

The Monroe Doctrine is mentioned in nearly every textbook that deals with the growth of the new nation in North America. It is often viewed as the United States' first attempt at imperialism. As with the War of 1812, there is a larger European and Latin American context in which to see this moment.

Great Britain

This British textbook offers a slightly different take on who should get credit for Latin American security. It is interesting to note that Great Britain still refers to "security," while most Latin American texts refer to "economic interests."

The French, firmly established in Spain after 1823, possessed the only fleet capable of transporting an invasion force. An attempt at Anglo-American co-operation floundered because of United States suspicion of Cannings' motives. In December 1823 the American President Monroe declared the American continent closed to further European colonization. This was directed against Britain and her Canadian claims as much as in defence of the South American states.

Canning had already obtained assurances from Polignac (the French ambassador) that France had no intention of assisting a Spanish assault on South America. The record of these conversations was made public as the Polignac Memorandum. Since the meeting preceded the Monroe Doctrine by two months, the Latin Americans were reminded that they owed their security to Canning and the Royal Navy, not the United States.*

---

*Martin, Howard. *Challenging History: Britain in the Nineteenth Century*. Surrey: Thomson, 1996, 212.

Brazil

In the following excerpts, the authors use the Monroe Doctrine to explain U.S. growth, U.S. interests in Latin America, and even U.S. recognition of Brazil's independence.

Consolidation and Expansion of the New State

The Napoleonic wars and the continental blockade in Europe indirectly affected the North-American trade with Latin America and some European countries, particularly with France. England, the main enemy of the French Empire, and also an American rival in the conquest of new markets, started to cause problems in order to block the commercial relations between the US and the European and Latin American countries.

Those commercial quarrels added to the North American expansionist ideas, which aspired to take Canada from England, leading to the **Second War of Independence** (1812–1814). The British wars in Europe and the North-American desire for a commercial rapprochement made possible the signing of the **Lasting Peace of Ghent**, confirming the Great Lakes region as a neutral zone and defining the borders between the US and British Canada.

The war led to the rise of American nationalist feeling related to territorial unity and also caused concern about the European threat to American commercial interests. One of the main US concerns was related to the growth of trade between the US and the independent Latin America countries, now threatened by a revival of colonization due to the intentions of the Holy Alliance. Those feelings were expressed by the **Monroe Doctrine** (1823) through US President Mr. James Monroe (1817–1825) in his address to Congress, the message of which can be summarized as "America for the Americans".

The Monroe Doctrine shaped, from the political point of view, an international economic expansion for the US. That policy would be essential for its commercial development. The internal expansion, through the conquest of territories in North America led to the **race west**. From the Atlantic coast, where the original 13 colonies started, the pioneers moved forward to the interior until they reached the western coast, the Pacific Ocean.*

The Independence of Latin America

What mattered for the Spanish American elites, represented by the *criollos* (Spanish descendents born in America), was breaking up the ties with the monopolist *métropole*,† which made trade difficult, especially trade with England, the main economic power at the time. In its colonies the Spanish crown reserved the most productive sectors for itself, besides limiting access to administrative and po-

---

*Vicento, Cláudio. *História geral*. São Paulo: Scipioine, 2002, 329–31.

†Editors' note: *Métropole* in the European sense means the homeland or the home country. Thus, for Latin America, Spain or Portugal is meant. For the British colonies, Great Britain would be the *métropole*.

litical positions to its own appointments. But England was interested in the colonies' independence which would eliminate the commercial barriers imposed by the Iberian monopolists thus activating new markets, indispensable for its industrial progress. *Criollos* and the British had intersecting interests that lead them to the same goal: the independence of the Spanish America.

Britain's support was decisive for Latin America's emancipation. With the Napoleonic defeat in 1815, the Iberian metropole returned to the old style colonialism, but they did not succeed because of the British support for the *criollo's* fight for independence from 1817 to 1825. The **Monroe Doctrine**, established by the US, also helped to consolidate Latin America's independence, aiding the *criollo's* war of independence.*

Recognition of Brazil

Another serious problem that Brazil had been facing was the recognition of its independence. The Latin American governments delayed the recognition of Brazil's independence because they were suspicious of the real intentions of the Brazilian monarchic government. They saw it as a typical European system, which was not compatible with the republican regime adopted by all the other newly independent Latin American countries. They also questioned the legitimacy of Brazilian sovereignty over the Cisplatina Province (now Uruguay) and the insistence of the Brazilian Emperor D. Pedro I on keeping it Brazilian.

The United States and the main European powers took their time in recognizing Brazilian independence since they wanted to take advantage of the situation to serve their interests. The United States was the first country to recognize Brazilian Independence in 1824. Although the recognition would have been coherent in the context of the Monroe Doctrine, the North Americans declared that they intended to amplify their international markets. Brazil would be a strong ally in a future anti-European commercial bloc. Thus commercial hegemony was the main aspiration for the North Americans.†

Caribbean

The Caribbean text is very explicit regarding the reasons for including such a warning in Monroe's speech: economic interests.

The Monroe Doctrine

The United States and Britain were both pleased at the revolt of Spain's colonies in South and Central America. The new countries set up by the Liberators were no longer bound to obey trading regulations made in Spain and they bought increasing amounts of goods from British and American traders. So Britain and the

---

*Vicento, Cláudio. *História geral*. São Paulo: Scipione, 2002, 323.
†Silva, Fransisco de Assis. *História do Brasil: Colônia, Imperio, República*. São Paulo: Moderna, 2002, 126.

USA were both alarmed when the King of Spain called on the rulers of other European countries to supply him with ships and troops to win back his colonies.

In 1823 the British Foreign Secretary, George Canning, asked the Americans to join in a warning that the United States and Britain would resist the scheme to reconquer Spain's colonies. The American President, Monroe, however, went further and issued an independent warning which also applied to Britain. It was delivered in his annual message to Congress in December 1823. The part of the speech which became known as the Monroe Doctrine said:

> The American continents by the free and independent conditions which they have assumed and maintained are henceforth not to be considered subjects for future colonisation by European powers.

He went on to say that any European attempt to interfere in 'any portions of this hemisphere' would be seen as 'the manifestation of an unfriendly disposition to the United States'. In other words, the Americans were making it clear that they were the major power in the American hemisphere—not any other European country, including Britain.*

Mexico
This Mexican text is decidedly more critical of the ambition of the U.S. government.

The Monroe Doctrine and the Thesis of Manifest Destiny
Within the first few decades of the 19th century, the US system had all the economic and political problems of a complete society that had grown from 4 million people in 1790 to 10 million in 1820, and was still growing. With such growth came the frequently heard slogan in the political discourse of the era, "The March West."

The territories of Kentucky, Tennessee, Ohio, Indiana and Illinois were quickly incorporated into the new nation by means of despoiling the indigenous populations. In order to continue this expansion, certain people like Moses and Stephen Austin penetrated Mexican territory under agreements of colonization, in which they promised to respect the sovereignty of the Mexican government in the province of Coahuila and Texas. Then, the senior administrators of the North American government went into action, playing their expansionist ambitions against the diplomatic slowness of the European powers.

In Europe in the meantime, Russia, Prussia and Austria, under the direction of the Chancellor of the latter, Clemente de Metternich (1815), had agreed to unify their interests under the so-called "Sacred Alliance," hoping to fortify the absolutist monarchies and, consequently, to combat the ideas of liberalism. For its part, Spain, led by Fernando VII, relied on the armies of this reactionary coalition and sought to defeat the Spanish liberals, defenders of the Constitución de Cádiz

*Claypole, William, and John Robottom. *Caribbean Story, Bk. 2: The Inheritors.* Kingston: Carlong, 1994, 167–168.

(1812). This same political strife tried to implant itself in the newly liberated ex-colonies of Spain.

In 1822 events occurred that brought about, as a consequence, the need for the North American government to take a position with respect to the power of the Sacred Alliance, over which France now ruled, led by Louis VIII. In August, the plenipotentiary ministry of the United States communicated the following: "The English government has invited us to make a joint declaration against the powers of the Sacred Alliance."

At the insistence of the Secretary of State, John Quincy Adams, the fifth president of the United States, James Monroe, included in the annual message delivered to Congress the second of December, 1823, the following statement: "With the existing colonies or dependencies of any European power we have not interfered and shall not interfere. But with the Governments who have declared their independence and maintained it, and whose independence we have, on great consideration and on just principles, acknowledged, we could not view any interposition for the purpose of oppressing them, or controlling in any other manner their destiny, by any European power in any other light than as the manifestation of an unfriendly disposition toward the United States."

The political and military events of the American continent demonstrated how such a declaration could be manipulated in order to justify the imperialistic comportment of the United States, itself. The principal manifestation of this tendency was to assume the role of protector of the young Hispano-American nations, and under this pretext, to intervene in their politics and determine their destinies. Along with this political act that helped the United States to obtain in practice its recognition as a capitalist power at the international level, it's worth mentioning the governing character that the Monroe Doctrine has held ever since in the relations of this great power with the Hispano-American nations.*

France

French textbooks rarely, if ever, mention the Monroe Doctrine. By 1823, France had lost its North American colonies. The following text comes from a supplemental history book used by many students and teachers in French classrooms.

In 1819 Spain was in the midst of colonial revolt. Taking advantage of the situation, the US, using both threats and persuasion, convinced Spain to cede the portion of the coast that they still possessed reaching from the Atlantic to the mouth of the Mississippi, including Florida. Through this action they achieved new, direct access to the Gulf of Mexico. President Monroe had Spain in mind, or more precisely, her rebelling colonies, when he gave his famous speech outlining the position of the United States and setting the new tone from America: the end justifies the means. A French expedition had just reestablished the authority of Ferdinand VII over Spain. The circumstances gave credibility to the rumors that the European

*Palacios, Mario Alfonso Rodriguez. *México en la historia: tercer grado, educación secundaria.* Mexico City: Editorial Trillas, 1992, 50–51.

powers intended to intervene in the Americas in order to reestablish their dominant authority over the rebelling colonies. What would the United States do? Everything about the situation begged for their intervention. Their sympathies were with the rebelling colonies that were only following in their footsteps. Their own proper interests certainly didn't include the return of European imperialistic powers in the near vicinity, but instead the maintenance of weaker states as neighbors. President Monroe decided then to recognize the insurgent governments and to give a warning to Europe. In a message to Congress he defined the principles of his administration, what would come to be known as the Monroe Doctrine. It reaffirmed the principle of neutrality put forth by Washington while providing more detail and extending its application to all the New World. The United States wished to remain on good terms with Europe and restated its desire to remain uninvolved in her internal conflicts. In return, they asked that Europe not interfere in any of the affairs in the American sphere. They refused to allow European colonization in areas previously untouched by European domination. Specifically, they would consider any action against a government having proclaimed its independence as an unfriendly act. The European governments hardly took notice of this declaration by the United States assuming it unsupportable. They considered it a bragging tool to be used as propaganda for some internal policies. But the text was not without value. It was the first attempt at a national doctrine formulating the motto or idea: Hands off the American Hemisphere! Through its broad definition of this new hemisphere, it also marked the beginning of a certain American hegemony over the larger American space.*

Manifest Destiny

Beginning in the 1830s and 1840s, many Americans came to view the U.S.'s westward expansion as ordained by God. Today, "Manifest Destiny" is often associated with imperialism and portrayed in a negative light in many history textbooks. The countries that give it the most coverage tend to be those most affected by it historically, i.e., Mexico, Canada, the Caribbean, and Latin America.

Canada

The Canadian text refers to "manifest destiny" in terms of the threat felt by Canadians toward their American neighbors to the south.

Political Developments to 1867

The expansionary goals of the United States provided a catalyst for British North American union. In the first half of the nineteenth century, the Americans had swept aside the Indians and Spanish to extend their borders to the Pacific. They argued that it was their God-given right, or "manifest destiny," to do so. If the bel-

*Rémond, René. *Histoire des États-Unis*. Paris: PUF—Que sais-je?, 1992, 40–41.

ligerent statements of politicians and pundits following the Civil War could be believed, the boundaries of the United States would soon extend to the North Pole as
well. Most British North Americans had little interest in becoming American citizens. In the 1860s they were proud members of the British Empire and intended
to stay that way. It was true that the mother country was tired of pouring money
into the defence of the struggling North American colonies, but by adopting a
tighter political framework, they could arguably better repel American aggression
and serve the interests of Great Britain as well as their own.*

This textbook details how the U.S. obtained the state of Washington.

In 1842 the Webster-Ashburton Treaty had sorted out the complex eastern
boundary issues along the Maine-New Brunswick border. The western boundary
west of the Rocky Mountains was settled in 1846. Under the Oregon Boundary
Treaty the border across the Rockies to the Pacific continued from the Great Lakes
at the 49th parallel to the Pacific (excluding Vancouver Island). This 'compromise' allowed the Americans to possess the state of Washington, in which they had
virtually no nationals and which had been occupied chiefly by the Hudson's Bay
Company. While the geographical interests of British North America may have
been sacrificed by the Oregon settlement, entente was good for business.†

Although the rush for gold in California is a common theme in U.S. textbooks,
what was taking place north of the border is not discussed.

Canadian Gold Rush

Meanwhile on the West Coast, sheer serendipity brought the region to the attention of the world. In 1857 the discovery of gold on the mainland, along the
Thompson and Fraser rivers, brought fortune-hunters scurrying from around the
world. The amount of gold easily available was quite small by earlier California
standards. The ensuing rush was a pale imitation of the American one. Nevertheless, hundreds of miners, mainly from California, made their way to the Fraser
River in the interior of British Columbia in the spring of 1858. The quiet village of
Victoria was transformed overnight into a major port. South of the 49th parallel,
talk of American annexation spread rapidly. The British government rushed legislation putting New Caledonia under the direct jurisdiction of the Crown. [. . .]
The miners, however rough in appearance, were not really badly behaved and accepted British authority readily enough.‡

This text further explains how American interest in British Columbia drove this
region to seek union with Canada.

While the question of Rupert's Land dragged slowly to its conclusion, the
Canadian government was presented with an unexpected (although not totally
unsolicited) gift. It consisted of a request from British Columbia—to which

---

*Finkel, Alvin, et al. *History of the Canadian Peoples: 1867 to the Present, v. 2*. Toronto: Copp Clark
Pittman, 1993, 12.
†Bumsted, J.M. *A History of the Canadian Peoples*. Toronto: Oxford University Press, 1998, 148.
‡Bumsted, J.M., ibid., 158–59.

Vancouver Island had been annexed in 1866—for admission into the new union. The initiative from the Pacific colony had originated with the Nova Scotia-born journalist, Amor De Cosmos (William Alexander Smith, 1825–97), a member of the colony's legislative council. As early as March 1867 he had introduced a motion that the British North America Act, then about to be passed by the British Parliament, allow for the eventual admission of British Columbia. Entry into Confederation would introduce responsible government, as well as resolving the colony's serious financial difficulties, which resulted partly from the interest on debts incurred for road building during the gold rushes. Union with Canada received an additional impetus when—conterminously with the passage of the British North America Act but quite independent of it—the American government purchased Alaska from the Russians. The purchase touched off demands in the American press for the annexation of British Columbia as well. Officially the British notified the colony in November 1867 that no action would occur on its relationship with Canada until Rupert's Land had been duly incorporated into the new nation.*

Mexico

Mexico lost a considerable amount of land to the U.S. in the 19th century, a fact which is given prominent treatment in Mexican textbooks.

The Expansionist Tendencies of the United States of America

The process of expansion of the USA intensified in the first half of the 19th century. The country appropriated Louisiana in 1803, West Florida in 1810, East Florida in 1819, Texas in 1845, New Mexico, California and Arizona between 1845 and 1848 and Oregon in 1847. In the second half of that century it incorporated into its territory La Mesilla (1853) and Alaska (1867).

The methods that this country utilized in the process of expansion were some of the following:

- The purchase or annexation of territories and the incorporation of certain regions in the USA.
- The negotiation of borderline treaties.
- The financing of separatist movements.
- Bribery and conspiracy, war, displacement, extermination and relocation of indigenous populations to reservations.

With all these strategies, the territories of the United States of America grew more than triple of what the country possessed in 1783. The US expansionism was based on the content of the **Monroe Doctrine** and **Manifest Destiny**. The former proclaimed that any intervention of the European powers in the independent countries of the American continent would be considered as a threat to the secu-

*Bumsted, J.M. *A History of the Canadian Peoples.* Toronto: Oxford University Press, 1998, 193–95.

rity of the USA and that America would no longer be a territory of colonization or conquest for said powers. In this way, the USA reserved for itself the right to intervene in the American continent when it felt its interests were threatened. Manifest Destiny consisted in the belief that the USA was the "country chosen by providence" to inhabit the American continent and that the US people had been chosen by divine will to cultivate and benefit from the land.

The USA demonstrated its expansionist politics toward our country from the beginning of the 19th century, and put it into practice through various strategies. For example, they tried to buy Mexican territories on several occasions. Then in 1821 and 1822, they obtained the means by which to populate Texas through the concessions granted to Moses and Stephen Austin. In 1825, the USA began a politics of intervention with Joel R. Poinsett, the representative of that country in Mexico. Anthony Butler, successor to Poinsett, tried to negotiate a new border treaty with the Mexican government and eventually to buy from our country the territory of Texas. For their part, the southern slave states of the American Union tried to seize some of the Mexican territory along the border, and founded in them other states with systems based on slavery. In such a way, they hoped to gain political predominance over the free-states in the US Congress.*

The Thesis of Manifest Destiny

In 1830 the Sacred Alliance was fading and its ideological principles were swept away in nearly all of Europe. In America, the process of expansion of capitalist North America required an ideological and political justification. It was a lawyer named John L. O'Sullivan who, in a series of newspaper articles which appeared in 1845, tried to justify the increasingly aggressive politics of the North American government concerning the territorial annexations, making them appear legal by "divine right."

The name given to this new application of Monroe-ism was *Manifest* or *Revealed Destiny*, a name which invoked Providence in an act similar to the feudal crusades. One phrase become well-known and symbolic for the success of its intentions: "The view of the map captivates the North Americans." It referred ever after to the American continent.

The briefest recounting of the interventions and actions of the United States, in America in the 19th century, would fill several pages of this unit. Let us limit ourselves to only the most general cases which were, unfortunately, neither the only nor the last.

Interventions in Mexico:

(a)   Open help for the Texan colonies in their separatist activities (1836).

(b)   Invasion of Mexican territories (1846) in order to obtain, by means of war, more than 2 million km^2 as booty.

*López, José de Jesús Nieto, et al. *Historia 3*. Mexico: Santillana, 2000, 108–109.

Interventions in Central America and the Caribbean:

(a)   Separation of Panama from the Republic of Colombia, to which it belonged, with the intent of opening an inter-oceanic canal.
(b)   Occupation of Puerto Rico and Cuba under the pretext of freeing them
from Spain who kept them as colonies.*

Brazil

*Brazil offers a concise summary of U.S. expansion after independence. This text is
careful to highlight the economic benefits of the expansion as well.*

In the middle of the 19th century, the country reached its continental dimensions through expropriation of lands from the native Indians and neighboring people, or by buying colonial possessions from European powers:

1803 — bought the territory of Louisiana which had belonged to France.
1819 — bought Florida, a Spanish possession, which gave to the US access to
the Antilles (Caribbean).
1848 — war against Mexico, in which Mexico lost 2 million km^2 of its territory
(treaty of Guadalupe-Hidalgo). From that new land were created the
states of Texas, California, New Mexico, Arizona, Utah and Nevada.
With those annexations, the US reached the Pacific Ocean.
1867 — bought Alaska from Russia.

The North-America territorial expansion was mainly justified by the Doctrine
of Manifest Destiny, in which the US carried out the annexation of areas between
the Atlantic and the Pacific Oceans. The North Americans were chosen by destiny
to dominate America. In reality the territorial advancement was in fact due to the
international capitalist goals of expansion. The conquest of the West to the Pacific
Ocean gave the US direct access to the Western world and gave the US access to
and a strategic position in the sought after markets of China and Japan. The annexation of Florida opened a way to the Mexican Gulf, the Antilles Sea and also to
Latin America.[†]

Mexico

This Mexican text is decidedly more critical of the ambition of the U.S. government.

The Monroe Doctrine and the Thesis of Manifest Destiny

Within the first few decades of the 19th century, the US system had all the economic and political problems of a complete society that had grown from 4 million
people in 1790 to 10 million in 1820, and was still growing. With such growth came
the frequently heard slogan in the political discourse of the era, "The March West."

*Palacios, Mario Alfonso Rodriguez. *México en la historia: tercer grado, educación secundaria.* Mexico
City: Editorial Trillas, 1992, 51–52.
[†]Vicento, Cláudio. *História geral.* São Paulo: Scipione, 2002, 329–31.

The territories of Kentucky, Tennessee, Ohio, Indiana and Illinois were quickly incorporated into the new nation by means of despoiling the indigenous populations. In order to continue this expansion, certain people like Moses and Stephen Austin penetrated Mexican territory under agreements of colonization, in which they promised to respect the sovereignty of the Mexican government in the province of Coahuila and Texas. Then, the senior administrators of the North American government went into action, playing their expansionist ambitions against the diplomatic slowness of the European powers.

In Europe in the meantime, Russia, Prussia and Austria, under the direction of the Chancellor of the latter, Clemente de Metternich (1815), had agreed to unify their interests under the so-called "Sacred Alliance," hoping to fortify the absolutist monarchies and, consequently, to combat the ideas of liberalism. For its part, Spain, led by Fernando VII, relied on the armies of this reactionary coalition and sought to defeat the Spanish liberals, defenders of the Constitución de Cádiz (1812). This same political strife tried to implant itself in the newly liberated ex-colonies of Spain.

In 1822 events occurred that brought about, as a consequence, the need for the North American government to take a position with respect to the power of the Sacred Alliance, over which France now ruled, led by Louis VIII. In August, the plenipotentiary ministry of the United States communicated the following: "The English government has invited us to make a joint declaration against the powers of the Sacred Alliance."

At the insistence of the Secretary of State, John Quincy Adams, the fifth president of the United States, James Monroe, included in the annual message delivered to Congress the second of December, 1823, the following statement: "With the existing colonies or dependencies of any European power we have not interfered and shall not interfere. But with the Governments who have declared their independence and maintained it, and whose independence we have, on great consideration and on just principles, acknowledged, we could not view any interposition for the purpose of oppressing them, or controlling in any other manner their destiny, by any European power in any other light than as the manifestation of an unfriendly disposition toward the United States."

The political and military events of the American continent demonstrated how such a declaration could be manipulated in order to justify the imperialistic comportment of the United States, itself. The principal manifestation of this tendency was to assume the role of protector of the young Hispano-American nations, and under this pretext, to intervene in their politics and determine their destinies. Along with this political act that helped the United States to obtain in practice its recognition as a capitalist power at the international level, it's worth mentioning the governing character that the Monroe Doctrine has held ever since in the relations of this great power with the Hispano-American nations.*

*Palacios, Mario Alfonso Rodriguez. *México en la historia: tercer grado, educación secundaria.* Mexico City: Editorial Trillas, 1992, 50–51.

Lapulapu and Magellan

–Steve Shalom

Stephen Rosskamm Shalom teaches political science at William Paterson University in Wayne, New Jersey, and writes political analysis and commentary. This piece originally appeared in Resistance in Paradise: Rethinking 100 Years of U.S. Involvement in the Caribbean and the Pacific, which was edited by Deborah Wei and Rachel Kammel and published by the American Friends Service Committee and Office of Curriculum Support, School District of Philadelphia, in 1998.

On the small island of Mactan in the central Philippines, there are two plaques commemorating the same historical event. One plaque was erected in 1941 and is entitled "Ferdinand Magellan's Death." It reads:

> On this spot Ferdinand Magellan died on April 27, 1521, wounded in an encounter with the soldiers of Lapulapu, chief of Mactan Island. One of Magellan's ships, the *Victoria*, under the command of Juan Sebastian Elcano, sailed from Cebu on May 1, 1521, and anchored at San Lucar de Barrameda on September 6, 1522, thus completing the first circumnavigation of the earth.

The second plaque was erected in 1951 and is entitled "Lapulapu." It reads:

> Here, on 27 April 1521, Lapulapu and his men repulsed the Spanish invaders, killing their leader, Ferdinand Magellan. Thus, Lapulapu became the first Filipino to have repelled European aggression.

Sometimes people say things that are simply untrue. But the information on both of these plaques is accurate: each one is describing a different aspect of the historical truth. Anyone who wants to study history has to learn to sort out truth from falsehood. Beyond that, however, it is also important to recognize that depending on their point of view, people might emphasize different aspects of an event.

Reprinted by permission from *Resistance in Paradise: Rethinking 100 Years of U.S. Involvement in the Caribbean and the Pacific*, Deborah Wei and Rachael Kamel, Eds. Philadelphia: American Friends Service Committee and Office of Curriculum Support, School District of Philadelphia, 1998.

In the case of the two plaques on Mactan, the first one was erected in 1941, when the Philippines was still a U.S. colony. The second plaque was put up in 1951, after the Philippines became a formally independent country. Think about the difference between these two plaques in how the facts are presented. How might the change in the political status of the Philippines have affected the wording of the plaques?

Mass Media: For the Many, by the Few

–Michael Parenti

Author and lecturer Michael Parenti received his Ph.D. in political science from Yale University and has taught at a number of colleges and universities in the United States and abroad. The following article is taken from his widely used college text, Democracy for the Few, *published by Thomson Wadsworth in 2002 and now in its seventh edition.*

The mainstream media claim to be free and independent, objective and neutral, the "watchdogs of democracy." A closer look suggests that they too often behave like the lapdogs of plutocracy.

He Who Pays the Piper

The major news media or press (the terms are used interchangeably here), consisting of newspapers, magazines, radio, films, and television, are an inherent component of corporate America, being themselves highly concentrated conglomerates. As of 2000, eight corporate conglomerates controlled most of the national media—down from twenty-three in 1989. About 80 percent of the daily newspaper circulation in the United States belongs to a few giant chains like Gannett and Knight-Ridder, and the trend in owner concentration continues unabated. Today less than 2 percent of U.S. cities have competing newspapers under separate ownership.[1]

Six major companies distribute virtually all the magazines sold on newsstands. Eight corporate conglomerates control most of the book-sales revenues, and a few bookstore chains enjoy over 70 percent of book sales. A handful of companies and banks control the movie industry. Four giant networks, ABC, CBS, NBC, and Fox, dominate the television industry, and a handful of corporations command most of the nation's radio audience.[2] NBC is owned by General Electric, Capital Cities/ABC by Disney, and CBS by Westinghouse. Jack Welch, CEO of General

From *Democracy for the Few*, 7th ed., by Michael Parenti. © 2002. Reprinted with permission of Wadsworth, a division of Thomson Learning: www.thomsonrights.com Fax 800 730-2215.

Electric, is a conservative who agreed to bankroll the rightist *McLaughlin Group.* Michael Jordan, head of CBS-Westinghouse, is a rightist who has spoken out against government regulations of the free market. Fox network is owned by right-wing billionaire and media mogul Rupert Murdoch, who bankrolls the *Weekly Standard,* a right-wing opinion magazine, and whose Fox News Channel reportedly quizzed journalistic applicants on whether they were registered Republicans or not.[3]

Banks such as Morgan Guaranty Trust and Citibank are among the major stockholders of networks. Representatives of powerful corporations—including IBM, Ford, General Motors, and Mobil Oil—sit on the boards of all the major networks and publications. The media conglomerates own not only television networks but other lucrative holdings such as cable companies, book publishing houses, magazines, newspapers, movie studios, satellite television, and radio stations.[4]

Over the last two decades, the broadcast industry has used its immense lobbying power to kill what few regulations were in place to protect diversity and public interest programming. It spent more than $100 million to secure passage of the 1996 Telecommunications Act, which permits a single company to own television stations serving more than one-third of the U.S. public. By lifting restrictions on the sale of media properties, the act was supposed to bring a flowing of competition that would give consumers greater choice, lower cable prices, and cheaper local phone service.

In fact, within three years, cable rates had risen 21 percent and local phone rates 10 percent. And now, one company can own up to six radio stations and two television stations in a single city (as opposed to the previous restriction of one radio and one TV outlet in any one market). Consequently, since 1996 there have been over a thousand mergers of radio companies, with over half of the nation's eleven thousand radio stations being bought up by large conglomerates. The upshot is fewer independent commentators with an alternative perspective on world affairs and community issues; and more "hate radio" types who spew their venom against feminists, ethnic minorities, the homeless, gays, labor unions, and environmentalists.[5]

Media owners do not hesitate to exercise control over news content. They frequently kill stories they dislike and in other ways inject their own preferences. As one group of investigators reported: "The owners and managers of the press determine which person, which facts, which version of the facts, and which ideas shall reach the public."[6] In recent times, media bosses have refused to run advertisements, stories, or commentaries that advocated single-payer health insurance, criticized U.S. military intervention in other countries, or opposed the North American Free Trade Agreement (NAFTA).

Corporate advertisers are another influential group who leave their political imprint on media content. They might cancel advertising accounts not only when they feel that the reporting reflects poorly on their product, but also when they disapprove of what they perceive as a "liberal" drift in news and commentary. Network bosses are keenly aware of the control exercised by business sponsors. To quote former president of CBS Frank Stanton, "Since we are advertiser-supported we must take into account the general objective and desires of advertisers as a whole."[7] The prize-winning *Kwitney Report*, a PBS news show that revealed U.S. backing of death squads and dictators in Central America and other hot issues, went off the air because it could not procure corporate funding.[8] Lowell Bergman, former producer of *60 Minutes*, says news producers "are finding it more and more difficult to do pieces that are critical of Fortune 500 companies, or of sponsors or suppliers to the network."[9]

Journalists can sometimes slip unusually critical information into stories, but if they persist, their reports are spiked, they are reassigned, and soon their careers are at risk. The media boss controls the journalist, not the other way around. Media chiefs have canceled radio and television shows, such as Michael Moore's *TV Nation*, that contained relatively mild and flippant critiques of big companies. Jim Hightower's populist commentaries played on more than two hundred ABC radio affiliates until canceled by Disney soon after it took over ABC in 1997. (Hightower has managed to reappear on a smaller number of independent stations.)

Television journalists Steve Wilson and Jane Akre lost their jobs after doing an investigative series on the dangers of hormones fed to cows, a report that Wilson and Akre say a Fox affiliate in Tampa, Florida, refused to run because it offended Monsanto. Mike Gallagher was let go by the *Cincinnati Enquirer* after reporting that Chiquita banana company sprayed its Latin American workers with pesticides, bribed Colombian officials, and smuggled cocaine in banana boats. Controversy developed around *how* Gallagher obtained his information (he pilfered some voicemail tapes), not whether the reports were true.[10]

There are other examples: An *Atlanta Journal-Constitution* reporter was forced to resign after running stories that annoyed Coca-Cola and Atlanta banks, whose racist practices had been exposed. A consumer reporter was let go by KCBS-TV in Los Angeles after automotive advertisers repeatedly complained to his bosses about his critical reports on car safety. A writer was pressured out of his job at *Fortune* magazine after publicizing the exorbitant income received by the head of Time Warner, *Fortune*'s owner. For a series of reports on the abuses of corporate America, Frances Cerra of the *New York Times* incurred the ire of her editors and was transferred to a Long Island beat. There she wrote articles on Shorham nuclear power plant that contained some information running counter to the pronuclear editorial stance of the *Times*. Her final story was suppressed as "biased"; it reported that the plant was in serious financial trouble—which proved true. Cerra was never given a new assignment.[11]

Compare the above cases to the treatment accorded ABC correspondent John Stossel, who suddenly announced that government regulation of business led to no good and that "it is my job to explain the beauties of the free market." Instead of being reprimanded for his lack of objectivity, Stossel was given a starring role in numerous TV specials to promote his laissez-faire ideology.[12]

Working journalists are instructed to remain "neutral" when performing their tasks. Meanwhile the openly active partisan role that media *owners* play in political affairs, including attending fundraisers and state dinners, contributing to campaigns, and socializing with high-ranking officeholders, is not seen as violating journalistic standards of independence and objectivity.

Newspeople who consistently support the worldview of global capitalism and the national security state are the ones more likely to be rewarded with choice assignments, raises, bonuses, and promotions to editor and bureau chief. There are additional blandishments, such as lucrative honoraria from moneyed interests. How objective can David Broder be about Wall Street corruption after receiving $6,000 for a speech to the American Stock Exchange? How alert can William Safire be to price-gouging among utility companies after pocketing a $15,000 speaker's fee from Southern Electric? One might recall how the Shah of Iran, a dictator and torturer detested by most of his people, received glowing press in the United States for twenty-five years. More than five hundred journalists, newscasters, editors, and publishers, including such notables as Marvin Kalb and David Brinkley, were recipients of the Shah's gifts and invited to his lavish parties. Journalists who wrote critically of him did not make the gift list.[13]

On infrequent occasions, the news media will go against a strong corporate interest and give tentative exposure to consumer and environmental issues, as with the exposés on how the tobacco industry conspired to hook smokers by inserting more nicotine in cigarettes, and how smoking causes cancer. Of course, we knew about the link between smoking and cancer for over half a century. The press and policymakers took their time in giving the issue the attention it deserved, even then only after a growing public outcry and numerous class action suits against Big Tobacco.

A host of other consumer issues such as carcinogens in cosmetics, radioactive materials in products sold on the market, the use of industrial waste sludge as fertilizers, and the unsafe quality of so many prescription and over-the-counter drugs, along with manifold issues relating to the environment, still do not get the attention they deserve.

The Ideological Monopoly

Across the country, newspapers offer little variety in perspective and editorial policy, ranging mostly from moderately conservative to ultraconservative, with a smaller number that are blandly centrist. Most "independent" dailies, along with the chains, rely heavily on the wire services and on big circulation papers for stories, syndicated columns, and special features.

Despite conservative complaints about a liberal media, surveys show that Washington journalists, while more liberal on "cultural issues" such as abortion and school prayer, are decidedly more conservative on economic issues. They are more than twice as likely to support NAFTA and free trade, and far more in favor of trimming Medicare and Social Security.[14] In any case, as already noted, more important than the working journalists in shaping news content are the rich conservatives who own and control the major media.

News reports on business rely almost entirely on business sources. The workings of the capitalist political economy remain virtually unmentioned. The tendency toward chronic instability, recession, inflation, and underemployment; the transference of corporate diseconomies onto the public—these and other such problems are treated superficially, if at all, by pundits who have neither the inclination nor the freedom to offer critical observations about our capitalist paradise. Poverty remains an unexplained phenomenon in the media. Whether portraying the poor as unworthy idlers or simple unfortunates, the press seldom if ever gives critical attention to the market forces that create and victimize low-income people.

The press has failed to explain the real impact of the national debt and how it has generated an upward redistribution of income, as working people must pay back the money that government borrows from the rich. Almost nothing has been said in the mainstream media about how corporate America feeds from the public trough or how it harasses environmental activists and whistle-blowing employees; almost nothing on how the oil, gas, and nuclear interests have stalled the development of alternative and renewable energy sources such as solar power.[15]

Media coverage of electoral campaigns also leaves much to be desired, focusing mostly on the contest per se, on who will run, who will win, and what campaign ploys are effective—with relatively little if any focus on policy content. News commentators act more like theater critics, reviewing the candidate's performance and style. One study found that more than two-thirds of campaign coverage centers on insider strategy and political maneuvering rather than substantive issues.[16]

Progressive candidates who try to develop a plausible image among the electorate find themselves dependent for exposure on mass media that are owned by the same conservative interests they are attacking. They compete not only against well-financed opponents but also against the media's many frivolous and stupefying distractions. Hoping to educate the public to the issues, they discover that the media allow little or no opportunity for them to make their position understandable to voters who might be willing to listen. The sheer paucity of information can make meaningful campaign dialogue nearly impossible. By withholding coverage of minor-party candidates while bestowing it lavishly on major-party ones, the media help perpetuate the two-party monopoly.

The press has helped create the "lock-'em-up" crime craze throughout America. Between 1993 and 1996 the nationwide homicide rate dropped by 20 percent, yet coverage of murders on the ABC, CBS, and NBC evening news leaped 721 percent. As a result, the number of U.S. residents who ranked crime as the prime problem jumped sixfold.[17] Corporate crime, however, is another story, largely an unreported one. Recent surveys show that mainstream media rarely express critical editorial opinions on corporate crimes.[18]

Instead of treating affirmative action as an attempt to redress the effects of long-standing racism and sexism, the media has consistently misled the public on the issue, overlooking the persistence of racism in many walks of life, and leaving people with the impression that African Americans are enjoying special privileges at the expense of Whites.[19]

Every evening, network news studios faithfully report stock-exchange averages, but stories deemed important to organized labor are scarcely ever touched. There are no daily reports about the number of workers injured or maimed on the job. Reporters seldom enlist labor's views on national questions. On the ABC opinion show *Nightline*, corporate leaders appeared seven times more frequently than labor representatives. Workers are virtually never interviewed as knowledgeable sources regarding work issues. Unions are usually noticed only when they go on strike, but the issues behind the strike, such as occupational safety or loss of benefits, are rarely acknowledged. The misleading impression is that labor simply turns down "good contracts" because it wants too much. Unions make "demands" while management makes "offers." Most newspapers have large staffs for business news but not a single labor reporter. Strikes and demonstrations are given sympathetic and generous coverage when they occur in communist countries.

The "expert" guests appearing on newscasts are predominantly government officials (or former officials), corporate heads, and members of conservative think tanks, along with a sprinkling of conservative "New Democrats," who sound not too different from the others. Likewise, of the hundreds of mainstream editorialists, TV pundits, radio talk-show hosts, and syndicated columnists who crowd the communication universe, a small number are lukewarm "liberals." A typical example would be syndicated columnist Anthony Lewis, who accurately describes himself as "a pro-capitalist, middle-of-the-road tepid centrist" who supported George Bush's destruction of Iraq and Clinton's destruction of Yugoslavia, and who denounced unions for lobbying against NAFTA.[20] Other media "liberal" commentators and columnists who are hailed as representing the "left," such as Sam Donaldson, Cokie Roberts, Juan Williams, and Bob Beckel (a corporate lobbyist) have virtually nothing to say about progressive issues and corporate profiteering. When not chattering endlessly and superficially about insider strategies and public personalities, most "liberal" pundits boost the blessings of globalization, and support the national security state and U.S. interventionism with a hawkish fervor that sometimes outdoes their conservative counterparts.[21]

Citizens who utilize their democratic rights under the First Amendment by launching protests usually are given short shrift by the news media. For instance, the tens of thousands of people who demonstrated against the World Trade Organization (WTO) in Seattle in 1999 were characterized as misinformed zealots, violence-prone marginal figures, and "flat-earthers." Globalization is treated as a benign, equitable, and inevitable process, rather than a transnational corporate strategy to roll back the public regulations and democratic protections of every domestic economy in the world.[22]

Official Manipulation

Scores of "independent" and "objective" journalists have moved back and forth in their careers between media and government, in what has been called the "revolving door." David Gergen served in the Nixon, Ford, Reagan, and Clinton administrations, and in between was an editor at *U.S. News and World Report* and a PBS commentator. Pat Buchanan was a Nixon staff writer, a columnist and TV opinion-show host for CNN, a Reagan staffer, then a CNN host again.[23] The CEO of National Public Radio, Kevin Klose, is a former chief of all the major government propaganda agencies: Voice of America, Radio Free Europe, Radio Liberty, and Radio Marti. NPR has little to say that is critical of U.S. foreign policy and the national security state. The head of the Corporation for Public Broadcasting, Robert Coonrod, has a resumé strikingly similar to Klose's, from Voice of America to Radio Marti.[24]

Press reports about State Department and Pentagon policies rely heavily on State Department and Pentagon releases. Press coverage of the space program is regularly supportive with scarcely a word given to the program's critics. Little if any positive exposure is afforded anti-imperialist struggles throughout the world or domestic protests against U.S. overseas interventions against Third World peoples. Demonstrators and agitators who violently attack democratically elected governments in countries that resist the total embrace of the free market, such as post-communist Bulgaria and Yugoslavia, are hailed as purveyors of democracy and given lavish coverage, and are never condemned for their violence. Far from being vigilant critics of government policy, most news organizations act more like mouthpieces for officialdom's counterrevolutionary, free-market globalism.

The corporate media, along with NPR and PBS, portrayed the Vietnam War, the invasion of Grenada, the invasion of Panama, the destruction of Iraq, the destruction of Yugoslavia, and the growing U.S. intervention against revolutionary guerrillas in Colombia as arising from noble intentions, with no mention given to the underlying class interests and little attention to the horrendous devastation wreaked by U.S. forces upon the peoples of those countries.

The U.S. press ignored the slaughter of some 500,000 Indonesians by the U.S.-supported militarists of that country, and the genocidal campaign waged by those same militarists in East Timor. The media made scant mention of the massive repression of dissident peasants, workers, clergy, students, and intellectuals in Uruguay, Guatemala, El Salvador, Zaire, the Philippines, and dozens of other U.S.-supported procapitalist regimes. Ever faithful to the official line, press coverage is energetically negative toward leftist movements and governments while being supportive of right-wing procapitalist ones and having little ill to say of the Central Intelligence Agency (CIA)–supported counterrevolutionary mercenary forces, as in Angola, Mozambique, and Nicaragua, whose campaigns have taken hundreds of thousands of lives.[25]

Also unreported is the widespread U.S.-supported terrorism in scores of countries, utilizing death squads, massacres, and mass detentions. Human rights violations in noncapitalist countries like China, Tibet, and North Korea are given wide play, while longstanding bloody and repressive violations in Turkey, Honduras, Indonesia, and dozens of other U.S.-supported, free-market countries receive scant notice.[26]

The media remain largely supportive when U.S. presidents invade or bomb other countries. The press often chooses to act "responsibly" by not informing the public about U.S. covert actions and other questionable policies abroad and at home. Journalistic responsibility should mean the unearthing of truthful information no matter how troubling it be to the established powers. But the "responsibility" demanded by government officials and often agreed to by the news media means the opposite—the burying of troublesome information precisely because it is true.

Sometimes media opinionmakers are quite blatant in their partisan expressions. During the 1999 U.S./NATO bombing of Yugoslavia, which killed hundreds of innocent civilians and wrecked that country's entire economy, without the loss of a single American life, CBS Evening News Anchor Dan Rather declared: "I'm an American, and I'm an American reporter. And yes, when there's combat involving Americans, you can criticize me if you must, damn me if you must, but I'm always pulling for us to win." Is Rather saying that he supports any U.S. one-sided slaughter regardless of the costs and immoral horrors perpetrated, regardless of the actual merits of the issues involved?[27] He sounds less like a dispassionate, objective newsperson and more like a jingoistic cheerleader.

More than four hundred U.S. journalists, including nationally syndicated columnists, editors, and some major publishers, have carried out covert assignments for the CIA over the last four decades, gathering intelligence abroad or publishing the kind of stories that create a climate of opinion supportive of the CIA's interventionist objectives. Included are personnel from the *Washington Post*, CBS, NBC, ABC, *Newsweek*, the *Wall Street Journal*, the Associated Press, and prominent press moguls such as William Paley, erstwhile head of CBS; Henry Luce, late owner of Time Inc.; and Arthur Hays Sulzberger, late publisher of the *New York Times*. The CIA has owned more than 240 media operations around the world, including newspapers, magazines, publishing houses, radio and television stations, and wire services. Many Third World countries get more news from the CIA and other such Western sources than from Third World news organizations.[28]

In a series of deeply researched articles in the *San Jose Mercury News*, Gary Webb exposed the CIA's involvement in the drug traffic between the contras (U.S.-supported mercenary troops in Central America) and inner-city dealers in the United States. The series confirmed the worst suspicions of African-American community leaders and set off a firestorm of controversy. Webb was swiftly subjected to a barrage of counterattacks from the *Washington Post, New York Times, Los Angeles Times*, and the major TV networks. They accused him of saying things he had not said. They focused on a few minor speculative points not firmly established while ignoring the more damning and well-substantiated heart of the investigation. And they unquestioningly accepted the CIA's claim that it was not involved in drug trafficking. Eventually, Webb's editor caved in to the pressure, making a public self-criticism for having published the series. Webb left the *Mercury News* soon after. A subsequent report by the CIA itself largely confirmed his charges.[29]

In 1998 CNN producers April Oliver and Jack Smith ran a story accusing the U.S. military of using sarin, a highly lethal nerve gas, in an operation behind enemy lines in Laos in 1970 that killed about one hundred people, including two American defectors. An immediate and vitriolic storm of abuse came down upon Oliver and Smith from the Pentagon and the major media. CNN hastily issued a fawning retraction and fired the two producers. The story's lead reporter, distinguished newsman Peter Arnett, was reprimanded and ultimately left the network because of the controversy. Oliver and Smith put together a seventy-seven-page document showing that their story was based entirely on testimony by U.S. airmen and other military personnel, including participants in the operation who stood by their stories.[30] Oliver has sued CNN for being wrongfully fired.

Government manipulation of the press is a constant enterprise. Officials give choice leads to sympathetic journalists and withhold information from troublesome ones. They meet regularly with media bosses to discuss or complain about specific stories. And every day the White House, the Pentagon, and other agencies release thousands of self-serving reports to the media, many of which are then uncritically transmitted to the public as news from independent sources.

The Justice Department won a Supreme Court decision allowing the government to issue subpoenas requiring newspeople to disclose their sources to grand-jury investigators, in effect reducing the press to an investigative arm of the very officialdom over whom it is supposed to act as a watchdog. The *New York Times* reassured its readers that "subpoenas are rarely issued to journalists in the United States." But one study found that more than 3,500 subpoenas were served on members of the news media in one year alone.[31] Dozens of reporters who wish to protect their sources have been jailed or threatened with prison terms for trying to protect their sources by refusing to hand over materials and tapes. Such government coercion creates a chilling effect, encouraging the press to avoid trouble from officialdom by censoring itself.

* * *

Room for Alternatives?

In sum, the media are neither objective nor honest in their portrayal of important issues. The news is a product not only of deliberate manipulation but of the ideological and economic power structure under which journalists operate and into which they are socialized.

The Fairness Law required that time be given to an opposing viewpoint after a station broadcasted an editorial opinion. But it made no requirement as to the diversity of the opposing viewpoints, so usually the range was between two only slightly different stances. The "Fairness Doctrine," as it was known, often was unfairly applied. The Federal Communications Commission (FCC) ruled that no broadcast time need be made available to "communists or the communist viewpoint" but only to "controversial issues of public importance on which persons other than communists hold contrasting views."[32] President Reagan vetoed Congress's attempt to extend the life of the Fairness Doctrine in 1987. Opponents of the law argue that it is an infringement on the freedom of the press, since it forces a private broadcaster to give time to an opposing viewpoint. Thus it also has a chilling effect on opinions, since owners will refrain from expressing their views because of the obligation to accommodate competing ones. But the airwaves are the property of the people of the United States and should be open to divergent views.

The Public Broadcasting Act of 1967 launched the Public Broadcasting System (PBS) as a public television alternative to commercial TV. Instead of being independently financed by a sales tax on television sets or by some other method, PBS was made dependent on annual appropriations from Congress and was run by a board appointed by the president. PBS and National Public Radio (NPR) are now required to match federal funds with money from other sources. Viewer or listener contributions are solicited to pay for operational costs. The programs themselves are financed by large corporations. Not surprisingly, both NPR and PBS offer public affairs shows populated by commentators and guest "experts" who are as ideologically conservative and politically safe as any found on the commercial networks.

Of the many interesting documentaries made by independent producers dealing with important and controversial political issues, few if any gain access to mainstream movie houses or major television networks. Thus, the documentary *Faces of War*, revealing the U.S.-supported counterinsurgency destruction visited upon the people of El Salvador, was denied broadcast rights in twenty-two major television markets. The award-winning *Building Bombs* and the exposé on the Iran-contra affair, *Coverup*, were denied access to PBS and all commercial channels. In 1991, *Deadly Deception*, a documentary critical of General Electric and the environmental devastation wreaked by the nuclear weapons industry, won the Academy Award, yet, with a few local exceptions, it was shut out of commercial and public television. So too with the Academy Award–winning documentary *Panama Deception*, which offered a critical exposé of the U.S. invasion of Panama.

Many areas of the country are awash in talk shows and news commentary that are outspokenly ultrarightist, procapitalist, militaristic, anti-union, anti-feminist, and anti-immigrant. Wealthy conservatives have poured millions of dollars into building the religious right's radio network, consisting of 1,300 local stations, and its television network, the Christian Broadcasting Network, which has as many affiliates as ABC. There is a significant religious left in this country, dedicated to peace and social justice issues, but it gets no substantial financial backing and therefore owns no major media outlets.

Denied access to major media, the political left has attempted to get its message across through small publications that suffer chronic financial difficulties and sometimes undergo harassment from police, the Federal Bureau of Investigation, rightist vigilantes, the Internal Revenue Service, and the U.S. Postal Service. Skyrocketing postal rates effect a real hardship on dissident publications. While defending such increases as economically necessary, the government continues to subsidize billions of pieces of junk mail sent out every year by business and advertising firms.

Pacifica network's five radio outlets and other community- and listener-sponsored stations sometimes offer alternative political perspectives (along with a great deal of cultural esoterica and conventional mainstream views). The Pacifica board of directors, as of 2000 dominated by persons unfriendly toward progressive radio, now seems determined to neutralize the few remaining dissident voices on the member stations and turn Pacifica into another NPR.[33]

A growing movement of mostly poor and inner-city individuals and communities across the country have set up unlicensed "microradio" FM stations, which have far less than one hundred watts of power and transmit in a limited radius of one to five miles. Microradio advocates argue that they are public space and their broadcast outlets are too small to interfere with the larger signals. The real threat they pose is that low-income people and other dissidents might use the airwaves to voice heterodox views. After much struggle by microradio broadcasters, the FCC reluctantly approved low-power FM signals in 2000. But the National Association of Broadcasters, the trade group representing most of the corporate media, lobbied hard to have all microstations suppressed. A measure was passed by Congress, prohibiting the FCC from licensing microstations until further study, supposedly to insure that microradio does not interfere with major broadcasting.[34]

There are sometimes limits to how the media can suppress and distort events since reality itself is radical. The Third World really is poor and exploited; the U.S. government really does side with the rich oligarchs; real wages actually have declined for many workers; corporations do wield enormous power, plunder and pollute the environment, and downsize their workforce while reaping record profits. To maintain its credibility, the press must occasionally report some of these realities. When it does, the rightists complain bitterly about a "liberal bias." Furthermore, the press is not entirely immune to more democratic and popular pressure. If, despite the media's misrepresentation and neglect, a well-organized and persistent public opinion builds around an issue, while not attacking the capitalist system as a system, it occasionally can break through the media sound barrier.

If we consider censorship to be a danger to our freedom, then we should not overlook the fact that the media are already heavily censored by those who own or advertise in them. Public television and radio should be funded by the public rather than by rich corporations and foundations who get to impose their own ideological preferences while writing off the costs as a tax deduction. Public law should require all newspapers and broadcasting stations to allot space and time to a diverse array of political opinion, including the most progressive and revolutionary. But given the interests the government serves, this is not a likely development.

Ultimately the only protection against monopoly control of the media is ownership by the people themselves, with legal provisions allowed for the inclusion of a broad spectrum of conflicting views. This is not as chimerical or radical as it sounds. In the early 1920s, before it was taken over by commercial interests, radio consisted primarily of hundreds of not-for-profit stations run mostly by colleges, universities, labor unions, and community groups.[35]

Today more community-supported radio stations and public access cable television stations are needed. The microradio station should be encouraged, for it is among the most democratic of media, requiring almost no capital while being relatively more accessible to the community in which it operates. The Internet also offers a wide range of progressive websites that provide information and opinion rarely accommodated by mainstream media.

Those who own the newspapers and networks will not relinquish their hold over private investments and public information. Ordinary citizens will have no access to the mass media until they can gain control over the material resources that could give them such access, an achievement that would take a different kind of economic and social system than the corporate "free market" we have. In the meantime, Americans should have no illusions about the "free and independent press" they are said to enjoy.

NOTES

1. Dean Alger, *Megamedia: How Giant Corporations Dominate Mass Media, Distort Competition, and Endanger Democracy* (Lanham, Md.: Rowman & Littlefield, 1998); Arthur Rowse, *Drive-By Journalism* (Monroe, Maine: Common Courage, 2000); Ben Bagdikian, *The Media Monopoly*, 5th ed. (Boston: Beacon, 1997).

2. For a partial list, see *Nation*, March 17, 1997, 23–26.

3. "From the Top," *Extra!*, July/August 1998.

4. Alger, *Megamedia*, passim. *Nation*, March 17, 1997. For a detailed account of a network takeover, see Dennis Mazzocco, *Networks of Power* (Boston: South End, 1994).

5. Daniel Zoll, "Radio Rat Poison," *San Francisco Bay Guardian*, September 20, 2000; Molly Ivins, "Surprise! Telecom Act Is a Disaster," *San Francisco Chronicle*, March 16, 1999.

6. Report by the Commission on Freedom of the Press, quoted in Robert Cirino, *Don't Blame the People* (New York: Vintage, 1972), 47; also Michael Parenti, *Inventing Reality: The Politics of News Media*, 2nd ed. (New York: St. Martin's, 1993), 33–35, 47, 59.

7. Quoted in Eric Barnouw, *The Sponsor* (New York: Oxford University Press, 1978), 57.

8. Jonathan Kwitney, telephone conversation with Michael Parenti, March 1992.

9. Interview with *MediaFile*, publication of Media Alliance, January/February 2000.

10. Herb Kaye, "'Freedom of the Press'—for Publishers," *People's Weekly World*, August 22, 1998.

11. "Where's the Power: Newsroom or Boardroom?" *Extra!*, July/August 1998; *Fear and Favor in the Newsroom*, documentary film, California Newsreel, San Francisco, KQED-TV, November 12, 1998.

12. "Where's the Power: Newsroom or Boardroom?" *Extra!*, July/August 1998.

13. Burling Lowrey, "The Media's Honoraria," *Washington Post*, April 26, 1989; William Dorman, "Favors Received," *Nation*, October 11, 1980.

14. David Croteau, "Challenging the 'Liberal Media' Claim," *Extra!*, July/August 1998.

15. Carl Jensen (ed.), *America's CENSORED Newsletter*, December 1992.

16. Todd Purdum in *New York Times*, January 13, 1999.

17. According to Vincent Schiraldi, director of Justice Policy Institute, cited in David McGowan, *Derailing Democracy* (Monroe, Maine: Common Courage, 2000), 60.

18. Survey by Morton Mintz in *Nieman Reports*, July 2000.

19. Robert Entman, "The Color Game: How Media Play the Race Card," *Newswatch*, Summer 1999.

20. "Who Gets to Speak?" *Extra!*, July/August 1998; Doug Ireland, "Unfit to Print," *Nation*, July 28–August 4, 1997; Norman Solomon and Jeff Cohen, *Wizards of Media Oz: Behind the Mainstream News* (Monroe, Maine: Common Courage, 1997).

21. "Field Guide to TVs Lukewarm Liberals," *Extra!*, July/August 1998.

22. William Solomon, "More Form Than Substance: Press Coverage of the WTO Protests in Seattle," *Monthly Review*, May 2000. On how the media misrepresented NAFTA, see Edward Herman, "Mexican Meltdown," Z *Magazine*, September 1995.

23. "Journalists at Work: Who's Watching the Watchdogs?" *Alternative Press Review*, Spring/Summer 1998, and ⟨http://www.pir.org⟩.

24. William Blum, *Rogue State* (Monroe, Maine: Common Courage, 2000), 10.

25. Parenti, *Inventing Reality*, passim; and Blum, *Rogue State*, passim.

26. See the discussion and citations in Chapter 7.

27. Rather quoted and criticized in Blum, *Rogue State*, 10.

28. Sean Gervasi, "CIA Covert Propaganda Capability," *CovertAction Information Bulletin*, December 1979/January 1980; Daniel Brandt, "Journalism and the CIA," *Alternative Press Review*, Spring/Summer 1998; Carl Bernstein, "The CIA and the Media," *Rolling Stone*, October 20, 1977.

29. Gary Webb, *Dark Alliance: The CIA, the Contras, and the Crack Cocaine Explosion* (New York: Seven Stories, 1998); and Jeffrey St. Clair et al., *The CIA, Drugs and the Press* (New York and London: Verso, 1998).

30. "Tailwind: Rebuttal to the Abrams/Kohler Report," posted July 22, 1998, ⟨http://www.freedomforum.org/fpfp/specialprograms/tailwind1.asp⟩; also April Oliver and Peter Arnett, "Did the U.S. Drop Nerve Gas?" *Time*, June 15, 1998.

31. *New York Times*, July 1, 1998; and study by Reporters Committee for Freedom of the Press, cited by Leib Dodell, letter to the editor, *New York Times*, July 8, 1998.

32. Federal Communications Commission, "Applicability of the Fairness Doctrine in the Handling of Controversial Issues of Public Importance," *Federal Register* 29, July 25, 1964, 10415 ff.

33. See bimonthly publication of *KPFA Folio*, Sonoma County Peace and Justice Center, California; also ⟨http://www.savepacifica.net/strike/⟩.

34. Ben Clarke, "NAB Moves to Kill Low Power FM," *San Francisco Bay Guardian*, September 20, 2000; see also ⟨http://www.freeradio.org⟩.

35. Robert McChesney, *Telecommunications, Mass Media and Democracy: The Battle for the Control of U.S. Broadcasting 1928–1935* (New York: Oxford University Press, 1993).

Questions for Thinking, Writing, and Discussion

1. What does it mean to say that maps are conventional? How does this impact on their accuracy and on their usefulness?

2. Why have critics suggested that the Mercator map was ethnocentric, colonialist, and racist? Explain why you agree and/or disagree with this characterization.

3. What, according to Janice Monk and Adriana Greenwood, are the gender issues with which we must be concerned when using certain kinds of statistics? Explain in detail how statistics can make women's participation in the economy invisible.

4. Both Chilla Bulbeck and Chandra Mohanty examine a number of terms which have been used to divide up the world. With respect to each of the terms or pairs of terms they consider, discuss the advantages and/or disadvantages of their use by considering to which aspects of reality they direct our attention.

5. Read several articles about international affairs in your daily newspaper and discuss the language they use to describe their topic in light of the essays by Chilla Bulbeck and Chandra Mohanty.

6. Article 6 illustrates how perspective and interests shape the way we see and describe events. Choose three moments in history and talk about the difference in the ways in which each of the participants might see and describe them.

7. In Article 8 Michael Parenti challenges the view that mainstream media in the United States are free, independent, neutral, and objective. What do you think are the most compelling pieces of evidence he offers in support of his claim that the media "often behaves like the lapdogs of plutocracy"? Do you think his article is persuasive?

8. What was the most interesting point or points made in this section of the book? Explain why you found it interesting and what additional questions it prompted you to ask or what research it prompted you to do.

Suggestions for Further Reading

Beneria, Lourdes. Toward a Greater Integration of Gender in Economics. *World Development*, Vol. 23 (1995), No. 11, pp. 1839–1850.

Beneria, Lourdes. The Enduring Debate over Unpaid Labor. *International Labour Review*, Vol. 138 (1999), No. 3, pp. 287–308.

Chomsky, Noam. *Media Control: The Spectacular Achievements of Propaganda*. Seven Stories Press, 2002.

Herman, Edward S. *Manufacturing Consent: The Political Economy of the Mass Media*. New York: Pantheon Books, 2002.

Huff, Darrell, and Irving Geis. *How to Lie with Statistics*. New York: W.W. Norton, 1993.

Kaiser, Ward L. *A New View of the World—A Handbook to The World Map: Peters Projection.* New York: Friendship Press, 1987.

Kaiser, Ward L., and Denis Wood. *Seeing Through Maps: The Power of Images to Shape Our View of the World.* Amherst, MA: ODT, Inc., 2001.

Loewen, James W. *Lies My Teacher Told Me: Everything Your American History Text Book Got Wrong.* New York: Touchstone Books, 1996.

McChesney, Robert, and John Nichols. *Our Media, Not Theirs: The Democratic Struggle Against Corporate Media.* Seven Stories Press, 2002.

Roy, Arundhati. "Peace Is War: The Collateral Damage of Breaking News." www.sarai.net/journal/reader.4.ht.

Thrower, Norman J.W. *Maps and Civilization: Cartography in Culture and Society.* Chicago: University of Chicago Press, 1999.

Turnbull, David. *Masons, Tricksters and Cartographers: Comparative Studies in the Sociology of Scientific and Indigenous Knowledge.* Harwood Academic Publishers, 2000.

Waring, Marilyn. *If Women Counted: A New Feminist Economics.* New York: Harper Collins, 1990.

Zinn, Howard. *A People's History of the United States.* New York: Perennial Classics, 2003.

part two

Colonialism and Its Legacy

The only thing worse than being occupied is being an occupier.
L. Paul Bremer III, Chief Administrator of Occupied Iraq

When I was a young girl going to school in the fifties, with the exception of Europe, we didn't spend a lot of time studying other parts of the world. I do remember, however, an assignment that we had in fifth grade. One day we were presented with a map of Africa and on the very next, we were given a map of Latin America. Although the borders of the countries were outlined, neither map included any place names. Our homework assignment? To indicate the natural resources in each country. I remember using a scrap of foil from a gum wrapper to stand for silver, some match sticks to indicate timber, and a variety of other ordinary things to stand for the wealth of minerals, gem stones, sugar, spices, oil, fruits, and other riches that each continent possessed. This fairly typical grade school assignment tells us a lot about U.S. foreign policy in the fifties and the relationship between the United States and certain other parts of the world. As I have written elsewhere, "having completed this survey of resources to exploit, we evidently had learned all that it was necessary to know about our neighbors near and far."*

Some 34 years later, while attending an afterschool conference with my daughter's second-grade teacher, I found myself staring at a world map that hung on the wall behind her desk. From a distance, I could see that while none of the continents were divided into countries, some parts of the world, namely Europe and the United States, were covered with the names of cities. Other parts of the map were virtually empty. For example, the entire continent of Africa was bare except for the names of a handful of cities along the coastline and the name "Johannesburg" printed down near the bottom of what I knew to be South Africa. In other words, part of the world, namely the West, was portrayed as alive with activity while other parts were portrayed as a vast and empty wasteland. When I questioned the teacher about the map, she explained that the children were too young to digest a lot of information, so only the names of important places were listed. How little things had changed! *Important* to whom one might ask? Evidently the important places in Africa (and in other parts of the world as well) continued to be port cities where ships could dock, their hulls filled with manufactured goods seeking a market and depart, their hulls filled with the raw materials of the continent.

It is no accident then that we begin our study of global issues by looking at colonialism and its legacy. As the articles in this section make clear, it is impossible to understand the world that we inhabit in the first decade of the twenty-first century without attending to the colonial past that has shaped it. The vast inequalities of wealth and power that orchestrate relations between countries in the world today, the unrelenting poverty that is the reality of life for the majority of the world's people, the vastly different access to health care, education, and other social services enjoyed by people by virtue of an accident of birth, cannot be understood unless we place them in the context of colonization and its consequences for development. In fact, as Jerry Kloby observes in Article 4, "many of the major development problems

---

*Paula Rothenberg. *Invisible Privilege*. University Press of Kansas, 2000, p. 16.

that exist in the world today can be traced to the colonial relationships and economic arrangements that were forged during the period of colonization." They hold the key to understanding the present and to formulating policies that will bring us closer to an equitable future.

Although there were voyages of exploration before Columbus set sail in 1492, the age of conquest and colonization is generally agreed to have begun at that time and to have lasted approximately four centuries. During this period, England, France, Spain, Portugal, and Holland, the major European powers of the day, were engaged in extending their control to large portions of the world. They established colonies in Africa, India, the Far East, Oceana, and throughout the Western Hemisphere. While the early period of empire building, during which Portugal and Spain were dominant, emphasized looting gold and silver, it rapidly evolved into a more sophisticated and institutionalized form of expropriation which Felix Green describes in Article 2 as "the pillage of other countries' wealth through unequal trade and through investment which draws out far more wealth than it puts in." In this part of the text and in later sections we will examine both forms of domination and their consequences.

This section begins with an essay by William Appleman Williams, "Empire as a Way of Life," that offers definitions of some key terms: colonialism, imperialism, and empire, and examines the way in which empire as a way of life shapes the foreign policy and national character of a people. Not one to mince words, Williams, with a nod to English philosopher John Locke, tells us that "empire as a way of life involves taking wealth and freedom away from others to provide for your own welfare, pleasure, and power."

The challenge that faced the English and other European empire builders and U.S. imperialism somewhat later, was to find a way to justify this process. The ideological justification of empire has remained essentially the same throughout much of modern history, even as its packaging has undergone a fashion makeover from time to time. On the one hand, we find a rationale that emphasizes the importance of color, maintaining that those who are not white are inferior in a variety of ways and will benefit from control by the imperial power, and on the other hand, we have the rationale that stresses Christianity and the need to either convert or destroy "heathens" who are portrayed as agents of the devil. In the end, these two approaches are very much related since it usually turns out that those who are identified as heathen and godless for the most part happen to be dark skinned. Note that in either case, the imperial power invades, subdues, subordinates, and often enslaves an independent people, but always, allegedly, for their own benefit or because of their own imperfections.

In Article 2, "How It Began," Felix Green reminisces about his childhood in Britain and the then unshakable belief he held, along with his schoolmates, that the "vast medley" of people around the globe (India, Canada, Australia, New Zealand, a huge part of Africa, Samoa, Burma, Malaya, Hong Kong, the West Indies, and Ceylon) were ruled by the British because they wanted to be. Echoing Williams' theme he writes: "People who run empires have to be disingenuous, and they must not ask themselves too many questions. They need to have at their command a rhetoric of justification that . . . [will convince them] that they are doing humanity good."

In Article 3 Samir Amin offers an account of Eurocentrism, the worldview that both underlies and attempts to justify much of the behavior of the West toward peoples and countries in other parts of the world. At the heart of Eurocentrism is the belief that the European West is the best of cultures that the world has ever known, that its values, its science, its literature, its political and economic institutions represent the highest stage of development known to humanity. It comes with the corollary view that neither the East nor the South has anything of value to offer in this regard.

But in the end, colonialism is all about economics. The greater part of Felix Greene's essay is devoted to elaborating the material conditions, the features of industrialization in Britain, that made it possible for Britain to develop a global empire. He cites the development of new technology that brought Britain into the age of industrialization, the "availability" of a large supply of "cheap" labor, the accumulation of capital (which he defines as "wealth produced by the workers but expropriated from them"), and the development of foreign markets and the slave trade.

While Greene provides an overview of the economics of empire with respect to changing conditions in the imperial power that produce the economic basis for expansion, the selections by Jerry Kloby, Walter Rodney, and Eduardo Galeano offer graphic accounts of the way colonization was carried out in specific parts of the world. Kloby begins by examining the methods used by King Leopold II of Belgium in colonizing the Congo Free State, which he offers as a classic example of colonial domination's brutality. He then goes on to describe the nature of colonization under the French in West Africa and Southeast Asia (Indochina), and the British in India, Ireland, and China. Rodney surveys colonial domination throughout Africa, focusing his attention on the claim by some that in some ways colonialism was actually good for Africans. Rodney finds this claim utterly without merit and goes into great detail to challenge it. The map of Africa, Article 6, which follows shows that by 1914 the African content was virtually divided among seven European nations.

In Article 7 Eduard Galeano writes movingly about the impact of colonization throughout Latin America, painting a picture of "the rape of accumulated treasure" and "the systematic forced exploitation of the forced labor of Indians and abducted Africans in the mines" and suggests that it was Latin American gold and silver that made Europe's economic development possible. His description of the extraordinary riches looted by the colonizing powers and the wealthy and sophisticated cities that grew up during that time period provides a sharp contrast to the underdevelopment and poverty that characterizes much of the region today. For example, using the figures in an essay by Alexander von Humbolt, Galeano projects that the economic surplus taken from Mexico between 1760 and 1809 in the form of silver and gold exports would total some five billion present day dollars (and this calculation was made in the early 1970s, so the figure today would be considerably higher). All of this underscores the central point of Galeano's piece. He writes: "For those who see history as competition, Latin America's backwardness and poverty are merely the result of its failure. We lost; others won. But the winners happen to have won thanks to our losing; the history of Latin America's underdevelopment is, as someone has said, an integral part of the history of world capitalism's development."

Although the Rodney piece explicitly talks about the impact of colonialism on African women, much colonial history that is written fails to examine gender relations or even acknowledge gender as a category relevant to historical scholarship. In Article 8, Jan Jindy Pettman sets out to correct the absence of women from most conventional histories of colonization by examining what she calls "the sexual politics of colonialism and the race politics of gender." By this she means that the colonial powers made use of certain ideas about women and sexuality to control women's bodies and to reinforce the boundaries of race. Refusing to treat either colonizer or colonized women as homogenous groups, she inquires into the different roles and relationships and choices available to women within each group and complicates traditional accounts of colonialism by insisting that in order to be accurate and complete, this history must take account of the sexual politics of colonization.

It is interesting to read Article 9, Maria Mies' classic essay "The Myth of Catching-Up Development," in the context of Amin's description of Eurocentrism. In her essay, Mies challenges the assumption that underlies most development strategies, namely, the belief that every society should strive to achieve "the good life" as it is defined by the affluent societies of the United States, Europe, and Japan. In the course of surveying the history of underdeveloped countries in such vastly different areas as regions of the South, East Europe, and East Germany, Mies argues that the catching-up development path is a myth that has not proved successful when applied throughout the developing world. This is so because the accumulation model that has been employed in the North depends upon colonial exploitation and colonizing. She writes "This catching-up policy of the colonies is always a lost game. Because the very progress of the colonizers is based on the existence and exploitation of the colonies." In a passage reminiscent of the words of Eduardo Galeano, Mies argues that "the poverty of underdeveloped nations is not a result of 'natural' lagging behind but the direct consequence of the development of rich industrial countries who exploit the so-called periphery in Africa, South America and Asia."

Part Two ends with Vandana Shiva's "The Second Coming of Columbus," which is subtitled "Piracy Through Patents." She argues that more than 500 years after the initial period of colonial exploitation, a new and secular form of colonization is being carried out through the General Agreement on Tariffs and Trade (GATT) and other recent international "agreements" which give Western corporations the right to patent indigenous knowledge. According to Shiva, this is simply a new way to give Western powers control over the wealth of non-Western peoples.

one

Empire as a Way of Life

–William Appleman Williams

William Appleman Williams was born in Iowa and attended the U.S. Naval Academy. After serving in the Pacific in World War II, he attended graduate school at the University of Wisconsin where he received a Ph.D. in history. During his academic career he taught at both Wisconsin and Oregon State. The following article is taken from his book Empire as a Way of Life, *which was published by Oxford University Press in 1980.*

In order to think seriously about empire as a way of life, we must first choose a strategy of inquiry that is appropriate to the subject. Then we must define the basic terms involved, and outline the process whereby the different elements of society are integrated into an overall outlook and culture.

Let us begin with the concept, way of life. There are many ways to define this seemingly soft and fuzzy but nevertheless very tangible aspect of human existence. All cultures have recognized the reality of the phenomenon, and many people—philosophers as well as sociologists, economists as well as historians, and anthropologists as well as political theorists and students of literature—have offered descriptions and definitions. Drawing upon a good many such efforts, I want here to work with this proposition: a way of life is the combination of patterns of thought and action that, as it becomes habitual and institutionalized, defines the thrust and character of a culture and society.

In the classic German word, it is a *Weltanschauung*, a conception of the world and how it works, and a strategy for acting upon that outlook on a routine basis as well as in times of crisis. If you prefer an Anglo-Saxon formulation, consider it this way: each society holds in common certain assumptions about reality, and every day those assumptions guide and set limits upon its members—their awareness and perception, their understanding of cause and consequence, their sense of options, and their range of action.

From *Empire as a Way of Life* by William Appleman Williams, copyright © 1980 by William Appleman Williams. Used by permission of Oxford University Press.

"We stabilize around a set of concepts . . . and hold them dear," explains one sociologist. "At each moment of each day, we make the same mistakes . . . we consider that our own personal consciousness *is* the world." Or, in the words of a historian, "those unconsciously accepted presuppositions which, in any age, so largely determine what men think about the nature of the universe and what can and cannot happen in it."

In thinking about empire as a way of life, we must consider the dynamics of the process as well as a static description of the empire at any particular moment. The empire as a territory and as activities dominated economically, politically, and psychologically by a superior power is the *result* of empire as a way of life. This is particularly important in the case of the United States because from the beginning the persuasiveness of empire as a way of life effectively closed off other ways of dealing with the reality that Americans encountered.

It is next necessary to clarify the key terms *empire* (and *imperial*), *colonialism*, and *imperialism*. As with many words that deal with primary human actions, *empire* has been used to name several kinds of activity, relationships, policies, and institutions. Any extended discussion of such denotations and connotations inevitably becomes an exercise in splitting ever more hairs until the central issue is lost in the mangy debris. All that said, it is nevertheless true that empire has consistently been used to specify two associated, but nevertheless different, relationships.

One is the union of initially separate but physically and politically and socially related units of population under one central authority. The resort to force by one or more of those entities may or may not be a major element in the process, but in either case the result is an empire governed as an imperial system. The will, and power, of one element asserts its superiority. This meaning of empire is illustrated by the United Kingdom of England, Scotland, and Wales; and, as I will argue a bit later, by the government created by the Constitution over the original and significantly independent states of America.

The other meaning of empire concerns the forcible subjugation of formerly independent peoples by a wholly external power, and their subsequent rule by the imperial metropolis. One thinks here of the First Americans and of the northern half of Mexico seized by conquest in the 1840s by the United States and integrated into its imperial system. Or of England's assault upon Ireland.

The term *colonialism* has been devalued by sloppy usage. Here again, therefore, we are wise to settle upon two basic meanings. The substance involves the large-scale transfer and subsequent rule of people from (or under the control of) the imperial metropolis to an area previously unoccupied, or populated by people who cannot resist the invasion and are therefore conquered or destroyed. Such examples include Great Britain colonizing North America (and Australia), and transferring and colonizing Africans to its southern regions—a system of slavery carried on by the United States after 1776.

The other meaning of colonialism is more complicated, and a case can be made for viewing it as a separate phenomenon that emerged during the transition from classic colonialism to imperialism. This kind of colonialism did involve, however, the shift of people from metropolis to the subjugated area as a matter of official policy, and for that reason it seems more useful to consider it as a particular kind of colonialism.

Here the crucial element concerns the *function* of the people sent out from the metropolis. Rather than being charged to settle and populate the area, they were (and still are) dispatched to rule an indigenous society by setting limits on the choices the natives *can* consider. Thus the form is often called *administrative colonialism.* Consider here the British in India and Africa, and the United States in Cuba and the Philippines.

The term *imperialism* is even more thoroughly muddled and confused. The semantic trouble began with the casual appropriation of the word *imperial,* originally associated with empire, to describe an evolving set of *different* relationships between advanced industrial societies and the rest of the world. It was then frazzled and fuzzied by an English Liberal named John A. Hobson and a Russian revolutionary who chose to call himself Lenin, both of whom employed it to explain those relationships as well as to prophesy the future. All in all, the word disappeared into a swamp of analysis, propaganda, projection, and nonsense.

But the term *imperialism* does have an irreducible meaning: the loss of sovereignty—control—over essential issues and decisions by a largely agricultural society to an industrial metropolis. Superior economic power subjects an inferior political economy to its own preferences. Adam Smith said it once and for all: the city enjoys and exploits a structural advantage over the country. The metropolis routinely displays and occasionally uses its military power, and metropolitan advisers (official and private, academic and corporate) are always on guard as supervisory personnel, but the essence of imperialism lies in the metropolitan domination of the weaker economy (and its political and social superstructure) to ensure the extraction of economic rewards. One thinks here of the relationship between Great Britain and Argentina between 1870 and 1914, between the United States and many countries in the western hemisphere (Canada as well as Cuba and Panama), and between all industrial powers and what has become known as the Third World.

If we accept that basic definition of imperialism, then we have no trouble dealing with similar relationships—superior over inferior—between industrial societies. That is a more complicated and fluctuating involvement, but it can and has produced serious tension and widespread violence. Indeed, the outbreak of World Wars I and II, as well as America's relationship with Western Europe and Japan after 1945, can be understood as manifestations of that variation on the theme of modern imperialism.

* * *

Locke said it as well as anyone and more honestly than most: empire as a way of life involves taking wealth and freedom away from others to provide for your own welfare, pleasure, and power. Even so, others like Henry VII were respectably candid. Elizabeth I may have been discreet in knighting Drake, but her general directive was straight to the point: conquer any "remote heathen and barbarous lands" and impose proper government upon such savages. And in 1607 the directors of the Virginia Company of London were properly blunt. Knowing the purpose of settlement, they warned their colonists that "you cannot carry yourselves so toward them [the First Americans] but they will grow discontented with your habitation."

In the broader sense, however, the English and other European empire builders developed a contradictory and convoluted (if at times sophisticated) argument that justified their imperial activities in India, Africa, Asia, and America. That elaborate ideology was not simply or only a callous or cynical rationalization. Whatever their roots in the mundane realities of greed, such overarching systems of ideas take on a life of their own and function (and become accepted) as engines of action.

Thus it is revealing and useful to explore them on their own terms. My emphasis here is on the English confrontation with the established seaboard, but it applies with equal force to the subsequent enslavement of Africans and the destruction of the First Americans west of the Appalachian Mountains. Both were the motifs of the imperial coin. . . .

The problem confronting the English (and other European) empire builders was very simple. Even by their own rules, the unilateral, uninvited, and unprovoked intrusion over thousands of miles by one culture into the life and affairs of another could not be explained or justified by an appeal to self-defense. That primal right could plausibly be invoked, even at best, *only after the initial penetration had occurred and was resisted.* Hence the initial invasion must be justified by some other logic. Over the years, scholars dealing with that problem have tended to separate into two groups: one emphasizes the importance of color (blacks and browns are inferior); the other stresses Christianity (heathens are agents of the Devil and so must be converted or destroyed).

Now in truth those explanations are less contradictory or exclusive than mutually supportive and reinforcing of empire as a way of life. Whatever its origins in the eastern Mediterranean, Christianity became a European phenomenon and, despite the brownish hue of some Mediterranean Catholics and Orthodox believers, they were generally lighter—"whiter" than the uninformed or unpersuaded in India, Asia, Africa, and America. Heathens were on sight generally darker than converts, and hence visually tainted by the domestic force of the Devil who was always presented as black.

That evidence, such as it was, was reinforced by other kinds of proof. Europeans were highly conscious—one might even say hypersensitive—of having come through an extremely difficult and perilous time of troubles. Not only had they been challenged by Islamic and other non-believers, but the infidels had probed close to the vitals of their own way of life. They had also been tested in horrendous trials by disease and other disasters. But they *had* survived. It was more than a bit like death and resurrection. Given their Christianity, that was understandably interpreted as a sign of the Grace of God. Their disputations and wars with each other about the nature of the true faith were tactical not strategic: not about the faith, but only about how best to interpret and extend it.

Thus it is important to realize that Jennings's perceptive remark about the Holy Church has to do with secular as well as religious ideology. It was not only that Christianity was the true religion. The faithful had survived and were moving toward the assertion of their superiority. They had developed better ships and more deadly weapons to subdue the Eastern infidels. They had triumphed over pestilence and poverty to build cities. They had controlled dissidence through the creation of centralized instruments of government. And they had organized economic activity well enough to generate a growing surplus (well, at least for some).

To employ the science and the language of a later century, there was a nonarticulated social Darwinism in all of that: a preview of the sense, if not the theory, of the superiority inherent in mere survival and continuation. It was not formulated in those terms, or with those footnotes, but it was nevertheless a very real and present and powerful element of the developing imperial way of life. There was, in short a secular Holy Church with its own doctrine of superiority.

Those complementary dogmas, sacred and secular, did not immediately or inevitably produce a hard-line racist outlook. There emerged instead a spectrum of attitudes, among both religious and lay thinkers, that can usefully be described in terms of two contradictory images: the Noble Savage and the Ignoble Savage. The former, a combination of romanticism and superciliousness, developed as the faith and idiom of the more humane group of English and American imperialists. They considered themselves superior, and justified the imposition of imperial power on that basis, but they modified such arrogance in several respects.

To begin with, they acknowledged that some aspects of "savage" life were worth serious consideration and perhaps even emulation. They were impressed, for example, by the significantly (even statistically) lower incidence of violence within First American societies, and by the limits generally imposed by those cultures upon inter-societal warfare. They responded favorably—or at least thoughtfully and tolerantly—to the more relaxed attitudes about sex, marriage, and divorce, and to the different idioms of personal hygiene (as in daily bathing) and medical treatment. And they recognized, however cautiously, that the religion of the First Americans—including its emphasis on dreams—bespoke a sense of awe and wonder that was related to their own belief in spirits and miracles.

Those more relaxed or benevolent imperialists also acknowledged the impressive skills of the First Americans. Not only were they good farmers (who cleared enough land to let half lie fallow), but they demonstrated a sophisticated understanding of how to create and sustain a symbiotic relationship with the land. They did not graze cattle or pigs, to be sure, but they did create pasture for deer. They also displayed an ability to organize a division of labor, both within and between cultures, that led to a remarkable system of trade over long distances that involved food, metals, and other commodities.

For all those reasons, the group of English people (and later Americans) that we can usefully call the soft imperialists—religious and secular—did not become racists. They were arrogant, supercilious, and patronizing, but they did separate themselves from the racists on three vital issues. First, they considered the First Americans human. Second, they acknowledged their achievements. And, third, on those grounds, they considered it possible and desirable to elevate the Noble Savage into at least partial civilization. They left the future open.

It would be pleasant, and surely uplifting, to report that such soft imperialists carried the day. They did not. Indeed not. But even so the soft imperialists were and remained important. If nothing else, they now and again prevented the hard-line imperialists from plunging joyfully into disaster. American historians, along with their fellow intellectuals, display their imperial temperament by cataloging people according to two categories: imperialists and anti-imperialists. It is a less than helpful filing system. We Americans, let alone our English forefathers, have produced very, very few anti-imperialists. Our idiom has been empire, and so the primary division was and remains between the soft and the hard.

It all comes down to the question of whether one conquers to transform the heathen into lower-class members of the empire or simply works them to death for the benefit of the imperial metropolis. Even if the softies win, empire is still the way of life.

But the truth of it is that the hard-liners won. And so in that sense, at any rate, the question of racism is secondary. The primary question has always been the control of wealth and the liberty for some to do as they choose. Racism, the product of the image of the Ignoble Savage, began and survived as the psychologically justifying and economically profitable fairy tale. It provided the gloss for the harsh truth that empire, soft or hard, is the child of an inability or an unwillingness to live within one's own means.* Empire as a way of life is predicated upon having more than one needs.

Think of it this way: the English-American empire builders went first for the land cleared and cultivated by the First Americans. It was simply too much hard work to chop those trees and root those stumps. Easier by far to take the land already cleared by the heathens. And take their food to survive. We have all heard, as children of children of children, how our ancestors in Virginia and Massachusetts were saved by the surplus produce from the gardens cultivated by those Ignoble Savages. And it is true. Hence it cannot be true that they were nomads who misused the land. John Winthrop of Massachusetts, churchman though he was, was simply wrong—if not worse—when he said that the First Americans "inclose noe land neither have any settled habitation." They treasured and cherished all the land they shared in common.

But, good Christian imperial lawyer that he was, Winthrop was making the best case for grabbing the land. After all, as Cromwell had said, all others were

---

*As Edmund S. Morgan has demonstrated in *American Slavery, American Freedom: The Ordeal of Colonial Virginia*, racism also came to be used as an instrument to control the domestic tension that was caused by the uneven distribution of the wealth acquired through imperial policies.

"sick." And you were sick if you did not sit on it all the time. No fences and no cattle meant "noe other but a naturall right to those countries." Hence, "if we leave them sufficient for their use we may lawfully take the rest." The "rest" meant wherever they were not located at any given moment, and the law was imperial fiat. Winthrop was a soft imperialist in that he hoped to convert the heathen to embrace their doom, but a hard imperialist in acquiring the loot.

There and elsewhere empire was ruthless. Even so, all such beliefs and rationalizations which prompted and sanctified numerous imperial wars killed fewer First Americans than the diseases imported by the European invaders. The gunfire removed the hardy. Prior to the appearance of the Europeans there were probably between 10 and 12 million people living north of the Rio Grande River. And it seems very likely, given the existence of surplus-producing agriculture, that the population was increasing on a regular basis.

Then came the first Spanish and French, followed by the fleets of fishermen to the north and the early colonies that failed to survive. The coughs, the sneezes, and the laying on of hands were like the bombs over Hiroshima and Nagasaki. The instruments of mass death were smallpox and other diseases. By the time of Jamestown and Plymouth, as Jennings observes, the "American land was more like a widow than a virgin."

Then the soft imperialists subverted their grand ideal. For it was impossible to preserve the Noble Savage and at the same time bring him into the imperial world. The consolidation of English settlements generated extremely powerful non-military forces of destruction. We are perhaps too preoccupied with the role of violence in imperial expansion. Having experienced violence, I do not discount its power or persuasion; or, in other respects, its convenience in the matter of conquest. It is difficult, for example, to discount the urge to mayhem generated by the discovery that tobacco earned significant profits. After all, no superior persons would weary themselves by clearing the brush and forests when rifles would drive the First Americans from land already prepared.

All that said, the disruption of First American cultures caused by ostensibly mundane and innocent economic exchange, let alone the fur industry, was a deadly scythe cutting devastating swathes through a complex and integrated way of life. As it was with smallpox, so it was with trade. Imperial philosophers are very serious about commerce for sound reasons: it subverts an established way of life and creates a dependency upon the metropolis. Trade between unequals is as harmless as a magnet around a compass.

The commerce in guns, knives, other tools, and blankets quickly altered preferences and destroyed indigenous skills among the First Americans. Even without the almost incalculable effect of huge amounts of alcohol (a major if neglected industry in all imperial expansion), that dependency was a progressively demoralizing force. And the fur trade was far more complex than the term *trade* indicates. It substituted commercial hunting for balanced cropping of the harvest and thus subverted the supply of food and clothing. It imposed upon the women an assembly-line system of preparing the pelts that disrupted family and tribal life, and it created a preview of the share-cropping system that later kept black Americans hostage to the imperial way of life even after they were ostensibly free.

As with the Africans who were colonized in the British-American empire as slaves, the First Americans made enormous contributions to the way of life developed by their conquerors. Their concern and generosity ensured the survival of the first English settlements. They taught the invaders how to explore and sustain themselves in the far reaches of the continent. And they had developed at least half of the crops that provided the imperial Americans with their sustenance. Indeed, they taught the Europeans how to be pioneers.

And for that they were destroyed. In the beginning as possessors of cultivated land and as pawns in the wars of empire between European powers, and ultimately as disposable commodities by erstwhile colonials expanding their own empire.

How It Began

—Felix Greene

In this excerpt from his book The Enemy: What Every American Should Know About Imperialism *(Vintage Books, 1971), British correspondent, film maker, and lecturer Felix Greene talks about empire from the perspective of a British national.*

It was formerly the custom in British schools, even during my own childhood, to hang a large map of the world on the wall of each classroom. The dominant color was red, for this was before the Russian Revolution, and red had not yet been appropriated by the Communists. India, Canada, Australia, New Zealand, huge areas of the African continent running from Cairo to the Cape of Good Hope, Samoa, Burma, Malaya, Hong Kong, the West Indies, Ceylon—all colored red. And

From *The Enemy* by Felix Greene, copyright © 1971 by Felix Greene. Used by permission of Random House, Inc.

scattered across every ocean hundreds of islands and small outposts, obscure harbors and refuelling stations—also red. Here on these maps, for the edification of British youth, was spread the British Empire in all its majesty. One-quarter of the land surface of the world, one-fifth of the human population intimately linked with or controlled by our own tiny island. It made us feel very superior.

We took for granted that this vast medley of people, of every possible creed and color, were under us because they wanted to be. Who better could they be under? We British were just; our rule was benign. The young men we sent out to administer the empire were hardworking, they lived on a pittance, had enormous self-reliance and were incorruptible. Were we not demonstrating to these backward peoples what good government was? Were we not leading them towards the infinite consolations of Christian civilization? Were we not teaching them, with the patience of a father toward his children, that it was part of God's plan that young men wear trousers and that the breasts of young women be covered? In our generosity we were even providing them with schools where they could learn English and could broaden their minds by reciting Shakespeare.* We built hospitals and clinics to improve their health, and agricultural colleges where they could learn how to grow their crops better. No wonder they respected us. It gave us a curious thrill, as we looked on these maps, to think that all these people scattered around the world saluted our flag and sang "God Save the King"—*our* king.

What was more, this admirable state of affairs was clearly destined to continue indefinitely because we British were more clever and more humane than the Romans and Spaniards and the others who had tried to run an empire and had made a mess of it. Besides, we were the richest people in the world, our fleet was by far the most powerful and so our empire would go on and on forever, Amen.

That, in all its fraudulent innocence, was the vision of the world entertained by our young minds and most of the British people not so many years ago.

No one of course mentioned such words as exploitation, expropriation or forced labor. No one told us that the schools "we" provided were paid for by the people we ruled; that the "medical services" on which we prided ourselves often provided only one doctor for 10 thousand or more people (and in one case, Nigeria, only one for 34 thousand people); and that the increased profits resulting from improved agricultural methods benefited the plantation owner and not those who labored for him. No one told us about the conditions of work in the African diamond mines or in the cotton fields of India. No one talked about relative infant mortality rates or expectancy of life. We heard a lot about the *cost* of running the

---

*Writing in the *New Statesman* (April 4, 1969), Sir Jock Campbell gives a marvelous example of the non-education that was provided, until quite recently, in the British colonies. "I was shown over a high school in British Guiana a year or two before it became independent Guyana. The English Literature class were reading an erotic short story in Cornish dialect; for Geography the children were studying the [English] Lake District; for Agriculture, the dust bowl of the American Middle West. They were doing sums in pounds, shillings and pence (when the 'colony' used dollars and cents). And the girls' domestic economy form room was bedecked with . . . posters showing how to buy, cook, serve, and carve beef: most of the class were Hindus."

empire, and the enormous effort it took (the "white man's burden" we called it). But we never heard a word about the millions of pounds sterling (far, far more than the visible budgetry costs) that flowed back each year to British investors in the form of interest and profit; or the millions made by the bankers who financed it all, and by the insurance and shipping companies; or of the salaries and pensions paid out to Britishers from the colonial funds. No one explained to us that much of the cost of the empire was borne by the colonial people themselves. Nor that the costs that were paid for were paid by the British people as a whole through taxation, while the *benefits*, the fabulous financial benefits, were being reaped by a relatively small handful of individuals.

People who run empires have to be disingenuous, and they must not ask themselves too many questions. They need to have at their command a rhetoric of justification that will shield them from realities. They need to be serenely confident that they are doing humanity good.

But why bother with justifications when none were needed? Words and ideas only get in the way, and can be disturbing. There, on the map, was something more real than words. The British Empire—solid and permanent as Gibraltar.

Those maps, of course, no longer hang in British classrooms. The old methods of empire have changed. Such control as the British ruling class still retains is more indirect, less visible. A new empire, the American Empire, has replaced the British Empire as the leading imperialist power. Exercising its power in a structurally different way, but nevertheless seeking the same ends and often with the same means, it is the American Empire which today bestrides the world. Though militarily and industrially vastly more powerful than the British Empire ever was, the new Empire is subject to greater challenge and greater uncertainty and is much less likely to last as long. . . .

Empires—domination of one power over another—have been a feature throughout recorded history.

China, Egypt, Greece, Rome—all exercised control over peoples outside their own formal borders. These empires of antiquity were primarily concerned with tribute or the plunder of wealth. It was for treasure that Spain sent her galleons and armed caballeros to Mexico and South America; it was plunder that made Spain the richest country in the world in the sixteenth century.

The emphasis then was on the looting of gold and silver. Our concern is not with the empires of long ago but of today. A central characteristic of modern imperialism is its emphasis on a different kind of plunder—the pillage of other countries' wealth through *unequal trade* and through *investment* which draws out far more wealth than it puts in.

The people of Britain (or more precisely, a relatively small controlling group within Britain) were the first to apply these new methods of plunder on a truly global scale. They became, before long, the real professionals of empire building. The system they developed, in its magnitude, diversity and in the complexity of its operations, dwarfed all previous empires. Never before had so many people—one-quarter of the entire human race—been subjugated and put to work for the enrichment of so few.

What were the conditions that made it possible for the British to develop such a wondrously profitable system? Of course, innumerable factors contributed to the success, but we can isolate four closely related conditions that were of basic importance:

1. The new technology of the industrial revolution.
2. The availability of an abundant supply of cheap labor.
3. The accumulation of capital.
4. The development of foreign markets.

The New Technology

As the new steam-powered factories increased their production capacity, the nations of Europe soon realized that commodities could be produced faster than they could be sold in the home market. This does not mean that there was a "surplus" productive capacity in any real sense. The workers themselves needed the goods, but their wages were so low that they did not have the money with which to buy. At this early stage capitalism was already confronted by its own fundamental contradiction—the capacity to expand production faster than the market can absorb it.

The fundamental, built-in, inescapable contradiction of capitalism can (even at the cost of over-simplification) be briefly summarized as follows: The profit an employer makes is secured by selling goods at a price higher than they cost him to make. The total earnings of workers can never match the full value of what they produce or there would be no profit. What is paid out in wages is therefore *never* sufficient to purchase all that is produced. This basic contradiction is hidden by the complexities of the economic process, and the consequences of the inability of purchasing power to absorb all that is produced can be postponed by enhancing consumer demand by buying on credit—but this merely stimulates demand today at the expense of tomorrow. There are other methods of boosting consumer demand, by stage-engendered monetary expansion, governmental consumption for military spending and so on. Ultimately, however, the decisive market factor is consumption by individuals. As long as the total amount paid out in wages and salaries is less than the value of the goods manufactured (and in a capitalist system based on profit it *must* be less) available purchasing power will never be able to absorb the output of consumer goods.

British industry, first in the field, was technically the most advanced and the most efficiently managed. In almost every branch of technical innovation British engineers led the way. Others merely followed. Thus the British gained a clear start over other industrializing countries of Europe.

* * *

Cheap Labor

Britain could not have advanced her industrialization so rapidly if, just when own-ers of factories needed it most, an abundant supply of cheap labor had not made it-self available.

Britain had been an agricultural country, but with wool becoming Britain's chief export, the landowners found raising sheep more profitable than renting land to tenants. Thousands of peasant farmers were evicted from their cottages, up-rooted, often with no warning, from the land that they and their fathers had used from time immemorial.

What caused even more widespread suffering were the Acts under which pub-lic or "common land" was enclosed. In accordance with age-old tradition all men were free to use these common lands for the grazing of sheep and goats; in the economy of the peasant farmers access to this land was an essential element without which they could not survive. Between 1760 and 1810 no fewer than 2,765 Enclosure Acts were passed. The human suffering they caused is beyond imagination.

Thus it happened that when the new factories that were springing up required labor, tens of thousands of homeless and hungry agricultural workers, with their wives and children, were forced into the cities in search of work, *any* work, under any conditions, that would keep them alive.

The emergence of a huge, property-less and impoverished working class was precisely what the new industrialists wished for. They could, and did, dictate their own conditions. The laboring people of Britain were subjected to treatment so in-human that today we would have difficulty in believing it if the official records were not there for us to read. For wages that would barely keep them alive workers were herded into huge slums that had no sewerage, no adequate water supply, no beauty, no cultural amenities, no playgrounds. The company-built hovels in which they had to live were of such meanness that today it would be illegal to use them to house animals. In the cotton mills near Manchester the workers were required to work fourteen hours a day in a temperature of eighty-four degrees. . . .

Children were cheaper to hire than adults, so children frequently became the wage earners while their parents remained unemployed. Pauper children, bought from the Guardians of the Poor, were cheaper still and were shipped in groups from London to the mining towns of South Wales and the northern cotton mills. Boys of nine were sent down the mines to work for fourteen hours a day hewing coal; and in the cotton mills of Lancashire girls of seven would work as "appren-tices" from five in the morning until eight at night—a fifteen-hour work day. . . .

In ways such as these did those with wealth and power achieve the continua-tion of the supply of cheap labor—the second of the 4 basic factors which made the development of the empire possible.

For those looking only at the statistics, Britain showed extraordinary advances during the industrial revolution. Production of cotton, of iron and coal and of every commodity was being multiplied tenfold. Profits were soaring. Wealth was pouring into Britain from all over the world. For the few it was a field day. Money, money, money . . . it was rolling in. Money for country mansions; money for huge London houses; money for carriages and servants and elegant clothes; money for weekend parties and tours around the Continent; money for plays and entertainment and fancy-dress balls; money for music and education and seaside holidays; money just for fun. This rich man's London might have been a million miles away from the dark cities where the great mass of the British people were existing in inconceivable degradation. In 1836, at a time of unprecedented "prosperity," thousands of people were literally starving.

This was the cost that successive generations of the British working class paid for Britain's industrial leadership, which made possible the "glories of empire."

* * *

The Accumulation of Capital

The third major factor which made possible the new methods of global plunder was the accumulation of capital. This derives from the exploitation of the workers which we have just described.

Capital is the wealth produced by the workers but expropriated from them. To put it differently, the worker produces a given amount of value but he is paid not the full amount he has produced but only a part — the existential minimum necessary to guarantee his return to the same work tomorrow. The value he produced but did not receive, that value which was appropriated (stolen would be the better word) is the source of all capital. "Capital," said Marx, "is but yesterday's frozen or dead labor." This is true whether the capital is represented by money, machinery, factories, or anything else. Accumulated capital, arising from the exploitation of workers yesterday, perpetuates the enslavement of the living workers today.

But there is one question on which we must be clear if we are to understand the workings of capitalism. At what stage is wealth created? The capitalist convinces himself that it is *he* who has created wealth, capital, when he sells an article for more than it cost him. But in actual fact wealth is not created at the time when a commodity is sold but when it is produced. It is true that it is only when he sells an article and gets paid for it that the capitalist can lay his hands on the excess value — that portion that was not paid to the worker. But this value was already *contained in the product itself* before it was marketed. The real issue is not whether the accumulation of capital is "wrong" — for capital is an essential element of progress — but who owns it, who controls it, and for whose benefit it is to be used.

The relatively small group of capitalists who developed British industry had no doubts as to the answers. The capital belonged to them, would be controlled by them and would benefit them. This was, as they saw it, the natural law of things. It never occurred to them to question it.

* * *

The Development of Foreign Markets

From the sixteenth century Britain had recognized the importance of the seas as her main trade highway, and had thereafter built a powerful fleet of merchant and war ships. The aim was trade, and particularly trade which exploited the profitability of cheap labor in the overseas territories. There was the slave trade, organized as a "business-like" operation, in which the British ships plied the "triangle" of trade. The ships transported slaves from Africa to America, carried tobacco and cotton from America to Bristol and Liverpool, and then returned with manufactured goods (including guns, whiskey and Bibles) to the African ports. There were also the products of the East which were handled by the East India Company—a powerful government organ in its own right.

Though the British took the lead in expanding their foreign markets, there was nevertheless a continuous bitter rivalry among the newly industrialized powers. The French, the Germans, the Belgians, the Dutch, as well as the British, were faced with the same problem (factories able to produce more goods than could be sold at home) and all were seeking the same solutions. The wars between France and Britain from 1792 to 1815 were essentially a struggle for markets and for sources of raw material which could be obtained at the least possible cost through the use of cheap labor.

The century from Britain's victory over France at Waterloo in 1815 to the start of World War I in 1914, the century during which Britain exercised to the highest degree her world-wide power and plundered her wealth of other nations most successfully, is often referred to as a peaceful period. *Pax Britannica* it is often called. It was a century of almost continuous strife. Only by the use of aggressive military force was Britain able to seize one after the other, her overseas possessions.

1814	British Guiana
1816	Gambia, Sikkim
1819	Singapore
1821	The Gold Coast
1826	Assam
1833	Falkland Islands
1839	Aden
1840	New Zealand
1841	Hong Kong
1842	Natal, Sind
1846	North Borneo
1849	The Punjab
1852	Burma
1853	Nagpur
1854	Baluchistan
1861	Nigeria
1868	Basutoland
1874	Fiji
1878	Cyprus

1882	Egypt
1884	Somaliland
1887	Zululand
1888	Southern Rhodesia, Sarawak
1890	Kenya, Zanzibar
1891	Northern Rhodesia, Nyasaland
1894	Uganda
1900	Transvaal, Orange Free State, Tonga
1906	Swaziland

The West Indies, India, Australia, Ceylon, Mauritius and part of North America were already colonized, and with the defeat of the French, Britain had assumed control over large areas of the North American continent. That was only the start. Here is the timetable of British penetration into almost every corner of the world during this century of "peace."

There were only fifteen years in that century when Britain was not engaged in some bloody military struggle. So much for Pax Britannica!

* * *

The development of Britain's global system of exploitation would have been impossible if the small group with capital had not learned to pool their resources, to gather together, to concentrate, to centralize large reserves of money—the capital that was never rightfully theirs in the first place.

Because of the volume of her trade, London became the financial center of the world. Merchant bankers combined the role of both merchants and bankers. A network of credit agencies was established throughout the empire whose sole purpose was to encourage British investments and trade and to increase profits. Branches of London banks were set up in all colonial territories. It was *capital* that enabled the factories and ships to be built, credits to be extended to cover purchases, the necessary reserves to be built up for insurance. At certain moments the immediate availability of large sums of money enabled the British to jump ahead of others. When, for example, the British Government heard that financial control of the Suez Canal could be seized (it was then owned by the French) if 4 million pounds were found immediately, the Government turned to the bankers and the money was provided overnight.

Those making commodities and selling them abroad, the bankers making money by extending credit, the insurance companies, the shipping companies, the entrepreneurs were not of course engaging in their activities for the "glory of empire" or "to bring civilization to the backward people"—this was merely the rhetoric. They were out for themselves, they were out for *profit*. And they made it. The empire, this intricate, complex system which was using the cheap labor in Britain and the still cheaper labor in the colonies as a means of amassing wealth, seemed foolproof. Outwardly it gave every appearance of stability and strength. Yet, even as it grew, there were intimations that the system contained its own built-in contradictions which must sooner or later prove fatal.

***

On the eve of World War I, Britain's foreign investment represented one-quarter of Britain's total national assets. One-half of Britain's annual savings were being placed abroad. This exported capital brought in huge annual revenues in the form of interest and profits, but it also brought consequences which were detrimental to the economy as a whole. Britain in this sense had become a parasite, drawing its nourishment from the toil of millions overseas. Capital that should have been invested to keep factories in Britain up-to-date went abroad where the returns were greater. Inevitably Britain's industrial plant began to suffer and her manufacturers were less and less able to produce goods in competition with other countries.

By 1870 Britain's industrial monopoly was lost. Germany and the United States, especially, were not ready to see Britain's position of supremacy continue unchallenged. Rising later on the industrial scene, they could take advantage of more advanced technology, more modern factories, and little by little these countries began to out-produce and under-sell Britain. Britain was saddled with old machinery and cheap labor scattered in distant colonies, while a growing imperialist rival, the United States, used "free" wage labor and slavery (a "colony" much more conveniently placed within her own territory) to amass sufficient capital eventually to render British factories obsolete.

On the eve of World War I Britain was still very powerful. The empire at that time consisted of fifty-five countries, 12 million square miles of territory, over 400 million people. The British navy was the most powerful in the world, and British merchant ships represented 50 per cent of the world's tonnage. The pound was the currency against which all other currencies were measured. But both the United States and Germany had out-stripped British industrial production, and Germany was challenging Britain's naval supremacy on the high seas.

In Germany Britain saw still another threat.

For several centuries Britain had realized that she would become vulnerable if ever Europe was unified under a single power. Britain had already fought three major continental wars to prevent such unification. She had fought Philip of Spain, Louis of France and Napoleon. Now, in 1914, she felt herself threatened again. Not only was Germany encroaching on Britain's commercial position overseas, but, with plans for a huge expansion of naval forces, her supremacy on the seas. Added to these fears was the possibility that if Germany were victorious in another war she might gain power over all of continental Europe.

Britain has no choice. Though in an already weakened position, Britain and her empire had to turn to meet this challenge in the first of two prolonged, destructive, costly and bloody wars. Britain was on the winning side of both, but they brought to an end her position of world supremacy.*

---

*Just how quickly Britain's military power was supplanted can be seen by the decline of her naval forces. Until after World War I the British navy was supreme; by 1922, under the Washington Treaty, she "granted" equality of naval strength to the United States. For a short period in 1947 the British navy was down to a total active strength of one cruiser and four destroyers.

* * *

Every empire at the height of its success has appeared indestructible and permanent. With such wealth and massive power at its disposal, such sophistication and administrative experience in its leadership, why should it ever be eclipsed? Yet within every empire there are built-in antagonisms which make its eventual decline inevitable. Today the world supremacy of the United States appears as unassailable as did that of Britain at the height of her imperial might. But America's present power and wealth cannot in any conceivable way prevent her economy from declining. For this very power and wealth require the continued economic enslavement of other peoples and these peoples (and not only in the poor countries) are no longer prepared to submit.

All empires rise and fall, and the American empire will be no exception. As the decline of Britain shows us, when empires begin to crumble they may crumble fast.

Eurocentrism

–Samir Amin

Samir Amin was born in Egypt and received his Ph.D. in economics in Paris. He is currently director of UNITAR, a United Nations research institute in Dakar, Senegal, and serves as economic consultant to many developing nations. In the following section he offers a succinct definition of the worldview known as "Eurocentrism." It is taken from a book by the same name that was published in 1989 by Monthly Review Press.

Eurocentrism is, like all dominant social phenomena, easy to grasp in the multiplicity of its daily manifestations but difficult to define precisely. Its manifestations, like those of other prevailing social phenomena, are expressed in the most varied of areas: day-to-day relationships between individuals, political information and opinion, general views concerning society and culture, social science. These expressions

Excerpts from *Eurocentrism* by Samir Amin, translated by Russell Moore, *Monthly Review Press.*
Copyright © 1989 by Monthly Review Press. Reprinted by permission of Monthly Review Foundation.

are sometimes violent, leading all the way to racism, and sometimes subtle. They express themselves in the idiom of popular opinion as well as in the erudite languages of specialists on politics, the Third World, economics, history, theology, and all the formulations of social science. I will therefore begin with this set of common ideas and opinions transmitted by the media, on which a broad consensus exists in the West, in order to summarize the Eurocentric vision.

The European West is not only the world of material wealth and power, including military might; it is also the site of the triumph of the scientific spirit, rationality, and practical efficiency, just as it is the world of tolerance, diversity of opinions, respect for human rights and democracy, concern for equality—at least the equality of rights and opportunities—and social justice. It is the best of the worlds that have been known up until this time. This first thesis, which simply repeats facts which are in themselves hardly debatable, is reinforced by the corollary thesis that other societies—the socialist East and the underdeveloped South—have nothing better to offer on any of the levels mentioned (wealth, democracy, or even social justice). On the contrary, these societies can only progress to the extent that they imitate the West. And this is what they are doing, in any case, even if they are doing it slowly and imperfectly, because of elements of resistance based on outmoded dogmatisms (like Marxism) or anachronistic motivations (like tribalism or religious fundamentalism).

Consequently, it becomes impossible to contemplate any other future for the world than its progressive Europeanization. For the most optimistic, this Europeanization, which is simply the diffusion of a superior model, functions as a necessary law; imposed by the force of circumstances. The conquest of the planet by Europe is thus justified, to the extent that it has roused other peoples from their fatal lethargy. For others, non-European peoples have an alternative choice: either they can accept Europeanization and internalize its demands, or, if they decide against it, they will lead themselves to an impasse that inevitably leads to their decline. The progressive Westernization of the world is nothing more than the expression of the triumph of the humanist universalism invented by Europe.

The Westernization of the world would impose on everyone the adoption of the recipes for European superiority: free enterprise and the market, secularism and pluralist electoral democracy. It should be noted that this prescription assumes the superiority of the capitalist system, as well as this system's capacity to respond, if not to every possible challenge in the realm of the absolute, at least to all potential demands on the conceivable horizon of the future. Marxism and the socialist regimes that it has inspired are only avatars of history, brief detours in the forward march toward Westernization and capitalism.

Under these circumstances, the European West has little to learn from others. The most decisive evolutions, destined to shape the future of humanity, continue to have their origin in the West, from scientific and technological progress to social advances like the recognition of the equality of men and women, from concern with ecology to the critique of the fragmented organization of labor. The tumultuous events that shake the rest of the world—socialist revolutions, anti-imperialist wars of liberation—are, despite the more radical appearance of the ambitions that nourish them, in fact less decisive for the future than the progress being made almost imperceptibly in the West. These tumultuous events are only the vicissitudes through which the peoples concerned have been compelled to pass in order to attempt to correct their backwardness.

The Legacy of Colonialism

–Jerry Kloby

"The Legacy of Colonialism" is excerpted from Jerry Kloby's book, Inequality, Power and Development, *which was published by Humanity Books in 2003 and is in its second edition. Kloby teaches political science at William Paterson University in New Jersey.*

One of the major reasons for the development problems that exist in much of the world today is the destruction of indigenous social relationships and productive economic practices, as well as the evolution of various patterns of relationships that were established during the era of colonialism. Generally, colonies fall into two categories. First, there are those colonies established primarily as a new homeland for settlers from the mother country, such as the British colonies in North America in the 1600s and 1700s; or in Rhodesia and the Cape of Africa, as well as Australia and New Zealand, in the nineteenth century; or the case of the Dutch in parts of southern African and, to some degree, the French in Algeria. Second, there are colonies that are procured for the enrichment of the mother country, especially the exploitation of natural resources but also for their labor. The prime example of this type is the Spanish conquest of much of the Americas. In the second type,

Excerpts from *Inequality, Power and Development: Issues in Political Sociology*, 2 ed., by Jerry Kloby (Amherst, NY: Humanity Books). Copyright © 2004 by Jerry Kloby. Reprinted with permission.

the relationship is more purely one of political and economic domination for the enrichment of the colonial power; however, this may also be a factor in the first type of colony, a fact that has often led to sharp conflicts between colonies and their mother country. The second type of colonialism is more common, and it is the type that we will examine here.

Colonialism may be best described as the formal political domination of one country by another in which the relationship between the two nations is always one of economic exploitation, although the dominant nation may pretend otherwise. The era of modern colonialism started shortly after the great boom in global exploration that is symbolized by the travels of Christopher Columbus, and it is generally agreed to have peaked in the late 1800s and the beginning of the twentieth century, although some European countries held on to their colonies for many decades after. However, the end of colonialism did not mean the end of exploitation. While many countries were granted formal political independence, the economic relationships did not necessarily undergo drastic change. This reality gave rise to the term *neocolonialism*, which designates a situation of formal independence coupled with continued economic exploitation by an external power.

The effects of colonialism are felt very strongly today in both the economic development of the Third World and its political development. Let us begin a somewhat detailed examination of colonialism by taking a look at the methods used to subjugate the people in an array of colonies and the long-lasting consequences these have had. A classic example of colonial domination and its brutality can be seen in the methods used by King Leopold II of Belgium in colonizing the Congo Free State, the portion of Africa now encompassed by the nation of the Democratic Republic of the Congo.

King Leopold's Congo

Using the services of the great explorer Sir Henry Morton Stanley (1841–1904) in the late 1870s, Leopold saw the potential for wealth that the Congo region of Africa held. But in order to secure control of the Congo, Leopold had to not only subjugate the native populations but defeat an Anglo-Portuguese attempt to colonize the Congo River basin. In 1885, Leopold consolidated his control over the region and gained the recognition of the major European powers and the United States as the sovereign of the Congo Free State, an area eighty times larger than Belgium itself.

The Congo was rich in natural rubber reserves, a fact that would quickly become a curse rather than a source of wealth for the native people in the region. For quite some time native Africans had been trading ivory, tin, palm oil, and other goods with the Europeans, but the invention of the rubber tire for bicycles, carts, and automobiles dramatically increased European demand for rubber. One of the first steps in securing the rubber for European interests was a decree by King Leopold that native rights were restricted to the actual sites of the towns and villages and a small area around them that was under cultivation. Other land was ruled "vacant" and property of the state, that is, of King Leopold. Of course, natives had used this land for hunting and other purposes, but this was of no concern to the king. The decree gave Leopold control over perhaps 90 percent of the land, and commercial activity in the king's territory would be permitted only after a tax was paid to the king's officials. Leopold also weakened the local economies and simultaneously strengthened his own position by forbidding the natives to trade with other Europeans. Exploitation of the Congo's resources was facilitated by the establishment of Belgian-owned concessions that used native labor to extract rubber and other resources. Official representatives of the Belgian king were rewarded through a system of sliding-scale bonuses for increased production of rubber and ivory in their districts.

The entire system of exploitation was enforced by the Belgian military and by the establishment of a native army. These soldiers were also rewarded if production increased in their districts. Enforcement of the system of exploitation became barbaric and, for the most part, people in Belgium and the rest of Europe were shielded from knowledge of the cruelty. As part of the system of control, women and children were often taken away to "hostage houses" where they were held to ensure the cooperation of the men in meeting rubber and ivory quotas. Soldiers sent out to get rubber and ivory often found that the most effective method was to raid villages, seize prisoners, and have them redeemed afterward for set quantities of ivory and rubber. In the late 1890s, a Swedish missionary disclosed that Belgian officers were requiring the native soldiers to bring in as "trophies" the hands and sexual organs of males, as proof that they had performed their missions to punish villagers for noncooperation. Belgian soldiers also took part in this barbarism. One wrote home telling how he had killed 150 men, cut off 60 hands, and crucified women and children.[1] Baskets of hands that had been smoked in order to keep them from rotting in the warm, moist climate would often be presented to the Belgian officials.

Occasionally, Congo courts—really no more than a tool of Belgian rule—would find a soldier guilty of crimes of cruelty but few, if any, ever served time in jail. The courts generally accepted the defense that the soldiers acted under orders of their superiors, but the courts never chose to initiate proceedings against the superiors.

The system of exploitation was also enforced by forbidding the natives to clear the ground for farming or to go hunting and fishing, because these activities took time from rubber extraction. Consequently, their villages deteriorated, their food supply diminished, and starvation ensued. The Congo River, to which Henry Morton Stanley had traveled just two decades earlier and seen large areas teeming with vibrant, productive human life, had become depopulated and, in places, reduced to desert-like conditions. Travelers' accounts in 1903 and afterward told of walking for weeks without seeing another human being. After twenty years of King Leopold's rule, an estimated ten million inhabitants of the Congo had died either directly at the hands of Belgian or native soldiers, or from starvation and disease brought about by colonial exploitation. Many had fled the Congo as well, but their fate may not have been much better. The French, seeing the economic advantage of King Leopold's system, constructed its likeness in the neighboring French Congo with similar results. It is likely that some Congo natives managed to flee as far as Rhodesia or South Africa only to work and perhaps die in the gold or diamond mines there. By 1900, almost every square mile of Africa had been colonized.

French West Africa

French colonialism in West Africa, while not taking quite the barbaric form of Leopold's rule in the Congo, may in the long run have had more severe consequences. It offers a very instructive lesson for understanding the roots of a variety of problems that exist in the Third World today.

In 1659, the French established a colonial outpost in what is now known as Senegal, and French traders made a steady profit dealing in slaves, ivory, animal skins, and gold.[2] By 1865, the area of modern Senegal had come under French colonial control, and later, along with Mauritania, Mali, and Niger, it became part of French West Africa. The French recognized that the area was suitable for growing peanuts and that this could benefit their slave trade. Peanut seeds were brought from Brazil by the slave ships, planted in Africa, and used as provisions for slaves on the journey to the Americas. As time went on, peanuts and peanut oil became more and more important commercially, and French colonial authorities were able to establish the peanut as the dominant cash crop in the Sahel region, the dry grasslands in western Africa.

Before the peanut became so dominant, the local people had grown a variety of crops and an ecologically sound system of crop rotation had been practiced. But the French, who had essentially imposed this crop on the people, had little interest in the consequences that the peanut would have on the local populations. Peanuts take a lot of nutrients from the soil, and farmland used for growing peanuts generally needs a long fallow period to recuperate. If peanuts are grown year after year on the same land, the organic material in the soil is sharply diminished, crop output consequently drops, the soil's ability to grow anything and hold water is reduced, and the region's susceptibility to drought and *desertification* increases.

It should be noted that the average West African peasant had little intrinsic incentive to grow peanuts. This is something that was forced on them, and the method of coercion provides an interesting lesson in the economics of colonialism. The French, after declaring the region their own, levied taxes on the peasants that had to be paid in cash. One of the few ways that peasants could come up with the cash was to produce crops that the French were willing to buy. In a sense, the peasant was exploited twice, first by selling his crop and then by handing over a part of the money made from the sale to the French government as tax payments. The reader should note how crucial the introduction of a money-based system of trade is to the development of a worldwide system of capitalism. West Africans were reduced to laboring on their own land for someone else's benefit.

This system of relationships set the stage for future economic and ecological problems. Over time, West Africans were producing less food for themselves. The soil was being farmed too intensely in an attempt to keep up the tax payments and earn money for other things they now had to buy. Overall food production was reduced, leaving less food available to be stored for emergency use. Periodic droughts and locust infestations led to numerous famines in the 1900s. By the time the French West African colonies received their independence in 1960, the region was on the verge of ecological disaster. A major drought and famine took place in the Sahel from 1969 to 1974, resulting in one of the great tragedies of the twentieth century. Disease and starvation were rampant, but a pattern of dependency had been established that required the continued production of cash crops for export. So although every single nation in the region was producing enough grain to feed its population, many people were dying of hunger and the region was exporting large amounts of food to feed foreigners.[3] From 1970 to 1974, the region exported approximately $1.25 billion worth of food. Even though formal colonialism had ended, the region was clearly tied to a world market system of unequal exchange. Colonialism in the past had laid the foundation for famine and environmental disaster in the present and future.

Colonialism in Indochina and India

Colonial policies similar to those in French West Africa were implemented by the French in Southeast Asia. From 1860 to 1931, France was able to convert approximately 40 percent of the potential food-producing land in Indochina (Laos, Cambodia, and Vietnam) to production for rubber, coffee, tea, and rice for export. Ironically, much of the rice was being exported to West Africa to help compensate for lower food production for domestic consumption among West Africans. Both regions, however, experienced a decrease in available food. Famines struck West Africa seven times between 1900 and 1930. In Vietnam, the colonial system of production for export, combined with Japanese occupation and war, resulted in two million deaths due to starvation between 1943 and 1945.[4]

British colonialism in India had a similar effect. A system of land revenue (essentially a tax) imposed on India meant that more production had to be shifted to exchange crops—crops that the British were willing to buy. For the most part this meant cotton. As Indian agriculture shifted more and more to cotton production, less land was used for food production, and the food that was produced also shifted more toward cash crops to suit British needs. British economic policy also took on extremely coercive forms:

> From the beginning of the 19th century, the British systematically destroyed the Indian textile industry by economic means (prohibition of imports into England) and also extra economic means (destruction of the industrial towns of Surat, Dacca, Murshidabad, and others). They imposed agricultural specialization, by creating from scratch a pattern of large landed property, reinforced by the exemption of the cotton fields from the tax.[5]

In essence, the British had industrialized their own textile production, destroyed the Indian textile industry, forced India to produce cotton and sell it at a low rate, shipped the raw materials to England where they were manufactured into clothes and other textiles, and then sold these goods back to the people of India who could afford them and to other markets around the world. British colonial policy was hardly benevolent to its colonial subjects or to the local economic systems. In fact, it went as far as forbidding "the establishment of modern industry in the colonies after having destroyed the crafts."[6]

In the mid-1800s, one of the world's chief exporters of cotton was the United States, which exploited an enslaved population of stolen Africans to harvest crops at minimal cost. During the 1860s, though, the American Civil War caused cotton production and exports to drop. The British attempted to fill the void in the world market by forcing greater production out of their Indian colony. The resulting increase in land used for growing cotton led to decreased food production; this, coupled with increased rice exports from India to Australia, caused a major famine in 1866. It has been estimated that one million people were victims of starvation in the region of Orissa alone.[7]

British rule in India had far-reaching effects. At first, the British appointed *revenue-farmers*, who were responsible for collecting the land taxes. Gradually, the revenue-farmers developed into large landlords. This followed the English pattern because, as India's first prime minister, Jawaharlal Nehru (1889–1964), pointed out, "It was far easier to deal with a few individuals than with a vast peasantry."[8] Under the British system, "The balance between industry and agriculture was upset, the traditional division of labor was broken up and numerous stray individuals could not be easily fitted into any group activity."[9] The British carefully cultivated their allies within Indian society and exploited existing differences, thereby worsening various rivalries. According to Nehru: "A new class, the owners of land, appeared; a class created by, and therefore to a large extent identified with, the British government. The breakup of the old system created new problems, and probably the beginnings of the new Hindu-Moslem problem can be traced to it. . . . British rule . . . consolidated itself by creating new classes and vested interests who were tied up with that rule and whose privileges depended on its continuance."[10]

Nehru went on to discuss how the British pursued policies deliberately designed to create divisions among sectors of Indian society and to encourage "one group at the cost of the other."[11] He also claimed that "nearly all of our major problems today have grown up during British rule and as a direct result of British policy."[12]

Colonialism in Ireland and China

British colonial policy had similar results in Ireland as the Irish were forced into an overdependency on the potato as a staple crop. In the 1800s, a high percentage of Irish land was being used to grow crops and raise livestock for export to England. Since the potato was a high-yield crop and a fairly nourishing and filling food source, it became popular for families to grow potatoes on the small amount of land available for domestic production. When the potato blight struck in 1845, the result was a devastating famine directly caused by colonialism. Out of a population of eight million, approximately one million people died of starvation, and about 1.5 million emigrated, mostly to the United States, as refugees from the devastation that the potato blight caused.[13]

British and other colonial powers also attempted with varying degrees of success to colonize China. China is one of the world's oldest civilizations and prior to its extensive contact with Europe in the 1700 and 1800s, China was more advanced in many ways. Chinese porcelain, silk, tea, and other products were highly desired in Europe, but the demand for European products in China was minimal. The British, in order to stimulate trade, embarked on a concerted policy of drug dealing in order to create a need for British currency. The British brought opium from India for sale in China, and when the Chinese authorities tried to put a stop to the drug trade the British declared war in the name of free trade. The first *opium war* was fought from 1839 to 1842, and victorious England was able to extract a number of concessions from China. England was awarded the territory of Hong Kong and granted access to five port cities.

The drug addiction that resulted from the opium trade contributed to the impoverishment of China and created an economic and chemical dependency from which Great Britain was able to benefit. A second opium war, in which France joined in on the side of the British, was fought from 1856 to 1860, and resulted in a further loss of Chinese sovereignty. China suffered a third major defeat at the hands of foreigners in 1895 when Japan overtook part of the Korean peninsula and the island of Taiwan.

The late 1800s witnessed a series of rebellions in China against the West, including the *Boxer Rebellion* in 1898–1900, which was put down by joint British, Russian, German, French, Japanese, and U.S. expeditions. The country was then divided into spheres of influence by the imperial powers. Nationalist sentiment continued to grow in China, as did the appeal of communist economic and political philosophy. The Chinese communist revolution eventually cast off foreign domination and established a communist government in China in 1949 that nationalized all foreign holdings, instituted extensive land reform, and initiated widespread education and health programs.[14]

These are just a few examples of how colonialism disrupted indigenous development and caused past and recent famines. The general relationship between the core nations and the Third World or peripheral nations is summed up nicely by the Indian scholar Ranjit Sau:

> To the extent there was any exchange of goods between the outer periphery and the metropolitan center of world capitalism throughout the four centuries, it had always been an unequal exchange to the detriment of the former. . . . They are poor partly because this natural wealth has been, and still is being, plundered by imperialism for the needs of its own industrialization at the expense of those countries from which it slips away in its raw state.[15]

NOTES

1. Much of the information on Leopold's rule in the Congo comes from E. D. Morel, *The Black Man's Burden* (New York: Monthly Review Press, 1969). Morel's book was first published in Great Britain in 1920; see esp. chaps. 9 and 10. See also Leften S. Stavrianos, *Global Rift: The Third World Comes of Age* (New York: William Morrow, 1981), pp. 301–303; and Adam Hochschild's superb and moving *King Leopold's Ghost* (Boston: Houghton Mifflin, 1999).

2. Richard W. Franke and Barbara H. Chasin, *Seeds of Famine* (Montclair, N.J.: Allanheld, Osmun, 1980), pp. 64–65.

3. Frances Moore Lappé and Joseph Collins, *World Hunger, Twelve Myths* (New York: Grove Press, 1986), p. 17.

4. Richard W. Franke, "Why Hunger? An Anthropologist's Viewpoint," paper presented at the Victor Johnson Symposium on World Hunger, Amherst College, Amherst, Massachusetts, December 3, 1981, p. 8.

5. Samir Amin, *Unequal Development* (New York: Monthly Review Press, 1976), p. 299.

6. Ibid., p. 199. This analysis of British colonialism's impact on India's development also applies to the nation of Bangladesh, which by the mid-1850s had become part of British India.

7. Marx, *Capital* (New York: International Publishers, 1967), 2:140–41; and Franke, "Why Hunger?" p. 6.

8. Jawaharlal Nehru, *The Discovery of India* (Garden City, N.Y.: Anchor Books, 1959), p. 219.

9. Ibid., p. 217.

10. Ibid., p. 219.

11. Ibid., p. 221.

12. Ibid.

13. The number of deaths and the immigration statistics come from *Encyclopedia Britannica*, vol. 17 (Chicago: Encyclopedia Britannica, 1985), p. 359.

14. James DeFronzo, *Revolutions and Revolutionary Movements*, 2d ed. (Boulder, Colo.: Westview Press, 1996); see chap. 3, "Revolution in China." See also *The World Guide 2001/02* (Oxford: New Internationalist Publications, 2001), pp. 165–67.

15. Sau, *Unequal Exchange, Imperialism, and Underdevelopment*, pp. 40–41.

How Europe Underdeveloped Africa

–Walter Rodney

Walter Rodney was born in Georgetown, Guyana, in 1942. At the age of 24, he received a Ph.D. with honors in African history. He taught in Tanzania and at the University of the West Indies and was a leading figure in the resistance movement in Guyana in the 1970s. Walter Rodney was assassinated in Georgetown, Guyana in 1980. The following is an excerpt from his book, How Europe Underdeveloped Africa, *published by Howard University Press in 1982.*

The black man certainly has to pay dear for carrying the white man's burden.

—*George Padmore (West Indian) Pan-Africanist, 1936*

In the colonial society, education is such that it serves the colonialist. . . . In a regime of slavery, education was but one institution for forming slaves.

—*Statement of Frelimo (Mozambique Liberation Front) Department of Education and Culture, 1968*

The Supposed Benefits of Colonialism to Africa
Socio-Economic Services

Faced with the evidence of European exploitation of Africa, many bourgeois writers would concede at least partially that colonialism was a system which functioned well in the interests of the metropoles. However, they would then urge that another issue to be resolved is how much Europeans did for Africans, and that it is necessary to draw up a balance sheet of colonialism. On that balance sheet, they place both the credits and the debits, and quite often conclude that the good outweighed the bad. That particular conclusion can quite easily be challenged, but attention should also be drawn to the fact that the process of reasoning is itself misleading. The reasoning has some sentimental persuasiveness. It appeals to the

Walter Rodney, excerpts from *How Europe Underdeveloped Africa*. Copyright © 1972 by Walter Rodney. Reprinted with the permission of Howard University Press. All rights reserved.

common sentiment that "after all there must be two sides to a thing." The argument suggests that, on the one hand, there was exploitation and oppression, but, on the other hand, colonial governments did much for the benefit of Africans and they developed Africa. It is our contention that this is completely false. Colonialism had only one hand—it was a one-armed bandit.

What did colonial governments do in the interest of Africans? Supposedly, they built railroads, schools, hospitals, and the like. The sum total of these services was amazingly small.

For the first three decades of colonialism, hardly anything was done that could remotely be termed a service to the African people. It was in fact only after the last war that social services were built as a matter of policy. How little they amounted to does not really need illustrating. After all, the statistics which show that Africa today is underdeveloped are the statistics representing the state of affairs at the end of colonialism. For that matter, the figures at the end of the first decade of African independence in spheres such as health, housing, and education are often several times higher than the figures inherited by the newly independent governments. It would be an act of the most brazen fraud to weigh the paltry social amenities provided during the colonial epoch against the exploitation, and to arrive at the conclusion that the good outweighed the bad.

Capitalism did bring social services to European workers—firstly, as a by-product of providing such services for the bourgeoisie and the middle class, and later as a deliberate act of policy. Nothing remotely comparable occurred in Africa. In 1934, long before the coming of the welfare state to Britain, expenditure for social services in the British Isles amounted to 6 pounds 15 shillings per person. In Ghana, the figure was 7 shillings 4 pence per person, and that was high by colonial standards. In Nigeria and Nyasaland, it was less than 1 shilling 9 pence per head. None of the other colonizing powers were doing any better, and some much worse.

The Portuguese stand out because they boasted the most and did the least. Portugal boasted that Angola, Guinea, and Mozambique have been their possessions for five hundred years, during which time a "civilizing mission" has been going on. At the end of five hundred years of shouldering the white man's burden of civilizing "African natives," the Portuguese had not managed to train a single African doctor in Mozambique, and the life expectancy in eastern Angola was less than thirty years. As for Guinea-Bissau, some insight into the situation there is provided by the admission of the Portuguese themselves that Guinea-Bissau was more neglected than Angola and Mozambique!

Furthermore, the limited social services within Africa during colonial times were distributed in a manner that reflected the pattern of domination and exploitation. First of all, white settlers and expatriates wanted the standards of the bourgeoisie or professional classes of the metropoles. They were all the more determined to have luxuries in Africa, because so many of them came from poverty in Europe and could not expect good services in their own homelands. In colonies like Algeria, Kenya, and South Africa, it is well known that whites created an infrastructure to afford themselves leisured and enjoyable lives. It means, therefore, that the total amenities provided in any of those colonies is no guide to what Africans got out of colonialism.

In Algeria, the figure for infant mortality was 39 per 1,000 live births among white settlers; but it jumped to 170 per 1,000 live births in the case of Alergians living in the towns. In practical terms, that meant that the medical, maternity, and sanitation services were all geared towards the well-being of the settlers. Similarly, in South Africa, all social statistics have to be broken down into at least two groups—white and black—if they are to be interpreted correctly. In British East Africa there were three groups: firstly, the Europeans, who got the most; then, the Indians, who took most of what was left; and thirdly, the Africans, who came last in their own country.

In predominantly black countries, it was also true that the bulk of the social services went to whites. The southern part of Nigeria was one of the colonial areas that was supposed to have received the most from a benevolent mother country. Ibadan, one of the most heavily populated cities in Africa, had only about 50 Europeans before the last war. For those chosen few, the British colonial government maintained a segregated hospital service of 11 beds in well-furnished surroundings. There were 34 beds for the half-million blacks. The situation was repeated in other areas, so that altogether the 4,000 Europeans in the country in the 1930s had 12 modern hospitals, while the African population of at least 40 million had 52 hospitals.

The viciousness of the colonial system with respect to the provision of social services was most dramatically brought out in the case of economic activities which made huge profits, and notably in the mining industry. Mining takes serious toll of the health of workers, and it was only recently in the metropoles that miners have had access to the kind of medical and insurance services which could safeguard their lives and health. In colonial Africa, the exploitation of miners was entirely without responsibility. In 1930, scurvy and other epidemics broke out in the Lupa goldfields of Tanganyika. Hundreds of workers died. One should not wonder that they had no facilities which would have saved some lives, because in the first place they were not being paid enough to eat properly.

South Africa's large working class African population was in a sad state. The Tuberculosis Commission of 1912 reported that in the shanty towns,

> Scarcely a single family exists in which at least one member is not suffering or dying from tuberculosis. Hospital services are so inadequate that incurable tuberculosis and other cases are simply sent home to die—and spread the infection. In some areas, a single doctor has to attend to the needs of 40,000 people. The natives must pay for medical treatment. There is no provision for pauper patients. About 65% of the native children die before reaching two years.

That was as early as 1912, when the basis of the South African gold and diamond empire was already laid. After this, the shanty towns increased, the slum conditions grew worse, and the government committed itself to pursuing the odious policy of apartheid, which meant separation of the races so as better to exploit the African people.

Many Africans trekked to towns, because (bad as they were) they offered a little more than the countryside. Modern sanitation, electricity, piped water, paved roads, medical services, and schools were as foreign at the end of the colonial period as they were in the beginning—as far as most of rural Africa was concerned. Yet, it was the countryside that grew the cash crops and provided the labor that kept the system going. The peasants there knew very little of the supposed "credits" on the colonial balance sheet.

Because even the scanty social services were meant only to facilitate exploitation, they were not given to any Africans whose labor was not directly producing surplus for export to the metropoles. That is to say, none of the wealth of exploited Africans could be deployed for the assistance of their brothers outside the money economy. . . .

The Arusha Declaration powerfully and simply expressed one of the deepest truths of the colonial experience in Africa when it stated: "We have been oppressed a great deal, we have been exploited a great deal, and we have been disregarded a great deal."

The combination of being oppressed, being exploited, and being disregarded is best illustrated by the pattern of the economic infrastructure of African colonies: notably, their roads and railways. These had a clear geographical distribution according to the extent to which particular regions needed to be opened up to import-export activities. Where exports were not available, roads and railways had no place. The only slight exception is that certain roads and railways were built to move troops and make conquest and oppression easier.

Means of communication were not constructed in the colonial period so that Africans could visit their friends. More important still, they were not laid down to facilitate internal trade in African commodities. There were no roads connecting different colonies and different parts of the same colony in a manner that made sense with regard to Africa's needs and development. All roads and railways led down to the sea. They were built to extract gold or manganese or coffee or cotton. They were built to make business possible for the timber companies, trading companies, and agricultural concession firms, and for white settlers. Any catering to African interests was purely coincidental. Yet in Africa, labor, rather than capital, took the lion's share in getting things done. With the minimum investment of capital, the colonial powers could mobilize thousands upon thousands of workers. Salaries were paid to the police officers and officials, and labor came into existence because of the colonial laws, the threat of force, and the use of force. Take, for instance, the building of railways. In Europe and America, railway building required huge inputs of capital. Great wage bills were incurred during construction, and added bonus payments were made to workers to get the job done as quickly as possible. In most parts of Africa, the Europeans who wanted to see a railroad built offered lashes as the ordinary wage and more lashes for extra effort.

* * *

As part of the hypocrisy of colonialism, it became fashionable to speak of how Europe brought Africa into the twentieth century. This assertion has implications in the socio-economic and political spheres, and it can be shown to be false not in some but in all respects.

So often it is said that colonialism modernized Africa by introducing the dynamic features of capitalism, such as private property in land, private ownership of the other means of production, and money relations. Here it is essential to distinguish between *capitalist elements* and *capitalism as a total social system.* Colonialism introduced some elements of capitalism into Africa. In general terms, where communalism came into contact with the money economy, the latter imposed itself. Cash-crop farming and wage labor led away from the extended family as the basis of production and distribution.

One South African saying put forward that "the white man has no kin, his kin is money." That is a profound revelation of the difference between capitalist and pre-capitalist societies; and when capitalism came into contact with the still largely communal African societies, it introduced money relations at the expense of kinship ties. However, colonialism did not transform Africa into a capitalist society comparable to the metropoles. Had it done that, one might have complained of the brutalities and inequalities of capitalism, but it could not then have been said that colonialism failed to advance Africa along the path of human historical development.

Capitalism as a system within the metropoles or epicenters had two dominant classes: firstly, the capitalists or bourgeoisie who owned the factories and banks (the major means for producing and distributing wealth); and secondly, the workers or proletariat who worked in the factories of the said bourgeoisie. Colonialism did not create a capital-owning and factory-owning class among Africans or even inside Africa; nor did it create an urbanized proletariat of any significance (particularly outside South Africa). In other words, capitalism in the form of colonialism failed to perform in Africa the tasks which it had performed in Europe in changing social relations and liberating the forces of production.

It is fairly obvious that capitalists do not set out to create other capitalists, who would be rivals. On the contrary, the tendency of capitalism in Europe from the very beginning was one of competition, elimination, and monopoly. Therefore, when the imperialist stage was reached, the metropolitan capitalists had no intention of allowing rivals to arise in the dependencies. However, in spite of what the metropoles wanted, some local capitalists did emerge in Asia and Latin America. Africa is a significant exception in the sense that, compared with other colonized peoples, far fewer Africans had access even to the middle rungs of the bourgeois ladder in terms of capital for investment.

Part of the explanation for the lack of African capitalists in Africa lies in the arrival of minority groups who had no local family ties which could stand in the way of the ruthless primary accumulation which capitalism requires. Lebanese, Syrian, Greek, and Indian businessmen rose from the ranks of petty traders to become minor and sometimes substantial capitalists. Names like Raccah and Leventis were well known in West Africa, just as names like Madhvani and Visram became well known as capitalists in East Africa.

There were clashes between the middlemen and the European colonialists, but the latter much preferred to encourage the minorities rather than see Africans build themselves up. For instance, in West Africa the businessmen from Sierra Leone were discouraged both in their own colony and in other British possessions where they chose to settle. In East Africa, there was hope among Ugandans in particular that they might acquire cotton gins and perform some capitalist functions connected with cotton growing and other activities. However, when in 1920 a Development Commission was appointed to promote commerce and industry, it favored firstly Europeans and then Indians. Africans were prohibited by legislation from owning gins.

Taking Africa as a whole, the few African businessmen who were allowed to emerge were at the bottom of the ladder and cannot be considered as "capitalists" in the true sense. They did not own sufficient capital to invest in large-scale farming, trading, mining, or industry. They were dependent both on European-owned capital and on the local capital of minority groups.

That European capitalism should have failed to create African capitalists is perhaps not so striking as its inability to create a working class and to diffuse industrial skills throughout Africa. By its very nature, colonialism was prejudiced against the establishment of industries in Africa, outside of agriculture and the extractive spheres of mining and timber felling. Whenever internal forces seemed to push in the direction of African industrialization, they were deliberately blocked by the colonial governments acting on behalf of the metropolitan industrialists. Groundnut-oil mills were set up in Senegal in 1927 and began exports to France. They were soon placed under restrictions because of protests of oil-millers in France. Similarly in Nigeria, the oil mills set up by Lebanese were discouraged. The oil was still sent to Europe as a raw material for industry, but European industrialists did not then welcome even the simple stage of processing groundnuts into oil on African soil.

Many irrational contradictions arose throughout colonial Africa as a result of the non-industrialization policy: Sudanese and Ugandans grew cotton but imported manufactured cotton goods, Ivory Coast grew cocoa and imported tinned cocoa and chocolate.

The tiny working class of colonial Africa covered jobs such as agricultural labor and domestic service. Most of it was unskilled, in contrast to the accumulating skills of capitalism proper. When it came to projects requiring technical expertise, Europeans did the supervision—standing around in their helmets and white shorts. Of course, in 1885 Africans did not have the technical know-how which had evolved in Europe during the eighteenth and nineteenth centuries. That difference was itself partly due to the kind of relations between Africa and Europe in the pre-colonial period. What is more significant, however, is the incredibly small number of Africans who were able to acquire "modern" skills during the colonial period. In a few places, such as South Africa and the Rhodesias, this was due to specific racial discrimination in employment, so as to keep the best jobs for whites. Yet, even in the absence of whites, lack of skills among Africans was an integral part of the capitalist impact on the continent.

***

In some districts, capitalism brought about technological backwardness in agriculture. On the reserves of Southern Africa, far too many Africans were crowded onto inadequate land, and were forced to engage in intensive farming, using techniques that were suitable only to shifting cultivation. In practice, that was a form of technical retrogression, because the land yielded less and less and became destroyed in the process. Wherever Africans were hampered in their use of their ancestral lands on a wide-ranging shifting basis, the same negative effect was to be found. Besides, some of the new cash crops like groundnuts and cotton were very demanding on the soil. In countries like Senegal, Niger, and Chad, which were already on the edge of the desert, the steady cultivation led to soil impoverishment and encroachment of the desert.

White racist notions are so deep-rooted within capitalist society that the failure of African agriculture to advance was put down to the inherent inferiority of the African. It would be much truer to say that it was due to the white intruders, although the basic explanation is to be found not in the personal ill-will of the colonialists or in their racial origin, but rather in the organized viciousness of the capitalist/colonialist system.

Failure to improve agricultural tools and methods on behalf of African peasants was not a matter of a bad decision by colonial policy-makers. It was an inescapable feature of colonialism as a whole, based on the understanding that the international division of labor aimed at skills in the metropoles and low-level manpower in the dependencies. It was also a result of the considerable use of force (including taxation) in African labor relations. People can be forced to perform simple manual labor, but very little else. This was proven when Africans were used as slaves in the West Indies and America. Slaves damaged tools and carried out sabotage, which could only be controlled by extra supervision and by keeping tools and productive processes very elementary. Slave labor was unsuitable for carrying out industrial activity, so that in the U.S.A. the North went to war in 1861 to end slavery in the South, so as to spread true capitalist relations throughout the land. Following the same line of argument, it becomes clear why the various forms of forced agricultural labor in Africa had to be kept quite simple, and that in turn meant small earnings.

Capitalists under colonialism did not pay enough for an African to maintain himself and family. This can readily be realized by reflecting on the amounts of money earned by African peasants from cash crops. The sale of produce by an African cash-crop farmer rarely brought in 10 pounds per year and often it was less than half that amount. Out of that, a peasant had to pay for tools, seeds, and transport and he had to repay the loan to the middleman before he could call the remainder his own. Peasants producing coffee and cocoa and collecting palm produce tended to earn more than those dealing with cotton and groundnuts, but even the ordinary Akwapim cocoa farmer or Chagga coffee farmer never handled money in quantities sufficient to feed, clothe, and shelter his family. Instead, subsistence farming of yams or bananas continued as a supplement. That was how the peasant managed to eat, and the few shillings earned went to pay taxes and to buy the increasing number of things which could not be obtained without money in the middlemen's shops—salt, cloth, paraffin. If he was extremely lucky, he would have access to zinc sheets, bicycles, radios, and sewing machines, and would be able to pay school fees. It must be made quite clear that those in the last category were extremely few.

One reason why the African peasant got so little for his agricultural crops was that his labor was unskilled. That was not the whole explanation, but it is true that a product such as cotton jumped in value during the time it went through the sophisticated processes of manufacture in Europe. Karl Marx, in clarifying how capitalists appropriated part of the surplus of each worker, used the example of cotton. He explained that the value of the manufactured cotton included the value of the labor that went into growing the raw cotton, plus part of the value of the labor that made the spindles, plus the labor that went into the actual manufacture. From an African viewpoint, the first conclusion to be drawn is that the peasant working on African soil was being exploited by the industrialist who used African raw material in Europe or America. Secondly, it is necessary to realize that the African contribution of unskilled labor was valued far less than the European contribution of skilled labor.

It has been observed that one hour of work of a cotton peasant in Chad was equivalent to less than one centimeter of cotton cloth, and he needed to work fifty days to earn what was needed to buy three meters of the cloth made from his own cotton in France. Yet, the French textile worker (using modern spindles) ran off three meters of cloth in a matter of minutes! Assuming that the Frenchman was not closer to God (who made the whole world in only six days and rested on the seventh), then there must be factors in the capitalist/colonialist system which permitted the great disparity in the relative value of labor in Chad and France. In the first place, the Chad peasant was defrauded through trade so that he sold cheap and bought dear, and therefore received a minute proportion of the value that he created with his labor. This was possible not because of mysterious "market forces" as bourgeois economists would like us to believe, but because of political power being vested entirely in the hands of the colonialists. It was a consequence of monopolistic domination, both economically and politically. Secondly, the quantity of time spent by the Chad peasant was longer because colonialism did not permit him to acquire the tools to shorten the hours required to produce a given quantity of raw cotton.

To a certain extent, it would have been in the interests of the colonial powers to have had better agricultural techniques in Africa, leading to increased volume and quality of production. All colonial regimes sponsored some scientific research into tropical agriculture. However, the research was almost entirely devoted to cash crops, it was limited in scope, and it was more easily adaptable by plantations than by African peasants who had no capital. The pitiable amount devoted to agricultural improvement in Africa during the colonial period contrasts sharply with the increasingly huge sums that were devoted to research in Europe over the same period—with enormous benefits to both industry and agriculture in the metropoles.

***

Negative Character of the Social, Political, and Economic Consequences

The argument so far has been aimed at showing that benefits from colonialism were small and they were not gifts from the colonialists, but rather fruits of African labor and resources for the most part. Indeed, what was called "the development of Africa" by the colonialists was a cynical shorthand expression for "the intensification of colonial exploitation in Africa to develop capitalist Europe." The analysis has gone beyond that to demonstrate that numerous false claims are made purporting to show that Europe developed Africa in the sense of bringing about social order, nationalism, and economic modernization. However, all of that would still not permit the conclusion that colonialism had a negative impact on Africa's development. In offering the view that colonialism was negative, the aim is to draw attention to the way that previous African development was blunted, halted, and turned back. In place of that interruption and blockade, nothing of compensatory value was introduced.

The colonization of Africa lasted for just over seventy years in most parts of the continent. That is an extremely short period within the context of universal historical development. Yet, it was precisely in those years that in other parts of the world the rate of change was greater than ever before. As has been illustrated, capitalist countries revolutionized their technology to enter the nuclear age. Meanwhile, socialism was inaugurated, lifting semi-feudal semi-capitalist Russia to a level of sustained economic growth higher than that ever experienced in a capitalist country. Socialism did the same for China and North Korea—guaranteeing the well-being and independence of the state as well as reorganizing the internal social arrangements in a far more just manner than ever before. It is against those decisive changes that events in Africa have to be measured. To mark time or even to move slowly while others leap ahead is virtually equivalent to going backward. Certainly, in relative terms, Africa's position via-à-vis its colonizes became more disadvantageous in the political, economic, and military spheres.

The decisiveness of the short period of colonialism and its negative consequences for Africa spring mainly from the fact that Africa lost power. Power is the ultimate determinant in human society, being basic to the relations within any group and between groups. It implies the ability to defend one's interests and if necessary to impose one's will by any means available. In relations between peoples, the question of power determines maneuverability in bargaining, the extent to which one people respect the interests of another, and eventually the extent to which a people survive as a physical and cultural entity. When one society finds itself forced to relinquish power entirely to another society, that in itself is a form of underdevelopment.

During the centuries of pre-colonial trade, some control over social, political, and economic life was retained in Africa, in spite of the disadvantageous commerce with Europeans. That little control over internal matters disappeared under colonialism. Colonialism went much further than trade. It meant a tendency towards direct appropriation by Europeans of the social institutions within Africa. Africans ceased to set indigenous cultural goals and standards, and lost full command of training young members of the society. Those were undoubtedly major steps backward.

The Tunisian, Albert Memmi, puts forward the following proposition:

> The most serious blow suffered by the colonized is being removed from history and from the community. Colonization usurps any free role in either war or peace, every decision contributing to his destiny and that of the world, and all cultural and social responsibility.

Sweeping as that statement may initially appear, it is entirely true. The removal from history follows logically from the loss of power which colonialism represented. The power to act independently is the guarantee to participate actively and *consciously* in history. To be colonized is to be removed from history, except in the most passive sense. A striking illustration of the fact that colonial Africa was a passive object is seen in its attraction for white anthropologists, who came to study "primitive society." Colonialism determined that Africans were no more makers of history than were beetles—objects to be looked at under a microscope and examined for unusual features.

The negative impact of colonialism in political terms was quite dramatic. Overnight, African political states lost their power, independence, and meaning—irrespective of whether they were big empires or small polities. Certain traditional rulers were kept in office, and the formal structure of some kingdoms was partially retained, but the substance of political life was quite different. Political power had passed into the hands of foreign overlords. Of course, numerous African states in previous centuries had passed through the cycle of growth and decline. But colonial rule was different. So long as it lasted, not a single African state could flourish. . . .

Sometimes, the African rulers who were chosen to serve as agents of foreign colonial rule were quite obviously nothing but puppets. The French and the Portuguese were in the habit of choosing their own African "chiefs"; the British went to Iboland and invented "warrant chiefs"; and all the colonial powers found it convenient to create "superior" or "paramount" rulers. Very often, the local population hated and despised such colonial stooges. There were traditional rulers such as the Sultan of Sokoto, the Kabaka of Buganda, and the Asantehene of Asante, who retained a great deal of prestige in the eyes of Africans, but they had no power to act outside the narrow boundaries laid down by colonialism, lest they find themselves in the Seychelles Islands as "guests of His Majesty's Government."

One can go so far as to say that colonial rule meant the effective eradication of African political power throughout the continent, since Liberia and Ethiopia could no longer function as independent states within the context of continent-wide colonialism. Liberia in particular had to bow before foreign political, economic, and military pressures in a way that no genuinely independent state could have accepted; and although Ethiopia held firm until 1936, most European capitalist nations were not inclined to treat Ethiopia as a sovereign state, primarily because it was African, and Africans were supposed to be colonial subjects.

The pattern of arrest of African political development has some features which can only be appreciated after careful scrutiny and the taking away of the blinkers which the colonizers put on the eyes of their subjects. An interesting case in point is that of women's role in society. Until today, capitalist society has failed to resolve the inequality between man and woman, which was entrenched in all modes of production prior to socialism. The colonialists in Africa occasionally paid lip service to women's education and emancipation, but objectively there was deterioration in the status of women owing to colonial rule.

A realistic assessment of the role of women in independent pre-colonial Africa shows two contrasting but combined tendencies. In the first place, women were exploited by men through polygamous arrangements designed to capture the labor power of women. As always, exploitation was accompanied by oppression; and there is evidence to the effect that women were sometimes treated like beasts of burden, as for instance in Moslem African societies. Nevertheless, there was a countertendency to insure the dignity of women to greater or lesser degree in all African societies. Mother-right was a prevalent feature of African societies, and particular women held a variety of privileges based on the fact that they were the keys to inheritance.

More important still, some women had real power in the political sense, exercised either through religion or directly within the politico-constitutional apparatus. In Mozambique, the widow of an Nguni king became the priestess in charge of the shrine set up in the burial place of her deceased husband, and the reigning king had to consult her on all important matters. In a few instances, women were actually heads of state. Among the Lovedu of Transvaal, the key figure was the Rain-Queen, combining political and religious functions. The most frequently encountered role of importance played by women was that of "Queen Mother" or "Queen Sister." In practice, that post was filled by a female of royal blood, who might be mother, sister, or aunt of the reigning king in places such as Mali, Asante, and Buganda. Her influence was considerable, and there were occasions when the "Queen Mother" was the real power and the male king a mere puppet.

What happened to African women under colonialism is that the social, religious, constitutional, and political privileges and rights disappeared, while the economic exploitation continued and was often intensified. It was intensified because the division of labor according to sex was frequently disrupted. Traditionally, African men did the heavy labor of felling trees, clearing land, building houses, apart from conducting warfare and hunting. When they were required to leave their farms to seek employment, women remained behind burdened with every task necessary for the survival of themselves, the children, and even the men as far as foodstuffs were concerned. Moreover, since men entered the money sector more easily and in greater numbers than women, women's work became greatly inferior to that of men within the new value system of colonialism: men's work was "modern" and women's was "traditional" and "backward." Therefore, the deterioration in the status of African women was bound up with the consequent loss of the right to set indigenous standards of what work had merit and what did not.

One of the most important manifestations of historical arrest and stagnation in colonial Africa is that which commonly goes under the title of "tribalism." That term, in its common journalistic setting, is understood to mean that Africans have a basic loyalty to tribe rather than nation and that each tribe still *retains* a fundamental hostility towards its neighboring tribes. The examples favored by the capitalist press and bourgeois scholarship are those of Congo and Nigeria. Their accounts suggest that Europeans tried to make a nation out of the Congolese and Nigerian peoples, but they failed, because the various tribes had their age-long hatreds; and, as soon as the colonial power went, the natives *returned* to killing each other. To this phenomenon, Europeans often attach the word "atavism," to carry the notion that Africans were returning to their primitive savagery. Even a cursory survey of the African past shows that such assertions are the exact opposite of the truth.

It is necessary to discuss briefly what comprises a tribe—a term that has been avoided in this analysis, partly because it usually carries derogatory connotations and partly because of its vagueness and the loose ways in which it is employed in the literature on Africa. Following the principle of family living, Africans were organized in groups which had common ancestors. Theoretically, the tribe was the largest group of people claiming descent from a common ancestor at some time in the remote past. Generally, such a group could therefore be said to be of the same ethnic stock, and their language would have a great deal in common. Beyond that, members of a tribe were seldom all members of the same political unit and very seldom indeed did they all share a common social purpose in terms of activities such as trade and warfare. Instead, African states were sometimes based entirely on part of the members of a given ethnic group or (more usually) on an amalgamation of members of different ethnic communities.

All of the large states of nineteenth-century Africa were multi-ethnic, and their expansion was continually making anything like "tribal" loyalty a thing of the past, by substituting in its place national and class ties. However, in all parts of the world, that substitution of national and class ties for purely ethnic ones is a lengthy historical process; and, invariably there remains for long periods certain regional pockets of individuals who have their own narrow, regional loyalties, springing from ties of kinship, language, and culture. In Asia, the feudal states of Vietnam and Burma both achieved a considerable degree of national homogeneity over the centuries before colonial rule. But there were pockets of "tribes" or "minorities" who remained outside the effective sphere of the nation-state and the national economy and culture.

In the first place, colonialism blocked the further evolution of national solidarity, because it destroyed the particular Asian or African states which were the principal agents for achieving the liquidation of fragmented loyalties. In the second place, because ethnic and regional loyalties which go under the name of "tribalism" could not be effectively resolved by the colonial state, they tended to fester and grow in unhealthy forms. Indeed, the colonial powers sometimes saw the value of stimulating the internal tribal jealousies so as to keep the colonized from dealing with their principal contradiction with the European overlords—i.e., the classic technique of divide and rule. Certainly, the Belgians consciously fostered that; and the racist whites in South Africa had by the 1950s worked out a careful plan to "develop" the oppressed African population as Zulu, as Xhosa, and as Sotho so that the march towards broader African national and class solidarities could be stopped and turned back.

The civil war in Nigeria is generally regarded as having been a tribal affair. To accept such a contention would mean extending the definition of tribe to cover Shell Oil and Gulf Oil! But, quite apart from that, it must be pointed out that nowhere in the history of pre-colonial independent Nigeria can anyone point to the massacre of Ibos by Hausas or any incident which suggests that people up to the nineteenth century were fighting each other because of ethnic origin. Of course there were wars, but they had a rational basis in trade rivalry, religious contentions, and the clashes of political expansion. What came to be called tribalism at the beginning of the new epoch of political independence in Nigeria was itself a product of the way that people were brought together under colonialism so as to be exploited. It was a product of administrative devices, of entrenched regional separations, of differential access by particular ethnic groups into the colonial economy and culture.

* * *

In recent times, economists have been recognizing in colonial and post-colonial Africa a pattern that has been termed "growth without development." That phrase has now appeared as the title of books on Liberia and Ivory Coast. It means that goods and services of a certain type are on the increase. There may be more rubber and coffee exported, there may be more cars imported with the proceeds, and there may be more gasoline stations built to service the cars. But the profit goes abroad, and the economy becomes more and more a dependency of the metropoles. In no African colony was there economic integration, or any provision for making the economy self-sustained and geared to its own local goals. Therefore, there was growth of the so-called enclave import-export sector, but the only things which developed were dependency and underdevelopment.

A further revelation of growth without development under colonialism was the overdependence on one or two exports. The term "monoculture" is used to describe those colonial economies which were centered around a single crop. Liberia (in the agricultural sector) was a monoculture dependent on rubber, Gold Coast on cocoa, Dahomey and southeast Nigeria on palm produce, Sudan on cotton, Tanganyika on sisal, and Uganda on cotton. In Senegal and Gambia, groundnuts accounted for 85 to 90 per cent of money earnings. In effect, two African colonies were told to grow nothing but peanuts!

Every farming people have a staple food, plus a variety of other supplements. Historians, agronomists, and botanists have all contributed to showing the great variety of such foods within the pre-colonial African economy. There were numerous crops which were domesticated within the African continent, there were several wild food species (notably fruits), and Africans had shown no conservatism in adopting useful food plants of Asian or American origin. Diversified agriculture was within the African tradition. Monoculture was a colonialist invention.

Those who justify the colonial division of labor suggest that it was "natural" and respected the relative capacities for specialization of the metropoles and colonies. Europe, North America, and Japan were capable of specializing in industry and Africa in agriculture. Therefore, it was to the "comparative advantage" of one part of the world to manufacture machines while another part engaged in simple hoe-culture of the soil. That kind of arrogant partition of the world was not new. In the fifteenth century, the feudal monarchies of Portugal and Spain wanted the whole world for themselves, and they got the Pope to draw a line around the globe, making the allocations. But Britain, Holland, and France suggested that they were not at all convinced that Adam had left a will which gave the earth to Portugal and Spain. In like manner, it can be questioned whether there is any testament which stated that the river Gambia should inherit groundnut growing while the river Clyde (of Scotland) should become a home of shipbuilding.

There was nothing "natural" about monoculture. It was a consequence of imperialist requirements and machinations, extending into areas that were politically independent in name. Monoculture was a characteristic of regions falling under imperialist domination. Certain countries in Latin America such as Costa Rica and Guatemala were forced by United States capitalist firms to concentrate so heavily on growing bananas that they were contemptuously known as "banana republics." In Africa, this concentration on one or two cash crops for sale abroad had many harmful effects. Sometimes, cash crops were grown to the exclusion of staple foods—thus causing famines. For instance, in Gambia rice farming was popular before the colonial era, but so much of the best land was transferred to groundnuts that rice had to be imported on a large scale to try to counter the fact that famine was becoming endemic. In Asante, concentration on cocoa raised fears of famine in a region previously famous for yams and other foodstuff.

Yet the threat of famine was a small disadvantage compared to the extreme vulnerability and insecurity of monoculture. When the crop was affected by internal factors such as disease, that amounted to an overwhelming disaster, as in the case of Gold Coast cocoa when it was hit by swollen-shoot disease in the 1940s. Besides, at all times, the price fluctuations (which were externally controlled) left the African producer helpless in the face of capitalist maneuvers.

From a capitalist viewpoint, monocultures commended themselves most because they made colonial economies entirely dependent on the metropolitan buyers of their produce. At the end of the European slave trade, only a minority of Africans were sufficiently committed to capitalist exchange and sufficiently dependent upon European imports to wish to continue the relationship with Europe at all costs. Colonialism increased the dependence of Africa on Europe in terms of the numbers of persons brought into the money economy and in terms of the number of aspects of socio-economic life in Africa which derived their existence from the connection with the metropole. The ridiculous situation arose by which European trading firms, mining companies, shipping lines, banks, insurance houses, and plantations all exploited Africa and at the same time caused Africans to feel that without those capitalist services no money or European goods would be forthcoming, and therefore Africa was in debt to its exploiters!

The factor of dependency made its impact felt in every aspect of the life of the colonies, and it can be regarded as the crowning vice among the negative social, political, and economic consequences of colonialism in Africa, being primarily responsible for the *perpetuation* of the colonial relationship into the epoch that is called neo-colonialism.

Finally, attention must be drawn to one of the most important consequences of colonialism on African development, and that is the stunting effect on Africans as a physical species. Colonialism created conditions which led not just to periodic famine but to chronic undernourishment, malnutrition, and deterioration in the physique of the African people.

* * *

Education for Underdevelopment

Education is crucial in any type of society for the preservation of the lives of its members and the maintenance of the social structure. Under certain circumstances, education also promotes social change. The greater portion of that education is informal, being acquired by the young from the example and behavior of elders in the society. Under normal circumstances, education grows out of the environment; the learning process being directly related to the pattern of work in the society. Among the Bemba of what was then Northern Rhodesia, children by the age of six could name fifty to sixty species of tree plants without hesitation, but they knew very little about ornamental flowers. The explanation is simply that knowledge of the trees was a necessity in an environment of "cut and burn" agriculture and in a situation where numerous household needs were met by tree products. Flowers, however, were irrelevant to survival.

Indeed, the most crucial aspect of pre-colonial African education was its *relevance* to Africans, in sharp contrast with what was later introduced. The following features of indigenous African education can be considered outstanding: its close links with social life, both in a material and spiritual sense; its collective nature; its many-sidedness; and its progressive development in conformity with the successive stages of physical, emotional, and mental development of the child. There was no separation of education and productive activity or any division between manual and intellectual education. Altogether, through mainly informal means, pre-colonial African education matched the realities of pre-colonial African society and produced well-rounded personalities to fit into that society.

Some aspects of African education were formal: that is to say, there was a specific program and a conscious division between teachers and pupils. Formal education in pre-colonial Africa was also directly connected with the purposes of society, just like informal education. The programs of teaching were restricted to certain periods in the life of every individual, notably the period of initiation or "coming of age." Many African societies had circumcision ceremonies for males or for both sexes, and for some time before the ceremonies a teaching program was arranged. . . .

The colonizers did not introduce education into Africa: they introduced a new set of formal educational institutions which partly supplemented and partly replaced those which were there before. The colonial system also stimulated values and practices which amounted to new informal education.

The main purpose of the colonial school system was to train Africans to help man the local administration at the lowest ranks and to staff the private capitalist firms owned by Europeans. In effect, that meant selecting a few Africans to participate in the domination and exploitation of the continent as a whole. It was not an educational system that grew out of the African environment or one that was designed to promote the most rational use of material and social resources. It was not an educational system designed to give young people confidence and pride as members of African societies, but one which sought to instill a sense of deference towards all that was European and capitalist.

* * *

One limitation of the educational system of colonial Africa which is obscured by statistical averages is the great variation in opportunity between different regions in the same colony. In many colonies, only Africans living in or near the principal towns had educational opportunities. For instance, in Madagascar the capital town of Tananarive had the most substantial school facilities; in Gambia literacy was high for Bathurst town but low outside; and in Uganda the urbanized region of Buganda practically monopolized education. Generally speaking, the unevenness in educational levels reflected the unevenness of economic exploitation and the different rates at which different parts of a colony entered the money economy. Thus, in Gold Coast, the Northern Territories were neglected educationally, because they did not offer the colonialists any products for export. In Sudan it was the huge southern region which was in a similar position. Inside Tanganyika, a map showing the major cotton and coffee areas virtually coincides with a map showing areas in which colonial education was available. It means that those whom the colonialists could not readily exploit were not offered even the crumbs of education. . . .

Africans were being educated inside colonial schools to become junior clerks and messengers. Too much learning would have been both superfluous and dangerous for clerks and messengers. Therefore, secondary education was rare and other forms of higher education were virtually non-existent throughout most of the colonial epoch. That which was provided went mainly to non-Africans. As late as 1959, Uganda spent about 11 pounds per African pupil, 38 pounds per Indian, and 186 pounds on each European child—the difference being due largely to the availability of secondary education for the children of the capitalists and the middlemen.

* * *

Early educational commissions also accorded high priority to religious and moral flavoring of instruction—something that was disappearing in Europe itself. The role of the Christian church in the educational process obviously needs special attention. The Christian missionaries were as much part of the colonizing forces as were the explorers, traders, and soldiers. There may be room for arguing whether in a given colony the missionaries brought the other colonialist forces or vice versa, but there is no doubting the fact that missionaries were agents of colonialism in the practical sense, whether or not they saw themselves in that light. The imperialist adventurer Sir Henry Johnston disliked missionaries, but he conceded in praise of them that "each mission station is an exercise in colonisation."

In Europe, the church had long held a monopoly over schooling from feudal times right into the capitalist era. By the late nineteenth century, that situation was changing in Europe; but, as far as the European colonizers were concerned, the church was free to handle the colonial educational system in Africa. The strengths and weaknesses of that schooling were very much to be attributed to the church.

Both inside and outside church and school, the personnel of the church were instrumental in setting values during the colonial epoch. They taught an ethic of human relations that in itself could appeal to the finer instincts of Africans, just as it had previously stirred other Europeans. Of course, there was a huge gap between European conduct and the Christian principles with which they were associated; and, on the part of the Africans, it was also true that motives for accepting Christianity often had nothing to do with the content of the religion. Indeed, the church as a source of education was probably more attractive to many converts than the church as a dispenser of religion.

Whatever the church taught in any capacity may be considered as a contribution to formal and informal education in colonial Africa, and its teachings must be

placed within a social context. The church's role was primarily to preserve the social relations of colonialism, as an extension of the role it played in preserving the
social relations of capitalism in Europe. Therefore, the Christian church stressed
humility, docility, and acceptance. Ever since the days of slavery in the West
Indies, the church had been brought in on condition that it should not excite the
African slaves with doctrines of equality before God. In those days, they taught
slaves to sing that all things were bright and beautiful, and that the slavemaster in
his castle was to be accepted as God's work just like the slave living in a miserable
hovel and working twenty hours per day under the whip. Similarly, in colonial
Africa, churches could be relied upon to preach turning the other cheek in the
face of exploitation, and they drove home the message that everything would be
right in the next world. Only the Dutch Reformed church of South Africa was
openly racist, but all others were racist in so far as their European personnel were
no different from other whites who had imbibed racism and cultural imperialism
as a consequence of the previous centuries of contact between Europeans and the
rest of the world. . . .

In the final analysis, perhaps the most important principle of colonial education was that of capitalist individualism. Like many aspects of the superstructure of
beliefs in a society, it had both its negative and positive sides, viewed historically.
The European bourgeoisie were progressive when they defended the individual
from the excessive control of the father in the family and against the collective regulations of the church and feudal society. However, the capitalist system then went
on to champion and protect the rights of the individual property owners against
the rights of the mass of exploited workers and peasants. When capitalism had its
impact on Africa in the colonial period, the idea of individualism was already in its
reactionary phase. It was no longer serving to liberate the majority but rather to enslave the majority for the benefit of a few.

When individualism was applied to land, it meant that the notions of private
ownership and the transfer of land through sale became prevalent in some parts of
the continent. Much more widespread was the new understanding that individual
labor should benefit the person concerned and not some wider collective, such as
the clan or ethnic group. Thus, the practice of collective labor and egalitarian social distribution gave way to accumulative tendencies. Superficially, it appeared
that individualism brought progress. Some individuals owned large coffee, cocoa,
or cotton *shambas*, and others rose to some prominence in the colonial administration through education. As individuals, they had improved their lot, and they became models of achievement within the society. Any model of achievement is an
educational model, which directs the thoughts and actions of young and old in the
society. The model of personal achievement under colonialism was really a model
for the falling apart and the underdevelopment of African society taken as a whole.

It is a common myth within capitalist thought that the individual through drive
and hard work can become a capitalist. In the U.S.A., it is usual to refer to an individual like John D. Rockefeller, Sr., as someone who rose "from rags to riches." To

complete the moral of the Rockefeller success story, it would be necessary to fill in the details on all the millions of people who had to be exploited in order for one man to become a multimillionaire. The acquisition of wealth is not due to hard work alone, or the Africans working as slaves in America and the West Indies would have been the wealthiest group in the world. The individualism of the capitalist must be seen against the hard and unrewarded work of the masses.

The idea of individualism was more destructive in colonial Africa than it was in metropolitan capitalist society. In the latter, it could be said that the rise of the bourgeois class indirectly benefited the working classes, through promoting technology and raising the standard of living. But, in Africa, colonialism did not bring those benefits—it merely intensified the rate of exploitation of African labor and continued to export the surplus. In Europe, individualism led to entrepreneurship and adventurism of the type which spearheaded Europe's conquest of the rest of the world. In Africa, both the formal school system and the informal value system of colonialism destroyed social solidarity and promoted the worst form of alienated individualism without social responsibility.

* * *

Most of what emerged from the colonial educational system was not unique. Educational systems are designed to function as props to a given society, and the educated in the young age groups automatically carry over their values when their turn comes to make decisions in the society. In Africa, the colonialists were training low-level administrators, teachers, NCOs, railroad booking clerks, for the preservation of colonial relations; and it is not surprising that such individuals would carry over colonial values into the period after independence was regained. The colonialists meanwhile took action wherever possible to insure that persons most favorable to their position continued to man African administrations and assumed new political and state police powers. Such a presentation of events would be termed one-sided by many Europeans and Africans, too. In a sense, that is true, and the one-sidedness is deliberate. It is a presentation of what the colonial educational system achieved *in terms of what it set itself to achieve*. The other side of the matter is not the good with which colonial educators can be credited, but rather the good that emerged in spite of the efforts and intentions of the colonizers and because of the struggles of African people.

Colonialism in Africa, 1914

The following map appeared originally in A History of the African People, *3rd edition, Waveland Press, 1992, which was written by Robert W. July, Professor Emeritus of Hunter College and the Graduate Center of the City University of New York.*

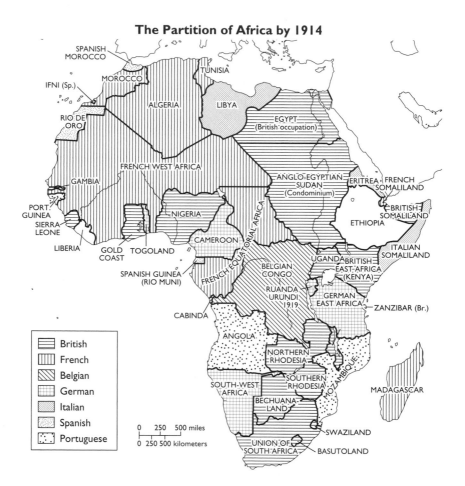

The Partition of Africa by 1914

Reprinted by permission of Waveland Press, Inc. from *A History of the African People,* 5th ed. (Long Grove, IL: Waveland Press, Inc., 1998). All rights reserved.

126

seven

Open Veins of Latin America

–Eduardo Galeano

Journalist and author Eduardo Galeano was born in Montevideo, Uruguay in 1940. After a military coup in 1973, he was imprisoned and later lived in exile in both Argentina and Spain. He returned to Uruguay in 1985. The selection that follows, "Open Veins of Latin America," is from his book by the same name, which was translated by Cedric Belfrage and published originally by Monthly Review Press in 1973.

The division of labor among nations is that some specialize in winning and others in losing. Our part of the world, known today as Latin America, was precocious: it has specialized in losing ever since those remote times when Renaissance Europeans ventured across the ocean and buried their teeth in the throats of the Indian civilizations. Centuries passed, and Latin America perfected its role. We are no longer in the era of marvels when fact surpassed fable and imagination was shamed by the trophies of conquest—the lodes of gold, the mountains of silver. But our region still works as a menial. It continues to exist at the service of others' needs, as a source and reserve of oil and iron, of copper and meat, of fruit and coffee, the raw materials and foods destined for rich countries which profit more from consuming them than Latin America does from producing them. The taxes collected by the buyers are much higher than the prices received by the sellers; and after all, as Alliance for Progress coordinator Covey T. Oliver said in July 1968, to speak of fair prices is a "medieval" concept, for we are in the era of free trade.

The more freedom is extended to business, the more prisons have to be built for those who suffer from that business. Our inquisitor-hangman systems function not only for the dominating external markets; they also provide gushers of profit from foreign loans and investments in the dominated internal markets. Back in 1913, President Woodrow Wilson observed: "You hear of 'concessions' to foreign capitalists in Latin America. You do not hear of concessions to foreign capitalists in the United States. They are not granted concessions." He was confident: "States that are obliged . . . to grant concessions are in this condition, that foreign interests are apt to dominate their domestic affairs . . . ," he said, and he was right.[1] Along

From "Open Veins of Latin America" by Eduardo Galeano. © 1997 Monthly Review Press. Reprinted by permission.

the way we have even lost the right to call ourselves Americans, although the Haitians and the Cubans appeared in history as new people a century before the *Mayflower* pilgrims settled on the Plymouth coast. For the world today, America is just the United States: the region we inhabit is a sub-America, a second-class America of nebulous identity.

Latin America is the region of open veins. Everything, from the discovery until our times, has always been transmuted into European—or later United States—capital, and as such has accumulated in distant centers of power. Everything: the soil, its fruits and its mineral-rich depths, the people and their capacity to work and to consume, natural resources and human resources. Production methods and class structure have been successively determined from outside for each area by meshing it into the universal gearbox of capitalism. To each area has been assigned a function, always for the benefit of the foreign metropolis of the moment, and the endless chain of dependency has been endlessly extended. The chain has many more than two links. In Latin America it also includes the oppression of small countries by their larger neighbors and, within each country's frontiers, the exploitation by big cities and ports of their internal sources of food and labor. (Four centuries ago sixteen of today's twenty biggest Latin American cities already existed.)

For those who see history as a competition, Latin America's backwardness and poverty are merely the result of its failure. We lost; others won. But the winners happen to have won thanks to our losing: the history of Latin America's underdevelopment is, as someone has said, an integral part of the history of world capitalism's development. *Our defeat was always implicit in the victory of others; our wealth has always generated our poverty by nourishing the prosperity of others—the empires and their native overseers. In the colonial and neocolonial alchemy, gold changes into scrap metal and food into poison.* Potosí, Zacatecas, and Ouro Prêto became desolate warrens of deep, empty tunnels from which the precious metals had been taken; ruin was the fate of Chile's nitrate pampas and of Amazonia's rubber forests. Northeast Brazil's sugar and Argentina's quebracho belts, and communities around oil-rich Lake Maracaibo, have become painfully aware of the mortality of wealth which nature bestows and imperialism appropriates. The rain that irrigates the centers of imperialist power drowns the vast suburbs of the system. In the same way, and symmetrically, the well-being of our dominating classes—dominating inwardly, dominated from outside—is the curse of our multitudes condemned to exist as beasts of burden.

* * *

When Christopher Columbus headed across the great emptiness west of Christendom, he had accepted the challenge of legend. Terrible storms would play with his ships as if they were nutshells and hurl them into the jaws of monsters; the sea serpent, hungry for human flesh, would be lying in wait in the murky depths. According to fifteenth-century man, only one thousand years remained before the purifying flames of the Last Judgment would destroy the world, and the world was then the Mediterranean Sea with its uncertain horizons: Europe, Africa, Asia. Portuguese navigators spoke of strange corpses and curiously carved pieces of wood that floated in on the west wind, but no one suspected that the world was about to be startlingly extended by a great new land.

America not only lacked a name. The Norwegians did not know they had discovered it long ago, and Columbus himself died convinced that he had reached Asia by the western route. In 1492, when Spanish boats first trod the beaches of the Bahamas, the Admiral thought these islands were an outpost of the fabulous isle of Zipango—Japan. Columbus took along a copy of Marco Polo's book, and covered its margins with notes. The inhabitants of Zipango, said Marco Polo, "have gold in the greatest abundance, its sources being inexhaustible. . . . In this island there are pearls also, in large quantities, of a red color, round in shape, and of great size, equal in value to, or even exceeding that of white pearls."[2] The wealth of Zipango had become known to the Great Kubla Khan, stirring a desire to conquer it, but he had failed. Out of Marco Polo's sparkling pages leaped all the good things of creation: there were nearly thirteen thousand islands in the Indian seas, with mountains of gold and pearls and twelve kinds of spices in enormous quantities, in addition to an abundance of white and black pepper.

Pepper, ginger, cloves, nutmeg, and cinnamon were as prized as salt in preserving meat against putrefaction and loss of flavor in winter. Spain's Catholic rulers decided to finance the adventure to get direct access to the sources and to free themselves from the burdensome chain of intermediaries and speculators who monopolized the trade in spices and tropical plants, muslins and sidearms, from the mysterious East. The desire for precious metals, the medium of payment in commercial dealings, also sparked the crossing of the sinister seas. All of Europe needed silver; the seams in Bohemia, Saxony, and the Tyrol were almost exhausted.

***

Between 1545 and 1558 the prolific silver mines of Potosí, in what is now Bolivia, and of Zacatecas and Guanajuato in Mexico, were discovered, and the mercury amalgam process, which made possible the exploitation of the lowest-grade silver, began to be used. The "silver rush" quickly eclipsed gold mining. In the mid-seventeenth century silver constituted more than 99 percent of mineral exports from Spanish America. Latin America was a huge mine, with Potosí as its chief center. Some excessively enthusiastic Bolivian writers insist that in three centuries Spain got enough metal from Potosí to make a silver bridge from the tip of the Cerro to the door of the royal palace across the ocean. This is certainly fanciful, but even the reality stretches one's imagination to the limit: the flow of silver achieved gigantic dimensions. The large-scale clandestine export of Latin American silver as contraband to the Philippines, to China, and to Spain itself is not taken into account by Earl Hamilton, who nevertheless cites, in his well-known work on the subject, astounding figures based on data from the Casa de Contratación in Seville.[3] Between 1503 and 1660, 185,000 kilograms of gold and

16,000,000 of silver arrived at the Spanish port of Sanlúcar de Barrameda. Silver shipped to Spain in little more than a century and a half exceeded three times the total European reserves—and it must be remembered that these official figures are not complete.

The metals taken from the new colonial dominions not only stimulated Europe's economic development; one may say that they made it possible. Even the effect of the Persian treasure seized and poured into the Hellenic world by Alexander the Great cannot be compared with Latin America's formidable contribution to the progress of other regions.

* * *

Plunder, internal and external, was the most important means of primitive accumulation of capital, an accumulation which, after the Middle Ages, made possible a new historical stage in world economic evolution. As the money economy extended, more and more social strata and regions of the world became involved in unequal exchange. Ernest Mandel has added up the value of the gold and silver torn from Latin America up to 1660, the booty extracted from Indonesia by the Dutch East India Company from 1650 to 1780, the harvest reaped by French capital in the eighteenth-century slave trade, the profits from slave labor in the British Antilles and from a half-century of British looting in India. The total exceeds the capital invested in all European industrial enterprises operated by steam in about 1800.[4] This enormous mass of capital, Mandel notes, created a favorable climate for investment in Europe, stimulated the "spirit of enterprise," and directly financed the establishment of manufactures, which in turn gave a strong thrust to the Industrial Revolution. But at the same time the formidable international concentration of wealth for Europe's benefit prevented the jump into the accumulation of industrial capital in the plundered areas: "The double tragedy of the developing countries consists in the fact that they were not only victims of that process of international concentration, but that subsequently they have had to try and compensate for their industrial backwardness—that is, realize the primitive accumulation of industrial capital—in a world flooded with articles manufactured by an already mature industry, that of the West."[5]

The Latin American colonies were discovered, conquered, and colonized within the process of the expansion of commercial capital. Europe stretched out its arms to clasp the whole world. Neither Spain nor Portugal received the benefits of the sweeping advance of capitalist mercantilism, although it was their colonies that substantially supplied the gold and silver feeding this expansion. As we have seen, while Latin America's precious metals made deceptive fortunes for a Spanish nobility living in a belated and contra-historical Middle Age, they simultaneously sealed the ruin of Spain in centuries to come. It was in other parts of Europe that modern capitalism could be incubated, taking decisive advantage of the expropriation of primitive American peoples. The rape of accumulated treasure was followed by the systematic exploitation of the forced labor of Indians and abducted Africans in the mines.

Europe needed gold and silver. The money in circulation kept multiplying and it was necessary to stimulate the movement of capitalism in the hour of birth: the bourgeoisie took control of the cities and founded banks, produced and exchanged merchandise, conquered new markets. Gold, silver, sugar: the colonial economy, supplying rather than consuming, was built in terms of—and at the service of—the European market. During long periods of the sixteenth century the value of Latin American precious metal exports was four times greater than the value of the slaves, salt, and luxury goods it imported. The resources flowed out so that emergent European nations across the ocean could accumulate them. This was the basic mission of the pioneers, although they applied the Bible almost as often as the whip to the dying Indians. The Spanish colonies' economic structure was born subordinated to the external market and was thus centralized around the export sector, where profit and power were concentrated.

During the process, from the metals stage to that of supplying foodstuffs, each region became identified with what it produced, and each produced what Europe wanted of it: *each product, loaded in the holds of galleons plowing the ocean, became a vocation and a destiny.* The international division of labor, as it emerged along with capitalism, resembled the distribution of function between a horseman and a horse, as Paul Baran put it. The markets of the colonial world grew as mere appendices to the internal market of invading capitalism.

Celso Furtado notes that while most of Europe's feudal seigneurs obtained an economic surplus from the people they dominated and used it in one way or another in the same areas, the chief aim of those Spaniards who received Latin American mines, lands, and Indians from the king was to extract a surplus to send to Europe.[6] This observation helps explain the ultimate goal of the Latin American colonial economy from its inception: although it showed some feudal characteristics, it functioned at the service of capitalism developing elsewhere. Nor, indeed, can the existence of wealthy capitalist centers in our own time be explained without the existence of poor and subjected outskirts: the one and the other make up the same system.

But not all of the surplus went to Europe. The colonial economy was run by merchants, by owners of mines and of big estates, who divided up the usufruct of Indian and black labor under the jealous and omnipotent eye of the Crown and its chief associate, the Church. Power was concentrated in the hands of a few, who sent metals and foodstuffs to Europe and received back the luxury goods to the enjoyment of which they dedicated their mushrooming fortunes. The dominant classes took no interest whatever in diversifying the internal economies or in raising technical and cultural levels in the population: they had a different function within the international complex they were acting for, and the grinding poverty of the people—so profitable from the standpoint of the reigning interests—prevented the development of an internal consumer market.

One French economist argues that Latin America's worst colonial legacy, which explains its backwardness today, is lack of capital.[7] But all the historical evidence shows that the colonial economy produced bountiful wealth for the classes connected internally with the colonial system of domination. The labor that was abundantly available for nothing or practically nothing, and the great European demand for Latin American products, made possible "a precocious and abundant accumulation of capital in the Iberian colonies. The hard core of beneficiaries, far from growing, became smaller in proportion to the mass of the population, as may be seen from the well-known fact that unemployed Europeans and Creoles constantly increased."[8] The capital that stayed in Latin America, after the lion's share went into the primitive accumulation process of European capitalism, did not generate a process similar to that which took place in Europe, where the foundations of industrial development were laid. It was diverted instead into the construction of great palaces and showy churches, into the purchase of jewels and luxurious clothing and furniture, into the maintenance of flocks of servants, and into the extravagance of fiestas. To an important extent this surplus was also immobilized in the purchase of new lands, or continued to revolve around speculative commercial activities.

In the twilight of the colonial era Alexander von Humboldt found in Mexico an enormous amount of capital in the hands of mine owners and merchants, while no less than half of Mexican real estate and capital belonged to the Church, which also controlled much of the remaining land through mortgages.[9] Mexican mine operators invested their surpluses in the purchase of great latifundia and in mortgage loans, as did the big exporters of Veracruz and Acapulco; the Church hierarchy multiplied its possessions in similar fashion. Palatial residences sprang up in the capital, and sumptuous churches appeared like mushrooms after rain; Indian servants catered to the golden luxuries of the powerful.

In mid-seventeenth-century Peru, capital amassed by *encomenderos*,* mine operators, inquisitors, and officials of the imperial government was poured into commercial projects. The fortunes made in Venezuela from growing cacao—begun at the end of the sixteenth century and produced by applying whips to the backs of black slaves—were invested in new plantations, other commercial crops, in mines, urban real estate, slaves, and herds of cattle.

The Silver Cycle: The Ruin of Potosí

Andre Gunder Frank, in analyzing "metropolis-satellite" relations through Latin American history as a chain of successive subjections, has highlighted the fact that the regions now most underdeveloped and poverty-stricken are those which in the past had had the closest links with the metropolis and had enjoyed periods of boom.[10] Having once been the biggest producers of goods exported to Europe, or later to the United States, and the richest sources of capital, they were abandoned

---

*An *encomienda* was an estate granted by the Crown to the Spanish conquistadores and colonists for their services to Spain. It included the services of the Indians living on it. The *encomendero* was thus the owner. (Trans.)

by the metropolis when for this or that reason business sagged. Potosí is the outstanding example of this descent into the vacuum.

In the sixteenth and seventeenth centuries the Cerro Rico of Potosí (Mexico's Guanajuato and Zacatecas silver mines had their boom much later) was the hub of Latin American colonial life: around it, in one way or another, revolved the Chilean economy, which sent it wheat, dried meat, hides, and wines; the cattle-raising and crafts of Córdoba and Tucumán in Argentina, which supplied it with draft animals and textiles; the mercury mines of Huancavelica; and the Arica region whence the silver was shipped to Lima, chief administrative center of the period. In the independence period the area, now a part of Bolivia, still had a larger population than what is now Argentina. A century and a half later Bolivia's population is almost six times smaller than Argentina's.

Potosían society, sick with ostentation and extravagance, left Bolivia with only a vague memory of its splendors, of the ruins of its churches and palaces, and of eight million Indian corpses. Any one of the diamonds encrusted in a rich *caballero*'s shield was worth more than what an Indian could earn in his whole life under the *mitayo*,* but the *caballero* took off with the diamonds. If it were not a futile exercise, Bolivia—now one of the world's most poverty-stricken countries—could boast of having nourished the wealth of the wealthiest. In our time Potosí is a poor city in a poor Bolivia: "The city which has given most to the world and has the least," as an old Potosían lady, enveloped in a mile of alpaca shawl, told me when we talked on the Andalusian patio of her two-century-old house. Condemned to nostalgia, tortured by poverty and cold, Potosí remains an open wound of the colonial system in America: a still audible "J'accuse."

The people live off the refuse. In 1640 the priest Alvaro Alonso Barba published in Madrid's royal printshop his excellent work on the art of metals.[11] Tin, he wrote, "is poison." He mentioned the Cerro, where "there is much tin, although few recognize it, and people throw it aside looking for the silver everyone seeks." Today the tin the Spaniards discarded like garbage is exploited in Potosí. Walls of ancient houses are sold as high-grade tin. Through the centuries the wealth has been drained from the five thousand tunnels the Spaniards bored into the Cerro Rico. As dynamite charges have hollowed it out, its color has changed and the height of its summit has been lowered. The mountains of rock heaped around the many tunnel openings are of all colors: pink, lilac, purple, ochre, gray, gold, brown. A crazy quilt of garbage. *Llamperos* break the rocks and Indian *palliris* in search of tin pick like birds, with hands skilled in weighing and separating, at the mineral debris. Miners still enter old mines that are not flooded, carbide lamps in hand, bodies crouching, to bring out whatever there is. Of silver there is none. Not a glint of it: the Spaniards even swept out the seams with brooms. The *pallacos* use pick and shovel to dig any metal out of the leavings. "The Cerro is still rich," I was blandly told by an unemployed man who was scratching through the dirt with his

---

*A *mitayo* is an Indian who pays a *mita*, or tribute, usually in the form of forced labor in public works, especially the mines. (Trans.)

hands. "There must be a God, you know: the metal grows just like a plant." Opposite the Cerro Rico rises a witness to the devastation: a mountain called Huakajchi, meaning in Quechua "the *cerro* that has wept." From its sides gush many springs of pure water, the "water eyes" that quench the miners' thirst.

* * *

In Huanchaca, another Bolivian tragedy, Anglo-Chilean capitalists in the past century stripped veins of highest-grade silver more than two yards wide; all that remains is dusty ruin. Huanchaca is still on the map as if it continued to exist— identified by crossed pick and shovel as a live mining center. Did the Mexican mines of Guanajuato and Zacatecas enjoy a better fate? On the basis of Alexander von Humboldt's figures in his already cited *Political Essay on the Kingdom of New Spain*, the economic surplus drained from Mexico between 1760 and 1809— barely half a century—through silver and gold exports has been estimated at some five billion present-day dollars.[12] In Humboldt's time there were no more important mines in Latin America. The great German scholar compared Guanajuato's Valenciana mine with the Himmelsfürst in Saxony, then the richest in Europe; the Valenciana was producing thirty-six times more silver at the turn of the century and its profits were thirty-three times as great for its investors. Count Santiago de la Laguna trembled with emotion in describing, in 1732, the Zacatecas mining district and "the precious treasures concealed in its deep womb," in mountains "graced with more than four thousand shafts, the better to serve both of Their Majesties," God and the King, "with the fruit of its entrails," and that "all might come to drink and participate of the great, the rich, the learned, the urban and the noble" because it was a "fount of wisdom, order, arms, and nobility."[13] The priest Marmolejo would later describe the city of Guanajuato, crisscrossed by rivers and bridges, with its gardens recalling those of Semiramis in Babylon and its ornate churches, theater, bullring, cockfight arenas, and towers and cupolas rising against the green mountainsides. But this was "the country of inequality," about which Humboldt could write: "Perhaps nowhere is inequality more shocking . . . The architecture of public and private buildings, the women's elegant wardrobes, the high-society atmosphere: all testify to an extreme social polish which is in extraordinary contrast to the nakedness, ignorance, and coarseness of the populace." The new veins of silver gobbled up men and mules in the *cordillera* foothills; the Indians, who "lived from day to day," suffered chronic hunger and epidemics killed them off like flies. In only one year, 1784, more than eight thousand died in Guanajuato when a lack of food, the result of a bad cold spell, set off a wave of disease.

Capital, far from accumulating, was squandered. There was a saying: "Father a merchant, son a gentleman, grandson a beggar." In a plea to the government in 1843 Mexican politician Lucas Alamán gave a sombre warning and insisted on the need to defend national industry by banning or imposing heavy duties on foreign imports. "We must proceed to develop industry as the only source of general prosperity," he wrote. "The riches of Zacatecas would bring no benefits to Puebla but for the former's consumption of the latter's manufactures, and if these decline again, as has happened before, that presently flourishing area will be ruined and the riches of the mines will not be able to save it from poverty." The prophesy proved true. In our time Zacatecas and Guanajuato are not even the most important cities in their own regions. Both languish amid the skeletons of the camps of the mining boom. Zacatecas, high and arid, lives from agriculture and exports labor to other states; its gold and silver are low in quality compared to former days. Of the fifty mines once exploited in the Guanajuato district, only two remain today. The population of the beautiful city does not grow, but tourists flock there to view the exuberant splendor of olden times. San Diego, La Valenciana, La Compañia, the cemetery in whose catacombs over one hundred mummies, preserved intact by the salinity of the soil, are on show. Half the families in Guanajuato state average more than five members and live today in one-room hovels.

A Flood of Tears and Blood: And Yet the Pope Said Indians Had Souls

In 1581 Philip II told the *audiencia** of Guadalajara that a third of Latin America's Indians had already been wiped out, and that those who survived were compelled to pay the tributes for the dead. The monarch added that Indians were bought and sold; that they slept in the open air; and that mothers killed their children to save them from the torture of the mines.[14] Yet the Crown's hypocrisy had smaller limits than the empire: it received a fifth of the value of the metals extracted by its subjects in all of the Spanish New World, as well as other taxes, and the Portuguese Crown was to have the same arrangement in eighteenth-century Brazil. Latin American silver and gold—as Engels put it—penetrated like a corrosive acid through all the pores of Europe's moribund feudal society, and, for the benefit of nascent mercantilist capitalism, the mining entrepreneurs turned Indians and black slaves into a teeming "external proletariat" of the European economy. Greco-Roman slavery was revived in a different world; to the plight of the Indians of the exterminated Latin American civilizations was added the ghastly fate of the blacks seized from African villages to toil in Brazil and the Antilles. The colonial Latin American economy enjoyed the most highly concentrated labor force known until that time, making possible the greatest concentration of wealth ever enjoyed by any civilization in world history.

The price of the tide of avarice, terror, and ferocity bearing down on these regions was Indian genocide: the best recent investigations credit pre-Columbian Mexico with a population between 30 and 37.5 million, and the Andean region is estimated to have possessed a similar number; Central America had between 10 and 13 million. Aztecs, Incas, and Mayas totaled between 70 and 90 million when

*An *audencia* was a judicial district as well as a judicial, administrative, and advisory body. In Mexico, it was the supreme court of administration and judgment. (Trans.)

the foreign conquerors appeared on the horizon; a century and a half later they had been reduced to 3.5 million. In 1685 only 4,000 Indian families remained of the more than 2 million that had once lived between Lima and Paita, according to the Marquis of Barinas. Archbishop Liñán y Cisneros denied that the Indians had been annihilated: "The truth is that they are hiding out," he said, "to avoid paying tribute, abusing the liberty which they enjoy and which they never had under the Incas."[15]

While metals flowed unceasingly from Latin American mines, equally unceasing were the orders from the Spanish Court granting paper protection and dignity to the Indians whose killing labor sustained the kingdom. The fiction of legality protected the Indian; the reality of exploitation drained the blood from his body. From slavery to the *encomienda* of service, and from this to the *encomienda* of tribute and the regime of wages, variants in the Indian labor force's juridical condition made only superficial changes in the real situation. The Crown regarded the inhuman exploitation of Indian labor as so necessary that in 1601 Philip III, banning forced labor in the mines by decree, at the same time sent secret instructions ordering its continuation "in case that measure should reduce production."[16] Similarly, between 1616 and 1619, Governor Juan de Solórzano carried out a survey of work conditions in the Huancavélica mercury mines (directly exploited by the Crown, in distinction to the silver mines, which were in private hands): "The poison penetrated to the very marrow, debilitating all the members and causing a constant shaking, and the workers usually died within four years," he reported to the Council of the Indies and to the king. But in 1631 Philip IV ordered that the same system be continued, and his successor Charles II later reaffirmed the decree.

In three centuries Potosí's Cerro Rico consumed eight million lives. The Indians, including women and children, were torn from their agricultural communities and driven to the Cerro. Of every ten who went up in to the freezing wilderness, seven never returned. Luis Capoche, an owner of mines and mills, wrote that "the roads were so covered with people that the whole kingdom seemed on the move." In their communities the Indians saw "many afflicted women returning without husbands and with many orphaned children" and they knew that "a thousand deaths and disasters" awaited them in the mines. The Spaniards scoured the countryside for hundreds of miles for labor. Many died on the way, before reaching Potosí, but it was the terrible work conditions in the mine that killed the most people. Soon after the mine began operating, in 1550, the Dominican monk Domingo de Santo Tomás told the Council of the Indies that Potosí was a "mouth of hell" which swallowed Indians by the thousands every year, and that rapacious mine owners treated them "like stray animals." Later Fray Rodrigo de Loaysa said: "These poor Indians are like sardines in the sea. Just as other fish pursue the sardines to seize and devour them, so everyone in these lands pursues the wretched Indians." Chiefs of Indian communities had to replace the constantly dying *mitayos* with new men between eighteen and fifty years old. The huge stone-walled corral where Indians were assigned to mine and mill owners is now used by workers as a football ground. The *mitayos'* jail—a shapeless mass of ruins—can still be seen at the entrance to Potosí. . . .

The *mita* labor system was a machine for crushing Indians. The process of using mercury to extract silver poisoned as many or more than did the toxic gases in the bowels of the earth. It made hair and teeth fall out and brought on uncontrollable trembling. The victims ended up dragging themselves through the streets pleading for alms. At night six thousand fires burned on the slopes of the Cerro and in these the silver was worked, taking advantage of the wind that the "glorious Saint Augustine" sent from the sky. Because of the smoke from the ovens there were no pastures or crops for a radius of twenty miles around Potosí and the fumes attacked men's bodies no less relentlessly.

Ideological justifications were never in short supply. The bleeding of the New World became an act of charity, an argument for the faith. With the guilt, a whole system of rationalizations for guilty consciences was devised. The Indians were used as beasts of burden because they could carry a greater weight than the delicate llama, and this proved that they were in fact beasts of burden. The viceroy of Mexico felt that there was no better remedy for their "natural wickedness" than work in the mines. Juan Ginés de Sepúlveda, a renowned Spanish theologian, argued that they deserved the treatment they got because their sins and idolatries were an offense to God. The Count de Buffon, a French naturalist, noted that Indians were cold and weak creatures in whom "no activity of the soul" could be observed. The Abbé De Paw invented a Latin America where degenerate Indians lived side by side with dogs that couldn't bark, cows that couldn't be eaten, and impotent camels. Voltaire's Latin America was inhabited by Indians who were lazy and stupid, pigs with navels on their backs, and bald and cowardly lions. Bacon, De Maistre, Monesquieu, Hume, and Bodin declined to recognize the "degraded men" of the New World as fellow humans. Hegel spoke of Latin America's physical and spiritual impotence and said the Indians died when Europe merely breathed on them.

In the seventeenth century Father Gregorio García detected Semitic blood in the Indians because, like the Jews, "they are lazy, they do not believe in the miracles of Jesus Christ, and they are ungrateful to the Spaniards for all the good they have done them." At least this holy man did not deny that the Indians were descended from Adam and Eve: many theologians and thinkers had never been convinced by Pope Paul III's bull of 1537 declaring the Indians to be "true men." When Bartolomé de las Casas upset the Spanish Court with his heated denunciations of the conquistadores' cruelty in 1557, a member of the Royal Council replied that Indians were too low in the human scale to be capable of receiving the faith. Las Casas dedicated his zealous life to defending the Indians against the excesses of the mine owners and *encomenderos*. He once remarked that the Indians preferred to go to hell to avoid meeting Christians.

Indians were assigned or given in *encomienda* to conquistadores and colonizers so that they could teach them the gospel. But since the Indians owed personal services and economic tribute to the *encomenderos*, there was little time for setting them on the Christian path to salvation.

Indians were divided up along with lands given as royal grants, or were obtained by direct plunder: in reward for his services, Cortés received twenty-three thousand vassals. After 1536 Indians were given in *encomienda* along with their descendants for the span of two lifetimes, those of the *encomendero* and of his immediate heir; after 1629 this was extended to three lifetimes and, after 1704, to four. In the eighteenth century the surviving Indians still assured many generations to come of a cozy life. Since their defeated gods persisted in Spanish memory, there were saintly rationalizations aplenty for the victors' profits from their toil; the Indians were pagans and deserved nothing better.

The past? Four hundred years after the papal bull, in September 1957, the highest court in Paraguay published a notice informing all the judges of the country that "the Indians, like other inhabitants of the republic, are human beings." And the Center for Anthropological Studies of the Catholic University of Asunción later carried out a revealing survey, both in the capital and in the countryside: eight out of ten Paraguayans think that "Indians are animals." In Caaguazú, Alta Paraná, and the Chaco, Indians are hunted down like wild beasts, sold at bargain prices, and exploited by a system of virtual slavery—yet almost all Paraguayans have Indian blood, and Paraguayans tirelessly compose poems, songs, and speeches in homage to the "Guaraní soul."

When the Spaniards invaded Latin America, the theocratic Inca empire was at its height, spreading over what we now call Peru, Bolivia, and Ecuador, taking in part of Colombia and Chile, and reaching northern Argentina and the Brazilian jungle. The Aztec confederation had achieved a high level of efficiency in the Valley of Mexico, and in Yucatan and Central America the remarkable civilization of the Mayas, organized for work and war, persisted among the peoples who succeeded them.

These societies have left many testimonies to their greatness despite the long period of devastation: religious monuments built with more skill than the Egyptian pyramids, technically efficient constructions for the battle against nature, art works showing indomitable talent. In the Lima museum there are hundreds of skulls which have undergone trepanning and the insertion of gold and silver plates by Inca surgeons. The Mayans were great astronomers, measuring time and space with astonishing precision, and discovered the value of the figure zero before any other people in history. The Aztecs' irrigation works and artificial islands dazzled Cortés—even though they were not made of gold.

The conquest shattered the foundations of these civilizations. The installation of a mining economy had direr consequences than the fire and sword of war. The mines required a great displacement of people and dislocated agricultural communities; they not only took countless lives through forced labor, but also indirectly destroyed the collective farming system. The Indians were taken to the mines, were forced to submit to the service of the *encomenderos*, and were made to surrender for nothing the lands which they had to leave or neglect. On the Pacific coast the Spaniards destroyed or let die out the enormous plantations of corn, yucca, kidney and white beans, peanuts, and sweet potato; the desert quickly devoured great tracts of land which the Inca irrigation network had made abundant. Four and a half centuries after the Conquest only rocks and briars remain where roads had once united an empire. Although the Incas' great public works were for the most part destroyed by time or the usurper's hand, one may still see across the Andean *cordillera* traces of the endless terraces which permitted, and still permit, cultivation of the mountainsides. A U.S. technician estimated in 1936 that if the Inca terraces had been built by modern methods at 1936 wage rates they would have cost some $30,000 per acre.[17] In that empire which did not know the wheel, the horse, or iron, the terraces and aqueducts were made possible by prodigious organization and technical perfection achieved through wise distribution of labor, as well as by the religious force that ruled man's relation with the soil—which was sacred and thus always alive. . . .

As Darcy Ribeiro puts it, the Indians were the fuel of the colonial productive system. "It is almost certain," writes Sergio Bagú, "that hundreds of Indian sculptors, architects, engineers, and astronomers were sent into the mines along with the mass of slaves for the killing task of getting out the ore. The technical ability of these people was of no interest to the colonial economy. They were treated as so many skilled workers." Yet all traces of those broken cultures were not lost: hope of the rebirth of a lost dignity sparked many Indian risings.

* * *

Exiled in their own land, condemned to an external exodus, Latin America's native peoples were pushed into the poorest areas—arid mountains, the middle of deserts—as the dominant civilization extended its frontiers. *The Indians have suffered, and continue to suffer, the curse of their own wealth; that is the drama of all Latin America.* When placer gold was discovered in Nicaragua's Río Bluefields, the Carca Indians were quickly expelled far from their riparian lands, and the same happened with the Indians in all the fertile valleys and rich-subsoil lands south of the Rio Grande. The massacres of Indians that began with Columbus never stopped. In Uruguay and Argentine Patagonia they were exterminated during the last century by troops that hunted them down and penned them in forests or in the desert so that they might not disturb the organized advance of cattle latinfundia. The Yaqui Indians of the Mexican state of Sonora were drowned in blood so that their lands, fertile and rich in minerals, could be sold without any unpleasantness to various U.S. capitalists. Survivors were deported to plantations in Yucatán, and the Yucatán peninsula became not only the cemetery of the Mayas who had been its owners, but also of the Yaquis who came from afar: at the beginning of our century the fifty kings of henequen had over one hundred thousand Indian slaves on their plantations. Despite the exceptional physical endurance of the strapping, handsome Yaquis, two-thirds of them died during the first year of slave labor. In our day henequen can compete with synthetic fiber substitutes only because of the workers' abysmally low standard of living. Things have certainly changed, but not as much—at least for the natives of Yucatán—as some believe: "The living conditions of these workers are much like slave labor," says one contemporary authority.[18] On the Andean slopes near Bogota the Indian peon still must give a day's work without pay to get the *hacendado*'s permission to farm his own plot on moonlit nights. As René Dumont says, "This Indian's ancestors, answering to no man, used once to cultivate the rich soil of the ownerless plain. Now he works for nothing to gain the right to cultivate the poor slopes of the mountain."[19]

REFERENCES

1. Woodrow Wilson, as quoted in Scott Nearing and Joseph Freeman, *Dollar Diplomacy* (1925; reprint ed., New York: Monthly Review Press, 1966).

2. *The Adventures of Marco Polo,* ed. Richard J. Walsh (New York: John Day, 1948), p. 143.

3. Earl J. Hamilton, *American Treasure and the Price Revolution in Spain, 1501–1650* (1934; reprint ed., New York: Octagon, 1965).

4. Ernest Mandel, *Marxist Economic Theory,* 2 vols. (New York: Monthly Review Press, 1968), 2: 443–444.

5. Ernest Mandel, "La teoría marxiana de la acumulación primitiva y la industrialización del Tercer Mundo," *Amaru* (Lima), April–June 1968.

6. Celso Furtado, *The Economic Development of Latin America: A Survey from Colonial Times to the Cuban Revolution* (Cambridge: Cambridge University Press, 1970), p. 11.

7. J. Beaujeau-Garnier, *L'économie de l'Amérique Latine* (Paris, 1949).

8. Sergio Bagú, *Economía de la sociedad colonial: ensayo de historia comparada de América Latina* (Buenos Aires, 1949).

9. Alexander de Humboldt, *Political Essay on the Kingdom of New Spain* (London, 1811), Book II, Chapter VII, p. 22.

10. Andre Gunder Frank, *Capitalism and Underdevelopment in Latin America* (New York and London: Monthly Review Press, 1967).

11. Alvaro Alonso Barba, *Arte de los metales* (Potosí, 1967).

12. Humboldt, *Political Essay,* Book IV, Chapter XI. See also Fernando Carmona, Introduction to Diego López Rosado, *Historia y pensamiento económico de México* (Mexico, 1968).

13. Don Joseph Ribera Bernárdez (Count Santiago de La Laguna), *Descripción breve de la muy noble y leal ciudad de Zacatecas,* in Gabriel Salinas de la Torre, *Testimonios de Zacatecas* (Mexico, 1946).

14. John Collier, *The Indians of the Americas* (New York: W. W. Norton, 1947), p. 138.

15. Emilio Romero, *Historia económica del Perú* (Buenos Aires, 1941).

16. Enrique Finot, *Nueva historia de Bolivia* (Buenos Aires, 1946).

17. According to a member of the United States Soil Conservation Service, cited in Collier, *The Indians of the Americas,* p. 53.

18. Arturo Bonilla Sánchez, "Un problema que se agrava: la subocupación rural," in *Neolatifundismo y explotación, de Emiliano Zapata a Anderson Clayton & Co.* (Mexico, 1968).

19. René Dumont, *Lands Alive* (New York: Monthly Review Press, 1965), p. 10.

ADDITIONAL BIBLIOGRAPHY

Aguilar Monteverde, Alonso. *Dialéctica de la economía mexicana.* Mexico, 1968.

Banco de Comercio. *La economía del estado de Guanajuato.* Mexico, 1968.

————. *La economía del estado de Zacatecas.* Mexico, 1968.

Baran, Paul A. *The Political Economy of Growth.* New York: Monthly Review Press, 1962.

Cañete y Domínguez, Pedro Vicente. *Potosí colonial: guía histórica, geográfica, política, civil y legal del gobierno e intendencia de la provincia de Potosí.* La Paz, 1939.

Capitan, L., and Lorin, H. *El trabajo en América, antes y después de Colón.* Buenos Aires, 1948.

Capoche, Luis. *Relación general de la Villa Imperial de Potosí.* Madrid, 1959.

Chávez Orozco, Luis. *Revolución industrial—revolución política.* Mexico: Biblioteca del Obrero y Campesino, n.d.

de Martínez Arzana y Vela, Nicolás. *Historia de la Villa Imperial de Potosí.* Buenos Aires, 1943.

Elliott, J. H. *Imperial Spain.* London, 1963.

Furtado, Celso. *The Economic Growth of Brazil.* Berkeley & Los Angeles: University of California Press, 1963.

Galeano, Eduardo. *Guatemala: Occupied Country.* New York and London: Monthly Review Press, 1969.

Gerbi, Antonio. *La disputa del Nuevo Mundo.* Mexico, 1960.

Halperin Donghi, Tullio. *Historia contemporánea de América Latina.* Madrid, 1969.

Hanke, Lewis. *Estudios sobre fray Bartolomé de Las Casas y sobre la lucha por la justicia en la conquista española de América.* Caracas, 1968.

Hawkes, Jacquetta. "Prehistoria." In *Historia de la Humanidad.* Buenos Aires: UNESCO, 1966.

Huamán Poma. "El primer nueva crónica y buen gobierno." In *El reverso de la conquista: relaciones aztecas, mayas, e incas,* edited by Miguel Léon-Portilla, Mexico, 1964.

Manchester, Allan K. *British Preeminence in Brazil: Its Rise and Fall.* Chapel Hill, N.C.: University of North Carolina Press, 1933.

Marmolejo, Lucio. *Efemérides guanajuatenses, o datos para formar la historia de la cuidad de Guanajuato.* Guanajuato, 1883.

Molins, Jaime. *La ciudad única.* Potosí, 1951.

Mora, José Maria Luis. *México y sus revoluciones.* Mexico, 1965.

Mousnier, Roland. *Los siglos xvi y xvii. Historia general de las civilizaciones,* edited by Maurice Crouzet, vol. 4. Barcelona, 1967.

Ots Capdequí, J. M. *El estado español en la Indias.* Mexico, 1941.

Quesada, Vicente G. *Crónicas potosinas.* Paris, 1890.

Ramos, Jorge Abelardo. *Historia de la nación latinoamericana.* Buenos Aires, 1958.

Ribeiro, Darcy. *The Americas and Civilization.* New York: Dutton, 1971.

Ruas, Eponina. *Ouro Prêto: sua história, seus templos e monumentos.* Rio de Janeiro, 1950.

Simonsen, Roberto S. *História econômica do Brasil, 1500–1820.* São Paulo, 1962.

Turner, John Kenneth. *Barbarous Mexico.* 1910; reprint ed. Austin: University of Texas Press, 1969.

Vázquez Franco, Guillermo. *La conquista justificada.* Montevideo, 1968.

Women, Colonisation, and Racism
–Jan Jindy Pettman

Jan Jindy Pettman lectures on political science at the Australian National University. The following piece is an excerpt from her book Worlding Women, *which was published by Routledge in 1996.*

European colonisation was a global process, involving the extraordinary imposition of European power over the rest of the world. The history of colonisation dominates the last 500 years, from the time of Columbus and the 'discoveries' literally making 'the world'. Colonisation was marked by formal political control, economic exploitation and cultural domination, and resistance.

Colonial power made use of certain ideas of women and sexuality to construct and police both women's bodies and racialised boundaries. It also set a racialised hierarchy in world politics, through structural relations of domination, subordination and exploitation. 'Whiteness' and 'non-white' are still significant political identities in the world today.

This selection explores the sexual politics of colonisation, and the 'race' politics of gender. It suggests that white women are ambiguously placed within contemporary constructions of global power, in ways different from white men, and from 'other' women. These differences draw attention to the gendered, and racialised, dimensions of international relations and of political identities (Doty, 1993). They continue to inform and complicate relations between women, and feminist theorising. . . .

Colonising Women
Within conventional histories of colonisation, women are largely absent. Empire and anticolonial nationalisms are told as conflicts and competitions between different men. Colonial histories may be romances of empire, of white conquest or of anticolonial resistance.

Women are further elided through a popular and revealing analogy between 'women' and the colonised. Here, women's oppression is compared with colonisation, and oppression is something women share with the colonised. This particular

Excerpts from *Worlding Women* by J. Pettman. Reprinted by permission of Taylor & Francis.

connection underscores the masculine character of 'control over' relations in general (Peterson, 1992), and ways in which dominated peoples, including the colonised, are feminised. But the colonised/women analogy leaves colonised women, and the gender politics of colonisation as it is constructed within both colonised and coloniser groups, unexamined. 'Women' become dominant-group women, in the metropole or less often in the colonies, while the feminisation of the colonised is seen as being done to colonised men. It is unclear where colonised women are in these representations.

In other representations, coloniser powers were associated with civilisation and culture, and the colonised with nature, as women were in the metropoles. The close associations between sex and power in the construction of dominant and imperial masculinities is revealed in the profusion of phallic imagery, for example, penetrating the dark continent and the eroticisation of conquest, leading one commentator to suggest that 'homosocial desire acts as a kind of textual unconscious for the entire discussion of empire' (Donaldson, 1992: 8). . . .

Within the boys' own adventure of empire and the colonies, white women were usually absent—invisible—or passive companions or victims of white men's actions. Occasionally they were made visible, especially in settler colonies as breeders of the white race. But there is another colonial story which locates women in rather different ways. Here, white women are given agency, but for bad. This is the story of the memsahib and other local variations, the gross stereotyping of white women as idle, pampered, petty, parasitic upon empire and tended by servants who are mistreated, spending time and energy only on gossip, complaint and concerns with status and display (Knapman, 1986; Strobel, 1991; Jolly, 1993). A variation of this image goes further, to lay the blame for 'loss of empire' at their feet. White women are here judged as more racist than their men, as disrupting formerly close relations between early colonists and the locals, and as drawing and defending raced boundaries through their snobbishness and sexual jealousy. Causal connections are made between deteriorating 'race relations' and increasing numbers of white women in the colonies—somehow these women are to blame for the ultimate 'loss of empire'.

There is now a growing literature on white women in the colonies, and in relation to empire. Much of this literature is of the 'retrieval' kind, 'women's adventures' and/or feminist stories. It tells us that (white) women were there, though in very different roles and relations over time and place, for example in larger numbers and crucial as reproducers of the race in settler colonies (de Lepervanche, 1989), or as unwelcome intruders in tropical colonies whose officials were concerned with administration and extraction of surplus (Callaway, 1987; Strobel, 1991). These writings are interventions, then, against an ungendered colonisation. They tell a different story of gender and race relations, seeking to refute the scapegoating of white-coloniser women and the trivialisation of their lives as decorative accessories of empire.

These retrieval feminist writings document coloniser women's lives to disrupt the stereotypes, to reveal the variety of coloniser women's lives, views and relations.

They demonstrate that life in the colonies was often extremely difficult, their work hard, and their isolation and loneliness frequent. Often, too, they argue that coloniser women were not more racist than 'their' men. Indeed, some had close relations with 'the locals', especially with colonised women, through a range of teaching, helping and missionary activities that were seen there, as elsewhere, as peculiarly women's work. Helen Callaway argues that unlike their image as harsher and more racist, coloniser women represented the humane and 'civilising' side of empire and enabled the emergence of a more equal relationship in the transition from empire to commonwealth (1987: 244).

Documenting the lives of coloniser women is part of a feminist project, to take women's own experiences seriously. It gives them a presence beyond their usual invisibility or stereotypic representation in masculinist tellings. It often reveals differences among women which caution us against homogenising them within a single category. It may or may not recognise class differences and other boundary politics, which privileged some and penalised other coloniser women in the structuring of colonial society. But critics of some retrieval herstories find fault in their valorising of white women's lives in ways that sanitise or release coloniser women from responsibility as part of the colonising force. For while colonisation was gendered, gender was racialised, and white women were ambiguously placed in terms of the colonial project. They were both oppressed in terms of patriarchal relations, and oppressors, or at least advantaged by 'race' relations in colonialism (Strobel, 1991: 41; Pettman, 1992). In this situation, innocence is not available as a position for coloniser women, and their stories cannot be told in relation to their men alone. Their relations with 'other' women become highly problematic. Questions of responsibility and complicity juggle with those of power and control.

Many coloniser women, especially missionary women, were engaged in helping and service work with colonised women. But even where the former saw the latter as sisters, in a precursor to global sisterhood, they retained notions of difference in race and cultural hierarchy that represented 'other' women as little sisters or surrogate daughters. Barbara Ramusack (1990) characterises these relations as 'maternal imperialism', with coloniser women a part of the civilising and Christianising project. Colonised women appear as victims of their culture and of their men (and at times, of white men)—to be saved by white women's interventions. So Margaret Jolly uses the label 'colonising women' to indicate these women's problematic location within the colonial project (1993: 104). These presumptions and hidden power relations between women have returned to haunt us, replicated in some contemporary western feminist representations of 'third-world women' as always already victims (Mohanty, 1988; Mani, 1990).

The maternalist trope sees women as connected through their similar women's bodies, maternity and family responsibilities, even though structured through big-sisterly or motherly responsibility and difference between women. But maternity is also used to divide women along lines of class, race and nation, to make good and bad mothers. Here there could be collusion between colonial authorities, colonising women and some local male authorities, seeking control of women's sexuality, fertility and marriage (Jolly, 1992). (There are clear parallels between the tasks 'at home' of public health and maternal education aimed at making white working-class mothers better mothers, and the kinds of education, surveillance and intervention directed at colonised women.) There were ambivalences, too: concern about 'over breeders', and very different attitudes towards the treatment of different women in terms of maternal health and reproductive rights.

Jane Haggis points to the role of colonising women as significant agents 'in articulating and conducting a project of domestication aimed at colonised women' (1992: 1). She explores the use of maternal imagery and language by missionary wives and single women missionaries of the London Missionary Society in South India as they constructed their relations with colonised women. They pursued their project of making good wives and mothers of colonised women in accordance with their own cultural and class notions of desirable family relations and sex roles. There was congruence, then, between their objectives in restructuring family life, sex roles and men's and women's work, and the cultural reconstruction and political economy of empire. They were engaged in a project of domestication, which involved a reproduction of the colonial order (Nair 1992: 42).

A different example of the complexities of raced gender relations in colonisation and women's work for and with other women is revealed in a study of African-American missionary women in southern Africa. They identified with African women in some ways not available to white women, but also felt set apart from them by their commitment to Christianity and a civilising mission, which was shaped by western notions of women's roles and family life (Jacobs, 1990).

Colonising women benefited from empire, as 'the inferior sex within the superior race' (Strobel, 1991: xi). Some had opportunities and choices in the colonies that they would not have found had they stayed at home. Yet while they were privileged in terms of race, cultural and often class power in the colonies, they were more or less constrained or exploited within their own family, social or institutional lives. They were culture carriers, and often shared with men of their family or group views of themselves and others. But they negotiated complex relations and contradictory pressures and identities, interpreting their worlds with reference to personal though socially located ideas and values.

Within structures of power and practices that were both racist and sexist, individual colonising women made their ways. They pursued a variety of relations, or refused relations, with colonised women. Recent feminist writings on colonising women tell of the very different choices and politics pursued, for example, by different British feminists in India (Paxton, 1990). Another compares Charlotte Geddie, a Presbyterian missionary in 'maternalist sympathy' for ni-Vanuatu women, with Beatrice Grimshaw, a traveller and journalist who represented Pacific women as downgraded and beyond redemption, promoting white-settler and planter interests against missionary endeavours (Jolly, 1993).

Colonised women, too, were never a homogenous group, even as contemporaries in any particular colony. There were always some differences among them that predated colonisation, whether of age and marital status in more egalitarian small-scale communities, or of hierarchy and, for example, caste, class or prior oc-cupation status. (Current rewritings of these differences, however, are informed by different political projects that construct certain understandings of women as more equal with men 'before', or of women's difference as emblematic of 'culture' de-fined against the colonising power—a politics I will pursue.) Colonised women, too, made their own decisions in the face of colonising power, some converting or collaborating, others resisting or subverting, others sidelined in competition or deals between different groups of men. The search for colonised women's stories often displays a familiar tension between recognising their agency as opposed to their relative powerlessness and at times atrocious treatment at the hands of colonisers. We still know little of most colonised women's lives, though feminist recastings of colonial stories are making more women visible.

Domestic Politics

Colonising and colonised women's relations were further complicated by their many personal encounters, especially in domestic service. The close proximity of the women in these relations was within households, in forms of family labour usually designated private, away from the public/political sphere attended to in po-litical science, sociology and much history. It is complicated by the gendered and often sexualised nature of domestic labour generally.

The politics of domestic-service work varied enormously, and in places was it-self part of the 'education' and domestication project targeted at colonised women. In Australia, for example, many young 'half-caste' Aboriginal girls were seized by the state and trained in domestic arts before being placed in white homes as do-mestic servants. Subject to supervision but rarely protected by state Aboriginal Protection Boards, they were a source of cheap labour for white families. They and other Aboriginal women who laboured in white city and country homes relieved white women of domestic labour and childcare responsibilities, even while some faced the removal of their own children on the grounds of being unsuitable moth-ers. The cruel irony here, as in other colonial situations, was that the very women whose sexuality and maternity, cleanliness and reliability were so often found wanting were responsible for childcare and house duties for 'superior' women. . . .

Domestic labour is often sexualised, and in colonial situations racialised gen-der stereotypes frequently represented colonised women as promiscuous or exotic. These representations connect in difficult and dangerous ways with other dimen-sions of the sexual politics of colonisation.

The Sexual Politics of Colonisation

Retrieval herstories challenge

> the extraordinary presumption that sexuality between white men and colonised
> women was indicative of racial harmony. Even when such sexual relations did not
> constitute rape, and when indigenous women embraced a sexual or love relation

with colonising men, there was still an element of conquest: sexual access to local women legitimised the colonial relation. Sexual relations between white women and 'men of colour' on the contrary betrayed the imperial accumulations of the power of race, class and sex (Jolly, 1993: 108).

Particular constructions of women and sexuality were used to police women's bodies, and the boundaries of race. Colonising women were distinguished from colonised women through racialised gender stereotypes which replicated the good mother/bad mother in the good woman/bad woman dichotomy (though colonising women could become bad women by unruly, unrespectable or sexually licentious behavior; and lower-class or independent single colonising women might likewise be perceived as beyond the bounds of protection). Colonising women were generally represented as pure, non-sexual, mothers, civilising influences on 'their' men. They were the property or possessions of their men and their community. Their fidelity and the restriction of their sexual relations to same-race men were essentially part of keeping the race pure. Any suggestion of a sexual relationship between a white woman and a colonised man was quickly read as rape, though in some cases white women were also blamed for 'encouraging' attention (Strobel, 1991; Bynum, 1992).

Colonised/black men's sexuality was constructed as savage, violent, voracious (though with specific characteristics attributed to different groups of men). This complicates the previous notion of colonised men as feminised. A contradictory bundle of images could be activated simultaneously or in different situations. Colonised/black men were seen to have too little of some masculine characteristics, such as responsibility and stability, and too much of others, especially in terms of a sexualised hypermasculinity, which was a threat to white women, and to black/colonised women too. So restrictions were placed on the movements and relations of black men—in the name of protecting white women (though they were more likely generated by white men's sexual anxieties and fears around appropriating the bodies of colonised women and the land and labour of colonised men. Indeed, it seems that the spectre of the black/colonised rapist against whom white womanhood must be protected arises especially at times when colonial authority is questioned, and black/colonised men must be 'put down' (Sharpe, 1993). Such panics over supposedly vulnerable white women allowed the far more common rape of colonised/black women by white men to go largely unnoted.

Colonised women's sexuality was variously represented, in racialised gender stereotypes that distinguished, for example, between African and Asian women, or between Melanesian and Polynesian women. Often they were seen as sexual creatures (using the word advisedly), more of nature and less controlled and chaste than good white women. As temptresses or as amoral, they could be held responsible for the seduction of white men. This image was complicated, though, by some missionary, humanitarian and early feminist representations of them as victims of their men's brutish natures, or savable through Christianising and domesticity. But this could have a related effect, in detaching women from 'their' men, and putting them under the 'protection' of white men and, sometimes, of white women.

In a complex sexual politics of colonisation, excluding and controlling boundaries were drawn around white women and black men, leaving white men free to transgress the boundaries, and use, abuse or even care for colonised women (Pettman, 1992). Even where concubinage was preferred to the importation of white women, as in early stages in some tropical colonies, the women involved remained dependent and vulnerable, and were policed in ways that maintained racialised boundaries and carefully determined who counted as white (Stoler, 1991; Baustad, 1994). The children of colonising men and colonised women usually stayed with the mother, thus keeping the white race pure. White men who lived with and loved colonised women were often persecuted or at least socially stigmatised—more so than those who were more secret and often more abusive in their relations across the line.

Tessie Lui argues that 'race is a *gendered* social category that rests on regulating sexuality and particularly on controlling the behaviour of women' (1991: 163). Distinctions between legitimate and illegitimate children are bolstered by norms and in many places legislation and sanctions condoning or prohibiting certain kinds of marriages and sexual relations, as in South Africa until very recently. These in turn relate to social entitlements, which in colonial and race power societies go far beyond rights to individual inheritance and social status. Sex is seen as the vulnerable link in maintaining group boundaries, so it is especially important for colonising—and, if they can, colonised—men to control same-group women's sexual behaviour and domestic lives. Sex, gender and women's bodies become part of the material for the construction of group boundaries. 'Women's bodies were the contested terrain on which men built their political regimes' (Lui, 1991: 163).

BIBLIOGRAPHY

Baustad, Suzanne 1994, 'Sex and Empire Building: Prostitution in the Making and Resisting of Global Orders', paper for the Citizenship, Identity, Community conference, York University, Ontario.

Bynum, Victoria 1992, *Unruly Women: The Politics of Social and Sexual Control in the Old South*, University of North Carolina Press, Chapel Hill.

Callaway, Helen 1987, *Gender, Culture and Empire: European Women in Colonial Nigeria*, Macmillan, London.

Donaldson, Laura 1992, *Decolonizing Feminism: Race, Gender and Responsibility*. University of North Carolina Press, Chapel Hill.

Doty, Roxanne Lynn 1993, 'The Bounds of "Race" in International Relations', *Millennium*, vol. 22, no. 3, pp. 443–62.

Haggis, Jane 1992, 'Good Wives and Mothers or Dedicated Workers: Contradiction of Domesticity in the Mission of Sister Hood' Gender Relations Project paper, Australian National University, Canberra.

Jacobs, Sylvia 1990, 'African-American Women Missionaries and European Imperialism in Southern Africa', *Women's Studies International Forum*, vol. 13, no. 4, pp. 381–94.

Jolly, Margaret 1992, 'Other Mothers: Material Insouciance and the Regulation Debate in Fiji and Vanuatu 1890–1930', Gender Relations Project paper, Australian National University, Canberra.

Jolly, Margaret 1993, 'Colonising Women: the Maternal Body and Empire' in *Feminism and Politics of Difference*, eds. S. Gunew and A. Yeatman, Allen & Unwin, Sydney.

Knapman, Claudia 1986, *White Women in Fiji 1835–1930: the Ruin of Empire?* Allen & Unwin, Sydney.

Lui, Tessie 1991, 'Race and Gender in the Politics of Group Formation', *Frontiers*, vol. 12, no. 2, pp. 155–65.

Mani, Lata 1990, 'Multiple Mediations: Feminist Scholarship in the Age of Multinational Reception', *Feminist Review*, no. 35, pp. 24–41.

Mohanty, Chandra 1988, 'Under Western Eyes: Feminist Scholarship and Colonial Discourses', *Feminist Review*, no. 30, pp. 61–88.

Nair, Janaki 1992, 'Uncovering the *Zenana*: Visions of Indian Womanhood in Englishwomen's Writing' in *Expanding the Boundaries of Women's History: Essays on Women in the Third World*, eds. C. Johnson-Odim and M. Strobel, Indiana University Press, Bloomington.

Paxton, Nancy 1990, 'Feminism under the Raj—Complicity and Resistance in the Writings of Flora Annie Steel and Annie Besant', *Womens Studies International Forum*, vol. 13, no. 4, pp. 333–46.

Peterson, V. Spike ed. 1992, *Gendered States: Feminist (Re)Visions of International Relations*, Lynne Rienner, Boulder.

Pettman, Jan 1992, *Living in the Margins: Racism, Sexism and Feminism in Australia*, Allen & Unwin, Sydney.

Ramusack, Barbara 1990, 'Cultural Missionaries, Maternal Imperialists, Feminist Allies: British Activists in India, 1865–1945', *Women's Studies International Forum*, vol. 13, no. 4, pp. 309–21.

Sharpe, Jenny 1993, *Allegories of Empire: the Figure of Woman in the Colonial Text*, University of Minnesota Press, Minneapolis.

Stoler, Ann 1991, 'Carnal Knowledge and Imperial Power: Gender, Race and Morality in Colonial Asia' in *Gender at the Crossroads of Knowledge*, ed. M. di Leonardo, University of California Press, Berkeley.

Strobel, Margaret 1991, *European Women and the Second British Empire*, Indiana University Press, Bloomington.

The Myth of Catching-up Development

–Maria Mies

Maria Mies is Professor of Sociology at the Fachhochschule in Cologne, Germany, but retired from teaching in 1993. She spent many years working in India and established the Women and Development Programme at the Institute of Social Studies in The Hague, Netherlands, in 1979. The following piece appeared in her book Ecofeminism *(Zeb books, 1993), which she co-authored with Vandana Shiva.*

Virtually all development strategies are based on the explicit or implicit assumption that the model of 'the good life' is that prevailing in the affluent societies of the North: the USA, Europe and Japan. The question of how the poor in the North, those in the countries of the South, and peasants and women worldwide may attain this 'good life' is usually answered in terms of what, since Rostow, can be called the 'catching-up development' path. This means that by following the same path of industrialization, technological progress and capital accumulation taken by Europe and the USA and Japan the same goal can be reached. These affluent countries and classes, the dominant sex—the men—the dominant urban centres and lifestyles are then perceived as the realized utopia of liberalism, a utopia still to be attained by those who apparently still lag behind. Undoubtedly the industrialized countries' affluence is the source of great fascination to all who are unable to share in it. The so-called 'socialist' countries' explicit aim was to catch up, and even to overtake capitalism. After the breakdown of socialism in Eastern Europe, particularly East Germany, the aim is now to quickly catch up with the lifestyle of the so-called market economies, the prototype of which is seen in the USA or West Germany.

A brief look at the history of the underdeveloped countries and regions of the South but also at present day East Europe and East Germany can teach us that this catching-up development path is a myth: nowhere has it led to the desired goal.

This myth is based on an evolutionary, linear understanding of history. In this concept of history the peak of the evolution has already been reached by some,

"The Myth of Catching-up Development" by Maria Mies and Vandana Shiva from *Ecofeminism.* Copyright 1993. Reprinted by permission of Zed Books.

namely, men generally, white men in particular, industrial countries, urbanites. The 'others'—women, brown and black people, 'underdeveloped' countries, peasants—will also reach this peak with a little more effort, more education, more 'development'. Technological progress is seen as the driving force of this evolutionary process. It is usually ignored that, even in the early 1970s, the catching-up development theory was criticized by a number of writers. Andre Gunder Frank,[1] Samir Amin,[2] Johan Galtung,[3] and many others have shown that the poverty of the underdeveloped nations is not as a result of 'natural' lagging behind but the direct consequence of the overdevelopment of the rich industrial countries who exploit the so-called periphery in Africa, South America and Asia. In the course of this colonial history, which continues today, these areas were progressively underdeveloped and made dependent on the so-called metropolis. The relationship between these overdeveloped centres or metropoles and the underdeveloped peripheries is a colonial one. Today, a similar colonial relationship exists between Man and Nature, between men and women, between urban and rural areas. We have called these the colonies of White Man. In order to maintain such relationships force and violence are always essential.[4]

But the emotional and cognitive acceptance of the colonized is also necessary to stabilize such relationships. This means that not only the colonizers but also the colonized must accept the lifestyle of 'those on top' as the only model of the good life. This process of acceptance of the values, lifestyle and standard of living of 'those on top' is invariably accompanied by a devaluation of one's own: one's own culture, work, technology, lifestyle and often also philosophy of life and social institutions. In the beginning this devaluation is often violently enforced by the colonizers and then reinforced by propaganda, educational programmes, a change of laws, and economic dependency, for example, through the debt trap. Finally, this devaluation is often accepted and internalized by the colonized as the 'natural' state of affairs. One of the most difficult problems for the colonized (countries, women, peasants) is to develop their own identity after a process of formal decolonization—identity no longer based on the model of the colonizer as the image of the true human being; a problem addressed by Fanon,[5] Memmi,[6] Freire,[7] and Blaise.[8] To survive, wrote Memmi, the colonized must oppress the colonization. But to become a true human being he/she, him/herself, must oppress the colonized which, within themselves, they have become.[9] This means that he/she must overcome the fascination exerted by the colonizer and his lifestyle and re-evaluate what he/she is and does.

To promote the elimination of the colonizers from within the colonized, it is useful to look more closely at the catching-up development myth.

It may be argued that those who have so far paid the price for development also look up to those at the top as their model of the future, as their concrete utopia; that this is a kind of universal law. But if we also consider the price nature had to pay for this model, a price that now increasingly affects people in the affluent societies too, it may be asked why do not these people question this myth? Because even in the North, the paradigm of unlimited growth of science and technology, goods and services—of capital—and GNP have led to an increasing deterioration in the environment, and subsequently the quality of life.

Divide and Rule: Modern Industrial Society's Secret

Most people in the affluent societies live in a kind of schizophrenic or 'double-think' state. They are aware of the disasters of Bhopal and Chernobyl, of the 'greenhouse' effect, the destruction of the ozone layer, the gradual poisoning of ground-water, rivers and seas by fertilizers, pesticides, herbicides, as well as industrial waste, and that they themselves increasingly suffer the effects of air pollution, allergies, stress and noise, and the health risks due to industrially produced food. They also know that responsibility for these negative impacts on their quality of life lies in their own lifestyles and an economic system based on constant growth. And yet (except for very few) they fail to act on this knowledge by modifying their lifestyles.

One reason for this collective schizophrenia is the North's stubborn hope, even belief, that they can have their cake and eat it: ever more products from the chemical industry *and* clean air and water; more and more cars and no 'greenhouse' effect; an ever increasing output of commodities, more fast- and processed- foods, more fancy packaging, more exotic, imported food *and* enjoy good health and solve the waste problem.

Most people expect science and technology to provide a solution to these dilemmas, rather than taking steps to limit their own consumption and production patterns. It is not yet fully realized that a high material living standard militates against a genuinely good quality of life, especially if problems of ecological destruction are clearly understood.

The belief, however, that a high material living standard is tantamount to a good or high quality of life is the ideological support essential to uphold and legitimize the constant growth and accumulation model of modern industrial society. Unless the masses of people accept this the system cannot last and function. This equation is the real ideological-political hegemony that overlies everyday life. No political party in the industrialized countries of the North dares question this schizophrenic equation, because they fear it would affect their election prospects.

We have already shown that this double-think is based on assumptions that there are no limits to our planet's resources, no limits to technological progress, no limits to space, to growth. But as, in fact, we inhabit a limited world, this limitlessness is mythical and can be upheld only by colonial divisions: between centres and peripheries, men and women, urban and rural areas, modern industrial societies of the North and 'backward', 'traditional', 'underdeveloped' societies of the South. The relationship between these parts is hierarchical not egalitarian, and characterized by exploitation, oppression and dominance.

The economic reason for these colonial structures is, above all, the *externalization of costs*[10] from the space and time horizon of those who profit from these divisions. The economic, social and ecological costs of constant growth in the industrialized countries have been and are shifted to the colonized countries of the South, to those countries' environment and their peoples. Only by dividing the international workforce into workers in the colonized peripheries and workers in the industrialized centres and by maintaining these relations of dominance even after formal decolonization, is it possible for industrial countries' workers to be paid wages ten times and more higher than those paid to workers in the South.

Much of the social costs of the reproduction of the labour force within industrial societies is externalized *within* those societies themselves. This is facilitated through the patriarchal-capitalist sexual division of labour whereby women's household labour is defined as non-productive or as non-work and hence not remunerated. Women are defined as housewives and their work is omitted from GNP calculations. Women can therefore be called the internal colony of this system.

The ecological costs of the industrial production of chemical fertilizers, pesticides, atomic energy, and of cars and other commodities, and the waste and damage for which they are responsible during both the production and the consumption process, are being inflicted on nature. They manifest themselves as air-, water-, soil-pollution and poisoning that will not only affect the present, but all future generations. This applies particularly to the long-term effects of modern high technology: atomic industry, genetic engineering, computer technology and their synergic effects which nobody can either predict or control. Thus, both nature and the future have been colonized for the short-term profit motives of affluent societies and classes.

The relationship between colonized and colonizer is based not on any measure of partnership but rather on the latter's coercion and violence in its dealings with the former. This relationship is in fact the secret of unlimited growth in the centres of accumulation. If externalization of all the costs of industrial production were not possible, if they had to be borne by the industrialized countries themselves, that is if they were internalized, an immediate end to unlimited growth would be inevitable.

Catching-up Impossible and Undesirable

The logic of this accumulation model, based on exploitation and colonizing divisions, implies that anything like 'catching-up development' is impossible for the colonies, for all colonies. This is because just as one colony may, after much effort, attain what was considered the ultimate in 'development', the industrial centres themselves have already 'progressed' to a yet more 'modern' stage of development; 'development' here meaning technological progress.What today was the TV is tomorrow the colour TV, the day after the computer, then the ever more modern version of the 'computer generation' and even later artificial intelligence machines and so forth.[11] This catching-up policy of the colonies is therefore always a lost game. Because the very progress of the colonizers is based on the existence and the exploitation of those colonies.

These implications are usually ignored when development strategies are discussed. The aim, it is usually stated, is not a reduction in the industrialized societies' living standards but rather that all the 'underdeveloped' should be enabled to attain the same level of affluence as in those societies. This sounds fine and corresponds to the values of the bourgeois revolutions: equality for all! But that such a demand is not only a logical, but also a material impossibility is ignored. The impossibility of this demand is obvious if one considers the ecological consequences of the universalization of the prevailing production system and lifestyle in the North's affluent industrial societies to everyone now living and for some further 30 years on this planet. If, for example, we note that the six per cent of the world's population who live in the USA annually consume 30 per cent of all the fossil energy produced, then, obviously, it is impossible for the rest of the world's population, of which about 80 per cent live in the poor countries of the South, to consume energy on the same scale.[12]

According to Trainer, those living in the USA, Europe and Japan, consume three-quarters of the world's energy production. 'If present world energy production were to be shared equally, Americans would have to get by on only one-fifth of the per capita amount they presently consume'.[13] Or, put differently, world population may be estimated at eleven billion people after the year 2050; if of these eleven billion people the per capita energy consumption was similar to that of Americans in the mid-1970s, conventional oil resources would be exhausted in 34–74 years;[14] similar estimations are made for other resources.

But even if the world's resource base was unlimited it can be estimated that it would be around 500 years before the poor countries reached the living standard prevailing in the industrialized North; and then only if these countries abandoned the model of permanent economic growth, which constitutes the core of their economic philosophy. It is impossible for the South to 'catch-up' with this model, not only because of the limits and inequitable consumption of the resource base, but above all, because this growth model is based on a colonial world order in which the gap between the two poles is increasing, especially as far as economic development is concerned.

These examples show that catching-up development is not possible for all. In my opinion, the powers that dominate today's world economy are aware of this, the managers of the transnational corporations, the World Bank, the IMF, the banks and governments of the club of the rich countries; and in fact they do not really want this universalization, because it would end *their* growth model. Tacitly, they accept that the colonial structure of the so-called market economy is maintained worldwide. This structure, however, is masked by such euphemisms as 'North-South relations', 'sustainable development', 'threshold-countries' and so on which suggest that all poor countries can and will reach the same living standard as that of the affluent countries.

Yet, if one tries to disregard considerations of equity and of ecological concerns it may be asked if this model of the good life, pursued by the societies in the North, this paradigm of 'catching-up development' has at least made people in the

North happy. Has it fulfilled its promises there? Has it at least made women and children there more equal, more free, more happy? Has their quality of life improved while the GDP grew?

We read daily about an increase of homelessness and of poverty, particularly of women and children,[15] of rising criminality in the big cities, of growing drug, and other addictions, including the addiction to shopping. Depression and suicides are on the increase in many of the affluent societies, and direct violence against women and children seems to be growing—both public and domestic violence as well as sexual abuse; the media are full of reports of all forms of violence. Additionally, the urban centres are suffocating from motor vehicle exhaust emissions; there is barely any open space left in which to walk and breathe, the cities and highways are choked with cars. Whenever possible people try to escape from these urban centres to seek relief in the countryside or in the poor South. If, as is commonly asserted, city-dwellers' quality of life is so high, why do they not spend their vacations in the cities?

It has been found that in the USA today the quality of life is lower than it was ten years ago. There seems to be an inverse relationship between GDP and the quality of life: the more GDP grows, the more the quality of life deteriorates.[16] For example: growing market forces have led to the fact that food, which so far was still prepared in the home is now increasingly bought from fast-food restaurants; preparing food has become a service, a commodity. If more and more people buy this commodity the GDP grows. But what also grows at the same time is the erosion of community, the isolation and loneliness of individuals, the indifference and atomization of the society. As Polanyi remarked, market forces destroy communities.[17] Here, too, the processes are characterized by polarizations: the higher the GDP the lower the quality of life.

But 'catching-up development' not only entails immaterial psychic and social costs and risks, which beset even the privileged in the rich countries and classes. With the growing number of ecological catastrophes—some man-made like the Gulf War or Chernobyl—material life also deteriorates in the rich centres of the world. The affluent society is one society which in the midst of plenty of commodities lacks the fundamental necessities of life: clean air, pure water, healthy food, space, time and quiet. What was experienced by mothers of small children after Chernobyl is now experienced by mothers in Kuwait. All the money of oil-rich Kuwait cannot buy people sunlight, fresh air, or pure water. This scarcity of basic common necessities for survival affects the poor and the rich, but with greater impact on the poor.

In short, the prevailing world market system, oriented towards unending growth and profit, cannot be maintained unless it can exploit external and internal colonies: nature, women and other people, but it also needs people as consumers who never say: 'IT IS ENOUGH'. The consumer model of the rich countries is not generalizable worldwide, neither is it desirable for the minority of the world's population who live in the affluent societies. Moreover, it will lead increasingly to wars to secure ever-scarcer resources; the Gulf War was in large part about the control of oil resources in that region. If we want to avoid such wars in future the only alternative is a deliberate and drastic change of lifestyle, a reduction of consumption and a radical change in the North's consumer patterns and a decisive and broad-based movement towards energy conservation.

These facts are widely known, but the myth of catching-up development is still largely the basis of development policies of the governments of the North and the South, as well as the ex-socialist countries. A TV discussion[18] in which three heads of state participated—Robert Mugabe of Zimbabwe, Vaclav Havel of the CSFR, and Richard von Weizsacker, President of the then FRG—is a clear illustration of this. The discussion took place after a showing of the film *The March*, which depicted millions of starving Africans trying to enter rich Europe. The President of the FRG said quite clearly that the consumption patterns of the 20 per cent of the world's population who live in the affluent societies of the industrialized North are using 80 per cent of the world's resources, and that these consumption patterns would, in the long run, destroy the natural foundations of life—worldwide. When, however, he was asked, if it was not then correct to criticize and relinquish the North's consumption patterns and to warn the South against imitating the North he replied that it would be wrong to preach to people about reducing consumption. Moreover, people in the South had the right to the same living standard as those in the North. The only solution was to distribute more of 'our' wealth, through development aid, to the poor in the South, to enable them to 'catch-up'. He did not mention that this wealth originated as a result of the North's plundering of the colonies, as has been noted.

The President of socialist Zimbabwe was even more explicit. He said that people in the South wanted as many cars, refrigerators, TV sets, computers, videos and the same standard of living as the people in the North; that this was the aim of his politics of development. Neither he nor von Weizsacker asked whether this policy of universalizing the North's consumption patterns through a catching-up strategy was materially feasible. They also failed to question the ecological consequences of such a policy. As elected heads of state they dared not tell the truth, namely that the lifestyle of the rich in the North cannot be universalized, and that it should be ended in these countries in order to uphold the values of an egalitarian world. . . .

In other parts of the world the collapse of the catching-up development myth leads to waves of fundamentalism and nationalism directed against religious, ethnic, racial, 'others' within and outside their own territory. The main target of both nationalism and fundamentalism, and communalism, is women, because religious, ethnic and cultural identity are always based on a patriarchy, a patriarchal image of women, or rather control over 'our' women, which, as we know from many examples, almost always amounts to more violence against women, more inequality for women.[19] Moreover, the collapse of the myth of catching-up development results in a further militarization of men. Practically all the new nationalisms and fundamentalisms have led to virtual civil war in which young, militarized men play the key role. As unacceptable as equals by the rich men's club and unable to share their lifestyle they can only show their manhood—as it is understood in a patriarchal world—by shouldering a machine-gun.

The myth of catching-up development, therefore, eventually leads to further destruction of the environment, further exploitation of the 'Third World', further violence against women and further militarization of men.

NOTES

1. Frank, A. G., *World Accumulation 1492–1789*. Macmillan, New York, 1978.

2. Amin, S., *Accumulation on a World Scale. A Critique of the Theory of Underdevelopment*. Monthly Review Press, New York, 1974.

3. Galtung, J., Eine Strukturelle Theorie des Imperialismus, in D. Senghaas (ed.) *Imperialismus und strukturelle Gewalt. Analysen über abhängige Reproduktion*. Suhrkamp, Frankfurt, 1972.

4. Mies, M., *Patriarchy and Accumulation on a World Scale, Women in the International Division of Labour*. Zed Books, London, 1989.

5. Fanon, F., *Peau Noire, Masques Blancs*. Edition du Seuil, Paris, 1952; English version: *Black Skin, White Masks*. Paladin, London, 1970.

6. Memmi, A., *Portrait du Colonise*. Edition Payot, Paris, 1973.

7. Freire, P., *Pedagogy of the Oppressed*. Penguin Books, Harmondsworth, 1970.

8. Blaise, S., *Le Rapt des Origines. ou: Le Meurtre de la Mere*. Maison des Femmes, Paris, 1988.

9. Memmi, op. cit., quoted in Blaise (1988) p. 74.

10. Kapp, W. K., Social Costs of Business Enterprise. Asia Publishing House, Bombay, 1963.

11. Ullrich, O., *Weltniveau. In der Sackgasse des Industriesystems*. Rotbuchverlag, Berlin, 1979, p. 108.

12. See *The Global 2000 Report to the President* US Foreign Ministry (ed.) Washington, Appendix, 1980, p. 59.

13. Trainer, F. E., *Developed to Death. Rethinking World Development*. Green Print, London, 1989.

14. Ibid., p. 61.

15. Sheldon, Danzinger and Stern.

16. Trainer, op. cit., p. 130.

17. Polanyi, K., *The Great Transformation*. Suhrkamp, Frankfurt, 1978.

18. This discussion took place under the title: 'Die Zukunft gemeinsam meistern' on 22 May 1990 in Norddeutscher Rundfunk (NDR). It was produced by Rolf Seelmann-Eggebert.

19. Chhachhi, A. 'Forced Identities: The State, Communalism, Fundamentalism and Women in India', in Kandiyoti, D. (ed.) *Women, Islam and the State*. University of California Press, 1991.

The Second Coming of Columbus
Piracy Through Patents

—Vandana Shiva

Vandana Shiva is a physicist, ecologist, activist, and editor. She directs the Research Foundation for Science, Technology and Natural Resource Policy in India, where she has established Navdanya, a movement for biodiversity conservation and farmers' rights. This excerpt is from her book Biopiracy: The Plunder of Nature and Knowledge. *It was published by South End Press in 1997.*

On April 17, 1492, Queen Isabel and King Ferdinand granted Christopher Columbus the privileges of "discovery and conquest." One year later, on May 4, 1493, Pope Alexander VI, through his "Bull of Donation," granted all islands and mainlands "discovered and to be discovered, one hundred leagues to the West and South of the Azores towards India," and not already occupied or held by any christian king or prince as of Christmas of 1492, to the Catholic monarchs Isabel of Castille and Ferdinand of Aragon. As Walter Ullmann stated in *Medieval Papalism*:

> The pope as the vicar of God commanded the world, as if it were a tool in his hands; the pope, supported by the canonists, considered the world as his property to be disposed according to his will.

Charters and patents thus turned acts of piracy into divine will. The peoples and nations that were colonized did not belong to the pope who "donated" them, yet this canonical jurisprudence made the christian monarchs of Europe rulers of all nations, "wherever they might be found and whatever creed they might embrace." The principle of "effective occupation" by christian princes, the "vacancy" of the targeted lands, and the "duty" to incorporate the "savages" were components of charters and patents.

The Papal Bull, the Columbus charter, and patents granted by European monarchs laid the juridical and moral foundations for the colonization and extermination of non-European peoples. The Native American population declined from 72 million in 1492 to less than 4 million a few centuries later.

Five hundred years after Columbus, a more secular version of the same project of colonization continues through patents and intellectual property rights (IPRs).

From *Biopiracy* by Vandan Shiva. Reprinted by permission of South End Press.

The Papal Bull has been replaced by the General Agreement on Tariffs and Trade (GATT) treaty. The principle of effective occupation by christian princes has been replaced by effective occupation by the transnational corporations supported by modern-day rulers. The vacancy of targeted lands has been replaced by the vacancy of targeted life forms and species manipulated by the new biotechnologies. The duty to incorporate savages into Christianity has been replaced by the duty to incorporate local and national economies into the global marketplace, and to incorporate non-western systems of knowledge into the reductionism of commercialized Western science and technology.

The creation of property through the piracy of other's wealth remains the same as 500 years ago.

The freedom that transnational corporations are claiming through intellectual property rights protection in the GATT agreement on Trade Related Intellectual Property Rights (TRIPs) is the freedom that European colonizers have claimed since 1492. Columbus set a precedent when he treated the license to conquer non-European peoples as a natural right of European men. The land titles issued by the pope through European kings and queens were the first patents. The colonizer's freedom was built on the slavery and subjugation of the people with original rights to the land. This violent takeover was rendered "natural" by defining the colonized people as nature, thus denying them their humanity and freedom.

John Locke's treatise on property[1] effectually legitimized this same process of theft and robbery during the enclosure movement in Europe. Locke clearly articulated capitalism's freedom to build as the freedom to steal; property is created by removing resources from nature and mixing them with labor. This "labor" is not physical, but labor in its "spiritual" form, as manifested in the control of capital. According to Locke, only those who own capital have the natural right to own natural resources, a right that supersedes the common rights of others with prior claims. Capital is thus defined as a source of freedom that, at the same time, denies freedom to the land, forests, rivers, and biodiversity that capital claims as its own and to others whose rights are based on their labor. Returning private property to the commons is perceived as depriving the owner of capital of freedom. Therefore, peasants and tribespeople who demand the return of their rights and access to resources are regarded as thieves.

These Eurocentric notions of property and piracy are the bases on which the IPR laws of the GATT and World Trade Organization (WTO) have been framed. When Europeans first colonized the non-European world, they felt it was their duty to "discover and conquer," to "subdue, occupy, and possess." It seems that the Western powers are still driven by the colonizing impulse to discover, conquer, own, and possess everything, every society, every culture. The colonies have now been extended to the interior spaces, the "genetic codes" of life-forms from microbes and plants to animals, including humans.

John Moore, a cancer patient, had his cell lines patented by his own doctor. In 1996, Myriad Pharmaceuticals, a U.S.-based company, patented the breast cancer gene in women in order to get a monopoly on diagnostics and testing. The cell lines of the Hagahai of Papua New Guinea and the Guami of Panama are patented by the U.S. commerce secretary.

The natural development and exchange of knowledge has, in effect, been criminalized by the Economic Espionage Act of 1996, which became U.S. law on September 17 and empowers U.S. intelligence agencies to investigate the ordinary activities of people worldwide. The act considers the intellectual property rights of U.S. corporations as vital to national security.

The assumption of empty lands, terra nullius, is now being expanded to "empty life," seeds and medicinal plants. The takeover of native resources during colonization was justified on the ground that indigenous people did not "improve" their land. As John Winthrop wrote in 1869:

> Natives in New England, they enclose no land, neither have they any settled habitation, nor any tame cattle to improve the land by soe have nor other but a Natural Right to those countries. Soe as if we leane them sufficient for their use, we may lawfully take the rest.[2]

The same logic is now used to appropriate biodiversity from the original owners and innovators by defining their seeds, medicinal plants, and medical knowledge as nature, as nonscience, and treating the tools of genetic engineering as the yardstick of "improvement." Defining Christianity as the only religion, and all other beliefs and cosmologies as primitive, finds its parallel in defining commercialized Western science as the only science, and all other knowledge systems as primitive.

Five hundred years ago, it was enough to be a non-christian culture to lose all claims and rights. Five hundred years after Columbus, it is enough to be a non-Western culture with a distinctive worldview and diverse knowledge systems to lose all claims and rights. The humanity of others was blanked out then and their intellect is being blanked out now. Conquered territories were treated as people-less in the patents of the 15th and 16th centuries. People were naturalized into "our subjects." In continuity with conquest by naturalization, biodiversity is being defined as nature—the cultural and intellectual contributions of non-Western knowledge systems are being systematically erased.

Today's patents have a continuity with those issued to Columbus, Sir John Cabot, Sir Humphrey Gilbert, and Sir Walter Raleigh. The conflicts that have been unleashed by the GATT treaty, by patents on life-forms, by the patenting of indigenous knowledge, and by genetic engineering are grounded in processes that can be summarized and symbolized as the second coming of Columbus.

At the heart of Columbus's "discovery" was the treatment of piracy as a natural right of the colonizer, necessary for the deliverance of the colonized. At the heart of the GATT treaty and its patent laws is the treatment of biopiracy as a natural right of Western corporations, necessary for the "development" of Third World communities.

Biopiracy is the Columbian "discovery" 500 years after Columbus. Patents are still the means to protect this piracy of the wealth of non-Western peoples as a right of Western powers.

Through patents and genetic engineering, new colonies are being carved out. The land, the forests, the rivers, the oceans, and the atmosphere have all been colonized, eroded, and polluted. Capital now has to look for new colonies to invade and exploit for its further accumulation. These new colonies are, in my view, the interior spaces of the bodies of women, plants, and animals. Resistance to biopiracy is a resistance to the ultimate colonization of life itself—of the future of evolution as well as the future of non-Western traditions of relating to and knowing nature. It is a struggle to protect the freedom of diverse species to evolve. It is a struggle to protect the freedom of diverse cultures to evolve. It is a struggle to conserve both cultural and biological diversity.

What is creativity? This is at the heart of the current debates about patents on life. Patents on life enclose the creativity inherent to living systems that reproduce and multiply in self-organized freedom. They enclose the interior spaces of the bodies of women, plants, and animals. They also enclose the free spaces of intellectual creativity by transforming publicly generated knowledge into private property. Intellectual property rights on life-forms are supposed to reward and stimulate creativity. Their impact is actually the opposite—to stifle the creativity intrinsic to life-forms and the social production of knowledge.

Science is an expression of human creativity, both individual and collective. Since creativity has diverse expressions, I see science as a pluralistic enterprise that refers to different "ways of knowing." For me, it is not restricted to modern Western science, but includes the knowledge systems of diverse cultures in different periods of history. Recent work in the history, philosophy, and sociology of science has revealed that scientists do not work in accordance with an abstract scientific method, putting forward theories based on direct and neutral observation. Scientific claims, like all others, are now recognized as arising not out of a verificationist model, but from the commitment of a specialized community of scientists to presupposed metaphors and paradigms, which determine the meaning of constituent terms and concepts as well as the status of observation and fact. These new accounts of science, based on its practice, do not leave us with any criteria to distinguish the theoretical claims of indigenous non-Western sciences from those of modern Western science. That it is the latter that is more widely practiced in non-Western cultures has more to do with Western cultural and economic hegemony than with cultural neutrality. Recognition of diverse traditions of creativity is an essential component of keeping diverse knowledge systems alive. This is particularly important in this period of rampant ecological destruction, in which the smallest source of ecological knowledge and insights can become a vital link to the future of humanity on this planet.

Indigenous knowledge systems are by and large ecological, while the dominant model of scientific knowledge, characterized by reductionism and fragmentation, is not equipped to take the complexity of interrelationships in nature fully into account. This inadequacy becomes most significant in the domain of life sciences, which deal with living organisms. Creativity in the life sciences has to include three levels:

1. The creativity inherent to living organisms that allows them to evolve, recreate, and regenerate themselves.
2. The creativity of indigenous communities that have developed knowledge systems to conserve and utilize the rich biological diversity of our planet.
3. The creativity of modern scientists in university or corporate labs who find ways to use living organisms to generate profits.

The recognition of these diverse creativities is essential for the conservation of biodiversity as well as for the conservation of intellectual diversity—across cultures and within the university setting.

Intellectual property rights are supposed to reward and provide recognition for intellectual creativity. Yet knowledge and creativity have been so narrowly defined in the context of IPRs that the creativity of nature and of non-Western knowledge systems has been ignored. IPRs are theoretically property rights to products of the mind. People everywhere innovate and create. If IPR regimes reflected the diversity of knowledge traditions that account for creativity and innovation in different societies, they would necessarily be pluralistic—also reflecting intellectual modes of property systems and systems of rights—leading to an amazing richness of permutations and combinations.

As currently discussed in global platforms, such as GATT and the Biodiversity Convention, or as unilaterally imposed through the Special 301 clause of the U.S. Trade Act, IPRs are a prescription for a monoculture of knowledge. These instruments are being used to universalize the U.S. patent regime worldwide, which would inevitably lead to an intellectual and cultural impoverishment by displacing other ways of knowing, other objectives for knowledge creation, and other modes of knowledge sharing.

The TRIPs treaty of the Final Act of GATT is based on a highly restricted concept of innovation. By definition, it is weighted in favor of transnational corporations, and against citizens in general and Third World peasants and forest dwellers in particular.

The first restriction is the shift from common rights to private rights. As the preamble of the TRIPs agreement states, intellectual property rights are recognized only as private rights. This excludes all kinds of knowledge, ideas, and innovations that take place in the "intellectual commons"—in villages among farmers, in forests among tribespeople and even in universities among scientists. TRIPs is therefore a mechanism for the privatization of the intellectual commons and a deintellectualization of civil society. The mind becomes a corporate monopoly.

The second restriction of intellectual property rights is that they are recognized only when knowledge and innovation generate profits, not when they meet social needs. According to Article 27.1, to be considered an IPR, innovation has to be capable of industrial application. This immediately excludes all sectors that produce and innovate outside the industrial mode of organization. Profits and capital accumulation are the only ends of creativity; the social good is no longer recognized. Under corporate control, there is a "deindustrialization" of small-scale production in the informal sectors of society.

By denying the creativity of nature and other cultures, even when that creativity is exploited for commercial gain, intellectual property rights becomes another name for intellectual theft and biopiracy. Simultaneously, people's assertion of their customary, collective rights to knowledge and resources is turned into "piracy" and "theft."

The U.S. International Trade Commission claims that U.S. industry is losing between $100 million and $300 million per year because of "weak" intellectual property protection in Third World countries.[3] When one takes into account the value of Third World biodiversity and intellectual traditions used freely by commercial interests in the United States, it is the United States—and not countries like India—that is engaged in piracy.

Even though many of the patents in the United States are based on Third World biodiversity and knowledge, it is falsely assumed that without IPR protection, creativity lies buried. As Robert Sherwood states, "Human creativity is a vast national resource for any country. Like gold in the hills, it will remain buried without encouragement for extraction. Intellectual property protection is the tool which releases that resource."[4]

This interpretation of creativity, as unleashed only when formal regimes of IPR protection are in place, is a total negation of creativity in nature as well as the creativity generated by nonprofit motives in both industrial and nonindustrial societies. It is a denial of the role of innovation in traditional cultures and in the public domain. In fact, the dominant interpretation of IPRs leads to a dramatic distortion in the understanding of creativity, and as a result, in the understanding of the history of inequality and poverty.

The economic inequality between the affluent industrialized countries and the poor Third World ones is a product of 500 years of colonialism, and the continued maintenance and creation of mechanisms for draining wealth out of the Third World. According to the United Nations Development Program, while $50 billion flows annually from the North to the South in terms of aid, the South loses $500 billion every year in interest payments on debts and from the loss of fair prices for commodities due to unequal terms of trade. Instead of seeing the structural inequality of the international economic system as lying at the roots of Third World poverty, IPR advocates explain poverty as arising from a lack of creativity, which, in turn, is seen as rooted in a lack of IPR protection.

NOTES

1. John Locke, *Two Treatises of Government*, ed. Peter Caslett (Cambridge University Press, 1967).

2. John Winthrop, "Life and Letters," quoted in Djelal Kadir, *Columbus and the Ends of the Earth* (Berkeley: University of California Press, 1992), p. 171.

3. Vandana Shiva, *Monocultures of the Mind* (London: Zed Books, 1993).

4. Robert Sherwood, *Intellectual Property and Economic Development* (Boulder, San Francisco, and Oxford: Westview Press).

Questions for Thinking, Writing, and Discussion

1. Early in Article 1, William Appleman Williams offers a one-sentence definition of what is meant by a "way of life." Explain Williams' use of this concept in more detail and by offering examples, then go on to explain what Williams means by "*empire* as a way of life."

2. What, according to Williams, is the role of racism in helping to rationalize or justify imperialism?

3. What, according to Williams, is the difference between "soft imperialists" and "hard imperialists"?

4. Williams draws a distinction between colonialism and imperialism. What, according to him, is the basis of this distinction and is this distinction useful?

5. Who, according to Felix Greene, bore the cost of empire in Britain? How does he make a case for his claim?

6. Compare and contrast the definition of colonialism offered by Jerry Kloby with that offered by Williams. What are the similarities and differences in the definitions they provide? Is one more adequate or useful than the other?

7. What, according to Jerry Kloby and Walter Rodney, has been the major impact of colonialism in shaping the modern world? What aspects of contemporary economic and political life can be explained or understood in light of it?

8. Why does Rodney dispute the claim that colonialism modernized Africa? Does he make a persuasive case for his position?

9. Compare and contrast Eduardo Galeano's and William Appleman Williams' accounts of the ideological justifications offered by the colonial powers for colonization. Why do you think these rationalizations were so effective?

10. Based on your readings of Kloby, Rodney, and Galeano, what would you identify as the key elements by which a colonial power dominates a colonized people? In your discussion, be sure to comment on how it is possible for a small foreign minority to take control of an entire population in their own native land.

11. What does Jan Pettman mean when she says "Within conventional histories of colonialism women are largely absent"? How does her attempt to reclaim women's history enrich or transform our understanding of colonialism?

12. Why is Maria Mies so pessimistic about the possibility that developing nations can "catch up" to the more developed nations by following the same path of industrialization, technological progress, and capital accumulation as that taken by the more affluent countries?

13. Why does Vandana Shiva refer to "piracy through patents" as the "second coming of Columbus?"

Suggestions for Further Reading

Bowen, John. "The Myth of Global Ethnic Conflict," *Journal of Democracy*. 7.4 (1996), 3–14.

Cesaire, Aime. *Discourse on Colonialism*. New York: New York University Press, 2000.

Memmi, Albert. *The Colonizer and the Colonized*. Boston: Beacon Press, 1991.

Frank, Andre Gunder. *Capitalism and Underdevelopment in Latin America*. New York: Monthly Review Press, 1969, pp. 281 or 296.

Galeano, Edward. *Open Veins of Latin America: Five Centuries of Pillage of a Continent*. New York: Monthly Review Press, 1973.

Hopkirk, Peter. *The Great Game: The Struggle for Empire in Central Asia*. Kodansha Globe, Reprint edition, 1994.

James, C. L. R. *The Black Jacobins*. New York: Random House, 1963.

Kaplan, Amy, and Donald E. Pease. *Cultures of U.S. Imperialism*. Durham and London: Duke University Press, 1993.

LaFeber, Walter. *Inevitable Revolutions: The United States and Central America*. New York: W. W. Norton & Company, 1983.

Loomba, Ania. *Colonialism Postcolonialism*. New York and London: Routledge, 2005.

Parsons, Timothy. *The British Imperial Century, 1815–1914*. Rowman and Littlefield, 1999.

Said, Edward W. *Culture and Imperialism*. New York: Vintage, 1994.

Said, Edward W. *Orientalism*. New York: Vintage, 1979.

Schoultz, Karl. *Beneath the United States: A History of U.S. Policy Toward Latin America*. Cambridge, MA: Harvard University Press, 1998.

Schlesinger, Stephen C. *Bitter Fruit: The Story of the American Coup in Guatemala*. Boston: Harvard University Press, 1999.

Shalom, Steve. *Imperial Alibis: Rationalizing U.S. Intervention After the Cold War*. Boston: South End Press, 1992.

Spurr, David. *The Rhetoric of Empire: Colonial Discourse in Journalism, Travel Writing, and Imperial Administration (Post-Contemporary Interventions Series)*. Durham: Duke University Press, 1993.

Wild, Antony. *The East India Company Trade and Conquest from 1600*. The Lyons Press, 2000.

Williams, Eric. *From Columbus to Castro: A Brief History of the Caribbean, 1492–1969*. New York: Vintage Books, 1984.

part three

Constructing Difference: Creating "Other" Identities

Power consists in the ability to make others inhabit your story of their
reality—even as is so often the case, when that story is written in their blood.
–Philip Gourevitch

As we have already seen, a critical element in the creation and maintenance of empire involves the ability to justify or rationalize the subordination of one group of people by another. This is necessary both because persuading the population in question that their subordinate status is deserved makes it easier to subdue them and because some members of the dominant group would be reluctant to participate without a relatively benign justification for what might appear to be an inhumane policy. Racism, sexism, heterosexism, and class divisions all benefit from the construction of difference—a difference that simultaneously explains and excuses the domination of one group by another.

It is, of course, most effective if the difference can be given some authoritative and seemingly independent grounding. For this reason, alleged differences are often said to be natural, universal, immutable, or eternal, based on biology or on god's teachings. In this respect both religion and science have played key roles at different times in history in rationalizing domination. Advocates of both white supremacy and male superiority have often cited passages in holy books that they claim support their view, and during the colonial period throughout the world the church often played a significant role in justifying the imposed racial hierarchy and in reconciling native peoples to their newly subordinate status and their servitude. Scientific racism and sexism were called upon to "prove" that certain groups, namely white people and men, were biologically superior by virtue of the size of their brains, the shape of their heads, and the general nature of their physiognomy. Differences in condition or achievement that some would recognize as the result of discrimination have often been excused by alleging innate differences.

But in spite of the demagoguery mobilized by some, in Article 1, "Assigning Value to Difference," Albert Memmi points out that "it is not the difference which always entails racism; it is racism which makes use of the difference." The key point here is not the existence of difference in itself—after all, we are surrounded by an infinite number of differences in the world—but the way in which the supremacist *interprets* difference, hence Memmi's definition of racism as " the generalized and final assigning of values to real or imaginary differences, to the accuser's benefit and at his victim's expense, in order to justify the former's own privileges or aggression." In the end, according to Memmi, racism is all about the need to justify aggression and injustice. Although his primary focus is on racism, many would argue that Memmi's analysis applies equally well to other forms of oppression and exploitation.

Taking Memmi's analysis a step further, in Article 2, "Hatred Written on the Body," Zillah Eisenstein provides us with a passionate analysis of the ways in which difference or "otherness" is constructed on bodies. She writes: "Because people grow othered by their racialized, sexualized, and engendered bodies, bodies are important to the writing of hatred on history." Beginning with the underlying assumption that human beings share much in common and that neither purity of blood nor purity of race exist, Eisenstein seeks to understand the kinds of extraordinary hatred that explode almost daily around the world, taking the form of attacks on individuals and conflicts between nations and national groups. Moving back and forth freely among racism, sexism, heterosexism, anti-semitism, and other forms of hatred, Eisenstein provides a graphic account of the construction of difference and its consequences. A strength of this piece is her insistence on showing how her analysis applies equally well to the way hatred gets constructed and acted out in the situation of Koreans, Blacks, and Jews in Los Angeles; the rape of Muslim women in Bosnia; attacks on lesbians and gays around the world, Vietnamese and African guest workers in Germany, and Palestinians massacred in Hebron.

In Article 3, "Stories from Rwanda," Philip Gourevitch provides an example of how the colonial powers, in this case Germany and Belgium, used the doctrine of racial superiority and the construction of difference to divide populations and shore up their rule. When Belgium replaced Germany as the colonial power in Rwanda, the Belgians quickly set about using the groundwork laid by the Germans to create a doctrine of racial superiority and difference that would divide the Hutus and the Tutsis. By radically reengineering Rwandan society along so-called ethnic lines, the colonizers insured that a once united population with a strong sense of national identity would be transformed into more easily controllable warring tribes. In this way, both the German and Belgian colonizers used difference to create hatred in ways that would facilitate colonial rule. The genocidal violence that occurred in Rwanda in 1994 is but one more legacy of colonialism.

In "Construction of an Enemy," Article 4, Eleanor Stein turns our attention to the United States and asks us to reflect on the ways in which the U.S. government constructed Arabs, South Asians, and Muslims as "the enemy" following the September 11, 2001 attacks. Stein argues that the policy of racial profiling adopted by the U.S. government and supported by media complicity has dehumanized members of these groups and has constructed them as the enemy of "America" in the twenty-first century. She writes: "given a dehumanized enemy, bombing its cities and sacking its history was presented on U.S. TV as an extreme sport." Stein places her discussion of current racial profiling in the context of a history of past nativist and xenophobic policies and legislation on the part of the U.S. government, in particular the internment of Japanese Americans in camps during World War II.

The next three articles examine the construction of otherness and difference from a somewhat different perspective. Chandra Mohanty was born in India and has lived and taught in the United States for many years; Ella Shohat was born in Iraq and like Mohanty now lives and works in the United States; and Stuart Hall was born in Jamaica but now lives and works in Great Britain. Each of these authors reflects on their changing sense of self and its relation to how others see them. They place their own evolving understanding of who they are and how they are perceived and categorized by others within the context of changing political events around the world that impact on this process.

Chandra Mohanty talks about what it means to be South East Asian in North America in Article 5. Her nuanced account of her evolving sense of self as she travels back and forth between India and the United States is ever mindful of the complications imposed on that project by issues of gender, race, and class and clearly illustrates the tension between how we see ourselves and how others see us. Mohanty takes us on her journey from "foreign student" to "student of color" to "resident alien," and then, green card in hand, back to Bombay at a time when relations between Muslims and Hindus were particularly volatile and called into question what it might mean to identify as a Hindu.

Ella Shohot embraces her complex identity as an Arab Jew and the rich history that comes with it, but she finds that many in North America have trouble with an identity that for them seems to contradict boundaries they regard as given. This raises interesting questions about the way difference is created and the permeability or lack thereof of its boundaries and whose interests they serve. As Shohat observes, "watching media images from the Middle East, one is led to believe that there are only Euro-American Jews in Israel and only Moslem Arabs in the rest of the Middle East." Like Chilla Bulbeck in Part Two, Shohot's essay implicitly cautions us against thinking in terms of binarisms and challenges the worldview that such thinking engenders.

In "Old and New Identities," Article 7, Stuart Hall offers us an account of how an identity that once had negative connotations can be co-opted and transformed by the population it was applied to and in that process lead to a change of consciousness. Hall tells us that he was not Black while growing up in Jamaica but learned to be Black in Britain during the 1960s and later found himself teaching the same identity to his young son. He focuses our attention on a moment in the 1970s (a moment that occurred in the United States as well), when people of color decided to embrace an identification with their Blackness and assert their right to define that identity in their own terms. Unlike the United States, where the term "Black" has a more limited application, in Britain people from the Asian subcontinent, Pakistan, Bangladesh, from different parts of India, as well as the Caribbean and East Africa, all identify as Black. They do so because Black serves as a political category that focuses on the commonalities these groups share in relation to a racist social-political system. On the other hand, Hall is quick to point out that this identity is not without its problems. For one thing, it has a way of silencing very specific experiences of Asian people and of some Black people as well. And, by failing to recognize gender difference, Hall points out "Black" reconstituted the authority of Black masculinity over Black women. His solution to the complicated nature of this identification is "the politics of living idenitity through difference." The realization that "all of us are composed of multiple social identities, not one," is a conclusion with which both Mohanty and Shohat would certainly agree.

In December 2004, Yahoo posted a news story entitled "Researchers Find Gay Penguins in Japanese Aquariums." According to the story, researchers had identified a number of same-sex pairs of penguins at 16 major aquariums and zoos throughout Japan. The first question that should come to mind, even before reading Chilla Bulbeck's article, "Sexual Identities: Western Imperialism?" is what kind of sense does it make to apply the category "gayness" to penguins. After all, the categories describing sexual behavior and characterizing people who engage in that behavior in particular ways are socially constructed, not given in nature; they change over time; and most importantly, they have evolved in relation to the behavior and life-style choices of human beings. There is something quite odd about projecting these terms on to the animal kingdom, just as it would be odd to describe a tomato as blushing simply because it is red. Some would contend that the claim says more about the peculiar preoccupation of contemporary society with gender identity and sexuality than it does about the penguins.

In her essay, Bulbeck reminds us that throughout much of history and across cultures people have performed a variety of sex acts without having those acts determine their sexual identity. For example, in Ancient China and in many parts of the modern world, a man could and can engage in so-called "homosexual acts" without undermining his heterosexual identity. It is the Western preoccupation with constructing fairly rigid gender differences, a preoccupation that we have exported around the world, that is transforming the relatively fluid sexual identities that exist within many cultures into a more rigid system of dual categories. Creating the sexual "other" or deviant is one more way of reinforcing gender difference and exercising control over individuals and groups.

one

Assigning Value to Difference

–Albert Memmi

Albert Memmi was born in Tunisia in 1920 and educated at the University of Algiers and the Sorbonne. Although Arabic was his mother tongue, much of his writing is in French. Because he was a Jew growing up in a predominantly Muslim colony, some might say he was strategically positioned to write about "difference." The following essay appears in his book Dominated Man, *which was published by Beacon Press in 1996.*

I. Definition

Racism is the generalized and final assigning of values to real or imaginary differences, to the accuser's benefit and at his victim's expense, in order to justify the former's own privileges or aggression.

II. Analysis of the Racist Attitude

This analysis reveals four essential elements:

1. Stressing the *real or imaginary differences* between the racist and his victim.
2. *Assigning values* to these differences, to the advantage of the racist and the detriment of his victim.
3. Trying to make them *absolutes* by *generalizing* from them and claiming that they are final.
4. *Justifying* any present or possible *aggression* or *privilege*.[1]

III. Commentary

The term "racism" is obviously not adequate to cover a mechanism so widespread. It is too narrow, just as "anti-Semitism" is, on the contrary, too broad. Strictly speaking, it would apply to a theory of biological differences. The Nazis, adding to

Excerpts from "Attempt at a Definition," from *Dominated Man* by Albert Memmi, copyright © 1968 by Albert Memmi. Used by permission of Viking Penguin, a division of Penguin Group (USA) Inc.

1. If further summary were necessary, I would say that racism seems to me to include three essential elements: insisting on a *difference*; putting it to *mythical use*; the *convenience* of such use.

the ideas of the apologists for the slave trade and for colonization, included a system for establishing a political, moral and cultural hierarchy of human groups according to their biological differences.

A Widespread Mechanism

The racist actually bases his accusation on a biological or a cultural difference, from which he generalizes to cover the whole of the defendant's personality, his life and the group to which he belongs. Sometimes the biological trait is unclear or even missing. We can see that the mechanism is infinitely more varied, more complex and—unhappily—more common than the term "racism" would imply. It ought to be replaced by another term or other words showing what varied and at the same time what interrelated forms racism can take.[1]

Stressing the Difference

The first form of racism consists of stressing a *difference* between the accuser and his victim. But revealing a characteristic differentiating two individuals or two groups does not in itself constitute a racist attitude. After all, this is part of what any student of the human sciences does. The assertion that there is a difference takes on a special *significance* in the racist context: by emphasizing the difference, the racist aims to intensify or cause the *exclusion*, the *separation* by which the victim is placed outside the community or even outside humanity.

The colonizer discriminates to demonstrate the impossibility of including the colonized in the community: because he would be too biologically or culturally different, technically or politically inept, etc. Anti-Semitism attempts, by depicting the Jew as radically foreign and strange, to explain the isolation of the Jew, the quarantine under which he is placed. Making use of the difference is an essential step in the racist process: *but it is not the difference which always entails racism; it is racism which makes use of the difference.*

The Difference Is Real or Imaginary

If the difference is missing, the racist invents one; if the difference exists, he interprets it to his own advantage. He emphasizes only those differences which contribute to his argument. In other words, the difference is real or imaginary, important or slight in itself.

One important point, however: contrary to the view commonly held by the sentimental anti-racist, I do not think that the difference singled out by the racist is always the work of imagination, sheer madness or a malevolent lie. The racist can base his argument on a *real trait*, whether biological, psychological,

---

1. Perhaps by a pair of terms: "aggression-justification," for instance, which sums up quite well the general mechanism we are about to describe.

cultural or social—such as the color of the black man's skin or the solid tradition of the Jew.[1]

Of course the racist can make up a difference, if he needs one to construct his argument, but his method is not confined to imagining more or less fantastic differential traits nor to the mere observation of sometimes genuine differences. It always adds an *interpretation* of such differences, a prejudiced attempt to *place a value* on them.[2] To put it briefly, the difference is assigned a value in such a way as to discredit the defendant and reflect credit on his accuser.

Placing a Value on the Difference

Here is certainly one of the key elements in the racist process. Explicitly or implicitly, the assigning of values is intended to prove two things: the inferiority of the victim *and* the superiority of the racist. Better still, it proves the one by the other: inferiority of the black race automatically means superiority of the white. Inferiority of the colonized vividly demonstrates the superiority of the colonizer. Thus, the assigning of values is negative and positive at the same time: negative value of the victim, therefore positive value of the accuser. It follows that:

1. any difference separating the victim from his accuser is likely to be suspect and deserve denunciation. Racism begins by assigning a negative value and, simply by changing a minus to a plus sign, can turn any difference, whether real or imagined, into a positive quality on the part of the accuser. In the racist way of thinking, *difference is evil.* This means, of course, the difference characterizing the victim in relation to the accuser, who is taken as the point of reference. It is not whiteness that differentiates the white man from the black; it is blackness that disastrously differentiates the black man from the white.

2. the racist will do his utmost to stretch the distance between the minus and the plus signs, to *maximize the difference.* The smaller he makes his victim, the bigger he becomes; the more drastically he marks the difference at the expense of his victim, the more drastically he turns it to his own advantage.[3]

That is why a simple biological or cultural difference, which is sometimes a real one, brings a whole crowd of meanings in its wake: the biology of the Jew becomes a repulsive biology, an unhealthful one. One step further, and it becomes heavy with a specific, harmful psychology, then with a metaphysical life of its

---

1. Or even at times a genuine *inadequacy.* Of course, the racist, far from viewing it as a result of the oppression to which he himself subjects his victim or at least of the objective conditions which the victim is made to endure, holds that inadequacy against him, as if it were a defect or flaw. Examples: the technical unpreparedness of the colonized, which is the result of colonization; or the high rate of absenteeism among working women, the result of their family duties.

2. I have run into a good deal of argument over this phrase, *"placing a value on the difference."* Here of course it has the strict meaning of assigning either a *negative* or a *positive* value.

3. See, in *The Colonizer and the Colonized* the notion of the *"Negro complex,"* which also includes this see-saw movement, both complementary and contradictory.

own, etc. . . . . We go from biology to ethics, from ethics to politics, from politics to metaphysics.

Once a value has been assigned, the coherence of the consequences emerges, and it is apparent that the noxious and inflammatory difference, overwhelming the victim and flattering his accuser, must be made *absolute*. If the accuser wants to be radically superior, then the difference must be made radical.

The Difference Is Generalized

So the discriminatory process enters the stage of generalization, "totalization." One thing leads to another until *all of the victim's personality* is characterized by the difference, and *all of the members* of his social group are targets for the accusation.

1. In this perspective it is easier to understand why biological racism is so successful; it fits in particularly well. The disastrous difference is echoed, as it were, in a substratum: it penetrates the flesh, the blood and the genes of the victim. It is transformed into fate, destiny, heredity. From then on, the victim's very *being* is contaminated, and likewise *every manifestation of that being*: behavior, body and soul. Rarely does biological racism fail to give rise to psychological and cultural racism. In fact, the whole might be called an *ethnism*.

2. If the difference penetrates so profoundly into the being of the victim, it must also penetrate *all his family*, who are part of the same being.[1]

This is not actually a generalization: the relation between the individual trait and the collective trait is, so to speak, dialectic. Each of the defendant's real or supposed defects is extended to all his equals, but it is in the name of an implied collective defect that the defendant is condemned. From the greed of one Jew the anti-Semite concludes that all Jews are greedy and decides that no single Jew can be trusted because all Jews are greedy. The same is true with the stereotype of the lazy colonized.

Racism, on whatever level it occurs, always includes this *collective* element which is, of course, one of the best ways of totalizing the situation: there must be no loophole by which any Jew, any colonized or any black man could escape this *social determinism*.

The Difference Is Final

It is easy to understand how the same movement also extends through *time*, back into the past and forward into the future. The Jew has always been greedy, the black man has always been inferior. Conclusion: the Jew will always be greedy, the black man will always be inferior; there is no hope of a change, no salvation to be expected. *Globalization, totalization, social generalization* and *temporal generalization* — all tend to a single purpose which, in the extreme, would be a substantiation of the difference, than of the victim as a figure. Thus, there is said to be a sort of absolute black man, a kind of absolute Jew. They are negative figures, of course;

1. See, ibid., *"the mark of the plural."*

definitively and absolutely negative. In the Middle Ages, as we know, the Jew finally became one of the incarnations of the devil, and in our own country he became the radical and antithetical enemy of the Nazis. In the same way the black man has become one of the inferior categories of the human species. *In the extreme, racism merges into myth.*

At this point the whole structure takes leave of reality, from which it had derived its strength for a time, and follows its own coherence, moving from mere accusation to myth through the successive stages by which the victim is stripped of value. Broadly speaking, the process is one of *gradual dehumanization.* The racist ascribes to his victim a series of surprising traits, calling him incomprehensible, impenetrable, mysterious, strange, disturbing, etc. Slowly he makes of his victim a sort of animal, a thing or simply a symbol.

As the outcome of this effort to expel him from any human community, the victim is chained once and for all to his destiny of misfortune, derision and guilt. And as a counterpart, the accuser is assured once and for all of keeping his role as rightful judge.

Justification of the Accuser

While racism moves toward myth, *the myth refers back to the racist.*

It is in the racist himself that the motives for racism lie. A superficial analysis is enough to reveal them, whether in individual or collective aggression.

I will not repeat the now classic analyses of two phenomena: the scapegoat, and the foreigner corrupting the national soul. We are already familiar with the way a group of human beings, in order to rid itself of certain guilt feelings, projects them onto an object, an animal, a man or another group, which it accuses and punishes in its own stead. Nor will I linger over the alibi type of racism, an excuse for individual aggression. Competition on the economic front, rivalry between intellectuals or artists—these can give rise to racism, as a way of justifying *a priori* every difficulty the accuser runs into and his behavior toward his adversary. There is even a less sordid, distinctly *individual motivation*[1] which has been largely overlooked so far. A certain embarrassment when faced with what is different, the anxiety which results, spontaneous recourse to aggression in order to push back that anxiety—all of these are to be found in children, and probably in a good many adults as well. Whatever is different or foreign can be felt as a disturbing factor, hence a source of scandal. The attempt to wipe it out follows naturally. This is a

---

1. Yet the fact of an individual motivation does not cancel out the mediation of the social factor, which I consider crucial in any racist process. Individual motivation does not become genuine racism until it is filtered through the culture and the ideologies of a group. In the prevailing stereotypes it seeks, and finds, the explanation of its own uneasiness, which is then turned into racism. The individual racist actually discovers discrimination all about him—in his education and his culture—as a potential mental attitude, and he adopts it when he feels the need to do so. The intermediary of society is felt on two levels: that of the victim, as member of a guilty and defective group, and that of the accuser, representative of a normal and healthy group.

primitive, virtually animal reaction, but it certainly goes deeper than we care to admit. We will have to give it more serious study instead of trying to sidestep it by optimistic moralizing. However that may be, the mechanism remains the same. By an accurate or a falsified characterization of the victim, the accuser attempts to explain and to *justify* his attitude and his behavior toward him.

Justifying Injustice

But what sort of attitude and behavior are these, that they need to be justified? Why does the accuser feel obliged to accuse in order to justify himself? *Because he feels guilty toward his victim.* Because he feels that his attitude and his behavior are essentially unjust and fraudulent. Here, in fact, we must turn the racist's argument inside out: he does not punish his victim because his victim deserves to be punished; he calls him guilty because he is *already* punished or, at best, because he, the accuser, is preparing to punish him.

Proof? *In almost every case, the punishment has already been inflicted.* The victim of racism is *already* living under the weight of disgrace and oppression. The racist does not aim his accusations at the mighty but at the vanquished. The Jew is already ostracized, the colonized is already colonized. In order to justify such punishment and misfortune, a process of rationalization is set in motion, by which to explain away the ghetto and the colonial exploitation.

Very often, the precarious nature of the victim's life, the injustice of it are independent of the will of any individual. *Racism is the objective counterpart of the victim's objective situation.* Examples: women suffer because they have deserved to suffer; the black man is a slave because he has been cast out. The individual can be tempted by this collective reasoning; it forms part of the values held by his peers and relieves him of the weight of any responsibility. Where everyone tolerates and condones scandal, scandal disappears.

Racism and Oppression

This is why racism accompanies almost every kind of oppression: *racism is one of the best justifications of and symbols for oppression.* I have found it in the colonial relationship, in anti-Semitism and in oppression of the black man. More or less explicitly, it is also found in the condition of the proletarian worker, the servant, and so on.

Of course it varies subtly, emerging differently from one social and historical context to another, from one form of oppression to another. The common denominator must not obscure the need, in each case, to look for the distinguishing features of each context: quite the contrary. As I have amply shown, the racist accusation, although it follows a relatively monotonous and banal pattern, should suggest something else: the precise context, the specific oppression which is the real cause of the racist alibi. The black man is labeled congenitally good-for-nothing so that he can be kept in economic bondage; the colonized is tagged as unfit to handle anything technical so that colonization can last; the proletarian as politically and socially childish so that the domination of the property-owning classes can continue unchallenged. To come to the end of each particular form of racism, we will have to tackle colonization or the social and political structure of our societies.

The fact remains that *we have discovered a fundamental mechanism*, common to all racist reactions: the *injustice of an oppressor toward the oppressed*, the former's permanent *aggression* or the aggressive act he is getting ready to commit, *must be justified*. And isn't privilege one of the forms of permanent aggression, inflicted on a dominated man or group by a dominating man or group? How can any excuse be found for such disorder (source of so many advantages) if not by overwhelming the victim? Underneath its masks, *racism is the racist's way of giving himself absolution.*

The Definition Once Again

Now we can come back to the definition offered in the beginning to summarize the essential points of this commentary:

Racism is the generalized and final assigning of values to real or imaginary differences, to the accuser's benefit and at his victim's expense, in order to justify the former's own privileges or aggression.

Hatred Written on the Body

–Zillah Eisenstein

Zillah Eisenstein is Professor of Politics at Ithaca College in Ithaca, New York, and an author and political activist. Eisenstein's discussion of how hatred gets written on the body is taken from her book Hatreds: Racialized and Sexualized Conflicts in the 21st Century, *which was published by Routledge in 1996.*

"Otherness" is constructed on bodies. Racism uses the physicality of bodies to punish, to expunge and isolate certain bodies and construct them as outsiders. The named "other" is a foreigner, immigrant, or stranger. Jews' and blacks' and women's bodies of all colors are used to mark the hatred of this "otherness." Racial hatred is not neat and separate; it is multiple and continuous. And much hatred spills over into the sexual aspects of racial meanings.

Yellow stars. White hoods. Both are symbols of specific hatreds and a grand narrative of hate, though the former marks those who are hated, while the latter marks those who do the hating. Hatred is unique and historically contextualized, but it also repeats itself as though it were intractable, as though it lay in our psyches ready to be pulled forward, outward from the deepest layers of our unconscious.

On the eve of the twenty-first century, hatreds explode in such places as sarajevo, argentina, chechnya, rwanda, los angeles, and oklahoma city. The hatred embodies a complex set of fears about difference and otherness. It reveals what some people fear in themselves, their own "differences." Hatred forms around the unknown, the difference of "others." And we have learned the difference that we fear through racialized and sexualized markings. Because people grow othered by their racialized, sexualized, and engendered bodies, bodies are important to the writing of hatred on history.

Hatred is not only color-coded but inscribed on such body parts as noses, hair, vaginas, eyes. I argue that physicality—our physical bodies—is key to constructing and seeing hatreds. Bodies are always in part psychic constructions of meaning symbolized through coloring hatred on sexualized sites. This psychic realm is a space of knowable and unknowable mental layerings that unconsciously and consciously frame our seeing. It is an unfathomable realm of desire and repression; of injury, hurt and fear, and imagination and fantasy. This non-corporeal arena of de-

Copyright © 1996 from *Hatreds* by Zillah Eisenstein. Reproduced by permission of Routledge/Taylor & Francis Books.

sire and escape is where one knows but does not know, sees but does not see. The psyche, our mind's eye, which *already* frames our experiencing of everyday life friendships, schools, neighborhoods, churches, mosques, is also constructed by this history. Within this psychic space we name and interpret what we think we see. Here we negotiate and renegotiate fear, desire, and difference itself. . . .

The unsettled psyches of borderless worlds and interconnected selves are localized in the fear and threat of women, semites, homosexuals, and colored people. These fears are repressed, and recast as hatreds. This hatred, in turn, orders and organizes the world. The repressed self requires the lies, the fantasized symbolizations. The fantasy framework is required by desires of the other as well as identification with the other.[1]

Jean-Paul Sartre calls this repression the "idea of the jew." It is the anti-semite who makes the jew.[2] But stereotypes are not merely false images. Rather, they are "ambivalent text[s] of projection and introjection . . . displacement, overdetermination, guilt, [and] aggressivity."[3] Racialized hatreds play back and forth between the mind's eye and its fears, and the peopled realities of daily life.

The chaos of the psychic realm has some people fearing in others what they most fear in themselves. These fears can elicit the different mindsets of colonialism, nationalism, orientalism, and imperialism.[4] The politics to be understood here extend from the real to layers of the unconscious. If serbs rape muslim women *as if* they are ethnic-cleansing, then the imaginary must be destroyed in order for life to be livable. Politics must allow people to embrace their own "radical strangeness" in an attempt to deny hatred.[5]

I do not view hatred as natural, or timeless, or homogenized, and yet it is something more than contextually specific. As a politics of "otherness," hatred calls forth the imaginings of unconscious fantasies. But the fantasies are changeable.

So I proceed cautiously here. There is no one kind of hate. No one kind of body. No one kind of psyche. Yet hatreds are reformulated continuously, and I keep wondering why. This leads me to focus more on those who hate than on those who are hated, or on those who hate those who hate them. I also say little about those who fight against hatred—those who fought, for example, against slavery, for civil rights, against nazism, against misogyny. I say little about them because they are not who I fear.

A problem with writing about hatred is that it makes the world seem completely hate-filled. Or, as Michael Taussig asks: "If life is constructed, how come it appears so immutable?"[6] Because we cannot make full sense of hate, because much of hate is unspeakable, or indescribable, it can seem untouchable.[7] By speaking hatred, I hope to touch it, and to begin to move through and past the trauma it creates.

Body Borders and Psychic Hatreds

Hate is fueled by fictive symbols, by pictures in the mind. Serbian nationalists, the right wing in russia, the anti-abortionists of operation rescue in the u.s., skinheads in germany, the ku klux klan, and religious fundamentalists around the globe are violently committed to controlling the borders in which we live. As the world becomes more economically unequal and transnational, this border-consciousness seems to be more and more evident. Racialized ethnic nationalisms are in part a response to transnational capital in eastern and central europe. Ex-communists reposition themselves for the new world order by using old hatreds and wounds.

In other parts of the world—rwanda, iran, algeria—violent wars erupt or continue. Women are raped as part of a systematic campaign of ethnic cleansing in the balkans. Muslims are massacred by a crazed militant jewish settler while praying in hebron. Khalid Abdul Muhammad of the nation of islam, in speaking of jews, "prays 'that God will kill my enemy and take him off the face of the planet Earth.'"[8] Snipers in sarajevo shoot at children. Maja Djokic, on her way home from a volleyball game in sarajevo, is hit by shrapnel and dies. Her father says, "There are perhaps 10,000 dead in Sarajevo, of whom 1,700 were children. So we cannot think that Maja's death was anything special. But of course, she was our Maja, so we think it is special."[9]

A truck bomb blows up a jewish community center in buenos aires.[10] A car bomb explodes near the israeli embassy in london, wounding thirteen.[11] More than sixty thousand have died in the war in chechnya.[12] Paramilitary right-wing groups and their fascist underworld are exposed by the bombing of the federal building in oklahoma city. Christopher Hitchens says that these "aryan fundamentalists" who present themselves as patriots and anti-government individualists are a thoroughly racist movement.[13] Hate does not seem specific to any one corner of the world.[14]

The hatred is global, *and* it is specifically racialized along religious, ethnic, and gender lines. In apprehending it, we must take into account particular geographies, histories, and cultures, as well as psychic mappings and layerings that may still make a grand narrative of otherness.

The psyche is mapped with a tension between the unlimited, unbordered desires of our bodies *and* the truncated multiple needs of our consciousness. Denial and repression underlie fear and loathing. This fear makes the unconscious, for psychoanalytic feminist Jacqueline Rose, utterly political at its core, so that right-wing ideologies thrive on and push against the "furthest limits of psychic fantasy."[15] Psychic sexual desire becomes the ground of political manipulation.

Desire is not easily controlled or erased. Fear of the unbridled self requires the construction of an "other" who/which must be shut out. Repression is recast as fear and hatred. For Mikkel Borch-Jacobsen, "unconscious desire is undoubtedly not (re)presented to consciousness." Consciousness is exceeded continuously. The realm of desire, and with it the forbidden, is always waiting to express itself. Repression negotiates the inadmissable.[16] There is a constant struggle to contain desire.

Ronald Takaki depicts a process of separation from the instinctual (sexual) self as integral to the racializing of identity. This cultural construction of race forms any individual's psychic construction. People of color are then identified with the body, not the mind. And to be in control of the instinctual body is to establish whiteness over the black, indian, mexican, asian.[17] Fear dominates in the realm of unconscious desire because racial and sexual fantasies are limitless in these arenas. As Rose argues, "Freedom may not be sexy, but fear of it is wholly determined by sex."[18]

Wilhelm Reich argued that fascism directs itself to the unconscious; that sexuality is repressed and located here; and that repressed desire is not open to conscious knowing.[19] Fear becomes a major resource of fascism.[20] If desire is structured sexually, and we come to our sexuality through racialized fantasies, then, as Frantz Fanon argues, the racist must create his/her inferior. As such, "the myth of the bad nigger is part of the collective unconscious."[21] Racism itself, for Paul Gilroy, becomes a part of the process of denying and repressing the historical and unconscious experience.[22]

Fear and hate bespeak anxiety about the borders of an individual's desires. Experiencing differences, or even just seeing them, challenges and uproots certainty about the self. Jonathan Rutherford views this realm of personal anxiety as a threat to the dissolution of the self which demands new boundaries. The right wing always plays with the anxiety about difference and the unknown,[23] using racialized fantasies of orderly patriarchal families to set the borders and boundaries of desire.

Psychic meanings, as the mind's eye, represent and (mis)interpret for us. We see, or do not see, accordingly. Those germans who claimed to have known nothing of the gas chambers during world war II did not let themselves know, or were not able to know, or could not fathom that they knew. I wonder what we will not let ourselves see today in sarajevo or rwanda. We see through an elaborate system of screens. And this seeing has only become more complicated with CNN coverage and the global communications network, which broadcast immediate and continual pictures of violence and hate. So we *think* we know; and yet we know only what is screened for us and what we allow ourselves to see.

Race (the often-times colored body), sex (the sexed/biological body), gender (the cultural/biological body), and sexuality (the various sexual/cultural desires of the body) inflect on each other. The lack of boundaries unsettles desire itself. We see body color(s) from bodies that are already marked by the phallus, or by the lack of it. We know the male muslim or jew by his circumcised penis, which bespeaks a partial lack of the true phallus, which in turns suggests the female. We know the black man by his oversized penis, which suggests the excess of black sexuality and a protectionism of white womanhood.[24] Or, as Judith Butler says, the black male body in the public psyche is always performing as a threat no matter what it is doing.[25]

Fanon wrote of the black man as a penis symbol, and of black men being lynched as a sign of sexual revenge. "We know how much of sexuality there is in all cruelties, tortures, beatings," he said. So the jew is killed or sterilized but the negro castrated.[26] Hitler spoke of the u.s. as a "niggerized jewish country," of jews and other minorities as guilty of the "syphilitization of our people," and of homosexuality as a "symptom of racial degeneracy."[27] Reich notes that the swastika, as a sign of racial superiority, was originally a sexual symbol.[28]

The writing of new-old borders through the racist, anti-semitic, misogynist history of the globe defines multiple nationalist struggles today. Michael Ignatieff writes that "the repressed has returned, and its name is nationalism." It is a nationalism defined by male resentment and a loathing of peace and domesticity.[29] Today's nationalisms represent a collective and individual paranoia resulting from unbridled fears and envy.[30] Serb nationalism is full of hate, and is completely bent on destroying the multicultural society of ex-yugoslavia with its fluid identities of muslim, croat, and serb. Zlata Filipovic, a thirteen-year bosnian girl now living in france, says that the war is "between idiots, not between Serbs and Croats and Muslims . . . They're crazy."[31] One could also say that Hitler too was crazy. And Stalin also.

But *crazy* is not quite helpful here, because illusion is a profound part of "othered" politics. Politics is very much about a symbolization that allows for, creates, and even sometimes demands that people live *as if* they believe in the representations, the distortions, even when they do not.[32] It makes no sense to speak of aryan or serbian racial purity when blood is mixed all the time. And yet we speak *as if* such racial lines exist, and then they do.

Serbs have married croats who have married muslims, and they have had children. Nada Salom, a journalist, is serb on her mother's side, slovenian on her father's, jewish in last name, and sarajevan through and through.[33] And yet we speak *as if* there is such a thing as a serb. When Lani Guinier was nominated for a position in the civil-rights division of the Clinton administration she was treated *as if* she were (only) black even though she has a white jewish mother. So is she a "light-skinned black or a dark-skinned jew"?[34] When Farrakhan pits black against jew, or when jews become fixated on black anti-semitism, they deny their shared otherness in order to draw boundary markers that let them feel safer. They imagine themselves in control.

* * *

Bordering Multiple Identities

Borders define and differentiate an inside from an outside. They are constituted through a construct of difference that is singular and exclusionary. American slavery defined racist borderlines between white and black. Civil-rights legislation rearranged the boundaries. Marriage defines the heterosexual borders between man and woman, and gays are outside them. The boundaries constructed through one's race, sex, gender, and sexuality cut apart and dissect the multiplicity of any one individual's identity. Any one identity embraces multiple borders: black women, muslim girls, gay men. Maria Lugones speaks of her multiple identity: "I realize that separation into clean, tidy things and beings is not possible for me because it would be the death of myself as multiplicitous and a death of community with my own." Whereas you can separate an egg yolk from the white of the egg, people exist in in-between spaces.[35]

Gays and lesbians represent uncomfortable identities for the heterosexual world. Gays and lesbians, particularly in their fantasized constructions, represent multiple, fluid, connected imaginings.[36] The homosexual is said to not "know the boundary of his own body—where his body ends and space begins."[37] Transvestites and transsexuals destroy the boundaries of gendered bodies. AIDS, although initially presented in the west as a gay disease, today knows no borders, crosses borders, breaks down old borders, creates new borders. It is a transnational disease that unsettles neat and tidy, singular identities.

But instead of radically pluralizing identities, singular difference is naturalized by the hetero/homo polarity. This normalizing of "difference" maintains a fantasmatic inside and outside for the increasingly complex global system. An inside space requires outsiders.[38] The division between homosexual (unnatural) and heterosexual (natural) is then written on the body through a system of signs: color, musculature, sex, gender, and so on. We are presented with a "body politic";[39] difference and otherness are inscribed on the body as fantasy.

The difference of *hetero*sexual is applauded while the sameness of *homo* is deplored. *Hetero* is naturalized by genitalia. Yet femaleness represents otherness as it is positioned against the white phallus. Homosexuality with its possible invisible (bodily) status is, ironically, marked by the phallus as danger itself.[40]

Difference—outside the construct of heterosexual—is treated as strangeness. And strangers are easy to distance and blame. The "other," as "woman" or "black" or "muslim," is translated and retranslated in relation to the changing world. So the world of transnational corporations attempts to adapt to a multicultural globe *as if* the borders of rich and poor did not still hold. And the u.s. speaks of protecting its borders, and limiting immigration, and maintains "difference" as strangeness, while insisting on a global vision.

* * *

Physicality and Body Construction

Physicality—body color, shape, size; facial structure, noses, eyes, hair; sexual body parts, penis, breasts, vaginas, clitoris—is symbolized as *the* body. The body is not a constant, but remains a constant site of political struggle. The female body operates as spectacle; its physicality is given meaning by marking its difference(s). Sandra Lee Bartky describes the female body as a "body on which an inferior status has been inscribed."[41] The meaning of a female body never exists outside context even though the body is never just contextual. As I have written elsewhere, "However contextualized, [the body] is also real. There is no innate body, but there are bodies."[42] There is no body, as fact, without interpretation, and yet the body according to Leslie Adelson "is more than a discursive sign."[43]

Identities are constructed on bodies, for bodies, by political discourse. Although a "history without bodies is unimaginable" for Adelson, it is a history made of "images of bodies imagined to be real." The body is then many things simultaneously: "It is a thing and a sign, an inside and an outside, a boundary constantly crossing itself."[44] Bodies absorb meaning and elicit meaning. Politics processes the definitions.

But the body also has meaning before we see it.[45] Fanon bespeaks this dilemma when he states: "My blackness was there, dark and unarguable." He is thus, he says, "overdetermined from without."[46] Lisa Jones writes that hair is already given meaning as the key racial signifier after skin.[47] In rwanda thousands were hacked to death according to the shapes of their noses. Tutsis tend to be taller with narrow features and high cheekbones; hutus tend to be shorter and have flatter, broader noses.[48]

The physicality of the body becomes a horribly powerful resource for those who wish to conquer, violate, humiliate, and shame.[49] The body's power—its intimacy, its creativity against systems of power, its physical dignity and integrity—is also its vulnerability.[50] We can feel our body as we can feel nothing else. Its pain, its illness, its thirst, its hunger demand strength in our attempt to meet their needs, and make us despairingly vulnerable in the process. The vulnerability inside our strength is why rape is so brutalizing. In the oppressor's hope of smashing the body's spirit people are starved, mutilated, tortured, shaved, and made deathly cold and sick. Our bodies have an enormous claim on us. They force us to know and feel what we otherwise would never allow ourselves to imagine. . . .

The body is a visual site, which makes it crucial for marking difference, and it is a felt site: one feels one's body. This utter intimacy makes the body unique as a location for politics. One hears the body cry out for its safety when one hears of torture, slavery, and death camps. Slavery bespeaks the "slow throttling and murder of nine millions of men [and women]" shackled, whipped, and beaten on the basis of the color of their bodies.[51] In the nazi death camps people craved warmth, food, water, medicine, and the list goes on and on. In the bosnian concentration camps the horrors sound too similar: filth, hunger, starvation, rape, death.[52] One begins to suspect that the destruction and annihilation of bodies are attempts to smash difference itself.

The body could, instead of marking "otherness," be a democratic site for politics. The body's utter variety and uniqueness is shared. After all, "the human body is common to us all."[53] It is ironic that the body, the one thing all human beings have in common, becomes a site for demarcating difference, hate, and pain. We each start with our bodies; no one can escape its reality. Yet we do not experience our physicality as an open potential of multiple meanings. Instead, we live in our bodies as they represent the fears of difference and strangeness. Color, vaginas, noses mark us as others.

Racializing the Sexualized Body

Purity of blood almost never exists, so neither does purity of race. Yet we live as if both were real qualities. The construction of the "other" or "others" depends on this notion of purity, of separateness. Yet racial purity is a construction of the mind's eye: a fantasy, a fiction. According to David Theo Goldberg, race has a "veneer of fixedness," yet is "almost, but not quite, empty in its own connotative capacity."[54] Race in this sense is never just biological. But the idea of race is always in part fixated on the body; hence the notion of "the" jew, or indian, or chicano. Race is, then, at once both fixed and utterly unstable. Its meaning is always contextualized, yet the meaning of race precedes its context. Colors, noses, and hair are defined before they are seen, yet one sees them only through the context of their world.

So I disagree with Etienne Balibar when he states that "racism has nothing to do with the existence of objective biological 'races'" if he means to completely contextualize racialized bodies.[55] Shirlee Taylor Haizlip pushes this point to its limits. She began the search for her mother's family assuming she would find black people passing for white. What she found instead was "black people who had become white. After all, if you look white, act white, live white, vacation white, go to school white, marry white, and die white, are you not 'white'?[56]

Racism may exist without race,[57] as when muslims were suspected of bombing the federal building in oklahoma city even after pictures of two white men were splashed across our TV screens as the suspects. However, racism was already in play and completely foregrounded the incident. Some people saw muslims as the terrorists, as if they were the actual bombers. Racism is constructed through fictions, which is not to say that race is a fiction. The concept of difference is so contaminated that we need to be cautious about how we choose to deconstruct it.

Nazism was built on the fiction of purity: the daughter born of a jewish father and an aryan mother was a jew in Hitler's germany even if the father had lost his life in world war I fighting for the fatherland. The jew is always in part a social construction: there are 1/2 jews, 1/4 jews, "decent" jews, "prominent" jews, "foreign" jews.[58]

Slobodan Milosevic depends on racialized fantasy in his construction of serb nationalism, while ex-yugoslavians look about for identities to justify the carnage. A bosnian muslim says, "banjaluka is our jerusalem." A bosnian serb says, "Like the jews . . . we will prevail in the end."[59] Complicating the racialized fantasies is the fact that it is often quite difficult to physically distinguish between serb and croat.

The nation of islam assumes racial purity while Lisa Jones writes how her (white) mother raised her to think politically about being a black woman. "African-american" might include people of african, native american, latin, and/or european descent.[60] There are no purist, singular visions here. French tennis star Yannick Noah, the son of a mixed marriage says, "In Africa I am white, and in France I am black."[61]

Color is an already "naturalized" sign for race. But color itself is never simply one thing. Haizlip says color is shadings of red to brown, and tan to pink. We call "ourselves honey, caramel, ivory, peaches-and-cream, mahogany, coal blue, red, bronze, amber, chocolate coffee."[62] According to Sander Gilman, color itself represents a quality of "otherness." So racialized meanings are represented through color and as though they mean color: black vs. white; ayran vs. non-white; oriental vs. non-oriental. The jew, the muslim, the roma, the algerian, all are/become "black." Dark skin as far back as ancient greece is a sign of illness.[63] W. E. B. Du Bois' color line—from light to dark skin—continues to demarcate the world system.[64] The foreigner, the stranger, the "other" is colored. And color, as symbol, connects the jew to the muslim to the african, to the generalized "other."

So there are multiple racial dimensions to the systemic system of racism. Balibar argues that there is "not merely a single invariant racism but a number of racisms." There are open series of situations and historical formations that define any particular racism. In this sense today's racism has little if anything to do with actual "objective biological 'races'." The biological theme has a "fictive essence." It is, and always has been a "pseudo-biological accounting."[65]

Today the theme of racism is less biological heredity and more the insurmountability of cultural differences. Historical cultures outline the "other"; the language of incompatibility displaces the superior/inferior divide.[66] Boundary lines are therefore being constantly redrawn and must remain flexible. Yet, "the cake of custom," as W. E. B. Du Bois calls it, remains very much in place.[67] This survival is easily seen in the revival of the hereditary bell-curve view of racial intelligence.[68]

So racism is both old and new, static and changing; tied to darkness of skin color and pluralized to encompass ethnic/cultural meanings that are not simply based on an inferior/superior divide. One can neither understand contemporary racism as simply a black/white divide nor as a system that has left the divide behind. This black/white divide is particularly true for western societies with a history of black slavery. Blackness sets the context for the meanings of otherness rooted in color.

If racism exists with and without race, anti-semitism exists with and without jews. Fictional constructions stand in for "real" blacks, jews, muslims. We hate on the basis of fictional beliefs about the "other," which is why truth does not matter much. So what if our neighbor is different from the stereotype of the boisterous jew, or terrorist muslim, or swarthy black? The rule, a fiction, still holds.

The west has characterized much of the bloodshed in bosnia as a morass of irresolvable ethnic hatred, and bosnia has become "the other."[69] This depiction ignores the intense ethnic/racial conflicts existing within the u.s., france, england, etc. I do not clearly demarcate race and ethnicity because they are so similarly constructed as fantasy at this particular time in history. Both are constructed from exclusionary conceptions of difference. Race and ethnicity interweave much the same way nature is mixed with culture, sex with gender, and the physical with the psychic. As such, race and ethnicity are constructed out of classifications based on ascriptions to the body, when the body is already imbricated in cultural/politicized meanings.

Racial conflict can be ethnically pluralized, and ethnic conflict can be polarized by racial fictions. The conflicts between koreans and blacks and jews and asians in los angeles or new york city reflect the tensions of a highly racialized society along cultural and colored lines. Race and ethnicity blur. This also is true of serbs and croats and muslims in bosnia.

Racializing the Phallus

Color is also symbolized by the phallus and the fear of sexual desire, given the intimate history of racializing sexuality and sexualizing racism. Thus racism and the phallus are intimately connected. Edward Said argues that there is always an undercurrent of sexual exaggeration when constructing racial others.[70] Winthrop Jordan describes how the black male is associated sexually with the bestiality of animals. His penis is large and unruly.[71] He also describes the sexualization of the racialized african female by seventeenth- and eighteenth-century european males. Calvin Hernton writes that black male sexuality is demonized as a "walking phallus."[72] Sander Gilman shows how the male jew is seen as effeminate with his circumcised (castrated) penis.[73] Faisal Fatehali Devji, discussing the circumcised muslim male, says: "Racism is when life hangs upon a foreskin."[74] The sexualized meanings of racial fears reflect the phallocratic construction of racism. Or as Bankimchandra Chattopadhyay states, "As the Europeans always allege, the 'Hindoos' are 'effeminate.'"[75]

Gilman explores the hypersexuality of the jew(ish male) and his circumcised penis as a marker of sexual threat. Circumcision and castration form a fantasy about the entire body.[76] The woman's clitoris was understood in viennese psychoanalytic circles at the turn of the century as a truncated penis. Interestingly, the clitoris was referred to, according to Gilman, as the "Jew" (Jud). Female masturbation was referred to as "playing with the Jew."[77]

Both the jewish male and female (jew and non-jew alike) with their defective sexual organs, are set apart from the phallic order. The body writing of the phallus is more visible than the writing of the clitoris, which is not seen. The invisibility underwrites the lacking.

Male jews share a particular otherness with male muslims and women and foreigners in general. Black men share the phallic space differently from the male jew or muslim; they are an unruly threat. They occupy the space as bestial "other." They too are the stranger, the foreigner.

Bosnia's muslims are said to be the new jews of europe,[78] while the blacks of somalia and haiti and south africa are pushed off the front pages of newspapers by the destruction of sarajevo. Nevertheless, the black/white transnational divide continues to construct the variations of ethnic "otherness." This divide is why vietnamese and african guest workers in germany are called "niggers," and why roma are hated for their dark skins.[79] According to Gilman, jews were metaphorically described as the negroes of europe in the 1920s writings of Milena Jesenka. In the late nineteenth century the views that jews had black skin or were "swarthy" and that their circumcised penises carried sexual diseases were general consensus in ethnological literature. Gilman concludes that "The Jews' disease is written on the skin." Their foreignness was a sign of racial otherness.[80] Color comes into play in Frau Anna Fest's denial that most germans think jews are cheats. She says, "The worst is the 'white Jew'; the 'white Jew' is a Christian."[81]

While color has marked the jew, this marking does not mean that the racial history of blacks and jews has been one and the same. Rather, this marking is very different from that which has characterized the racial history of blacks. Yet the hatreds of blacks, jews, and muslims are deeply tied to signs and fictions that are color-coded according to sexualized meanings. Signs of race and color are easily transposed to signs of sex and gender.

Race is encoded in and through the uncontrollable arena of sex. Racial fears bespeak the openness of sexual desire. Black male slaves were viewed as potential rapists of white women, while white masters raped their black female slaves. Jewish men were depicted as vile and effeminate while nazi officers starved and raped jewish women. Serb and croatian nationalists speak of racial purity and ethnic cleansing and systematically rape muslim women. Serbs describe Tito as not-a-man; they say, "He was a woman," which represents the serbs' sense of having been emasculated by history.[82]

To speak of the war in bosnia as one of simply ethnic/religious hatred masks the fantasy structures of racialized sexuality and the significance of women within nationalist struggles. When a serb general demands that a woman be raped "first before the eyes of those whom she bore, then before the eyes of those who bore her, then before the eyes of her husband who fathered children with her,"[83] we see woman defined as the fulcrum through which the "other" gets continually reproduced. Traumatize and destroy her children, her parents, her husband, the nation, by conquering her.

Border Writings on Women

In nazi germany, green triangles noted criminals; black triangles noted anti-socials; red triangles noted politicals; yellow stars noted jews; pink triangles noted homosexuals. There was no colored triangle or star for women, no marking as such. Jewish women wore the yellow star; their identity was marked by yellow. Their identity as women was not specified. They were just jews. It is usually not mentioned that at least half of those persecuted on racial grounds in nazi germany were women.[84]

Aryan women were identified as women, as mothers of the race. Their job was described as kinder, kuche, and kirche (children, kitchen, and church). They were expected to be dutiful wives and mothers and "receptacles of the seed of the race."[85] Policies directed at these women focused on creating a "racial consciousness." Procreation was the responsibility of aryan women; abortion and sterilization were required for non-aryan women.[86]

Women throughout time and place have been used to reproduce "the" race: as breeders, as mothers, and sometimes as wives. Aryan women were defined as reproducers of the race in nazism through their racial status as "pure." As "mother of the nation" she defined the racial borders against non-aryan women and men.

Women, as female, are naturalized as "mothers" and as such can never be named as complete outsiders, like "the" jew, or black, or muslim. Their bodies are used to normalize "the" race, or family, or nation. They mark the inside, by reproducing it and naturalizing it, and in doing so are made invisible as border markers. They remain visibly invisible though present; systematically and perpetually semioticized. This symbolization is unsettled by the visibility of non-docile women. The unruly behavior of women, symbolized as a (feminist) sisterhood, makes women visible in unsettling ways for the nation.

Women are symbolized and represented according to Sandra Lee Bartky as "docile bodies" that are used as "ornamental surfaces."[87] As symbol, the woman is not-man, not-citizen, not-phallus. She is not-outside and not-inside; she is the invisible border. She represents our deepest fears and longings of sexual desire, obligation and duty, uncontrolled passion, and reproductive capacities.

Women, *as a fantasmatic*, construct the very meaning of stranger because they are different *from* men, strangers to them. They, as a homogenized fantasy, are the absolute other while never being named specifically as such. They represent the unnamed, the absence, in order to name the "other" others. Woman is in the nation but not of it; she is present but not seen; she is named, but not for what she is. Woman as translator of the bloodline constructs the nation, but through the naturalness of blood has no specified significance. The nationalizing of identity makes the woman visible while ascribing invisibility to her.

Women of color are the double foreigner, the double stranger. Their absence is twice effected, their presence twice negated. They are held up to the fantasmatic and found doubly wanting.

Women bear the new bodies for the nation state, and/or their rape represents conquered territories. Although the nation is psychically positioned against women, it is also reproduced through them. Women exist within as a male fantasy: silenced, conquered, soft. Women, though not-men, are included as "mother" of the nation. The insider/outsider status of women is necessary because the mother can comfort while she keeps borders intact. Women, as mothers and daughters, are distanced, silenced, without making them the outside.

The veil worn by muslim women elicits the psychic borders differentiating east from west, innocence from sex, availability from denial. The veil symbolizes the purity of denial, and also a rape fantasy.[88] In western fantasy, the veil hides, separates, marks a border and a forbidden space. It also sometimes comforts the muslim man as a "time-mirror"; it reassures him of "his" traditions.[89]

For muslim women the veil can liberate or confine. In sarajevo during world war II muslim women shrouded their jewish neighbors in their veils to protect them from the nazis. Today, the western media depicts muslim culture through its veiled women as backward and anti-modern. Such pictures during the gulf war and the war in bosnia reproduce "otherness" as part of the meaning of war itself. And western women are supposed to feel free and liberated compared to the "orient."

Women are symbolized in homogenized form; differences among them are denied in order to make them the "sign" of the authentic nation. Women become the absolute fiction and the transnational desire/fear. This hatred, written on the body, is then written on the nation.

NOTES

1. Slavoj Zizek, *The Sublime Object of Ideology* (London: Verso, 1989), p. 118.

2. Jean-Paul Sartre, *Anti-Semite and Jew* (New York: Schocken Books, 1948), pp. 17, 69.

3. Homi K. Bhabha, *The Location of Culture* (New York: Routledge, 1994), p. 82.

4. Aijaz Ahmad, *In Theory, Classes, Nations, Literatures* (London: Verso, 1992).

5. Julia Kristeva, *Strangers to Ourselves*, trans. by Leon Roudiez (New York: Columbia University Press, 1991), p. 195. See also: *Nations Without Nationalism*, trans. by Leon Roudiez (New York: Columbia University Press, 1993).

6. Michael Taussig, *Mimesis and Alterity* (New York: Routledge, 1993), p. xvi.

7. See the fabulous discussion of the unspeakability of hate in Shoshana Felman and Dori Laub, *Testimony* (New York: Routledge, 1992).

8. As quoted in Robert D. McFadden, "Islam Speaker in New Tirade Against Jews," *New York Times*, February 28, 1994, p. B1. See also The Nation of Islam, *The Secret Relationship Between Blacks and Jews*, vol. 1 (Boston: Latimer Associates, 1991); and Tony Martin, *The Jewish Onslaught* (Dover, Mass.: The Majority Press, 1993).

9. As quoted in Roger Cohen, "Sarajevo Girl Killed, Yet Serbs Suffer," *New York Times*, April 26, 1995, p. A8.

10. James Brooke, "Boom! Suddenly, The Chldren See Life Starkly," *New York Times*, July 27, 1994, p. A4.

11. James Brooke, "Car Bomb Outside the Israeli Embassy in London Wounds 13," *New York Times*, July 27, 1994, p. A8.

12. Sergei Kovalev, "Death in Chechnya," *New York Review of Books*, vol. XLII, no. 10 (May 11, 1995), p. 12.

13. Christopher Hitchens, "Minority Report," *The Nation*, vol. 260, no. 20 (May 22, 1995), p. 711.

14. Mark Thompson, "The Final Solution of Bosnia-Hercegovina," in Rabia Ali and Lawrence Lifschultz, eds., *Why Bosnia? Writings on the Balkan War* (Connecticut: The Pamphleteer's Press, 1993), p. 164.

15. Jacqueline Rose, *Why War?* (Oxford: Blackwell, 1993), pp. 5, 10.

16. Mikkel Borch-Jacobsen, *The Freudian Subject* (Stanford: Stanford University Press, 1988), pp. 5, 4, 2.

17. Ronald Takaki, *Iron Cages, Race and Culture in 19th Century America* (New York: Alfred Knopf, 1979), pp. 13, 148.

18. Jacqueline Rose, p. 33.

19. Wilhelm Reich, *The Mass Psychology of Fascism* (New York: Farrar, Straus and Giroux, 1970), pp. 41, 20. Also see: Lee Baxandall, ed., *Sex-Pol, Essays, 1929–34* (New York: Vintage Books, 1966).

20. T. W. Adorno, Else Frenkel-Brunswik, Daniel Levinson, and R. Nevitt Sanford, *The Authoritarian Personality* (New York: W.W. Norton and Co., 1950), p. 976.

21. Frantz Fanon, *Black Skin, White Masks* (New York: Grove Press, 1967), pp. 92, 93.

22. Paul Gilroy, *There Ain't No Black in the Union Jack: The Cultural Politics of Race and Nation* (London: Hutchinson, 1987), p. 12.

23. Jonathan Rutherford, "A Place Called Home: Identity and the Cultural Politics of Difference," in Jonathan Rutherford, ed., *Identity, Community, Culture, Difference* (London: Lawrence & Wishart), pp. 11, 13.

24. Michael Kimmelman, "Constructing Images of the Black Male," *New York Times*, November 11, 1994, p. C1.

25. Judith Butler, "Endangered/Endangering: Schematic Racism and White Paranoia," in Robert Gooding-Williams, ed., *Reading Rodney King, Reading Urban Uprising* (New York: Routledge, 1993), p. 19.

26. Frantz Fanon, pp. 159, 162.

27. Adolf Hitler, *Mein Kampf* (New York: Reynal & Kitchcock, 1940), pp. 26, 111.

28. Wilhelm Reich, pp. 101–103.

29. Michael Ignatieff, *Blood and Belonging* (New York: Farrar, Straus and Giroux, 1993), pp. 5, 246.

30. Danilo Kis, "On Nationalism," in Ali and Lifschultz, eds., *Why Bosnia?* p. 126.

31. As quoted in Alan Riding, "From Sarajevo, A Girl and A Diary," *New York Times*, January 6, 1994, p. A1. See also Zlata Filopovic, *Zlata's Diary: A Child's Life in Sarajevo* (New York: Viking/Penguin, 1994).

32. Zizek, *The Sublime Object of Ideology*; and his *For They Know Not What They Do; Enjoyment as a Political Factor* (London: Verso, 1991).

33. Zlatko Dizdarevic, *Portraits of Sarajevo* (New York: Fromm International Pub. Corp., 1994), p. 96.

34. Steven Holmes, "You're Smart If You Know What Race You Are," *New York Times*, October 23, 1994, p. E5.

35. Maria Lugones, "Purity, Impurity and Separation," *Signs: Journal of Women in Culture and Society*, vol. 19, no. 2 (Winter 1994), p. 469. See also Gloria Anzaldua, *Borderlands, La Frontera* (San Francisco: aunt lute books, 1987).

36. Douglas Crimp, "Right on, Girlfriend," in Michael Warner, ed., *Fear of a Queer Planet* (Minneapolis: University of Minnesota Press, 1993), p. 316.

37. Lauren Berlant and Elizabeth Freeman, "Queer Nationality," in Warner, ed., *ibid.*, p. 205.

38. Anna Marie Smith, *New Right Discourse on Race and Sexuality*, p. 40.

39. Renate Bridenthal, Atina Grossmann, and Marion Kaplan, *When Biology Became Destiny: Women in Weimar and Nazi Germany* (New York: Monthly Review Press, 1984), p. xiv.

40. See: Judith Butler, *Bodies That Matter* (New York: Routledge, 1993), especially chapter 2, for an interesting discussion of the lesbian phallus.

41. Sandra Lee Bartky, "Foucault, Femininity, and the Modernization of Patriarchal Power," in Irene Diamond and Lee Quinby, ed., *Feminism and Foucault* (Boston: Northeastern University Press, 1988), p. 71.

42. Zillah Eisenstein, *The Female Body and the Law* (Berkeley: University of California Press, 1988), p. 80.

43. Leslie A. Adelson, *Making Bodies, Making History* (Lincoln: University of Nebraska, 1993), p. 19.

44. *Ibid.*, pp. 1, 2, 34.

45. See Linda Nicholson, "Interpreting Gender," *Signs*, vol. 20, no. 1 (Autumn 1994), pp. 70–103, for a provocative discussion of the meanings of sex, gender, and bodies.

46. Frantz Fanon, pp. 117, 116.

47. Lisa Jones, *bulletproof diva* (New York: Doubleday, 1994), p. 296.

48. William Schmidt, "Refugee Missionaries From Rwanda Speak of Their Terror, Grief and Guilt," *New York Times*, April 12 1994, p. A6.

49. See the discussion by Judith Lewis Herman, *Trauma and Recovery* (New York: Basic Books, 1992).

50. Dorinda Outram, *The Body and the French Revolution* (New Haven: Yale University Press, 1989), p. 23.

51. W. E. B. Du Bois, *The Souls of Black Folk* (New York: Signet Classic, 1969), p. 94.

52. Ali & Lifshultz, eds., *Why Bosnia?*, p. 113.

53. Mary Douglas, *Natural Symbols* (New York: Pantheon, 1982), p. vii.

54. David Theo Goldberg, *Racist Culture* (Oxford: Blackwell, 1993), pp. 81, 80.

55. Etienne Balibar, "Racism and Nationalism," in Etienne Balibar and Immanuel Wallerstein, *Race, Nation, Class* (London: Verso, 1991), p. 37.

56. Shirlee Taylor Haizlip, *The Sweeter the Juice* (Simon & Schuster, 1994), p. 266.

57. Etienne Balibar, "Is There a 'Neo-Racism'?" in Balibar and Wallerstein, p. 23.

58. Hannah Arendt, *Eichmann in Jerusalem: A Report on the Banality of Evil* (New York: Penguin, 1963), pp. 113, 169.

59. Roger Cohen, "Bosnian Foes Gaze at History's Mirror and See a Jew," *New York Times*, October 2, 1994, p. E3.

60. Lisa Jones, p. 31.

61. As quoted in Sharon Begley, "Race Is Not Enough," *Newsweek*, vol. CXXV, no. 7 (February 13, 1995), p. 68.

62. Shirlee Taylor Haizlip, pp. 14, 30.

63. Sander L. Gilman, *Jewish Self-Hatred* (Baltimore: Johns Hopkins, 1986), p. 207.

64. W. E. B. Du Bois, p. 54.

65. Etienne Balibar, "Is There a 'Neo-Racism'?" and "Racism and Nationalism," in Balibar and Wallerstein, pp. 40, 37, 26.

66. *Ibid.*, p. 21.

67. W. E. B. Du Bois, "Fifty Years After" edition of *The Souls of Black Folk* (New York: Blue Heron Press, 1953) and reprinted in *Monthly Review*, vol. 45, no. 7 (December 1993), p. 34.

68. Richard Herrnstein and Charles Murray, *The Bell Curve: Intelligence and Class Structure in American Life* (New York: The Free Press, 1994).

69. Zlatko Dizdarevic, *Sarajevo, A War Journal* (New York: Fromm International, 1993), p. 21.

70. Edward W. Said, *Orientalism* (New York: Vintage Press, 1978), pp. 311–12.

71. Winthrop D. Jordan, *White Over Black: American Attitudes Toward the Negro, 1550–1812* (New York: W.W. Norton, 1968), pp. 238, 151.

72. Calvin C. Hernton, *Sex and Racism in America* (New York: Grove Press, 1965), p. 245.

73. Sander L. Gilman, *Freud, Race, and Gender* (Princeton: Princeton University Press, 1993), pp. 36–58.

74. Faisal Fatehali Devji, "Hindu/Muslim/Indian," *Public Culture*, vol. 5, no. 1 (Fall 1992), p. 12.

75. As stated in Partha Chatterjee, *Nationalist Thought and the Colonial World* (Minneapolis: Univ. of Minnesota Press, 1993), p. 54.

76. Sander Gilman, *Freud, Race, and Gender*, pp. 49, 172, 163.

77. *Ibid.*, p. 38–39.

78. Ali & Lifshultz, eds., *Why Bosnia?*, p. xix.

79. Paul Hockenos, *Free to Hate: The Rise of the Right in Post-Communist Eastern Europe* (New York: Routledge, 1993), pp. 25, 27.

80. Sander Gilman, *Freud, Race, and Gender,* p. 19–20.

81. Alison Owings, *Frauen: German Women Recall the Third Reich* (New Brunswick, N.J.: Rutgers University Press, 1993), p. 341.

82. Ali & Lifshultz, eds., *Why Bosnia?,* p. 56.

83. *Ibid.,* p. 123.

84. Bridenthal, Grossmann, and Marion Kaplan, p. 272. Also see: Cornelie Usborne, *The Politics of the Body in Weimer Germany* (Ann Arbor: University of Michigan Press, 1992).

85. George L. Mosse, *The Crisis of German Ideology* (New York: Schocken Books, 1981), p. 141.

86. Bridenthal, Grossmann, and Kaplan, pp. 24, 272, 288.

87. Sandra Lee Bartky, pp. 62, 64.

88. Faisal Devji, p. 9.

89. Fatima Mernissi, *The Veil and the Male Elite,* trans. by Mary Jo Lakeland (New York: Addison-Wesley, 1987), pp. 93, 195.

Stories from Rwanda

–Philip Gourevitch

Philip Gourevitch is editor of The Paris Review. *He has reported from Africa, Asia, and Europe for a number of magazines. His book* We Wish to Inform You That Tomorrow We Will Be Killed with Our Families, *Farrar Straus, 1998, won the National Book Award for Nonfiction in 1999.*

In the famous story, the older brother, Cain, was a cultivator, and Abel, the younger, was a herdsman. They made their offerings to God—Cain from his crops, Abel from his herds. Abel's portion won God's regard; Cain's did not. So Cain killed Abel.

Rwanda, in the beginning, was settled by cave-dwelling pygmies whose descendants today are called the Twa people, a marginalized and disenfranchised group

Chapter 4 from *We Wish to Inform You That Tomorrow We Will Be Killed with Our Families: Stories from Rwanda* by Philip Gourevitch. Copyright © 1998 by Philip Gourevitch. Reprinted by permission of Farrar, Straus & Giroux, LLC.

that counts for less than one percent of the population. Hutus and Tutsis came later, but their origins and the order of their immigrations are not accurately known. While convention holds that Hutus are a Bantu people who settled Rwanda first, coming from the south and west, and that Tutsis are a Nilotic people who migrated from the north and east, these theories draw more on legend than on documentable fact. With time, Hutus and Tutsis spoke the same language, followed the same religion, intermarried, and lived intermingled, without territorial distinctions, on the same hills, sharing the same social and political culture in small chiefdoms. The chiefs were called Mwamis, and some of them were Hutus, some Tutsis; Hutus and Tutsis fought together in the Mwamis' armies; through marriage and clientage, Hutus could become hereditary Tutsis, and Tutsis could become hereditary Hutus. Because of all this mixing, ethnographers and historians have lately come to agree that Hutus and Tutsis cannot properly be called distinct ethnic groups.

Still, the names Hutu and Tutsi stuck. They had meaning, and though there is no general agreement about what word best describes that meaning—"classes," "castes," and "ranks" are favorites—the source of the distinction is undisputed: Hutus were cultivators and Tutsis were herdsmen. This was the original inequality: cattle are a more valuable asset than produce, and although some Hutus owned cows while some Tutsis tilled the soil, the word Tutsi became synonymous with a political and economic elite. The stratification is believed to have been accelerated after 1860, when the Mwami Kigeri Rwabugiri, a Tutsi, ascended to the Rwandan throne and initiated a series of military and political campaigns that expanded and consolidated his dominion over a territory nearly the size of the present Republic.

But there is no reliable record of the precolonical state. Rwandans had no alphabet; their tradition was oral, therefore malleable; and because their society is fiercely hierarchical the stories they tell of their past tend to be dictated by those who hold power, either through the state or in opposition to it. Of course, at the core of Rwanda's historical debates lie competing ideas about the relationship between Hutus and Tutsis, so it is a frustration that the precolonical roots of that relationship are largely unknowable. As the political thinker Mahmood Mamdani has observed: "That much of what passed as historical fact in academic circles has to be considered as tentative—if not outright fictional—is becoming clear as postgenocidal sobriety compels a growing number of historians to take seriously the political uses to which their writings have been put, and their readers to question the certainty with which many a claim has been advanced."

So Rwandan history is dangerous. Like all of history, it is a record of successive struggles for power, and to a very large extent power consists in the ability to make others inhabit your story of their reality—even, as is so often the case, when that story is written in their blood. Yet some facts, and some understandings, remain unchallenged. For instance, Rwabugiri was the heir to a dynasty that claimed to trace its lineage to the late fourteenth century. Five hundred years is a very long life for any regime, at any time, anywhere. Even if we consider the real possibility that the rememberers of the royal house were exaggerating, or marking time differently than we do, and that Rwabugiri's kingdom was only a few centuries old—that's still a ripe age, and such endurance requires organization.

By the time Rwabugiri came along, the Rwandan state, having expanded gradually from a single hilltop chieftaincy, administered much of what is now southern and central Rwanda through a rigorous, multilayered hierarchy of military, political, and civil chiefs and governors, subchiefs, and deputy governors, sub-subchiefs, and deputy deputy governors. Priests, tax collectors, clan leaders, and army recruiters all had their place in the order that bound every hill in the kingdom in fealty to the Mwami. Court intrigues among the Mwami's sprawling entourage were as elaborate and treacherous as any Shakespeare sketched, with the additional complications of official polygamy, and a prize of immense power for the queen mother.

The Mwami himself was revered as a divinity, absolute and infallible. He was regarded as the personal embodiment of Rwanda, and as Rwabugiri extended his domain, he increasingly configured the world of his subjects in his own image. Tutsis were favored for top political and military offices, and through their public identification with the state, they generally enjoyed greater financial power as well. The regime was essentially feudal: Tutsis were aristocrats; Hutus were vassals. Yet status and identity continued to be determined by many other factors as well—clan, region, clientage, military prowess, even individual industry—and the lines between Hutu and Tutsi remained porous. In fact, in some areas of modern-day Rwanda that Mwami Rwabugiri failed to conquer, these categories had no local significance. Apparently, Hutu and Tutsi identities took definition only in relationship to state power; as they did, the two groups inevitably developed their own distinctive cultures—their own set of ideas about themselves and one another—according to their respective domains. Those ideas were largely framed as opposing negatives: a Hutu was what a Tutsi was not, and vice versa. But in the absence of the sort of hard-and-fast taboos that often mark the boundaries between ethnic or tribal groups, Rwandans who sought to make the most of these distinctions were compelled to amplify minute and imprecise field marks, like the prevalence of milk in one's diet, and, especially, physical traits.

Within the jumble of Rwandan characteristics, the question of appearances is particularly touchy, as it has often come to mean life or death. But nobody can dispute the physical archetypes: for Hutus, stocky and round-faced, dark-skinned, flat-nosed, thick-lipped, and square-jawed; for Tutsis, lanky and long-faced, not so dark-skinned, narrow-nosed, thin-lipped, and narrow-chinned. Nature presents countless exceptions. ("You can't tell us apart," Laurent Nkongoli, the portly vice president of the National Assembly, told me. "*We* can't tell us apart. I was on a bus in the north once and because I was in the north, where they"—Hutus—"were, and because I ate corn, which they eat, they said, 'He's one of us.' But I'm a Tutsi from Butare in the south.") Still, when the Europeans arrived in Rwanda at the end of the nineteenth century, they formed a picture of a stately race of warrior kings, surrounded by herds of long-horned cattle and a subordinate race of short, dark peasants, hoeing tubers and picking bananas. The white men assumed that this was the tradition of the place, and they thought it a natural arrangement.

"Race science" was all the rage in Europe in those days, and for students of central Africa the key doctrine was the so-called Hamitic hypothesis, propounded in 1863 by John Hanning Speke, an Englishman who is most famous for "discovering" the great African lake that he christened Victoria and for identifying it as the source of the Nile River. Speke's basic anthropological theory, which he made up out of whole cloth, was that all culture and civilization in central Africa had been introduced by the taller, sharper-featured people, whom he considered to be a Caucasoid tribe of Ethiopian origin, descended from the biblical King David, and therefore a superior race to the native Negroids.

Much of Speke's *Journal of the Discovery of the Source of the Nile* is devoted to descriptions of the physical and moral ugliness of African's "primitive races," in whose condition he found "a strikingly existing proof of the Holy Scriptures." For his text, Speke took the story in Genesis 9, which tells how Noah, when he was just six hundred years old and had safely skippered his ark over the flood to dry land, got drunk and passed out naked in his tent. On emerging from his oblivion, Noah learned that his youngest son, Ham, had seen him naked; that Ham had told his brothers, Shem and Japheth, of the spectacle; and that Shem and Japheth had, with their backs chastely turned, covered the old man with a garment. Noah responded by cursing the progeny of Ham's son, Canaan, saying, "A slave of slaves shall he be to his brothers." Amid the perplexities of Genesis, this is one of the most enigmatic stories, and it has been subjected to many bewildering interpretations—most notably that Ham was the original black man. To the gentry of the American South, the weird tale of Noah's curse justified slavery, and to Speke and his colonial contemporaries it spelled the history of Africa's peoples. On "contemplating these sons of Noah," he marveled that "as they were then, so they appear to be now."

Speke begins a section of his *Journal*, headed "Fauna," with the words: "In treating of this branch of natural history, we will first take man—the true curly-head, flab-nosed, pouch-mouthed negro." The figure of this subspecies confronted Speke with a mystery even greater than the Nile: "How the negro has lived so many ages without advancing seems marvelous, when all the countries surrounding Africa are so forward in comparison; and, judging from the progressive state of the world, one is led to suppose that the African must soon either step out from his darkness, or be superseded by a being superior to himself." Speke believed that a colonial government—"like ours in India"—might save the "negro" from perdition, but otherwise he saw "very little chance" for the breed: "As his father did, so does he. He works his wife, sells his children, enslaves all he can lay hands upon, and unless when fighting for the property of others, contents himself with drinking, singing, and dancing like a baboon, to drive dull care away."

This was all strictly run-of-the-mill Victorian patter, striking only for the fact that a man who had so exerted himself to see the world afresh had returned with such stock observations. (And, really, very little has changed; one need only lightly edit the foregoing passages—the crude caricatures, the question of human inferiority, and the bit about the baboon—to produce the sort of profile of misbegotten Africa that remains standard to this day in the American and European press, and in the appeals for charity donations put out by humanitarian aid organizations.) Yet, living alongside his sorry "negroes," Speke found a "superior race" of "men who were as unlike as they could be from the common order of the natives" by virtue of their "fine oval faces, large eyes, and high noses, denoting the best blood of Abyssinia"— that is, Ethiopia. This "race" comprised many tribes, including the Watusi— Tutsis—all of whom kept cattle and tended to lord it over the Negroid masses. What thrilled Speke most was their "physical appearances," which despite the hair-curling and skin-darkening effects of intermarriage had retained "a high stamp of Asiatic feature, of which a marked characteristic is a bridged instead of a bridge- less nose." Couching his postulations in vaguely scientific terms, and referring to the historical authority of Scripture, Speke pronounced this "semi-Shem-Hamitic" master race to be lost Christians, and suggested that with a little British education they might be nearly as "superior in all things" as an Englishman like himself.

Few living Rwandans have heard of John Hanning Speke, but most know the essence of his wild fantasy—that the Africans who best resembled the tribes of Europe were inherently endowed with mastery—and, whether they accept or re- ject it, few Rwandans would deny that the Hamitic myth is one of the essential ideas by which they understand who they are in this world. In November of 1992, the Hutu Power ideologue Leon Mugesera delivered a famous speech, calling on Hutus to send the Tutsis back to Ethiopia by way of the Nyabarongo River, a tribu- tary of the Nile that winds through Rwanda. He did not need to elaborate. In April of 1994, the river was choked with dead Tutsis, and tens of thousands of bodies washed up on the shores of Lake Victoria.

Once the African interior had been "opened up" to the European imagination by explorers like Speke, empire soon followed. In a frenzy of conquest, Europe's monarchs began staking claims to vast reaches of the continent. In 1885, represen- tatives of the major European powers held a conference in Berlin to sort out the frontiers of their new African real estate. As a rule, the lines they marked on the map, many of which still define African states, bore no relationship to the political or territorial traditions of the places they described. Hundreds of kingdoms and chieftaincies that operated as distinct nations, with their own languages, religions, and complex political and social histories, were either carved up or, more often, lumped together beneath European flags. But the cartographers at Berlin left Rwanda, and its southern neighbor Burundi, intact, and designated the two coun- tries as provinces of German East Africa.[*]

No white man had ever been to Rwanda at the time of the Berlin conference. Speke, whose theories on race were taken as gospel by Rwanda's colonizers, had

---

[*]Because Rwanda and Burundi were administered as a joint colonial territory, Ruanda-Urundi; because their languages are remarkably similar; because both are populated, in equal proportions, by Hutus and Tutsis; and because their ordeals as postcolonial states have been defined by violence between those groups, they are often considered to be the two halves of a single political and historical experience or "problem." In fact, although events in each country invariably influence events in the other, Rwanda and Burundi have existed since precolonial times as entirely distinct, self-contained nations. The differences in their histories are often more telling than the similarities, and comparison tends to lead to confusion unless each country is first considered on its own terms.

merely peered over the country's eastern frontier from a hilltop in modern-day Tanzania, and when the explorer Henry M. Stanley, intrigued by Rwanda's reputation for "ferocious exclusiveness," attempted to cross that frontier, he was repulsed by a hail of arrows. Even slave traders passed the place by. In 1894, a German count, named von Götzen, became the first white man to enter Rwanda and to visit the royal court. The next year, the death of Mwami Rwabugiri plunged Rwanda into political turmoil, and in 1897, Germany set up its first administrative offices in the country, hoisted the flag of Kaiser Wilhelm's Reich, and instituted a policy of indirect rule. Officially, this meant placing a few German agents over the existing court and administrative system, but the reality was more complicated.

Rwabugiri's death had triggered a violent succession fight among the Tutsi royal clans; the dynasty was in great disarray, and the weakened leaders of the prevailing factions eagerly collaborated with the colonial overlords in exchange for patronage. The political structure that resulted is often described as a "dual colonialism," in which Tutsi elites exploited the protection and license extended by the Germans to pursue their internal feuds and to further their hegemony over the Hutus. By the time that the League of Nations turned Rwanda over to Belgium as a spoil of World War I, the terms Hutu and Tutsi had become clearly defined as opposing "ethnic" identities, and the Belgians made this polarization the cornerstone of their colonial policy.

In his classic history of Rwanda, written in the 1950s, the missionary Monsignor Louis de Lacger remarked, "One of the most surprising phenomena of Rwanda's human geography is surely the contrast between the plurality of races and the sentiment of national unity. The natives of this country genuinely have the feeling of forming but one people." Lacger marveled at the unity created by loyalty to the monarchy—"I would kill for my Mwami" was a popular chant—and to the national God, Imana. "The ferocity of this patriotism is exalted to the point of chauvinism," he wrote, and his missionary colleague Father Pages observed that Rwandans "were persuaded before the European penetration that their country was the center of the world, that this was the largest, most powerful, and most civilized kingdom on earth." Rwandans believed that God might visit other countries by day, but every night he returned to rest in Rwanda. According to Pages, "they found it natural that the two horns of the crescent moon should be turned toward Rwanda, in order to protect it." No doubt, Rwandans also assumed that God expressed himself in Kinyarwanda, because few Rwandans in the insular precolonial state would have known that any other language existed. Even today, when Rwanda's government and many of its citizens are multilingual, Kinyarwanda is the only language of all Rwandans, and, after Swahili, it is the second most widely spoken African language. As Lacger wrote: "There are few people in Europe among whom one finds these three factors of national cohesion: one language, one faith, one law."

Perhaps it was precisely Rwanda's striking Rwandanness that inspired its colonizers to embrace the absurd Hamitic pretext by which they divided the nation against itself. The Belgians could hardly have pretended they were needed to bring order to Rwanda. Instead, they sought out those features of the existing civilization that fit their own ideas of mastery and subjugation and bent them to fit their purposes. Colonization is violence, and there are many ways to carry out that violence. In addition to military and administrative chiefs, and a veritable army of churchmen, the Belgians dispatched scientists to Rwanda. The scientists brought scales and measuring tapes and calipers, and they went about weighing Rwandans, measuring Rwandan cranial capacities, and conducting comparative analyses of the relative protuberance of Rwandan noses. Sure enough, the scientists found what they had believed all along. Tutsis had "nobler," more "naturally" aristocratic dimensions than the "coarse" and "bestial" Hutus. On the "nasal index," for instance, the median Tutsi nose was found to be about two and a half millimeters longer and nearly five millimeters narrower than the median Hutu nose.

Over the years, a number of distinguished European observers became so carried away by their fetishization of Tutsi refinement that they attempted to one-up Speke by proposing, variously, that the Rwandan master race must have originated in Melanesia, the lost city of Atlantis, or—according to one French diplomat—outer space. But the Belgian colonials stuck with the Hamitic myth as their template and, ruling Rwanda more or less as a joint venture with the Roman Catholic Church, they set about radically reengineering Rwandan society along so-called ethnic lines. Monsignor Léon Classe, the first Bishop of Rwanda, was a great advocate of the disenfranchisement of Hutus and the reinforcement of "the traditional hegemony of the well-born Tutsis." In 1930, he warned that any effort to replace Tutsi chiefs with "uncouth" Hutus "would lead the entire state directly into anarchy and to bitter anti-European communism," and, he added, "we have no chiefs who are better qualified, more intelligent, more active, more capable of appreciating progress and more fully accepted by the people than the Tutsi."

Classe's message was heeded: the traditional hill-by-hill administrative structures which had offered Hutus their last hope for at least local autonomy were systematically dismantled, and Tutsi elites were given nearly unlimited power to exploit Hutus' labor and levy taxes against them. In 1931, the Belgians and the Church deposed a Mwami they considered overly independent and installed a new one, Mutara Rudahigwa, who had been carefully selected for his compliance. Mutara promptly converted to Catholicism, renouncing his divine status and sparking a popular rush to the baptismal font that soon turned Rwanda into the most Catholicized country in Africa. Then, in 1933–34, the Belgians conducted a census in order to issue "ethnic" identity cards, which labeled every Rwandan as either Hutu (eighty-five percent) or Tutsi (fourteen percent) or Twa (one percent). The identity cards made it virtually impossible for Hutus to become Tutsis, and permitted the Belgians to perfect the administration of an apartheid system rooted in the myth of Tutsi superiority.

So the offering of the Tutsi herdsman found favor in the eyes of the colonial lords, and the offering of the Hutu cultivators did not. The Tutsi upper crust, glad for power, and terrified of being subjected to the abuses it was encouraged to inflict against Hutus, accepted priority as its due. The Catholic schools, which dominated the colonial educational system, practiced open discrimination in favor of Tutsis, and Tutsis enjoyed a monopoly on administrative and political jobs, while Hutus watched their already limited opportunities for advancement shrink. Nothing so vividly defined the divide as the Belgian regime of forced labor, which required armies of Hutus to toil en masse as plantation chattel, on road construction, and in forestry crews, and placed Tutsis over them as taskmasters. Decades later, an elderly Tutsi recalled the Belgian colonial order to a reporter with the words "You whip the Hutu or we will whip you." The brutality did not end with the beatings; exhausted by their communal labor requirements, peasants neglected their fields, and the fecund hills of Rwanda were repeatedly stricken by famine. Beginning in the 1920s, hundreds of thousands of Hutus and impoverished rural Tutsis fled north to Uganda and west to the Congo to seek their fortunes as itinerant agricultural laborers.

Whatever Hutu and Tutsi identity may have stood for in the precolonial state no longer mattered; the Belgians had made "ethnicity" the defining feature of Rwandan existence. Most Hutus and Tutsis still maintained fairly cordial relations; intermarriages went ahead, and the fortunes of *"petits Tutsis"* in the hills remained quite indistinguishable from those of their Hutu neighbors. But, with every school-child reared in the doctrine of racial superiority and inferiority, the idea of a collective national identity was steadily laid to waste, and on either side of the Hutu-Tutsi divide there developed mutually exclusionary discourses based on the competing claims of entitlement and injury.

Tribalism begets tribalism. Belgium itself was a nation divided along "ethnic" lines, in which the Franchophone Walloon minority had for centuries dominated the Flemish majority. But following a long "social revolution," Belgium had entered an age of greater demographic equality. The Flemish priests who began to turn up in Rwanda after World War II identified with the Hutus and encouraged their aspirations for political change. At the same time, Belgium's colonial administration had been placed under United Nations trusteeship, which meant that it was under pressure to prepare the ground for Rwandan independence. Hutu political activists started calling for majority rule and a "social revolution" of their own. But the political struggle in Rwanda was never really a quest for equality; the issue was only who would dominate the ethnically bipolar state.

In March of 1957, a group of nine Hutu intellectuals published a tract known as the *Hutu Manifesto*, arguing for "democracy"—not by rejecting the Hamitic myth but by embracing it. If Tutsis were foreign invaders, the argument went, then Rwanda was by rights a nation of the Hutu majority. This was what passed for democratic thought in Rwanda: Hutus had the numbers. The *Manifesto* firmly rejected getting rid of ethnic identity cards for fear of "preventing the statistical law from establishing the reality of facts," as if being Hutu or Tutsi automatically signified a person's politics. Plenty of more moderate views could be heard, but who listens to moderates in times of revolution? As new Hutu parties sprang up, rallying the masses to unite in their "Hutuness," the enthusiastic Belgians scheduled elections. But before any Rwandans saw a ballot box, hundreds of them were killed.

On November 1, 1959, in the central Rwandan province of Gitarama, an administrative subchief named Dominique Mbonyumutwa was beaten up by a group of men. Mbonyumutwa was a Hutu political activist, and his attackers were Tutsi political activists, and almost immediately after they finished with him, Mbonyumutwa was said to have died. He wasn't dead, but the rumor was widely believed; even now, there are Hutus who think that Mbonyumutwa was killed on that night. Looking back, Rwandans will tell you that some such incident was inevitable. But the next time you hear a story like the one that ran on the front page of *The New York Times* in October of 1997, reporting on "the age-old animosity between the Tutsi and Hutu ethnic groups," remember that until Mbonyumutwa's beating lit the spark in 1959 there had never been systematic political violence recorded between Hutus and Tutsis—anywhere.

Within twenty-four hours of the beating in Gitarama, roving bands of Hutus were attacking Tutsi authorities and burning Tutsi homes. The "social revolution" had begun. In less than a week, the violence spread through most of the country, as Hutus organized themselves, usually in groups of ten led by a man blowing a whistle, to conduct a campaign of pillage, arson, and sporadic murder against Tutsis. The popular uprising was known as "the wind of destruction," and one of its biggest fans was a Belgian colonel named Guy Logiest, who arrived in Rwanda from the Congo three days after Mbonyumutwa's beating to supervise the troubles. Rwandans who wondered what Logiest's attitude toward the violence might be had only to observe his Belgian troops standing around idly as Hutus torched Tutsi homes. As Logiest put it twenty-five years later: "The time was crucial for Rwanda. Its people needed support and protection."

Were Tutsis not Rwandan people? Four months before the revolution began, the Mwami who had reigned for nearly thirty years, and was still popular with many Hutus, went to Burundi to see a Belgian doctor for treatment of a venereal disease. The doctor gave him an injection, and the Mwami collapsed and died, apparently from allergic shock. But a deep suspicion that he had been poisoned took hold among Rwanda's Tutsis, further straining their fraying relationship with their erstwhile Belgian sponsors. In early November, when the new Mwami, a politically untested twenty-five-year old, asked Colonel Logiest for permission to deploy an army against the Hutu revolutionaries, he was turned down. Royalist forces took to the field anyway, but though a few more Hutus than Tutsis were killed in November, the counteroffensive quickly petered out. "We have to take sides," Colonal Logiest declared as Tutsi homes continued to burn in early 1960, and later he would have no regrets about "being so partial against the Tutsis."

Logiest, who was virtually running the revolution, saw himself as a champion of democratization, whose task was to rectify the gross wrong of the colonial order he served. "I ask myself what was it that made me act with such resolution," he would recall. "It was without doubt the will to give the people back their dignity. And it was probably just as much the desire to put down the arrogance and expose the duplicity of a basically oppressive and unjust aristocracy."

That legitimate grievances lie behind a revolution does not, however, ensure that the revolutionary order will be just. In early 1960, Colonel Logiest staged a coup d'état by executive fiat, replacing Tutsi chiefs with Hutu chiefs. Communal elections were held at midyear, and with Hutus presiding over the polling stations, Hutsus won at least ninety percent of the top posts. By then, more than twenty thousand Tutsis had been displaced from their homes, and that number kept growing rapidly as new Hutu leaders organized violence against Tutsis or simply arrested them arbitrarily, to assert their authority and to snatch Tutsi property. Among the stream of Tutsi refugees who began fleeing into exile was the Mwami.

"The revolution is over," Colonel Logiest announced in October, at the installation of a provisional government led by Grégoire Kayibanda, one of the original authors of the *Hutu Manifesto*, who gave a speech proclaiming: "Democracy has vanquished feudalism." Logiest also gave a speech, and apparently he was feeling magnanimous in victory, because he issued this prophetic caution: "It will not be a democracy if it is not equally successful in respecting the rights of minorities. . . . A country in which justice loses this fundamental quality prepares the worst disorders and its own collapse." But that was not the spirit of the revolution over which Logiest had presided.

To be sure, nobody in Rwanda in the late 1950s had offered an alternative to a tribal construction of politics. The colonial state and the colonial church had made that almost inconceivable, and although the Belgians switched ethnic sides on the eve of independence, the new order they prepared was merely the old order stood on its head. In January of 1961, the Belgians convened a meeting of Rwanda's new Hutu leaders, at which the monarchy was officially abolished and Rwanda was declared a republic. The transitional government was nominally based on a power-sharing arrangement between Hutu and Tutsi parties, but a few months later a UN commission reported that the Rwandan revolution had, in fact, "brought about the racial dictatorship of one party" and simply replaced "one type of oppressive regime with another." The report also warned of the possibility "that some day we will witness violent reactions on the part of the Tutsis." The Belgians didn't much care. Rwanda was granted full independence in 1962, and Grégoire Kayibanda was inaugurated as President.

So Hutu dictatorship masqueraded as popular democracy, and Rwanda's power struggles became an internal affair of the Hutu elite, very much as the feuds among royal Tutsi clans had been in the past. Rwanda's revolutionaries had become what the writer V. S. Naipaul calls postcolonial "mimic men," who reproduce the abuses against which they rebelled, while ignoring the fact that their past masters were ultimately banished by those they enchained. President Kayibanda had almost certainly read Louis de Lacger's famous history of Rwanda. But instead of Lacger's idea of a Rwandan people unified by "national sentiment," Kayibanda spoke of Rwanda as "two nations in one state."

Genesis identifies the first murder as a fratricide. The motive is political—the elimination of a perceived rival. When God asks what happened, Cain offers his notoriously barbed lie: "I do not know; am I my brother's keeper?" The shock in the story is not the murder, which begins and ends in one sentence, but Cain's shamelessness and the leniency of God's punishment. For killing his brother, Cain is condemned to a life as "a fugitive and a wanderer on the earth." When he protests, "Whoever finds me will slay me," God says, "Not so! If anyone slays Cain, vengeance shall be taken on him sevenfold." Quite literally, Cain gets away with murder; he even receives special protection, but as the legend indicates, the blood-revenge model of justice imposed after his crime was not viable. People soon became so craven that "the earth was filled with violence," and God regretted his creation so much that he erased it with a flood. In the new age that followed, the law would eventually emerge as the principle of social order. But that was many fratricidal struggles later.

Construction of an Enemy
–Eleanor Stein

Eleanor Stein teaches courses on telecommunications law at Albany Law School and women and law at the State University of New York in Albany. The following article appeared originally in Monthly Review, *July/August, 2003.*

> Remember the Nazi technique: "pit race against race, religion against religion, prejudice against prejudice. Divide and conquer!"
>
> —President Franklin D. Roosevelt (January 1942) admonishing Americans not to discriminate against aliens, weeks before he signed the Japanese exclusion order (Greg Robinson, By Order of the President, 2001).

The aggressive measures instituted by the Bush administration against immigrants and visitors of Muslim faith, or from primarily Muslim Arab and South Asian countries, seem aimed less at their putative foreign targets than at the hearts and minds of our domestic population. Packaged as post-September 11 law enforcement, the new racial profiling has netted few if any prosecutions for terrorist acts,

"Construction of an Enemy" by Eleanor Stein, *Monthly Review*, July/August 2003. Copyright 2003. Reprinted by permission.

but has done a great deal to demonize Arabs, South Asians, and Muslims, to dehumanize them, and to construct them as the enemy of America in the twenty-first century. Once the state successfully constructs an enemy group, it can justify detentions without charge, military occupation, and other drastic means of waging war against that other, the enemy.

Nativist and xenophobic identification of immigrants with national security threats is a theme coincident with the history of the United States. The Naturalization Act of 1790 prohibited citizenship and civil rights to immigrants of disfavored ethnicity. The Alien and Sedition Acts of 1798 placed restrictions on which ethnicities or nationalities could apply for citizenship, and authorized the president to order the deportation of all immigrants judged dangerous to national security. The "sedition" of concern in 1798 were the ideas of the French Revolution. The Chinese Exclusion (Geary) Act of 1882, in violation of the express terms of a treaty in force between China and the United States, forbade Chinese laborers from entering the United States.

The National Origins Act of 1924 established immigration quotas privileging "Nordic" immigrants. The Smith Act of 1940, required registration and fingerprinting of aliens, and added vague classifications of "subversives" and "excludables" to the list of deportable persons. The McCarran-Walter Act of 1952 empowered the Department of Justice to deport immigrants or naturalized citizens engaging in "subversive" activities. The Anti-Terrorism and Effective Death Penalty Act of 1996, granted the executive the authority, based upon secret evidence, to designate any foreign organization a terrorist group and to deport noncitizens as terrorists.

But it was the internment of Japanese Americans during the Second World War that elevated xenophobia into national policy. And it was in the internment cases that the Supreme Court, upholding the internment as a matter of military necessity, wrote the requirement of strict judicial scrutiny of "invidious" distinction into American jurisprudence.

Based upon reports by the military that it had intercepted radio and light signals between offshore locations and the California coast, the evacuation and internment orders forced persons of Japanese descent to leave their homes in specified control areas in California, Arizona, Oregon, and Washington, and move to internment camps. Over 120,000 persons, two-thirds of them U.S.-born citizens, spent the years of the war in such camps.

The internment order was rationalized not only by military necessity—the fear of sabotage and espionage—but also by the military's claim that the normal criminal investigatory work of the Justice Department had been overly slow and inadequate to guarantee U.S. security. The racist hysteria in which the roundups took place was fed by the Hearst press and by California economic interests—such as the White American Nurserymen—in competition with small entrepreneurs of Japanese descent.

Two brave individuals, Fred Korematsu and Gordon Hirabayashi, refused to report for internment and sought to challenge the order in the Federal Courts. In a shameful decision, the U.S. Supreme Court upheld as constitutional this mass internment; included were 80,000 citizens deprived of library solely by reason of their ethnic origin. Forty years later, when the two whose refusal to report for internment had led to Supreme Court cases sought (and received) judicial exoneration, it was discovered that the military report, which was the justification for the internment order and the Supreme Court decision, was a complete fabrication. An archival researcher, working in conjunction with a congressional commission appointed to investigate the internment, found the original report. The supposed intercepted radio and light signals, dutifully repeated in the Supreme Court opinion, had never occurred.

The shadow of Manzanar—the California internment camp—looms today over all of the current measures being taken against Arab and Muslim immigrants. These measures can be seen as internment for the twenty-first century—or to coin a more accurate term, externment.

Shortly after September 11, 2001, the "Ashcroft Raids" occurred, the secret detention and deportation of up to a thousand or more Arab or Muslim men. Some were held for months, even as long as one year, without access to lawyers and in some cases, to families. Ashcroft stated he intended to jail every terrorist he could find, and that net included thousands of Muslim noncitizens. What were the results of this dragnet? Not a single person charged with involvement in the September 11 attacks, and four indicted on charges of support for terrorism, with none of the indictments including any specific violent acts. The Justice Department now admits that at least 766 persons were detained on "special interest" charges after September 11 and held incommunicado; of these, 511 have been deported. The Justice Department claims that among those deported were some who could have been—*but have not been*—charged with terrorism offenses. This in turn has led to reported speculation that one purpose of the mass detention policy was the recruitment of intelligence agents (www.law.com/jsp/article.jsp?id=1052440755868). An additional six thousand were deported for violations of immigration status. Eight thousand were called for interviews on the sole ground that they were recent male immigrants from Arab countries.

The USA Patriot Act, enacted within six weeks of September 11, permits the Attorney General to detain noncitizens without a hearing; to bar foreign citizens from entering the United States because of their political opinions; and authorizes deportation based upon support of a disfavored group. None of these restrictions is tied to participation in any terrorist act. On April 29, 2003, the Supreme Court approved mandatory detention of "criminal aliens" pending deportation—that is, permanent resident aliens convicted of any of a list of crimes who are subject to deportation have no entitlement to a hearing to consider bail for the period they contest or await deportation.

Also coming soon may be Patriot Act II, which modifies the definition of "foreign power" to include all persons, regardless of whether they are affiliated with an international terrorist group, who engage in international terrorism; and defines any person who engages in clandestine intelligence gathering activities for a foreign power as an agent of that power, regardless of whether those activities are federal crimes.

One of the most far-reaching forms of racial profiling is the requirement of the Immigration and Naturalization Service, now merged into the Office of Homeland Security, termed Special Registration. These new rules apply to any male, over the age of sixteen, who is not currently a permanent resident (green card holder), from twenty-five countries: Afghanistan, Algeria, Bahrain, Eritrea, Iran, Iraq, Lebanon, Libya, Morocco, North Korea, Oman, Qatar, Somalia, Sudan, Syria, Tunisia, United Arab Emirates, Yemen, Pakistan, Saudi Arabia, Bangladesh, Egypt, Indonesia, Jordan, and Kuwait. These men were required to register in person at an immigration office during February and March 2003 on a few weeks notice, to be photographed, fingerprinted, and interviewed, in many cases about their political beliefs and associations. More than 125,000 registered; over 2,000 were detained. All must re-register annually and any time they leave the United States. A widespread panic resulted in immigrant communities, and thousands in the New York and New England areas traveled with their families to the Canadian border to seek asylum; however, the United States had closed the border. Hundreds were detained there, their families left without shelter or resources in the bitter New England winter. Local refugee assistance organizations, overwhelmed, were forced to close their doors.

Government profiling also contributed to a wave of popular violence against Arab, South Asian, and Muslim communities. The number of reported U.S. hate crimes against Muslims and Arabs in 2002 increased 1600 percent over the previous years.

The construction of an enemy, through government targeting with media complicity and a popular echo, endangers and dehumanizes millions of Arabs, Asians, and Muslims. Given a dehumanized enemy, bombing its cities and sacking its history was presented on U.S. TV as an extreme sport. The construction of an enemy provides an effective means of control of the domestic population, which visits its fears and frustrations on its Arab and Muslim neighbors. This control is, however, contested. In communities all over the country, towns and cities have passed local government resolutions criticizing and even refusing to enforce the Patriot Act.

Fred Korematsu and Gordon Hirabayashi waited forty years for vindication and reparations; and few outside the Japanese-American community, with the notable exception of the Quakers, had opposed internment. Hopefully we are doing better this time.

Interfaith groups are building bridges to Muslim communities. In upstate New York, Women Against War organized a toy drive for children of detainees and deportees to celebrate Eid, the end of Ramadan and, with national civil liberties organizations, recruited attorneys and other volunteers to assist men reporting for Special Registration and their families. And shortly after September 11 the National Asian Pacific American Legal Consortium invited Arab Americans to join them at the National Japanese American Memorial to show solidarity in anticipation of racial profiling. Resistance as ever is based on acts of individual decency, which in these sad times appear as acts of courage. But the liberty interests of all U.S. residents are implicated; if we do not stand by our Muslim neighbors in their registration, detention, and deportation nightmare we will have a yet harder time when these techniques are more widely applied.

On Being South Asian in North America

–Chandra Talpade Mohanty

Chandra Talpade Mohanty is professor of Women's Studies and Dean's Professor of the Humanities at Syracuse University. Born in India, Mohanty holds a Ph.D. and master's degree from the University of Illinois at Urbana-Champaign and a master's degree and bachelor's degree from the University of Delhi, India. Her autobiographical reflection, "On Being South Asian in North America," appeared originally in Our Feet Walk the Sky: Women of the South Asian Diaspora, *which was edited by The Women of South Asian Descent Collective and published by Aunt Lute Books, 1993.*

My local newspaper tells me that worldwide migration is at an all-time high in the early 1990s. Folks are moving from rural to urban areas in all parts of the Third World, and from Asia, Africa, the Caribbean and Latin America to Europe, North America and selected countries in the Middle East. Apparently two percent of the world's population no longer lives in the country in which they were born. Of course, the newspaper story primarily identifies the "problems" (for Europe and the USA) associated with these transnational migration trends. One such "problem" is taking jobs away from "citizens." I am reminded of a placard carried by Black and Third World people at an anti-racism rally in London: We Are Here Because You Were There. My location in the USA, then, is symptomatic of large

"On Being South Asian in North America," from *Our Feet Walk the Sky: Women of the South Asian Diaspora.* Copyright © 1993 by the Women of the South Asian Descent Collective. Reprinted by permission of Aunt Lute Books.

numbers of migrants, nomads, immigrants, workers across the globe for whom notions of home, identity, geography and history are infinitely complicated in the late
twentieth century. Questions of nation(ality), and of "belonging" (witness the situation of South Asians in Africa), are constitutive of the Indian diaspora. This essay
is a personal, anecdotal meditation on the politics of gender and race in the construction of South Asian identity in North America.

On a TWA flight on my way back to the U.S. from a conference in the
Netherlands, the professional white man sitting next to me asks: (a) which school
do I go to? and (b) when do I plan to go home?—all in the same breath. I put on
my most professional demeanor (somewhat hard in crumpled blue jeans and cotton T-shirt—this uniform only works for white male professors, who of course
could command authority even in swimwear!) and inform him that I teach at a
small liberal arts college in upstate New York, and that I have lived in the U.S. for
fifteen years. At this point, my work is in the U.S., not in India. This is no longer
entirely true—my work is also with feminists and grassroots activists in India, but
he doesn't need to know this. Being "mistaken" for a graduate student seems endemic to my existence in this country—few Third World women are granted professional (i.e., adult) and/or permanent (one is always a student!) status in the U.S.,
even if we exhibit clear characteristics of adulthood, like grey hair and facial lines.
He ventures a further question: what do you teach? On hearing "women's studies,"
he becomes quiet and we spend the next eight hours in polite silence. He has decided that I do not fit into any of his categories, but what can you expect from a
Feminist (an *Asian* one!) anyway? I feel vindicated and a little superior—even
though I know he doesn't really feel "put in his place." Why should he? He has a
number of advantages in this situation: white skin, maleness and citizenship privileges. From his enthusiasm about expensive "ethnic food" in Amsterdam, and his
J. Crew clothes, I figured class difference (economic or cultural) wasn't exactly
an issue in our interaction. We both appeared to have similar social access as
"professionals."

I have been asked the "home" question (when are you going home) periodi-
cally for fifteen years now. Leaving aside the subtly racist implications of the question (go home—you don't belong), I am still not satisfied with my response. What
is home? The place I was born? Where I grew up? Where my parents live? Where
I live and work as an adult? Where I locate my community—my people? Who are
"my people"? Is home a geographical space, an historical space, an emotional, sen-
sory space? Home is always so crucial to immigrants and migrants—I even write
about it in scholarly texts, perhaps to avoid addressing it as an issue that is also very
personal. Does two percent of the world's population think about these questions
pertaining to home? This is not to imply that the other ninety-eight percent does
not think about home. What interests me is the meaning of home for immigrants
and migrants. I am convinced that this question—how one understands and defines home—is a profoundly political one.

Since settled notions of territory, community, geography, and history don't
work for us, what does it really mean to be "South Asian" in the USA? Obviously I

was not South Asian in India—I was Indian. What else could one be but "Indian" at a time when a successful national independence struggle had given birth to a socialist democratic nation-state? This was the beginning of the decolonization of the Third World. Regional geographies (South Asia) appeared less relevant as a mark of identification than citizenship in a post-colonial independent nation on the cusp of economic and political autonomy. However, in North America, identification as South Asian (in addition to Indian, in my case) takes on its own logic. "South Asian" refers to folks of Indian, Pakistani, Sri Lankan, Bangladeshi, Kashmiri, and Burmese origin. Identifying as South Asian rather than Indian adds numbers and hence power within the U.S. State. Besides, regional differences among those from different South Asian countries are often less relevant than the commonalities based on our experiences and histories of immigration, treatment and location in the U.S.

Let me reflect a bit on the way I identify myself, and the way the U.S. State and its institutions categorize me. Perhaps thinking through the various labels will lead me back to the question of home and identity. In 1977, I arrived in the USA on an F1 visa—a student visa. At that time, my definition of myself—a graduate student in Education at the University of Illinois, and the "official" definition of me (a student allowed into the country on an F1 visa) obviously coincided. Then I was called a "foreign student," and expected to go "home" (to India—even though my parents were in Nigeria at the time) after getting my Ph.D. Let's face it, this is the assumed trajectory for a number of Indians, especially the post-independence (my) generation, who come to the U.S. for graduate study.

However, this was not to be my trajectory. I quickly discovered that being a foreign student, and a woman at that, meant being either dismissed as irrelevant (the quiet Asian woman stereotype), treated in racist ways (my teachers asked if I understood English and if they should speak slower and louder so that I could keep up—this in spite of my inheritance of the Queen's English and British colonialism!), or celebrated and exoticized (you are so smart! your accent is even better than that of Americans—a little Anglophilia at work here, even though all my Indian colleagues insist we speak English the Indian way!).

The most significant transition I made at that time was the one from "foreign student" to "student of color." Once I was able to "read" my experiences in terms of race, and to read race and racism as it is written into the social and political fabric of the U.S., practices of racism and sexism became the analytic and political lenses through which I was able to anchor myself here. Of course, none of this happened in isolation—friends, colleagues, comrades, classes, books, films, arguments, and dialogues were constitutive of my political education as a woman of color in the U.S.

In the late 1970s and early 1980s feminism was gaining momentum on American campuses—it was in the air, in the classrooms, on the streets. However, what attracted me wasn't feminism as the mainstream media and white Women's Studies departments defined it. Instead, it was a very specific kind of feminism, the feminism of U.S. women of color and Third World women, that spoke to me. In thinking through the links between gender, race and class in their U.S. manifestations, I was for the first time enabled to think through my own gendered, classed post-colonial history. In the early 1980s, reading Audre Lorde, Nawal el Sadaawi, Cherrié Moraga, bell hooks, Gloria Joseph, Paula Gunn Allen, Barbara Smith, Merle Woo and Mitsuye Yamada, among others, generated a sort of recognition that was intangible but very inspiring. A number of actions, decisions and organizing efforts at that time led me to a sense of home and community in relation to women of color in the U.S. Home not as a comfortable, stable, inherited and familiar space, but instead as an imaginative, politically charged space where the familiarity and sense of affection and commitment lay in shared collective analysis of social injustice, as well as a vision of radical transformation. Political solidarity and a sense of family could be melded together imaginatively to create a strategic space I could call "home." Politically, intellectually and emotionally I owe an enormous debt to feminists of color—and especially to the sisters who have sustained me over the years. . . .

For me, engagement as a feminist of color in the U.S. made possible an intellectual and political genealogy of being Indian that was radically challenging as well as profoundly activist. Notions of home and community began to be located within a deeply political space where racialization and gender and class relations and histories became the prism through which I understood, however partially, what it could mean to be South Asian in North America. Interestingly, this recognition also forced me to re-examine the meanings attached to home and community in India.

What I chose to claim, and continue to claim, is a history of anti-colonialist, feminist struggle in India. The stories I recall, the ones that I retell and claim as my own, determine the choices and decisions I make in the present and the future. I did not want to accept a history of Hindu chauvinist (bourgeois) upward mobility (even though this characterizes a section of my extended family). We all choose partial, interested stories/histories—perhaps not as deliberately as I am making it sound here. But consciously, or unconsciously, these choices about our past(s) often determine the logic of our present.

Having always kept my distance from conservative, upwardly mobile Indian immigrants for whom the South Asian world was divided into green-card holders and non-green-card holders, the only South Asian links I allowed and cultivated were with Indians with whom I shared a political vision. This considerably limited my community. Racist and sexist experiences in graduate school and after made it imperative that I understand the U.S. in terms of its history of racism, imperialism and patriarchal relations, specifically in relation to Third World immigrants. After all, we were into the Reagan-Bush years, when the neo-conservative backlash made it impossible to ignore the rise of racist, anti-feminist, and homophobic attitudes, practices and institutions. Any purely culturalist or nostalgic/sentimental definition of being "Indian" or "South Asian" was inadequate. Such a definition fueled the "model minority" myth. And this subsequently constituted us as "outsiders/ foreigners" or as interest groups who sought or had obtained the American dream.

In the mid-1980s, the labels changed: I went from being a "foreign student" to being a "resident alien." I have always thought that this designation was a stroke of inspiration on the part of the U.S. State, since it accurately names the experience and status of immigrants—especially immigrants of color. The flip side of "resident alien" is "illegal alien," another inspired designation. One can be either a resident or illegal immigrant, but one is always an alien. There is no confusion here—no melting pot ideology or narratives of assimilation—one's status as an "alien" is primary. Being legal requires identity papers. (It is useful to recall that the "passport"—and by extension the concept of nation-states and the sanctity of their borders—came into being after World War I.)

One must be stamped as legitimate (that is, not-gay-or-lesbian and not-communist!) by the Immigration and Naturalization Service (INS). The INS is one of the central disciplinary arms of the U.S. State. It polices the borders and controls all border crossings—especially those into the U.S. In fact, the INS is also one of the primary forces which institutionalizes race differences in the public arena, thus regulating notions of home, legitimacy and economic access to the "American dream" for many of us. For instance, carrying a green card documenting resident alien status in the U.S. is clearly very different from carrying an American passport, which is proof of U.S. citizenship. The former allows one to enter the U.S. with few hassles; the latter often allows one to breeze through the borders and ports of entry of other countries, especially countries which happen to be trading partners (much of Western Europe and Japan, among others) or in an unequal relationship with the U.S. (much of the noncommunist Third World). At a time when notions of a capitalist free-market economy seem (falsely) synonymous with the values attached to democracy, an American passport can open many doors. However, just carrying an American passport is no insurance against racism and unequal and unjust treatment within the U.S. It would be important to compare the racialization of first-generation immigrants from South Asia to the racialization of second-generation South Asian Americans. For example, one significant difference between these two generations would be between experiencing racism as a phenomenon specific to the U.S., versus growing up in the ever-present shadow of racism in the case of South Asians born in the U.S. This suggests that the psychic effects of racism would be different for these two constituencies. In addition, questions of home, identity and history take on very different meanings for South Asians born in North America. But to be fair, this comparison requires a whole other reflection that is beyond the scope of this essay.

Rather obstinately, I have refused to give up my Indian passport and have chosen to remain as a resident alien in the U.S. for the last decade or so. Which leads me to reflect on the complicated meanings attached to holding Indian citizenship while making a life for myself in the USA. In India, what does it mean to have a green card—to be an expatriate? What does it mean to visit Bombay every two to four years, and still call it home? Why does speaking in Marathi (my mother-tongue) become a measure and confirmation of home? What are the politics of being a part of the majority and the "absent elite" in India, while being a minority and a racialized "other" in the U.S.? And does feminist politics, or advocating feminism, have the same meanings and urgencies in these different geographical and political contexts?

Some of these questions hit me smack in the face during my last visit to India, in December 1992—post-Ayodhya (the infamous destruction of the Babri Masjid in Ayodhya by Hindu fundamentalists on 6 December 1992). In earlier, rather infrequent visits (once every four or five years was all I could afford), my green card designated me as an object of envy, privilege and status within my extended family. Of course the same green card has always been viewed with suspicion by left and feminist friends who (quite understandably) demand evidence of my ongoing commitment to a socialist and democratic India. During this visit, however, with emotions running high within my family, my green card marked me as an outsider who couldn't possibly understand the "Muslim problem" in India. I was made aware of being an "outsider" in two profoundly troubling shouting matches with my uncles, who voiced the most incredibly hostile sentiments against Muslims. Arguing that India was created as a secular state and that democracy had everything to do with equality for all groups (majority and minority) got me nowhere. The very fundamentals of democratic citizenship in India were/are being undermined and redefined as "Hindu."

Bombay was one of the cities hardest hit with waves of communal violence following the events in Ayodhya. The mobilization of Hindu fundamentalists, even paramilitary organizations, over the last half century and especially since the mid-1980s had brought Bombay to a juncture where the most violently racist discourse about Muslims seemed to be woven into the fabric of acceptable daily life. Racism was normalized in the popular imagination such that it became almost impossible to publicly raise questions about the ethics or injustice of racial/ethnic/religious discrimination. I could not assume a distanced posture towards religion any more. Too many injustices were being done in my name.

Although born a Hindu, I have always considered myself a non-practicing one—religion had always felt rather repressive when I was growing up. I enjoyed the rituals but resisted the authoritarian hierarchies of organized Hinduism. However, the Hinduism touted by fundamentalist organizations like the RSS (Rashtriya Swayamsevak Sangh, a paramilitary Hindu fundamentalist organization founded in the 1930s) and the Shiv Sena (a Maharashtrian chauvinist, fundamentalist, fascist political organization that has amassed a significant voice in Bombay politics and government) was one that even I, in my ignorance, recognized as reactionary and distorted. But this discourse was real—hate-filled rhetoric against Muslims appeared to be the mark of a "loyal Hindu." It was unbelievably heart-wrenching to see my hometown become a war zone with whole streets set on fire, and a daily death count to rival any major territorial border war. The smells and textures of Bombay, of home, which had always comforted and nurtured me, were violently disrupted. The scent of fish drying on the lines at the fishing village in

Danda was submerged in the smell of burning straw and grass as whole bastis (chawls) were burned to the ground. The very topography, language and relationships that constituted "home" were quietly but surely exploding. What does community mean in this context? December 1992 both clarified as well as complicated for me the meanings attached to being an Indian citizen, a Hindu, an educated woman/feminist, and a permanent resident in the U.S. in ways that I have yet to resolve. After all, it is often moments of crisis that make us pay careful attention to questions of identity. Sharp polarizations force one to make choices (not in order to take sides, but in order to accept responsibility) and to clarify our own analytic, political and emotional topographies. . . .

Let me now circle back to the place I began: the meanings I have come to give to home, community and identity. By exploring the relationship between being a South Asian immigrant in America and an expatriate Indian citizen in India, I have tried, however partially and anecdotally, to clarify the complexities of home and community for this particular feminist of color/South Asian in North America. The genealogy I have created for myself here is partial, interested and deliberate. It is a genealogy that I find emotionally and politically enabling—it is part of the genealogy that underlies my self-identification as an educator involved in a pedagogy of liberation. Of course, my history and experiences are far messier and not at all as linear as this narrative makes them sound. But then the very process of constructing a narrative for oneself—of telling a story—imposes a certain linearity and coherence that is never entirely there. But that is the lesson, perhaps, especially for us immigrants and migrants: i.e., that home, community and identity all fall somewhere between the histories and experiences we inherit and the political choices we make through alliances, solidarities and friendships.

One very concrete effect of my creating this particular space for myself has been my recent involvement in two grassroots organizations, one in India and the other in the U.S. The former, an organization called *Awareness*, is based in Orissa and works to empower the rural poor. Their focus is political education (similar to Paolo Friere's notion of "conscientization"), and they have recently begun to very consciously organize rural women. *Grassroots Leadership of North Carolina* is the U.S. organization I work with. It is a multiracial group of organizers (largely African American and White) working to build a poor and working peoples movement in the American South. While the geographical, historical and political contexts are different in the case of these two organizations, my involvement in them is very similar, as is my sense that there are clear connections to be made between the work of the two organizations. In addition, I think that the issues, analyses and strategies for organizing for social justice are also quite similar. This particular commitment to work with grassroots organizers in the two places I call home is not accidental. It is very much the result of the genealogy I have traced here. After all, it has taken me over a decade to make these commitments to grassroots work in both spaces. In part, I have defined what it means to be South Asian by educating myself about, and reflecting on, the histories and experiences of African American,

Latina, West Indian, African, European American, and other constituencies in North America. Such definitions and understandings do provide a genealogy, but a genealogy that is always relational and fluid as well as urgent and necessary.

> *This essay is dedicated to the memory of Lanubai and Gauribai Vijaykar, maternal grandaunts, who were single, educated, financially independent, and tall (over six feet) at a time when it was against the grain to be any one of these things; and to Audre Lorde, teacher, sister, friend, whose words and presence continue to challenge, inspire, and nurture me.*

Dislocated Identities
Reflections of an Arab Jew

–Ella Shohat

Ella Shohat is professor of cultural studies at New York University. She has lectured and published extensively on the intersection of gender, postcolonialism, and multiculturalism, as well as on Zionist discourse and the Arab-Jewish and Mizrahi questions. Her essay "Dislocated Identities: Reflections of an Arab Jew" appeared originally in Movement Research Journal, *volume 5, Fall/Winter 1992.*

I am an Arab Jew. Or, more specifically, an Iraqi Israeli woman living, writing, and teaching in the U.S. Most members of my family were born and raised in Baghdad, and now live in Iraq, Israel, the U.S., England, and Holland. When my grandmother first encountered Israeli society in the '50s, she was convinced that the people who looked, spoke, and ate so differently, the European Jews, were actually European Christians. Jewishness for her generation was inextricably associated with Middle Easternness. My grandmother, who still lives in Israel and still communicates largely in Arabic, had to be taught to speak of "us" as Jews and "them" as Arabs. For Middle Easterners, the operating distinction had always been

Ella Shohat "Dislocated Identities: Reflections of an Arab Jew," *Movement Research Journal*, 5, Fall/Winter 1992. Reprinted by permission of the author.

"Muslim," "Jew," "Christian," not Arab versus Jew. The assumption was that "Arabness" referred to a common shared culture and language, albeit with religious differences.

Americans are often amazed to discover the existentially nauseating or charmingly exotic possibilities of such a syncretic identity. I recall a well-established colleague who despite my elaborate lessons on the history of Arab Jews still had trouble understanding that I was not a tragic anomaly, the daughter of an Arab (Palestinian) and an Israeli (European Jew). Living in North America makes it even more difficult to communicate that we are Jews and yet entitled to our Middle Eastern difference. And that we are Arabs and yet entitled to our religious difference, like Arab Christians and Arab Muslims. It was precisely the policing of cultural borders in Israel that led some of us to escape into the metropolises of syncretic identities. Yet, in an American context, we face again a hegemony that allows us to narrate only a single Jewish memory, i.e., a European one. For those of us who don't hide our Middle Easternness under one Jewish "we," it becomes tougher and tougher to exist in an American context hostile to the very notion of Easternness.

As an Arab Jew, I am often obliged to explain the "mysteries" of this oxymoronic entity. That we have spoken Arabic, not Yiddish: that for millennia our cultural creativity, secular and religious, had been largely articulated in Arabic (Malmonides being one of the few intellectuals to "make it" into the consciousness of the West); and that even the most religious of our communities in the Middle East and North Africa never expressed themselves in Yiddish-accented Hebrew prayers, nor did they practice liturgical-gestural norms and sartorial codes favoring the dark colors of centuries-ago Poland. Middle Eastern Jewish women similarly never wore wigs; their hair covers, if worn, consisted of different variations on regional clothing (and in the wake of British and French imperialism, many wore Western-style clothes). If you go to our synagogues, even in New York, Montreal, Paris, or London, you'll be amazed to hear the winding quarter-tones of our music, which the uninitiated might imagine to be coming from a mosque.

Now that the three cultural topographies that compose my ruptured and dislocated history—Iraq, Israel, and the U.S.—have been involved in a war, it is crucial to say that we exist. Some of us refuse to dissolve so as to facilitate "neat" national and ethnic divisions. My anxiety and pain during a Scud attack on Israel, where some of my family lives, did not cancel out my fear and anguish for the victims of the bombardment of Iraq, where I also have relatives.

But war is the friend of binarisms, leaving little place for complex identities. The Gulf War intensified a pressure already familiar to the Arab Jewish diaspora in the wake of the Israeli-Arab conflict: a pressure to choose between being a Jew and being an Arab. For our families, who have lived in Mesopotamia since at least the Babylonian exile, who have been Arabized for millennia, and who were abruptly dislodged to Israel 40 years ago, to be suddenly forced to assume a homogeneous European Jewish identity based on experiences in Russia, Poland, and Germany, was an exercise in self-devastation. To be a European or an American Jew has hardly been perceived as a contradiction, but to be an Arab Jew has been seen as a kind of logical paradox, even an ontological subversion. This binarism has led many Oriental Jews (our name in Israel referring to our common Asian and African countries of origins) to a profound and visceral schizophrenia, since for the first time in our history Arabness and Jewishness have been imposed as antonyms.

Intellectual discourse in the West highlights a Judeo-Christian tradition, yet rarely acknowledges the Judeo-Muslim culture of the Middle East, of North Africa, or of pre-Expulsion Spain (1492) and of the European parts of the Ottoman Empire. The Jewish experience in the Muslim world has often been portrayed as an unending nightmare of oppression and humiliation. Although I in no way want to idealize that experience—there were occasional tensions, discriminations, even violence—on the whole, we lived quite comfortably within Muslim societies. Despite George Bush's facile assimilation of Hussein to Hitler, for Jews in the Muslim world there was no equivalent to the Holocaust. In the case of the Inquisition (1492), both Jews and Muslims were the victims of Christian zealotry. Our history simply cannot be discussed in European Jewish terminology. As Iraqi Jews, while retaining a communal identity, we were generally well-integrated and indigenous to the country, forming an inseparable part of its social and cultural life. Thoroughly Arabized, we used Arabic even in hymns and religious ceremonies. The liberal and secular trends of the 20th century engendered an even stronger association of Iraqi Jews and Arab culture, which brought Jews into an extremely active role in public and cultural life. Prominent Jewish writers, poets and scholars played a vital role in Arab culture, distinguishing themselves in Arabic-speaking theater, in music, as singers, composers, and players of traditional instruments. In Egypt, Morocco, Syria, Lebanon, Iraq, and Tunisia, Jews became members of legislatures, of municipal councils, of the judiciary, and even occupied high economic positions. (The finance minister of Iraq in the '40s was Ishak Sasson, and in Egypt, James Sanua—higher positions, ironically, than those our community has generally achieved within the Jewish state.)

The same historical process that dispossessed Palestinians of their property, lands, and national-political rights, was linked to the dispossession of Middle Eastern and North African Jews of their property, lands, and rootedness in Muslim countries. As refugees, or mass immigrants (depending on one's political perspective), we were forced to leave everything behind and give up our Iraqi passports. The same process also affected our uprootedness or ambiguous positioning within Israel itself. In Israel we have been systematically discriminated against by institutions that deployed their energies and material resources to the consistent advantage of European Jews and to the consistent disadvantage of Oriental Jews. Even our physiognomies betray us, leading to internalized colonialism or physical misperception. Sephardic Oriental women often dye their dark hair blond, while the men have more than once been arrested or beaten when mistaken for Palestinians. What for Ashkenazi immigrants from Russia and Poland was a social *aliya* (literally "ascent") was for Oriental Sephardic Jews a *yerida* ("descent").

Stripped of our history, we have been forced by our no-exit situation to repress our collective nostalgia, at least within the public sphere. The pervasive notion of "one people" reunited in their ancient homeland actively disauthorizes any affectionate memory of life before Israel. We have never been allowed to mourn a trauma that the images of Iraq's destruction only intensified and crystallized for some of us. Our cultural creativity in Arabic, Hebrew, and Aramaic is hardly studied in Israeli schools, and it is becoming difficult to convince our children that we actually did exist there, and that some of us are still there in Iraq, Morocco, and Yemen.

The notion of "in-gathering from exile" does not permit to narrate the exile of Arab Jews in the Promised land. My parents and grandparents, 30 or 40 years after they left Baghdad, still long for its sights and sounds. Oriental Jews in Israel are enthusiastic consumers of Jordanian, Lebanese, and Egyptian television programs and films, just as our Oriental-Arabic music is consumed in the Arab world often without being labeled as originating in Israel. The Yemenite-Israeli singer Ofra Haza has been recognized by the Yemenites as continuing a Yemeni cultural tradition. Back in the days before the horrific bombing of Baghdad, we used to play a bittersweet game of scanning the television to spot changes in the city's urban topography. But the impossibility of ever going there once led me to contemplate an ironic inversion of the Biblical expression: "By the waters of Zion, where we sat down, and there we wept, and when we remembered Babylon."

In the U.S., watching media images of the Middle East, one gets the impression that there are only Euro-American Jews in Israel and only Muslim Arabs in the rest of the Middle East. In the media, one finds few images of Palestinian-Israelis or of Iraqi, Moroccan, or Ethiopian Israelis even though we compose the majority of the population in Israel. During the Gulf War, most Israelis interviewed by American reporters tended to be Euro-Israelis, often speaking English with an American accent. The elision was especially striking when the missiles hit Iraqi Jewish neighborhoods in the south of Tel Aviv (television networks referred to "working-class neighborhoods," the equivalent of calling Harlem a working-class neighborhood, effacing its ethnic/racial cultural identity) and in Ramat Gan, a city well known for its Iraqi population, popularly nicknamed "Ramat Baghdad." (A local joke had it that the Scuds fell there because they smelled the *amba*, an Iraqi mango pickle.) Furthermore, some Iraqi Jews living in the U.S., Britain, and Israel still have families in Iraq. The media showed images of prayers in the mosques, and even in the churches of Baghdad, but there was no reference to prayers in the synagogue of Baghdad. In the American context too, it is only the story of European Jews that is narrated, denying Arab Jews the possibility of self-representation.

As an Iraqi Jew, I cannot but notice the American media's refusal to value Iraqi life. The crippled animals in the Kuwait Zoo received more sympathetic attention than civilian victims in Iraq. The media much prefer the spectacle of the triumphant progress of Western technology to the survival of the peoples and cultures of the Middle East. The case of Arab Jews is just one of many elisions. From the outside, there is little sense of our community, and even less sense of the diversity of our political perspectives. Oriental-Sephardic peace movements, from the Black Panthers of the '70s to the more recent East for Peace and the Oriental Front in Israel. Perspectives Judeo-Arabes in France, and the New York-based World Organization of Jews from Islamic Countries, not only call for a just peace for Israelis and Palestinians, but also for the cultural, political, and economic integration of Israel/Palestine into the Middle East. And thus an end to the binarisms of war, an end to a simplistic charting of Middle Eastern identities.

seven

Old and New Identities

–Stuart Hall

Stuart Hall was born in Kingston, Jamaica in 1932 and moved to England 19 years later, where he studied at Oxford University as a Rhodes Scholar. A major figure in cultural studies, Hall, now Retired Professor of Sociology at The Open University, was associated with the Center for Contemporary Cultural Studies at Birmingham University in England for many years. This brief excerpt is from his essay "Old and New Identities," which appears in Culture, Globalization and the World-System, *edited by Anthony D. King and published by the University of Minnesota Press in 1997.*

I was brought up in a lower middle class family in Jamaica. I left there in the early fifties to go and study in England. Until I left, though I suppose 98 per cent of the Jamaican population is either Black or colored in one way or another, I had never ever heard anybody either call themselves, or refer to anybody else as "Black." Never. I heard a thousand other words. My grandmother could differentiate about fifteen different shades between light brown and dark brown. When I left Jamaica, there was a beauty contest in which the different shades of women were graded according to different trees, so that there was Miss Mahogany, Miss Walnut, etc.

Stuart Hall, "Old and New Identities, Old and New Ethnicities," in Anthony D. King, editor, *Culture, Globalization and the World-System: Contemporary Conditions for the Representation of Identity.* Copyright © 1997. University of Minnesota Press. Reprinted by permission.

People think of Jamaica as a simple society. In fact, it had the most complicated color stratification system in the world. Talk about practical semioticians; anybody in my family could compute and calculate anybody's social status by grading the particular quality of their hair versus the particular quality of the family they came from and which street they lived in, including physiognomy, shading, etc. You could trade off one characteristic against another. Compared with that, the normal class stratification system is absolute child's play.

But the word "Black" was never uttered. Why? No Black people around? Lots of them, thousands and thousands of them. Black is not a question of pigmentation. The Black I'm talking about is a historical category, a political category, a cultural category. In our language, at certain historical moments, we have to use the signifier. We have to create an equivalence between how people look and what their histories are. Their histories are in the past, inscribed in their skins. But it is not because of their skins that they are Black in their heads.

I heard Black for the first time in the wake of the Civil Rights movement, in the wake of the de-colonization and nationalistic struggles. Black was created as a political category in a certain historical moment. It was created as a consequence of certain symbolic and ideological struggles. We said, "You have spent five, six, seven hundred years elaborating the symbolism through which Black is a negative factor. Now I don't want another term. I want that term, that negative one, that's the one I want. I want a piece of that action. I want to take it out of the way in which it has been articulated in religious discourse, in ethnographic discourse, in literary discourse, in visual discourse. I want to pluck it out of its articulation and rearticulate it in a new way."

In that very struggle is a change of consciousness, a change of self-recognition, a new process of identification, the emergence into visibility of a new subject. A subject that was always there, but emerging, historically.

You know that story, but I do not know if you know the degree to which that story is true of other parts of the Americas. It happened in Jamaica in the 1970s. In the 1970s, for the first time, Black people recognized themselves as Black. It was the most profound cultural revolution in the Caribbean, much greater than any political revolution they have ever had. That cultural revolution in Jamaica has never been matched by anything as far-reaching as the politics. The politics has never caught up with it.

You probably know the moment when the leaders of both major political parties in Jamaica tried to grab hold of Bob Marley's hand. They were trying to put their hands on Black; Marley stood for Black, and they were trying to get a piece of the action. If only he would look in their direction he would have legitimated them. It was not politics legitimating culture, it was culture legitimating politics.

Indeed, the truth is I call myself all kinds of other things. When I went to England, I wouldn't have called myself an immigrant either, which is what we were all known as. It was not until I went back home in the early 1960s that my mother who, as a good middle-class colored Jamaican woman, hated all Black people, (you know, that is the truth) said to me, "I hope they don't think you're an immigrant over there."

And I said, "Well, I just migrated. I've just emigrated." At that very moment, I thought, that's exactly what I am. I've just left home—for good.

I went back to England and I became what I'd been named. I had been hailed as an immigrant. I had discovered who I was. I started to tell myself the story of my migration.

Then Black erupted and people said, "Well, you're from the Caribbean, in the midst of this, identifying with what's going on, the Black population in England. You're Black."

At that very moment, my son, who was two and half, was learning the colors. I said to him, transmitting the message at last, "You're Black." And he said, "No. I'm brown." And I said, "Wrong referent. Mistaken concreteness, philosophical mistake. I'm not talking about your paintbox, I'm talking about your head." That is something different. The question of learning, learning to be Black. Learning to come into an identification.

What that moment allows to happen are things which were not there before. It is not that what one then does was hiding away inside as my true self. There wasn't any bit of that true self in there before that identity was learnt. Is that, then, the stable one, is that where we are? Is that where people are?

I will tell you something now about what has happened to that Black identity as a matter of cultural politics in Britain. That notion was extremely important in the anti-racist struggles of the 1970s: the notion that people of diverse societies and cultures would all come to Britain in the fifties and sixties as part of that huge wave of migration from the Caribbean, East Africa, the Asian subcontinent, Pakistan, Bangladesh, from different parts of India, and all identified themselves politically as Black.

What they said was, "We may be different actual color skins but vis-à-vis the social system, vis-à-vis the political system of racism, there is more that unites us than what divides us." People begin to ask "Are you from Jamaica, are you from Trinidad, are you from Barbados?" You can just see the process of divide and rule." No. Just address me as I am. I know you can't tell the difference so just call me Black. Try using that. We all look the same, you know. Certainly can't tell the difference. Just call me Black. Black identity." Anti-racism in the seventies was only fought and only resisted in the community, in the localities, behind the slogan of a Black politics and the Black experience.

In that moment, the enemy was ethnicity. The enemy had to be what we called "multi-culturalism." Because multi-culturalism was precisely what I called previously "the exotic." The exotica of difference. Nobody would talk about racism but they were perfectly prepared to have "International Evenings," when we would all come and cook our native dishes, sing our own native songs and appear in our own native costume. It is true that some people, some ethnic minorities in Britain, do have indigenous, very beautiful indigenous forms of dress. I didn't. I had to rummage in the dressing-up box to find mine. I have been de-racinated for four hundred years. The last thing I am going to do is to dress up in some native Jamaican costume and appear in the spectacle of multi-culturalism.

Has the moment of the struggle organized around this constructed Black identity gone away? It certainly has not. So long as that society remains in its economic, political, cultural, and social relations in a racist way to the variety of Black and Third World peoples in its midst, and it continues to do so, that struggle remains.

Why then don't I just talk about a collective Black identity replacing the other identities? I can't do that either and I'll tell you why.

The truth is that in relation to certain things, the question of Black, in Britain, also has its silences. It had a certain way of silencing the very specific experiences of Asian people. Because though Asian people could identify, politically, in the struggle against racism, when they came to using their own culture as the resources of resistance, when they wanted to write out of their own experience and reflect on their own position, when they wanted to create, they naturally created within the histories of the languages, the cultural tradition, the positions of people who came from a variety of different historical backgrounds. And just as Black was the cutting edge of a politics vis-à-vis one kind of enemy, it could also, if not understood properly, provide a kind of silencing in relation to another. These are the costs, as well as the strengths, of trying to think of the notion of Black as an essentialism.

What is more, there were not only Asian people of color, but also Black people who did not identify with that collective identity. So that one was aware of the fact that always, as one advanced to meet the enemy, with a solid front, the differences were raging behind. Just shut the doors, and conduct a raging argument to get the troops together, to actually hit the other side.

A third way in which Black was silencing was to silence some of the other dimensions that were positioning individuals and groups in exactly the same way. To operate exclusively through an unreconstructed conception of Black was to reconstitute the authority of Black masculinity over Black women, about which, as I am sure you know, there was also, for a long time, an unbreakable silence about which the most militant Black men would not speak.

To organize across the discourses of Blackness and masculinity, of race and gender, and forget the way in which, at the same moment, Blacks in the under class were being positioned in class terms, in similar work situations, exposed to the same deprivations of poor jobs and lack of promotion that certain members of the white working class suffered, was to leave out the critical dimension of positioning.

What then does one do with the powerful mobilizing identity of the Black experience and of the Black community? Blackness as a political identity in the light of the understanding of any identity is always complexly composed, always historically constructed. It is never in the same place but always positional. One always has to think about the negative consequences of the positionality. You cannot, as it were, reverse the discourses of any identity simply by turning them upside down. What is it like to live, by attempting to valorise and defeat the marginalization of the variety of Black subjects and to really begin to recover the lost histories of a variety of Black experiences, while at the same time recognizing the end of any essential Black subject?

That is the politics of living identity through difference. It is the politics of recognizing that all of us are composed of multiple social identities, not of one. That we are all complexly constructed through different categories, of different antagonisms, and these may have the effect of locating us socially in multiple positions of marginality and subordination, but which do not yet operate on us in exactly the same way.

Sexual Identities: Western Imperialism?

–Chilla Bulbeck

Chilla Bulbeck is the Foundation Chair in Women's Studies at the University of Adelaide. She holds the only named chair of women's studies in Australia and is part of a three-university women's/gender studies research and teaching community in Adelaide. The selection that follows is from her book Re-Orienting Western Feminisms: Women's Diversity in a Post Colonial World. *It was published by Cambridge University Press in 1997.*

Homosexual Acts and Homosexual Lives

Almost exclusive to the west is the notion of homosexual identity forged through shared lifestyles. With the rise of western individualism, 'perverse' practices increasingly became identities, leading ultimately to the development of gay communities or lesbian lifestyles, so that one became what one did, for example a homosexual (Plummer 1984:234; Foucault 1980:43). By contrast, in ancient China, 'One can *engage* in homosexual, sadistic or masochistic practises; one *is*

From *Re-Orienting Western Feminism: Women's Diversity in a Post Colonial World* by Chilla Bulbeck. Copyright 1998. Reprinted with permission of Cambridge University Press.

not defined as a sadist, a masochist, a homosexual' (Kristeva 1974:63). This distinction adds weight to the claim that gender identity is central in the west's dominant discourses. Furthermore, as Eve Sedgwick (1990:8) points out, it is in fact not the sodomite identity, the hysterical woman or the masturbating child which has emerged as the definition of sexual orientation but the gender of object choice. So central is (hetero)sexual identity that the defence 'homosexual panic' has been developed, a pathological psychological condition possibly brought on by homosexual advances. A woman approached by a man cannot plead 'gender panic', and nor can one plead 'race panic' when one beats black (or white) people (Sedgwick 1990: 18–19).

Although a central identity, the identity based on sexual orientation is much more open to ambiguity and rearrangement than identities founded on ethnicity or biological sex, for example (but perhaps not class, which is not considered) (Sedgwick 1990:34). While ambiguity makes sexual orientation identity more performative in the postmodern sense, it also makes it harder to prove, so that a response to coming out is often 'How do you know you're really gay?' (see Sedgwick 1990:75–89). Sedgwick's (1990:68) examples also demonstrate that, although western societies contain homosexual subcultures, they also contain intense homophobia and contradictory attitudes to the expression of a gay identity. Courts in the United States rule that one is allowed to be gay, but sometimes as long as you do not tell anyone, at other times as long as you warn prospective employers; at some times as long as you keep it in the bedroom where it belongs, at other times as long as you do not do certain acts even in the bedroom (for example sodomy is outlawed in a number of states). Such confusion and homophobia is a result of two contradictory beliefs, sometimes held simultaneously: that there is a distinct population of persons who are 'really gay' and that all sexual identities have aspects of both same-sex and cross-sex desires. The latter is sometimes repressed and expressed in a scapegoating of the 'really gay' (Sedgwick 1990:36–8, 84–9).

Stephen Murray's (1992) cross-cultural survey identifies four forms of homosexuality, in addition to the lifestyle choice variety attributed to the west. Only three will be discussed here since the fourth form, homosexual acts purely to earn money, adds little to explorations of masculinity. Age-graded homosexuality is part of a rite of passage to manhood in which young boys graduate to male roles in the homosexual exchange. Profession-defined homosexuality occurs among performers and prostitutes who cross-dress or cross-gender as part of their occupations. Examples include shamans, dancing boys, transvestite singers and prostitutes, and the actors of the Noh and Kabuki theatres in Japan from the fourteenth century (Murray 1992:119–22; Kaplan and Rogers 1990:222–4). In the third form, the man who takes the 'passive' (insertee) role is defined as committing a homosexual act but not the man who takes the 'dominant' (inserter) role. We will explore the relationship of these different forms of homosexuality to masculinity.

Age-graded homosexuality means that older men have sexual relations with younger men, often to mark passages in the younger men's lives or as part of a wider mentoring role. Historically age-graded homosexuality has been discovered in ancient Athens, China, Byzantium and medieval Persia (Adam 1986:22). Its most famous contemporary manifestation in ethnographic accounts is in the Papua New Guinea Highlands. Once considered all of a piece, homosexual practices differ, basically between highly ritualised and age-graded homosexual encounters, for example among the Kiman (Gray 1986:55, 61) to more intimate, apparently loving relations among the Big Nambas or Orokaivans (Jackson 1991:81). One question asked from a western perspective is whether men derive erotic pleasure from these rituals. While some observers suggest they do (Adam 1986:29; Moore 1993:138), one Sambian informant discussed his embarrassment at his preference for homosexual encounters when he was culturally expected to feel 'fear and shame'. He was unable to form a lasting relationship with any of the four wives he was assigned (Herdt 1992:50–9), which points to the expectation that age-graded homosexuality is something men do because of ritual, not something they are because of sexual orientation. Melanesian homosexuality has been explained along monstrous feminine lines (Adam 1986:25; Jackson 1991:81; Strathern 1988:89–114), although sometimes inflected with men's awe and respect for women's birth-giving powers (Strathern 1988:98–100). Such justifications for age-graded ritual homosexuality would explain the absence of ritualised female homosexuality. According to one observer, 'the only relatively clearly documented instance of "institutionalized" lesbianism in Melanesia comes from Malekula Island in the New Hebrides' (Murray 1992:397).

Generally profession-defined homosexuality has involved younger boys and older men in all-male cultures, like the Buddhist monks and samurais in Japan from the ninth century and the monasteries of Europe in the eleventh century. Although Buddhist monks described homosexual love as *shudo*, short for 'way of the gods' (Murray 1992:xvi–xxv), commentators say it was clearly eroticised (Jackson 1991:78–9). 'China boasts a longer continuous recorded history of male homosexuality than any other nation', dating back to 722–221 BC, and including male brothels, homoerotic art and stories of tender and erotic relations between emperors and their male lovers (Dynes and Donaldson 1992:xii; Connell 1993:604). The decline in ancient homosexual practices is attributed to the rise of religious or moralistic homophobia, including western influences in more recent times (Dynes and Donaldson 1992:xiv).

As opposed to western cultures, where homosexual acts denote homosexual lives, in some other cultures men may perform homosexual acts without this being a threat to their heterosexual identity. There appears to be considerable cross-cultural convergence that the role of inserter, as opposed to insertee, retains the aura of masculinity. Ritual homosexuality in Melanesia is said to involve a progression from the less desirable subordinate position of insertee or fellator to the dominant position of inserter or fellated, akin to English public schools (Jackson 1991:79, 83). In Brazil a strong distinction is drawn between the *bicha* (which means worm, internal parasite and is also the name for a female animal), who acts as the insertee, and the *macho* or *homem* or *homem mesmo* (man or real man), who acts as the inserter. The *bicha* is dominated like a woman, chooses female occupations and is referred to as *ela* although he has less status than a woman because of biological lack. Sexual encounters between two *bichas* are regarded as deviant and classed *lesbianismo*. For women the terms are *sapato* (big shoe) or *coturno* (army boot) reflecting an unacceptable masculinity (Fry 1986:141–2; Parker 1986:157, 274). On the other hand, among some homosexual subcultures in the anglophone west at least, both inserter and insertee remain masculine. Thus homosexual identity formation among men in Sydney is consolidated around a relationship with the male body (of both self and other). The men are 'very straight' in this sense of valuing masculine bodies (Connell 1992:743).

The studies discussed above focus on male homosexual acts rather than female homosexuality. This may be an artefact of predominantly male observers, who were less likely to be told of lesbian behaviour. Thus a 1951 study found lesbian behaviour in only 17 out of 76 societies, while a 1984 study found lesbian behaviour in as many as 95 cultures, although one-third were Native North American (Blackwood 1986:9). Out of 99 American Indian tribes who kept written records, 88 mention male homosexuality and 20 refer to lesbianism (Grahn 1986:43). It may be that gender ascription was usually less demanding for women, who therefore did not need to escape their destiny in cross-gender roles. Thus the bedarche (see below) has been explained as the American Indian man who cringes from the role of warrior. But women also chose third genders to become hunters or warriors, while others formed erotic attachments to women (Williams 1993:181, 183). It may be that testosterone and morphology have real effects, whatever cultures do to limit and channel them, so that female anatomy dictates no stark choice between passivity and activity (Mead in Blackwood 1986:7). But the terms passivity and activity are culturally loaded, even if we have seen some cross-cultural adherence to this dichotomy.

Another question which can be asked of this literature is whether the distinction between homosexual acts and homosexual lives is as clear as Murray's classification suggests. It can certainly be questioned by the following examples. In Australia, there were three reports in early 1993 of men forced to have oral and anal sex performed on them, while statistics suggest that men are 6.4 per cent of rape victims and 30 to 35 per cent of sexual assault survivors. The assailants are mostly self-identified as heterosexual, for whom the gender of the victim was immaterial (Burdack 1993:148–7). Both Kinsey (Giddens 1990:13) and more recently Shere Hite (1994:290) discovered extensive homosexual encounters between adolescents in the United States. Practices appear to have shifted from mutual masturbation in the 1970s to fellatio in the 1990s, reported by 36 per cent of Hite's respondents, although only a minority kiss. Relatively few boys seemed concerned that these practices might indicate homosexuality, although one said, 'At present, I go to a psychiatrist for help in deciding my sexuality' (Hite 1994:290, 293). Thus in the west, too, it would appear that men can perform 'homosexual' acts without seeing themselves as homosexual.

Perhaps, in societies which do not recognise homosexuality publicly, young men and women engage in more public intra-sex physical contact, which might also be associated with intense friendships (Yu and Carpenter 1991:195 for

Taiwan). At student dances in Beijing in 1991, the men unselfconsciously danced with each other, as did the women; there were a lesser number of mixed-sex couples (see also Thubron 1987:184 for Shanghai; McQueen 1991:49, 123 for Japan). In Hong Kong in 1979, but not in 1991, and only very rarely in Beijing in 1993, young men could be seen walking with their arms around each other's shoulders. Thus the practice does appear to have lessened as homosexuality has achieved some public recognition. One young man in Beijing told me that girls with arms interlinked did not make him think of lesbianism but that physical contact between boys did make him think of homosexuality. Professor Choi Po-king of the Chinese University of Hong Kong confirmed changing male practices in her society, while other Hong Kong women academics noted that, in comparison with Taiwanese women, Hong Kong women were much less effusive, possibly because lesbianism was more overtly recognised (for example see the study by Lieh-Mak et al. 1992:102–3 of Hong Kong women who self-identified as lesbians).

However, in the Philippines, described as 'one of the most tolerant nations on earth' (Dynes and Donaldson 1992:xii), intense same-sex friendships are common, and may be homosexual (Hart 1992b:216–19), although this is not necessarily assumed (Agnes Whiten, interview 1 June 1994). As opposed to Chinese culture, there are clear adult homosexual roles, for both men and women. The terms *bayot* (transvestite man, although cross-dressing is confined to the cities) and *lakin-on* lack the pejorative connotations of homosexuality in the west. *Lakin-on* are women who are tough, flat-chested, muscular, challenge men, have a brave look, ride horses or plough fields; they mostly 'only love women' and wear tight-fitting men's trousers. They pick up young college girls and may stab men who try to get too close to them (Whitam 1992:236–7, 242; Hart 1992a:204–9). Young girls may also become 'tomboys' or *callaheras* (girls who love to roam the streets) (de Dios 1994:31), engaging in physical fights and playing boys' ball games. Of one such tomboy, a neighbour said to her mother, 'You were not gifted with a boy child but you had a boy within you' (Del Douglas, interview 21 June 1994).

This review of the literature on homosexual practices reveals that a sharp distinction between westerners 'having' homosexual identities and non-westerners 'doing' homosexual acts does not cover the complexity of practice. But it may well be the case that homosexual subcultures are more prolific in western nations, particularly in large cities. Thus it is claimed that in Turkey, despite a long history of pederasty, only in Istanbul is there a homosexual subculture; elsewhere in the Islamic world homosexuality is defined as taking the receptor role (Dynes and Donaldson 1992:x–xi). In Japan there were no gay bars until the American occupation; homosexuality has 'remained something that men do, rather than something they become' (Murray 1992:368). According to Dennis Altman (1992:37),

> in many Third World cities—Bangkok, Rio de Janeiro and Mexico City above all, but also in Soweto, Seoul and Santiago—there are a number of men (though fewer women) who conceive of themselves as 'gay', as we use that term. However, they probably make up a smaller proportion of the homosexually active population than is true in, say, Sydney, Hamburg or Toronto.

In Brazil, under white western influences, homosexuality has changed from the appellation of *bicha* and *sapato* (still common in the countryside) to be defined as a sickness, as occurred in America and Britain at the turn of the century (discussed above). From the late 1960s, homosexuality was increasingly conceived as a chosen lifestyle (Fry 1986:151; Parker 1988:277; Parker 1986:158), indicated by new labels, *homens* and *entendidos* (literally those who know, and have adopted a gay identity). An *entendido* may be either passive or active in sexual encounters but is 'fundamentally homosexual in terms of his sexual object choice' (Parker 1986:158).

Neo-Confucian, Mongol, Manchu and western proscriptions against homosexuality repressed it from the language if not the practice of prerevolutionary China. Thus, lacking the term homosexual, one of Amy Tan's (1991:350–1) semi-fictional informants uses *zibuyong* meaning 'something like "hens-chicks-and-roosters"' to describe a man who she later understands was possibly gay. While the communist regime was also puritan in matters of sex, by the late 1980s a group of Chinese men, speaking the forbidden language of homosexual desire, expressed their needs in western terms: the right to express their sexuality, freedom to interact with other homosexuals, and a medical scientific explanation for their condition. But their letters also express romantic yearnings: 'The pain in my heart makes me extremely despair', the desire for 'a strong man [to] lie right next to me', as well as misogyny, distaste for women's bodies and their 'irrationality, gossiping, cursing, dependency' (Ruan and Tsai 1992:181, 182, 183).

In Thailand a translation of customary transvestite practices has produced drag shows which borrow heavily from western associations with homosexuality, for example Marilyn Monroe as a gay icon (Hardacre and Manderson 1990:33–4), while a blending of western and traditional Thai tropes has produced 'gym-toned Thai gay men' and *gay-quing*, a sexually versatile homosexual whose partner is a 'Gay-queen'. However, categories are distinguished in terms of masculine or feminine gender position, construed largely in terms of active or passive homosexuality and applying both to the definition of gay women and men (Jackson 1996:110, 115, 117–18).

While these appear to be examples of western sexual identities 'invading' eastern subjectivities, the invasion is built on indigenous understandings and practices of sexuality. In some countries these understandings once confined homosexuality to the role of the insertee, as in South America; in other countries homosexuality has been connected with particular professions, as in the Noh and Kabuki theatres; in other countries there are roles for women and men who choose not to follow the usual feminine and masculine role prescriptions, as in the Philippines. It is to this issue that we now turn, to investigate the idea that sexual identities are more fluid in some non-western cultures, thus providing a challenge to the construction of dualistic identities in the west's dominant discourses. This requires us to consider two assertions: that there is something like a 'third gender' in some non-western cultures, and that western sexual identities are organised around rigid dualisms like man and woman, gay and straight.

Third Genders

> Anthropologists have never assumed that the western concepts of the person and the self are universal, and, almost uniquely among academic disciplines, they have the data to show that this is the case.
>
> —Moore 1994a:29

The term gender identity was invented in the United States and is not found in other cultures (Nanda 1990:138). It suggests both the centrality of gender to one's identity and the fixed nature of that identity. Robert Stoller defines 'core' gender identity as an identity established early in life, although one which may be discrepant with the biologically given sex (Stoller 1968:30–5, 40; Hausman 1992:296). 'I am a male' suggests biological signals, while 'I am manly' is a more subtle and complicated response to social cues. Thus male transvestites retain the core gender identity of a man, but male-to-female transsexuals (the vast majority are male to female) have a core gender identity as women. The concept of 'core' gender identity refers us to humanist notions of the self, a single individual without ambiguity or contradiction. The term would clearly be criticised by postmodernists who focus on gender performance. It is also criticised by social constructionists like Connell (1994), who notes that gender identity is accomplished not only individually but also socially.

The significance of western sexual identities is suggested by the widespread belief that only the very old or very young would choose to be celibate. Indeed women beyond their childbearing years are offered hormone replacement therapy so they can retain their sexual appeal (described by one doctor as their very 'personality' being at stake: in Sybylla 1990:98). Rigid bifurcation also seems to characterise western sexual identities: body/mind, male/female, homosexual/heterosexual. Within these oppositions, western feminists in the 1970s developed another dualism, a distinction between sex as a biological attribute of the body and gender as a social construction of the mind. Thus surgical and other medical intervention in babies maintains a clear biological sex for those born with ambiguous characteristics (Kessler 1990:10), and without which the inevitable question, 'Is it a boy or a girl?,' must provoke discomfort. For Tahitians, by contrast, sexual identity is so insignificant that the sex of newborn infants may not be related as a part of the information which describes the birth (Nanda 1990:141). In much of island Southeast Asia, one does not ask how many brothers and sisters a person has but how many younger and older siblings (Errington 1990:50).

Corrective surgery is also offered to the male-to-female transsexual, but only on condition that s/he demonstrates that he always was a woman inside. The operation is thus performed to reveal 'true' sexual identity (Nanda 1990:143, 138; Raymond 1980), which must not include 'lesbianism, feminism or anal sex', although it appears that clinics are now less rigid in this regard, responding more to 'perseverance and consistency' than appropriate identification as feminine (Lewins 1995:94, 96). Legal access to passports, bank accounts and so on is also denied in a woman's name unless surgery is undertaken to make a 'functional woman'. A functional woman is defined by the fact that her vagina can accept three fingers and thus presumably a penis, aligning 'functional woman' with 'sexual utility' (McColl 1995:51–2, 48, 52).

Male-to-female transsexuals do not usually see themselves as a third sexual category; they are women, and may spurn self-help groups during their liminal stage as a hindrance to this new identity (Nanda 1990:138; see also Hausman 1992:293; Lewins 1995:97–8, who however notes that half the transsexuals in his sample had some association with support groups). But some of them also see that being a woman is a performance, just as being a man required 'pretending' to be male. However it is not pretending or passing to which they aspire, but invisibility, *really* 'being' a woman (McColl 1995:51; Lewins 1995:111). They also understand that gender is inscribed on the whole body rather than merely in the genitals (Lewins 1995:126, 125).

In most traditional societies, and in western society in former times, there were jobs or roles for men and other roles and jobs for women. One did not have to be 'essentially' a woman or man in terms of looks or temperament because the social role defined one's sex. Furthermore, the roles in which one acted may be at least as important as the sex enacted within them. Thus 'a woman acting in the capacity of sister is quite different from a woman acting in the capacity of wife', so that there is not a strong sense of 'the' status of women or their collective definition in contrast to men (Errington 1990:7 for some parts of island Southeast Asia). In such societies, neither biological determinism (sex) nor social constructionism (gender) prevails, but rather women and men are basically the same, although women 'tend not to become prominent and powerful' because of their social activities. Thus a 'Wana woman who becomes a powerful shaman has not broken the rules but beaten the odds' (Errington 1990:40, although Atkinson 1990:84, 90–3 suggests that men's genitals give them a biological edge in becoming shamans). But where there are no specific activities for men and women, sexual difference must perhaps be asserted through notions of essential difference between the sexes. These may be expressed hierarchically — men are superior to women — and driven home with physical force as men become more anxious about the dissolution of gender-role segregation (Johnson 1988;123; Jaggar 1994:144; Moore 1994a:33, 37, 47). In contrast is the acceptance in some cultures of lesbian relations, as long as women also perform their socially assigned role of motherhood (see for example Gandhi and Shah 1992:327 for India; Williams 1993:88 for southern Mexico; and Duncker 1992:70 discussing Audre Laude for the older African-American generation).

Furthermore, the western 'folk model' or 'local philosophy' of identity-formation sees the body as the source and locus of identity, which carries the authentic and 'interior self' (Moore 1994a:47, 33). The body is used to express sexual difference. Homophobic sexuality is expressed in 'poofter-bashing' and heterosexual superiority in physical aggression (on the roads, in bikie gangs, in some cases against women who do not know their place) (Connell 1991:159, 167 for Australia; Kopytoff 1990 for the United States; James and Saville-Smith 1989:14 for New Zealand). In contrast with western preoccupation with the body, 'many of the differences which concern people around the world are internal to bodies, that is within them rather than between them' (Moore 1994b:82–3), and may be shared by both male and female bodies. This is sometimes expressed in the construction of third genders.

It is claimed that some societies allow a third gender, a status which is that of neither man nor woman, and not homosexual either, but 'a distinct and autonomous social status on par with the status of men and women' (Roscoe 1994:370). Ambiguous sexuality or sexual identities are inscribed in Indian religion. Shiva can be both ascetic and erotic; his *linga* or phallus is set in the *yoni* or female symbol; he is often united with his female half or *shakti*. Ancient Hinduism identified a third sex internally divided into four categories (Nanda 1990:20–1). In India today the third sex of *hijras* are a religious community of men who undergo an operation in which the penis and the testicles are removed but no vagina is constructed. The ceremony mimics elements of a woman's wedding (Nanda 1990:26). Dressed in women's clothing, *hijras* perform ceremonies and dances at weddings, at temple festivals, and to celebrate the birth of a child. The dances involve 'an aggressively displayed female sexuality' (Nanda 1990:5). They are also homosexual prostitutes, and may be in social terms wives, mothers or grandmothers (Nanda 1990:xv–xvi). *Hijras* are neither man (because they have demonstrated their impotence and had their genitals removed) nor woman (because they lack the capacity to give birth and act outrageously in ways inappropriate for ordinary women) (Nanda 1990:26, 15–18).

Similarly, in Polynesian societies, like Tahiti, Hawaii, New Zealand, the Marquesas Islands (as well as the *fa'afafine* in Samoa), *mahus* have been described as a 'kind of third entity' who do women's work, and have sex with men. *Mahus* are assumed to be born thus, but can cast off the role 'as one can discontinue being a chief'. In Hawaii and Tahiti, *mahus* are distinguished from gay men because they have a spiritual rather than sexual identity (Nanda 1990:134–7). According to Timon Screech (1993), Japanese culture insistently asserted racial purity (apart from the 'honorary' Japanese, the Chinese) and gave more weight to function (or occupation) than to gender: 'If in the West gender is the *primary* and *least mutable* social division, in Japan that role was played by 'function'. In the West it is easier to switch class than gender[;] one can be classless, but to be genderless is impossible. In Japan the reverse was true' (Screech 1993:134). Thus the Japanese word for person, *hito*, is genderless; Buddhists and monks were accounted neither as men nor women but simply as 'clerics', although the function from which they hailed was always noted in biographies. Where homosexuals and others were categorised as cross-gendered or confused, the *kagema* were 'gender-added boys', an extra gender catering for the sexual desires of either men or women, including monks who were debarred from consorting with women (but could consort with *kagema* because this did not question monks' severance of family ties). The *kagema*, it appears from the evidence, always took the passive role and often wore the purple headcover worn by the female-impersonators of the Kabuki. Thus Screech sees the monks as a third gender where other interpretations describe this as profession-defined homosexuality (see above). This example points to the significance of the gaze through which cultural practices are understood, as does the example of the *xanith*.

In Oman, an Islamic society, the *xanith* (meaning impotent, effeminate, soft) do not undergo castration and have all the legal rights of men. But they dress as women, perform women's household chores and join women on festive occasions, in gossip and at meals (all forbidden to men). *Xanith* are homosexual prostitutes, a role perhaps made necessary by the high moral standard imposed on women (Garber 1992:349). In sexual encounters *xanith* take the passive role, which is considered the woman's role. At any time they can choose to become 'real' men, marrying and proving their virility by displaying a bloodied handkerchief after the wedding night (Wikan 1992; Nanda 1990:130–1; see also Williams 1988:258–9). Unni Wikan who described the *xanith* in 1977, called them 'transsexuals' because they wore some female and some male clothing, and were juridically and grammatically men but took on the woman's sexual position. However, Garber (1992:349, 351) asks whether the term 'transsexual', coined in 1949 to describe the condition of certain European and Anglo-American men, can be translated 'back into a culture which had been closed to the outside world (by Wikan's account) until 1971'.

This question must be asked of all cross-cultural analysis. To describe these third genders as 'homosexual' or 'transvestite' is to neglect the context in which they construct and perform their sexuality. They take on socially inscribed roles rather than gender identities (Moore 1994b:83, 91). Physical characteristics are the sign or effect of sexual difference rather than the cause of gender identity. Morphology is a consequence (not a cause) of behaviour, which then has its own consequences. 'Third gender' roles do not necessarily require a same-sex sexual orientation. Examples include the *bedarche* role for men in American Indian societies who could marry a woman and still remain a *bedarche* and the Chinese sisterhoods of silk weavers who initially took husbands (Blackwood 1984; Williams 1993:186). Neither are these third-gender roles a humanist insistence on revealing one's 'true' sexual inclination nor a dualist insistence on being either a man or a woman. Thus the *mahu* and *xanith* can throw off their roles and become men.

Instead, according to Moore, in traditional cultures 'gender identity' is 'performative' rather than 'categorical' and 'fixed' as in the west (Moore 1994b:91). Does this mean that we can explain such gender roles appropriately within postmodernist discourse? And does this mean that genders are fluid among the postmodernist cognoscenti of the west, performed in a variety of combinations? While 'gender benders' like Boy George have become popular and accepted in the west, their fascination *is* as benders of gender, who remain 'really' either male or female, a point Marjorie Garber (1992:390) also makes for transvestism or cross-gender role performance (see also Butler 1993:237). McColl (1995:45) suggests that the cross-dresser expresses anxieties about sex and gender roles 'that arise from the changes that body-building and genetic engineering have wrought on cultural ideas of the "naturalness" of sex and gender'. Thus gender bending is bound to the dualisms of male and female, heterosexual and homosexual, even as it challenges the widely assumed connections between body and gender.

Finally, western feminists have made their own attempts to disrupt dualisms like male and female, mind and body, gender and sex. Genevieve Lloyd (1989:20–1) suggests that the mind is the 'idea of the body', and so is also 'sexed' by the body which gives it sense impressions (see also Gatens 1991:25). Luce Irigaray recommends that women envisage their sexuality as 'These Two Lips Which are Not One'. Where men know their sexual pleasure comes from one solitary organ, women feel it coming from two sides, and many places. Women's 'two lips' which 'are one and two *simultaneously*' produce a new representation of women's sexuality. Not having 'one', a penis, may not mean having 'nothing' as Freud suggested. Rather it may mean having one and more than one at the same time (Grosz 1989:115, 116). Similarly some lesbians have rejected what they see as essentialist or humanist explanations for becoming lesbian, explanations which require them to conform to 'monogamous' and 'motherly' heterosexual tropes of femininity. In the 1980s, and influenced by postmodern ideas, a 'queer' self-definition was proposed as a challenge to the fixed and opposite identities produced within and against heterosexuality, asserting practices which destabilise both the female body and masculine identity (Martin 1992:109).

To summarise, while there clearly is a greater fluidity of sexual identity in some cultures, very possibly connected to a lesser salience of sexual identity, in all the examples discussed here sexual relations and gender roles are at issue. Societies have developed different ways of negotiating sexual difference, so that in some societies the sexes are very different and in others less so; in white western culture gender seems more mechanically built on the body, while in other cultures roles serve to support gender. In societies less focused on sex, especially sex defined in binary dualisms, third genders allow for a more fluid and changing expression of role performances which are not centrally gender performances, as such gender bending appears to be in the west. We will explore these issues a little further in the Conclusion, but first let us return to the claim made of homosexual lifestyle choices, that, as with economic and political invasion, contemporary colonialism involves the invasion of the very subjecthood of those dwelling in post-colonies.

Sexual Identities Invade the Interior of Colonised Subjects?

'How do you know these things?' she gasped. 'Porn', he informed her gravely. 'I study the porn magazine'. She laughed. Thank God for pornography, then, she thought, in the absence of holy erotic temple sculptures, we need secular inspirations.

—Inez Baranay 1995:352 *describing a white woman and a
Balinese man's sexual encounter*

As with the constructions of 'effeminate' Asian and hyper-masculine Latino machismo masculinities, some women of colour are seen as too passive, some too promiscuous. The white woman is seen as at the centre, a reasonable self-possessed balanced sexuality. Clearly 'other' cultures are no strangers to sexual practice or sexual discussions, as the above analysis has revealed. To pose the question of this section is to ask, not whether sex is discussed, practised, enjoyed, but whether it is constructed in terms which reveal the influence of western obsessions with sexual identity or western medicalisation of sex as *scientia sexualis*. Kalpana Ram (1991:92) claims that a 'colonial subjectivity' arises from the invasion of the west into the very 'interiority' of the colonial subject (see also Nandan 1992:196 for the South Pacific nations). Thus when Ted Turner launched CNN, he claimed that 'we're gonna take the news and put it on the satellite . . . and we're gonna bring world peace, and we're gonna get rich in the process'. The culture-makers of women's magazines in the west are market researchers and advertisers. They are selling commodities like clothing and make-up in particular ways, as an expression of freedom, individuality, leisure, international sophistication, heterosexual attractiveness and even premarital expression, ideas which apparently challenge the conventional social order in countries like India, China and Japan (Rosenberger 1996:2, 24 speaking of women's magazines in Japan). But are the watchers and readers of western images mere passive recipients of a promised bag of goodies where democratic values and consumerist desires are indistinguishable? Two case studies reveal the hybridisation of sexual identities in China, Singapore, India and Japan.

Little Honeys in China: Prostitutes or Concubines?

In 1991 a student class in Beijing presented a skit which contrasted western sexual desire (represented by a male) and eastern reticence and modesty (represented by a female). During the May Fourth Movement particularly, Chinese intellectuals grappled with western concepts, adopting neologisms for society, culture, intellectuals, individualism. A sexological perspective also suggested a new word for woman, *nüxing*, literally 'female sex' but suggesting 'sex opposition and sex attraction'. *Nüxing* was deemed unsuitable by communist writers, who saw it as 'febrile' and indicating 'bourgeois women's preoccupations'. They invented the 'kin-inflected category of' *funü*, a womanhood achieved through 'revolutionary practice' (Barlow 1994:263–9). With the easing of communist ideological control, *nüxing* has reappeared, but now suggests 'biologically inferior', subject to romantic love, pertaining to gender psychology and so on (Barlow 1994:277).

From a western perspective, the asexual nature of Chinese society struck me forcibly when I was there in 1979, so that I suffered my own version of 'gender vertigo' (Connell 1990:470–1). Professor Wang Jiaxiang, while comfortable using the English words for 'the lower part of the body', rarely reads or says those words in Chinese. Foreign literature translated into Chinese is censored of the explicit sexual scenes, as are the movies. One of my friends, a woman in her mid-twenties, suffered considerable embarrassment when I asked her to translate the Chinese terms for various methods of contraception (this required her to use terms like condom, IUD, sterilisation and, most difficult for her, *coitus interruptus*). This may be a function of marital status or personality, as another of my friends of the same age, but married, blithely told me about the unreliability of free government-made condoms available from clinics. In 1991 tales of illegitimate pregnancies and students' affairs with married men were communicated in hushed and horrified tones. By 1993, however, Chinese-language newspapers were bemoaning the phenomenon of 'little honeys'. These women, often college-educated, become mistresses of Chinese businessmen (often from Taiwan or Hong Kong). Some are calculating and save enough money for a comfortable retirement when replaced. Others fall in love and commit suicide when their lover loses interest in them. The same mixture of responses seems to characterise the 'Chinese girlfriends' of the young (and sometimes not so young) western bucks who teach in Beijing's universities. Some girlfriends say they are open-eyed, but are willing to risk their virginity for a chance, however slight, to emigrate to the west. Some deeply regret falling in love and giving up their virginity in a lost cause. Aware of women's calculus in sexual matters, some young Chinese men complain of the growing demands by girlfriends for material tokens in exchange for sexual favours ('We throw our money after them . . . Sometimes my friends spend *half a month's salary* on one meal. That's to get the girls to do what they want': Thubron 1987:60–1).

Clearly sexual practices and orientations have changed in China; superficially they have become more 'westernised'. Thus in classes for newlyweds, instructors now suggest that women can approach the relationship as a source of enjoyment and not merely a duty, while commercialised and eroticised images of the female body are becoming more common (Evans 1995:383, 389), as are abortions among unmarried women, at least in Beijing and Shanghai (Xiao et al. 1995:245). Ding Xiaoqi (1991:112) bemoans the trend towards divorce, women demanding orgasms (ten years ago a survey suggested that 97 per cent of women never experienced orgasm), wearing bikinis and entering the fashion industry, attracted by 'the allure of the self-expression involved in this profession'.

Additionally since the 1980s, sexual issues are dealt with in 'scientific' discourses, in sexual disorder clinics, in marriage guidance counselling, in research on 'sexual psychology' and sexual crime (like 'peeping toms'), in sex education for adolescents (Xiao 1987:17; Fennell and Jeffry 1992:20–1; Lin Shiwei, 'Centre Solves Problems that are all in the Mind', *China Daily* 26 October 1993:5). On the other hand, young women told me that 'true equality', such as they believe western women have, makes women deny their real essence: their femininity and their dependence on men. Thus although there is now greater emphasis on sexual self-definition, and some of it arises from western influences, Chinese femininity is still a thing apart, drawing on a history of romantic tragedy, concubinage and the competent revolutionary woman as well as on western fashions.

Women's Magazines in Singapore and India[1]

The standard of female beauty as white, western and wealthy is promulgated by magazines like *Cosmopolitan*, which is translated into seventeen languages (Chapkis 1994:230). In white society largeness is no longer associated with largesse but with lack of self-control (Bordo 1990:94), and there are signs that these new meanings of ample figures are seeping into the minds of younger middle-class women in other cultures. Today Maori tourist shows concentrate on 'fineness and fairness, along with an affected delicacy of movement' instead of the 'big women, really big, and graceful' who once performed 'forceful dance styles'. These gifted performers have internalised Pakeha myths that they are 'too fat', 'too black' or need to shave their legs (Awekotuku 1991:92, 132–3). Indrani Ganguly's (1992:2–3) survey of immigrants to Australia found that many upper-class Argentinians believed women were ideally 'slim' or 'thin', although Tongan women disagreed. Vietnamese women thought a 'flat, thin' body the ideal, although a little more weight after marriage was a good sign: 'A moon face is the sign of graciousness' (Ganguly n.d.:17). Fair skin was considered preferable by women from most countries surveyed, in contrast with an acquired darker skin preferred by Anglo-Australians and Argentinians. Some Vietnamese women favoured cosmetic surgery to make their eyes look 'more western' (Ganguly 1992:3).

There is both cultural resistance and accommodation to white western standards of beauty in this sample of immigrants to Australia. Thus western standards are often integrated with traditional images. In Singapore *Her World* reproduces glamorous images of women who are recognisably Asian but who are 'Europeanised' in terms of low-cut attire, make-up and eye shape. In October 1994 ('If I Were a Young Woman', *Her World* 1994:117–26), a number of leading Singapore women gave advice to young women. These women were bank vice-presidents, company managing directors, senior public servants and professional women. They advised young women on how to combine motherhood and career, both being deemed an expected part of a woman's life (although only one adviser suggested life might be possible without marriage and motherhood). Younger women were advised to use the government's matchmaking agency, to use condoms if engaging in premarital sex, to deliver their babies normally (some women choose Caesarean sections because they think normal delivery loosens muscles and produces a 'less exciting sex life') and to use HRT in menopause (from Mary Rauff, gynaecologist, *Her World* 1994:125). Readers were also advised to 'stay away from heavy make-up', 'chunky accessories—and gold, gold, gold' and to 'Change your spectacle frames every year' (Sylvia Lian, *Her World* 1994:125). Indirect methods of conflict resolution were suggested, for example accepting that an argument with mother has been forgiven if she warms up your dinner when you come home, or leaving your husband in charge of the household for a while if he denigrates the way you run it (Esther Tzer Wong, *Her World* 1994:118). While Singaporean female university students want more equally shared housework and family decision-making, they phrase this not in terms of 'love' but 'mutual respect' and mutual obligations (Lyons 1994:3–4).

The ideal woman on Delhi television is as charming as western women, but she produces sons to ensure patriliny, engages in traditional rites and rituals and dies unsullied, if abandoned (Krishnan and Dighe 1990:51–2). A deviant male does not care for the family, puts self above community and country, is violent towards women, is not an income earner and allows his wife to dominate him (Krishnaraj and Chanana 1990). An article on 'Modern Day Marriages' in the Indian magazine *Feminina* (its masthead declaring it to be 'For The Woman of Substance') notes the influence of western thinking in marriage choice. Religion and lineage have been displaced for 'interpersonal vibes', education, financial independence and emotional responsibility for oneself (Ritu Bhatia in Sand 1994:18). Such marriages may be preceded by living together and end in divorce or single parenthood. In a current affairs magazine, an article entitled 'The Changing Woman' describes women who 'are becoming the kind of men they wanted to marry' (Jain 1992:36). Changing women include fourteen airline pilots of Indian Airlines, deans of hospitals, politicians who made it without the help of male political relatives, and the 130,000 women in 1988–89 who set up small-scale industries. Prahlad Kakkar notes that films and women's magazines like *Savvy* encourage more explicit sexual talk of 'the need for sexual fulfilment', 'impotence and perversions', 'adultery, wife abuse and her sex life', and women's willingness to ask for what she wants in love-making (Jain 1992:41, 43).

Sexually degrading representations of women have been attacked—literally with eggs, cowdung and tar thrown at offending billboards. Women's movement activists have engaged in critiques of beauty contests and 'chick charts' and 'uglies' lists drawn up by male students at a college in Delhi (Gandhi and Shah 1992:69, 75, 50). When two women police constables married in a Hindu ceremony, most women's groups refused to comment publicly beyond saying it was a personal matter, possibly fearing a backlash. There was much private discussion, but Nadita Gandhi and Nandita Shah (1992:158) ask, 'Why have we not been able to discuss the compulsory nature of heterosexuality, non-penetrative sexual methods and lesbianism?' Is it cultural reluctance or a belief that these issues are far removed from the daily struggle of most Indian women? One answer is that mainstream Indian political life (as in many countries in both west and east) more readily accommodates women's interventions in defence of the dignified or victimised woman, as attacks on pornography suggest, rather than producing an Indian woman who seeks sexual expression apart from men (Rajan 1993:136–8).

To some Chinese observers, western constructions of sexuality are overdetermined, focused on the romantic dyad and constantly verbalised (Sun 1991:12, 28, 11; Chen Zhingming et al. 1990:113). The same point is made for Japan, where most people distinguish the fleeting nature of romance (expressed in extramarital affairs by both sexes) from the long-term arrangement of marriage (Iwao 1993:111, 61). In contrast, the demands placed on an American marriage must make it 'full of sustained tension and energy, which could be quite strenuous'. A good Japanese marriage, on the other hand, is 'like air', vital for survival but hardly felt (Iwao 1993:77, 75). Women hope for the 'three highs' in marriage: high income, higher education and physical height (Iwao 1993:67), but not high love.[2] As with the Chinese reluctance to discuss personal matters, in Japan putting feelings into words is thought to diminish them so that there is much reading between the lines (Iwao 1993:98). The divorce rate is rising as in China, but remains well below the United States rate (1.26 per cent compared with 4.8 per cent: Iwao 1993:113). The pressures on marriage in Japan include women's greater financial independence, and greater assertiveness and impatience with men who are 'bright and well educated, gentle and kind, but vulnerable and spoiled' (Iwao, 1993:273–4). But the generation educated after World War II has taken on some notions of dyadic companionship, so that a lecture series, School for Bridgegrooms, trains men in how to be 'good husbands and wise fathers' (Iwao 1993:66–7), while more young couples marry for love or companionship, wives expecting husbands to share leisure interests and childrearing (Imamura 1996:3). Seven men have formed a men's liberation movement which offers a critical reading of the heroic samurai and addresses the problems of the early-dying overworked salary-man (Connell 1994). Some men have become primary carers of children; some seek new family-oriented roles as they worry about their future after retirement; some have formed the Association of Men Opposed to Prostitution in Asia. Such men tend to be viewed as 'oddities, "drop-outs" from the competition for success, or as traitors to the male sex' (Yamaguchi 1995:253).

The history of colonialism, the seductive power of media images from the west, and the alignment of material commodities with progress, means that western images probably have an advantage over indigenous ones. Both invasion and hybridisation are at work in the powers of persuasion and resistance across cultural borders. Western forms of sexual identity and expression are derided, devalued or transformed. Commitment to kin connections rather than the exclusive love dyad, to rational calculations in sexual exchanges rather than helpless romanticism, and to indigenous styles of fashion and beauty persist.

Conclusion: Post-Sex

> The seeds of hegemony are never scattered on barren ground. They might establish themselves at the expense of prior forms, but they seldom succeed in totally supplanting what was there before.
>
> —*Comaroff and Comaroff 1991:25*

The so-called third genders of non-western societies are made up of elements of male and female roles and biologies. They are not something entirely different, like kangaroos for example. Similarly, postmodernists do not, on the whole, suggest that westerners should challenge gender identities by presenting asexual images. If this were so, Madonna would hardly be one of the most written-about icons of sexual disruption. Thus she stops short of outright contestation of sexuality as a mechanism of desire (Kaplan 1993:161, 155). Nor do postmodernists suggest that instead of defining ourselves through our sex we choose another medium, for example our spirituality. To indigenous people in Australia, 'humans are more spirit than matter'. Women in white western culture are so defined by their sexual being that rape is a total abnegation of their selfhood. For Murris, while rape is not pleasant, it does not violate a woman's spirit (Watson 1994). Indeed, speaking of women reclaiming the monstrous feminine but perhaps equally applicable to gender performances like Madonna's, Marina Warner (1994;11) is sceptical of women's power to perform their sexuality in parody: 'these postmodern strategies all buckle in the last resort under the weight of culpability the myth has entrenched'. Like Victorian attempts to repress sex, attempts at inversion merely magnify the demons of female pollution or the significance of sex in our lives.

Thus white western women and men might learn something about the sexual prison in which they construct their identities from considering other attitudes towards sex, many of which are far more liberating than the compulsive obsession with youth, looks and sexual activity in the west (at least for women who lack these!). Just as western sexualised images invade Japan, China and Singapore, so too have Japanese gay and lesbian groups appropriated the erotic histories of homosexual practices by monks or actors to explore their sexual identities and expressions. Instead of their preoccupation with sexual identity, westerners might also consider the performative aspects of gender flexibility which suggest that sexual practice and orientation can be picked up and put aside, and is often a relatively insignificant definition of the self in society. Perhaps, too, western society is developing its own mechanisms for moving beyond the requirements of compulsive sexual expression. 'Post-sex', possibly provoked by the threat of AIDS but also interpreted in the light of postmodernist ideas, does not view sex with disgust, as did the medieval Christians, but rather with 'a trendy indifference' (Arcand 1994:241). Post-sex also suggests a lighthearted attack on sexual preoccupation while allowing greater space for other avenues of identity construction—spiritual, kin-related, cerebral, and so on.

NOTES

1.   My thanks to Lenore Lyons-Lee and Indrani Ganguly for providing me with the magazines on which this section is based.

2.   A comparative survey of American and Japanese couples reveals these differences. Where 84 per cent of American men and 87 per cent of American women rated being in love as very important, only 67 per cent of Japanese men and 68 per cent of Japanese women did so (Iwao 1993:70).

BIBLIOGRAPHY

Note: Books cited by surname and short title only occur in full elsewhere in the bibliography. Chinese names are generally used with family name first. In the text Chinese authors have been cited in full because the small number of Chinese family names would make them difficult to distinguish; where a name appears in the Bibliography without a comma between family and given names, that is the order which appears in the original work.

Adam, Barry D. (1986) 'Age, Structure, and Sexuality: Reflections on the Anthropological Evidence on Homosexual Relations', *Journal of Homosexuality* 11(3/4):19–33

Altman, Dennis (1992) 'AIDS and the Discourses of Sexuality' in R. W. Connell and G. W. Dowsett, eds, *Rethinking Sex: Social Theory and Sexuality Research.* Melbourne: Melbourne University Press

Arcand, Bernard (1994) *The Jaguar and the Anteater: Pornography Degree Zero*, transl. Wayne Grady. London: Verso [first published Montreal, 1991]

Atkinson, Jane Monnig (1990) 'How Gender Makes a Difference in Wana Society' in Jane Monnig Atkinson and Shelly Errington, eds, *Power and Difference: Gender in Island Southeast Asia.* Stanford: Stanford University Press

Atkinson, Jeff (1995) 'Child Labour', *Horizons*, newsletter of Community Aid Abroad, 3(4):8–9

Awekotuku, Ngahuia Te (1991) *Mana Wahine Maori: Selected Writings on Maori Women's Art, Culture and Politics.* Auckland: New Women's Press

Baranay, Inez (1995) 'The Edge of Bali' in Robyn Gerster, ed., *Hotel Asia: An Anthology of Australian Literary Travelling to Asia.* Melbourne: Penguin

Barlow, Toni E. (1994) 'Theorizing Woman: *Funü, Guojia Jiating*' in Angelo Zito, ed., *Body, Subject and Power in China.* Chicago: University of Chicago Press

Barrett, Michèle (1992) 'Words and Things: Materialism and Method in Contemporary Feminist Analysis' in Michèle Barrett and Anne Phillips, eds, *Destabilizing Theory: Contemporary Feminist Debates.* Cambridge: Polity Press

Blackwood, Evelyn (1986) 'Breaking the Mirror: The Construction of Lesbianism and the Anthropological Discourse on Homosexuality', *Journal of Homosexuality* 11(3/4):1–18

Bordo, Susan (1990) 'Reading the Slender Body' in Mary Jacobus et al., eds, *Body/Politics: Women and the Discourses of Science.* New York: Routledge

Brettell, Caroline B. and Carolyn F. Sargent (1993) 'Gender, Ritual and Religion' in Caroline B. Brettell and Carolyn F. Sargent, eds, *Gender in Cross-Cultural Perspective.* Englewood Cliffs, New Jersey: Prentice Hall

Burdack, Mark (1993) review of *Male Victims of Sexual Assault* by Mezey and King, eds, *Alternative Law Journal* 18(3):146–8

Butler, Judith (1993) *Bodies That Matter: On the Discursive Limits of "Sex".* New York: Routledge

Chapkis, Wendy (1994) 'Skin Deep' in Alison M. Jaggar, ed., *Living With Contradictions: Controversies in Feminist Social Ethics.* Boulder, Col.: Westview Press

Chen Zhingming, Wang Xiao'ou and Chang Yuemin (1990) 'The Melting Pot and the Mosaic: A Comparison of Americans and Canadians' in Wang Jianguang, *Westerners Through Chinese Eyes*

Comaroff, Jean and John Comaroff (1991) *Of Revelation and Revolution: Christianity, Colonialism and Consciousness in South Africa* vol. 1. Chicago: University of Chicago Press

Connell, Robert W. (1990) 'A Whole New World: Remaking Masculinity in the Context of the Environmental Movement', *Gender and Society* 4(4):452–78

Connell, Robert W. (1991) 'Live Fast and Die Young: The Construction of Masculinity among Young Working-Class Men on the Margin of the Labour Market', *Australian and New Zealand Journal of Sociology* 27(2):141–71

Connell, R. W. (1992) 'A Very Straight Gay: Masculinity, Homosexual Experience, and the Dynamics of Gender', *American Sociological Review* 57(6):735–51

Connell, R. W. (1993) 'The Big Picture: Masculinities in Recent World History', *Theory and Society* 22:597–623

Connell, R. W. (1994) 'Masculinities: The Big Picture', seminar presented to Department of Anthropology and Sociology, University of Queensland, 28 October

de Dios, Aurora Javate (1994) 'Triumphs and Travails: Women's Studies in the Academy' in Lazarus et al., *Women's Studies, Women's Lives*

Ding Xiaoqi (1991) 'Feminism in China', *Asian Studies Review* 15(1):111–13

Duncker, Patricia (1992) *Sisters and Strangers: An Introduction to Contemporary Feminist Fiction*. Oxford: Blackwell

Dynes, Wayne R. and Stephen Donaldson (1992) Introduction to Wayne R. Dynes and Stephen Donaldson, eds, *Lesbianism*. New York: Garland

Dynes, Wayne R. and Stephen Donaldson, eds (1992) *Asian Homosexuality*. New York: Garland

Errington, Shelly (1990) 'Recasting Sex, Gender and Power: A Theoretical and Regional Overview' in Jane Monnig Atkinson and Shelly Errington, eds, *Power and Difference: Gender in Island Southeast Asia*. Stanford: Stanford University Press

Evans, Harriet (1995) 'Defining Difference: The "Scientific" Construction of Sexuality and Gender in the People's Republic of China', *Signs* 20(2):357–94

Fennell, Vera and Lyn Jeffry (1992) 'To Increase the Quality of Women: A Preliminary Assessment of Women's Studies in Beijing'. Beijing: Ford Foundation

Foucault, Michel (1980) *The History of Sexuality* vol. 1. New York: Random House [first published in 1976]

Fry, Peter (1986) 'Male Homosexuality and Spirit Possession in Brazil', *Journal of Homosexuality* 11(3/4):137–53

Fujimura-Fanselow, Kumiko and Atsuko Kameda, eds (1995) *Japanese Women: New Feminist Perspectives on the Past, Present and the Future*. New York: Feminist Press

Gandhi, Nadita and Nandita Shah (1992) *The Issues at Stake: Theory and Practice in the Contemporary Women's Movement in India*. New Delhi: Kali for Women

Ganguly, Indrani (1992) 'Cross-Cultural Body Image', *MediaMatters* 2(3):2–3 news-sheet of MediaSwitch Queensland

Garber, Marjorie (1992) *Vested Interests: Cross-Dressing Cultural Anxiety*. New York and London: Routledge

Gatens, Moira (1991) *Feminism and Philosophy: Perspectives on Difference and Equality*. Cambridge: Polity Press

Giddens, Anthony (1990) *The Transformation of Intimacy: Sexuality, Love and Eroticism in Modern Societies*. Cambridge: Polity Press

Grahn, Judy (1986) 'Strange Country This: Lesbianism and North American Indian Tribes', *Journal of Homosexuality* 11(3/4):43–54

Gray, J. Patrick (1986) 'Growing Yams and Men: An Interpretation of Kimam Male Ritualized Homosexual Behavior', *Journal of Homosexuality* 11(3/4):55–68

Grosz, Elizabeth (1989) *Sexual Subversions: Three French Feminists.* Sydney: Allen & Unwin

Hardacre, Helen and Lenore Manderson (1990) The Hall of Mirrors: Sex and the Representation of Asia. Paper prepared for the International Workshop on the Construction of Gender and Sexuality in East and Southeast Asia, University of California, Los Angeles, 9–11 December

Hart, Donn V. (1992a) 'The Cebuano Bayot and Lakin-On' in Murray, *Oceanic Homosexualities*

Hart, Donn V. (1992b) 'Homosexuality and Transvestism in the Philippines: The Cebuan Filipino Bayot and Lakin-On' in Dynes and Donaldson, *Asian Homosexuality*

Hausman, Bernice L. (1992) 'Demanding Subjectivity: Transsexualism, Medicine, and the Technologies of Gender', *Journal of the History of Sexuality* 3(2):270–302

Herdt, Gilbert H. (1992) 'Semen Depletion and the Sense of Maleness' in Murray, *Oceanic Homosexualities*

Hite, Shere (1994) *The Hite Report on the Family Growing Up Under Patriarchy.* London: Bloomsbury

Imamura, Anne E. (1996) Introduction to Anne E. Imamura, ed., *Re-Imaging Japanese Women.* Berkeley: University of California Press

Iwao, Sumiko (1993) *The Japanese Woman: Traditional Image and Changing Reality.* New York: Free Press

Jackson, Graham (1991) *The Secret Lore of Gardening: Patterns of Male Intimacy.* Toronto: Inner City Books

Jackson, Peter A. (1996) 'The Persistence of Gender: From Ancient Indian *Pandakas* to Modern Thai *Gay-Quings*' in Chris Berry and Annamarie Jagose, eds, *Australia Queer.* Special issue of *Meanjin* 55(1):110–20

Jaggar, Alison M., ed. (1994) *Living With Contradictions: Controversies in Feminist Social Ethics.* Boulder, Col.: Westview Press

Jain, Madhu (1992) 'The Changing Woman', *India Today* 15 July:36–43

James, Bev and Kay Saville-Smith (1989) *Gender, Culture and Power: Challenging New Zealand's Gendered Culture.* Auckland: Oxford University Press

Johnson, Miriam M. (1988) *Strong Mothers, Weak Wives.* Berkeley: University of California Press

Kaplan, E. Ann (1993) 'Madonna Politics: Perversion, Repression, or Subversion? Or Masks and/asMaster-y' in Cathy Schwichtenberg, ed., *The Madonna Connection: Representational Politics, Subcultural Identities, and Cultural Theory.* Sydney: Allen & Unwin

Kaplan, Gisela T. and Lesley J. Rogers (1990) 'Scientific constructions, cultural productions: scientific narratives of sexual attraction' in Terry Threadgold and Anne Cranny-Francis, eds, *Feminine/Masculine and Representation.* Sydney: Allen & Unwin

Kopytoff, Igor (1990) 'Women's Roles and Existential Identities' in Peggy Reeves Sanday and Ruth Gallagher Goodenough, eds, *Beyond the Second Sex: New Directions in the Anthropology of Gender.* Philadelphia: University of Pennsylvania Press

Krishnan, Prabha and Anita Dighe (1990) *Affirmation and Denial: Construction of Femininity on Indian Television.* New Delhi: Sage

Krishnaraj, Maithreyi and Karuna Chanana (1990) *Gender and the Household Domain: Social and Cultural Dimensions.* London: Sage

Kristeva, Julia (1974) *About Chinese Women*, transl. Anita Barrows. London: Marion Boyars

Lazarus, Barbara et al., eds (1994) *Women's Studies Women's Lives: Theory and Practice in South and Southeast Asia*. Melbourne: Spinifex Press in association with Kali for Women

Lewins, Frank (1995) *Transsexualism in Society: A Sociology of Male-to Female Transsexuals*. Melbourne: Macmillan

Lieh-Mak, F., K. M. O'Hoy and S. L. Luk (1992) 'Lesbianism in the Chinese of Hong Kong' in Dynes and Donaldson, *Asian Homosexuality*

Lloyd, Genevieve (1989) 'Woman as Other: Sex, Gender and Subjectivity', *Australian Feminist Studies* 10:13–22

Longley, Kateryna O. (1992) 'Fifth World' in Sneja Gunew and Kateryna O. Longley, eds, *Striking Chords: Multicultural Literary Interpretations*. Sydney: Allen & Unwin

Lyons, Lenore (1994) Report on the Feminist Reading Workshop Conducted on the AWARE Premises in December 1993. Unpublished paper

McColl, G. C. (1995) 'Posing: Questions About Cross-Dressing', *Meanjin* 54(1):44–53

McQueen, Humphrey (1991) *Tokyo World: An Australian Diary*. Melbourne: Heinemann

Martin, Biddy (1992) 'Sexual Practice and Changing Lesbian Identities' in Barrett and Phillips, *Destabilizing Theory*

Moore, Clive (1993) 'The Abominable Crime: First Steps Towards a Social History of Male Homosexuals in Colonial Queensland, 1859–1900' in Robert Aldrich, ed., *Gay Perspectives II: More Essays in Australian Gay Culture*. Sydney: Department of Economic History, University of Sydney, with the Australian Centre for Gay and Lesbian Research

Moore, Henrietta L. (1994a) *A Passion for Difference: Essays in Anthropology and Gender*. Cambridge: Polity Press

Moore, Henrietta (1994b) '"Divided We Stand": Sex, Gender and Sexual Difference', *Feminist Review* 47(Summer):78–95

Murray, Stephen O., ed. (1992) *Oceanic Homosexualities*. New York and London: Garland

Nanda, Serena (1990) *Neither Man Nor Woman: The Hijras of India*. Belmont, Calif.: Wadsworth Publishers

Nandan, Satendra (1992) 'Artists and Islands in the Pacific' in Longley, *Striking Chords*

Parker, Richard (1988) 'Youth, Identity and Homosexuality: The Changing Shape of Sexual Life in Contemporary Brazil', *Journal of Homosexuality* 17(3/4):269–89

Parker, Richard (1986) 'Masculinity, Feminity, and Homosexuality: On the Anthropological Interpretation of Sexual Meanings in Brazil', *Journal of Homosexuality* 11(3/4):155–63

Rajan, Rajeswari Sunder (1993) *Real and Imagined Women: Gender, Culture and Post-Colonialism*. London: Routledge

Ram, Kalpana (1991) '"First" and "Third World" feminisms: a new perspective?', *Asian Studies Review* 15(1):91–6

Roscoe, Will (1994) 'How to Become a Bedarche: Toward a Unified Analysis of Gender Diversity' in Gilbert Herdt, eds, *Third Sex, Third Gender: Beyond Sexual Dimorphism in Culture and History*. New York: Zone Books

Rosenberger, Nancy R. (1996) 'Fragile Resistance, Signs of Status: Women Between State and Media in Japan' in Imamura, *Re-Imaging Japanese Women*

Ruan, Fang-fu and Yung-mei Tsai (1992) 'Male homosexuality in Contemporary Mainland China' in Dynes and Donaldson, *Asian Homosexuality*

Screech, Timon (1993) 'Race and Gender? Human Categorisation in Japan' in Sunil Gupta, ed., *Disrupted Borders: An Intervention in Definitions and Boundaries*. London: Rivers Oram Press

Sedgwick, Eve Kosofsky (1990) *Epistemology of the Closet*. Berkeley and Los Angeles: University of California Press

Stoller, Robert J. (1968) *Sex and Gender or The Development of Masculinity and Femininity*. New York: Science House

Strathern, Marilyn (1988) *Gender of the Gift*. Berkeley: University of California Press

Sun, Lung-kee (1991) 'Contemporary Chinese Culture: Structure and Emotionality', *Australian Journal of Chinese Affairs* 26:1–25

Sybylla, Roe (1990) 'Old Plans, New Specifications: A Reading of the Medical Discourse of Menopause', *Australian Feminist Studies* 12:95–107

Tan, Amy (1991) *The Kitchen God's Wife*. New York: G. P. Putnam's Sons

Thubron, Colin (1987) *Behind the Wall: a Journey Through China*. London: Heinemann

Wang Jianguang, ed. (1990) *Westerners Through Chinese Eyes*. Beijing: Foreign Languages Press

Warner, Marina (1994) *Managing Monsters: Six Myths of Our Time: The 1994 Reith Lectures*. Vintage: London

Watson, Lilla (1994) keynote address at the Australian Women's Studies Association Conference: Women and the Politics of Change. Australian Women's Research Centre, Deakin University, Geelong, 4–6 December

Whitam, Frederick L. (1992) 'Bayot and Caliboy: Homosexual–Heterosexual Relations in the Philippines' in Murray, *Oceanic Homosexualities*

Wikan, Unni (1992) 'Man Becomes Woman: Transsexualism in Oman as a Key to Gender Roles' in Dynes and Donaldson, *Asian Homosexuality*

Williams, Walter L. (1993) 'Amazons of America: Female Gender Variance' in Brettell and Sargent, *Gender in Cross-Cultural Perspective*

Xiao Ding (1987) 'Sex Therapy Chalks Up Successes', *Women of China* April:16–17

Xiao Yang et al. (1995) 'An Analysis of Induced Abortions' in Tao Chungfang and Xiao Yang, eds, *Research on Women's Reproductive Health in China*. Beijing: New World Press

Yamaguchi, Masanori (1995) 'Men on the Threshold of Change' in Fujimura-Fanselow and Kameda, *Japanese Women*

Yu, Lucy C. and Lee Carpenter (1991) 'Women in China' in Leonore Loeb Adler, ed., *Women in Cross-Cultural Perspective*. Westport, Conn.: Praeger.

Questions for Thinking, Writing, and Discussion

1. Do you think Albert Memmi's definition and analysis of racism can be applied to other forms of oppression? Try applying his analysis to sexism, heterosexism and homophobia, or classism, and discuss the ways in which it is useful and/or the ways in which it is not applicable.

2. What does Zillah Eisenstein mean when she writes "because people grow othered by their racialized, sexualized, engendered bodies, bodies are important to the writing of hatred on history."

3. How does Zillah Eisenstein's discussion support or challenge Memmi's analysis of racism?

4. How does Philip Gourevitch's account of the ethnic reengineering of Rwandan society support or challenge Memmi's analysis of racism? How does it support or challenge Eisenstein's account of the process of "othering" and writing hatred on the body?

5. According to Eleanor Stein, what have been the consequences of constructing Arabs, South Asians, and Muslims as "the other" in the United States?

6. Do some research to find out how the press depicted Japanese Americans during World War II and how they portrayed Arabs, South Asians, and Muslims during the Gulf War and after 9/11, and then write an essay in which you discuss the similarities and differences in these portrayals.

7. Using the essays by Chandra Mohanty, Ella Shohot, and Stuart Hall, write an essay in which you reflect on your sense of self and discuss the various factors that come into play in shaping your own sense of who you are and where you feel at home.

8. Chilla Bulbeck argues that sexual identities are constructed, not given. Explain what this means and agree or disagree with her.

9. Does Bulbeck make a good argument for her claim that "sexual identities are more fluid in some western cultures, thus providing a challenge to the construction of dualistic identities in the West's dominant discourses"? Discuss in some detail.

10. What are the implications of the West's preoccupation with dualistic sexual identities for the creation of difference. Use this notion to discuss Eisenstein's essay.

Suggestions for Further Reading

Butler, Judith P. *Bodies That Matter: On the Discursive Limits of "Sex."* New York and London: Routledge, 1993.

Eisenstein, Zillah. *Hatreds: Racialized and Sexualized Conflicts in the 21st Century.* New York and London: Routledge, 1996.

Fausto-Sterling, Anne. *Sexing the Body: Gender Politics and the Construction of Sexuality.* New York: Basic Books, 2000.

Johnston, Allan G. *Privilege, Power and Difference.* New York: McGraw-Hill, 2001.

Mamdani, Mahoud. *When Victims Become Killers: Colonialism, Nativism, and the Genocide in Rwanda.* Princeton, NJ: Princeton University Press, 2002.

Ore, Tracey C. *The Social Construction of Difference and Inequality.* New York: McGraw-Hill, 2002.

Rosenbaum, Karen, and Toni-Michelle C. Travis. *The Meaning of Difference: American Constructions of Race, Sex and Gender, Social Class, Sexual Orientation.* New York: McGraw-Hill, 2002.

Patriarchy and Domination

Patriarchy itself is an expression of socioeconomic oppression.

Nawal El Saadawi

Women do two-thirds of the world's work, yet they earn only one-tenth of the world's income and own less than one percent of the world's property. Human Rights Watch tells us that "millions of women throughout the world live in conditions of abject deprivation of, and attacks against, their fundamental human rights for no reason other than that they are women." Amnesty International calls violence against women "the greatest human rights scandal of our times." In virtually every country in the world women are paid less than men for comparable work. In some parts of the world women still can't own property (in the United States the right to do so is little more than 150 years old), in some countries they are not allowed to drive a car; in other parts of the world they are not allowed to vote; in others they can vote but are disproportionately underrepresented in government. In some parts of the world infant girls are routinely put to death and girl children are sold into sex slavery; they receive less food and less education than their brothers and other male relatives and have less control over every aspect of their lives. In this section of the book we examine the system of domination whereby men have exercised control over women and children throughout much of history and have used their power to their own advantage. That system is called patriarchy.

As we have already seen, the subordination of one group by another requires a rationale that justifies the resulting unequal distribution of resources and opportunity and reconciles those who are subordinated to their position. In the same way that colonialism both invokes and reinforces the doctrine of white supremacy, patriarchy both invokes male supremacy and institutionalizes male privilege. It cites biology or scripture or a combination of both as the justification for gender hierarchy, beginning with the Bible's story that Eve was made from Adam's rib in order to keep him company and serve him. Science is called upon to "prove" that men are superior and hence suited to rule and women are inferior, hence suited to obey. A host of alleged physical and mental "differences" between men and women are cited, which, as in the case of racism, are used to construct all women as "other." Here difference is constructed as deviant, deficient, even pathological. Portrayed as overly emotional, weak, irrational, and a victim of their biology, many women around the globe are consigned by gender difference to a life of dependency and suffering. For women of color who must contend with the power of both patriarchy and white supremacy, the burden is even more onerous and the consequences even more devastating.

What does it mean to claim that societies all over the world, including U.S. society, are organized around patriarchal values and institutionalize male privilege? Does it mean that women *never* occupy positions of power? No, it does not. Does it mean that *all* men are better off than all women in some absolute sense? No, it does not. It does mean that gender privilege is woven into the normal operation of everyday society in such a way that the organization of society and its institutions reflects and perpetuates male power. And it does so quite apart from the desires or intentions of any individual male. Sociologist Allan G. Johnson describes it this way: "In patriarchy, power is culturally gendered in that it is associated primarily with men." He goes on to explain: "This kind of thinking supports a structure that allocates most power to men. In almost every organization, the farther down you look, in the power structure, the more numerous women are; the higher up you go, the fewer women you'll find. That's what a male dominated system looks like."[1]

Of course, the particular privileges or benefits that any man may enjoy or may forfeit depend upon a complex set of interlocking factors such as his race/ethnicity, class, and sexual orientation, along with other variables, for example, religion, age, and physical condition. The same holds true for women. While patriarchy as a system works to the detriment of all women, how it impacts on *individual* women will vary with respect to differences in class, race/ethnicity, sexual orientation, and so forth. For example, a woman who is victim of patriarchy in some respects may be the beneficiary of her own skin privilege and/or of her own or her partner's or husband's class privilege. How patriarchy impacts on the lives of individual women will be the result of many different factors coming together and it is important to bear in mind that an individual may be privileged in some respects but not in others. Insofar as privilege is both complicated and often invisible, it can be a difficult concept to come to terms with.

In Article 1, Gerda Lerner defines patriarchy as a system of rules, customs, and values that institutionalize male control. Lerner suggests that at a certain point in time, women began to function both as a kind of resource for men and as the source of social status for them in ways that paralleled the acquisition of property. She explains this in terms of the commodification of women or, more correctly, the commodification of women's sexuality: the idea that women's sexual and reproductive capacities and services became a commodity or a thing to be controlled and exchanged by men as part of the economic and social relationships between individuals and between tribes. Throughout her discussion of the evolution of gender roles, Lerner pays careful attention to the ways in which gender intersects with race and class and suggests that class is not separate from gender but is itself always expressed in gendered terms.

While the patriarchal family has displayed an amazing ability to assume a variety of different forms at different times and in different places—for example, polygamy in some parts of the world, monogamy in others—Lerner points out that all forms of the patriarchal family have included a double standard for men and women with respect to sexual behavior and that standard always disadvantages women. Further, while in some forms of the family, sexual relations become more egalitarian but economic relations remain patriarchal and in other cases this pattern is reversed, regardless of variations in relations between men and women within the family, men retain their positions of dominance in public institutions and government.

Many of the very characteristics that Lerner ascribes to patriarchy and the patriarchal family are illustrated concretely in the accounts of women's lives on the West Bank that are included in Article 2. In "The Foundation of Gender Identity: *Garaba*, Relational Connectivity, and Patriarchy," women of different ages, educational backgrounds, and economic status, Muslim and Christian, talk about their lives and the cultural rules and expectations that shape their existence. Cheryl Rubenberg intersperses these first-person accounts with an analysis of the meaning of "identity" and the importance of kinship relations or *garaba* in the Arab world in general. Unlike much of the West, where identity is about becoming an individual, in the Arab world and in many other cultures, identity is about "relational connectivity" or group membership. Rubenberg maintains that understanding the connection between patriarchy and kinship is crucial to understanding the relations, roles, and hierarchies that exist within these societies. Here patriarchy is reflected and reinforced in every social institution and decisions about every aspect of a woman's life are made within the web of patriarchal kinship connectivity.

While some in the West may find it easy to recognize and deplore the operation of patriarchy in the lives of some Arab women, it may be more difficult for them to recognize the role of patriarchy in daily life closer to home. In Article 3, "Gender, Race, and Class in Silicon Valley," Karen Hossfeld examines the role of patriarchal ideology in the on-the-job exploitation of women workers in California. Among the techniques used to control these workers is a work culture predicated on traditional gender roles. By encouraging women workers to identify with their femininity rather than their role as workers, management uses traditional patriarchal values to devalue the women's sense of their own productive worth, making it easier to pay them low wages. The patriarchal assumption that the man is and should be the breadwinner in the family, an assumption shared by many of the married women and their husbands, also makes it easier to pay women less. As with women on the West Bank, Hossfeld's discussion of factory work in Silicon Valley points out that if a woman earns more than her husband or partner, it can destabilize a relationship and provoke a violent response from a man if he believes that this undermines his manhood. Hossfeld's article provides numerous other examples of the way management uses patriarchal values in the workplace to control women workers in the interest of keeping wages low and profits high.

In "Daughters and Generals in the Politics of the Globalized Sneaker," Article 4, Cynthia Enloe explores this same theme by examining the ways in which corporations like Nike, Reebok, Adidas, and Puma, which began moving their factories off shore in the 1970s, have used local constructions of femininity to cheapen women's labor throughout the developing world. Enloe focuses most of her attention on the production of sneakers in South Korea beginning in the 1970s and traces the changes in conceptions of femininity encouraged by the Seoul regime and their impact on women's labor. In order to encourage young women on small farms to migrate to cities, where they became part of the industrialization of South Korea, the government encouraged them to see themselves as patriots. At the same time, they encouraged parents of young women to redefine the appropriate behavior expected of a "respectable daughter" and a "respectable woman" in order to make it compatible with the new labor-force needs of industrialization. Enloe's analysis takes us through a series of changes in the prevailing conception of femininity that were generated and manipulated by both the government and corporations in order to keep women's labor costs low. At the same time, she acknowledges and describes some of the interests and strategies that the women workers themselves brought to the process.

Enloe's account ends with the shift of sneaker production from Korea to Indonesia when the Korean government decided to redirect production from light (feminized) to heavy (masculinized) industry. As a result of this decision, factory women lost their jobs and the state used its power to modify the prevailing cultural definition of "femininity" once again to help reconcile these jobless women to their new status. For a parallel account of how the prevailing conception of femininity was modified in the United States during and after World War II in order to move women into the workforce when men went to war and then out of the workforce when the men came home and wanted their jobs back, see Chapter 2 of Betty Friedan's *The Feminine Mystique*.

According to the World Health Organization's report on "Violence Against Women," Article 5, at least 1 out of every 5 women in the world has been physically or sexually abused at some point in her life by some man or men. A recent report issued by UNICEF suggests that the figure is closer to 1 in 2. These studies show that domestic violence is the most common form of violence experienced by women. In fact, the WHO report documents the reality that "a woman is more likely to be injured, raped, or killed by a current or former partner than by any other person." The role that violence plays in subordinating women around the world can be inferred from the list of acts of violence that are directed against women and girls at every stage of the life cycle that are enumerated in the report. While cataloguing this violence, which has reached epidemic proportions, the report also faults governments around the world for their response to it. By adopting definitions of what constitutes a crime that generally reflect patriarchal values, governments around the world are complicitous both in failing to identify acts of violence against women as crimes and in failing to prosecute these attacks. As the articles in this section make clear, shame, fear of reprisal, or both are among the major factors that keep women from reporting domestic violence and seeking help.

Article 6, "Culture of Honor, Culture of Change," offers us an analysis of one of the most extreme forms of violence practiced against women—honor killings. Honor killings are acts of murder in which a woman is killed by family members, based on an allegation, suspicion, or proof that she has engaged in immoral behavior. Such "immoral behavior" has a wide range of definition. Honor killings have been carried out against women who have gone to the movies without permission, refused to submit to an arranged marriage, married against their family's wishes, or failed to serve a meal on time, or against women who have "allowed themselves" to be raped. In this article, Aysan Sev'er and Gökçeçiçek Yurdakul examine the dynamics of honor killings in Turkey within the context of a patriarchal system. In a challenge to those who blame honor killings on the teachings of the Muslim religion, they report that their study failed to demonstrate a clear or direct connection between Islam and such crimes and suggest that it is a cultural understanding of honor rather than a religious one that is invoked by those who kill. They suggest that social change and globalization are factors that are responsible for an increase in honor killings, as women around the globe are bombarded with images of a different life than the one they have always known. Although this article focuses on honor killings in Turkey, such killings have been reported in Afghanistan, Bangladesh, Great Britain, Brazil, Ecuador, Egypt, India, Iraq, Iran, Israel, Italy, Jordan, Pakistan, Morocco, Sweden, and Uganda and undoubtedly occur elsewhere in the world as well.

The last two articles in this section take up a topic that is touched upon earlier in the WHO Report (Article 4) as well, the increased violence against women during armed conflict and in refugee situations. In "The Connection Between Militarism and Violence Against Women," Article 7, Lucinda Marshall suggests that a key element that underlies this violence is the process by which women are defined or constructed as "other" in a way that demeans and dehumanizes them. Here it may be useful to refer back to Zillah Eisenstein's account of writing hatred on the body that appears in Part Three, as well as Albert Memmi's account of how groups are "othered." Because, as we have already seen, women in patriarchal society are often viewed as possessions of men, the rape and brutalization of women in war is often carried out as part of the attack on male combatants and their honor.

In Article 8, "The Impact of Political Conflict on Women: The Case of Afghanistan," by Sima Wali, Elizabeth Gould, and Paul Fitzgerald, we are asked to consider the condition of women refugees worldwide. Statistics show that the majority of refugees and displaced persons in the world are women and that these women suffer life-long trauma as a result. Written from a public health perspective, this essay uses the case of Afghanistan to look at the impact of war and displacement on women and to make a plea for efforts to understand the relationship between the humanitarian disasters that marked the last decade of the twentieth century and that now characterize the beginning of the twenty-first and the political circumstances that have caused them. Unlike previous articles that situate violence against women exclusively in the context of culture, this article asks us to look at the political decisions that have been made by governments and transnational agencies and recognize how they have created the humanitarian crises that mark our world.

NOTE

1. Allan G. Johnson, *Privilege, Power and Difference*. (Mountain View, CA: Mayfield, 2001), p. 97.

The Patriarchial Family

–Gerda Lerner

Gerda Lerner was born in Vienna, Austria, in 1920. Forced to flee the Nazis during World War II, Lerner settled in the United States. In 1958, at the age of 38, she returned to college and received her Ph.D. in history from Columbia University in 1966. A pioneer in the field of women's history, Lerner's discussion of the patriarchal family is taken from her book The Creation of Patriarchy, *which was published by Oxford University Press in 1987.*

Patriarchy is a historic creation formed by men and women in a process which took nearly 2500 years to its completion. In its earliest form patriarchy appeared as the archaic state. The basic unit of its organization was the patriarchal family, which both expressed and constantly generated its rules and values. We have seen how integrally definitions of gender affected the formation of the state. Let us briefly review the way in which gender became created, defined, and established.

The roles and behavior deemed appropriate to the sexes were expressed in values, customs, laws, and social roles. They also, and very importantly, were expressed in leading metaphors, which became part of the cultural construct and explanatory system.

* * *

The patriarchal family has been amazingly resilient and varied in different times and places. Oriental patriarchy encompassed polygamy and female enclosure in harems. Patriarchy in classical antiquity and in its European development was based upon monogamy, but in all its forms a double sexual standard, which disadvantages women, was part of the system. In modern industrial states, such as in the United States, property relations within the family develop along more egalitarian lines than those in which the father holds absolute power, yet the economic and sexual power relations within the family do not necessarily change. In some cases, sexual relations are more egalitarian, while economic relations remain patriarchal; in other cases the pattern is reversed. In all cases, however, such changes within the family do not alter the basic male dominance in the public realm, in institutions and in government.

"The Creation of Patriarchy," from *The Creation of Patriarchy* by Gerda Lerner, copyright © 1986, 1987 by Gerda Lerner. Used by permission of Oxford University Press, Inc.

The family not merely mirrors the order in the state and educates its children to follow it, it also creates and constantly reinforces that order.

It should be noted that when we speak of relative improvements in the status of women in a given society, this frequently means only that we are seeing improvements in the degree in which their situation affords them opportunities to exert some leverage within the system of patriarchy. Where women have relatively more economic power, they are able to have somewhat more control over their lives than in societies where they have no economic power. Similarly, the existence of women's groups, associations, or economic networks serves to increase the ability of women to counteract the dictates of their particular patriarchal system. Some anthropologists and historians have called this relative improvement women's "freedom." Such a designation is illusory and unwarranted. Reforms and legal changes, while ameliorating the condition of women and an essential part of the process of emancipating them, will not basically change patriarchy. Such reforms need to be integrated within a vast cultural revolution in order to transform patriarchy and thus abolish it.

The system of patriarchy can function only with the cooperation of women. This cooperation is secured by a variety of means: gender indoctrination; educational deprivation; the denial to women of knowledge of their history; the dividing of women, one from the other, by defining "respectability" and "deviance" according to women's sexual activities; by restraints and outright coercion; by discrimination in access to economic resources and political power; and by awarding class privileges to conforming women.

For nearly four thousand years women have shaped their lives and acted under the umbrella of patriarchy, specifically a form of patriarchy best described as paternalistic dominance. The term describes the relationship of a dominant group, considered superior, to a subordinate group, considered inferior, in which the dominance is mitigated by mutual obligations and reciprocal rights. The dominated exchange submission for protection, unpaid labor for maintenance. In the patriarchal family, responsibilities and obligations are not equally distributed among those to be protected: the male children's subordination to the father's dominance is temporary; it lasts until they themselves become heads of households. The subordination of female children and of wives is lifelong. Daughters can escape it only if they place themselves as wives under the dominance/protection of another man. The basis of paternalism is an unwritten contract for exchange: economic support and protection given by the male for subordination in all matters, sexual service, and unpaid domestic service given by the female. Yet the relationship frequently continues in fact and in law, even when the male partner has defaulted on his obligation.

It was a rational choice for women, under conditions of public powerlessness and economic dependency, to choose strong protectors for themselves and their children. Women always shared the class privileges of men of their class *as long as they were under "the protection" of a man.* For women, other than those of the lower classes, the "reciprocal agreement" went like this: in exchange for your sexual, economic, political, and intellectual subordination to men you may share the power of men of your class to exploit men and women of the lower class. In class society it is difficult for people who themselves have some power, however limited and circumscribed, to see themselves also as deprived and subordinated. Class and racial privileges serve to undercut the ability of women to see themselves as part of a coherent group, which, in fact, they are not, since women uniquely of all oppressed groups occur in all strata of the society. . . .

Women have for millennia participated in the process of their own subordination because they have been psychologically shaped so as to internalize the idea of their own inferiority. The unawareness of their own history of struggle and achievement has been one of the major means of keeping women subordinate.

The connectedness of women to familial structures made any development of female solidarity and group cohesiveness extremely problematic. Each individual woman was linked to her male kin in her family of origin through ties which implied specific obligations. Her indoctrination, from early childhood on, emphasized her obligation not only to make an economic contribution to the kin and household but also to accept a marriage partner in line with family interests. Another way of saying this is to say that sexual control of women was linked to paternalistic protection and that, in the various stages of her life, she exchanged male protectors, but she never outgrew the childlike state of being subordinate and under protection.

Other oppressed classes and groups were impelled toward group consciousness by the very conditions of their subordinate status. The slave could clearly mark a line between the interests and bonds to his/her own family and the ties of subservience/protection linking him/her with the master. In fact, protection by slave parents of their own family against the master was one of the most important causes of slave resistance. "Free" women, on the other hand, learned early that their kin would cast them out, should they ever rebel against their dominance. In traditional and peasant societies there are many recorded instances of female family members tolerating and even participating in the chastisement, torture, even death of a girl who had transgressed against the family "honor." In Biblical times, the entire community gathered to stone the adulteress to death. Similar practices prevailed in Sicily, Greece, and Albania into the twentieth century. Bangladesh fathers and husbands cast out their daughters and wives who had been raped by invading soldiers, consigning them to prostitution. Thus, women were often forced to flee from one "protector" to the other, their "freedom" frequently defined only by their ability to manipulate between these protectors.

The Foundation of Gender Identity
Garaba, Relational Connectivity, and Patriarchy

—Cheryl A. Rubenberg

Cheryl A. Rubenberg is an independent analyst and a former associate professor of political science at Florida International University. The article that follows is an excerpt from her book Palestinian Women: Patriarchy and Resistance in the West Bank, *which was published by Lynne Rienner Publishers in 2001.*

I've worked since I got married. I love working and I love my job. If I stay at home it's as if I've dropped out of life. Getting out of the house gives me opportunities for different ways of seeing the world. Working is very important for women. It builds character and gives a woman self-esteem. . . . If my husband told me to stop working I would accept his decision passively and stay at home. I might try to talk with him gently but I wouldn't carry it further than that because I wouldn't want it to reach the stage of divorce. The problem, you see, isn't just between my husband and me; the problem is the whole society. If I were to go to my parents and complain in such a situation, everyone—my father, my brothers, my uncles—would tell me that the issue [of my working] is my husband's responsibility. He is the man of the house. It's his right to make all decisions concerning me, I shouldn't even try to discuss his decision with him, and I should be contented at home. This is not the way I think it should be, but it doesn't matter what I think, it's much bigger than me. Here the norm of male dominance is extremely strong—no matter what class, educational level, social or geographic location, it's the same, and it's overwhelming.

—Rasha, 28, married with three children, camp resident, "moderately religious" Muslim, tawjihi plus two-year diploma

A battered woman couldn't tell any of her friends or neighbors, much less her children, because of the community. We live with the community. I have a sister who was beaten black and blue every day by her husband. Once he pulled all her hair out and once he punched her eye out. Even I didn't know about any of this for many years— he's an educated man. But she was quiet and patient, and little by little, over the years, he began to appreciate her and to behave better with her. If a woman were to speak about violence outside, the man would react even more violently. And, instead

Chapter 3 from "Women as Individuals: The Structure, Shaping and Maintenance of Women's Gendered Identities," from *Palestinian Women: Patriarchy and Resistance in the West Bank* by Cheryl Rubenberg. Coyright 2001. Reprinted by permission of Lynne Reinner Publishers.

of helping him as she should, she would be damaging him by tarnishing his and his family's reputation. If the man or his family heard about her talk, she would be severely punished by both. Remember, most of the marriages here link families together. So if she hurts her husband and his family, she hurts herself and her family. This means that women must keep their mouths shut. Do I think this is right? It doesn't matter what I think. This is our society. I suffer. I sacrifice. But this is the life God gave me so I accept it.

— Marwa, 45, married with three children, village resident,
"very religious" Christian, tawjihi

Our marriage is very difficult. My husband beats me nearly every day. He doesn't like me — he was forced to marry me as I was forced to marry him. I tried to talk to my family about my problems when we were first married but all that accomplished was creating more problems, especially with his family. So I decided not to tell anyone about my problems — just to keep them to myself . . . I don't even see my parents anymore . . . I don't know what God wants from me but to be honest, I don't care anymore. I don't care anything about my husband. All I care about is to have children and to take care of them.

— Nada, 17, married, pregnant with twins, camp resident,
"not very religious" Muslim, completed sixth grade.

Marriage. Work. Violence. Silence. The voices of Rasha, Marwa, and Nada from three different decades, both Muslim and Christian, bring to life the dynamics of women in West Bank society and some of the dilemmas they face. . . .

The Foundation of Gender Identity: *Garaba*, Relational Connectivity, and Patriarchy

In the West Bank (and the Arab world in general), identity signifies something quite different than it does in Western societies. Identity among camp and village women is firmly grounded in *garaba* (kinship) and in the connective web of relations that bonds kin groupings together.[1] In the West, we experience the individuating (separating) process; in Palestinian society, identity is experienced as "relational connectivity." Palestinians live and conceptualize their lives not as individuals but as members of a family group. Kinship relations give rise to identity through relationality and connectivity within the family group. As Suad Joseph explains, "Relationality is a process by which socially oriented selves are produced under different regimes of political economy. . . . In the Arab world . . . various forms of relationality are highly valued and institutionally supported."[2]

Building on the concept of relationality, Joseph further expands our understanding of kinship dynamics by refining it in the concept of "connectivity." Connectivity involves relationships in which a person's personal boundaries are relatively fluid so that the individual understands her "self" to be constituted by "significant others" — overwhelmingly patrilineal agnates — that is, paternal relatives. Connectivity, Joseph argues, should be understood as an activity or intention (rather than a state of being) that acts to reinforce family solidarity.[3] Thus, in the first moment, kinship is deeply inscribed in identity; and relationality is intertwined with patriarchy so that connectivity is structured into a system of domination and subordination.[4]

Apprehending the connection between patriarchy and kinship is crucial to the comprehension of all the relations, roles, and hierarchies growing out of kinship in this particular social environment. Patriarchy involves "the privileging of males and seniors and the mobilization of kin structures, kin morality, and kin idioms to legitimate and institutionalize gendered and aged domination."[5] It gives rise to a group of ideological principles and social relations that privilege the primacy of paternal agnates in all social, economic, and political associations. These principles, in turn, define individual identity, roles (the gendered division of labor), social practices (such as marriage patterns and the preference for sons), and obligations; they also sanction personal connections.[6] Patriarchy is legitimized by the discourse of "honor and shame."[7]

The basic relations in a patriarchal system are control by, and submission to, those who rank higher in terms of age and gender: duties and obligations are strictly defined along these two axes.[8] They are marked by inequality but legitimized through the concept of "complementarity," which means that while roles and responsibilities are dissimilar and unequal, they are idealized as reciprocal and therefore of equal value. The institutionalization of hierarchies of age and gender signifies that older men have more power than do younger men, and men in general have more power than women.

Patriarchy originates in the family and is reflected and reinforced in every social institution. It gives rise to particular "truths" that distinctly position women and signify to them the "reality" of their situation. Several such truths, here expressed in common proverbs, include: "Women are too emotional, they think from their hearts; that is why men should make all the decisions in the house." "Woman's role in life is to be an obedient wife and good mother." "Women's most important place is in the home—men have the right to go out and do whatever they wish." "Women should not humiliate their husbands by 'talking' outside the home." "Fathers have the right to decide about their daughters' education." "Husbands have the right to determine whether or not their wives may work outside the home." "If a wife disobeys her husband, he has the right to beat her."

Second only to functional hierarchies, "factionalism" is the preeminent dynamic of the *garaba* structure. It involves the fundamental separation of self from other, based on blood ties, and supersedes every other kind of social relation. Factionalism implies that individuals and families will behave differently with relatives than with outsiders (*gharibah*). Within families, ties are permanent and characterized by mutual support, caring, material assistance, individual sacrifice for the family good, and trust. Conversely, distrust, exclusion, competitiveness, suspicion, advantage seeking, a balance in obligations, an absence of concern, and frequent conflict typically mark relations among non-kin.[9]

The village women in my research community tended to regard with suspicion and distrust all *gharibah* women—especially those from within their particular village. This division was more blurred, yet clearly present, in the refugee camps. Non-kinswomen were treated formally and were usually contacted only when there was a very specific reason: weddings, wakes, and other formal occasions in which every village family was expected to participate. In terms of general deportment, my observations suggest that while kinswomen can and do laugh and joke together, dance in each other's company, and may even engage in ribaldry on occasion, in the presence of non-kin women, their behavior is proper and constrained. With regard to the inherent distrust, I often heard a woman exclaim to a sister regarding a visit by a non-kin woman: "What did she want?" "Why do you imagine she came by?" The sense of distrust felt by kinswomen toward non-kin women stems, in part, from the fear of the outsider gaining information about the family that could become gossip and then be used against the family. It is also related, at the most basic level, to the binary distinction between self and other—the factionalism inherent in this particular kinship configuration.

Kinship identity among Palestinian camp and village individuals is conceived of in terms of *hamayel* (clans), an ambiguous construction but roughly defined as a semiorganized collection of extended families (*'ailah*) based on patrilinality from one eponymous ancestor. *Hamayel* are usually, though not always, geographically contiguous. Historically, some Palestinian *hamayel* were large, spreading over several villages, while many were smaller, forming only part of the population of one village. After the *nakba* in 1948, many *hamayel* were widely dispersed—often to distant countries. However, regardless of size or contiguity, *hamayel* were, and in the main continue to be, the fundamental structure in Palestinian sociopolitical organization and the basis of individuals' most significant social connections. Today, *hamayel* are most clearly observed within village society. In the camps, because the population is usually composed of refugees from more than one pre-1948 village, they are less distinct. Nevertheless, even in the camps, social organization, memory, marriage patterns, and other aspects of social life are organized around enduring clan structures as well as memories of village society that existed prior to 1948. This is apparent in women's everyday conversations about their former lives in their original village, in the hierarchy of their present social relations, and in various other ways.[10] Moreover, even when a *hamulah* is widely geographically dispersed, patrilineal affiliational and social ties remain in force.[11]

The *'ailah*, or functionally extended family, has specific characteristics and broad meaning for individuals in this society. Most significant is that kinship relations supersede every other kind of social relation. Kinship constitutes the dominant social institution through which persons or groups inherit their religious, class, and social affiliations, as well as providing security and support in the face of societal distress. Today loyalty and commitment to the family are the minimum expectations of every family member, while family interests almost always transcend those of individuals. In short, the traditional West Bank family constitutes both an economic and a social unit, and all members are expected to cooperate to ensure its continuation and advancement. It is the primary focus of loyalty, allegiance, and identity.[12] Traditionally, its strength and durability has derived from its ability to provide its members with all their basic needs—material, physical, and psychological. However, as a consequence of changing political and economic circumstances since the *nakba*, the Palestinian *'ailah* has become less and less able to meet the economic and security needs of its members, while at the same time and for the same reasons, many individuals have increasingly needed to rely on their clans.

In West Bank camp and village society, family solidarity has been necessary for social, economic, and political survival. The particular political and economic circumstances that have bounded the West Bank in the past century have reinforced connectivity and have made women's choices—even those that support this dynamic—both rational and functional. Nevertheless, patriarchal kinship, in the particular context of West Bank rural village and refugee camp society, is a system for monopolizing resources, maintaining kinship status, reproducing the patriline, controlling women's sexuality and bodies, legitimating violence, and appropriating women's labor. Two women's stories illustrate some of the ways patriarchal kinship affects women.

Mona grew up in a refugee camp in Jordan and was 18 and living in a refugee camp in the West Bank when I talked with her. Mona's father's family was originally from Ramale. They became refugees in 1948; some family members migrated to West Bank camps while others, like Mona's father, went to Jordanian camps. Mona had completed her secondary education with a 98 percent average, passed the *tawjihi*, and had been accepted at the University of Jordan, where she intended to study medicine. During the summer before she was to start, the wife of one of her father's brothers came to Jordan from the West Bank for a visit. When she saw Mona, she decided Mona would be a perfect bride for her son. Over Mona's objections, the marriage contract was written—without the bride ever having seen her soon-to-be husband. Her aunt promised Mona's father that Mona could continue her education once she married and came to the West Bank. But the promises were not written into the marriage contract since the prospective husband was "family"—he and Mona are patrilateral parallel cousins—and it would have been socially shameful to question the family's word (honor) by requiring such a stipulation. The wedding party was set for two months hence; however, before the appointed time, Mona learned that her husband had been in prison for a violent criminal offense. She wanted to break the engagement but her father refused, insisting that she proceed with the marriage. He argued that since the marriage contract had been signed, if Mona backed out then, she would be considered a divorced woman with all the attendant negative connotations.

Mona had been married for ten months and was three months pregnant when we spoke. She described herself as an "observant" (Muslim) and in a "poor" economic situation. Since she married, she has not seen any of her family in Jordan. She could not even phone them, as there are few telephones in either camp and none in either family's home. Her mother-in-law forced her to leave the nursing school in the camp in which she had enrolled before coming to the West Bank. She did not allow Mona to leave her (the mother-in-law's house where she and her husband lived in one room) without either the mother-in-law or a sister-in-law in accompaniment. Additionally, Mona stated that she had been regularly beaten by her mother-in-law and forced to do all the housework. The physical distance and formalities involved in international travel made a temporary return to her natal home extremely difficult. Divorce was even more out of the question, especially since her husband did not want one. Should she go to court seeking a divorce, a Sharia judge would have inevitably refused her petition because her situation did not fall within any of the legal definitions that allow women to initiate divorce. Further deterrence came from her father's opposition since he did not want the shame that he would incur having agreed to give Mona to his brother's son. Mona cried throughout the interview but ended by saying: "I guess my situation isn't that unique. I simply have to learn to be patient and accept it."

Mona's story is a poignant illustration of the geographically wide-ranging consequences of patriarchal connectivity for women. It is a particularly revealing example of the meaning of the functionally extended family. Felicia's situation is also highly relevant in this context. Though all her paternal relatives reside in one village, her story captures very concisely the dynamics of gender, identity, kinship, and patriarchal connectivity and the negative consequences this matrix of constructs can have on women. Felicia is a 27-year-old mother of three, a village resident who completed *tawjihi*. She is employed as a caregiver in a child daycare center and is an "observant" Muslim, in a "poor" economic situation.

> *I was 20 when I got married; I had just completed my first year of university and wanted to continue. My cousin* [father's brother's son] *was released after four years in prison from the intifada. I didn't know him but I accepted him as a husband—it was a traditional marriage. But I wanted to finish university before I married. My husband wanted to get married right away. He promised to let me finish my education, and my father didn't want to anger his older brother, so he insisted I do what my cousin wanted. I wanted to write in my marriage contract that I could continue my education but my father said no, that it was unnecessary because it was all in the family and it would appear that we didn't trust his word. After we got married—I got pregnant right away—he told me to leave the university. He said I could choose either to continue studying or to stay with him, but not both. He also said there was no reason for me to go on studying because he would never permit me to work. So I left the university. Then there were serious problems between my father and my husband's father* [they are brothers] *over the inheritance my grandfather left them, and their quarrel had a serious negative impact on my relationship with my husband. I also had many problems with my in-laws from the beginning of the marriage. My aunt* [mother-in-law] *used to beat me and shout bad words at me and humiliate me. Many times I went back to my family in despair. My first son was born in my parents' home. Once I stayed with my family for eight months and took a decision not to return to my husband. But the families interfered, especially my father who said I had to go back, because the family problems would get worse if I didn't. . . . Yes, my husband beat me*

frequently when we were first married, but now since I've come back the last time
things are a little better. . . . I've been working for six years but only because our eco-
nomic circumstances are so bad and because his mother said yes, and so he said okay.
I don't mind the job; the pay isn't much, what I like most is getting out of the house
and away from the family problems. My husband is seldom able to find work and we
need my income, small as it is, just to feed the family. I do all the housework, child
care, cooking, and cleaning. My husband refuses to do anything—he expects me to
wait on him totally. My mother-in-law doesn't help me—I have to help her. My father
and father-in-law are still quarreling and my mother-in-law still treats me badly, but
I've learned to accept things more and to be more patient. All I really care about now
are my children. All my hopes and dreams are with them. . . . I see the situation of
women in this society as quite good, they have freedom, they get their education, they
can work, they are in all the professions—even politics. I think the only problem
Palestinian women face is their families.

Neither Mona's or Felicia's story is unusual. Both reveal many of the issues
that patriarchal kinship connectivity raises for women: selection of marriage partner, education, employment, in-laws, violence, and limitation of options.

Patriarchal patrilinality affects women in other specific ways. The necessity of
producing paternal agnates in the context of patriarchal kinship mandates that
women be fertile and bear "fruit," specifically sons. Within West Bank camp and
village society, as in all Arab societies, there is a well-known preference for boys
over girls that is explained by the importance of patrilinality combined with the
son's obligations to his parents and sisters inherent in the relations of patriarchal
kinship. . . .

There is great discrimination between boys and girls, and between men and women in
our society. When a woman gives birth to a boy, the father and everyone celebrates.
But if she gives birth to a daughter, it's practically a shame—women comfort her and
tell her "Inshallah, next time a boy." Yet it is women who give birth, nurture children,
provide emotional support—how can they be devalued so much?
            —*Jenna, 32, single, village resident, "observant" Muslim, tawjihi*

NOTES

1. Lila Abu-Lughod, *Veiled Sentiments: Honor and Poetry in a Bedouin Society*
(Berkeley: University of California Press, 1986), pp. 39–77, esp. pp. 40–41. Also see Suad
Joseph, "Introduction: Theories and Dynamics of Gender, Self, and Identity in Arab Fami-
lies," Joseph, ed., *Intimate Selving in Arab Families: Gender, Self, and Identity* (Syracuse:
Syracuse University Press, 1999), p. 12.

2. Joseph, "Introduction," p. 9. Joseph's work in this area has been pioneering. In ad-
dition to the sources in note 3, see Joseph, "Family as Security and Bondage: A Political
Strategy of the Lebanese Urban Working Class," in Helen I. Safa, ed., *Towards a Political
Economy of Urbanization in Third World Countries* (London: Oxford University Press,
1982), pp. 151–174; Joseph, "Gender and Citizenship in Middle Eastern States," *Middle East
Report* 26, no. 1 (January-March 1996): 4–10; Joseph, "Elite Strategies for State Building:

Women, Family, Religion and the State in Iraq and Lebanon," in Deniz Kandiyoti, ed., *Women, Islam and the State* (Philadelphia: Temple University Press, 1991), pp. 176–200.

3. The concepts of "relationality" and "connectivity" have been specifically articulated and developed by Suad Joseph in many contexts. Here see Joseph, "Introduction," pp. 9–15; Joseph, "Gender and Relationality among Arab Families in Lebanon," *Feminist Studies* 19, no. 3 (Fall 1993): 465–486; Joseph, "Problematizing Gender and Relational Rights: Experiences from Lebanon," *Social Politics* (Fall 1994): 271–272.

4. Abu-Lughod, *Veiled Sentiments*, pp. 39–77.

5. Suad Joseph, "Gender and Relationality," p. 468; Joseph, "Introduction"; Joseph, *Intimate Selving in Arab Families*, p. 12.

6. Abu-Lughod, *Veiled Sentiments*, pp. 39–77.

7. Hisham Sharabi, *Neopatriarchy: A Theory of Distorted Change in Arab Society* (New York: Oxford University Press, 1988), pp. 31–32.

8. Sharabi, *Neopatriarchy*, 1988.

9. Several good analyses of interfamily and intrafamily relations may be found in Lawrence Rosen, *Bargaining for Reality: The Construction of Social Relations in a Muslim Community* (Chicago: University of Chicago Press, 1984), pp. 18–163; Andrea B. Rugh, *Within the Circle: Parents and Children in an Arab Village* (New York: Columbia University Press, 1997), pp. 214–246; and Suad Joseph, *Gender and Family in the Arab World* (Washington, DC: Middle East Research and Information Project, 1994).

10. See, for example, the study by Subhi Jawabreh "Al-Arroub Refugee Camp Case Study; The Pre-'48 Homeland and Social Organization Today," *Jerusalem Times* (Jerusalem, Palestinian weekly, English), May 29, 1998, p. 9.

11. Some observations concerning Palestinian *hamulah* may be found in Kitty Warnock, *Land Before Honor: Palestinian Women in the Occupied Territories* (New York: Monthly Review Press, 1990), pp. 19–32.

12. Halim Barakat, *The Arab World: Society, Culture, and State* (Berkeley: University of California Press, 1993), pp. 97–98.

Gender, Race, and Class in Silicon Valley

–Karen J. Hossfeld

Karen J. Hossfeld received a Ph.D. in sociology from the University of California at Santa Cruz in 1988 and currently is Associate Professor of Sociology at San Francisco State University. Her essay on gender, race, and class in Silicon Valley appeared originally in Women Workers and Global Restructuring, *edited by Kathryn Ward and published by the ILR Press at Cornell University in 1990.*

A growing number of historical and contemporary studies illustrate the interconnections between patriarchy and capitalism in defining both the daily lives of working women and the nature of work arrangements in general. Sallie Westwood, for example, suggests that on-the-job exploitation of women workers is rooted in part in patriarchal ideology. Westwood states that ideologies "play a vital part in calling forth a sense of self linked to class and gender as well as race. Thus, a patriarchal ideology intervenes on the shopfloor culture to make anew the conditions of work under capitalism" (1985:6).

One way in which patriarchal ideology affects workplace culture is through the "gendering" of workers—what Westwood refers to as "the social construction of masculinity and femininity on the shop floor" (page 6). The forms of work culture that managers encourage, and that women workers choose to develop, are those that reaffirm traditional forms of femininity. This occurs in spite of the fact that, or more likely because, the women are engaged in roles that are traditionally defined as nonfeminine: factory work and wage earning. My data suggest that although factory work and wage earning are indeed traditions long held by working-class women, the dominant *ideology* that such tasks are "unfeminine" is equally traditional. For example, I asked one Silicon Valley assembler who worked a double shift to support a large family how she found time and finances to obtain elaborate manicures, makeup, and hair stylings. She said that they were priorities because they "restored [her] sense of femininity." Another production worker said that factory work "makes me feel like I'm not a lady, so I have to try to compensate."

Reprinted from Karen Hossfeld, "Their Logic Against Them: Contradictions in Sex, Race, and Class in Silicon Valley," in *Women Workers and Global Restructuring*, edited by Kathryn Ward. Copyright © 1990 Kathryn Ward. Used by permission of the publisher, Cornell University Press.

This ideology about what constitutes proper identity and behavior for women is multileveled. First, women workers have a clear sense that wage earning and factory work in general are not considered "feminine." This definition of "feminine" derives from an upperclass reality in which women traditionally did not need (and men often did not allow them) to earn incomes. The reality for a production worker who comes from a long line of factory women does not negate the dominant ideology that influences her to say, "At work I feel stripped of my womanhood. I feel like I'm not a lady anymore. It makes me feel . . . unattractive and unfeminine."

Second, women may feel "unwomanly" at work because they are away from home and family, which conflicts with ideologies, albeit changing ones, that they should be home. And third, earning wages at all is considered "unwifely" by some women, by their husbands, or both because it strips men of their identity as "breadwinner."

On the shop floor, managers encourage workers to associate "femininity" with something contradictory to factory work. They also encourage women workers to "compensate" for their perceived loss of femininity. This strategy on the part of management serves to devalue women's productive worth. . . .

An example of a company policy that divides workers by gender is found in a regulation one large firm has regarding color-coding of smocks that all employees in the manufacturing division are required to wear. While the men's smocks are color-coded according to occupation, the women's are color-coded by sex, regardless of occupation. This is a classic demonstration of management's encouragement of male workers to identify according to job and class and its discouragement of women from doing the same. Regardless of what women do as workers, the underlying message reads, they are nevertheless primarily women. The same company has other practices and programs that convey the same message. Their company newsletter, for example, includes a column entitled "Ladies' Corner," which runs features on cooking and fashion tips for "the working gal." A manager at this plant says that such "gender tactics," as I call them, are designed to "boost morale by reminding the gals that even though they do unfeminine work, they really are still feminine." But although some women workers may value femininity, in the work world, management identifies feminine traits as legitimation for devaluation.

In some places, management offers "refeminization" perks to help women feel "compensated" for their perceived "defeminization" on the job. A prime example is the now well-documented makeup sessions and beauty pageants for young women workers sponsored by multinational electronics corporations at their Southeast Asian plants (Grossman 1979; Ong 1985). While such events are unusual in Silicon Valley, male managers frequently use flirting and dating as "refeminization" strategies. Flirting and dating in and of themselves certainly cannot be construed as capitalist plots to control workers; however, when they are used as false compensation for and to divert women from poor working conditions and workplace alienation, they in effect serve as a form of labor control. In a society where women are taught that their femininity is more important than other aspects of their lives—such as how they relate to their work—flirting can be divisive. And when undesired, flirting can also develop into a form of sexual harassment, which causes further workplace alienation.

One young Chinese production worker told me that she and a coworker avoided filing complaints about illegal and unsafe working conditions because they did not want to annoy their white male supervisor, whom they enjoyed having flirt with them. These two women would never join a union, they told me, because the same supervisor told them that all women who join unions "are a bunch of tough, big-mouthed dykes." Certainly these women have the option of ignoring this man's opinions. But that is not easy, given the one-sided power he has over them not only because he is their supervisor, but because of his age, race, and class. . . .

The women I interviewed rarely pose their womanhood or their self-perceived femininity as attributes meriting higher pay or better treatment. They expect *differential* treatment because they are women, but "differential" inevitably means lower paid in the work world. The women present their self-defined female attributes as creating additional needs that detract from their financial value. Femininity, although its definition varies among individuals and ethnic groups, is generally viewed as something that subtracts from a woman's market value, even though a majority of women consider it personally desirable.

In general, both the women and men I interviewed believe that women have many needs and skills discernible from those of male workers, but they accept the ideology that such specialness renders them less deserving than men of special treatment, wages, promotions, and status. Conversely, both the men and women viewed men's special needs and skills as rendering men *more* deserving. Two of the classic perceived sex differentials cited by employers in electronics illustrate this point. First, although Silicon Valley employers consistently repeat the old refrain that women are better able than men to perform work requiring manual skills, strong hand-eye coordination, and extreme patience, they nonetheless find it appropriate to pay workers who have these skills (women) less than workers who supposedly do not have them (men). Second, employers say that higher entry-level jobs, wages, and promotions rightly belong to heads of households, but in practice they give such jobs only to men, regardless of their household situation, and exclude women, regardless of theirs.

When a man expresses special needs that result from his structural position in the family—such as head of household—he is often "compensated," yet when a woman expresses a special need resulting from her traditional structural position in the family—child care or *her* position as head of household—she is told that such issues are not of concern to the employer or, in the case of child care, that it detracts from her focus on her work and thus devalues her productive contribution. This is a clear illustration of Heidi Hartmann's definition of patriarchy: social relationships between men, which, although hierarchical, such as those between employer and worker, have a material base that benefits men and oppresses women (1976). . . .

Central to gender-specific capital logic is the assumption that women's paid work is both secondary and temporary. More than 70 percent of the employers and 80 percent of the women workers I interviewed stated that a woman's primary jobs are those of wife, mother, and homemaker, even when she works full time in the paid labor force. Because employers view women's primary job as in the home, and they assume that, prototypically, every women is connected to a man who is bringing in a larger paycheck, they claim that women do not need to earn a full living wage. Employers repeatedly asserted that they believed the low-level jobs were filled only by women because men could not afford to or would not work for such low wages.

Indeed, many of the women would not survive on what they earned unless they pooled resources. For some, especially the nonimmigrants, low wages did mean dependency on men—or at least on family networks and household units. None of the women I interviewed—immigrant or nonimmigrant—lived alone. Yet most of them would be financially better off without their menfolk. For most of the immigrant women, their low wages were the most substantial and steady source of their family's income. *Eighty percent of the immigrant women workers in my study were the largest per annum earners in their households.*

Even when their wages were primary—the main or only family income—the women still considered men to be the major breadwinners. The women considered their waged work as secondary, both in economic value and as a source of identity. Although most agreed that women and men who do exactly the same jobs should be paid the same, they had little expectation that as women they would be eligible for higher-paying "male" jobs. While some of these women—particularly the Asians—believed they could overcome racial and class barriers in the capitalist division of labor, few viewed gender as a division that could be changed. While they may believe that hard work can overcome many obstacles and raise their *families'* socioeconomic class standing, they do not feel that their position in the gender division of labor will change. Many, of course, expect or hope for better jobs for themselves—and others expect or hope to leave the paid labor force altogether—but few wish to enter traditional male jobs or to have jobs that are higher in status or earnings than the men in their families.

The majority of women who are earning more than their male family members view their situation negatively and hope it will change soon. They do not want to earn less than they currently do; rather, they want their menfolk to earn more. This was true of women in all the ethnic groups. The exceptions—a vocal minority—were mainly Mexicanas. Lupe, a high-tech worker in her twenties, explained:

> Some of the girls I work with are ridiculous—they think if they earn more than their husbands it will hurt the men's pride. They play up to the machismo. . . . I guess it's not entirely ridiculous, because some of them regularly come in with

black eyes and bruises, so the men are something they have to reckon with. But, my God, if I had a man like that I would leave. . . .

My boyfriend's smart enough to realize that we need my paycheck to feed us and my kids. He usually brings home less than I do, and we're both damn grateful for every cent that either of us makes. When I got a raise he was very happy—I think he feels more relieved, not more resentful. But then, he's not a very typical man, no? Anyway, he'd probably change if we got married and had kids of his own—that's when they start wanting to be the king of their castle.

A Korean immigrant woman in her thirties told how her husband was so adamant that she not earn more than he and that the men in the household be the family's main supporters that each time she cashed her paycheck she gave some of her earnings to her teenaged son to turn over to the father as part of his earnings from his part-time job. She was upset about putting her son in a position of being deceitful to his father, but both mother and son agreed it was the only alternative to the father's otherwise dangerous, violent outbursts.

As in the rest of America, in most cases, the men earned more in those households where both the women and men worked regularly. In many of the families, however, the men tended to work less regularly than the women and to have higher unemployment rates. While most of the families vocally blamed very real socioeconomic conditions for the unemployment, such as declines in "male" industrial sector jobs, many women also felt that their husbands took out their resentment on their families. A young Mexicana, who went to a shelter for battered women after her husband repeatedly beat her, described her extreme situation:

He knows it's not his fault or my fault that he lost his job: they laid off almost his whole shift. But he acts like I keep my job just to spite him, and it's gotten so I'm so scared of him. Sometimes I think he'd rather kill me or have us starve than watch me go to work and bring home pay. He doesn't want to hurt me, but he is so hurt inside because he feels he has failed as a man.

Certainly not all laid-off married men go to the extreme of beating their wives, but the majority of married women workers whose husbands had gone through periods of unemployment said that the men treated other family members significantly worse when they were out of work. When capitalism rejects male workers, they often use patriarchal channels to vent their anxieties. In a world where men are defined by their control over their environment, losing control in one arena, such as that of the work world, may lead them to tighten control in another arena in which they still have power—the family. This classic cycle is not unique to Third World immigrant communities, but as male unemployment increases in these communities, so may the cycle of male violence.

Even some of the women who recognize the importance of their economic role feel that their status and identity as wage earners are less important than those of men. Many of the women feel that men work not only for income but for respect and dignity. They see their own work as less noble. Although some said they derive satisfaction from their ability to hold a job, none of the women considered her job to be a primary part of her identity or a source of self-esteem. These women see themselves as responsible primarily for the welfare of their families: their main identity is as mother, wife, sister, and daughter, not as worker. Their waged work is seen as an extension of caring for their families. It is not a question of *choosing* to work—they do so out of economic necessity.

When I asked whether their husbands' and fathers' waged work could also be viewed as an extension of familial duties, the women indicated that they definitely perceived a difference. Men's paid labor outside the home was seen as integral both to the men's self-definition and to their responsibility vis-à-vis the family; conversely, women's labor force participation was seen as contradictory both to the women's self-image and to their definitions of female responsibility.

Many immigrant women see their wage contribution to the family's economic survival not only as secondary but as *temporary*, even when they have held their jobs for several years. They expect to quit their production jobs after they have saved enough money to go to school, stay home full time, or open a family business. In actuality, however, most of them barely earn enough to live on, let alone to save, and women who think they are signing on for a brief stint may end up staying in the industry for years.

That these workers view their jobs as temporary has important ramifications for both employers and unions, as well as for the workers themselves. When workers believe they are on board a company for a short time, they are more likely to put up with poor working conditions, because they see them as short term. A Mexican woman who used to work in wafer fabrication reflected on the consequences of such rationalization:

> I worked in that place for four years, and it was really bad—the chemicals knocked you out, and the pay was very low. My friends and me, though, we never made a big deal about it, because we kept thinking we were going to quit soon anyway, so why bother. . . . We didn't really think of it as our career or anything—just as something we had to do until our fortune changed. It's not exactly the kind of work a girl dreams of herself doing.
>
> My friend was engaged when we started working there, and she thought she was going to get married any day, and then she'd quit. Then, after she was married, she thought she'd quit as soon as she got pregnant. . . . She has two kids now, and she's still there. Now she's saying she'll quit real soon, because her husband's going to get a better job any time now, and she'll finally get to stay home, like she wants.

Ironically, these women's jobs may turn out to be only temporary, but for different reasons and with different consequences than they planned. Industry analysts predict that within the next decade the majority of Silicon Valley production jobs may well be automated out of existence (Carey 1984). Certainly for some of the immigrant women, their dreams of setting aside money for occupational training or children's schooling or to open a family business or finance relatives' immigration expenses do come true, but not for most. Nonetheless, almost without exception, the women production workers I interviewed—both immigrant and nonimmigrant—saw their present jobs as temporary.

Employers are thus at an advantage in hiring these women at low wages and with little job security. They can play on the women's *own* consciousness as wives and mothers whose primary identities are defined by home and familial roles. While the division of labor prompts the workers to believe that women's waged work is less valuable than men's, the women workers themselves arrive in Silicon Valley with this ideology already internalized.

REFERENCES

Carey, Pete. 1984. "Tomorrow's Robots: A Revolution at Work." *San Jose Mercury News*, February 8–11.

Grossman, Rachel. 1979. "Women's Place in the Integrated Circuit." *Southeast Asia Chronicle 66—Pacific Research* 9:2–17.

Hartmann, Heidi. 1976. "Capitalism, Patriarchy, and Job Segregation by Sex." In *Women in the Workplace*, ed. Martha Blaxall and Barbara Reagan, 137–70. Chicago: University of Chicago Press.

Ong, Aihwa. 1985. "Industrialization and Prostitution in Southeast Asia." *Southeast Asia Chronicle* 96:2–6.

Westwood, Sallie. 1985. *All Day, Every Day: Factory and Family in the Making of Women's Lives*. Champaign: University of Illinois Press.

Daughters and Generals in the Politics of the Globalized Sneaker[1]

–Cynthia Enloe

Cynthia Enloe has served as chair of Clark University's Government Department and Director of Women's Studies. She is currently a research professor in the IDCE Department at Clark University in Massachusetts and teaches the intensive seven-week seminar, "Gender, Militarization, and Development." Her widely reprinted essay, "Daughters and Generals in the Globalized Sneaker," first appeared in Rethinking Globalizations(s): From Corporate Transnationalism to Local Interventions, *edited by Preet S. Aulakh and Michale G. Schechter and published by St. Martin's Press in 2000.*

All of us who have come together for these discussions are trying to chart the basic dynamics of late twentieth-century globalization: the specific processes, the complexities of those processes, the resistances to those processes.

What I thought I would do is talk a bit about one global industry as a way of clarifying what asking feminist questions can reveal. Some of you may try to put a good deal of distance between yourself and feminism, but what I'd like you to do is just imagine what a feminist set of questions yields in terms of making sense of globalization—what it is, who benefits, who loses, and what are the prospects for it. I'm really here to urge a kind of feminist curiosity. I began to realize after being a political scientist for about fifteen or twenty years (I was a little slow) that in fact I was missing a lot. The main thing I realize I was missing was politics; I was not asking enough questions about where power is and how it operates. By not asking feminist questions, I had underestimated power.

> So let's start locally. With whom does Michigan State have their sporting goods logo franchise?
> Audience: Reebok.
> Is that because Nike has The University of Michigan's clothing and shoe contract?

The competition among not just football rivals, but sporting goods corporations today is fierce—and it is global. Due to how this franchise system works, American

Excerpts from *Rethinking Globalization: Corporate Transnationalism to Local Interventions* by Preet S. Aulakh and Michale G. Schechter (eds.). Copyright 2000. Reprinted by permission of Palgrave Macmillan.

universities are now deeply involved in the international politics of clothing and the international politics of sneakers.

How many of you have ever seen the fine print of Michigan State's franchise agreement with Reebok? In their contract with the University of Wisconsin, Reebok's fine print initially stated that no members—no student, no member of any sports team—of the University could remove or in any way deface the company logo. If you don't want to have the telltale Reebok symbol on your sneaker or on your sports outfit when you are playing in front of the television cameras and your parents, you would be breaking a legal contract if you tried to take out the stitching or painted it a different colour.

The reason I raise this on the one hand is the connection between American 1990s university politics in an era of shrinking public funding and, on the other, the globalization of sporting goods manufacture. It is this connection that links Michigan State University athletes, administrators and fans to the Asian women who stitch sneakers and the investment-hungry governments that try to control them.

One-third of all athletic shoes produced in the world today now are coming from China. The other principal sources are Indonesia and Vietnam. If we were having this discussion about the international politics of sneakers in 1980, it would be South Korea that would be demanding our analytical attention. That is, the particular dynamics between American universities, American state officials, Asian factory women, Asian state officials and companies such as Reebok and Nike must be historicized. Globalizing sneakers is not a political process that began yesterday. In 1998, we are standing in a very particular moment in the long-developing and on-going gendered globalization of sneakers.

The offshore manufacture of sneakers really began in South Korea and to some extent Taiwan and it was infused with the politics of the Cold War.[2] The Nike, Reebok, Adidas, Puma and other sneaker companies began moving offshore. Nike's executives based in Oregon closed their last US factory in Saco, Maine (one of America's poorest states) in 1975. They chose for their new factory sites two countries whose statuses were very closely allied to the US state in the Cold War. This is not insignificant. Go home and line up your oldest and newest sneakers historically. I suggest that those sneakers that you could date back to the 1970s, no matter what colour they are, are khaki. That is, that pair is militarized. Those sneakers are militarized by the kinds of agreements between the states whose private industries were the sites of the production of sneakers in the 1970s and the United States state and the major shoe manufacturing companies like Nike and Reebok and Adidas.

The politics of women in the globalization of sneakers is not simply the impact of that globalization *on* women. Rather, women at several points have shaped globalization. Insofar as the sneaker industry—like the garment industry, like the tea industry, like the textile industry—depends for its bottom-line profits on the ability to make labour cheap and keep it cheap, insofar as the sneaker industry depends on being able to make the labour of its assembly workers cheap, those corporations in their global strategizing are dependent upon local constructions of femininity. That is, it was not simply Nike's people in Beaverton, Oregon, having an impact on women in South Korea in the 1970s. Those Korean women who became the assembly workers had their own conceptions of femininity and Nike was in part dependent on those constructions. What Nike executives, their Korean male sub-contractors, the militarized officials of the 1970s Seoul regime each—and together—had to try to do was to exert pressure on those women so that their constructions of femininity would be such that would make their labour cheap.

Cheap labour. It's an analytically dreadful phrase. It hides politics. To casually (lazily) say 'cheap labour' was what lured Nike to South Korea is to tempt us to imagine the labour of a Korean woman stitching a sneaker in 1975 is automatically ('naturally') cheap—as if it takes nothing to cheapen her labour. More politically accurate is 'cheapened labour.' It prompts you to ask what and who does it take, operating in concert, to cheapen labour?

To answer this question, one has to become curious about the gendering of politics in a highly militarized South Korean society in the 1970s. First, a lot of young women on small farms are being encouraged by the central government to see their futures as migrating from their small towns to cities and there participating in the industrialization of South Korea. South Korea's then highly militarized state was encouraging young women to see themselves as patriots, contributing to the nation by leaving their homes and going to work in factories without their parents' supervision. Simultaneously, government officials were encouraging parents to redefine daughterhood. It takes a lot to encourage parents to so radically reimagine what a respectable daughter is, a still marriageable daughter is. An otherwise thoroughly patriarchal regime pursued their statist, nationalist goal of internationally funded industrialization by launching a campaign to redefine the meaning of the 'respectable woman'. Insofar as a Korean woman depends in the long run for her financial security on a good marriage (Jane Austen would have felt pretty much at home in 1970s Korea or Koreans would have felt pretty much at home in early 1800s England) her parents must adopt a strategy to keep their daughter seen as respectable. If she loses her respectability, she may be doomed to a life of poverty. So it is not to be taken lightly when a government presses parents to redefine daughterly respectability, thus allowing their daughters to come from the countryside without parental supervision and work in these new factories— electronics factories, garment factories, textile factories, and athletic shoe factories. Inside every 1970s computer chip and every elaborately stitched sneaker is a complex web of cold war militarized, feminized respectability and daughterly patriotism.

The women themselves have also had their own strategies. A recent book by University of Maryland Women's Studies Scholar Seungkeung Kim takes seriously the strategizing by 1980s South Korean factory women.[3] Kim worked on the assembly line with women who answered the cold war Korean regime call to work for long hours at low wages. Most of these women, Kim found, understood that the pay they were getting from various multinational corporations was inadequate to meet their multiple responsibilities. For the South Korean women who served as the backbone of the 'South Korean miracle' by assembling electronics and garments and sneakers were not just autonomous female citizens. They were daughters. They saw themselves as daughters. You are a 'daughter' insofar as, when you get your paycheque, you feel as though part of your paycheque has to go home to your farming parents who need some of your salary to make ends meet and to pay for your brother's continued scholarship. Thus when we look at a pair of Nikes produced in 1970s–80s South Korea, we should see there in the elaborate stitching the maintenance of farm families in a time of government-favoured industrialization; we should see there, too, the education of boys paid for by the early school-leaving of their factory-working sisters. When these women talked to Kim, all of them, despite the differences amongst them, described a strategy of saving of money for their dowries. In South Korea by the 1970s young women were expected to bring their own money into a marriage. They couldn't count on their parents.

Now, at this point, let me indulge in an autobiographical aside. When I was at Berkeley in the 1960s, studying in political science nobody—nobody—told me that I should be interested in dowries. Nobody said, 'If you really want to be a keen observer of the international political economy and the militarization of the state you should spend a little time thinking about dowries.' So I'm a little late in thinking about all of this, and what I notice now—belatedly—is that I have to be curious about, learn about, things for which I really have few skills. I have belatedly begun to see that the companies now producing sneakers and electronics for export *depended* on these women thinking of themselves as daughters and as potential fiancées.

It is with this in mind that we need to analyse South Korean factory women's likelihood of unionizing. We need to look afresh also at what was at stake when in the early 1980s university women such as Insook Kwon were urging factory women to join them in their public demands for democracy. It would have been perfectly logical for a woman sewing sneakers for Nike or Reebok in 1970s–80s South Korea to hesitate. She would strategically calculate that she needed to continue to send money home to her parents in order to maintain her reputation as a 'good daughter' and to continue to put some money weekly into a savings account in order to accumulate enough to offer a suitable young man a dowry. For most of the women working in the factories around Seoul and Pusan a suitable husband was a man a little further up the redesigned class hierarchy—for instance, men who worked for Hyundai Shipping or had low-level government civil service jobs. Work in the sneaker factory was many young women's strategy to rise a notch on the class ladder. But it entailed constantly thinking about what do the young urban men want in a marriage. Those men want fiancées who will bring decent dowries into a marriage.[4]

Sneaker companies depended on this. The South Korean government depended on this. These elite men knew that women who were focused on their daughterly responsibilities of sending part of their paycheque home and saving money for dowries were not women who were likely to strike for decent pay, for the right to unionize, for wider democratic reforms. Thus when we think about globalization—and resistances to more exploitive dynamics—we need to take women factory workers' own strategies seriously. We need to craft a new analytical curiosity, a curiosity that seeks to unravel the Gordian knot tying together sneaker design, sneaker company calculations, local regime's ideologies of femininity, working-class men's marital expectations, middle-class pro-democracy alliance-building efforts and factory women's complex—and evolving—strategies.

South Korea is one of the success stories of democratization. To explain that success we have to consider what it took in the mid-1980s for a Korean factory woman to reimagine herself so that she could, for instance, see it as reasonable to take the risk of attending a union rally. The democratization of labour unions came to be seen by many Koreans as integral to the democratization of the whole political system.

What do these insights imply for how we investigate the state, the foreign corporation and its local capitalist subcontracting factory owner? Should we imagine that Nike executives in Oregon, generals and finance ministry economists in Seoul and factory managers in Pusan each write memos about 'the good daughter' and dowry practices? Well, we should *assume* nothing. But we should devise research approaches which make these elite calculations visible when they *do* exist.

Korean feminist activists and researchers have found that a number of factory owners, perhaps for subconscious motivations, set up dating services in the 1970s–80s. Why did they do that? Regularly replacing newly married women with unmarried novices insured turnovers. Turnover undercuts seniority. Thus regular departures due to marriage helps a factory owner cheapen labour. Sometimes, of course, employers have a great stake in seniority. It depends on what skills are necessary to produce the product for the profit level desired. Sometimes turnover drives capitalist employers crazy because they need workers who will stay on and become more and more skilled making the product a very good product. But in other industries, sneakers for instance, turnover enhances the bottom-line because it means that managers are constantly taking in new workers, employees who can be paid at the so-called training pay rate. Promoting the myth and practice of the good marriage had two advantages for these capitalist allies of their own government's cold warrior officials and foreign executives relying on their factories to produce high quality goods at minimal cost. Promoting their women workers' dating prospects would, managers hoped, keep the women on the assembly line focused on themselves as just daughters and 'respectable', well-dowried wives—keep them, that is, from seeing themselves as *citizens*, as autonomous individuals with public voices, with rights.

In the mid-1980s thousands of Korean factory women began to take themselves seriously as citizens. It was then that the sneaker executives began to shut down their factories in Pusan. They began to look instead toward Indonesia, to Indonesian women as still-daughterly potentially cheapened labour.[5] It may not be coincidental that it also was the mid-80s that South Korea's masculinized state elite decided that the time had come in the process of industrialization to shift the state's economic incentives: hereafter, the government would press Korean entrepreneurs to eschew light industry—feminized industry—and, instead, put their capitalist eggs in the basket marked heavy—read masculinized—industry. Called 'restructuring', this policy, when combined with the sneaker corporations' flight—from democratization—translated into factory women losing their jobs in South Korea. At the time, officials in Seoul tried to persuade those newly jobless women that their giving up their paid employment was good for the Korean nation: resigning themselves to a return to an earlier version of womanhood as unpaid dependent was an act of feminized 'patriotism'. As Korean feminist Choi Soung-ai has recently explained, this massive loss of women's employment in the name of the state-designed 'restructuring' was deemed good for the nation; it was only when the economic collapse of late 1997–8 compelled many *men* to lose their jobs that the South Korean elite (now democratically elected) deemed it a 'national crisis'.[6]

The sneakers produced today in Indonesia are like their older counterparts, tinted khaki. What we now have in Indonesia is also a militarized state. They seem to go together quite nicely.[7] Thus our understanding of women's participation in industrializing processes that is so central to globalization should provide more questions about the process of militarization. Indonesian researchers have noted that it's not at all uncommon for factory owners, owners who are producing for export, to bring retired generals on to their boards of directors. Now to any of you who have studied Thailand, this is old hat. You can't make sense of Thai banking unless you understand the retired generals' syndrome. Similarly, since the 1980s, some overseas manufacturing factory owners have made explicit alliances with particular members of the Indonesian armed forces as a way of building the sorts of political networks presumed valuable for doing profitable business under the Suharto regime. Women-as-daughters sewing the sneakers plus generals-as-company board members opening the right garment doors—it has been a winning strategy for certain sneaker companies in 1980s–90s Indonesia. A lot of discussions that went on about local resistance to the Suharto regime were surprisingly ungendered.[8] Who was doing the marching? Who was walking out from factories to protest unliveable wages and denial of the rights to independent union organizing? If you take a really good look at photographs, you'll see that oftentimes those demonstrations are composed of women. These are also women who, according to researchers such as Diane Wolf, have been brought into factories as daughterly women workers here too so they could serve to cheapen labour enough to maximize profits in the making of athletic shoes.[9] Here too, just as in 1970s South Korea, a masculinized, militarized state officialdom used the rhetoric of 'patriotic' daughterly womanhood as a cornerstone of their industrializing strategy. Here too, statist nationalism, structural militarism and selective local and foreign capitalist entrepreneurship were deemed an insufficient tripod on which to build a globally competitive industrial project. What the Indonesian elite decided, just as had the South Korean elite before them, was that a fourth big leg had to be constructed— and maintained. That fourth leg was an updated form of patriarchy. Making visible that state-maintained fourth leg, revealing the reliance of the other three legs of nationalist industrialism on that fourth leg—these have been among the central efforts of both South Korean and Indonesian feminists.

Reebok or Nike can only permeate the international market if local societies do not change their ideas about what is a 'respectable young woman'. Nike has a global advertising/marketing strategy that is calling for the world to be one big homogenized market. But Nike executives also do *not* want the world in practice to lose its heterogeneity of constructions of 'respectable' femininity. Insofar as women in Indonesia or South Korea—or Vietnam or China—challenge on their own terms what it means to be a 'respectable daughter', what it means to be a 'good wife', they become women who are harder to manage and harder to *keep* cheap. So Nike, on the one hand, is perhaps one of the best known symbols of globalization; on the other, however, it depends on the impenetrability of alternative notions of women-as-citizen into those societies where it produces its products. It shares this dependence with the local authoritarian state elites that keep patriarchal order in those societies. Consequently, while Nike, Reebok and other sneaker giants may celebrate the globalized girl athlete in their own advertisements, they simultaneously rely on regimes to undermine the legitimacy of local feminists' challenging critiques with claims that those women activists are mere dupes of Western neo-imperialism.

NOTES

1. This chapter is based on an oral presentation delivered at Michigan State University on April 3, 1998 as part of a conference, 'Globalization and its (Dis)Contents: Multiple Perspectives' and later revised; but some of its original oral qualities have been deliberately retained here. This format accords with a variety of methodologies currently being employed, including oracy and personal narratives.

2. For an elaboration on this argument, see: Cynthia Enloe, 'Feminists Try on the Post-Cold War Global Sneaker', in Nancy Hewitt, Jean O'Barr and Nancy Rosebaugh, (eds), *Talking Gender* (Chapel Hill, University of North Carolina Press, 1996): 176ff.

3. Seung-Kyng Kim, *Class Struggle or Family Struggle? The Lives of Women Factory Workers in South Korea* (New York: Cambridge University Press, 1997).

4. See also Insook Kwon, 'The "New Women" in 1920's Korea: Rethinking Feminism, Nationalism and Imperialism', *Gender and History*, forthcoming in 1999.

5. For an elaboration on this phenomenon, see: Indrasari Tjandraningshih, 'Between Factory and Home: Problems of Women Workers', in Ballinger and Olsson, (eds), *Behind the Swoosh* (Uppsala, Sweden: International Coalition for Development Action, 1997): 145–59.

6. Choi Soung-ai, 'Whose Honor, Whose Humiliation? Women, Men, and the Economic Crisis', *Asian Women Workers Newsletter* (Hong Kong), vol. 17, no. 2, 1998, pp. 6–7.

7. On this and related points, see Jeff Ballinger and Claes Ollson (eds), *Behind the Swoosh: The Struggle of Indonesians Making Nike Shoes* (Uppsala, Sweden, International Coalition for Development Action, 1997).

8. But note Ines Smyth and Mies Grijns, '*Unjuk Rasa* or Conscious Protest? Resistance Strategies of Indonesian Women Workers', *Bulletin of Concerned Asian Schools*, vol. 29, no. 4, 1997, pp. 13–22.

I am also indebeted to an Indonesian feminist from whose research on the recent political discourse among Indonesians on the contested meaning of 'the working woman' I learned a great deal. Because of the intimidation recently practised by the Suharto regime against independent critics, her name must be withheld.

9. Diane Lauren Wolf, *Factory Daughters: Gender, Household Dynamics, and Rural Industrialization in Java* (Berkeley: University of California Press, 1992).

Violence Against Women
–World Health Organization

The World Health Organization, the United Nations specialized agency for health, was established in 1948 with the mission of securing the highest level of health for all people. It issues reports on a variety of health-related topics on a regular basis. The report on violence against women that was issued in July 1997 is available online, as are a number of other useful publications and fact sheets. For more information visit www.who.int

Definition and Scope of the Problem

Violence against women and girls is a major health and human rights issue. At least one in five of the world's female population has been physically or sexually abused by a man or men at some time in their life. Many, including pregnant women and young girls, are subject to severe, sustained or repeated attacks.

Worldwide, it has been estimated that violence against women is as serious a cause of death and incapacity among women of reproductive age as cancer, and a greater cause of ill-health than traffic accidents and malaria combined.[1]

The abuse of women is effectively condoned in almost every society of the world. Prosecution and conviction of men who beat or rape women or girls is rare when compared to numbers of assaults. Violence therefore operates as a means to maintain and reinforce women's subordination.

United Nations Definition

The Declaration on the Elimination of Violence Against Women, adopted by the United Nations General Assembly in 1993, defines violence against women as "any act of gender-based violence that results in, or is likely to result in, physical, sexual, or psychological harm or suffering to women, including threats of such acts, coercion or arbitrary deprivation of liberty, whether occurring in public or private life".[2] It encompasses, but is not limited to, "physical, sexual and psychological violence occurring **in the family**, including battering, sexual abuse of female children in the household, dowry related violence, marital rape, female genital mutilation and other traditional practices harmful to women, nonspousal violence and violence related to exploitation; physical, sexual and psychological vi-

Reprinted by permission of WHO.

278

olence occurring **within the general community**, including rape, sexual abuse, sexual harassment and intimidation at work, in educational institutions and elsewhere; trafficking in women and forced prostitution; and physical, sexual and psychological violence **perpetrated or condoned by the state**, wherever it occurs." . . .

Violence Across the Life Span

Violence has a profound effect on women. Beginning before birth, in some countries, with sex-selective abortions, or at birth when female babies may be killed by parents who are desperate for a son, it continues to affect women throughout their lives. Each year, millions of girls undergo female genital mutilation. Female children are more likely than their brothers to be raped or sexually assaulted by family members, by those in positions of trust or power, or by strangers. In some countries, when an unmarried woman or adolescent is raped, she may be forced to marry her attacker, or she may be imprisoned for committing a "criminal" act. Those women who become pregnant before marriage may be beaten, ostracized or murdered by family members, even if the pregnancy is the result of a rape.

After marriage, the greatest risk of violence for women continues to be in their own homes where husbands and, at times, in-laws, may assault, rape or kill them. When women become pregnant, grow old, or suffer from mental or physical disability, they are more vulnerable to attack. Women who are away from home, imprisoned or isolated in any way are also subject to violent assaults. During armed conflict, assaults against women escalate, including those committed by both hostile and "friendly" forces. . . .

Violence Against Women Throughout the Life Cycle

Phase	Type of Violence
Pre-birth	Sex-selective abortion; effects of battering during pregnancy on birth outcomes
Infancy	Female infanticide; physical, sexual and psychological abuse
Girlhood	Child marriage; female genital mutilation; physical, sexual and psychological abuse; incest; child prostitution and pornography
Adolescence and adulthood	Dating and courtship violence (e.g. acid throwing and date rape); economically coerced sex (e.g. school girls having sex with "sugar daddies" in return for school fees); incest; sexual abuse in the workplace; rape; sexual harassment; forced prostitution and pornography; trafficking in women; partner violence; marital rape; dowry abuse and murders; partner homicide; psychological abuse; abuse of women with disabilities; forced pregnancy
Elderly	Forced "suicide" or homicide of widows for economic reasons; sexual, physical and psychological abuse

In Families

The most common form of violence against women is domestic violence, or violence against women in families. Research consistently demonstrates that a woman is more likely to be injured, raped or killed by a current or former partner than by any other person.[3]

Men may kick, bite, slap, punch or try to strangle their wives or partners; they may burn them or throw acid in their faces; they may beat or rape them, with body parts or sharp objects; and they may use deadly weapons to stab or shoot them. At times, women are seriously injured, and in some cases they are killed or die as a result of their injuries.

The nature of violence against women in families has prompted comparisons to torture.[4] The assaults are intended to injure women's psychological health as well as their bodies, and often involve humiliation as well as physical violence. Also like torture, the assaults are unpredictable and bear little relation to women's own behaviour. Finally, the assaults may continue week after week, for many years.

Physical Abuse

In every country where reliable, large-scale studies have been conducted, results indicate that between 16% and 52% of women have been assaulted by an intimate partner. Although national data are scarce, there are a growing number of community-based and small-scale studies which indicate widespread violence against women is an important cause of morbidity and mortality.

It is likely that these studies, from both industrialized and developing countries, underestimate the problem for many reasons. Some women may believe that they deserve the beatings because of some wrong action on their part. Other women refrain from speaking about the abuse because they fear that their partner will further harm them in reprisal for revealing "family secrets", or they may be ashamed of their situation. Furthermore, in many countries there are no legal or social sanctions against violence by an intimate partner. Considering these factors, estimates of the prevalence of physical abuse by a partner are probably conservative.

Rape in Intimate Relationships

Physical attacks by a partner may include rape and sexual violence. Women in many societies, however, do not define forced sex as rape if they are married to, or living with, the attacker. Although some countries have now recognized marital rape as a criminal offence, others still argue that husbands have a legal right to unlimited sexual access to their wives.

Surveys in a number of countries show that from 10% to 15% of women report being forced to have sex by their intimate partner. Among women who are physically assaulted in their relationship, the figures are higher.

Pyschological or Mental Violence

Psychological violence includes repeated verbal abuse, harassment, confinement, and deprivation of physical, financial and personal resources. For some women, the incessant insults and tyrannies which constitute emotional abuse may be more painful than the physical attacks because they effectively undermine women's security and self-confidence. A single occurrence of physical violence may greatly intensify the meaning and impact of emotional abuse. Women have been reported as saying that the worst aspect of battery was not the violence itself but the "mental torture" and "living in fear and terror".

Failures of Detection

There has been a failure in most countries to identify and provide support to women suffering from domestic violence. This is due, in part, to the fact that if women do seek help it is from neighbours or family members, not the police or health services. A number of studies have shown that shame or fear of reprisal often prevents women from reporting an attack to authorities, or even speaking to friends about it. Some fear that if their injuries are reported, their children will be taken away by child protection services. Those services which could provide support, such as the police or health care, often do not identify women suffering from violence, or they are unable to respond adequately. They may not be trained to deal with the problem or know where to refer women seeking help. They may be afraid of confronting the problem, or be ill-equipped to deal with the complex situation surrounding the woman who has suffered violence. . . .

Rape and Sexual Assault

Large-scale studies of rape and sexual assault are scarce. Those that do exist, however, consistently report high prevalence rates. Research conducted in industrialized countries has shown that the likelihood of a woman being raped or having to fight off an attempted rape is high. In developing countries, research suggests that rape is an ever-present threat and reality for millions of women.

Six separate investigations suggest that between 14% and 20% of women in the United States will experience a completed rape at least once in her lifetime.[5,6]

In a random sample of 420 women in Toronto, Canada, 40% reported at least one episode of forced sexual intercourse since the age of 16.[7]

Although rape and sexual assault may be perpetrated by strangers, evidence from many sources indicates that a high percentage of rapists are acquaintances, "friends", relatives, and those in positions of trust or power. Another consistent finding is the high percentage of young, and often very young, rape victims (see following table). Many sexual assaults are perpetrated by more than one attacker. "Gang rape", where two or more men subdue and penetrate their victims, is not uncommon.

Statistics on Sex Crimes[a]

Country	Attackers Known to Victim (%)	Victims Aged 15 or Less (%)	Victims Aged 10 or Less (%)
Peru (Lima)	60	—	18[b]
Malaysia	68	58	18[c]
Mexico (City)	67	36	23
Panama (City)	61	40	—
Papua New Guinea	—	47	13[d]
Chile (Santiago)	72	58	32
United States	78	62	29

Adapted from: Heise, L. Violence against women: the hidden health burden. *World health statistics quarterly*, 1993, **46**(1): 78–85.
[a]Includes attempted and completed rape and sexual assaults such as molestation, except for the US data which is for completed rape only.
[b]Percentage of survivors aged nine or less.
[c]Percentage of survivors aged six or less.
[d]Percentage of survivors aged seven or less.

Women are also subject to what has been termed "non-contact" sexual abuse in which, for example, men expose their penises or make obscene telephone calls. Where non-contact abuse has been studied, it has been discovered that a high percentage of women have experienced this type of abuse; in some cases up to 50% of all women questioned.

Women in Custody

Often, women who enter prisons are already victims of violence.

In a study of more than 300 women in federal prisons in Canada, 68% of all women, and 90% of Aboriginal women reported physical abuse at some time in their lives.[8]

Violence against women who are in custody in institutions and prisons may be widespread. The nature of abuse ranges from physical or verbal harassment to sexual and physical torture. Various reports on women in custody have shown that women are stripped, shackled and their body cavities searched by male guards. Women from many countries report being raped while in detention centres.[9] Incarceration, intended as a time for reform from criminal activities, then becomes one more episode of victimization. The psychological and physical sequelae of this violence are further compounded by feelings of helplessness, and a general unavailability of medical care and support services.

Trafficking in Women, Forced Prostitution

Each year, thousands of women throughout the world are tricked, coerced, abducted or sold into slavery-like conditions and forced to work as prostitutes, domestic workers, sweatshop labourers or wives. Reports of involvement in international trafficking by state officials and police were routinely received by the United Nations Special Rapporteur on violence against women during her investigation into this issue.[10]

Violence Against Women Domestic Workers

Domestic workers are vulnerable to violent assaults, including physical abuse and rape, by their employers. Migrant women are especially at risk as employers may withhold salaries, passports and personal documents. This limits workers' movement in those countries where aliens are required to carry proof of their legal status, thus impeding any attempts to claim protection at their embassies.

In some countries, domestic workers are not covered by labour laws. Where laws are in place, workers may not be informed of their rights, especially in countries where the host language is unknown to them or they are separated from their social group.[11]

Many Women Keep the Violence a Secret

Women who are the victims of sexual violence are often reluctant to report the crime to police, family or others. In countries where a woman's virginity is associated with family honour, unmarried women who report a rape may be forced to marry their attacker. Some may be murdered by their shamed fathers or brothers, as a way of restoring family honour. In some countries, a woman who has been raped may be prosecuted and imprisoned for committing the "crime" of sex outside of marriage, if she cannot prove that the incident was in fact rape.

The Girl Child

The earliest years of a person's life are supposed to be a time of carefree exploration, growth and support. For millions of girls around the world the reality is quite different. Violence against the girl child includes physical, psychological and sexual abuse, commercial sexual exploitation in pornography and prostitution, and harmful practices such as son preference and female genital mutilation.

Sexual Abuse of Children

Child sexual abuse is an abuse of power that encompasses many forms of sexual activity between a child or adolescent (most often a girl) and an older person, most often a man or older boy known to the victim. The activity may be physically forced, or accomplished through coercive tactics such as offers of money for school fees or threats of exposure. At times, it may take the form of breach of trust in which an individual, such as a religious leader, teacher or doctor, who has the confidence of the child, uses that trust to secure sexual favours.

Studies have shown that between 36% and 62% of all sexual assault victims are aged 15 or less (see table in the preceding section, page 282). Research suggests that the sexual abuse of children is commonplace.

Incest, sexual abuse occurring within the family, although most often perpetrated by a father, stepfather, grandfather, uncle, brother or other male in a position of family trust, may also come from a female relative. As with sexual abuse, incest is accomplished by physical force or by coercion. Incest takes on the added psychological dimension of betrayal by a family member who is supposed to care for and protect the child.

Research in Kingston, Jamaica, reported that 17% of a random sample of 452 primary school girls, ages 13–14, had experienced attempted or completed rape, half before the age of 12.[12]

In a study of 1193 randomly selected ninth grade students in Geneva, Switzerland, 20% of girls and 3% of boys reported experiencing at least one incident of sexual abuse involving physical contact.[13]

A general unwillingness to acknowledge the extent of child sexual abuse exists in many societies. Attempts to downplay the prevalence and nature of child abuse often blame the victim or the victims' mother for the violence. Accusations against the child include the idea that the child invites the abuse or that she imagines it. The mother may be blamed for "causing" the abuse by refusing to have sex with the abuser, or for "colluding" by not realising or reporting what was going on.

Attention is often focused on commercialized paedophilia, which while important, distracts attention from the more widespread problem of incest and sexual abuse.

Commercial Exploitation

The commercial exploitation of children occurs in many settings. The problem includes child prostitution and pornography, the trafficking of children for sexual purposes, and bonded labour.

Many factors can conspire to push children into exploitative and abusive situations. Well documented cases show that families are often deceived by the promise of job opportunities for their children. Sometimes, girls are sent away from home to work and become subject to physical and sexual abuse.

Street children may be at particular risk. With no means of economic or social support, they may be forced to rely on prostitution for survival. They also lack the basic protection that a home and family can offer, thus making them more vulnerable to violent attack on the street.[14]

Female Genital Mutilation (FGM)

Today, the number of girls and women who have been subjected to FGM is estimated at more than 130 million individuals worldwide, and a further two million girls are at risk of this practice.[15]

FGM, a form of violence against the girl child that affects her life as an adult woman, is a traditional cultural practice. In those societies where it is practised, it is believed that FGM is necessary to ensure the self-respect of the girl and her family and increases her marriage opportunities.

FGM constitutes all procedures that involve partial or total removal of the external female genitalia or other injury to the female genital organs whether for cultural or any other nontherapeutic reasons. FGM is discussed extensively in the WHO document, *Female Genital Mutilation.*

Son Preference

In most societies, a higher value is placed on sons. In extreme cases, the reduced status of daughters may result in violence. Prenatal sex selection can result in a disproportionate number of abortions of female, as compared with male, foetuses. After birth, in families where the demand for sons is highest, infanticide of female infants may be practised.[16]

Other Forms of Discrimination

Son preference may manifest in other practices which are discriminatory against girls. These practices include:

- neglect of girls, more so than boys, when they are sick;
- differential feeding of girls and boys;
- a disproportionate burden of housework for girls, from a very young age;
- less access to education for girls than their brothers.[17]

In Situations of Armed Conflict and Displacement

Armed conflict and uprootedness bring their own distinct forms of violence against women with them. These can include random acts of sexual assault by both enemy and "friendly" forces, or mass rape as a deliberate strategy of genocide.[18–21]

Some Forms of Violence Resulting from Conflict/Refugee Situations

- Mass rape, military sexual slavery, forced prostitution, forced "marriages" and forced pregnancies
- Multiple rapes and gang rape (with multiple perpetrators) and the rape of young girls
- Sexual assault associated with violent physical assault
- Resurgence of female genital mutilation, within the community under attack, as a way to reinforce cultural identity
- Women forced to offer sex for survival, or in exchange for food, shelter, or "protection"

Increased Violence Against Women During Conflict

The general breakdown in law and order which occurs during conflict and displacement leads to an increase in all forms of violence. The tensions of conflict, and the frustration, powerlessness and loss of traditional male roles associated with displacement may be manifested in an increased incidence of domestic violence against women. Alcohol abuse may also become more common and exacerbate the situation.

The underlying acceptance of violence against women which exists within many societies becomes more outwardly acceptable in conflict situations. It can, therefore, be seen as a continuum of the violence that women are subjected to in peacetime. The situation is compounded by the polarization of gender roles which frequently occurs during armed conflict. An image of masculinity is sometimes formed which encourages aggressive and misogynist behaviour. On the other hand, women may be idealized as the bearers of a cultural identity and their bodies perceived as 'territory' to be conquered. Troops may also use rape and other forms of violence against women to increase men's subjugation and humiliation.

Who Is Most Vulnerable?

Some groups of women and girls are particularly vulnerable in conflict and displacement situations. These include targeted ethnic groups, where there is an official or unofficial policy of using rape as a weapon of genocide. Unaccompanied women or children, children in foster care arrangements, and lone female heads of households are all frequent targets. Elderly women and those with physical or mental disabilities are also vulnerable, as are those women who are held in detention and in detention-like situations including concentration camps.

SOURCES

1. World Bank. *World Development Report 1993: investing in health*. New York, Oxford University Press, 1993.

2. *Declaration on the elimination of violence against women*. New York, United Nations, 23 February 1994 (Resolution No. A/RES/48/104).

3. Council on Scientific Affairs, American Medical Association, Violence against women: relevance for medical practitioners, *Journal of the American Medical Association*, 1992, **267**(23):3184–3189.

4. United Nations Economic and Social Council, *Report of the Special Rapporteur on violence against women*, E/CN.4/1996/53, February 1996.

5. Koss M, Gidyez C A, Wisniewski N, The scope of rape: incidence and prevalence of sexual aggression and victimization in a national sample of higher education students. *Journal of consulting and clinical psychology*, 1987, **55**.

6. Kilpatrick DG, Edmunds CN, Seymour AK, *Rape in America: a report to the nation*. Arlington, VA, The National Victim Center, 1992.

7. Randall M, Haskell L. Sexual violence in women's lives: findings from The Women's Safety Project, a community-based survey. *Violence against women*, March 1995, 6–31.

8. Shaw M. *The survey of federally sentenced women*, as cited in The Arbour Report, Correctional Services of Canada, 1996.

9. United Nations, Economic and Social Council, *Report of the Special Rapporteur on violence against women, its causes and consequences*, 22 November 1994, E/CN.4/1995/42.

10. United Nations, Economic and Social Council, *Report of the Special Rapporteur on violence against women, its causes and consequences*, 12 February 1997, E/CN.4/1997/47.

11. *Punishing the victim, rape and mistreatment of Asian maids in Kuwait.* Middle East Watch, Women's Rights Project, August, 1992, 4(8).

12. Walker S et al. *National and health determinants of school failure and dropout adolescent girls in Kingston, Jamaica.* Washington, DC: International Center for Research on Women. Nutrition of Adolescent Girls Research Program, No. 1, 1994.

13. Halpérin D et al. Prevalence of child sexual abuse among adolescents in Geneva: results of a cross sectional survey. *British Medical Journal*, 1996, **312**:1326–9.

14. World Health Organization. *Commercial sexual exploitation of children: the health and psychosocial dimensions.* Paper presented at the World Congress Against Sexual Exploitation of Children, Stockholm, Sweden, 27–31 August, 1996.

15. World Health Organization. *Female genital mutilation: report of a WHO technical working group, Geneva, 17–19 July 1995.* Geneva, World Health Organization, 1996, WHO/FRH/WHD/96.10.

16. Ravindran S. *Health implications of sex discrimination in childhood*, World Health Organization, UNICEF, 1986.

17. Ravindran S. *Health implications of sex discrimination in childhood*, World Health Organization, UNICEF, 1986.

18. *Sexual violence against refugees, Guidelines on prevention and response.* Geneva, United Nations High Commission for Refugees, 1995.

19. Swiss S, Giller J. Rape as a crime of war: a medical perspective. *Journal of the American Medical Association*, 1993, **270**:612–615.

20. *Working with victims of organized violence from different cultures.* The International Federation of Red Cross and Red Crescent Societies, 1995.

21. Zwi A, Ugalde A. Towards an epidemiology of political violence in the Third World. *Social science and medicine*, 1989, **28**(7):649–657.

Culture of Honor, Culture of Change
A Feminist Analysis of Honor Killings in Rural Turkey

–Aysan Sev'er and Gökçeçiçek Yurdakul

Aysan Sev'er, a first generation Turkish-Canadian, is Professor of Sociology at the University of Toronto in Scarborough. Gökçeçiçek Yurdakul is a Ph.D. candidate in Sociology at the same university. Their article, "Culture of Honor, Culture of Change: A Feminist Analysis of Honor Killings in Rural Turkey," appeared in Violence Against Women *in September 2001.*

The Fourth World Conference on Women in Beijing ("Long Talks," 1995) turned the global spotlight on a wide range of violence that women and girls suffer throughout the world and approved an Action Plan to enhance women's status (Bunch & Frost, 1997). Unquestionably, one of the most extreme forms in the continuum of violence is honor killings. An *honor killing*[1] is a generic term used to refer to the premeditated murder of preadolescent, adolescent, or adult women by one or more male members of the immediate or extended family. These killings are often undertaken when a family council decides on the time and form of execution due to an allegation, suspicion, or proof of sexual impropriety by the victim (Amnesty International, 1999; Pervizat, 1998). The family council typically includes the father and brother(s) of the victim, and may also include uncles, grandfathers, and male in-laws. Definitions of impropriety can be extremely amorphous, often subsuming sexual or sensual acts, allegations, or rumors. Acts or accusations may range from going to the movies without approval or a chaperon to kissing,

AUTHORS' NOTE: We wish to thank Vappu Tyyska and an anonymous reviewer for their insightful comments on an earlier version of this article. We are also grateful to the Social Sciences and Humanities Research Council of Canada (SSHRC) for its generous support of the primary author's research on violence.

"Culture of Honor, Culture of Change" by Aysan Sev'er in *Violence Against Women*, Vol. 7, No. 9, September, 2001. Copyright © 2001. Reprinted by permission of Sage Publications.

holding hands, dating, or having intercourse with a man who is not one's culturally or legally sanctioned husband (Pervizat, 1998). In one extreme case, the husband dreamed about the unfaithfulness of his wife and used his dream as a justification to arrange her murder (Amnesty International, 1999). The decision for executions may be given in cases of eloping with a lover, even if the girl/woman may have legally married the man. Executions may also take place after an incestuous, acquaintance, or stranger rape, even if the girl/woman was extremely young or was forced to marry the offender after the rape. Executions may even be carried out when the rape victim is mentally challenged or seriously injured during the assault (Amnesty International, 1999).

Indeed, since the mid-1990s, numerous humanitarian organizations—such as Amnesty International, the United Nations, and its branch that deals with women's issues (UNIFEM)—have devoted time, energy, and money to raise awareness about these gendered atrocities. Respected news media have joined the compassionate chorus by publishing newspaper articles, news reports, and television series on honor killings (e.g., Sawyer, 1999). Thus far, the hub of the international inquiry and media attention has been honor killings in Pakistan, Jordan, Egypt, Aman, and a few other Islamic states.[2] This attention is well placed when one considers the estimate of 200 to 300 women annually falling victim to honor killings in Pakistan alone. It is reported that Jordan, Egypt, and Aman each record 25 to 30 honor killings a year (Goodenough, 1999; Sati, 1997). However, these numbers may grossly underrepresent the reality. Like most other violent crimes against women and girls (e.g., wife abuse, rape, child sexual abuse), the reported cases of honor killings may constitute only a small fraction of a culturally submerged iceberg (Amnesty International, 1999; Sev'er, 1998; Solomon, 1992).

Another bias in the humanitarian reports also needs to be mentioned. Although these reports are written with sensitivity toward religious differences, they nevertheless leave the impression that there may be something wrong with Islam or its practice. Especially in the televised reports, a sobering discussion about honor killings is frequently juxtaposed over a silhouette of a mosque or a soundtrack of a Moslem call for prayer. The outcome of these visual and auditory cues is to inseparably tie the crime with the already negatively stereotyped Moslem world. In fact, honor killings predate Islam and are not consistent with the Qur'an (Goodenough, 1999; Muslim Women's League, 1999; Queen Noor, 1999; Rodgers, 1995; Sati, 1997; Turgut, 1998).[3] Moreover, we argue in this article that honor killings are not confined to a few, fragile, nonsecular democracies such as Pakistan or to patriarchal monarchies such as Jordan. Honor killings are one extreme in the worldwide patriarchal violence against women. They also occur in better established, developing, democratic, and secular states, and regretfully the incidence of such killings may be on the rise. We do not need to single out Islam (or another religion) to understand the epistemology of killing women for honor.[4] Instead, we can seek an in-depth understanding of honor killings (as well as other ways of killing women and female children) through a careful application of feminist perspectives without invoking religiosity or religion. We will use Turkey to exemplify these assertions.

Turkey: Contradictions Between True Modernization and Patriarchal Control of Women

Surge in Modernization in Women's Status in the 1920s

To most of the general public and many academics in North America, Turkey is a little-understood enigma in the global puzzle. With the exception of negative stereotypes fueled by controversial films such as *Midnight Express* and, more recently, some pity due to the wrenching images of three devastating earthquakes in its heartland, Turkey remains obscure.

In fact, Turkey is a vibrant democracy (Arat, 1996). Within the past 77 years, Turkey has moved away from an imperialist, nonsecular, patriarchal, and increasingly corrupt Ottoman empire and its successive male sultans to a democratic, secularized (since 1924) republic (since 1923) with a modern constitution (since 1924). Both the multiparty political governance and the educational institutions (since 1924) have been completely dissociated from Islamic rule and law (Shari'ah), despite the fact that more than 99% of the Turkish population is Moslem (*Worldmark*, 1998, p. 790).

For the purpose of this article, the social, cultural, and legal modernization of Turkey is as important as its political transformation. Between 1926 and 1928, Turkey adopted (with modifications) and successfully implemented civil, family, and contract laws from Switzerland, criminal law from Italy, business administration laws from France, and commerce laws from Germany. Again, this systematic Westernization in political and legal thought and practice has set Turkey apart from other primarily Moslem states that have retained much closer links between religion and other institutions including politics, education, and justice systems (Arat, 1996; Orucu, 1996). Moreover, the modernization in Turkish women's rights should be underscored (Arin, 1996). Through the adaptation and implementation of the Swiss-originated civil and family laws (1926), polygamy, betrothal, and bride-price—common practices under Ottoman rule and in many contemporary Islamic countries because they are permitted under Shari'ah—have been outlawed in Turkey. The modernized civil and family laws provide equal rights to women and men in education, employment, and inheritance, and equalize women's and men's rights and obligations in divorce (see Arin, 1996). In contrast, under Ottoman rule and in the majority of the Islamic world, divorce was/is strictly a male prerogative, with devastating social, cultural, and economic consequences for women.

Turkish law sees the family as the cradle of the society, and thus harshly criminalizes violence among close family members. For example, assault of a family member increases the codified term of punishment for common assault anywhere between one third to one half (Arin, 1996, p. 132). This means that if killing a nonfamily member will bring a 10-year sentence, killing a family member may bring up to 15 years. Turkish law even protects women (and young men) from public harassment and stalking by criminalizing both of these activities (Arin, 1996, p. 134).

In the political arena, Turkish women received the right to vote and be elected in municipal, state, and federal elections between 1930 and 1934. After the 1935 national elections, there were 18 elected women ministers in the Turkish Parliament.[5] This number translates into 4.5% women parliamentarians in 1935, as opposed to only 1.7% women parliamentarians in 1991 (Kidog, 1997, p. 8). These are noteworthy developments if one considers that women's right to vote was legalized in England in 1928. French women had to wait until 1944, and their Quebec sisters until 1940 for the same political right (Kislali, 1996; Nelson & Robinson, 1999). It should also be noted that in the early 1990s Turkey had a female prime minister (Tansu Ciller), even before an advanced society such as Canada had one[6] and in contrast to the United States, which has yet to elect a female president or vice president.

Inhibiting Forces Against Modernization in Women's Status

Nevertheless, the head start of the 1920s has not assured Turkey a secure place among the First World countries, nor has it assured Turkish women parity with their male counterparts. Some of the lag can be understood in terms of disadvantages in the country's demographics. Turkey occupies a land equal to 7.8% the size of Canada or 8.3% of the United States, with a population density of 78.2 people per square kilometer. The population is approximately 64 million, and the country is plagued with a very high growth rate (see United Nations, 1997). Per capita annual income is around US$1,400, and the per capita gross domestic product is slightly more than US$2,200. Like other economically struggling nations, the population distribution is flat and disproportionately bottom-heavy, with approximately 30% of the total population consisting of people younger than age 15, and less than 4% of the population older than 65 years of age. Life expectancy remains substantially lower than in highly industrialized societies (66 for women and 63 for men), and infant mortality rates remain high (39.9 per 1,000 live births) (see United Nations, 1997). Although the literacy rate is reported as 80% for people older than 6 years (89% for men and 72% for women) (Kidog, 1998; United Nations Educational, Scientific, and Cultural Organization, 1999), older people, rural residents, and women are significantly more likely to be illiterate.[7]

Correlated with the disadvantages in education, women's labor force participation is also problematic for two reasons. First, although the participation rates reach 50% in rural areas, women's work frequently involves unpaid contributions to the family farm or small business that are under men's control (Orucu, 1996). Second, although the labor participation rate for men reaches 98% in urban areas, women's rate is only 35% and women work in gender-segregated, low-paying service jobs (Kidog, 1998). Turkish customs explicitly emphasize the family roles of women and deem secondary any work or career aspirations women may have (Orucu, 1996). Having been carefully socialized into gendered divisions of labor, most girls/women learn to curb their career involvement or revisit their level of commitment after marriage. Until 1999, the legal retirement age for women was

45 years. Even for educated and career-oriented women, this young retirement age left very little time to establish independence after the natural process of childbearing and rearing that almost all Turkish women see as a must (Orucu, 1996). Although the age of retirement for women now has been raised to 58 (*Sabah*, 1999), the cultural expectations that cast women in a tangential relationship with the work world will continue to impact their choice (or lack of choices) for many generations to come.

Inhibiting forces to modernization can also be understood in terms of cultural factors, especially (but not exclusively) those that are rooted in law and customs. Although the official stance of the republic is committed to gender equality and secularism, these professed ideologies have not been able to dismantle the strong customary expectations about the mutual exclusivity of the public and private domains. Despite the rhetoric of equality, an overwhelming emphasis is placed on the caregiving, nurturing, and self-sacrificing roles of women. Marriage and motherhood are still the ultimate path to status attainment. According to Arat (1996), 49% of men who reside in western Turkey and 60% of those in eastern Turkey still believe that they are smarter than women; 56% of men residing in western Turkey and 73% in eastern Turkey believe that they should have absolute authority over women and 36% of western Turkish men and 57% of eastern Turkish men believe that they have the right to punish women if they are challenged by them. These are far from egalitarian attitudes.

Not surprisingly, there is a cultural preoccupation with female propriety. Many patriarchal mechanisms and rituals exist for sexual and reproductive control of women (Yurdakul, 1999). Although patriarchal expectations (such as insistence on virginity before marriage) color all Turkish gender relations, they are particularly fierce and unforgiving among rural populations. Rural populations, especially in eastern regions, often occupy the lowest rungs on the socioeconomic ladder, are most likely to be undereducated or illiterate, and are most vulnerable to religious and cultural misconceptions or even extremism.

The Turkish legal system, which was progressive and revolutionary at the time of its inception in 1926, has grown stagnant, and thus has not kept up with the gender-based advances taking place in the modern world. Men are still considered to be the providers for the family. Although rape is considered a very serious offense, marital rape is not covered unless corroborated by serious injury (Kaya, 1996). Until very recently, the victim was the only one who could lay charges against an abusive partner (Arin, 1996). In a patriarchal society, this requirement assured women's silence in abuse cases. Although the onus of reporting abuse is now shared by the state prosecutor and the penalty for not reporting has been raised from 3 to 6 months ("Article 23233," 1998), patriarchal norms are likely to continue to protect abusing men rather than victimized women.

In Turkish law, nontraditional family arrangements have no recognition or protection. In legal marriages, the principle of property is one of separate ownership during and after marriage unless contractually stipulated otherwise by the partners (Arin, 1996). In practice, almost all property is registered in the man's name. Because separate contracts within marriage are seen as contrary to cultural norms, women's dependence on men is legally entrenched by separate ownership legislation. The existing family law also gives greater weight to the father's decision in disputed custody cases and still considers the sexual propriety of women (even after a legal separation) a factor in sustaining paternal rights over children (Kidog, 1997). A deep legal division continues to differentiate children from legal marriages from those born out of wedlock (*pic* translates as "bastard" and is a degrading insult as well as a derogatory legal term for children born out of wedlock). Such designations, despite the overarching equality principle in Turkish law, continue to restrict women's sexual freedom and reproductive choice.

The process of law enforcement is even more problematic than the gender ramifications of legal statutes. The front liners, such as the police or gendarme (federal police/army combination), and the major players of the criminal justice system are either exclusively (the police and gendarme) or disproportionally (lawyers, judges, and legislators) male. Most of these men hold strong patriarchal stereotypes and expectations. Even in clearly abusive situations, a father's or a husband's right over his children or wife is seldom questioned and rarely criminalized. In a recent study, 66% of the police stated that women are responsible for attacks against them because they dress or act in provocative ways ("Polis Tecavuzde," 2000). In Turkey, the total respect for the privacy of the family and men's culturally legitimized superiority within it is an iron cage for many women and children. In extreme cases, the privacy of the family hides even the darkest customs, such as honor killings (Farac, 1998). Patriarchal discretions about family honor allow men to receive reduced sentences of one fourth to one eighth of the prescribed term ("Campaign," 1999; Turgut, 1998). The irony of this needs emphasis in terms of the contradictions in the Turkish law: As mentioned earlier, violence toward a family member (man or woman) increases the punishment anywhere from one third to one half. However, if it is honor-related violence (i.e., an honor killing of women), the sentences may be reduced by as much as seven eighths (Arin, 1996).

Detrimental Forces Against Modernization in Women's Status: The Cultural Equation of Men's Honor, Family Honor, and Sexual Propriety of Women and Girls

In the West, honor is often defined as moral integrity, the esteem accorded to virtue or talent. Both the depth and the breadth of an eastern understanding of honor is very different (Abu-Lughod, 1986). In its purest and most desirable form, honor is an integral dimension of Eastern culture, where one's honorable deeds are looked on as a valued possession. In a way, neither the rich nor the poor are exempt from trying their very best to lead honorable lives and to protect their own as well as the family name from insinuations or open charges of dishonor.

In its positive manifestation, honor is a nontangible path for social status that can equate a very poor man or woman with a very rich one, at least on one culturally esteemed dimension. The negative side of this generally admirable Eastern tradition is when honor becomes an obsession, a biased scale men use to judge other men, and men and women use to judge women (Brooks, 1995; Goodwin, 1994; Yurdakul, 1999). Interestingly, the poor are even more possessive about their honor, because they have little else in the rigidly stratified societies in which they live. At the extreme end of this continuum, judgments about honor can and do become fatal.

Similar to other Middle Eastern and primarily Islamic cultures (Abou-Zeid, 1974; Abu-Lughod, 1986), Turkish culture is also tightly wrapped around sentiments of honor. The richness of the Turkish language in providing many different words for *honor* attests to its cultural importance. The term *onur* closely corresponds to the North American understanding of honor. *Seref* is linked to the glory derived from a man's own or one's male kin's accomplishments (Abou-Zeid, 1974, pp. 245–246) and thus represents an honor that is derived from an achieved status. In that sense, seref is almost exclusively possessed and controlled by men, an honor that they can increase or lose through their own or their male kin's accomplishments. *Haysiyet* is linked with an internal ability to feel shame, whereas *haysiyetsiz* refers to the absence of this quality. *Yuzsuz* literally translates as faceless, which makes a visual connotation to the absence of honor with the ability to feel shame. *Ar* is yet another word that links the ability to feel shame with the blood that circulates in the body. *Ar damari catlamis* are words that imply the symbolic event of a burst artery, where all honor has spilled. *Nam* and *san* are words for an honorable renown, *gurur* is an honorable pride, *prestij* is a borrowed term to refer to the Western concept of prestige, and *izzet* is the type of honor derived from being able to show generosity to others. Gurur, onur, ar, prestij, and izzet are usually gender neutral in their application, whereas seref is androcentric.

In contrast, *namus* is a type of sexual honor that presupposes physical and moral qualities that women ought to have. This type is associated with the shame of women and women's families (Yurdakul, 1999). Women must protect their namus for the duration of their lives—more specifically, before, during, and after marriage. Women are also expected to protect the namus of other women and girls related to them, for example, their daughters and granddaughters. Moreover, namus has an additional hereditary quality, whereby "the shame of mother is transmitted to the children, and a person's lack of [namus] may be attributed to his birth, hence the power of insults, the most powerful of all [relating] to the purity of the mother. After this, the greatest dishonor of a man derives from the impurity of his wife" (Pitt-Rivers, 1974, p. 52). Even after marriage dissolution[8] men may feel threatened by the sexual behavior of their former wives and how it may cast a shadow on their namus. A woman's sexuality, therefore, is deemed a force to be controlled by the woman herself. However, namus is much too important to be trusted to women alone (Brooks, 1995). Fathers and other male kin before marriage exercise full rights to sanction women who deviate. Husbands and their male kin assume this task during marriage and even after its dissolution.

North American research provides ample documentation of men's control of women's sexual behavior because of jealousy and possessiveness (see DeKeseredy & Hinch, 1991; Dobash & Dobash, 1979, 1998; Sev'er, 1997, 1998). Yet namus-related control is substantially more all-encompassing, because it is derived directly from cultural perceptions, expectations, and judgments and is not based on the controlling behavior of an individual man. Presumably, a shamed man and his (or his wife's) kin, neighbors, sometimes whole communities, and the agents of law enforcement act as biased judges and juries against the offending woman by actively enforcing severe sanctions, remaining stoic witnesses, or failing to investigate wrongdoings (Farac, 1998; Turgut, 1998).

Even though other types of honor can be related to a variation of acts or deeds, namus is related to virginity and chastity of women before marriage or being the subservient recipient (not the initiator) of the sexual desires and advances of husbands during marriage. Brooks (1995) links this fear of women's sexual desire to a Qur'anic interpretation that women are endowed with nine parts of sexual desire (as opposed to one part in men). Women are expected to protect their own as well as their husband's namus even if the husband may have died. The Islamic commonality among the Middle Eastern cultures[9] contributes to the association of honor with women's bodies and selected men's rights over them. A more secular understanding of the same phenomenon is the commodification of women.

Commodification of women is reflected in the preoccupation with virginity. In Turkish, *bakire* means untouched and refers to a virgin (regardless of age). The term *kiz* means a girl but also infers virginity. The language differentiates kiz from *kadin*, which means woman (a married woman) by connoting lack of virginity in the latter. There are no comparable words to differentiate virginal and nonvirginal men or married and unmarried men, because the sexuality and marital status of men are not stringently monitored. The culture is exclusively consumed with women's sexuality. Words such as *kizligini bozmak* or *kizligini kaybetmek* translate as breaking or spoiling a girl's virginity or losing virginity. Both terms imply the irreversibility of the status passage. Terms such as *kizin bozuk cikti* imply lack of virginity (translated as "your daughter was spoiled or broken"). In short, the value of a girl is judged by the actual (as well as expected) intactness of her hymen.

The word *dusmek* (fall) signifies a woman's sharp descent on the continuum of namus. The only way a fallen woman can clean the namus of her family is through killing the man who defiled her or by taking her own life. In a well publicized case, 32-year-old Sukran Gonenc drenched herself in gasoline and burned herself to death in the presence of the Turkish media and hundreds of onlookers. The reason for this public suicide was her lover's refusal to marry her because she was not a virgin. In an interview, her lover said, "How can she expect me to marry a woman like that? My family would never allow such a thing!" ("Cakmagi Cakdigi An," 1999). Even when women kill themselves they will remain unclean, but their death helps clean the namus of their families. Men can also clean family namus by killing the woman who brought them shame.

The cultural obsession about women's sexuality in general and virginity in particular has created rich—and by Western standards, demeaning—rituals around men's initiation of the first sexual experience through marriage. Although there are wide variations according to class and geographic region, either symbolic or actual droplets of blood on *gerdek* (the culturally sanctioned nuptial night of losing virginity) are linked to the evaluation of the worthiness of women. In western Turkey and most other affluent urban areas, the rituals are symbolic, such as wearing white (only virgins wear white wedding gowns), or tying a scarlet belt around the bride's waist (signifying the blood to be shed through penetration of the hymen). In more remote regions, the rituals can be much more graphic, such as girls being subjected to arbitrary virginity examinations (Turgut, 1998) or the bloodiest sheets from gerdek being displayed on a clothesline or presented to the inlaws to prove virginity. There are reported cases of reversal of marital contracts due to lack of proof. Such reversals are deemed a grave dishonor to the woman and a greater insult to the namus of her male kin. In such cases, young women are known to have taken their own lives. Others kill children born out of wedlock ("Bebegini Kurtlara Yedirdi," 1995). Some are killed by their male kin (Turgut, 1998).

The cultural obsession with virginity also manifests itself in an obsession with women's infidelity. In Iran, adulterous women can still be buried to their chest and stoned to death, and even the size of stones is carefully regulated: not too small to unduly prolong the suffering, but not too large to end it too quickly (Brooks, 1995; "Iste, Seriatin Gercek," 1997). Secular and modernized Turkish laws have banned such barbaric practices since the 1920s, but the existence of laws is not necessarily a safeguard against male aggression.

In sum, according to cultural mores, men cannot have namus by themselves, because their namus is always determined by the namus of their mothers, wives, daughters, and sisters. Stated differently, men are vulnerable to the violations of their own namus through the impropriety of women in their current, extended, or even former families. Turkish language again richly reflects the ceaseless fear about losing namus and men's predatory prerogative to make a restoration. *Namusa laf gelmek* translates as other people's gossip about one's namus. *Namusu kirlenmek* or *lekelenmek* refers to one's namus being dirtied or stained, and *namusunu temizlemek* is a man's attempt (and obligation) to clean it. *Namussuz* signals a total loss of namus and, within the honor-saturated nature of Turkish culture, it is the equivalent of a moral purgatory. The amorphous moral quality of namus has led patriarchal societies in general, and rural parts of Turkey in particular, to develop extreme sanctions to control the sexual behavior of women (Delaney, 1987; Farac, 1998). Under rare circumstances, these extreme sanctions include premeditated murder as an attempt to clean a dirtied namus, but perhaps more important to reestablish men's brotherhood with other men and to deter other women from engaging in similar behavior (Sati, 1997). Nevertheless, despite the overemphasis on honor,

> The problem of "honor" killings is not a problem of morality or of ensuring that women maintain their own personal virtue; rather, it is a problem of domination, power and hatred of women who, in these instances, are viewed as nothing more than servants to the family, both physically and symbolically. (Muslim Women's League, 1999)

* * *

Some Examples of Recent Honor Killings in Rural Turkey

As discussed earlier, honor in Turkey plays a forceful role in all types of relationships, especially the relationship of women to men. Either real or presumed violations of namus may produce severe sanctions, especially among the rural segments of the population where people are much more likely to be traditional, patriarchal, nonsecularly married at an early age, and illiterate or undereducated (Acar, 1996; Arat, 1996; Elmaci, 1996). As Pitt-Rivers (1974) observes, "The ultimate vindication of honor lies in violence" (p. 29; see also Farac, 1998; Ilkaracan, 1999). According to Pervizat's (1999) careful research on this topic, there were at least 20 reported honor killings between 1997 and 1998, but because this is not the type of crime that can be easily identified, the number may be higher. Although this number may not seem too alarming in relation to what is happening in India, Pakistan, and Bangladesh, we argue that even one case is too many. We now review some of the incidents that have found their way into the social-scientific literature or the mass media.

Vezire Kaya, aged 36, miraculously survived a murder attempt by her husband of 10 years. After a family council decision about her sexual impropriety (alleged adultery), she was driven to a remote place, her hands were tied, her eyes were covered, and she was choked until she passed out. When her persecutors thought she was dead, they threw her into Firat (the Euphrates), which is notorious for its rapid-flow and strong currents. She survived her ordeal and went to the police. Her husband expressed no remorse and claimed that "he was just cleaning his namus" ("Aile Meclisinin," 1998).

Gonul Arslan, aged 21, was raised in a relatively modern way in a southern Turkish resort, but her father arranged her marriage to her cousin even though Gonul was in love with another man. The cousin was from a conservative village of SanliUrfa. Gonul ran away from her husband/cousin, but she was hunted down and returned to her father by her male kin. When she refused to go back to her husband, she was forcefully taken for a ride by her husband and other male relatives, strangled until she was presumed dead, and thrown into Firat. She survived and is currently living under an assumed name under state protection (Farac, 1998, pp. 81–98). Her father, husband, and two other relatives stand charged.

Rabia Oguz, aged 25, was considered a spinster in a village of SanliUrfa where girls are married in their early teens. When her family found out about a romantic relationship she was having, her brother was instructed to arrange a mock car-tractor accident to kill her ("Koy Meydaninda," 1995). Two cousins helped stage the accident. They killed Rabia in the marketplace by repeatedly driving the tractor over her body. As it turns out, Rabia and her mother were taken for a ride, but the mother was dropped off shortly before the murder. At first, no witnesses came forward and the killers went free. The police reopened the case when anonymous tips they received revealed that Rabia had initially escaped the mock accident and ran into a small shop crying for help. Unfortunately, her brother and a cousin grabbed her by her long hair and literally dragged her under the moving wheels of the tractor. After the Kafkaesque deed, the three men celebrated their success by shooting bullets into the air. An autopsy showed that Rabia was still a virgin, but the killers received reduced sentences (from life to 12.5 years) due to "severe provocation" (Farac, 1998, pp. 39–53).

Fatma Geyik, aged 22, was shot to death in the middle of the street. The execution order was given by a family council on allegations of Fatma's sexual relationship with a man and was carried out by her father ("Tore Icin Kizini," 1998). What is extremely interesting in this case is that Fatma had moved far away from her family of origin (from the eastern to the western part of Turkey), had gotten herself a job, and was fully self-sufficient and independent at the time of her death. Her father and uncle had traveled from one end of the country to the other to hunt her down. In her uncle's words, "Whatever happened happened after she got herself a job. She 'reduced our namus to a penny's worth'" ("Tore Icin Kizini," 1998).

Sevda Gok, aged 17, was publicly executed in the market area of SanliUrfa immediately after a midday Friday prayer (a particularly holy time in Islam) at the local mosque. Allegedly, she was running away from home to go to the movies (Kuyas, 1996). Her adolescent cousin, aged 14, cut her throat with a bread knife "like slaughtering sheep" (Farac, 1998, p. 63). Her executioner was caught a few blocks away with blood-soaked clothes and a knife. An autopsy showed that Sevda was a virgin ("Bir Namus Cinayeti," 1996). The adolescent cousin claimed that he loved Sevda and had intentions of marrying her, but it was his duty to clean the family honor. At least 100 people coming out of the mosque may have—indeed, must have—observed the slaughter, but no one volunteered details of the crime (Farac, 1998, pp. 57–65). Although this murder was premeditated and the cousin expressed no remorse, he received only a 7-year sentence.

Hatice, aged 12, and two of her female relatives had gone to a movie house in the middle of the day. Her jealous and suspicious husband, aged 17, "cut her throat like a chicken" and seriously wounded one of the other girls (Farac, 1998, pp. 73, 77). Although the surviving girls claimed that they went to the movie house only to use its washroom facilities, the husband claimed that his wife was turning tricks, and he had to clean his namus. His sentence was reduced for "mild provocation" (Farac, 1998, pp. 69–77).

Oruc Serin, aged 16, was shot to death by her brother in the market area of the rural town of Gaziantep (a southeastern province). The weapon was a hunting rifle. Just before her murder, Oruc had given birth out of wedlock and in a wheat field; she had buried the infant among the crop. The baby was still alive when local farmers found her, approximately 36 hours after the birth. Oruc was taken into police custody for attempted infanticide, and the judge imposed a particularly large bail, suspecting that she herself was in danger of honor killing. Nevertheless, her family managed to bail her out, locked her up without food or water for 3 days, and, when she eventually managed to escape, shot her to death ("Torelerin Kurbani," 1996).

Semse Kaynak, aged 19, was killed after allegedly falling under a farm tractor that was being driven by her brother in a rural town of SanliUrfa ("Yine Tore Vahseti," 1998). At the time of the incident, the victim's father, two brothers, sister-in-law, and the latter's infant son were also on board. First, her brother was charged with "reckless driving" and was released after a single day in gendarme custody (Farac, 1998, pp. 101–112). Only after following an anonymous tip did the gendarme establish that this was yet another honor killing. In fact, the tractor had backed up a few times over Semse's body. Just before her murder, Semse was found to be pregnant and had claimed that she was raped by her cousin. When confronted, the cousin agreed to marry Semse in a religious ceremony[10] and had actually done so. However, when Semse's pregnancy became visible right after marriage, her male kin sought an abortion for her to end this embarrassment. When their request for an abortion was refused because the pregnancy was in its 6th month, the father and brothers decided to stage an accident to kill her. The fact that so many people were riding the tractor at the time of her murder (including the sister-in law and her baby) was done to reduce Semse's legitimate fear of her male kin and to provide numerous false witnesses of the "accident" (Farac, 1998).

Hacer Felhan was one of 11 children of Mustafa, who eked out a very marginal existence for his large family. However, through the radio and neighbors' television, Hacer was increasingly tempted by a different, more colorful, and affluent existence. She sought out friends who gave her a glimpse of this "other" life, which involved fashion jewelry, high heels, and colorful dresses. When one of her (female) friends dedicated a love song to her on a local radio program, her family considered it to be an insult to their honor. Fearing falling victim to an honor killing, Hacer staged a mock suicide by leaving a note and her slippers beside a well in her back yard and sought refuge at a friend's house. However, police found out where she was and returned her to her family, despite her protest that her family would kill her. Indeed, the family had decided to clean their namus, and the executioner chosen was her 13-year-old brother, Muhammed. At his trial, Muhammed claimed that he did what he was told and, without emotion, related the long debate about which weapon he should use to ensure her death. The brother's sentence was reduced to 10 years due to his age and provocation. He was released after serving 2 years (Farac, 1998, pp. 25–36).

Aysel Dikmen, aged 18, was executed by her father. She had run away with the man she loved but was caught and placed in an orphanage by police because she was underage. When she was released to the custody of her father, he promptly took her life ("Campaign," 1999).

Cezvet Murat killed two of his sisters, Ayten and Gulten, because they came home late and he assumed they were seeing men ("Campaign," 1999). He said he was protecting his honor.

Suspecting infidelity, Abdullah Karadeve cut his pregnant wife's throat with a knife. She was expecting their eighth child ("Campaign," 1999).

Salih Esmer, aged 28, killed his sister, Semra, for dating. He also killed their mother for not keeping an eye on his sister ("Campaign," 1999).

Hulya Yakar was killed by her 11-year-old son for going out a lot ("Campaign," 1999). The son claimed that his mother was smearing his family name.

Selma Demir, aged 29, was stabbed 30 times by her father. The father said that he had to clean his namus because Selma was coming home late and she was separated from her husband ("Eve Gec Gelen," 1998).

Discussion

Although there are numerous other examples, the summarized cases we have presented show several patterns. First, cultural elaborations of honor are gender based. Honor killings occur only on the basis of women's behavior and, in nearly all cases, women are the only ones who are killed, even though their assumed or acted on impropriety always includes a male partner. However, women who may help or be around the target may also get hurt or killed (e.g., Hatice's friend, Semra's mother).

Second, family councils and the actual killers invoke a cultural understanding of honor rather than a religious one (at least in Turkey). Of course, the sociological meaning of culture subsumes all forms of belief systems, but any connection between Islam and this heinous crime is by no means clear or direct. International coverage of honor killings that overemphasizes the role of religion fails to look at the more prevalent patriarchal legitimization behind violence against women. After all, femicide is a worldwide occurrence, whether it manifests itself as acid throwing or "kitchen deaths" in Bangladesh and India, female infanticide in China, rape-and-kill rampages in Bosnia and Kosovo, or wife murders in every other part of the world, including North America (see Note 4). The only common denominator among these diverse crimes against women is the talons of an aggressive patriarchal culture that subjugates women by depriving them of free choice and economic independence and by commodifying their bodies.

Third, the plans for the honor murders are made and executed almost exclusively by men. Often, the killer is chosen as the youngest male member of the family to obtain the sympathy of the courts in case of a criminal trial. Hatice's killer was 17, Sevda's 14, Hacer's 13, and Hulya's 11. Ironically, patriarchy also victimizes very young men by forcing them to commit heinous crimes against their loved ones (Gunenc, 1991). In addition, in pockets of rural Turkey, very immature youth are still being pushed to play adult family roles. Although it contravenes the secular laws of Turkey, early arranged marriages through religious ceremonies and even polygamy are common (Elmaci, 1996). These patterns are related to lack of opportunities, education, and an acceptable standard of living, ... Moreover, . . . there is a continuing powerlessness of women relative to men and an ease in transgressing women's rights. In sum, there are areas in Turkey that seem to be caught in a time warp of destructive gender relations.

Fourth, the discussed cases strongly challenge the link between subjugation of women and accumulation of private property. Indeed, if there is any similarity between most male perpetrators and women victims, it is their sheer poverty. In these tragedies, the only property that men seem to have is the lives and bodies of their women. Indeed, these observations give support to the radical and socialist feminist perspectives of gendered subjugation rather than a strictly materialistic explanation.

Fifth, all victims are young. Semse was 19, Aysel 18, Sevda 17, Oruc 16, and Hatice 12 when they were killed. It is almost as if the patriarchal culture seems to be frightened by the emerging sexuality of young women and their (potential) challenge to male rules. As the radical feminist theory implies, cutting down a few women in the prime of their youth is expected to deter other young women from expressing themselves in a sensual way (Sati, 1997). The two clear messages are that women are untrustworthy and women are dispensable. If other women partake in these tragedies at all, they are there for tertiary purposes, such as providing distraction, creating a false sense of hope or safety for the victim, or serving as deceitful witnesses to the crime. Semse's sister-in-law and her infant son were taken for the murderous tractor ride just to provide a false sense of safety for Semse and to serve as a false witness to her murder. Rabia's mother was also taken for the ride for similar reasons, but then dropped off just before her daughter's murder. Both Semra and her mother were killed, the latter for not keeping an eye on her daughter. In other words, either as victims or as accomplices, women in these tragedies possess no personal, social, or structural power to ask for justice or accountability. They are terrified victims or reluctant accomplices in male domination. They have neither the ideology of equality nor an economic independence to confront men.

Sixth, . . . men who engage in honor killings act within the boundaries of male camaraderie. They get male kin support, community support (at least in the form of silence), and even support from the lower level police/gendarme and lawyers and judges (Krau, 1998; Muslim Women's League, 1999). Fathers, uncles, brothers, cousins, and other male kin take roles ranging from very active (e.g., in Fatma's, Rabia's, Semse's, and Vezire's cases) to quietly supportive. Some murderers make a rudimentary attempt to disguise their acts (e.g., the staged tractor accident in Semse's and Rabia's cases, or throwing Vezire and Gonul into the Firat after erroneously thinking they were dead). However, the deeply entrenched but misguided cultural norms and values that provide fertile ground for these murders also make some men extremely blunt (e.g., Fatma was shot and Hatice's throat was slashed in the middle of a street; Sevda and Oruc were executed in the market-places of their respective towns).

There are additional layers of patriarchy. . . . The state is not generally benign; it is often a biased force in preserving male domination and privilege. When women run away to hide (such as Hacer), police find and deliver them back to their parents, even when they are warned by the victim or know from experience that her life is in danger (e.g., Oruc's and Aysel's cases; see "Ayse Ve Oglunu," 1996). When suspicious accidents or drownings are reported, police usually release men who may have played a role in the incident (e.g., Rabia's and Vezire's

cases). The police may even fail to carry out full investigations unless there is public pressure to do so (e.g., Rabia's case). If these cases come to trial, male judges
are inclined to accept the honor dilemma of the murderers as a mediating factor.
Often, killers receive a light sentence and further benefit from reduced jail terms
under the auspices of provocation or tender age (e.g., Sevda's, Hatice's, and
Hacer's cases). The fact that these killings are decided and condoned by a group of
men (family elders) but carried out by younger members of the family also allows a
diffusion of responsibility and provides further cover and legitimacy for killers of
women. The killers may even receive a hero's treatment during incarceration
("Campaign," 1999; Cancel, 1999). Sati (1997) suggests that the level of respect
shown to the killer is proportional to the brutality of the killing.

Finally, the aspect of social change may be considered one of the most important elements in honor killings in a country that has been on its way to modernization since the 1920s. As discussed, Turkish laws leave no place for blatant
discrimination against women, let alone condoning their murder. Yet many
women die horrible deaths at the hands of family members. It is our contention
that the only way to make sense of this diabolic contradiction is to look at the perceived threat of social change, especially in backward, structurally disadvantaged,
and rabidly patriarchal rural areas. A recent *New York Times* article addressed the
severe impact of ethnic strife and internal migration on Turkish women's lives.
According to the article, women in the southeastern part of Turkey are twice as
likely to kill themselves as their male counterparts because of the resistance of
their families to any kind of social change. For instance, a 22-year-old woman
killed herself after being severely beaten by her parents for wearing a tight skirt,
and a 20-year-old woman killed herself to protest her arranged marriage. According to experts, "They cannot control their lives, only their deaths" ("Turkish
Women," 2000).

Through technological achievements and globalization, even extremely isolated parts of the globe are being bombarded with images of a different world than
the one they have always known. Despite the burdens of her arranged child marriage and the economic destitution surrounding her life, Hatice wanted to go
to the movies with her friends. Sevda was also infatuated with the movies and, at
the cost of running away from her home, wanted to experience the different life
they portrayed. Gonul, who was raised in a tourist haven, challenged her arranged
marriage to her cousin from the rural SanliUrfa and insisted on pursuing a love relationship. Hacer, unlike many generations of women before her, had the opportunity to listen to a radio and experience the dangerous pleasure of hearing a love
song dedicated to her. Fatma moved away from her repressive home, changed her
city, found herself a job, and became totally self-sufficient. Yet none could escape
the patriarchal web. In rigidly codified patriarchal systems, the awakening wants,
desires, and independence of women are considered threats. There may indeed be
a rise in crimes against women by men who resist these challenges and changes.
Like a wounded dinosaur, the patriarchal strongholds are extracting a few more
victims in the hope of preserving the status quo.

NOTES

1. Even the term *honor killing* is an oxymoron, because honor and killing should be mutually exclusive rather than interrelated concepts. A more appropriate term to refer to these murders is patriarchal killings.

2. Wife burnings (*suttee*) in India have also received attention (see Daly, 1989). Wife burnings share some similarities with honor killings. For example, in both cases, the victims are young or older women and the perpetrators are members of the immediate or extended family. However, there are also important differences. In their most traditional form, wife burnings are initiated (at least on the surface, although the entrenched customs may not give women alternatives) by the widow of a recently deceased man who throws herself on the funeral pyre of her husband. More recent variations are found to be related to dowry disputes where women suffer "accidental" deaths such as kitchen fires, while the husband and his family are conveniently freed to search for a new wife (and presumably a better dowry).

3. According to Yusuff (1998), even if women commit adultery, its proof is virtually impossible under Islamic Law because the proof requires "four witnesses who would have to testify that they actually witnessed the sexual offense, i.e., copulation." Suspicions, rumors, or hearsay are legally (according to the Shari'ah) inadmissible.

4. Historically, systematic murder of women has been common in different cultures. For example, women and girls have been systematically raped and killed during ethnic wars. In recent cases, such as in Bosnia and Kosovo, the victims were Moslems, but the perpetrators were not (MacKinnon, 1993). In China, female children are at risk (Landsberg, 1995, 1996; "Small Steps," 1996). Bangladeshi women are frequently disfigured by acid attacks ("Acid Attacks," 1999; "Vicious Twist," 2000). According to a 1991 Human Rights Watch report, there are similar practices in Brazil (Sati, 1997). In India, female children are systematically aborted, and some women are still subjected to ritualized deaths ("Ritual Death," 1999). In Saudi Arabia, adulterous women are stoned to death ("Zina Yapan," 1995). Even in so-called highly advanced societies such as the United States, Great Britain, and Canada, many women are stalked and killed by husbands, lovers, and ex-partners (Sev'er, 1997, 1998).

5. A detailed summary of Ataturk's political, social, legal, and educational reforms can be found online (http://members.tripod.com/tarihweb/ and http://www.Ataturk.com/index2.html/). Lest the before-their-time nature of these reforms goes unnoticed, one needs to be reminded that Canadian women were not considered "persons" and were not allowed to be elected to the Senate until 1929.

6. Kim Campbell was never elected to office and served only 3 months after Brian Mulroney resigned as Prime Minister of Canada.

7. See United Nations (1997), United Nations Educational, Scientific, and Cultural Organization (1999), and http://www.Turkey.org/f_library.htm for additional information. Also see Arat (1996) for a discussion of the higher rate of illiteracy of rural women.

8. At 5 per 1,000 marriages, divorce is still rare in Turkey (United Nations, 1997).

9. Myths about and fear of women's unchecked sexuality and men's legitimacy to curb that sexuality are not unique to Islam; they are a recurring theme in all patriarchal, monotheistic religions. Although the emphasis here is on Middle Eastern culture in general and Turkey in particular, it should be emphasized that the control of women's sexuality and cultural obsession with virginity and sexual purity are not confined to the Middle East. A glaring example of the overemphasis on women's purity is the 2,000-year-old attribution of virginity to Mary, mother of Jesus Christ.

10. Although marriages through a religious ceremony are not considered legal according to the secular Turkish laws, they are common among rural people.

REFERENCES

Abou-Zeid, A. (1974). Honor and shame among Bedouins of Egypt. In J. G. Peristiany (Ed.), *Honor and shame: The values of Mediterranean society* (pp. 243–260). Chicago: University of Chicago Press.

Abu-Lughod, L. (1986). *Veiled sentiments: Honor and poetry in a Bedouin society.* Berkeley: University of California Press.

Acar, F. (1996). Turkiye'de kadinlarin yuksek ogrenim deneyimi (New insights into women's higher education in Turkey). In N. Arat (Ed.), *Turkiye'de Kadin Olmak* (pp. 195–211). Istanbul, Turkey: Say.

Acid attacks brutalize the women who say "no." (1999, February 6). *Toronto Star*, p. A20.

Aile meclisinin namus cinayeti (Honor-related murder by the family council). (1998, June 14). *Hurriyet*, p. 1.

Amnesty International. (1999). *Pakistan: Violence against women in the name of honor.* London: Author.

Arat, N. (Ed.). (1996). *Turkiye'de Kadin Olmak* (Being a woman in Turkey). Istanbul, Turkey: Say.

Arin, C. (1996). Kadina yonelik siddet acisindan Turk Hukuku'nun kadina yaklasimi (The stance of the Turkish Law in relation to violence against women). In Mor Cati (Ed.), *Evdeki terror* (pp. 130–139). Istanbul, Turkey: Mor Cati.

Article 23233. (1998, January 17). *Resmi Gazete.*

Ayse ve oglunu kim kurtaracak? (Who is going to save Ayse and her son?) (1996, December 13). *Milliyet*, p. M1.

Bebegini kurtlara yedirdi (She fed her baby to the wolves). (1995, February 27). *Aksam*, p. 1.

Bir namus cinayeti (An honor-related murder). (1996, April 13). *Pazartesi*, p. 1.

Brooks, G. (1995). *Nine parts of desire: The hidden world of Islamic women.* New York: Doubleday.

Bunch, C., & Frost, S. (1997). *Women's human rights: An introduction* [Online]. Available: http://www.cwgl.rutgers.edu/whr.html

Cakmagi cakdigi an (The moment the cigarette lighter was flicked). (1999, June 25). *Hurriyet*, p. 1.

Campaign against honor killings in Turkey [Online]. (1999). Available: http://www.gn.apc.org/honour_killings/honour.htm

Cancel, C. M. (1999). *Women's issues—3rd world: Honor killings* [Online]. Available: wysiwyg://128/http://women3rdworld.minin...omen3rdworld/library/weekly/aa011299.htm

Daly, M. (1989). Indian suttee: The ultimate consummation of marriage. In L. Richardson & V. Taylor (Eds.), *Feminist frontiers II: Rethinking sex, gender and society* (pp. 429–431). New York: McGraw-Hill.

DeKeseredy, W. S., & Hinch, R. (1991). *Woman abuse: Sociological perspectives.* Toronto, Canada: Thompson.

Delaney, C. (1987). Seeds of honor, fields of shame. In D. D. Gilmore (Ed.), *Honor and shame and the unity of the Mediterranean* (pp. 35–48). Washington, DC: American Anthropological Association.

Dobash, E. R.,, & Dobash, R. (1979). *Violence against wives: A case against patriarchy.* New York: Free Press.

Dobash, E. R., & Dobash, R. (Eds.). (1998). *Rethinking violence against women.* Thousand Oaks, CA: Sage.

Elmaci, N. (1996). Poligami: Cok esli evlilikler (Polygamy: Marriage to multiple partners). In N. Arat (Ed.), *Turkiye'de Kadin Olmak* (pp. 79–124). Istanbul, Turkey: Say.

Eve gec gelen kizini 30 yerinden bicakladi (He stabbed his daughter 30 times for coming home late). (1998, May 31). *Hurriyet*, p. 1.

Farac, M. (1998). *Tore Kiskacinda Kadin* (Women caught in the honor vice). Istanbul, Turkey: Cagdas Yayinlari.

Goodenough, P. (1999). Middle East women campaign against "family honor" killings [Online]. Available: http://www.conservativenews.net/InDepth/archive/199903/IND19990308e.html

Goodwin, J. (1994). *Price of honor: Muslim women lift the veil of silence on the Islamic world*. Boston: Little, Brown.

Gunenc, H. S. (1991). *Representative responsibility of the male child and its manifestation in homicidal events*. Unpublished master's thesis, Bogazici University, Istanbul, Turkey.

Ilkaracan, P. (1999). Extra-marital relationships and honor killings in eastern Turkey [e-mail message to the UNIFEM List: Women and Women's Rights].

Iste, Seriatin gercek yuzu (The true face of shari'a). (1997, March 8). *Sabah*, p. 1.

Kaya, A. (1996). Turk Ceza Hukuku'nda evlilik ici tecavuz (Assault within marriage according to the Turkish Criminal Law). In Mor Cati (Ed.), *Evdeki terror* (pp. 140–142). Istanbul, Turkey: Mor Cati.

Kidog. (1997). *Education, legal status, reproductive health: Women in Turkey*. Istanbul, Turkey: Kidog (NGO Advocacy Network for Women).

Kidog. (1998). *In light of international declarations: Women in Turkey*. Istanbul, Turkey: Kidog (NGO Advocacy Network for Women).

Kislali, A. T. (1996). Ulusal egemenlik ve siyasette kadin (National independence and women in politics). In N. Arat (Ed.), *Turkiye'de Kadin Olmak* (pp. 73–78). Istanbul, Turkey: Say.

Koy meydaninda infaz (Execution in the village center). (1995, October 1). *Aksam*, p. 1.

Krau, N. (1998). Honor killings threaten dozens [Online]. Available: http://www.gsnonweb.com/gsnlib_a/gsnbase/98_08/980803/17359.html

Kuyas, N. (1996, May 8). Hedef: Siddete sifir hosgoru (Goal: Zero tolerance for violence). *Milliyet*, p. 22.

Landsberg, M. (1995, September 17). Scandal of China's unwanted baby girls. *Toronto Star*, p. A1.

Landsberg, M. (1996, January 6). Orphans left to die. *Toronto Star*, p. A16.

Long talks get compromise on U.N. women's action plan. (1995, September 15). *Toronto Star*, p. A2.

MacKinnon, C. (1993). Race, genocide, and women's human rights. In A. Stiglmayer (Ed.), *The war against women in Bosnia-Herzegovina* (pp. 183–196). Lincoln: University of Nebraska Press.

Muslim Women's League. (1999). *Position paper on honor killings* [Online]. Available: http://www.mwlusa.org/pub_hk.shtml

Nelson, E. D., & Robinson, B. W. (1999). *Gender in Canada*. Toronto, Canada: Prentice Hall.

Orucu, E. (1996). Hukukta Kadin ve Son Gelismeler (Women within the law and the latest developments). In N. Arat (Ed.), *Turkiye'de Kadin Olmak* (pp. 21–42). Istanbul, Turkey: Say.

Pervizat, L. (1998). *Honor killings*. Paper presented at the 54th session of the United Nations Commission on Human Rights.

Pervizat, L. (1999, April). *Honor killings in Turkey: Untold stories of women's human rights violations.* Paper presented at the Women Transforming the Public conference, University of California, Santa Barbara.

Pitt-Rivers, J. (1974). Honor and social status. In J. G. Peristiany (Ed.), *Honor and shame: The values of Mediterranean society* (pp. 19–77). Chicago: University of Chicago Press.

Polis tecavuzde kadini sucluyor (For sexual assaults, police blame women). (2000, October 15). *Bizim Anadolu,* p. 13.

Queen Noor, H. M. (1999). Women press releases [Online]. Available: http://www.accessme.com/QNoorjo/main/honorcrm.htm

Ritual death of widow spurs uproar in India. (1999, November 20). *Toronto Star,* p. A18.

Rodgers, W. (1995). *Honor killings: A brutal tribal custom* [Online]. Available: http://www2.cnn.com/WORLD/9512/honor_killings/

Sabah [Online]. (1999, August 15). Available: http://garildi.sabah.com.tr/cgi-bin/sayf...ysabah/9908/15/t/p06.html+emeklilik+yasi

Sati, N. (1997). *The dark side of honor: ArabiaCulture* [Online]. Available: http://arabia.com/content/culture/11_97/honor11.16.97.shtml

Sawyer, D. (Reporter). (1999, January 22). Honor killings. *20/20.* New York: ABC.

Sev'er, A. (Ed.). (1997). *A cross-cultural exploration of wife abuse.* Lewiston, NY: Mellen.

Sev'er, A. (1998). Separation and divorce and violence against women. In A. Sev'er (Ed.), *Frontiers in women's studies: Canadian and German perspectives* (pp. 167–195). Toronto: Canadian Scholars' Press.

Small steps to stop the killing of girls. (1996, January 18). *Toronto Star,* p. A17.

Solomon, J. C. (1992). Child sexual abuse by family members: A radical feminist perspective. *Sex Roles, 27,* 473–485.

Tore icin kizini oldurdu (He killed his daughter for honor). (1998, May 9). *Milliyet,* p. 14.

Torelerin kurbani (Victim of honor). (1996, June 20). *Yeni Yuzyil,* p. 4.

Turgut, P. (1998). *Loss of honor means death in Turkish region* [Online]. Available: http://metimes.com/issue98-17/reg/honor.htm

Turkish women who see death as a way out. (2000, November 3). *The New York Times,* p. A3.

United Nations. (1997). *United Nations demographic yearbook.* New York: Author.

United Nations Educational, Scientific, and Cultural Organization. (1999). *UNESCO statistical yearbook.* Lanham, MD: Author.

Vicious twist in war on wives. (2000, March 5). *Toronto Star,* p. B3.

Worldmark: Encyclopedia of cultures and daily life. (1998). (Vol. 3). Detroit, MI: Gale.

Yine tore vahseti (Another honor-related violence). (1998, February 27). *Sabah,* p. 11.

Yurdakul, G. (1999). *Construction of honor: Reflections in women's status in Turkey.* Unpublished paper, Middle East Technical University, Ankara, Turkey.

Yusuff, M. K. (1998). *Honor killings in the name of religion* [Online]. Available: http://www.geocities.com/~ahmanraj/topics/honor_killings.html

Zina yapan kadin taslayarak olduruluyor (An adulterous woman was killed by stoning). (1995, August 21). *Milliyet,* p. 15.

The Connection Between Militarism and Violence Against Women

–Lucinda Marshall

Lucinda Marshall is a feminist artist, writer, and activist. She is the founder of the Feminist Peace Network, www.feministpeacenetwork.org, *which publishes* Atrocities, *a bulletin documenting violence against women throughout the world. Her article "The Connection Between Militarism and Violence Against Women" appeared on* Z-Net.

With no end in sight to the horribly misguided and damaging 'War on Terrorism', it is increasingly urgent to recognize the effects of war on women. There can be no true peace while the pandemic of violence against women continues, a pandemic that is greatly exacerbated by militarism. Making the connection between militarism and violence against women is critical to ending the siege of violence under which all women live.

The theory of Power Over an 'other' provides the common thread between military campaigns and assaults against women. What this theory says is that it is allowable for a person, ethnic group, government, etc. to get what they want by way of power over an other. This modus operandi has led us to a point where, as Patricia Evans points out, we as a civilization have assumed so much power over people and resources, that we now have the power to wipe out the world.[1]

In order for the power over theory to work, an 'other' must be defined by creating distinctions (no matter how false) between people, cultures and so on. The other can be a person, country, ethnic group, etc. This theory is the lifeblood of militarism, which depends on the creating of an other by declaring distinctions between two groups. The other is then asserted to be 'less than'. Once that definition is made, then the other must be protected or destroyed.

All too commonly, whether implicitly or explicitly, women are the 'other'. Consequently, it becomes necessary in the eyes of those who seek Power Over to control and belittle women, and all aspects of womanhood. In many cultures,

"The Connection Between Militarism and Violence Against Women" by Lucinda Marshall is reprinted by permission of the author.

women are viewed as the possessions of their men. Therefore, when a woman is raped, it is effectively an attack on the manhood of her man. Using this reasoning, women become the targets of war in order to attack the honor of the men of a particular culture, ethnic group or country. For these reasons, rape and other forms of sexual assault against women are always a part of war and conflict. When women are assumed to be possessions that can be attacked, stolen and dishonored, they become a means of feminizing and degrading the enemy.

Many types of violence against women are exacerbated by militarism, including the indirect effects on civilian populations and post-conflict situations. These include:

- Rape/sexual assault and harassment both within the military and perpetrated on civilian populations.
- Domestic violence.
- Prostitution, pornography and trafficking.

Since the beginning of the patriarchal age, women have been considered the spoils of war, invisibilized under the euphemistic phrase, 'collateral damage'. In Rwanda, at least 250,000 women were raped in the 1994 genocide. During the 1990's, more than 20,000 Muslim women were raped as part of an ethnic cleansing campaign in Bosnia.[2] And as recently as 2003, the U.N. reported thousands of women and girls had been raped during fighting in the Democratic Republic of Congo. **Gang rape was so widespread and brutal that doctors began classifying vaginal destruction as a combat-related crime.**[3]

Military training frequently encourages the hatred and belittling of women. The use of gender slurs motivate men to act aggressively, both toward women within their own culture and women of the 'other' culture. Pornography and prostitution have always been unofficially sanctioned forms of entertainment for soldiers. Until 1999, pornography could easily be purchased by servicemen at U.S. military base commissaries, which were one of the largest purchasers of hard core pornography. Its removal cost the commissaries at least $10 million.[4]

Prostitution is another perennial side effect of military action. There has always been an unspoken U.S. military policy of keeping the men happy. An active sex industry for military R and R has been consistently allowed and encouraged to flourish, in direct violation of U.S. and international law. Women are forced into prostitution as de facto sex slaves for the military in a variety of ways, such as false employment promises, being sold by their families, abduction, etc. It is no surprise that trafficking routes tend to spring up near military bases. More than 5000 women, mainly from the Philippines and the former Soviet Union, were trafficked into South Korea in the mid 1990's, primarily to work as 'entertainers' at bars near U.S. military bases.[5]

Women within the military are also considered fair targets. In a recent study, 30% of female veterans reported experiencing rape or attempted rape by U.S. servicemen. According to a Department of Defense survey, one in five female cadets at the Air Force Academy said they had been sexually assaulted during their time there.[6] Unfortunately many of these assaults were not reported when they occurred because the victims feared retaliation, such as damage to their careers or being accused of being disloyal or unpatriotic.[7,8]

Sexual harassment has long plagued women in the military. The Tailhook Scandal illustrates the depth of the problem. In that case, over 50 officers were implicated in making women run a gauntlet where they were man-handled in a variety of sexual ways. Six other officers were accused of blocking the investigation into the scandal. What is most significant is that despite Congressional hearings and massive news coverage, none of those implicated were ever court martialed or prosecuted in civilian courts.[9]

There is also a long history of domestic violence within the military culture. There have been 218 domestic murders in the U.S. Military since 1995. While there are services available for military families who experience domestic violence, the system makes it hard for military wives to report DV.

In general there are very few safeguards for the victim. Batterers are rarely prosecuted or even barred from getting near their victims. The attitude of commanders when told of domestic violence incidents has tended to be, "I'll take care of it, he's my soldier", rather than one of protecting the victim. It is not uncommon for commanders to ignore orders for anger management counseling and the like when it conflicts with military assignments. In fact, the military has handled most cases of domestic violence by administrative actions rather than by court martial. In sharp contrast, in 1990, 80% of civilian cases were referred for prosecution.[10]

The effects of militarism during post-conflict periods are also quite grave. Men returning from 'war' frequently transfer their entitlement to commit violence from the battlefield to their own communities. For example, after the supposed end to the war in Afghanistan, the condition for women in that country has worsened considerably. Rape, forced prostitution and marriages, acid burnings, the bombing of girls' schools, and the sale of women are daily atrocities.[11] And here in the U.S., 3 soldiers returning from duty in Afghanistan promptly killed their wives at Fort Bragg, North Carolina.

The time has come when we can no longer deny that misogynist violence is a major component of militaristic power over thinking, as well as a significant part of the global pandemic of violence against women. But we must go beyond that and recognize the reality that men's violence against women is so prevalent, that even in 'peacetime', there is no peace for women. According to a recent UNIFEM report, one in three women will be sexually assaulted during their lifetime.[12] According to the U.S. Justice Department, every ninety seconds, a person over the age of 12 is sexually assaulted. 89% of the victims are female, 99% of the perpetrators are male.[13] It is therefore critical that those who are working to raise awareness about misogynist violence and those who are working to end militarism recognize the intersection of their agendas and find ways to work together.

NOTES

1. Evans, Patricia. *The Verbally Abusive Relationship: How to recognize it and how to respond*, Avon Media Corporation, Avon, Massachusetts, 1996, p. 29. It is interesting to note that this book focuses on power over women in personal relationships, yet right at the beginning, she makes the connection between the personal and political.

2. Women, War, Peace and Violence Against Women, www.womenwarpeace.org/issues/violence.htm

3. Rape So Common in D.R.C., It Is Considered Combat Injury", *U.N. Wire*, October 27, 2003, http://www.unwire.org/UNWire/20031027/449_9787.asp

4. "The Pentagon Takes Aim on Pornography", *Kentucky Citizen Digest.* March, 1999, www.tffky.org/articles/1999/199903dc.htm

5. Raja, Kanaga. "Women From Philippines And Former USSR Trafficked Into South Korea For Sex", Third World Network Features, September, 2002, www.twnside.org/sg/title/2396.htm

6. Herdy, Amy and Moffeit, Miles. "Female GIs Report Rapes in Iraq War: 37 Seek Aid After Alleging Sex Assaults By U.S. Soldiers", *Denver Post*, January 25, 2004. In just the last few months, we have learned that 88 cases of sexual assault have been reported by soldiers in the Gulf region during the U.S.'s current invasion of Iraq, with 37 women seeking assistance upon returning from active duty. The women reported not being able to get appropriate help when the incidents occurred.

7. Herdy, Amy and Moffeit, Miles. "Betrayal In The Ranks: For Crime Victims, Punishment", *Denver Post*, Nov. 16, 2003. This is one of an excellent series of articles. The reporters have continued to report on this story as it unfolds.

8. "Air Force Academy: Few Cases Resolved", *Kansas City Star*, February 5, 2003. Since new leadership took over in April, 2003, 21 cases of sexual misconduct have been reported at the Air Force Academy. Only four cases have been resolved with only one case resulting in criminal prosecution. In that case the perpetrator was sentenced to 100 hours of community service.

9. "The Tailhook Scandal", 1994, www.galegroup.com/free.resources/whm/trials/tailhook.htm

10. Also from Herdy and Moffeit's "Betrayal In The Ranks: For Crime Victims, Punishment".

11. See www.rawa.org for numerous reports.

12. "One In Three Women Worldwide Could Suffer Violence Directed At Her Simply Because She Is Female", UNIFEM, November 24, 2003, http://www.unifem.org/pressreleases.php?f_page_pid=6&f_pritem_pid=149

13. "Sexual Assault Statistics", www.stopfamilyviolence.org

The Impact of Political Conflict on Women: The Case of Afghanistan

–Sima Wali, Elizabeth Gould, and Paul Fitzgerald

Sima Wali is president and CEO of Refugee Women in Development, Inc. (RefWID), an international nonprofit institution focusing on women in conflict, post-conflict rein-tegration, and human rights. She is a native of Afghanistan. American journalists Elizabeth Gould and Paul Fitzgerald went to Afghanistan in 1981 to cover the war for CBS news and later produced a documentary for PBS. The article that follows is a col-laboration among all three and first appeared in the American Journal of Public Health *in October 1999.*

The recent war in Kosovo has forced the plight of refugee women on the world's attention. Rape, torture, forced prostitution, and an endless string of unnameable atrocities awaited many of the victims of the conflict in Kosovo. But as the West rallies to shoulder the burden of the displaced Kosovars after a short military engagement, it should be understood that a larger and longer-standing human tragedy continues in Afghanistan—a tragedy that is a direct legacy of America's Cold War foreign policy of the 1970s (P. Fitzgerald and E. Gould, unpublished data, 1999).

Now that the Soviet Union has been defeated through the US policy that in-tentionally trapped the Soviet Union in its own Vietnam, the legacy of that policy for the Afghan people remains. In Afghanistan, as in no other crisis spot in the world, women have been made to pay a special and painful price. To understand the tragedy of Afghanistan, and of the unprecedented levels of strife and violence throughout the decade of the 1990s in many parts of the developing world, it is es-sential to grasp the inextricable link between these humanitarian disasters and the political circumstances that caused them. Without such an understanding, a solu-tion to the worldwide crises in women's health and human rights is unattainable.

"The Impact of Political Conflict on Women: The Case of Afghanistan" by Sima Wali, Elizabeth Gould, and Paul Fitzgerald from *American Journal of Public Health*, October 1999. Copyright © 1999. Reprinted by permission of the American Public Health Association.

A Wall of Silence

It is hard to believe that 20 years after the Communist coup that overthrew the Afghan Republic, the basic human rights of Afghan women are still being violated. But then, the Afghan war began behind a wall of silence that separated the political events of that era from their human consequences. Today, it is this wall of silence that forbids the linking of humanitarian crises to the larger political issues that provoked them. It is this wall of silence that divides the peace negotiator from the humanitarian activist and the activist from the solution. It is this wall of silence that perpetuates humanitarian crises and frustrates relief workers and activists in their efforts to end crimes against humanity. And it is this wall of silence that, like the Berlin Wall, must come down if we are not to be overwhelmed by the long-term dependence of war victims on outside relief assistance.

As a consequence of the division between humanitarian crises and the political discourse that would alter them, conflicts remain unresolved, leaving the victims exposed to multiple abuses. Today, instead of working toward a common goal, relief and human rights workers must compete in an environment of conflicting empowerment models. The continuum of humanitarian involvement—from relief efforts to assistance with social and economic development—is not defined, and the concept of empowerment of victims does not exist. The absence of such a concept perpetuates warlordism and levels of destructiveness that threaten in some regions to altogether undo established societies and cultures.

Health, Mental Health, Gender, and Human Rights in Conflict Situations

In the Afghanistan crisis, a multitude of women have undergone war-related trauma.[1] Worldwide, women and girls make up more than half of the estimated 44 million refugees, asylum seekers, and internally displaced persons.[2] These women and girls suffer lifelong trauma from such abuses as multiple rape, forced prostitution, slavery, and other forms of gender-related violence. In addition, sexual violence substantially increases women's risk for sexually transmitted diseases. Although women are not immune to violence in times of peace, female victims of war are subjected to violence in the most extreme forms.

The World Health Organization (WHO) defines health as a state of complete physical, mental, and social well-being, and not merely the absence of disease or infirmity.[3] WHO's definition of health for women includes not only their physical well-being but also the ability to exercise more control over their lives and relationships and the ability to access information and resources that will allow them to take responsibility for their own health and that of their family. But since the Taliban militia took over Afghanistan in 1996, these goals have been unattainable; instead, Afghan women have been brutally and systematically suppressed.

Poverty and unequal access to resources are often at the heart of women's neglect and abuse, and this is especially true in war economies. Resources such as food and medical attention are often withheld from women and directed to male soldiers. The results are high levels of malnutrition, hunger, and hunger-related diseases that will affect that society for generations.[4] Sixty-two percent of Afghan women—both residents of Kabul and refugees in Pakistan—who were surveyed by the organization Physicians for Human Rights reported that they were employed before the Taliban takeover; only 20% of these women were employed during their last year in Kabul.[5]

The war in Afghanistan has devastated the lives not only of women but of children as well. A majority of Afghan children surveyed by UNICEF are suffering from severe stress as a result of witnessing acts of violence, including the killings of their parents or relatives. Between 1992 and 1996, 72% of the children surveyed had lost a family member, and 40% of those children had lost a parent.[6] According to the 1996 International Committee for the Red Cross, Afghanistan is the world's most heavily land-mined country. The Afghan Campaign to Ban Land Mines reports that 10 to 12 Afghans, many of them children, are killed or maimed by land mines every day. Afghan women bear the responsibility of caring for these disabled children, while they themselves are traumatized and malnourished.

The already inadequate resources assigned to health services for women have been further reduced since the advent of the Taliban regime, which actively denies women care in hospitals and clinics [see reference 5]. This discrimination against Afghan women has long-term consequences and threatens a worsening of already poor health indicators. Maternal and infant mortality rates, for example, are already high as a result of unhealthy birth spacing to replenish lost fighting forces. Afghanistan is the lowest-ranking country of 130 nations listed on both the United Nations Human Development Index[7] and the United Nations Development Program Gender Disparity Index. Its maternal mortality rates are among the highest in the world.[8]

The United Nations' (UN's) 1990 Human Development Report defines human development as a process of widening the range of people's choices.[9] The 1994 report expands this definition, stating that human development should "empower people enabling them to design and participate in the process and events that shape their lives."[10] However, women victimized by conflict cannot avail themselves of even the basics of human survival, and world institutions have failed to protect them from the most fundamental human rights violations. With hundreds of regional conflicts taking the place of the monolithic East vs West conflict of the Cold War, the world community has not evolved to meet today's challenges, a fact that not only hinders the resolution of existing problems but threatens to institutionalize these problems for future generations.

For example, critics of the UN claim that Afghan women's rights have been placed after the UN's need to ensure its presence, maintain its operations, and continue a dialogue with the Taliban in Afghanistan. Although they may be well intentioned, deals that diminish or deny Afghan women's rights—to a safe and productive livelihood; to access to education, health, and mental health services; to freedom from hunger; to safety; to freedom of expression; to access to international

and human rights entities; to participation in peace discourses; to freedom of association; and to freedom of movement—disillusion those who put their trust in
global institutions and the rule of law. Furthermore, the lack of external monitoring permits the Taliban to flout international covenants signed by previous governments in Afghanistan.

There has been much discussion about reforming existing institutions or creating new ones to meet today's challenges. There is a critical need for an institution
that is responsive to the needs of war-affected people, that operates under the auspices of the United Nations, and that works in partnership with Afghan-led civil institutions, international human rights entities, and women's organizations. Such
an institution must be prepared to acknowledge newly emerging human rights
concerns and elevate them to higher levels of importance. For example, the violation of women and girls has historically been dismissed as a byproduct of warfare.
However, during the 1980s in Cambodia and Vietnam, mass rape was used as a
calculated weapon of terror.[11] The practice of "ethnic breeding" (forcible impreg-
nation of women and girls by opposing factions) imposed on Bosnian Muslims in
the early 1990s set the stage for the current abuses against Albanian Kosovar
women. Thus, the international community must adopt an entirely new standard.
The public violence directed against Afghan women who do not conform to the
Taliban's view of Islamic practices must be challenged.

Conclusion

The United Nations Development Program's 1994 Human Development Report
describes "human security" as a necessary condition to peace. The report states:
"The world can never be at peace unless people have security in their daily lives.
The search for security in such a milieu lies in development, not in arms" [see reference 10, p. 1].

As the majority of the displaced and refugee populations, women who are war
victims hold a major stake in securing peace. Across the globe, women are among
the first to engage in dialogue, to effect reconciliation, and to promote values
aimed at creating a culture of justice and peace.

The health and human rights crisis in Afghanistan was brought about by the
Cold War between superpowers and must now be analyzed in the context of that
war. In this context, it is imperative that the gender apartheid policies and practices of the Taliban and the current level of violence against Afghan women be
linked to the larger geopolitical decisions made at the start of this conflict. In particular, it must be fully recognized that the United States' support for the most radical elements of Islamic fundamentalism throughout the 1980s slowly brought
about the destruction of the cultural framework that defined and maintained the
time-honored role of Afghan women. For Afghanistan to be at peace, this role
must be returned to Afghan women, and that is something only the United States
and the world community have the power to do.

REFERENCES

1. Women in Afghanistan: A Human Rights Catastrophe. New York, NY: Amnesty International; November 3, 1995.

2. World Refugee Survey. Washington, DC: US Committee for Refugees; 1995.

3. Cook RJ. Women's Health and Human Rights. Geneva, Switzerland: World Health Organization; 1994.

4. Wali S. Hunger among uprooted women and children. In: Hunger 1993: Uprooted People. Third Annual Report on the State of World Hunger. Washington, DC: Bread for the World Institute; 5992:54–59.

5. Rasekh Z, Bauer H, Manos M, Iacopino V. Women's health and human rights in Afghanistan. JAMA. 1998;280:449–455.

6. Gupta L. Survey on Afghan Children. New York, NY: United Nations Children's Fund (UNICEF): October 1997.

7. Human Development Report 1996. New York, NY: United Nations Development Program; 1996.

8. Human Development Report 1995. New York, NY: United Nations Development Program; 1995.

9. Human Development Report 1990. New York, NY: United Nations Development Program; 1990.

10. Human Development Report 1994. New York, NY: United Nations Development Program; 1994, p. 4.

11. Mollica R. The trauma story: the psychiatric care of refugee survivors of violence and torture. In: Ochberg F, ed. Post-Traumatic Therapy and Victims of Violence. New York, NY: Brunner/Mazel; 1998:295–314.

Questions for Thinking, Writing, and Discussion

1. What, according to Gerda Lerner, are the main components of patriarchy? Can you identify aspects of patriarchy at work in contemporary society?

2. In her essay, Gerda Lerner suggests that gender is always expressed in class terms. Discuss this claim in light of Allan Johnson's insight, quoted in the introduction, that in patriarchal society, power is culturally gendered. Explain what each thinker means and agree or disagree with them, offering concrete examples to illustrate your conclusion.

3. Compare and contrast the concept of identity that is dominant in the West with the concept of identity that is used in the Arab world. How does this concept of identity impact on women's lives?

4. Based on your readings, discuss the economic basis of honor killings and violence against women in general.

5. What role do women play in perpetuating patriarchal values and rule?

6. In their essay, Aysan Sev'er and Gökçeçiçek Yurdakul suggest that honor killings are not connected to Islam but instead grow out of a cultural understanding of honor. Do you think they have made a good case for this conclusion? What role do you think religion in general plays in relationship to the status of women in society? Illustrate your response with specific examples.

7. Using either or both Zillah Eisenstein's and Albert Memmi's articles in Part Three, select one article in this section and analyze it in terms of their discussions of racism, sexism, and other forms of hatred and violence against women.

8. Compare and contrast the accounts offered by Karen Hossfeld and Cynthia Enloe of how patriarchal values have been used to manipulate and control women factory workers. Do you think this analysis applies to women in other job categories?

9. Using the articles by Lucinda Marshall and by Sima Wali, Elizabeth Gould, and Paul Fitzgerald, discuss the impact of war and militarism on the lives of women and children.

Suggestions for Further Reading

Bart, Pauline B., and Eileen Geil Moran. *Violence Against Women: The Bloody Footprints.* Sage Publications, 1992.

Disch, Estelle. *Reconstructing Gender: A Multicultural Anthology.* New York: McGraw-Hill, 2002.

El Sadaawi, Nawal. *Love in the Kingdom of Oil.* Saqi, 2001.

Freeman, Carla. *High Tech and High Heels in the Global Economy: Women, Work and Pink-Collar Identities in the Caribbean.* Durham: Duke University Press, 2000.

French, John D., and Daniel James. "The Gendered Worlds of Latin American Women Workers," *Household and Factory to the Union Hall and Ballot Box.* Durham: Duke University Press, 1997.

Johnson, Allan G. *The Gender Knot: Unraveling Our Patriarchal Legacy.* Philadelphia: Temple University Press, 2005.

Kimmel, Michale S. *The Gendered Society.* Oxford University Press, 2003.

Lerner, Gerder. *The Creation of Patriarchy.* New York: Oxford University Press, 1987.

Mies, Maria. *Patriarchy and Accumulation on a World Scale.* Zed Books, 1999.

Narayan, Uma. "Cross-Cultural Connections, Border-Crossings, and 'Death by Culture,'" *Dislocating Cultures.* New York: Routledge, 1997.

Newell, Katherine S., et al. *Discrimination Against the Girl Child: Female Infanticide, Genital Cutting, Honor Killings.* Youth Advocacy Program International, 2000.

Ogasawa, Yuko. *Office Ladies and Salaried Men: Power, Gender, and Work in Japanese Companies.* University of California Press, 1998.

Rubenberg, Cheryl A. *Palestinian Women: Patriarchy and Resistance in the West Bank.* Boulder, Colorado: Lynne Rienner Publishers, Inc., 2001.

Salzinger, Leslie. *Genders in Production: Making Workers in Mexico's Global Factories.* University of California Press, 2003.

Tiano, Susan. "Patriarchy on the Line," *Labor, Gender and Ideology in the Mexican Maquila Industry.* Philadelphia: Temple University Press, 1994.

Poverty, Inequality, and Structural Violence

20% of the population in the developed nations consume 86%
of the world's goods.
–*1998 Human Development Report, United Nations Development Programme*

A mere 12% of the world's population uses 85% of its water, and these 12%
do not live in the Third World.
–*Maude Barlow, National Chairperson, Council of Canadians*

It is difficult to know how to covey the extraordinarily unequal nature of the distribution of wealth in the world today. Speaking on the International Day for the Eradication of Poverty in October 2000, U.N. Secretary General Koffi Anan told his audience: "Almost half the world's population lives on less than two dollars a day, yet even this statistic fails to capture the humiliation, powerlessness and brutal hardship that is the daily lot of the world's poor." According to the U.N.'s 1999 Human Development report, the gap between rich and poor is growing at an alarming rate. Figures show that in 1960, 20% of the world's people in the richest countries had 30 times the income of the poorest 20%. By 1997 that figure had increased to 74 times as much. In the United States the gap between rich and poor has been growing since 1973 and is currently the greatest it has been in 70 years.

People who study development and those of us who want to think critically about global issues are faced with the difficult task of trying to decide what constitutes an accurate measure of world poverty and how we can make accurate judgments about whether development initiatives are having an impact on it. The World Bank has adopted the practice of measuring poverty in terms of the number of people who live on one or two dollars a day. This measure is predicated on the assumption that people would be able to purchase the same amount of goods in any country for the same amount of money, but many dispute this assumption. And many believe that defining poverty in terms of living on one or two dollars a day leaves out far too many people who are indeed poor. For example, in the United States the poverty line for a family of four has been set at approximately eleven dollars a day. Where do they appear on the World Bank's poverty chart? What about people who live on three dollars a day, or four or five a day? Do they qualify as poor?[1] Many economists and political scientists argue that using a more realistic criterion for defining poverty would send the world poverty figures soaring. But while there is considerable disagreement about how to define poverty, there is little disagreement over the reality that the gap between rich and poor between and within nations is very large and that this unequal distribution of wealth is having a devastating impact on the health and well being of a large portion of humanity.

The articles in Part Five adopt a variety of approaches to studying poverty and enumerating some of its consequences at the same time as they struggle with the difficulties in collecting and interpreting poverty statistics. In Article 1, "Inequality in the Global Village," Jan Knippers Black confronts head on the contradictory picture of international development at the close of the twentieth century that emerges from a disparate collection of statistics, what she refers to as "development's mixed message." Some of the statistics that Black reviews suggest a degree of progress in combating things like malnutrition and communicable diseases and in improving school enrollment and literacy, while other data, mostly focused on economic growth trends, paint a more pessimistic future. How does one decide on the relative weight to give to competing data such as these? Black chooses to slip between horns of the dilemma. She argues that, even if it were the case that the standard of living were found to be improving for the majority of the world's people over the long run, whatever progress we can detect over time has hardly followed a steady enough course to leave us sanguine. And, more significantly, she points out that all of us live in the short run and in the short run living standards in many countries and for most of the people in the world at this moment in time are simply intolerable.

In Article 2, "Poverty and Inequality in the Global Economy," Michael Yates sets out to examine poverty and inequality in three different contexts: in the United States, in the poor countries of the world, and with regard to the gap between the richest and poorest countries globally. Yates, who believes that the official poverty level of income in the United States has been set misleadingly high, is disturbed by the contradiction he sees between the rhetoric of U.S. democracy's promise of equality of opportunity for all and the reality that current statistics show a large and increasing inequality of wealth in U.S. society. But however disturbing this inequality may be, he contends that it is nothing when compared to the levels of both poverty and inequality that exist in the rest of the world. As do other authors in this section, Yates challenges the methodology that the World Bank uses in arriving at its poverty calculations, calculations that he believes seriously understate the extent of the crisis. But most disturbing is his contention that the vast and growing inequality around the world is not an accident but rather the inevitable outcome of the operation of capitalism. According to Yates, the necessity of "inequality in income and wealth . . . are a profound contradiction of the capitalist mode of production." For this reason, like Maria Mies in Part Two, Yates rejects the possibility that "catching up development" can be successful and suggests that the contradictions of capitalism that create and require the continuous existence of vast inequalities of wealth are likely to produce social unrest in the years ahead.

The question of the accuracy of poverty data produced by the World Bank is confronted head on by Angus Deaton in Article 3, "Is World Poverty Falling?" which originally appeared in *Finance and Development*, a quarterly publication of the International Monetary Fund. Deaton's question is prompted specifically by conclusions published in two reports issued by the World Bank within a period of less than two years. The reports, which according to Deaton used the same data, arrived at contradictory conclusions about whether world poverty was actually rising or falling. Stressing the importance of an accurate poverty account, Deaton subjects some of the World Bank data to critical scrutiny and recommends greater transparency and perhaps independent oversight as a way of guaranteeing the accuracy and insuring the credibility of World Bank poverty figures.

One of the major indicators that is currently used to calculate the success of development initiatives and to compare the progress being made in different societies is the Gross Domestic Product (GDP). Article 4, "A Critical Look at Measurements of Economic Progress," an excerpt from a report issued by The International Forum on Globalization, offers a scathing critique of this measure. According to this critique, the GDP, which measures a society's performance exclusively in terms of the rate at which resources are converted to commodities and sold, and the activities that accompany that process, begs the question because it adopts the perspective of corporate globalization by assuming that all growth is good. By assuming that *everything* that is produced is good, the GDP fails to look at the human cost of production and fails to ask who benefits from it. For example, strip mining and constructing toxic dumps show up as positive indicators in the GDP, while growing food within communities and caring for the sick and elderly do not. But the health of people forced to live near a toxic dump—inevitably those who are poor and already vulnerable—will be further compromised and in the end the society as a whole will end up paying the costs of either or both the need for increased health and other social services and the costs of cleaning up the environment. By treating growth in and of itself as a positive, without asking what that growth will mean to the long-term health and well being of the population and of future generations, the GDP simply incorporates the assumption that fuels globalization, namely, that all growth is good. Further, by failing to distinguish between the production of goods and services that can help alleviate poverty and those that simply produce luxuries for the rich, the authors contend that this economic indicator is biased against the developing world and the poor. In fact, as they point out, it is common for the poor to lose ground during periods of rapid economic growth.

What, then, is a good indicator of the health and well being of a society? Many would agree with the authors of the preceding article that looking at the condition of the most vulnerable members of a society rather than its wealthiest members is a good way to gauge quality of life. The next two articles in this section, a 2004 report from the World Health Organization and the text of a speech delivered by Jeffrey Sachs, take a look at the state of world health and in doing so paint a disturbing picture of life in the global village. They describe a world of vastly unequal access to basic health care, where, in the words of the WHO report, "deep economic inequalities and social injustices continue to deny good health to many. . . ." Both this report and Sachs' comments reflect a deep pessimism about the likelihood that current initiatives are likely to improve world health in the coming decades. While the WHO report in Article 5 points to inadequacies in the health systems themselves in developing countries as key constraints to the implementation of major global health initiatives, Jeffrey Sachs argues in Article 6 that poor countries have so little money to spend on their health systems that there is no way those systems can be successful, hence the subtitle of his talk: "No Health Available at $7.50 per Person per Year." In his concluding remarks, Sachs calls upon the rich countries of the world, countries he describes as "unimaginably rich even by standards of twenty years ago" to increase their support of health for the poorest of the poor, which he says is at "shockingly low levels."

But, as Paul Farmer correctly observes, statistics in themselves are unable to adequately convey the extent and the experience of suffering, so in Article 7, "Suffering and Structural Violence," Farmer offers us the stories of two Haitian youths, Acéphie Joseph and Chouchou Louis, whose stories provide a heartbreaking picture of the impact of structural violence on people who occupy "the bottom rung of the social ladder in inegalitarian societies." In seeking to focus our attention on "structural violence," Farmer asks us to understand the ways in which interlocking economic, political, and social forces operate in the ordinary life of the poorest of the poor to deny them the possibility of making meaningful life choices. He writes, "for many, including most of my patients and informants, choices both large and small are limited by racism, sexism, political violence, *and* grinding poverty." It is this grinding poverty that, according to Farmer, assures that the poorest of the poor will be victims of wholesale rights violations and the most extreme forms of suffering.

One of the "axes of oppression" acknowledged by Farmer is homophobia. Article 8 presents the testimony of lesbian rights activist FannyAnn Eddy before the U.N. Commission on Human Rights. In her remarks, Eddy talks about the vulnerability of the lesbian, gay, bisexual, and transgendered community in Sierra Leone and throughout Africa. She speaks out against the silence and denial that contributes to an atmosphere of fear and violence and connects the failure of many African leaders to acknowledge the existence of this community with the spread of HIV/AIDS throughout the continent. In September 2004 Eddy was found dead on the floor of the Sierra Leone Lesbian and Gay Association office where she had been working alone the previous night. She had been raped repeatedly, stabbed, and her neck was broken.

Eddy's testimony is followed by two U.N. fact sheets—Article 9 by the International Labour Organization, which provides statistics on child labor, and Article 10, which gives a snapshot of world poverty and hunger.

In Article 11, the concluding article in this section, "Women and the Poor: The Challenge of Global Justice," Nawal El Saadawi poses the question "Why do we have inequality and poverty in the world?" It is to this question that we will turn more directly in the remaining sections of this book. For now, the Saadawi piece provides us with an interesting overview that weaves together many of the topics and issues that have already been discussed in this text.

NOTE

1. Globalissues.org

Inequality in the Global Village
–Jan Knippers Black

Jan Knippers Black is a professor in the Graduate School of International Policy Studies at the Monterey Institute of International Studies in California. She has traveled widely, beginning with a stint in the Peace Corps in Chile and including Fulbright and Mellon Fellowships for work in South America, the Caribbean, and India. The following selection is taken from her book Inequality in the Global Village, *which was published by Kumarian Press in 1999.*

Archeologists discovered long ago that the most promising place to dig for the major temple of a particular era was directly beneath the major temple of the subsequent era. Consecutive waves of conquerors have chosen to construct the sacred places of their new civilization directly over the ruins of the old. Is it any wonder, then, that in the heart of so many of the sacred sites and best-preserved historic districts around the world, one finds the golden arches of McDonald's hamburgers. McDonald's now has establishments in more than one hundred countries, an empire that would have been the envy of Genghis Khan.

For those who would understand and/or promote international development, the end of the twentieth century must be seen as both the best of times and the worst of times. The United Nations Development Programme (UNDP) reported in 1997 that poverty has fallen more in the past fifty years than it had in the previous five hundred. Life expectancy and infant mortality rates have improved markedly over the past quarter century, largely as a consequence of the spread of modern medical and sanitation practices. Child death rates in developing countries have been cut in half since 1960 and malnutrition rates have declined by almost one-third. It is estimated that oral dehydration therapy alone saves more than a million children annually and perhaps a few million more have been protected by inoculation from a variety of diseases.

The International Food Policy Research Institute reported that food production increased on average 2.6 percent each year between 1961 and 1985 while annual world population growth dropped from a high of about 2 percent in the early 1960s to 1.6 percent in the mid-1980s. UNDP figures show an increase in per capita food production in developing countries of 22 percent between 1980 and

From *Inequality in the Global Village* (West Hartford, Conn.: Kumarian Press, 1999, Chapter 2, pp. 11–17). Reprinted by permission.

1997, despite a 3 percent decline in Sub-Saharan Africa. Meanwhile, human fertility rates had fallen over the last quarter of the twentieth century by 40 percent. The proportion of children in the developing countries who were underweight declined from 41 percent in 1975 to 22 percent in 1996. UNICEF (United Nation's Children's Fund) has seen increases in school enrollment—from less than 40 percent of school age children in the 1950s to some 70 percent in the mid-1980s—as one of the greatest achievements in the developing world. Literacy rates reportedly continued their climb as well. Between 1970 and 1995 the worldwide adult illiteracy rate was nearly cut in half, from 57 percent to 30 percent.

Development's Mixed Message

Juxtaposed with such indicators of progress are equally well-established indicators of retrogression. Some of these indicators represent the negative effects of indisputably worthwhile endeavors. Overpopulation, for example, owes much to the spreading benefits of modern medicine. Others, like rural landlessness and urban unemployment, are attributable to long-term trends, like the spread of export-oriented agribusiness and capital-intensive technology, that have been beneficial to some and damaging to a great many others. And finally, there are shorter term trends, like international capital flows, that turned extremely disadvantageous for Third World countries in general and the Third World poor in particular in the 1980s.

Much of the bad news at the beginning of the 1990s had to do with economic growth trends that, having been positive for most of the previous twenty to thirty years, turned sharply negative in the 1980s. World GDP growth rates dropped in the late 1980s, from 4.3 percent in 1988 to 3.0 percent in 1989 to 1.0 percent in 1990.[1] During the last half of the 1980s in Latin America and the Caribbean, Africa, and much of Asia, foreign aid and new loans and investments did not begin to compensate for the amounts flowing, as debt service payments, from those areas into the coffers of First World banks. The terms of trade for traditional Third World products also declined sharply. Commodity prices worldwide plummeted in the 1980s and GDP dropped by 8 percent during the decade in Latin America and by 20 percent in Africa.[2]

The US Agency for International Development (USAID) reported that 70 percent of the world's ninety-five least developed countries suffered overall economic decline in the 1980s. Faltering growth rates meant falling wages and rising unemployment. In times of economic decline, the affluent are far better able to defend their share of income and assets, so the belts that are tightened will be those already around the narrowest waists. Such belt-tightening normally takes the forms not only of wage freezes, layoffs, and foreclosures, but also of cutbacks in subsidies and services and protections for workers and consumers. UNICEF reported that the world's thirty-six poorest countries slashed budgets for education and health by 25 percent and 50 percent, respectively, during the last half of the 1980s. Food production also fell in most of those countries. Infant mortality worsened in two-thirds of them. Overall life expectancy declined in a few, and diseases thought to have been eradicated, like smallpox and polio, reappeared.[3] Changes consistent throughout most of the world in budget priorities and other areas of economic policy left no doubt that the debts incurred in the 1970s, in many cases by military dictatorships, were being serviced in the 1980s by the classes and sectors that benefited least from the loans.

What is one to conclude from such seeming discrepancies with respect to progress and retrogression, apart from the fact that one can "prove" anything one wishes with statistics? How should we explain aggregate data showing long-term gains but short-term losses, increasing production but also increasing hunger, increasing educational levels for increasingly unemployed work forces? It may be that standards of living are improving for the majority of the world's population over the long term, although that remains subject to dispute on various grounds, subject most decidedly to some means of coming to terms with the contradiction between ecological limitations and the production and consumption requisites of an economic growth model, and subject finally to policy decisions yet to be made. At any rate, the short term is the term we live in, and, in the short term, living standards are definitely intolerable for a growing absolute number in the Third World, and since the 1980s, in the First World as well.

Economic recovery between 1987 and 1993 was such as to register, in accordance with World Bank criteria, a decline from 34 percent to 32 percent in the proportion of the people in developing countries living in income poverty. However, it is estimated that the actual number of income-poor people increased by almost 100 million during that period from 1.2 billion to 1.3 billion, and the number appeared to be growing in every region except Southeast Asia and the Pacific. According to the human development index drawn up by the UNDP, living standards declined more in thirty countries in 1996–97 than in any other year since the UNDP's *Human Development Report* was first issued in 1990. The average incidence of income poverty for Eastern Europe and the offspring states of the Soviet Union increased sevenfold between 1988 and 1994, from 4.7 percent to 32 percent. The number of people in the region who had become impoverished increased from 14 million to more than 119 million. Oxfam, one of the major international relief and development agencies, maintains that in cereal grains alone, the world food supply offers 2,200 calories per person per day; yet more than 840 million people are chronically hungry.

Progress on a Zig-Zag Course

Advances in living standards since the dawn of the industrial revolution have not followed a steady course, nor have they been uniform across geographic and cultural regions. Advances in some areas have come at the expense of decline in others — in colonial or neocolonial centers, for example, at the expense of colonized or client states. And periods of progress have been interspersed with periods of retrogression, consequent not only to the creation of wealth through technologically more efficient exploitation of material and human resources but also to development of social and political mechanisms for equitable allocation of responsibility and benefit. The distribution of progress and retreat in poverty reduction across time and region during the second half of the twentieth century is represented in Figure 1.

Following on the widespread, and in some regions very deep, recession of the 1980s, the 1990s have appeared to most analysts (and more important, to creditors and investors) to be a decade of recovery. In fact, growth in some regions and countries had been dramatic enough to inspire talk of economic miracles and to cause creditors and others in a position to set conditions and exercise leverage over state policy to insist on a uniform set of policy changes generally known as economic restructuring or structural adjustment. The miracles were gushers of foreign currency coming in as bankrupt governments staged going-out-of-business sales. It might have been guessed that if the prescriptions were the same (i.e., bleeding) for countries whose ills were as diverse as those of Haiti, Mexico, Russia, and South Korea, the needs being met were not those of the patients but rather of the doctors.

Such restructuring is designed to attract capital as credit or investment. As countries, all undergoing the same process, compete for capital, obligations and offerings to creditors take precedence over obligations to domestic constituencies. These policy changes, which have had the effect of shifting costs downward on the social pyramid and benefits upward and outward, to foreign stakeholders, have sharply increased the already growing wealth and income gaps between regions and countries and within them.

In 1994, the ratio of the income of the wealthiest 20 percent of the world population to that of the poorest 20 percent was 78 to 1, up from 30 to 1 in 1960. Globally, the number of billionaires increased between 1989 and 1996 from 157 to 447. The net worth of the world's ten wealthiest individuals amounts to more than 1.5 times the total national income of all of the least developed countries, as designated by the UNDP. In Mexico, where in the late 1980s and early 1990s economic miracles alternated with economic meltdowns, the holdings of the richest individual among many new billionaires is equal to the combined income of seventeen million poor Mexicans.[4]

Nor was such income disparity limited to the Third World. Pockets of poverty had been growing in the developed world as well since the early 1980s, particularly in the United Kingdom and the United States. By the early 1990s more than 100 million people in the industrialized countries were found to be income poor. In the United States, one-fifth of the aged and one-fourth of the children live beneath the poverty line. The boom of the 1990s had come largely at the expense of workers, most of whom were earning less in real wages in 1997 than they had in 1989. In fact, wages had been essentially flat in the US since the 1970s. The minimum wage bought less in 1998 than in 1968 and fewer employees had adequate health insurance or pensions.[5]

Income poverty is generally found in combination with other deprivations, since the poor are less able to defend their rights to services, to personal security, even to the "best things in life" that we used to believe were free, like relatively

FIGURE 1
Progress and Setbacks in Income Poverty Reduction Since 1950

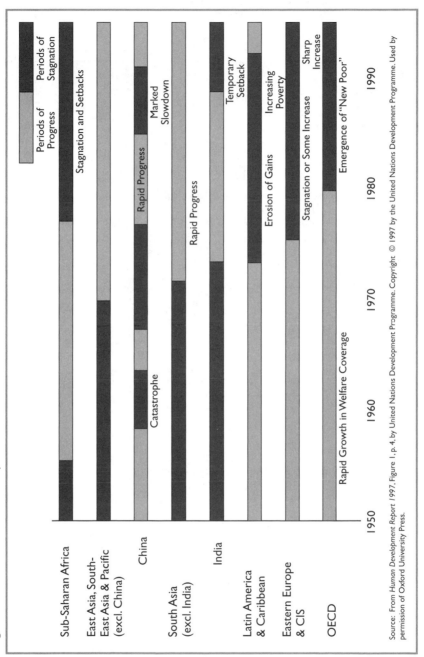

Source: From *Human Development Report 1997*, Figure 1, p. 4, by United Nations Development Programme. Copyright © 1997 by the United Nations Development Programme. Used by permission of Oxford University Press.

FIGURE 2
Global Income Distribution

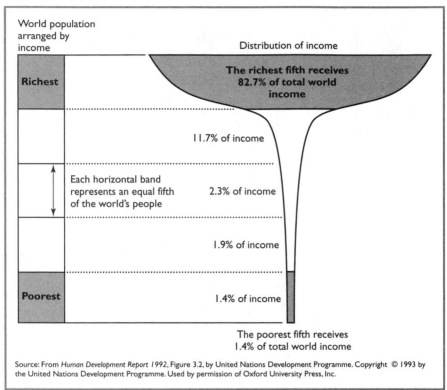

Source: From *Human Development Report 1992*, Figure 3.2, by United Nations Development Programme. Copyright © 1993 by the United Nations Development Programme. Used by permission of Oxford University Press, Inc.

unpolluted air and water. The water supply per capita in developing countries is only a third in the late 1990s of what it was in 1970, and 40 percent in those countries lack proper sanitation.

More than a billion people in the Third World lack adequate shelter, and worldwide it is estimated that 100 million are homeless. In New York City alone, 250,000 people have sought public shelter at some time in the past five years.[6] Education and health care are among the services that have suffered from recent changes in the dominant economic model. Between 1990 and 1993, Zambia spent thirty-five times as much on debt payment as it did on education.[7] In developing countries, seventeen million people die each year from curable infections and parasite diseases. HIV/AIDS afflicts another twenty-three million, fourteen million of them in Sub-Saharan Africa, where half the population lacks access to medical services. In the United States, where more money is spent on health care than in any other country, more than forty-seven million people are effectively denied care as they lack health insurance.

Worldwide, some 800 million people lack access to health care. Many, especially in Eastern Europe and the offspring states of the Soviet Union, are newly deprived. Malnutrition and premature deaths of both children and adults are on the rise. In the Ukraine average daily caloric intake dropped precipitously from about 3,500 in 1989 to 2,800 in 1994. By 1996, the new Moscow stock market was up 150 percent, making it one of the world's most attractive emerging markets.[8] (That was before it crashed in 1998.) But new cases of diphtheria among Russian children had increased twenty-nine-fold, from five hundred in 1989 to fifteen thousand in 1993. Cases of orphaned or abandoned children were also rising steeply. Children were entering the orphanages at the rate of 30,000 a year, amounting to 160,000 institutionalized by 1998.

School enrollment rates have dropped in that region and violent crime, on the rise almost everywhere in the past two decades, has increased even faster there. Crime rates have tripled, for example, since 1989 in Hungary and the Czech Republic.[9] Rising crime in turn means rising demand for police and prisons, which are even more costly than teachers and schools with which they compete for funds from shrinking public budgets. Since 1994, the United States has had more than a million people in its prisons, the highest per capita rate of any industrialized country. The American Association of State Colleges and Universities reports a five hundred-dollar-per-student decline between 1980 and 1995 in state appropriations for public universities and colleges, largely a result of increased state costs for prisons and health care.

NOTES

1. United Nations, Department of International Economic and Social Affairs, *World Economic Survey 1991* (New York: United Nations, 1991), p. 10.

2. Inter-American Development Bank, *The IDB*, Vol. 16, Nos. 9–10 and 11, 1989; and Jeff Drumtra and Thomas George, "The 1980s: A Lost Decade," *Worldview*, Vol. 2:3, Fall 1989, pp. 8, 11–12.

3. Drumtra and George, *loc. cit.*

4. UNDP, 1997, *loc. cit.*

5. Op. cit. Julianne Malveaux, "Trying to Put the Dream Back in View," *San Francisco Examiner*, Aug. 31, 1997, p. D-2; "When Gephardt Speaks," (editorial) *The Nation*, Dec. 29, 1997, p. 3.

6. UNDP, 1997, *loc. cit.*

7. Larry Elliot, "Caught on the Horns of a Global Dilemma," *The Manchester Guardian Weekly*, July 7, 1996, p. 13. Former President Kenneth Kaunda told this author, in conversation at the Oxford Union, Oxford University, Nov. 10, 1997, that his government, in order to stop such a capital drain, had severed relations in 1986 with the IMF and cut debt payments service to 10 percent of foreign exchange earnings. Economic growth shot

up to 8 percent the following years, but by 1989 the country was suffering from a liquidity crisis and was forced to submit once again to the IMF regimen.

    8.   Thomas L. Friedman, "Russians: Clear Destination, Unclear Map, Arrival Probable," *International Herald Tribune*, July 8, 1996, p. 8.

    9.   UNDP, 1997, *loc. cit.*

Poverty and Inequality in the Global Economy

–Michael D. Yates

Michael D. Yates is associate editor of Monthly Review *and a former professor at the University of Pittsburgh at Johnstown. His article "Poverty and Inequality in the Global Economy" appeared in* Monthly Review *in February 2004.*

Capitalism is hundreds of years old and today dominates nearly every part of the globe. Its champions claim that it is the greatest engine of production growth the world has ever seen. They also argue that it is unique in its ability to raise the standard of living of every person on earth. Because of capitalism, we are all "slouching toward utopia,"—the phrase coined by University of California at Berkeley economist J. Bradford DeLong—slowly but surely heading toward a world in which everyone will have achieved a U.S.-style middle-class life.[1]

    Given the long tenure of capitalism and the unceasing contentions of its adherents, it seems fair to ask if it is true that we are "slouching toward utopia." Let us look at three things: the extent of poverty and inequality in the richest capitalist economy—that of the United States; the extent of poverty and inequality in the

"Poverty and Inequality in the Global Economy" by Michael D. Yates. Copyright 2004 by Monthly Review Press. Reprinted by permission of Monthly Review Foundation.

poor countries of the world; and the gap between those countries at the top of the capitalist heap and those at the bottom.

The United States is often referred to as a nation dominated by the middle class and one in which it is relatively easy for a poor person to become a person of means. Here, it is said, equality of opportunity rules. It is hard to know what phrases like "middle class" and "equality of opportunity" mean, but it is fair to think that such a society ought not to be one in which there is widespread poverty and ought to be one in which people do indeed have a great deal of economic mobility.

The data on poverty and inequality of income and wealth do not square very well with this image. In the United States, the federal government had defined a "poverty level of income," one below which families are defined to be poor. It is an income below which families would find it difficult to live without serious problems and which would place them in real danger when faced with any sort of economic crisis, such as a sick child or an injury at work. This official poverty level of income is equal to three times the minimum food budget calculated by the Department of Agriculture, a very modest standard with numerous restrictive and unrealistic assumptions built into it, for example, that poor families will be able to buy food at the lowest unit price and will know how to convert the cheapest food into nutritious meals. In 2002, this was $18,392 for a family of four, or $12.60 per person per day. In 2002, 34.6 million persons lived in poverty, 12.1 percent of the population. The incidence of poverty was 24 percent for blacks and 21.8 percent for Hispanics. In 2001 (I don't have data for 2002), 35.2 percent of black children under six lived in poverty, as did 29.1 percent of Hispanic children under six. These numbers rise and fall over time and while they have been higher in the recent past, they are still remarkably high when we consider the enormous productive capacity of the U.S. economy and the more than 200 years in which this capacity has steadily risen. And if we used a more realistic definition of poverty—such as one-half the median income, a poverty definition typically used to compare the rich capitalist economies—the incidence of poverty would increase dramatically to 17 percent (in 1997), or more than 45 million persons.[2]

What are the chances that this extensive poverty could be eliminated? Not very high, given that this poverty coincides with large and growing inequality of both income and wealth, inequalities ingrained in the laws of motion of capitalism.

In the United States in 2000, income inequality was greater than at any time since the 1920s, with the richest 5 percent of all households receiving six times more income than the poorest 20 percent of households, up from about four times in 1970. A study by economist Paul Krugman (who has been skillfully assailing the Bush administration in his *New York Times* column) estimated that perhaps as much as 70 percent of all of the income growth in the United States during the 1980s went to the richest 1 percent of all families. With respect to wealth, in the United States in 1995, the richest 1 percent of all households owned 42.2 percent of all stocks, 55.7 percent of all bonds, 44.2 percent of all trusts, 71.4 percent of all noncorporate businesses, and 36.9 percent of all nonhome real estate. As with income inequality, this inequality has been increasing, at least for the past 20 years.[3]

Great and growing inequality mocks the notion of equality of opportunity. Consider a thought experiment:

> In Pittsburgh, Pennsylvania, . . . there is an extraordinarily wealthy family, the Hillman's, with a net worth of several billion dollars. One of their homes, along once fashionable Fifth Avenue, is a gorgeous mansion on a magnificent piece of property. About three miles east of this residence is the Homewood section of the city, whose mean streets have been made famous by the writer, John Edgar Wideman. On North Lang Street there is a row of three connected apartments. One of the end apartments has been abandoned to the elements—to the rodents and the drugs users. . . . Poverty, deep and grinding, is rampant on this street and in this neighborhood, which has one of the nation's highest infant mortality rates.
>
> Consider two children, one born in the Hillman house and another born in the North Lang Street apartment. In the former, there are two rich and influential parents, and in the latter there is a single mother working nights with three small children. Let us ask some basic questions. Which mother will have the best health care, with regular visits to the doctor, medicine if needed, and a healthy diet? Which child is more likely to have a normal birth weight? Which child is more likely to get adequate nutrition and have good health care in early childhood? If the poor child does not have these things, who will return to this child the brain cells lost as a consequence? Which child is more likely to suffer the ill effects of lead poisoning? . . . If the two children get ill in the middle of the night, which one will be more likely to make it to the emergency room in time? . . .
>
> As the two children grow up, what sort of people will they meet? Which will be more likely to meet persons who will be useful to them when they are seeking admission to college or looking for a job or trying to find funding for a business venture? . . . Which will go to the better school? Which will have access to books, magazines, newspapers, and computers in the home? . . . Which one will be more likely to have caring teachers who work in well-equipped and safe schools? Which one will be afraid to tell the teacher that he does not have crayons and colored paper at home? . . . When these two children face the labor market [or course, the rich child will never have to face the labor market in the sense the poor child will], which one will be more productive?[4].

We can buttress our thought experiment with empirical evidence. It now appears clear that in the United States—whose politicians and pundits are always touting the myth that "you can be anything you want to be,"—it is "increasingly apparent that the secret to success is to have a successful parent." Recent studies tell us that if your parents' income is in the top 20 percent of the distribution of family incomes, you have a 42.3 percent chance of ending up at the top too, but only a 6.3 percent chance of falling into the bottom 20 percent. If your parents' income is in the bottom 20 percent, you have only a 7.3 percent chance of ending up in the top 20 percent. No doubt these correlations would be still stronger if we considered wealth as well as income. If your parents were in the top 1 percent of the income distribution (and therefore certainly had a lot of wealth, something which might not be true parents at the lower end of the top 20 percent), the chances of you ending up in the top 20 percent would surely be higher than 42.3 percent.[5]

Compounding the unlikelihood of eliminating poverty is the fact that inequality in and of itself generates many socially undesirable outcomes. Inequality research has found that it we consider two states in the United States or two countries, each with the same average income, what we might call "social health" will be poorer in the state or country with the greater income inequality. Put another way, equally poor people will be worse off in terms of many social indicators if they live in the state or country with the greater income inequality. Using as a measure of inequality the share of income going to the poorest 50 percent of households in each U.S. state, researchers found that this share varied inversely (in the opposite direction) with the state's mortality rate. In addition,

> This measure of inequality was also tested against other social conditions besides health. States with greater inequality in the distribution of income also had higher rates of unemployment, higher rates of incarceration, a higher percentage of people receiving income assistance and food stamps, and a greater percentage of people without medical insurance. Again, the gap between rich and poor was the best predictor, not the average income in the state.
>
> Interestingly, states with greater inequality of income distribution also spent less per person on education, had fewer books per person in the schools, and had poorer educational performance, including worse reading skills, worse math skills and lower rates of completion of high school.
>
> States with greater inequality of income also had a greater proportion of babies born with low birth weight; higher rates of homicide; higher rates of violent crime; a greater proportion of the population unable to work because of disabilities; a higher proportion of the population using tobacco; and a higher proportion of the population being sedentary (inactive).[6]

Great and growing inequality saps the political power of those at the bottom, making it more likely that the social welfare programs which help to alleviate the harmful consequences of poverty will be gutted, while at the same time making it more likely that policies which further favor the rich will be put in place. The poor are increasingly filled with hopelessness and despair as they contemplate the yawning gap between them and those at the top.[7]

Although there is great poverty and inequality in the richest capitalist country, this cannot compare to the levels of both of these to be found in the vast majority of the world's economies, which are both capitalist and poor. The World Bank estimates the number of persons in different countries and in the world as a whole who subsist on less than $1 and $2 per day. In Nigeria, for example, in the early 1990s, 90.8 percent of the population lived on $2 per day or less; in India the figure was 86.2 percent in 1997. In a world population of some 6 billion persons, the World Bank estimates that 2.8 billion survive on $2 per day or less (about 45 percent); 1.2 billion lived on $1 (about 20 percent) per day or less.

The World Bank also uses a number comparable to the U.S. poverty level of income. Remember that the U.S. level for 2002 translates into $12.60 per person per day. The Bank's level for poor countries is now a little more than $1 per day. Using this number, it claims that poverty diminished worldwide over the 1990s. However, this claim is suspect. It is true that $1 per day might go further in a poor country because prices are cheaper, so that while $1 per day in the United States makes a person obviously destitute, such may not be the case in a very poor country. If over time, prices fall in a poor country, then, other things equal, the number of persons living in poverty will fall. The problem, however, is that when the World Bank speaks of prices in a poor country, it means an index of all prices and not the prices of the things very poor people buy. In general, the prices which are relatively lowest and which have declined most in poor countries are those of services unlikely to be consumed by the poor. As journalist George Monbiot tells us, "[The World Bank's] estimate of the purchasing power of the poor is based on the measure of their ability to buy any of the goods and services an economy has to offer: not only food, water and shelter but also airline tickets, pedicures and personal fitness training. The problem is that while basic goods are often more expensive in poor nations than they are in rich ones, services tend to be much cheaper [reflecting the tremendous pool of surplus labor in poor nations]. . . ." He goes on to say, "But the extremely poor, of course, do not purchase the services of cleaners, driver or hairdressers." Two researchers at Columbia University estimated that if corrections were made for the problems in the World Bank's methodology, the number of persons living in absolute poverty would rise by 30 to 40 percent, completely eliminating the alleged decrease in poverty.[8]

It should be noted in connection with the World Bank's poverty level that the World Bank has been instrumental in promoting large-scale export agriculture in poor countries. Many persons living below the World Bank poverty level are subsistence peasants operating outside the money economy. Their economic well-being is often greater than a dollar a day would indicate. As they are in effect dispossessed by Bank-promoted agriculture and move into urban areas, their money income may exceed the World Bank poverty level, but, in fact, they are considerably worse off than they were in the countryside.

Poverty on a global scale is matched by an enormous and growing inequality of incomes. . . . In China and India, the world's most populous nations and two of its fastest growing economies, inequality is growing rapidly. In China, once an extremely egalitarian country, income inequality is now barely distinguishable from that in the United States. China has witnessed perhaps the greatest income redistribution in history. In India, "Most of the benefits of . . . rapid economic growth are going to the wealthiest 20% of society." There, "350 million [persons] — more than a third of the population — live in dire poverty . . . In Calcutta alone, an estimated 250,000 children sleep on the sidewalks each night."[9]

World Bank economist Branco Milanovic has overseen the most sophisticated attempt to measure income inequality worldwide. Using a massive household survey covering the entire world, he found that,

> the richest 1 percent of people in the world get as much income as the poorest 57 percent. The richest 5 percent had in 1993 an average income 114 times greater than that of the poorest 5 percent, rising from 78 times in 1988. The poorest 5 percent grew poorer, losing 25 percent of their real income, while the richest 20 percent saw their real incomes grow by 12 percent, more than twice as high as average

world income. World inequality grew because inequality grew between and within countries. The rich nations grew richer and the poor nations grew poorer; the rich within each country grew richer at the expense of the poor. Milanovic calculated that the world income gini coefficient [a measure of inequality which increases from zero to one as inequality increases] was between .66 and a staggering .80, depending on the way you converted one currency into another.[10]

Buttressing Milanovic's findings, the United Nation's most recent *Human Development Report* tells us that the income of the richest 25 million Americans is the equivalent of nearly 2 billion of the world's poorest persons (2 billion is 80 times 25 million). In 1820, per capita income in western Europe was three times that in Africa; by the 1990s it was more than 13 times as high. Adding human meaning to these numbers, the report says, "The statistics today are shaming: more than 13 million children have died through diarrhoeal disease in the past decade. Each year over half a million women, one for every minute of the day, die in pregnancy and childbirth. More than 800 million suffer from malnutrition." In addition, "For many countries the 1990s were a decade of despair. Some 54 countries are poorer now than in 1990. In 21, a larger proportion is going hungry. In 14, more children are dying before the age of five. In 12, primary school enrollments are shrinking. In 34, life expectancy has fallen. Such reversals in survival were previously rare." Economist James Galbraith tells us that, "Looking at the broad range of developing countries, the University of Texas Inequality Project finds rising inequality in most of them, falling inequality in only a few." In Vietnam, in just two years, between 1999 and 2001, the gap between the richest and the poorest nearly doubled.[11]

Just as capitalism's proponents proclaim the reality of equality of opportunity, so too do they say that today's poor national economies have every chance of someday becoming rich. Can this be so?

The gap between the rich and the poor within countries is paralleled by that among countries. Since countries have widely different populations, a common way to compare countries is by their gross domestic product (GDP) per capita. Such a comparison shows extremely large differences among countries. At the top are what we can call "rich countries"; these are for the most part those capitalist nations which first industrialized and which early on took command, largely through conquest and colonization, of much of the rest of the world, from Latin America to Africa to Southeast Asia. At the bottom are the poorest of "poor countries," those nations on the receiving end of the forced expansion of the rich nations. Countries such as the United States, Norway, Japan, Germany, and France have per capital GDPs 20 to more than 100 times greater than countries like Ethiopia, Malawi, Afghanistan, and Bolivia. It is remarkable to observe that most of the rich countries are those where capitalism first arose, while most of the poor countries have long histories of colonial and imperial domination. In terms of per capita GDP, no Latin American country ranks in the top 35, and no African country ranks in the top 55. More than one-half of the poorest 50 countries are in Africa. Sixty percent of the top 50 are either in Europe or North America.

If we use nonmoney measures of how nations are faring, we see similar differences. In the United States, life expectancy at birth for women is about 80 years, in Switzerland 82; but in Afghanistan it is 46, in Sierra Leone 39. Infant mortality per 1,000 births is 3.98 in Norway, but it is 101 in Ethiopia.[12]

Mainstream economists have argued that the poor nations are simply on a low rung of a "development ladder," and that over time, especially if they adopt "free market" principles (basically the elimination of all barriers to the freedom of employers to try to make money, such as protective trade barriers, protective labor laws, subsidies to the poor, public enterprises, and limitations on the sale of land), they will become rich countries too. This convergence hypothesis is difficult to demonstrate. While a very few formerly poor nations, mostly in Asia, have become relatively rich ones (South Korea, for example), most have remained poor. In fact, Lance Pritchett, a World Bank economist, has persuasively argued that the world's poorest countries diverged in terms of per capita income from 1870 to 1960. The logic underlying Pritchett's methodology is interesting. He compared one of the world's richest nations, the United States, to one of its poorest, Ethiopia. He took the per capita GDP ratio for the United States and Ethiopia for 1960 (U.S. GDP per capita divided by Ethiopia GDP per capita) and noted that there could only have been convergence if the per capita GDP ratio had been larger in 1870. But for this to be true, Ethiopia's per capita GDP in 1870 would have been too low to sustain life! Therefore Pritchett concluded that there must have been divergence.

We also have good evidence that divergence continued after 1960, accelerating after 1980 when "free market" policies were introduced throughout the world on an increasing scale. Between 1980 and 2000, those countries with the highest GDPs per capita grew the most, implying that inequality among nations increased. The British magazine, *The Economist*, citing economists who believe that international inequality has decreased, argued that we need to weight each country's per capita GDP by its population. When we do this, we note that the two most populous countries, India and China, had very high average growth rates over this period, suggesting that in terms of population-weighted growth rates, worldwide inequality decreased. However, what *The Economist* failed to note was that, as we have seen, inequality within India and China rose, most notably in China. China's and India's per capita GDP grew rapidly, but the incomes of the average Chinese and Indian did not. So, in the face of this fact, it is hard to argue that inequality has fallen.

Even if we consider a poor nation that has grown more rapidly than a rich one, this relatively greater growth will have to continue for a very long time for per capita incomes to converge. Pritchett has this to say about India, a country which grew faster than the United States for a while and which is growing rapidly now:

> . . . a few developing countries were actually "converging," that is, they were growing faster than the United States. When are these lucky "convergers" going to overtake the United States? India, for example, registered an annual average growth rate of 3 percent between 1980 and 1993. If India could sustain this pace for another

100 years, its income would reach the level of high-income countries today. And, if India can sustain this growth differential for 377 years, my great-great-great-great-great-great-great-great-great-great-great-grandchildren will be alive to see India's income level "converge."[13]

Given all of this, it is difficult not to conclude that inequality, both within and among nations, must be endemic to capitalism. It is not very hard to see why. Wealth in a capitalist economy is unevenly divided by definition: Capitalism is an economic system in which the nonhuman means of production (what mainstream economists call "capital") are owned by a small minority of all persons. Wealth inequality in a market economy must, again as a consequence of the nature of the system, generate income inequality. A capitalist system always "builds" on the best, that is, other things equal, those with the most to start with continue to reap the lion's share of the annual income. So, when capitalist economies are not subject to constraints and regulations, inequality will inevitably grow.

In other words, what underlies inequality is the class nature of capitalism. The owning minority has a built-in advantage compared to the nonowning minority, both in terms of economic power inside the workplace and political power in the larger society. Whenever they can, they will press their advantage to secure a still larger share of society's income. Examples are too numerous to mention.

What then sustains the growing inequality both among nations and within nations is the rising power of the owners and the declining power of the workers (and in poor countries, of the peasants, as well). If we look at the world objectively, the income of a nation tends to be more equally divided the more powerful are the workers and peasants. Where they are weak in poor countries, these countries are pulled more tightly into the grip of the rich nations and intercountry inequality rises. Inequality also rises within these nations, while the incomes of the poor sink to levels barely able to sustain life, if that. This is true even when per capita GDP rises at a high rate. Similarly, in the rich countries, the weaker the workers, the greater the inequality, and the less likely it is that workers will reach out in solidarity with their brothers and sisters in the poor nations. It is no accident that the United States has both the weakest labor movement and the most unequal income of any rich country.

Inequality in income and wealth (and all of the social indicators which are linked to these inequalities) are a profound contradiction of the capitalist mode of production. Workers and their employers presumably meet as equals in the labor market, each free to make a bargain. Yet the results of this bargain favor the employers to a striking degree.

In capitalist economies, everyone is free to make money, but it is remarkable how few do. Capitalist economies espouse egalitarian values, but the consequences of their normal operations are extraordinarily inegalitarian. The same contradiction is apparent in relationships among nations. Countries enter into free trade relationships, but the consequences of this trade are enormous disparities in per capita GDP.

A contradiction so blatant requires resolution. On the one hand, workers and peasants have been forming diverse types of organizations to reverse the system-generated inequalities. These have had varying degrees of success, managing sometimes to wring concessions from the owners and on rarer occasions succeeding in making a revolution that transforms the entire system. But on the other hand, capitalists and their multitude of hired guns try to keep the contradiction from generating actions that threaten their existence. Needless to say, force and violence are critical elements in the ruling-class arsenal, especially when revolution threatens. However, there are many other weapons, including cooptation of working-class and peasant leaders, making strategic concessions (best exemplified by the "social pact" between employers and unions in Western Europe and to a lesser degree the United States), and a vast ideological apparatus geared to convincing people that there is no contradiction at all. With respect to the last of these, we are fed a daily diet of procapitalist propaganda, complete with missing or distorted information: workers are really "associates"; the suggestion that the rich benefit in this system at the expense of the poor is denounced as the "politics of hate"; poor nations are falling further behind the rich ones because they have not sufficiently embraced the free market; and on and on.

The glaring and growing inequalities everywhere apparent in the capitalist world have yet to spawn massive resistance. In fact, in the United States, working people often support government policies clearly inimical to their interests, such as the repeal of the estate tax and income tax cuts strongly biased toward the rich.[14] However, there are indications that troubles might be brewing for the rich and powerful. Under the radar screen, a kind of "social war" is being waged in poor neighborhoods around the world. While this war often involves intraclass violence, it has also terrified the elite. Writing in *Le Monde Diplomatique*, Ignacio Ramonet tells us:

> Faced with this rising tide of what the media calls insecurity, several countries—including Mexico, Colombia, Nigeria and South Africa—now spend more on fighting this social war than on national defence. Brazil spends 2% of GDP on its armed forces and more than 10.6% on protecting the rich against the despair of the poor.[15]

More publicized have been a wide range of social movements aimed in one way or another at addressing global inequality: armed revolutionary struggles in Colombia and Nepal; peasant movements throughout Latin America, most recently in Bolivia; movements of the poor and unemployed in countries as disparate as Argentina and South Africa; and a far-flung and wide-ranging global justice movement, encompassing campaigns against third world debt, child labor, sweatshops, trade agreements, land theft, and environmental destruction, among others.

It is impossible to tell how all of this "primitive" and more conscious protest will play out. But one gets the feeling that political struggle in the next decades might be intimately tied to the glaring and unconscionable inequality which has become the hallmark of contemporary capitalism. Under these conditions the system is unlikely to be entirely successful at keeping the lid on the boiling discontent underneath.

NOTES

1. Details of DeLong's contentions, including draft material for a book, *Slouching Toward Utopia* can be found at http://econ161.berkeley.edu/TCEH/Slouch_title.html.

2. For details on poverty, see Lawrence Mishel, Jared Bernstein, and Heather Boushey, *The State of Working America, 2002–2003* (Ithaca, N.Y.: Cornell University Press, 2003), 309–56. For the most recent U.S. Census Bureau data see http://www.census.gov. For international comparisons using the 50 percent of median income definition, see Mishel, *State*, 416.

3. On income inequality, see Mishel, Berstein, & Bolushey, *State*, 33–112. The income data in the paragraph are taken from http://www.census.gov. The wealth data are from Doug Henwood, "Distributing the Booty," http://www.panix.com/~dhenwood/Wealth_distrib.html. The Krugman data are from Paul Krugman, "The Rich, the Right, and the Facts," *The American Prospect* 11 (fall 1992), 19–31.

4. Michael D. Yates, *Naming the System: Inequality and Work in the Global Economy* (New York: Monthly Review Press, 2003), 58–59.

5. Economist Alan B. Krueger reports on the relevant studies in "The Apple Falls Close to the Tree, Even in the Land of Opportunity," *New York Times*, November 14, 2002.

6. The quote is from Yates, *Naming*, 60. It is taken from Peter Montague, "Economic Inequality and Health," http://www.korpios.org/resurgent/Inequality&Health.htm.

7. See Helen Epstein, "Enough to Make You Sick?," *New York Times Magazine*, October 12, 2003.

8. For World Bank data on poverty, see the Bank's World Development Reports, http://www.worldbank.org. On the inadequacies of the World Bank's methods for calculating poverty rates, see articles available at http://www.columbia.edu-sr793/. The quote is from George Monbiot, "Poor but Pedicured," *The Guardian*, May 6, 2003.

9. Paul Watson, "In India, No Job is Too Small," *Los Angeles Times*, October 25, 2003.

10. The quote is from Yates, *Naming*, 57–58. The original article is Branko Milanovic, "True World Income Distribution, 1988 and 1993: First Calculations Based on Household Surveys Alone," *The Economic Journal* 112 (January 2002), 51–92.

11. For a summary of the UN Report, see Larry Elliot, "The Lost Decade," *The Guardian*, July 9, 2003. The Galbraith quote is from James Galbraith, "Globalisation and Inequality: the Economist Gets it Wrong," http://www.opendemocracy.net/debates/article-7-30-1483.jsp. On inequality in Vietnam, see "Vietnamese Earn More but Rich-Poor Gap Widens," http://www.globalpolicy.org/socecon/inequal/2003/0114vietnam.htm.

12. For a wide range of statistics on output, health, life expectancy, labor markets, and other economic indicators, see International Labor Office, *Key Indicators of the Labour Market 2001–2002* (Geneva, Switzerland: International Labour Office, 2002).

13. Pritchett's methodology and the quote are in Lance Pritchett, "Forget Convergence: Divergence Past, Present, and Future," http://www.worldbank.org/fandd/english/0696/articles/090696.htm. For a discussion of the growth of per capita GDPs, see Galbraith, "Globalisation."

14. For examples, see Alan B. Krueger, "Cloudy Thinking on Tax Cuts," *New York Times*, October 16, 2003.

15. Ignacio Ramonet, "The Social Wars," *Le Monde Diplomatique*, November 2002, available in English at http://mondediplo.com/2002/11/.

Is World Poverty Falling?

–Angus Deaton

Angus Deaton is Dwight D. Eisenhower Professor of International Affairs and Professor of Economics and International Affairs at the Woodrow Wilson School, Princeton University. A British citizen, he has also taught at Cambridge University and the University of Bristol. His article "Is World Poverty Falling?" appeared in Finance and Development, a quarterly magazine of the IMF, in June 2002.

The first table of the World Bank's *World Development Report 2000/2001: Attacking Poverty* shows that the number of people living on less than $1 a day grew from 1.18 billion in 1987 to 1.20 billion in 1998—an increase of 20 million. Less than two years later, a headline chart in another major World Bank publication, *Globalization, Growth, and Poverty: Building an Inclusive World Economy,* showed that the number of people living in poverty fell by 200 million from 1980 to 1998 and showed no trace of an increase between 1987 and 1998. The poverty decrease was reaffirmed in the press release accompanying "The Role and Effectiveness of Development Assistance," a World Bank research paper issued before the March 2002 UN Financing for Development Conference in Monterrey, Mexico: "Over the past 20 years, the number of people living on less than $1 a day has fallen by 200 million, even as the world's population grew by 1.6 billion."

Can these statements be reconciled? Has there been a marked reduction in poverty in the last two years? Or has the Bank revised its interpretation of history?

Getting an accurate poverty count is important. The Bank sails under the banner "Our dream is a world free of poverty," which not only invites the use of the poverty count as a measure of the extent to which the dream is being fulfilled but also raises the issue of whether the organization's success can be convincingly measured by its own numbers. We also need an accurate poverty count to assess whether the international community is achieving one of the Millennium Development Goals endorsed by 189 countries at the September 2000 UN Millennium Summit—to "halve, between 1990 and 2015, the proportion of people whose income is less than one dollar a day." A lot depends on whether the scorecard is

"Is World Poverty Falling Apart?" by Angus Deaton in *Finance and Development:* A Quarterly Magazine of the IMF, June 2002, Vol. 39, No. 2. Copyright © 2002 International Monetary Fund. Reprinted by permission of the International Monetary Fund.

being credibly tallied, and the apparent discrepancies in the Bank's numbers deserve serious scrutiny. That scrutiny produces some genuinely good news about poverty declining but also raises some serious concerns about the numbers. With respect to the production of data, still greater transparency on the Bank's part is called for.

Poverty in India

Take the case of India. Its poverty counts are important not only because they have a large direct effect on world poverty counts—more than one-fourth of the world's poor live in India—but also because the world debate on globalization, poverty, and inequality has been echoed in an intense domestic debate.

India's economic liberalization in the early 1990s was followed by historically high rates of growth. But did this growth help or hurt the poor? Were their numbers reduced or did economic growth benefit only an increasingly wealthy urban elite?

The political debate has been fueled by questions about the accuracy of poverty measurements in light of the discrepancies between estimates of consumption growth based on national accounts statistics (NAS) and those based on household surveys carried out by the National Sample Survey (NSS). According to the NAS, real per capita consumption has been growing at about 3.2 percent a year since the reforms, while, at least until recently, the NSS data have shown little or no growth throughout the 1990s. Reform opponents resolutely quote the NSS data, while reform advocates back the NAS growth estimates, questioning the accuracy and the integrity of the NSS data and arguing that, because the poor's share of the national pie is more or less fixed, growth *must* reduce poverty.

The controversy only deepened last year with the release of the 1999–2000 consumption survey, the first major survey since 1993–94, when reforms had barely begun to take effect. In the intervening years, there had been a series of smaller ("thin") household surveys showing little or no growth in per capita consumption and, if anything, a rise in poverty. Accurate or not, they provided the only numbers in town and were widely used outside India—for example, in the World Bank's Attacking Poverty, albeit with due acknowledgment of uncertainty. Hence the belief that poverty in India had been increasing.

Unfortunately, in a decision whose timing could hardly have been worse, the NSS made major changes to the questionnaire design for the 1999–2000 survey. Although the new survey design is sensible in itself, it is not comparable with earlier designs and almost certainly leads to more consumption being reported, especially among the poor. As a result, measured poverty was lower than it would have been with the previous design. So when the Planning Commission issued its poverty estimates in February 2001, showing a dramatic fall in poverty—from 36 percent of the population to 26 percent—many cried foul. Pleas to have the survey redone to make it consistent with earlier surveys were ignored, and the ruling Bharatiya Janata Party was in no hurry to challenge estimates that showed rapid

FIGURE 1
Who's right?
Unofficial calculations ("thin" rounds) based on small household surveys show poverty rising in the late 1990s, while official estimates (planning commission head counts) based on National Accounts Statistics and author's own calculations (fully adjusted head counts) show poverty declining.

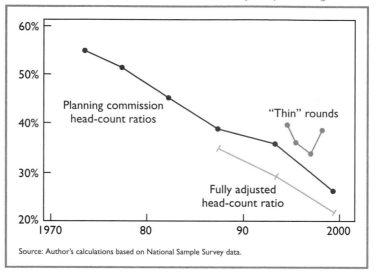

Source: Author's calculations based on National Sample Survey data.

progress in dealing with India's most intractable and longstanding social and economic problem.

The chart [Figure 1] shows the official estimates (the planning-commission head-count ratios) going back to 1973–74; each circle comes from a large consumption survey. The points labeled "thin" rounds show the (unofficially calculated) poverty estimates from recent smaller surveys. If the final point is blanked out, we can imagine the situation immediately prior to February 2001. From that perspective, the 1999–2000 estimate is nothing short of astonishing: the Indian poverty rate fell by 12.8 percent over 18 months, removing 60 million persons from poverty. Progress indeed!

Over the past year or so, I and others have been working with the data to try to sort out what happened. Although the questionnaire design was changed for most of the goods in the survey, data on an important group of expenditures were collected in the same way in all of the surveys. Fortunately, nearly all households purchase these goods, and the total amount they spend on them is a good predictor of whether a household is poor or not. The latest data show a marked increase in real expenditures on these goods, which indicates a substantial reduction in poverty overall. The extent of the increase also allows us to estimate how much poverty has fallen. Much to my surprise, most of the officially claimed reduction in poverty appears to be real. I estimate that poverty fell from 36 percent in 1993–94, not to 26 percent as in the official numbers, but to 28 percent. These calculations, although necessarily speculative, are supported by analysis carried out by K. Sundaram and Suresh Tendulkar at the Delhi School of Economics, who obtain very similar results using entirely different methods.

Another complication is the questionable quality of the Indian price indexes used to update the poverty lines. With some correction to the price indexes, as well as an allowance for the noncomparable survey design, the head-count ratio shows a fairly steady decline from 1987–88 through 1999–2000. Indeed, since the 1970s India has made more or less steady progress in reducing poverty. (The "fully adjusted" estimates in the figure also correct for overestimation of urban poverty in the official counts, and thus start from a lower base in 1987–88.) Even so, the estimates based on the "thin rounds" raise unanswered questions. Although the last of these, which is the most egregious, is relatively easy to challenge—if only because the survey ran for only six months—there is at present no obvious reason to dismiss the three earlier observations.

Can we conclude that the reforms helped reduce poverty? Neither consumption growth nor poverty reduction shows much sign of having been more rapid after the reforms. But neither is there any sign of general impoverishment as a result of the reforms—indeed, quite the reverse. What about inequality? Again, the change in survey design precludes any simple, uncontroversial answer. But the adjustment procedures applied to the poverty counts can also be used to estimate inequality, which has been increasing in recent years, particularly between states—the states in the south and west that were originally better off have grown most rapidly—as well as within urban areas, which have been the greatest beneficiaries of growth.

Because of this growing inequality, consumption by the poor did not rise as fast as average consumption, and poverty reduction was only about two-thirds of what it would have been had the distribution of consumption remained unchanged.

World Poverty at the Bank

India's story was not available to the authors of *Attacking Poverty*, whose estimates of the decline in world poverty would have been less pessimistic if, instead of a 50 million increase in the number of poor from 1993–94 to 1998, they had used the current estimate of a 50 million decline up to 1999–2000. Because China has also made continuing progress in reducing poverty, it is possible to paint a rosier picture of the decline of world poverty today than it was one year ago. Indeed, according to recent calculations by Shaohua Chen and Martin Ravallion (2000) of the World Bank using all of the household survey data since around 1980, and with due recognition of the data's many inadequacies, the best current estimate is that there are indeed around 200 million fewer people living in poverty now than 20 years ago. So it seems that both *Attacking Poverty* and *Globalization* were right: poverty rose a little from 1987 to 1998 but fell substantially from 1980 to 1998.

Yet there remains much in this story to make one uneasy. Most obvious is the discomfort of having to rely on data whose margin of uncertainty is enough to allow, over a period of two years, such discordant views about what is happening to poverty in the world.

Attacking Poverty, whose preparation was much influenced by nongovernmental organizations and groups opposed to globalization, frequently takes a skeptical view of the role of economic growth in promoting poverty reduction. *Globalization* takes a much more sanguine view. A chart showing the number of people living on less than $1 a day from 1820 to 1998 shows a decline from about 1980 that accelerates in the latest years. The historical data in this chart were assembled by François Bourguignon and Christian Morrisson in a paper that is to appear in the *American Economic Review*. They derive their estimates by applying (sometimes sketchy and outdated) distributional information to the consumption figures from national accounts data, a technique that is almost certainly the only methodology that would allow the construction of data for a century and a half. But as we have seen from India's statistics, such methods can sometimes beg the question of whether growth reduces poverty. After 1993, when the Bourguignon and Morrisson data end, *Globalization* uses the poverty estimates that were assembled by Shaohua Chen and Martin Ravallion prior to *Attacking Poverty*. But Chen and Ravallion's data from 1987 to 1993, which is when poverty increased, are dropped from the chart. In consequence, and without any new information, we go from an assessment that the number of poor people in the world was showing little or no decline from 1987 to 1998 in *Attacking Poverty* to an assessment, in *Globalization*, of a continuous and accelerating decline from 1980 to 1998.

One of the Bank's greatest achievements over the past 20 years has been its extensive investment in primary data, particularly the household surveys on which the poverty counts are based. Before the late 1980s, the Bank calculated and forecast poverty from data on aggregate consumption, together with whatever distributional information might be available, sometimes from an earlier period or even from a different, but "similar," country. Since they were first calculated in 1987, the $1 a day poverty counts have been based on direct observations of what poor people earn or consume, using the several hundred income and consumption surveys that are now available to the Bank. This statistical advance is what makes it possible for us to have a serious debate about what is happening to poverty in the world. And it is clear that the Bank's best economists do the calculations to the highest standards, and there has never been any suggestion that the counts are anything other than what the data show. But as the case of *Attacking* versus *Globalization* shows, it is possible for these underlying data to be used in ways that seem to support very different factual statements about trends in world poverty.

Although external access has improved over time, most of the data used in the count are not available to independent researchers or to agencies outside the Bank.

Nor, given the arrangements that the Bank makes with member countries, is it possible for the Bank to make all of the data available. So the Bank is effectively the only producer of world poverty counts. National governments around the world carefully separate and insulate the production of data from the policymakers who rely on them and are often judged by them. A similar arrangement would surely be wise for the world poverty counts, if only to protect those who create the statistics. Perhaps there should be an independent outside agency or auditor who either produces the numbers under a carefully specified contract or verifies their construction. Second best would be for the Bank to continue to calculate the numbers but to visibly insulate them from the internal policy debate and to institute a process of collection and production that is fully transparent to outside observers. The Bank's very success in producing these numbers, and in making them a central part of the policy debate, argues for an upgrading in the way they are produced and maintained. Otherwise, if its reports continue to contradict each other, the Bank risks losing the authority to monitor its own success, and no one will know whether or not the Millennium Development Goals are being achieved.

REFERENCES

François Bourguignon and Christian Morrisson, 2002, "Inequality among World Citizens: 1820–1992," DELTA Working Paper (Paris), American Economic Review, forthcoming.

Shaohua Chen and Martin Ravallion, 2000, "How did the world's poorest fare in the 1990s?" World Bank Research Paper (Washington); http://econ.worldbank.org/docs/1164.pdf

Angus Deaton, 2001, "Computing prices and poverty rates in India, 1999–2000," Research Program in Development Studies Working Paper, Princeton University; http://lnweb18.worldbank.org/sar/sa.nsf/Attachments/adp/$File/prices+poverty+55thRound+all.pdf

World Bank, 2001a, Globalization, Growth, and Poverty: Building an Inclusive World Economy (New York: Oxford University Press for the World Bank).

———, 2001b, World Development Report 2000/2001: Attacking Poverty (New York: Oxford University Press for the World Bank).

———, 2002, "The Role and Effectiveness of Development Assistance," World Bank Research Paper (Washington); http://econ.worldbank.org

A Critical Look at Measurements
of Economic Progress
—The International Forum on Globalization

"A Critical Look at Measurements of Economic Progress" is an excerpt from a report is-
sued by The International Forum on Globalization called Alternatives to Economic
Globalization. *The Forum is an alliance of leading activists, scholars, economists, re-*
searchers, and writers representing 60 organizations in 25 countries that was formed in
1994 in response to economic globalization. The report was published in 2002 by
Berrett-Koehler Publishers, Inc.

Not surprisingly, the primary unit that currently measures our success—Gross Domestic Product (GDP)—does so in terms that are compatible with the expansive
goals of corporate-driven globalization while marginalizing all other ways of judging how we are progressing as a society. This gives corporate globalization a powerful tool to convince us that the direction we are going in is a good one when it
isn't. By other standards, we are doing poorly.

Gross National Product and Gross Domestic Product
The GDP came into use in the mid-1980s, when it replaced the previous Gross
National Product (GNP). We will come back to that important difference a little
later in this section.

   Both measurements are rooted in the World War II period, when U.S. economists were trying to find a way to measure the speed at which productive capacity
in the country was increasing to meet war production needs. It was a useful measure at that time for that purpose, but its continued application is leading to distorted analyses and conclusions that exacerbate all the problems described in the
earlier sections of this chapter.

   GDP measures societal performance by one economic standard, the market
value of the aggregate of all economic production—that is, the rate at which resources are converted to commodities and sold, the activities that go into that

From "A Critical Look at Measurements of Economic Progress." Copyright © 2002. Reprinted by
permission of the International Forum on Globalization.

process, and all other paid services and activities in the formal economy. The assumption is that as GDP grows, society is better off: GDP growth brings progress and national well-being. Politicians run for office promising to increase GDP, and most domestic and international agencies use it as their standard of success.

However, the system is tragically flawed because it measures the wrong things and does not measure what it should measure. Clear-cutting of forests, strip-mining of mountaintops, construction of toxic dumpsites: all show up in GDP as positive indicators. So does expansion of military hardware and activities, prison construction, war, crime (and resources devoted to prevent it), as well as reconstruction from natural disasters.

Long-distance shipping of goods across oceans is seen as a good thing because it adds many layers of economic activity, from production to port to shipment to delivery. Local production for local consumption, involving less shipment (and less environmental impact), is seen as less productive because it does not contribute as much to GDP.

Unpaid household labor, care for the sick and elderly, self-sufficient food growing within communities—activities often carried out by women—do not contribute to GDP because little money changes hands, so they do not get counted. The same is true when anyone decides to keep land, forests, or other pristine areas as biodiversity preserves. This does not show up as a positive act. Razing the forests or putting copper mines on that land or converting it to mechanized agriculture or housing developments would add to GDP.

As David Korten likes to point out, using GDP as the standard of economic or social health "makes no more sense than taking the rapid expansion of one's personal girth as an indicator of improved personal health. Applying such a standard to society's economic priorities has led to a gross distortion of economic priorities and resource allocation that is helping to lead the world toward social and environmental collapse."

In their article "The Need for New Measurements of Progress," which appears in Jerry Mander and Edward Goldsmith's *The Case Against the Global Economy*, authors Clifford Cobb and Ted Halstead (then of Redefining Progress, an organization that has been a leading voice critiquing the GDP measurement) point out: "GDP is the statistical distillation of the worldview of conventional economics. It basically assumes that *everything* produced is good by definition. It is a balance sheet with no cost side of the ledger; it does not differentiate between costs and benefits, between productive and destructive activities, or between sustainable or unsustainable ones. It is a calculating machine that adds but does not subtract. It treats everything that happens in the market as a gain for humanity while ignoring everything that happens outside the realm of monetized exchange regardless of its importance to well-being." The authors conclude: "To do otherwise, economists generally say, would be to make 'value judgments.' But refusing to make such judgments is a judgment in itself."

The Importance of Including the Negative

GDP not only excludes beneficial nonmonetized economic activity but conveniently (for corporations) leaves out the actual costs to society of some activities—now and in the future—of this growth. Most alarming is the failure of GDP to account for the *depletion* of natural capital—topsoil, minerals, forests, rivers, life in the seas, the atmosphere—whose diminishment impoverishes the future of any society. Herman Daly of the University of Maryland, a former World Bank official, bemoans this failure of GDP and points out that natural capital is the basis of all real wealth in the world.

Cobb and Halstead agree: "When a timber company harvests an ancient redwood forest, the GDP rises by the market value of the wood. But it takes no account of the economic, environmental, and social costs involved in the loss of the forest." GDP actually treats resource overuse as *income* rather than *depletion*, thus creating a spectacular distortion in any effort to make judgments about the long-term health of any economy.

Similarly, the changeover of food-growing activity from small-scale, local, organic systems to industrial agriculture has increased pesticide use and fossil fuels and the need for long-distance transport. All are positive indicators for GDP. But they have serious health effects, causing illnesses of all kinds. Amazingly, however, these health effects also show up as positives in the GDP because they increase doctors' fees, hospital services, ambulances, medical machinery, drugs, and so on. (The messes created by the use of pesticides and oil require expensive cleanup operations, but these too are positive for GDP.) So from the point of view of GDP, public health problems are a good thing, not a bad one.

Particularly in higher-income countries, a significant portion of economic growth (increased GDP) comes from sales of such things as bottled water, which is actually a response to the *decline* in the purity and safety of water supplies. Another example is the increased demand for security systems to compensate for what is also a negative trend in society.

In the perverse world of GDP accounting, even a strong, stable family life contributes nothing to the economy. A divorce, however, generates lawyers' fees and probably means that at least one more new household will need to be furnished and fitted with commodities—a plus for GDP. A woman who bears her own child counts for nothing to GDP, but if she hires a surrogate to bear her child, that fee adds to GDP—as do the commissions and fees for lawyers, doctors, and other intermediaries. A parent who stays home to care for his or her own children counts for nothing. Parents who take a job to pay for day care add to GDP. All too often, GDP growth is actually a measure of social or environmental deterioration, not progress.

There are also countless cases of mining companies that extract gold and other minerals from the lands of indigenous peoples, using methods that kill topsoil, poison local water, and dump enormous piles of rocky waste into riverbeds. Human and natural losses can be enormous, and the sources of livelihood of the local people may be destroyed for generations to come, but GDP accounts record only the returns from the sale of the ore and the costs of mining it.

Military activity provides the supreme example. All additions to military hardware or personnel salaries or university research on weapons systems add to GDP, though they surely also add to the instability and insecurity in society. Once this hardware is actually used in war, then great destruction takes place, which requires later redevelopment and reconstruction—yet another plus for GDP, although the entire cycle of activity has been negative from start to finish. Death and destruction and pollution from this activity are not measured at all. So a country that becomes warlike may be assumed to be in better economic health as a result, receiving increased investment and other financial benefits.

GDP's Bias Against the Third World and the Poor

The Gross Domestic Product Index is designed to be helpful in measuring economic growth from year to year, and most economists argue that growth is crucial to lifting the world's poorest countries and peoples. We believe that this assumption is false and misleading. Ecological degradation of the kind that is measured as positive by GDP actually has devastating impacts on the poor because it reduces the resources—forests, lands, water, biodiversity—that poor people depend on, reducing their ability to live self-sufficiently and increasing their poverty. In any case, GDP reveals nothing about *who benefits* from growth, which is an essential question.

GDP makes no distinction between the production of goods and services that might actually help the poor—basic foods, health services, water, housing, education, job training, and so on—and the production of more luxuries for the rich—fancy foods, hotels, golf courses. This is yet another way in which GDP is useless as an indicator for society's performance. It is all too common for the deprivation of the poor to actually *increase* during periods of rapid economic expansion, because such growth often results from a systematic transfer of productive resources from the weaker elements of society to the rich and powerful. This is a common experience in low-income countries today, where many development projects—often financed with loans from the World Bank and its regional sister development banks—involve appropriating the lands on which poor people depend for their livelihoods and converting them to use for dams, tourist resorts, industrial agriculture and forestry estates, housing developments, and so on, which are designed to benefit people already better off than those displaced. Through this process, control of productive assets is consolidated in the hands of the capital-owning classes, and wages are depressed as the pool of wage labor expands among the displaced peoples. By the logic of economic growth and the GDP index, all this counts as progress.

The numbers clearly bear this out. In a recent report by the International Forum on Globalization, titled *Does Globalization Help the Poor?* more than one hundred quotes from economists, researchers, scholars, and journalists show that during the thirty-year period of the world's most accelerated economic growth (1960 to 1990), the gap between the rich and poor within countries and among countries greatly increased. (See Box 1.) Many of the sources for these data were actually from the institutions that have pushed for rapid economic growth via globalization, including the World Bank, the IMF, the United Nations, and even the CIA.

Box I   Global Economic Apartheid

By Robin Broad, American University, and John Cavanagh, Institute for Policy Studies

A careful analysis of social and economic data from the United Nations, the World Bank, the IMF, and other sources offers a shocking picture of trends in the global economy and the gap between rich and poor countries. There are two ways to measure what is happening economically between North and South. The first is to measure which is growing faster, and therefore whether the gap between them is growing or shrinking. The second is to measure financial resource flows between the two.

On the first issue the picture is clear: the North-South gap widened dramatically in the decade after 1982 as the Third World debt crisis drained financial resources from poor countries to rich banks. Between 1985 and 1992, Southern nations paid some $280 billion more in debt service to Northern creditors than they received in new private loans and government aid. Gross national product (GNP) per capita rose an average of only 1 percent in the South in the 1980s (in sub-Saharan Africa it fell 1.2 percent), while it rose 2.3 percent in the North.

Situating the lost decade of the 1980s within a longer time period reveals similar trends for some regions. According to the United Nations Development Program, per capita incomes in Africa were one-ninth of those in Northern countries in 1960; they had fallen to one-eighteenth by 1998. Per capita incomes in most of the rest of the developing world (Latin America and the Caribbean, and South Asia) remained at about one-tenth of Northern levels at the beginning and end of these four decades. Only in East Asia have developing countries closed the gap with the North.

Likewise, a look at various resource flows between North and South is instructive. Despite the perception of an easing of the debt crisis, the overall Third World debt stock swelled by around $100 billion each year during the 1990s (reaching $2.4 trillion in 2001). Southern debt service (which reached $331 billion in 2000) still exceeds new lending, and the net outflow remains particularly crushing in Africa. Although it is true that a series of debt reschedulings and the accumulation of arrears by many debtors have reduced the net negative financial transfer from South to North over the last few years, the flows remain negative.

Part of the reason why some analysts now argue that the debt crisis is no longer a problem is that since the early 1990s these outflows of debt repayments have been matched by increased inflows of foreign capital. Here too, however, a deeper look at disaggregated figures underlines the disconcerting reality. According to World Bank figures, roughly half of the new foreign direct investment by global corporations into the South in 1992 quickly left those countries as profits. In addition, foreign investment flows primarily to only ten to twelve Third World nations that are viewed as new profit centers by Northern corporations and investors. According to World Bank figures, more than 70 percent of investment flows in 1998 went to just ten of the so-called emerging markets: China, followed by Brazil, Mexico, Singapore, Thailand, Poland, Argentina, South Korea, Malaysia, and Chile.

The inescapable conclusion is that the North-South economic gap is now narrowing for about a dozen countries but continues to widen for well over one hundred others. Hence, without a major shift in policy, the world of the twenty-first century will be one of economic apartheid. There will be two dozen richer nations, a dozen or so poorer nations that have begun to close the gap with the rich, and approximately 140 poor nations slipping further and further behind.

Continued

Box 1: Continued

As U.S. firms have shifted from local to national and now to global markets over the past half-century, a new division of winners and losers has emerged in all countries. The book *Global Dreams,* by Richard Barnet, co-founder of the Institute for Policy Studies, and John Cavanagh, chronicles how powerful U.S. firms and their counterparts from England, France, Germany, and Japan are integrating only about one-third of humanity (most of those in the rich countries plus the elite of poor countries) into complex chains of production, shopping, culture, and finance.

Although there are enclaves in every country that are linked to these global economic webs, others are left out. Wal-Mart is spreading its superstores throughout the Western Hemisphere; millions in Latin America, though, are too poor to enjoy anything but glimpses of luxury. Citibank customers can access automated teller machines around the world; the vast majority of people nevertheless borrow from the loan shark down the road. Ford Motor Company pieces together its new "global car" in Kansas City from parts made all over the globe; executives in Detroit worry about who will be able to afford it.

Thus, although on one level the North-South gap is becoming more pronounced for most Third World countries, on another these global chains blur distinctions between geographical North and South. These processes create another North-South divide: the roughly one-third of humanity who make up a "global North" of beneficiaries in every country, and the two-thirds of humanity from the slums of New York to the favelas of Rio who are not hooked into the new global menu of producing, consuming, and borrowing opportunities in the "global South."

Source: Adapted and updated from Robin Broad and John Cavanagh, "Development: The Market Is Not Enough." *Foreign Policy* 101, Winter 1995–96.

GDP measurements have another direct negative impact on the South. Much of the production there takes place in the informal sector—community and household collaboration and exchange—and in subsistence agriculture. None of it appears in national accounting ledgers. The net effect of the invisibility of this activity is to open the door to development agencies that can argue for more "productive" economic approaches, such as increased foreign investment for capital-intensive infrastructures, industrial agriculture, high-tech assembly operations, and the like. All of these might create better numbers for GDP purposes and add to the illusion of progress, but they directly undermine traditional economies, cultures, and self-reliant systems. A type of small-scale financial support for local activities would make less of a splash for World Bank development figures but be far more beneficial for local people.

Finally, we mention an even more subtle though insidious manipulation that occurred in the mid-1980s, when the official measurement system switched from Gross National Product (GNP) to GDP. According to Clifford Cobb and Ted Halstead, this switch produced a "fundamental shift that exaggerated the contributions of multinational corporations. Under the old GNP, the profits of multinationals were attributed to the nation in which the corporations were based. If Goodyear owned a factory in Indonesia, the profits generated there were included in the

U.S. GNP figures. Now, however, under GDP, the profits are included in Indonesia's figures, *even though the profits come back to the U.S.*"

This shift in strategy has made it seem as if Southern countries were growing in wealth, when actually the multinationals have been walking off with the profits for the benefit of their Northern investors. Southern countries get nothing. According to Cobb and Halstead, "Suddenly, multinationals seemed an unqualified boon. . . . It has brought an even greater social and ecological cover-up for the social and ecological costs of globalization."

Measuring What Matters

Recently there has been a trend toward using indices like the Dow Jones Industrial Average and the Nikkei Index; in some quarters they are replacing GDP as the most closely watched economic indicators. TV and radio stations in some countries issue hourly reports on market fluctuations, with significant commentaries. However, stock prices are an even less meaningful indicator of human well-being than GDP. Only a tiny portion of the world's people own stock (although roughly half do in the United States), and as the recent collapse of the stock bubbles along with corporate scandals have revealed, there may be little connection between stock prices and substantive value. A rise in share prices increases the financial power of those who own the shares relative to the financial power of those who don't, but this is largely negative for society—a source of growing injustice—if there is no corresponding increase in productive capacity.

But we have also had a burst in very promising new efforts to develop new and better sets of indicators that would more accurately measure the things that matter. Readers can learn more details about some of them by contacting the International Institute for Sustainable Development of Canada, Environment Canada, the United Nations Development Program, or Redefining Progress (U.S.). These organizations have also joined with the World Bank and the U.N. Division for Sustainable Development in a comprehensive listing of some of these initiatives. (See http://iisdl.iisd.ca/measure/compindex-asp.) We offer a brief review of their suggestions here.

Genuine Progress Indicator

This is one of the better-known alternatives to the GDP, developed by Redefining Progress, of Berkeley, California. The GPI would include many factors now left out of GDP: resource depletion, pollution, long-term environmental damage, housework and nonmarket transactions, positive adjustments for growth in leisure time, negative adjustments for unemployment and underemployment, income distribution (positive adjustment for greater equity in the system, negative adjustment for greater disparity), positive adjustment for greater life span of durables and infrastructure, negative adjustment for defensive expenditures (those that try to maintain a given level of service without adding anything, such as pollution control devices and medical and material costs of auto accidents), and sustainable investment (which encourages domestic over foreign investment and investment from savings rather than borrowing).

Results from the GPI index compared with the GDP index vary from country to country but generally show that GPI rose more or less in tandem with GDP until about 1980. Then it sharply declined. The GPI is a big improvement over conventional GDP accounting because it begins to make visible the negative consequences of pursuing growth without accounting for costs and depletions.

Community Accounting Systems

Building on the work of Philippine economist Sixto Roxas, his country has become an important center of efforts to create true community accounting systems that take the household, rather than the enterprise, as the basic accounting unit. The differences are fundamental because in many instances the interests of the individual firm are at odds with the interests of the household and community. For example, a business benefits economically by hiring the fewest possible workers at the lowest possible wage. In contrast, the household benefits economically from having its members fully employed at the highest possible wage. The business benefits from selling its products at a high price, the household from buying at a low price.

Many investment projects may be highly profitable to a firm or individual yet very costly for the community—clear-cut logging for export, for example, or so-called export processing zones. The latter expropriate land, dominate local government decision making, enjoy tax holidays, demand fully developed infrastructure that must be paid for by local taxpayers, make priority claims on local water supplies and power generation, have few linkages to the local economy other than hiring labor at low wages, and contaminate local land and water supplies with their toxic wastes. Firms that operate in export-processing zones generate handsome profits that immediately go abroad, without compensating the community for the costs it incurs.

In contrast, community accounting systems take the household and community as the basic accounting unit and assess the costs and benefits of economic activity from a community perspective. At all levels, the community-based accounting system defines an economy that is inseparable from its habitat and corresponds to a local government responsible for managing the economy and its natural resource base.

The community balance sheet shows local natural resource stocks as *assets*. Production processes, such as in agriculture, forestry, mining, fisheries, trade, and services, create flows between asset accounts, firms, and households to reveal the consequences in terms of resource depletion and the distribution of benefits. Clear-cutting a forest is reflected immediately in the reduction of relevant community asset accounts. Unmet household needs are identified; resource flows into and out of the community are revealed; and the link between the community's well-being and the health of its local ecosystem is highlighted. This results in a perspective on investment decisions that is very different from the one provided by conventional methods of project assessment. Communities can more accurately assess the impact of proposed investments on the community balance sheet and negotiate with outside investors and trade interests accordingly.

Community-based accounting systems are also an important tool for implementing the principle of subsidiarity, because they allow local jurisdictions to see more clearly when trade offers real advantages to the community over local production—and when it does not. A substantial degree of self-reliance is encouraged, yet the community also remains open to beneficial trade and outside investment.

Local Indicators Initiatives

Many communities around the world have undertaken local initiatives to compile indicators of community social and environmental health. Redefining Progress identifies more than two hundred such efforts in the United States alone. Citizen led, they tend to focus on the kinds of communities in which people want to live. Recognizing the complexity of the human and natural systems involved, these initiatives make no effort to arrive at a single indicator. Many of those chosen reflect a highly sophisticated appreciation of the interplay between natural and human systems. Rarely do they include economic growth.

For example, the main indicator of social and environmental health chosen by Sustainable Seattle is the size of the seasonal spawning run of wild salmon. There is an almost primordial recognition that the condition of the wild salmon is a measure of the health of the watersheds on which all of the region's life depends. Toxic chemicals, loss of forest cover, disruption of stream flows, and urban sprawl all contribute to diminishing the salmon runs.

Sustainable Seattle's measure of stream quality is equally sophisticated. Rather than using a conventional test of the presence or absence of contaminants, it uses what is known as a benthic index of biological integrity, a measure of the diversity and density of bottom-dwelling (benthic) invertebrates. These are the mayflies, stoneflies, worms, mussels, and other groups of insects and invertebrates on which fish, birds, amphibians, and others rely for their food. The cleaner the water, the more they thrive.

Indicators of the number of pedestrian- and bicycle-friendly streets, open spaces near urban villages, reduction of fuel consumption and vehicle miles traveled, increased participation in gardening, and library and community center use all reflect a concern with the physical and social quality of urban life. Indicators of local farm production, employment concentration, and community reinvestment reveal the value placed on economic diversification and local ownership. A strong equity thrust is revealed in the decision to include indicators of unemployment, personal income distribution, number of hours of work required to meet basic needs, and the prevalence of low birthweight infants, children living in poverty, adult literacy, and racial equity in justice (disparities in the rate of arrests by race, for example).

All of the new indicators described here, and others, reject the argument that the well-being of society depends mainly on economic growth. Only the interests of economists, financiers, corporation heads, and others like them are served by economic expansion. When the poor speak for themselves, they speak of their need for secure rights to the land and waters on which they depend for their livelihoods, decent jobs that pay a living wage, and health care and education for their children. Some say they need money, but rarely, if ever, do they say, "We need economic growth and rising share prices."

One of the best ways to assess the health of any society may be with indicators that show the condition of the most vulnerable among us—children, the poor, the elderly. When infant mortality rates are low, everyone is literate, the poor and elderly are nourished and housed, crime rates are low, voter turnout is high, and community events are well attended, then we are probably looking at a healthy society—no matter the GDP, GNP, or Dow Jones average.

SOURCES

Daly, Heman E. *Beyond Growth: The Economics of Sustainable Development.* Boston: Beacon Press, 1996.

International Forum on Globalization. *Does Globalization Help the Poor?* San Francisco, 2001.

Korten, David C. *The Post-Corporate World: Life After Capitalism.* San Francisco: Berrett-Koehler and West Hartford, CT: Kumarian Press, 1999.

——. *When Corporations Rule the World.* 2d ed. West Hartford, CT: Kumarian Press and San Francisco: Berrett-Koehler, 2001.

Mander, Jerry, and Edward Goldsmith. *The Case Against the Global Economy: And for a Turn Toward the Local.* San Francisco: Sierra Club Books, 1996.

The Current State of Global Health

–World Health Organization, 2004

The World Health Organization, the United Nations specialized agency for health, was established in 1948 with the mission of securing the highest level attainable of health for all people. It issues reports on a variety of health-related topics on a regular basis. This report on global health was issued by the WHO in 2004.

The Problem: Current State of Global Health

The right to health is set forth in international human rights treaties and the WHO Constitution as the right to the "highest attainable standard of health". This right was reiterated in the Alma-Ata declaration, which was drafted in 1978 at the International Conference on Primary Health Care in the former USSR.

Today, the goals of Alma-Ata seem even more distant than they were a quarter of a century ago. Deep economic inequalities and social injustices continue to deny good health to many and persist as obstacles to continued health gains worldwide (1,2,3). There is also great variation in the pace and level of health achievements both between and within countries around the world. To illustrate these points, Table 1 shows regional disparities, Figure 1 shows inequities between countries, Figure 2 inequities within countries based on socio-economic level and Figure 3 inequities by gender.

One possible explanation is that health sector reforms that began in the late 1980s as part of the structural adjustment programmes of the World Bank have not been conclusively shown to improve inequities; in some cases they may have worsened them (4). Attempts to foster equity by targeting services, fee exemptions and free insurance for the poor have shown mixed results. Moreover, the push towards privatization and user fees has sometimes undermined public health systems and public health, and may well have accentuated rather than attenuated health inequities.

Looking forward, there is a risk that inequities will become worse, not better. Rapid progress in biomedical sciences, for example, is threatening to widen the equity gap. A WHO report on genomics and world health (5) in 2002, expressed concern about the risk that genetic research will exacerbate global health inequalities by creating a "genomics divide". Will the designer drugs of the future and other benefits that result from market-driven genomics research be unavailable to all but the wealthy few?

Reprinted by permission of WHO.

Table 1   Regional Disparities in Selected Health Indicators

World Regions	Under-Five Mortality Rate per 1,000 Live Births (2001)	Infant Mortality Rate per 1,000 Live Births (2000)	Maternal Mortality Rate per 100,000 Live Births (2001)	Prevalence of Tuberculosis per 100,000 Population (2001)
Developed regions	9	8	20	23
Developing regions	90	63	440	144
Northern Africa	43	39	130	27
Sub-Saharan Africa	172	106	920	197
Latin America and the Caribbean	36	29	190	41
Eastern Asia	36	31	55	184
South-Central Asia	95	70	520	218
South-Eastern Asia	51	39	210	108
Western Asia	62	51	190	40
Oceania	76	66	240	215

Source: United Nations Development Programme, 2003.

FIGURE 1
Under-5 Mortality Rates by Income Groups of Countries

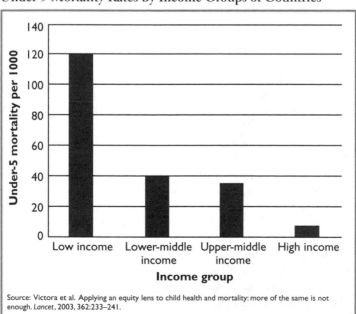

Source: Victora et al. Applying an equity lens to child health and mortality: more of the same is not enough. *Lancet*, 2003, 362:233–241.

FIGURE 2
Under-5 Mortality Rates by Socioeconomic Quintile of
the Household for Selected Countries

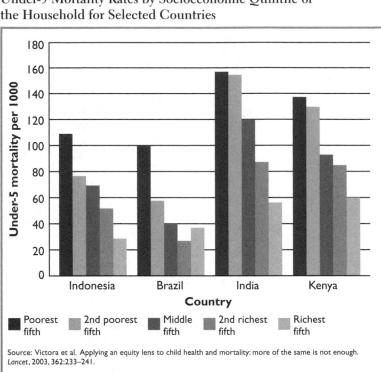

Source: Victora et al. Applying an equity lens to child health and mortality: more of the same is not enough. *Lancet*, 2003, 362:233–241.

The burden of disease has been reduced, quality of life improved and life expectancy increased. But as impressive as the achievements of health research have been, they are not reflected in the current state of global health. While one fifth of the world's population enjoys an average life expectancy approaching 80 years of age and a life comparatively free of disability, two thirds of the world's population living in the least well-off countries of Africa, Asia and Latin America suffer overwhelmingly from the world's burden of illness and premature death. Each year an estimated 15 million children—40,000 children per day—die from infection or malnutrition. Average life expectancy has dropped below 40 in some African countries because of HIV/AIDS. The toll of preventable and curable illness, early death and lifelong disability in developing countries from both communicable and noncommunicable diseases is unjust, immoral and a critical impediment to economic development and social stability.

Appropriate and effective interventions—such as diagnostic tests, drugs, vaccines, environmental and socio-behavioural interventions—and prevention strategies have led to enormous opportunities to improve health for all in the last

FIGURE 3
Maternal Mortality per 100,000 Live Births

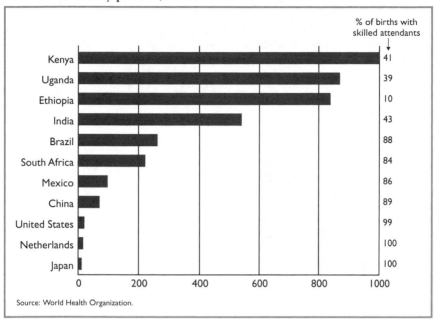

Source: World Health Organization.

50 years. Many argue that the knowledge already exists to save lives and improve the health of millions of people around the world. But this is not entirely true: the knowledge that an intervention works is only half the equation of improved health. What is standing in the way of improved health is the knowledge about how to effectively implement and use the interventions (6). This was the conclusion reached by the Bellagio Child Survival Study group (7), which has estimated that almost two thirds of under-five child mortality in the developing world could be prevented by applying simple, cost-effective interventions (see Figure 4). . . .

In an attempt to improve the state of global health, programmes and initiatives have been launched to better diagnose, treat, control or even eradicate diseases and other health problems. Principal among these are the Millennium Development Goals (MDGs) (8), three of which (goals 4, 5 and 6) are directly health-related: reduce child mortality, improve maternal health, and combat HIV/AIDS, malaria and other diseases. However, there are some concerns that health-related MDGs may not be achieved for most of the world's population by 2015 (9). Analysis of the reasons for such unsatisfactory progress suggest the existence of system-wide barriers and formidable challenges in implementation and scaling up because of weak health systems (10).

FIGURE 4
Actual and Preventable Under-5 Deaths by Country Profiles for
42 Countries with 90% of Under-5 Deaths, 2000

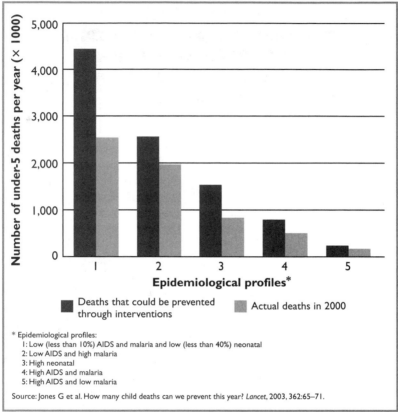

* Epidemiological profiles:
  1: Low (less than 10%) AIDS and malaria and low (less than 40%) neonatal
  2: Low AIDS and high malaria
  3: High neonatal
  4: High AIDS and malaria
  5: High AIDS and low malaria

Source: Jones G et al. How many child deaths can we prevent this year? *Lancet*, 2003, 362:65–71.

It is now a global imperative to find effective ways to strengthen health systems in order to improve the lives of people, to meet the MDGs and to prepare for what is to come. Health systems in developing countries are being identified as a key constraint to the implementation of major programmes such as the Global Fund to Fight AIDS, Tuberculosis and Malaria, the Global Alliance for Vaccines and Immunization (GAVI), and the 3 by 5 initiative to accelerate access to antiretroviral therapy to three million people by 2005. The systems constraints relate not only to the realization that inadequate information or human resources may slow progress but also that the focus on priority problems may be distorting the existing systems with unintended negative consequences to "non-" or "low-priority" health problems. In Haiti, for example, it has been observed that babies born to mothers

---

Box 1 Health System Constraints in Haiti

The tragic breakdown of health systems in the developing world is starkly illustrated by the fact that in some countries babies born to mothers on antiretroviral drugs die three weeks later from congenital syphilis.

This is the case in Haiti, where preliminary findings of a study by WHO, the London School of Hygiene and Tropical Medicine and GHESKIO (Groupe Haïtien d'Étude du Sarcome de Kaposi et des Infections Opportunistes) showed that about 20% of babies, born to mothers in Haiti who receive the Prevention of Mother-to-Child Transmission (PMTCT) package to prevent HIV/AIDS, die. In contrast, mother-to-child HIV transmission in Thailand was reduced to 1% after PMTCT programmes were introduced.

An estimated 720,000 infants are born HIV-positive every year around the world. In sub-Saharan Africa, only 30% of pregnant women are screened for syphilis even though the disease is responsible for more than 30% of perinatal deaths. There are some 492,000 cases of congenital syphilis in Africa every year.

Observations in many affected countries indicate that the epidemiology and transmission of HIV and syphilis are closely linked and that screening for both infections would lead to better health outcomes. Yet in much of the developing world, PMTCT programmes do not routinely include syphilis screening. This is a tragedy as congenital syphilis is pre-ventable if infected mothers are identified and treated by the middle of the second trimester of their pregnancy.

In many countries, health-care systems are severely limited, struggling with poor co-ordination, the conflicting agendas of different donor agencies and dire shortages of trained health-care workers and medical technicians.

In a country already suffering from such severe constraints in its health system, the ill-conceived integration of vertical programmes, or those focused on single diseases, into the broader health system may hamper what little health care is available already.

This tragedy is compounded by the fact that an inexpensive and rapid diagnostic test and an effective oral treatment for syphilis are available. It is the old story of effective interventions not reaching those in need, particularly in the developing world.

Clearly a more widespread application of rapid diagnosis and oral treatment for syphilis is needed, perhaps as part of the PMTCT or sentinel surveillance programmes for HIV. Such efforts must be informed by more research to determine the feasibility and sustainability of using these interventions in the local context and to address a key health systems research challenge of how to improve the integration of vertical programmes, such as those on HIV/AIDS, within broader health system functions.

Source: Peeling R et al. Surviving HIV and dying of syphilis. *Lancet*, 2004, in press.

---

successfully treated with antiretroviral drugs to prevent mother-to-child transmission of HIV/AIDS may then die of congenital syphilis (see Box 1).

As the health system struggles to deal with a massive single-disease initiative, and workers are diverted into high-profile programmes, screening and treatment for what is an eminently treatable and easily diagnosed condition, as Box 1 illustrates, is neglected with tragic consequences. But if resource-poor health systems are having difficulty dealing with current challenges, how are they to cope with the relentless march towards noncommunicable and chronic diseases?

The huge burden of communicable diseases is well known (*11*) but as populations age and risk exposures shift, noncommunicable diseases are rapidly becoming a leading cause of disability and premature death in developing nations (see Figure 5). For example, there were 151 million cases of diabetes worldwide in 2001, a figure that is expected to increase by 46% to 221 million cases in 2010, with the steepest growth in the developing world (*12*). The prevalence of obesity, cancer, cardiovascular disease and mental health disorders are also on the rise; WHO estimates that by 2020, noncommunicable diseases will account for about two thirds of the global disease burden.

In the absence of an adequate health system, how will people receive the long-term care they require? How can the impact of noncommunicable diseases be reduced if appropriate and culturally relevant programmes aimed at primary prevention, early diagnosis and secondary prevention are not designed and implemented? Efforts to stem the burden will, of course, be important but even with more appropriate primary prevention and early diagnostic tools, will systems be able to deliver these opportunities to those in need?

FIGURE 5
Mortality Attributable to 20 Leading Risk Factors, 2001

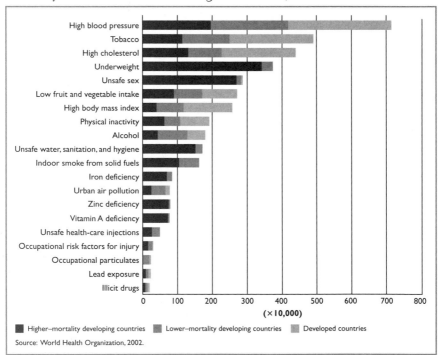

Source: World Health Organization, 2002.

REFERENCES

1. Evans T, Whitehead M, Diderichsen F et al. (eds). *Challenging inequities in health: from ethics to action.* New York, Oxford University Press, 2001.

2. Sen G, George A, Ostlin P (eds). *Engendering international health: the challenge of equity.* Cambridge, MA, MIT Press, 2002.

3. Marmot M. *Status syndrome: how your social standing directly affects your health and life expectancy.* London, Bloomsbury, 2004.

4. Labonte L, Schrecker R. *Fatal indifference: The G8, Africa and global health.* Ottawa, International Development Research Centre, 2004.

5. *Genomics and world health.* Geneva, World Health Organization, 2002.

6. Jha P et al. Improving the health of the global poor. *Science,* 2002, 295:2036–2039.

7. Jones G et al. How many child deaths can we prevent this year. *Lancet,* 2003, 362:65–71.

8. Millennium Development Goals (MDGs). http://www.who.int/mdg/en/

9. Wagstaff A, Claeson M. *The Millennium Development Goals for health: rising to the challenges.* Washington, DC, The World Bank, 2004.

10. Travis P et al. Overcoming health-systems constraints to achieve the millennium development goals. *Lancet,* 2004, 364:900–906.

11. Morens DM et al. The challenge of emerging and re-emerging infectious diseases. *Nature,* 2004, 430:242–249.

12. Zimmett P et al. Global and societal implications of the diabetes epidemic. *Nature,* 2001, 414:782–787.

Macroeconomics of Health:
No Health Available at $7.50 per Person per Year

Jeffrey D. Sachs is the director of The Earth Institute, Quetelet Professor of Sustainable
Development, and Professor of Health Policy and Management at Columbia Univer-
sity. He is also director of the U.N. Millennium Project and Special Advisor to United
Nations Secretary General Kofi Annan on the Millennium Development Goals, the in-
ternationally agreed-upon goals to reduce extreme poverty, disease, and hunger by the
year 2015. The following is the text of a plenary presentation Sachs made at the Mas-
sive Effort Advocacy Forum held in Winterthur, Switzerland, in October 2000.

Perhaps three million people, mostly children, die annually from diseases readily preventable by vaccination. Millions more die of diseases that are preventable by other means, or that are likely targets of new technologies in the next few years. Health is of course an end in itself, and humanity must not stand by as millions of people suffer unnecessary, often easily preventable deaths. But health is also an investment—in the economic well-being of people at the edge of survival. Without an improvement in public health in the poorest countries, all of the economic reform agenda, all of the potential benefits of a fast-growing world economy, are likely to bypass hundreds of millions of people, and leave them and their children in utter impoverishment.

Poor Health Cripples Poor Societies in Numerous Ways

Most directly, the burdens of illness and death rob society of productive healthy workers. This is most starkly the case in the HIV/AIDS pandemic, which is robbing Africa of the millions of the societies' most productive members in the prime of their lives. But the burden works through less obvious channels as well. Children surviving multiple bouts of diarrhoeal disease, respiratory infection, helminthic infections, and malaria, may well suffer lifetime impairments in physical and

"The Horrific Disease Burden of the Poorest Countries—Claiming Millions of Lives Every Year and Billions of Days of Sickness—Is a Fundamental Barrier to Economic Improvement of the World's Poorest." Copyright 2000. Reprinted by permission of Gordon McCord.

cognitive capacities. They are more likely to drop out of school early after repeated absences. The lifetime burdens of illness and under-nutrition, we have learned, can start with nutrient deficiencies in-utero, so that pre-natal care is an investment in a lifetime of health and productivity of the yet unborn child.

Ironically, the evidence strongly suggests that the massive number of early deaths among children—especially from malaria, diarrhoeal disease, and respiratory infections—actually speeds population growth, rather than slows it, with all of the attendant complications for society. This occurs because in societies with high rates of infant and child deaths, parents compensate the risk of death by having large numbers of children. And because they want insurance that at least one son will reach adulthood, they may have as many as six children when the expectation is that two will die. Insurance for the parents, though, translates into unmanageably fast population growth for the society, and low levels of school and health investments in each individual child.

When Health Is Looked upon as an Investment in the Future of Today's Poorest People, We Must Stand Shocked at the Extent of the Underinvestment That We Are Making

In the world's poorest countries, the national investments are a mirror of national impoverishment.When a country at $250 per capita makes an investment in public health of 3 percent of GDP, that translates into annual spending of just $7.50 per person per year. This compares with public health spending of $3,000 to $5,000 per person in the rich countries. Critics of foreign assistance sometimes mistakenly argue that the basic problem of health care in the poorest countries is mismanagement of health systems. I want to reject that view categorically: there is no way to manage an efficient health system at $7.50 per capita. And there is no way that the world's poorest societies, just barely surviving at current income levels, or perhaps not surviving, can manage much more than that out of their own resources. This is especially true when debt service payments to governments, the World Bank, and the International Monetary Fund, are draining more than the annual budgets for health care. Yes, by all means, countries like India and Nigeria which are spending around $3.00 in public funds per year in public health could do more themselves. And yes, by all means, countries should strive to maintain efficiency and honesty in health care delivery. But no, the poorest of the poor cannot be blamed for the disastrous state of public health. They simply lack the resources to do better.

And globalization is not making matters easier in this regard. Through Africa, highly mobile doctors are leaving their countries to work in Europe, the Middle East, and the United States. The market for skilled workers, including skilled workers in health, has become global. Poor countries, like it or not, will have to pay a competitive wage to their doctors if they expect to keep them in Kano, Nigeria, or Arusha, Tanzania, or Kerala State in India. The squeeze on skilled labor will therefore get worse, not better, unless we do something about it.

The Rich Countries Will Have to Help Square the Circle Through a Massive Effort of Support at Disease Control

The numbers can not add up in any other way. But thank goodness, very modest efforts by the standards of the rich countries can make a manifold difference for the poorest of the poor. The rich countries today are unimaginably rich even by standards of twenty years ago. The U.S. average income is $30,000 per year, signifying a $10 trillion dollar economy. The capital gains in the U.S. stock markets in the past five years are an astounding $8 trillion. There are now 1 billion people in rich countries enjoying a standard of living unrivalled in world history. Make no mistake about it, however, despite thirty years of public pronouncements about disease control, despite an international pledge of "Health for All in the Year 2000" made a generation ago, the rich-country support of health for the poorest of the poor is at shockingly low levels. These levels are even below what you might imagine.

The Organization for Economic Cooperation and Development (OECD), in Paris, keeps careful records of all official development assistance (ODA) by the rich countries and by the international institutions on behalf of the poorest countries. The numbers are shocking. In the category of Basic Health, which includes provisions for infectious disease control and support for primary health clinics, the total grants in 1998 from all donors—both governments and international agencies—for all 619 million people in the least developed countries was $209 million, or around 30 cents per person in the poorest countries. Even this exaggerates the real aid, however, since $21 million of this was tied aid and $88 million was so-called technical assistance, paying experts in the rich countries rather than providing cash-support to the poor countries. In fact, only $78 million came in the form of untied cash support for the poorest countries, around 13 cents per person in the recipient countries, and around three ten-thousandths of one percent of the income of the rich countries, . . . one or two minutes per year worth of rich-country income.

The level of support for HIV/AIDS is equally shocking, totaling a few tens of millions of dollars per year for the poorest countries, while the greatest pandemic in modern history, perhaps in world history, has unfolded before our eyes.

The Work of the Commission on Macroeconomics and Health

The work of the commission established by the WHO is devoted to understanding the areas of highest social return to new international investments in public health in the poorest countries, and to providing a serious estimate of the sums that will be needed as well as potential delivery mechanisms. That work will not be completed for one year, but we are far advanced in several aspects of the undertaking. We have identified major disease areas—including HIV/AIDS, malaria, TB, diarrhoeal disease, acute respiratory infection, helminthic infections, nutritional disorders, reproductive health–as the likely targets of effective intervention, and have begun to prepare detailed cost estimates for providing the population with existing technologies of prevention and treatment, as well as cost estimates for new research priorities where new technologies are urgently needed. I can safely say, speaking personally and with preliminary data, that international support for disease control can and should reach $10 to $20 billion per year from the richest countries, still a mere $10 to $20 per person per year in the rich countries. This must be accompanied by comprehensive debt cancellation for the world's highly indebted poor countries. With debt cancellation and a greatly increased level of spending, millions of lives can be saved, untold suffering can be relieved, and economic development prospects of the world's poorest countries can be enormously enhanced. And even the sum of $10 to $20 billion per year would be less than one-tenth of one percent of the incomes of the rich countries.

Increased spending should be combined with new methods of healthy delivery—drawing on the new information technologies, the schools, and the communities—in innovative ways. So too, the world's scientific community and the leading pharmaceutical and biotechnology companies must be induced, often through novel means such as "guaranteed purchase funds for vaccines" to devote much more of their astounding scientific prowess to the urgent, life-and-death needs of the world's poorest peoples. The donors will also need a new form of cooperation, not simply more funding. They will need to pool resources, rather than segregate them in pet projects. They will need to give up turf in a common battle against disease. They will need to turn to the independent scientific community for intensive, high-level, ongoing scrutiny, at every stage of the process. Independent panels of scientific experts should review disease control proposals coming from the international community, especially welcoming proposals coming from the affected countries themselves. These panels should emphasize scientific rigor, peer-review, and independence, to ensure the highest scientific standards in our new Massive Effort against disease. The World Health Organization has a unique role to play in this in convening this expertise, since WHO is the leader of global public health and the world's foremost bridge between the official donor community and the worlds of medical science and public health.

Suffering and Structural Violence
–Paul Farmer

Paul Farmer is Professor of Medical Anthropology in the Department of Social Medicine at the Harvard Medical School. He holds both an M.D. and a Ph.D. He divides his clinical time between the Brigham and Women's Hospital in Boston and a charity hospital in Rural Haiti, the Clinique Bon Saveur, where he serves as medical co-director. The selection that follows is from his book Pathologies of Power: Health, Human Rights and the New War on the Poor, *which was published by the University of California Press in 2003.*

> Growth of GNP or of industrial incomes can, of course, be very important as *means* to expanding the freedoms enjoyed by the members of the society. But freedoms depend also on other determinants, such as social and economic arrangements (for example, facilities for education and health care) as well as political and civil rights (for example, the liberty to participate in public discussion and scrutiny).
>
> *Amartya Sen,* Development as Freedom

> Where do people earn the Per Capita Income? More than one poor starving soul would like to know.
>
> In our countries, numbers live better than people. How many people prosper in times of prosperity? How many people find their lives developed by development?
>
> *Eduardo Galeano, "Those Little Numbers and People"*

Everyone knows that suffering, violence, and misery exist. How to define them? Given that each person's pain has for him or her a degree of reality that the pain of others can surely never approach, is widespread agreement on the subject possible? And yet people do agree, as often as not, on what constitutes extreme suffering: premature and painful illnesses, say, as well as torture and rape. More insidious assaults on dignity, such as institutionalized racism and gender inequality, are also acknowledged by most to cause great and unjust injury.

Chapter One, "On Suffering and Structural Violence" from *Pathologies of Power: Health, Human Rights and the New War on the Poor* by Paul Farmer. Copyright © 2003 The Regents of the University of California. Reprinted by permission of the University of California Press.

So suffering is a fact. Now a number of corollary questions come to the fore. Whenever we talk about medicine or policy, a "hierarchy of suffering" begins to take shape, for it is impossible to relieve every case at once. Can we identify the worst assaults? Those most at risk of great suffering? Among persons whose suffering is not fatal, is it possible to identify those most at risk of sustaining permanent and disabling damage? Are certain "event" assaults, such as torture or rape, more likely to lead to later sequelae than is sustained and insidious suffering, such as the pain born of deep poverty or racism? Are certain forms of insidious discrimination demonstrably more noxious than others?

Anthropologists and others who take these as research questions study both individual experience and the larger social matrix in which it is embedded in order to see how various social processes and events come to be translated into personal distress and disease. By what mechanisms, precisely, do social forces ranging from poverty to racism become *embodied* as individual experience?[1] This has been the focus of most of my own research in Haiti, where political and economic forces have structured risk for AIDS, tuberculosis, and, indeed, most other infectious and parasitic diseases. Social forces at work there have also structured risk for most forms of extreme suffering, from hunger to torture and rape.

Working in contemporary Haiti, where in recent decades political violence has been added to the worst poverty in the hemisphere, one learns a great deal about suffering. In fact, the country has long constituted a sort of living laboratory for the study of affliction, no matter how it is defined.[2] "Life for the Haitian peasant of today," observed the anthropologist Jean Weise some thirty years ago, "is abject misery and a rank familiarity with death."[3] The biggest problem, of course, is unimaginable poverty, as a long succession of dictatorial governments has been more engaged in pillaging than in protecting the rights of workers, even on paper. As Eduardo Galeano noted in 1973, at the height of the Duvalier dictatorship, "The wages Haiti requires by law belong in the department of science fiction: actual wages on coffee plantations vary from $.07 to $.15 a day."[4]

In some senses, the situation has worsened since. When in 1991 international health and population experts devised a "human suffering index" by examining several measures of human welfare ranging from life expectancy to political freedom, 27 of 141 countries were characterized by "extreme human suffering."[5] Only one of them, Haiti, was located in the Western hemisphere. In only three countries on earth was suffering judged to be more extreme than that endured in Haiti; each of these three countries was in the midst of an internationally recognized civil war.

Suffering is certainly a recurrent and expected condition in Haiti's Central Plateau, where everyday life has felt, often enough, like war. "You get up in the morning," observed one young widow with four children, "and it's the fight for food and wood and water." If initially struck by the austere beauty of the region's steep mountains and clement weather, long-term visitors come to see the Central Plateau in much the same manner as its inhabitants do: a chalky and arid land hostile to the best efforts of the peasant farmers who live here. Landlessness is widespread and so, consequently, is hunger. All the standard measures reveal how tenuous is the peasantry's hold on survival. Life expectancy at birth is less than fifty years, in large part because as many as two of every ten infants die before their first birthday.[6] Tuberculosis and AIDS are the leading causes of death among adults; among children, diarrheal disease, measles, and tetanus ravage the undernourished.[7]

But the experience of suffering, it's often noted, is not effectively conveyed by statistics or graphs. In fact, the suffering of the world's poor intrudes only rarely into the consciousness of the affluent, even when our affluence may be shown to have direct relation to their suffering. This is true even when spectacular human rights violations are at issue, and it is even more true when the topic at hand is the everyday violation of social and economic rights.[8] Because the "texture" of dire affliction is better felt in the gritty details of biography, I introduce the stories of Acéphie Joseph and Chouchou Louis.[9] Since any example begs the question of its relevance, I will argue at the outset that the stories of Acéphie and Chouchou are anything but "anecdotal." In the eyes of the epidemiologist as well as the political analyst, they suffered and died in exemplary fashion. Millions of people living in similar circumstances can expect to meet similar fates. What these victims, past and present, share are not personal or psychological attributes. They do not share culture or language or a certain race. What they share, rather, is the experience of occupying the bottom rung of the social ladder in inegalitarian societies.

Acéphie's Story

For the wound of the daughter of my people is my heart wounded,
I mourn, and dismay has taken hold of me.
Is there no balm in Gilead? Is there no physician there?
Why then has the health of the daughter of my people not been restored?
O that my head were waters, and my eyes a fountain of tears, that
I might weep day and night for the slain of the daughter
of my people!

Jeremiah 8:22–9:1

Kay, a community of fewer than three thousand people, stretches along an unpaved road that cuts north and east into Haiti's Central Plateau. Striking out from Port-au-Prince, the capital, it can take several hours to reach Kay, especially if one travels during the rainy season, when the chief thoroughfare through central Haiti turns into a muddy, snaking path. But even in the dry season, the journey gives one an impression of isolation, insularity. The impression is misleading, as the village owes its existence to a project conceived in the Haitian capital and drafted in Washington, D.C.: Kay is a settlement of refugees, substantially composed of peasant farmers displaced more than forty years ago by the construction of Haiti's largest dam.[10]

Before 1956, the village of Kay was situated in a fertile valley, and through it ran the Rivière Artibonite, Haiti's largest river. For generations, thousands of families had farmed the broad and gently sloping banks of the river, selling rice, bananas, millet, corn, and sugarcane in regional markets. Harvests were, by all reports, bountiful; life there is now recalled as idyllic. When the valley was flooded, the majority of the local population was forced up into the stony hills on either side of the new reservoir. By all the standard measures, the "water refugees" became exceedingly poor; the older people often blame their poverty on the massive buttress dam a few miles away, bitterly noting that it brought them neither electricity nor water.

In 1983, when I began working in the Central Plateau, AIDS was already afflicting an ever-increasing number of city dwellers but was unknown in areas as rural as Kay. Acéphie Joseph was one of the first villagers to die of the new syndrome. But her illness, which ended in 1991, was merely the latest in a string of tragedies that she and her parents readily linked together in a long lamentation, by now familiar to those who tend the region's sick.

The litany begins, usually, down in the valley, now hidden under the still surface of the lake. Both Acéphie's parents came from families who had made a decent living by farming fertile tracts of land—their "ancestors' gardens"—and selling much of their produce. Her father tilled the soil, and his wife, a tall and wearily elegant woman not nearly as old as she looks, was a "Madame Sarah," a market woman. "If it weren't for the dam," he once assured me, "we'd be just fine now. Acéphie, too." The Josephs' home was drowned, along with most of their belongings, their crops, and the graves of their ancestors.

Refugees from the rising water, the Josephs built a miserable lean-to on a knoll of high land jutting into the new reservoir. They remained poised on their knoll for some years; Acéphie and her twin brother were born there. I asked what had induced them to move higher up the hill, to build a house on the hard stone embankment of a dusty road. "Our hut was too near the water," replied their father. "I was afraid one of the children would fall into the lake and drown. Their mother had to be away selling; I was trying to make a garden in this terrible soil. There was no one to keep an eye on them."

Acéphie attended primary school in a banana-thatched and open shelter in which children and young adults received the rudiments of literacy in Kay. "She was the nicest of the Joseph sisters," recalled one of her classmates. "And she was as pretty as she was nice." Acéphie's beauty—she was tall and fine-featured, with enormous dark eyes—and her vulnerability may have sealed her fate as early as 1984. Though still in primary school then, she was already nineteen years old; it was time for her to help generate income for her family, which was sinking deeper and deeper into poverty. Acéphie began to help her mother by carrying produce to a local market on Friday mornings. On foot or with a donkey, it takes over an hour and a half to reach the market, and the road leads right through Péligre, site of the dam and a military barracks. The soldiers liked to watch the parade of women on Friday mornings. Sometimes they taxed them, literally, with haphazardly imposed fines; sometimes they levied a toll of flirtatious banter.

Such flirtation is seldom rejected, at least openly. In rural Haiti, entrenched poverty made the soldiers—the region's only salaried men—ever so much more attractive. Hunger was a near-daily occurrence for the Joseph family; the times were as bad as those right after the flooding of the valley. And so when Acéphie's good looks caught the eye of Captain Jacques Honorat, a native of Belladère formerly stationed in Port-au-Prince, she returned his gaze.

Acéphie knew, as did everyone in the area, that Honorat had a wife and children. He was known, in fact, to have more than one regular partner. But Acéphie was taken in by his persistence, and when he went to speak to her parents, a long-term liaison was, from the outset, a serious possibility:

> What would you have me do? I could tell that the old people were uncomfortable, worried; but they didn't say no. They didn't tell me to stay away from him. I wish they had, but how could they have known? . . . I knew it was a bad idea then, but I just didn't know why. I never dreamed he would give me a bad illness, never! I looked around and saw how poor we all were, how the old people were finished. . . . What would you have me do? It was a way out, that's how I saw it.

Acéphie and Honorat were sexual partners only briefly—for less than a month, according to Acéphie. Shortly thereafter, Honorat fell ill with unexplained fevers and kept to the company of his wife in Péligre. As Acéphie was looking for a *moun prensipal*—a "main man"—she tried to forget about the soldier. Still, it was shocking to hear, a few months after they parted, that he was dead.

Acéphie was at a crucial juncture in her life. Returning to school was out of the question. After some casting about, she went to Mirebalais, the nearest town, and began a course in what she euphemistically termed a "cooking school." The school—really just an ambitious woman's courtyard—prepared poor girls like Acéphie for their inevitable turn as servants in the city. Indeed, becoming a maid was fast developing into one of the rare growth industries in Haiti, and, as much as Acéphie's proud mother hated to think of her daughter reduced to servitude, she could offer no viable alternative.

And so Acéphie, twenty-two years old, went off to Port-au-Prince, where she found a job as a housekeeper for a middle-class Haitian woman who worked for the U.S. embassy. Acéphie's looks and manners kept her out of the backyard, the traditional milieu of Haitian servants. She was designated as the maid who, in addition to cleaning, answered the door and the phone. Although Acéphie was not paid well—she received thirty dollars each month—she recalled the gnawing hunger in her home village and managed to save a bit of money for her parents and siblings.

Still looking for a *moun prensipal*, Acéphie began seeing Blanco Nerette, a young man with origins similar to her own: Blanco's parents were also "water refugees," and Acéphie had known him when they were both attending the parochial school in Kay. Blanco had done well for himself, by Kay standards: he chauffeured a small bus between the Central Plateau and the capital. In a setting in which the unemployment rate was greater than 60 percent, he could command considerable respect, and he turned his attentions to Acéphie. They planned to marry, she later recalled, and started pooling their resources.

Acéphie remained at the "embassy woman's" house for more than three years, staying until she discovered that she was pregnant. As soon as she told Blanco, she could see him becoming skittish. Nor was her employer pleased: it is considered unsightly to have a pregnant servant. And so Acéphie returned to Kay, where she had a difficult pregnancy. Blanco came to see her once or twice. They had a disagreement, and then she heard nothing more from him. Following the birth of her daughter, Acéphie was sapped by repeated infections. A regular visitor to our clinic, she was soon diagnosed with AIDS.

Within months of her daughter's birth, Acéphie's life was consumed with managing her own drenching night sweats and debilitating diarrhea while attempting to care for the child. "We both need diapers now," she remarked bitterly, toward the end of her life. As political violence hampered her doctors' ability to open the clinic, Acéphie was faced each day not only with diarrhea but also with a persistent lassitude. As she became more and more gaunt, some villagers suggested that Acéphie was the victim of sorcery. Others recalled her liaison with the soldier and her work as a servant in the city, by then widely considered to be risk factors for AIDS. Acéphie herself knew that she had AIDS, although she was more apt to refer to herself as suffering from a disorder brought on by her work as a servant: "All that ironing, and then opening a refrigerator." She died far from refrigerators or other amenities as her family and caregivers stood by helplessly.

But this is not simply the story of Acéphie and her daughter, also infected with the virus. There is also Jacques Honorat's first wife, who each year grows thinner. After Honorat's death, she found herself desperate, with no means of feeding her five hungry children, two of whom were also ill. Her subsequent union was again with a soldier. Honorat had at least two other partners, both of them poor peasant women, in the Central Plateau. One is HIV-positive and has two sickly children. And there is Blanco, still a handsome young man, apparently in good health, plying the roads from Mirebalais to Port-au-Prince. Who knows if he carries the virus? As a chauffeur, he has plenty of girlfriends.

Nor is this simply the story of those infected with HIV. The pain of Acéphie's mother and twin brother was manifestly intense. But few understood her father's anguish. Shortly after Acéphie's death, he hanged himself with a length of rope.

Chouchou's Story

I never found the order
I searched for
but always a sinister
and well-planned disorder
that increases in the hands
of those who hold power
while the others
who clamor for
a more kindly world

a world with less hunger
and more hopefulness
die of torture
in the prisons.
Don't come any closer
there's a stench of carrion
surrounding me.
                        Claribel Alegría,
                        "From the Bridge"

Chouchou Louis grew up not far from Kay, in another small village in the steep and infertile highlands of Haiti's Central Plateau. He attended primary school for a couple of years but was forced to drop out when his mother died. Then, in his early teens, Chouchou joined his father and an older sister in tending their hillside garden. In short, there was nothing remarkable about Chouchou's childhood. It was brief and harsh, like most in rural Haiti.

Throughout the 1980s, church activities formed Chouchou's sole distraction. These were hard years for the Haitian poor, beaten down by a family dictatorship well into its third decade. The Duvaliers, father and son, ruled through violence, largely directed at people whose conditions of existence were similar to those of Chouchou Louis. Although many tried to flee, often by boat, U.S. policy maintained that Haitian asylum-seekers were "economic refugees." As part of a 1981 agreement between the administrations of Ronald Reagan and Jean-Claude Duvalier (known as "Baby Doc"), refugees seized by the U.S. Coast Guard on the high seas were summarily returned to Haiti. During the first ten years of the accord, approximately twenty-three thousand Haitians applied for political asylum in the United States. Eight applications were approved.[11]

A growing Haitian pro-democracy movement led to the flight of Duvalier in February 1986. Chouchou Louis, who must have been about twenty years old when "Baby Doc" fell, shortly thereafter acquired a small radio. "All he did," recalled his wife, years later, "was work the land, listen to the radio, and go to church." On the radio, Chouchou heard about the people who took over after Duvalier fled. Like many in rural Haiti, Chouchou was distressed to hear that power had been handed to the military, led by hardened *duvaliéristes*. It was this army that the U.S. government termed "Haiti's best bet for democracy." (Hardly a disinterested judgment: the United States had created the modern Haitian army in 1916.) In the eighteen months following Duvalier's departure, more than $200 million in U.S. aid passed through the hands of the junta.[12]

In early 1989, Chouchou moved in with Chantal Brisé, who was pregnant. They were living together when Father Jean-Bertrand Aristide—by then considered the leader of the pro-democracy movement—declared his candidacy for the presidency in the internationally monitored elections of 1990. In December of that year, almost 70 percent of the voters chose Father Aristide from a field of almost a dozen presidential candidates. No run-off election was required—Aristide won this plurality in the first round.

Like most rural Haitians, Chouchou and Chantal welcomed Aristide's election with great joy. For the first time, the poor—Haiti's overwhelming majority, formerly silent—felt they had someone representing their interests in the presidential palace. This is why the subsequent military coup d'état of September 1991 stirred great anger in the countryside, where most Haitians live. Anger was soon followed by sadness, then fear, as the country's repressive machinery, which had been held at bay during the seven months of Aristide's tenure, was speedily reactivated under the patronage of the army.

One day during the month after the coup, Chouchou was sitting in a truck en route to the town of Hinche. Chouchou offered for the consideration of his fellow passengers what Haitians call a *pwen*, a pointed remark intended to say something other than what it literally means. As they bounced along, he began complaining about the condition of the roads, observing that, "if things were as they should be, these roads would have been repaired already." One eyewitness later told me that at no point in the commentary was Aristide's name invoked. But his fellow passengers recognized Chouchou's observations as veiled language deploring the coup. Unfortunately for Chouchou, one of the passengers was an out-of-uniform soldier. At the next checkpoint, the soldier had him seized and dragged from the truck. There, a group of soldiers and their lackeys—their *attachés*, to use the epithet then in favor—immediately began beating Chouchou, in front of the other passengers; they continued to beat him as they brought him to the military barracks in Hinche. A scar on his right temple was a souvenir of his stay in Hinche, which lasted several days.

Perhaps the worst after-effect of such episodes of brutality was that, in general, they marked the beginning of persecution, not the end. In rural Haiti, any scrape with the law (that is, the military) led to a certain blacklisting. For men like Chouchou, staying out of jail involved keeping the local *attachés* happy, and he did this by avoiding his home village. But Chouchou lived in fear of a second arrest, his wife later told me, and his fears proved to be well-founded.

On January 22, 1992, Chouchou was visiting his sister when he was arrested by two *attachés*. No reason was given for the arrest, and Chouchou's sister regarded as ominous the seizure of the young man's watch and radio. He was roughly marched to the nearest military checkpoint, where he was tortured by soldiers and the *attachés*. One area resident later told us that the prisoner's screams made her children weep with terror.

On January 25, Chouchou was dumped in a ditch to die. The army scarcely took the trouble to circulate the *canard* that he had stolen some bananas. (The Haitian press, by then thoroughly muzzled, did not even broadcast this false version of events; fatal beatings in the countryside did not count as news.) Relatives carried Chouchou back to Chantal and their daughter under the cover of night. By early on the morning of January 26, when I arrived, Chouchou was scarcely recognizable. His face, and especially his left temple, was deformed, swollen, and lacerated; his right temple was also scarred. His mouth was a coagulated pool of dark blood. Lower down, his neck was peculiarly swollen, his throat collared with bruises left by a gun butt. His chest and sides were badly bruised, and he had several fractured ribs. His genitals had been mutilated.

That was his front side; presumably, the brunt of the beatings had come from behind. Chouchou's back and thighs were striped with deep lash marks. His buttocks were macerated, the skin flayed down to the exposed gluteal muscles. Already some of these stigmata appeared to be infected.

Chouchou coughed up more than a liter of blood in his agonal moments. Although I am not a forensic pathologist, my guess is that the proximate cause of his death was pulmonary hemorrhage. Given his respiratory difficulties and the amount of blood he coughed up, it is likely that the beatings caused him to bleed, slowly at first, then catastrophically, into his lungs. His head injuries had not robbed him of his faculties, although it might have been better for him had they done so. It took Chouchou three days to die.

Explaining Versus Making Sense of Suffering

> When we come to you
> Our rags are torn off us
> And you listen all over our naked body.
> As to the cause of our illness
> One glance at our rags would
> Tell you more. It is the same cause that wears out
> Our bodies and our clothes.
>
> The pain in our shoulder comes
> You say, from the damp; and this is also the reason
> For the stain on the wall of our flat.
> So tell us:
> Where does the damp come from?
>   Bertolt Brecht, "A Worker's Speech to a Doctor"

Are these stories of suffering emblematic of something other than two tragic and premature deaths? If so, how representative is either of these experiences? Little about Acéphie's story is unique; I have told it in some detail because it brings into relief many of the forces restricting not only her options but those of most Haitian women. Such, in any case, is my opinion after caring for hundreds of poor women with AIDS. Their stories move with a deadly monotony: young women—or teenage girls—fled to Port-au-Prince in an attempt to escape from the harshest poverty; once in the city, each worked as a domestic; none managed to find the financial security that had proven so elusive in the countryside. The women I interviewed were straightforward about the nonvoluntary aspect of their sexual activity:

in their opinions, poverty had forced them into unfavorable unions.[13] Under such conditions, one wonders what to make of the notion of "consensual sex."

What about the murder of Chouchou Louis? International human rights groups estimate that more than three thousand Haitians were killed in the year after the September 1991 coup that overthrew Haiti's first democratically elected government. Almost all were civilians who, like Chouchou, fell into the hands of the military or paramilitary forces. The vast majority of victims were poor peasants, like Chouchou, or urban slum dwellers. But note that the figures just cited are conservative estimates; I can testify that no journalist or human rights observer ever came to count the body of Chouchou Louis.[14]

Thus the agony of Acéphie and Chouchou was, in a sense, "modal" suffering. In Haiti, AIDS and political violence are two leading causes of death among young adults. These afflictions are not the result of accident or a *force majeure*; they are the consequence, direct or indirect, of human agency. When the Artibonite Valley was flooded, depriving families like the Josephs of their land, a human decision was behind it; when the Haitian army was endowed with money and unfettered power, human decisions were behind that, too. In fact, some of the same decision makers may have been involved in both cases.

If bureaucrats and soldiers seemed to have unconstrained sway over the lives of the rural poor, the agency of Acéphie and Chouchou was, correspondingly, curbed at every turn. These grim biographies suggest that the social and economic forces that have helped to shape the AIDS epidemic are, in every sense, the same forces that led to Chouchou's death and to the larger repression in which it was eclipsed. What's more, both of these individuals were "at risk" of such a fate long before they met the soldiers who altered their destinies. They were both, from the outset, victims of structural violence. The term is apt because such suffering is "structured" by historically given (and often economically driven) processes and forces that conspire—whether through routine, ritual, or, as is more commonly the case, the hard surfaces of life—to constrain agency.[15] For many, including most of my patients and informants, choices both large and small are limited by racism, sexism, political violence, *and* grinding poverty.

While certain kinds of suffering are readily observable—and the subject of countless films, novels, and poems—structural violence all too often defeats those who would describe it. There are at least three reasons. First, the "exoticization" of suffering as lurid as that endured by Acéphie and Chouchou distances it. The suffering of individuals whose lives and struggles recall our own tends to move us; the suffering of those who are "remote," whether because of geography or culture, is often less affecting.

Second, the sheer weight of the suffering makes it all the more difficult to render: "Knowledge of suffering cannot be conveyed in pure facts and figures, reportings that objectify the suffering of countless persons. The horror of suffering is not only its immensity but the faces of the anonymous victims who have little voice, let alone rights, in history."[16]

Third, the dynamics and distribution of suffering are still poorly understood. Physicians, when fortunate, can alleviate the suffering of the sick. But explaining its distribution requires many minds and resources. Case studies of individuals reveal suffering, they tell us what happens to one or many people; but to explain suffering, one must embed individual biography in the larger matrix of culture, history, and political economy.

In short, it is one thing to make sense of extreme suffering—a universal activity, surely—and quite another to explain it. Life experiences such as those of Acéphie and Chouchou, and of other Haitians living in poverty who shared similar social conditions, must be embedded in ethnography if their representativeness is to be understood. These local understandings must be embedded, in turn, in the historical system of which Haiti is a part.[17] The weakness of such analyses is, of course, their great distance from personal experience. But the social and economic forces that dictate life choices in Haiti's Central Plateau affect many millions of individuals, and it is in the context of these global forces that the suffering of individuals acquires its own appropriate context. . . .

Making Sense of Structural Violence

> Events of massive, public suffering defy quantitative analysis. How can one really understand statistics citing the death of six million Jews or graphs of third-world starvation? Do numbers really reveal the agony, the interruption, the questions that these victims put to the meaning and nature of our individual lives and life as a whole?
>
> Rebecca Chopp, The Praxis of Suffering

> My apologies to chance for calling it necessity.
> My apologies to necessity if I'm mistaken, after all.
> Please, don't be angry, happiness, that I take you as my due.
> May my dead be patient with the way my memories fade.
> My apologies to time for all the world I overlook each second.
> Wisława Szymborska, "Under One Small Star"

How might we discern the nature of structural violence and explore its contribution to human suffering? Can we devise an analytic model, one with explanatory and predictive power, for understanding suffering in a global context? This task, though daunting, is both urgent and feasible if we are to protect and promote human rights.

Our cursory examination of AIDS and political violence in Haiti suggests that analysis must, first, be *geographically broad*. The world as we know it is becoming increasingly interconnected. A corollary of this fact is that extreme suffering—especially when on a grand scale, as in genocide—is seldom divorced from the actions of the powerful.[18] The analysis must also be *historically deep*: not merely deep enough to remind us of events and decisions such as those that deprived Acéphie's parents of their land and founded the Haitian military, but deep enough to recall that modern-day Haitians are the descendants of a people kidnapped from Africa in order to provide our forebears with sugar, coffee, and cotton.[19]

Social factors including gender, ethnicity ("race"), and socioeconomic status may each play a role in rendering individuals and groups vulnerable to extreme human suffering. But in most settings these factors by themselves have limited explanatory power. Rather, *simultaneous* consideration of various social "axes" is imperative in efforts to discern a political economy of brutality. Furthermore, such social factors are differentially weighted in different settings and in different times, as even brief consideration of their contributions to extreme suffering suggests. In an essay entitled "Mortality as an Indicator of Economic Success and Failure," Amartya Sen reminds us of the need to move beyond "the cold and often inarticulate statistics of low incomes" to look at the various ways in which agency—what he terms the "capabilities of each person"—is constrained:

> There is, of course, plenty of [poverty] in the world in which we live. But more awful is the fact that so many people—including children from disadvantaged backgrounds—are forced to lead miserable and precarious lives and to die prematurely. That predicament relates in general to low incomes, but not just to that. It also reflects inadequate public health provisions and nutritional support, deficiency of social security arrangements, and the absence of social responsibility and of caring governance.[20]

To understand the relationship between structural violence and human rights, it is necessary to avoid reductionistic analyses. Sen is understandably concerned to avoid economic reductionism, an occupational hazard in his field. But numerous other analytic traps can also hinder the quest for a sound analytic purchase on the dynamics of human suffering.

The Axis of Gender

Acéphie Joseph and Chouchou Louis shared a similar social status, and each died after contact with the Haitian military. Gender helps to explain why Acéphie died of AIDS and Chouchou from torture. Gender inequality helps to explain why the suffering of Acéphie is much more commonplace than that of Chouchou. Throughout the world, women are confronted with sexism, an ideology that situates them as inferior to men. In 1974, when a group of feminist anthropologists surveyed the status of women living in disparate settings, they could agree that, in every society studied, men dominated political, legal, and economic institutions to varying degrees; in no culture was the status of women genuinely equal, much less superior, to that of men.[21] This power differential has meant that women's rights are violated in innumerable ways. Although male victims are clearly preponderant in studies of torture, females almost exclusively endure the much more common crimes of domestic violence and rape. In the United States alone, the number of such aggressions is staggering. Taking into account sexual assaults by both intimates and strangers, "one in four women has been the victim of a completed rape and one in four women has been physically battered, according to the results of recent community-based studies."[22] In many societies, crimes of domestic violence and rape are not even discussed and are thus invisible.

In most settings, however, gender alone does not define risk for such assaults on dignity. It is *poor* women who are least well defended against these assaults.[23] This is true not only of domestic violence and rape but also of AIDS and its distribution, as anthropologist Martha Ward points out: "The collection of statistics by ethnicity rather than by socioeconomic status obscures the fact that the majority of women with AIDS in the United States are poor. Women are at risk for HIV not because they are African-American or speak Spanish; women are at risk because poverty is the primary and determining condition of their lives."[24]

Similarly, only women can experience maternal mortality, a cause of anguish around the world. More than half a million women die each year in childbirth, but not all women face a high risk of this fate. In fact, according to analyses of 1995 statistics, 99.8 percent of these deaths occurred in developing countries.[25] Recent reported maternal mortality rates for Haiti vary, depending on the source, with numbers ranging from 523 deaths per 100,000 live births to the much higher rates of 1,100 and even as high as 1,400 deaths per 100,000 live births. Needless to say, these deaths are almost entirely registered among the poor.[26] Gender bias, as Sen notes, "is a general problem that applies even in Europe and North America in a variety of fields (such as division of family chores, the provision of support for higher training, and so on), but in poorer countries, the disadvantage of women may even apply to the basic fields of health care, nutritional support, and elementary education."[27]

The Axis of "Race" or Ethnicity

The idea of "race," which most anthropologists and demographers consider to be a biologically insignificant term, has enormous social currency. Racial classifications have been used to deprive many groups of basic rights and therefore have an important place in considerations of human inequality and suffering. The history of Rwanda and Burundi shows that once-minor ethnic categories—Hutu and Tutsi share language and culture and kinship systems—were lent weight and social meaning by colonial administrators who divided and conquered, deepening social inequalities and then fueling nascent ethnic rivalry. In South Africa, one of the clearest examples of the long-term effects of racism, epidemiologists report that the infant mortality rate among blacks may be as much as ten times higher than that of whites. For black people in South Africa, the proximate cause of increased rates of morbidity and mortality is lack of access to resources: "*Poverty* remains the primary cause of the prevalence of many diseases and widespread hunger and malnutrition among black South Africans."[28] The dismantling of the apartheid regime has not yet brought the dismantling of the structures of oppression and inequality in South Africa, and persistent social inequality is no doubt the primary reason that HIV has spread so rapidly in sub-Saharan Africa's wealthiest nation.[29]

Significant mortality differentials between blacks and whites are also registered in the United States, which shares with South Africa the distinction of being one

of the two industrialized countries failing to record mortality data by socioeconomic status. In 1988 in the United States, life expectancy at birth was 75.5 years
for whites, 69.5 years for blacks. In the following decade, although U.S. life expectancies increased across the board, the gap between whites and blacks widened
by another 0.6 years.[30] While these racial differentials in mortality have provoked a
certain amount of discussion, public health expert Vicente Navarro recently
pointed to the "deafening silence" on the topic of class differentials in mortality in
the United States, where "race is used as a *substitute* for class." But in 1986, on
"one of the few occasions that the U.S. government collected information on mortality rates (for heart and cerebrovascular disease) by class, the results showed that,
by whatever indicators of class one might choose (level of education, income, or
occupation), mortality rates are related to social class."[31]

Indeed, where the major causes of death (heart disease and cerebrovascular
disease) are concerned, class standing is a clearer indicator than racial classification. "The growing mortality differentials between whites and blacks," Navarro
concludes, "cannot be understood by looking only at race; they are part and parcel
of larger mortality differentials—class differentials."[32] The sociologist William
Julius Wilson makes a similar point in his landmark study *The Declining Significance of Race*, where he argues that "trained and educated blacks, like trained and
educated whites, will continue to enjoy the advantages and privileges of their class
status."[33] Although new studies show that race differentials persist even among the
privileged, it is important to insist that it is the African American poor—and an
analysis of the mechanisms of their impoverishment—who are being left out. At
the same time, U.S. national aggregate income data that do not consider differential mortality by race and place miss completely the fact that African American
men in Harlem have shorter life expectancies than Bangladeshi men.[34] Again, as
Sen remarks, race-based differences in life expectancy have policy implications,
and these in turn are related to social and economic rights:

> If the relative deprivation of blacks transcends income differentials so robustly, the
> remedying of this inequality has to involve policy matters that go well beyond just
> creating income opportunities for the black population. It is necessary to address
> such matters as public health services, educational facilities, hazards of urban life,
> and other social and economic parameters that influence survival chances. The pic-
> ture of mortality differentials presents an entry into the problem of racial inequality
> in the United States that would be wholly missed if our economic analysis were to
> be confined only to traditional economic variables.[35]

Other Axes of Oppression

Any distinguishing characteristic, whether social or biological, can serve as a pretext for discrimination and thus as a cause of suffering. Refugee or immigrant status is one that readily comes to mind, when thinking of the poor and the
powerless. Sexual preference is another obvious example; homosexuality is stigma-
tized to varying degrees in many settings. "Gay bashing," like other forms of violent criminal victimization, is sure to have long-term effects. But crimes against
gay men and women are again felt largely among the poor.

Questions about the relationship between homophobia and mortality patterns have come to the fore during the AIDS pandemic. In regard to HIV disease, homophobia may be said to lead to adverse outcomes if it "drives underground" people who would otherwise stand to benefit from preventive campaigns. But gay communities, at least middle-class ones in affluent nations, have been singularly effective in organizing a response to AIDS, and those most closely integrated into these communities are among the most informed consumers of AIDS-related messages in the world.[36]

Homophobia may be said to hasten the development of AIDS if it denies services to those already infected with HIV. But this phenomenon has not been widely observed in the United States, where an "AIDS deficit"—fewer cases than predicted—has been noted among gay men, though not in other groups disproportionately afflicted with HIV disease in the early years of the epidemic: injection drug users, inner-city people of color, and persons originally from poor countries in sub-Saharan Africa or the Caribbean.[37] Those engaged in sex work have not benefited from the AIDS deficit. However, males involved in prostitution are almost universally poor, and it may be their poverty, rather than their sexual preference, that puts them at risk of HIV infection. Many men involved in homosexual prostitution, particularly minority adolescents, do not necessarily identify themselves as gay.

None of this is to deny the ill effects of homophobia, even in a country as wealthy as the United States. The point is rather to call for more fine-grained, more systemic analyses of power and privilege in discussions about who is likely to have their rights violated and in what ways.

* * *

Structural Violence and Extreme Suffering

> At night I listen to their phantoms
> shouting in my ear
> shaking me out of lethargy
> issuing me commands
> I think of their tattered lives
> of their feverish hands
> reaching out to seize ours.
> It's not that they're begging
> they're demanding
> they've earned the right to order us
> to break up our sleep
> to come awake
> to shake off once and for all
> this lassitude.
> Claribel Alegría, "Nocturnal Visits"

Clearly, no single axis can fully define increased risk for extreme human suffering. Efforts to attribute explanatory efficacy to one variable lead to immodest claims of causality, for wealth and power have often protected individual women, gays, and ethnic minorities from the suffering and adverse outcomes associated with assaults on dignity. Similarly, poverty can often efface the "protective" effects of status based on gender, race, or sexual orientation. Leonardo Boff and Clodovis Boff, liberation theologians writing from Brazil, insist on the primacy of the economic:

> We have to observe that the socioeconomically oppressed (the poor) do not simply exist alongside other oppressed groups, such as blacks, indigenous peoples, women—to take the three major categories in the Third World. No, the "class-oppressed"—the socioeconomically poor—are the infrastructural expression of the process of oppression. The other groups represent "superstructural" expressions of oppression and because of this are deeply conditioned by the infrastructural. It is one thing to be a black taxi-driver, quite another to be a black football idol; it is one thing to be a woman working as a domestic servant, quite another to be the first lady of the land; it is one thing to be an Amerindian thrown off your land, quite another to be an Amerindian owning your own farm.[38]

This is not to deny that sexism or racism has serious negative consequences, even in the wealthy countries of North America and Europe. The point is simply to call for more honest discussions of who is likely to suffer and in what ways.

The capacity to suffer is, clearly, a part of being human. But not all suffering is equivalent, in spite of pernicious and often self-serving identity politics that suggest otherwise. Physicians practice triage and referral daily. What suffering needs to be taken care of first and with what resources? It *is* possible to speak of extreme human suffering, and an inordinate share of this sort of pain is currently endured by those living in poverty. Take, for example, illness and premature death, the leading cause of extreme suffering in many places in the world. In a striking departure from previous, staid reports, the World Health Organization now acknowledges that poverty is the world's greatest killer: "Poverty wields its destructive influence at every stage of human life, from the moment of conception to the grave. It conspires with the most deadly and painful diseases to bring a wretched existence to all those who suffer from it."[39]

Today, the world's poor are the chief victims of structural violence—a violence that has thus far defied the analysis of many who seek to understand the nature and distribution of extreme suffering. Why might this be so? One answer is that the poor are not only more likely to suffer; they are also less likely to have their suffering noticed, as Chilean theologian Pablo Richard, noting the fall of the Berlin Wall, has warned: "We are aware that another gigantic wall is being constructed in the Third World, to hide the reality of the poor majorities. A wall between the rich and poor is being built, so that poverty does not annoy the powerful and the poor are obliged to die in the silence of history."[40]

The task at hand, if this silence is to be broken, is to identify the forces conspiring to promote suffering, with the understanding that these are differentially weighted in different settings. If we do this, we stand a chance of discerning the causes of extreme suffering and also the forces that put some at risk for human rights abuses, while others are shielded from risk. No honest assessment of the current state of human rights can omit an analysis of structural violence.

NOTES

1. The embodiment paradigm, for which we are to some extent indebted to Merleau-Ponty (e.g., 1945), has been used widely in medical anthropology. For a helpful review, see Csordas 1990 and 1994.

2. Sidney Mintz reminds us of the non-newness of many of the global phenomena under study today. More specifically, the history of Haiti and much of the Caribbean presages current critiques concerning transnationalism:

> Why, then, has the vocabulary of those events become so handy for today's transnationalists? Is one entitled to wonder whether this means that the world has now become a macrocosm of what the Caribbean region was, in the 16th century? If so, should we not ask what took the world so long to catch up—especially since what is happening now is supposed to be qualitatively so different from the recent past? Or is it rather that the Caribbean experience was merely one chapter of a book being written, before the name of the book—world capitalism—became known to its authors? (Mintz 1997, p. 120).

3. Weise 1971, p. 38.

4. Galeano 1973, p. 122. It's worth noting that those with miserable jobs are nonetheless considered fortunate in a country where unemployment is estimated, by the omniscient Central Intelligence Agency, at about 70 percent (U.S. Central Intelligence Agency 2001). It's no wonder that the CIA is interested in the matter: Haiti was, until quite recently, one of the world's leading assemblers of U.S. goods. For more on the conditions of Haitian workers in U.S.-owned offshore assembly plants, see Kernaghan 1993. Of course, U.S. industries are not alone in exploiting cheap Haitian labor, as evidenced by a recent report on labor conditions on the orange plantations that lend Grand Marnier liqueur its distinctive tang; see Butler 2000.

5. In addition to standard indices of well-being and development, the "human suffering index" takes into account such factors as access to clean drinking water, daily caloric intake, religious and political freedom, respect for civil rights, and degree of gender inequality. For information about the human suffering index and how it was derived, see the Web site at *http://www.basics.org/programs/basics1/haiti.html.*

6. Depending on the source, the demographic statistics vary. According to the World Health Organization's *World Health Report 2000*, life expectancy at birth is 52.8 years, while the mortality rate for children under five is 115.5 per 1,000 births (World Health Organization 2000). The CIA, which should know, reports even grimmer statistics: life expectancy of 47.5 years for men and 49.2 years for women (U.S. Central Intelligence Agency 2000). Life expectancy is likely lower and mortality rates are likely higher in the Central Plateau than elsewhere in Haiti. See also United Nations Development Programme 2001.

7. For reviews of morbidity and mortality in Haiti, see the reports from the World Health Organization (WHO) and the United Nations Development Programme (UNDP) mentioned in note 6. The Pan American Health Organization (PAHO) regularly updates its data on Haiti (see Pan American Health Organization 2001). For a review of health trends in central Haiti, see Farmer and Bertrand 2000 as well as Farmer 1999; the latter volume

also presents pertinent information on HIV and tuberculosis in Haiti. Those seeking the latest available data on HIV should consult UNAIDS/World Health Organization 2000, with updated information on the Web. Underreporting, in large part a result of weak surveillance, is a major hindrance to those seeking to interpret official data and its echoes by the PAHO or the WHO. For example, the PAHO noted that Haiti reported 10,237 cases of tuberculosis in 1991, giving an estimated incidence of 154.7 per 100,000 population. In that same period (May 1990 to August 1992), Desormeaux and colleagues performed a house-to-house survey in Cité Soleil, an urban slum, and came up with a figure of 2,281 per 100,000 population. Among the HIV-infected, TB prevalence exceeded 5,770 per 100,000 population. See Pan American Health Organization 2001; Desormeaux, Johnson, Coberly, et al. 1996.

8. It's hard to think of a more compelling example than the 1981 massacre of all the inhabitants of El Mozote, El Salvador, by U.S.-trained and U.S.-funded troops. Leigh Binford lays out the challenges faced by those who would bring such events to broader attention:

> From January 1983 through December 1989, "El Mozote" was cited in a mere fifteen articles published in major U.S. and Canadian newspapers. (During this same period the U.S. government provided the Salvadoran military with more than $500 million in direct military assistance.) . . . The coverage of El Mozote shows us that for the journalists, no less than for most people of the West, the daily lives of billions of people in the rest of the world do not exist outside the parameters of crisis or scandal: hurricanes, earthquakes, volcanic eruptions, droughts, crop failures, and civil wars (1996, p. 4).

9. The names of the Haitians cited here have been changed, as have the names of their home villages.

10. There is a large literature concerning the impact of dams on the lives of those displaced. In anthropology, a classic example would be the 1971 study by Elizabeth Colson. Alaka Wali (1989) charts the fate of those displaced by a hydroelectric dam in eastern Panama. Two different, more recent books on this subject provide poignant examples of the consequences of building big dams: Arundhati Roy's *Cost of Living* (1999) includes a passionate protest against the Sardar Samovar Dam in the Narmada Valley of India; Patrick McCully's *Silenced Rivers: The Ecology and Politics of Large Dams* (1996) details the specific effects of big dams on the health of the displaced (see esp. McCully's chapter "Dams and Disease," pp. 86–100). Michael Ignatieff outlines the links between human rights and dam projects in specific terms:

> A human rights perspective on development, for example, would be critical of any macroeconomic strategy that purchased aggregate economic growth at the price of the rights of significant groups of individuals. A dam project that boosts electro-generation capacity at the price of flooding the lands of poor people without compensation and redress is an injustice, even if the aggregate economic benefit of such a measure is clear (2001, p. 167).

11. For a comprehensive and well-documented overview of the plight of Haitian refugees, see "Symposium: The Haitian Refugee Crisis: A Closer Look" 1993, a special issue of the *Georgetown Immigration Law Journal*. In an excellent overview of the roots of human rights violations in Haiti, an essay in that issue describes the Reagen-Duvalier pact (Executive Order 12,324 issued by Ronald Reagan on September 29, 1981) as follows:

> The Interdiction Program worked with grim efficiency during the Duvalier era. From its inception in late 1981, thousands of Haitians have been stopped and forcibly repatriated to Haiti. In every case, the Coast Guard destroyed the Haitian vessel and the Coast Guard cutter

returned crowded with Haitian asylum-seekers to Port-au-Prince. Despite well-documented evidence of gross and systematic human rights abuses during the Duvalier era and under the succeeding military governments, all but eight of the approximately 23,000 interdicted Haitians were returned to Haiti from October 1981 to September 1991 when President Aristide was overthrown in a military coup. Interviews conducted on the Coast Guard cutters were inherently flawed and help explain the blanket finding that all those interdicted were "economic refugees" (O'Neill 1993, p. 96).

O'Neill also provides a figure of 24,559 Haitian refugees applying for asylum during this period.

12. For more on U.S. aid to the military "governments" of post-Duvalier Haiti, see Farmer 1994 and Ridgeway 1994. Hancock (1989) also discusses the impact of U.S. aid to the Duvalier regimes.

13. This topic is discussed, at greater length and in general terms, in Farmer, Connors, and Simmons 1996. Concerning the expanding epidemic of HIV in Haiti and its relationship to structural violence, see Farmer 1992 and 1999. For more on the situation currently confronted by Haitian women, most of whom live in poverty, see the review by Neptune-Anglade (1986) and the testimonies collected by Racine (1999). More recently, Beverly Bell (2001) documents stories of Haitian women's struggles for survival as well as resistance against tyranny and terror.

14. For an overview of the human rights situation after the 1991 coup, see Americas Watch and the National Coalition for Haitian Refugees 1993 and O'Neill 1993. For a review of these and other reports, see Farmer 1994. Additional reports include Inter-American Commission on Human Rights 1994 and United Nations Human Rights Commission 1995 as well as the report on internal displacement issued in 1994 by Human Rights Watch/ Americas, Jesuit Refugee Service/USA, and the National Coalition for Haitian Refugees.

Toward the end of the Cédras-led coup, which led to thousands of outright murders, the army and paramilitary began a campaign of politically motivated rape. One survey terms this campaign "arguably the greatest crime against womankind in the Caribbean since slavery" (Rey 1999, p. 74). See also Human Rights Watch/Americas and National Coalition for Haitian Refugees 1994. It was during these years that our clinic received its first rape victims (Farmer 1996); one of my patients went on to testify about politically motivated rapes in a hearing on this topic held by the Organization of American States.

15. Some would argue that the relationship between individual agency and supraindividual structures forms the central problematic of contemporary social theory. I have tried, in this discussion, to avoid what Pierre Bourdieu has termed "the absurd opposition between individual and society," and here acknowledge the influence of Bourdieu, who has contributed enormously to the debate on structure and agency. For a concise statement of his (often revised) views on this subject, see Bourdieu 1990. That a supple and fundamentally nondeterministic model of agency would have such a deterministic—and pessimistic— "feel" is largely a reflection of my topic, suffering, and my "fieldwork site," which is Haiti. The relationship between agency and human rights is traced by Ignatieff, among others:

> We know from historical experience that when human beings have defensible rights—when their agency as individuals is protected and enhanced—they are less likely to be abused and oppressed. On these grounds, we count the diffusion of human rights instruments as progress even if there remains an unconscionable gap between the instruments and the actual practices of states charged to comply with them (2001, p. 4).

16. Chopp 1986, p. 2.

17. I have made this argument at greater length elsewhere; see Farmer 1992, chap. 22. The term "historical system" is used following Immanuel Wallerstein, who for many years has argued that even the most far-flung locales—Haiti's Central Plateau, for example—are part of the same social and economic nexus: "By the late nineteenth century, for the first time ever, there existed only one historical system on the globe. We are still in that situation today" (Wallerstein 1987, p. 318). See also his initial, magisterial formulation, *The Modern World-System: Capitalist Agriculture and the Origins of the European World-Economy in the Sixteenth Century* (1974).

18. The connections between the fecklessness of the powerful and the fates of the fragile have been well traced. The political economy of genocide is explored in Simpson 1993; see also Aly, Chroust, and Pross 1994. On the transnational political economy of human rights abuses, see Chomsky and Herman 1979a and 1979b, a two-volume study. When Mike Davis explores "late Victorian holocausts," which led to some fifty million deaths, he concludes that "we are not dealing, in other words, with 'lands of famine' becalmed in stagnant backwaters of world history, but with the fate of tropical humanity at the precise moment (1870–1914) when its labor and products were being dynamically conscripted into a London-centered world economy. Millions died, not outside the 'modern world system,' but in the very process of being forcibly incorporated into its economic and political structures" (2001, p. 9).

19. For historical background on Haiti, see James 1980, Mintz 1974, and Trouillot 1990.

20. Sen 1998, p. 2.

21. Rosaldo and Lamphere 1974. For differing views, see Leacock 1981.

22. Koss, Koss, and Woodruff 1991, p. 342. From November 1995 to May 1996, the National Institute of Justice and the Centers for Disease Control jointly conducted a national telephone survey that confirmed the high rates of assault against U.S. women (Tjaden and Thoennes 1998). See also Bachman and Saltzman 1995.

23. It is important to note, however, that in many societies upper-class or upper-caste women are also subject to laws that virtually efface marital rape. The study by Koss, Koss, and Woodruff (1991) includes this crime with other forms of criminal victimization, but such information is collected only through community-based surveys.

24. Ward 1993, p. 414.

25. A recent joint report by WHO, UNICEF, and UNFPA on estimated maternal mortality for 1995 notes that of the 515,000 estimated maternal deaths worldwide, only 0.2 percent, or 1,200, occurred in industrialized countries. The lifetime risk of maternal death for women in such countries is calculated at 1:4,085, whereas for women in developing nations, the risk is much higher, at 1:61. In fact, for the subgroup of countries characterized as "least developed"—of which Haiti is one—the estimated risk of maternal death is, tragically, even higher, at 1:16 (World Health Organization, United Nations Children's Fund, United Nations Population Fund 2001, p. 48).

26. The maternal mortality rate (MMR) of 523 deaths is for the year 2000 and is based on reports from the national health authority to PAHO; see Pan American Health Organization 2001. The much higher rate of 1,100 maternal deaths per 100,000 live births comes from the joint report published by WHO, UNICEF, and UNFPA; see World Health Organization, United Nations Children's Fund, United Nations Population Fund 2001 (p. 44). These numbers are likely to be even higher if one measures maternal mortality at the community level. The only community-based survey done in Haiti, conducted in 1985 around the town of Jacmel in southern Haiti, found that maternal mortality was 1,400 per 100,000 live births (Jean-Louis 1989). During that same period, "official" statistics reported much

lower rates for Haiti, ranging from an MMR of 230 for the years 1980–87 (United Nations Development Programme 1990, p. 148) and an MMR of 340 for 1980–85 to a higher estimate in the years that followed, 1987–92, of 600 maternal deaths per 100,000 live births (World Bank 1994, p. 148). For additional maternal mortality data from that period, see World Health Organization 1985.

27. Sen 1998, p. 13. For an in-depth discussion of the population-based impact of gender bias in poor countries, see Sen's classic essay on "missing women" (Sen 1992).

Sen summarizes the potential impact of public action in poor regions by examining Kerala state:

> Kerala's experience suggests that "gender bias" against females can be radically changed by public action—involving both the government and the public itself—especially through female education, opportunities for women to have responsible jobs, women's legal rights on property, and by enlightened egalitarian politics. Correspondingly, the problem of "missing women" can also be largely solved through social policy and political radicalism. Women's movements can play a very important part in bringing about this type of change, and in making the political process in poor countries pay serious attention to the deep inequalities from which women suffer. It is also interesting to note, in this context, that the narrowly economic variables, such as GNP or GDP per head, on which so much of standard development economics concentrates, give a very misleading picture of economic and social progress (1998, p. 15).

28. Nightingale, Hannibal, Geiger, et al. 1990, p. 2098; emphasis added. For a more in-depth account, and a more complicated view of the mechanisms by which apartheid and the South African economy are related to disease causation, see Packard 1989.

29. Although HIV is said to have recently "taken off" among South Africa's black population, it has been, from the beginning, an epidemic disproportionately affecting black people in that country. South African data indicate that in 1994, when seventeen white women were diagnosed with AIDS, almost fifteen hundred black women—nearly one hundred times as many—had the disease (Department of Health, Republic of South Africa 1995, p. 67).

Even after the dismantling of the apartheid system, HIV continues to disproportionately affect black South Africans (Lurie, Harrison, Wilkinson, et al. 1997). As Chapman and Rubenstein (1998) note in a report for the American Association for the Advancement of Science and Physicians for Human Rights, "the epidemiology of the HIV/AIDS epidemic . . . demonstrates the link between poverty, low status and vulnerability to infection" (p. 20). They report the "rigid segregation of health facilities; grossly disproportionate spending on the health of whites as compared to blacks, resulting in world-class medical care for whites while blacks were usually relegated to overcrowded and filthy facilities; public health policies that ignored diseases primarily affecting black people; and the denial of basic sanitation, clean water supply, and other components of public health to homelands and townships" (p. xix). Along with being denied medical services, many black South Africans were forced to relocate to townships and were later forced, by economic conditions, to live in squatter settlements on the outskirts of cities, creating a culture of migration and disrupted family ties (pp. 18–20). As Lurie and colleagues note, "migrant labour was a central tenet of apartheid, which sought to create a steady flow of cheap black labour to South Africa's mines, industries and farms. A myriad of laws prohibited black South Africans from settling permanently in 'whites only' areas, and as a result, migration patterns in South African tend to be circular, with men maintaining close links with their rural homesteads" (1997, p. 18).

This forced system of migration has had a distinct impact on the shaping of the AIDS epidemic. As Carol Kaufman explains, "the system of labor migration remains deeply entrenched, and women who have partners involved in labor circulation are especially vulnerable to unprotected sexual intercourse as well as STDs and HIV/AIDS transmission" (1998, p. 432). Quarraisha and Salim Abdool-Karim cite a 1998 study conducted in rural South Africa which found that "women whose partners spent 10 or fewer nights per month at home had an HIV prevalence of 13.7% compared with 0% in women who spent more than 10 nights in a month with their partners" (1999, p. 139). See Lurie, Harrison, Wilkinson, et al. 1997 for further documentation of this link. Furthermore, data from 1994 reveal that poverty is rampant in South Africa, with close to two-thirds of black households surviving below the minimum subsistence level (Chapman and Rubenstein 1998, p. 20).

30. The National Center for Health Statistics (1998) reported life expectancies at birth in 1996 as 76.8 years for whites and 70.2 years for blacks. Two years later, the same sources suggest a heartening trend: reported life expectancies increased to 77.3 for whites and 71.3 for blacks (National Center for Health Statistics 2000). But the discrepancy is still on the order of 9 to 10 percent of lifespan. For a detailed discussion of recent health status disparities and leading causes of death for African Americans, see Byrd and Clayton 2002, pp. 519–45.

31. Navarro 1990, p. 1238.

32. Ibid., p. 1240.

33. Wilson 1980, p. 178.

34. McCord and Freeman 1990.

35. Sen 1998, p. 17.

36. Although class differences between physicians and university students are not as significant as others examined here, it is notable that a study reported in the *American Journal of Psychiatry* (Klein, Sullivan, Wolcott, et al. 1987) observed that gay psychiatrists were much more likely than students to adopt effective risk reduction. Clearly, many factors—age, educational level, and so on—may be significant here. In the United States, we still lack economically informed studies of risky behavior among gay men; for gay men in France, one study (Pollak 1988) suggests that economic status is important in determining access to information and services.

39. These data are reviewed in Farmer, Walton, and Furin 2000. See also Aalen, Farewell, De Angelis, et al. 1999.

38. Boff and Boff 1987, p. 29.

39. World Health Organization 1995, p. 5.

40. Richard is cited in Nelson-Pallmeyer 1992, p. 14.

BIBLIOGRAPHY

Aalen, O. O., V. T. Farewell, D. De Angelis, et al. 1999. "New Therapy Explains the Fall in AIDS Incidence with a Substantial Rise in Number of Persons on Treatment Expected." *AIDS* 13 (1): 103–8.

Abdool-Karim, Q., and S. S. Abdool-Karim. 1999. "South Africa: Host to a New and Emerging HIV Epidemic." *Sexually Transmitted Infections* 75 (3): 139–40.

Aly, G., P. Chroust, and C. Pross. 1994. *Cleansing the Fatherland: Nazi Medicine and Racial Hygiene*. Baltimore: Johns Hopkins University Press.

Americas Watch and the National Coalition for Haitian Refugees. 1993. *Silencing a People: The Destruction of Civil Society in Haiti*. New York: Human Rights Watch.

Bachman, R., and L. Saltzman. 1995. *Violence Against Women: Estimates from the Re-designed Survey.* Washington, D.C.: U.S. Department of Justice, Office of Justice Programs, Bureau of Statistics.

Bell, B. 2001. *Walking on Fire: Haitian Women's Stories of Survival and Resistance.* Ithaca, N.Y.: Cornell University Press.

Binford, L. 1996. *The El Mozote Massacre.* Tucson: University of Arizona Press.

Boff, L., and C. Boff. 1987. *Introducing Liberation Theology.* Maryknoll, N.Y.: Orbis Books.

Bourdieu, P. 1990. *In Other Words: Essays Toward a Reflexive Sociology.* Cambridge: Polity.

Butler, K. 2000. "Grand Marnier Workers Toil for 2 Pounds a Day on Haiti Planta-tion." *Independent* (London), 16 July, p. 3.

Byrd, W. M., and L. A. Clayton. 2002. *An American Health Dilemma.* Vol. 2, *Race, Medicine, and Health Care in the United States, 1900–2000.* New York: Routledge.

Chapman, A., and L. Rubenstein, eds. 1998. *Human Rights and Health: The Legacy of Apartheid.* Washington, D.C.: American Association for the Advancement of Science.

Chomsky, N., and E. Herman. 1979a. *After the Cataclysm.* Boston: South End Press.

———. 1979b. *The Washington Connection and Third World Fascism.* Boston: South End Press.

Chopp, R. S. 1986. *The Praxis of Suffering: An Interpretation of Liberation and Political Theologies.* Maryknoll, N.Y.: Orbis Books.

Colson, E. 1971. *The Social Consequences of Resettlement: The Impact of the Kariba Re-settlement upon the Gwembe Tonga.* Manchester, England: Manchester University Press.

Csordas, T. 1990. "Embodiment as a Paradigm for Anthropology." *Ethos* 18 (1): 5–47.

———, ed. 1994. *Embodiment and Experience: The Existential Ground of Culture and Self.* New York: Cambridge University Press.

Davis, M. 2001. *Late Victorian Holocausts.* London: Verso.

Department of Health, Republic of South Africa. 1995. *Health Trends in South Africa 1994.* Pretoria: Department of Health.

Desormeaux, J., M. P. Johnson, J. S. Coberly, et al. 1996. "Widespread HIV Counsel-ing and Testing Linked to a Community-Based Tuberculosis Control Program in a High-Risk Population." *Bulletin of the Pan American Health Organization* 30 (1): 1–8.

Farmer, P. E. 1992. *AIDS and Accusation: Haiti and the Geography of Blame.* Berkeley: University of California Press.

———. 1994. *The Uses of Haiti.* Monroe, Maine: Common Courage Press.

———. 1996. "Haiti's Lost Years: Lessons for the Americas." *Current Issues in Public Health* 2: 143–51.

———. 1999. *Infections and Inequalities: The Modern Plagues.* Berkeley: University of California Press.

Farmer, P. E., and D. Bertrand. 2000. "Hypocrisies of Development and the Health of the Haitian Poor." In *Dying for Growth: Global Inequality and the Health of the Poor,* edited by J. Y. Kim, J. V. Millen, A. Irwin, and J. Gershman, pp. 65–89. Monroe, Maine: Common Courage Press.

Farmer, P. E., M. Connors, and J. Simmons, eds. 1996. *Women, Poverty, and AIDS: Sex, Drugs, and Structural Violence.* Monroe, Maine: Common Courage Press.

Farmer, P. E., D. A. Walton, and J. J. Furin. 2000. "The Changing Face of AIDS: Im-plications for Policy and Practice." In *The Emergency of AIDS: The Impact on Immunology,*

Microbiology, and Public Health, edited by K. Mayer and H. Pizer, pp. 139–61. Washington, D.C.: American Public Health Association.

Galeano, E. 1973. *Open Veins of Latin America: Five Centuries of the Pillage of a Continent.* New York: Monthly Review Press.

Hancock, G. 1989. *The Lords of Poverty: The Power, Prestige, and Corruption of the International Aid Business.* New York: Atlantic Monthly Press.

Human Rights Watch/Americas, Jesuit Refugee Service/USA, and National Coalition for Haitian Refugees. 1994. "Fugitives from Injustice: The Crisis of Internal Displacement in Haiti." Report 6 (10).

Human Rights Watch/Americas and National Coalition for Haitian Refugees. 1994. "Terror Prevails in Haiti: Human Rights Violations and Failed Diplomacy." *Haiti Insight* 6 (5): 1–47.

Ignatieff, M. 2001. *Human Rights as Politics and Idolatry.* Princeton: Princeton University Press.

Inter-American Commission on Human Rights. 1994. *Report on the Situation of Human Rights in Haiti.* Washington, D.C.: Inter-American Commission on Human Rights.

James, C. L. R. 1980. *The Black Jacobins.* London: Allison and Busby.

Jean-Louis, R. 1989. "Diagnostic de l'état de santé en Haïti." *Forum Libre* 1 (*Médecine, Santé et Démocratie en Haïti*): 11–20.

Kaufman, C. 1998. "Contraceptive Use in South Africa Under Apartheid." *Demography* 35 (4): 421–34.

Kernaghan, C. 1993. *Haiti After the Coup: Sweatshop or Real Development.* New York: U.S. National Labor Committee.

Klein, D. E., G. Sullivan, D. L. Wolcott, et al. 1987. "Changes in AIDS Risk Behaviors Among Homosexual Male Physicians and University Students." *American Journal of Psychiatry* 144 (6): 742–47.

Koss, M., P. Koss, and J. Woodruff. 1991. "Deleterious Effects of Criminal Victimization on Women's Health and Medical Utilization." *Archives of Internal Medicine* 151 (2): 342–47.

Leacock, E. B. 1981. *Myths of Male Dominance.* New York: Monthly Review Press.

Lurie, M., A. Harrison, D. Wilkinson, et al. 1997. "Circular Migration and Sexual Networking in Rural Kwazulu/Natal: Implications for the Spread of HIV and Other Sexually Transmitted Diseases." *Health Transition Review* 7 (Supplement 3): 17–27.

McCord, C., and H. Freeman. 1990. "Excess Mortality in Harlem." *New England Journal of Medicine* 322 (3): 173–77.

McCully, P. 1996. *Silenced Rivers: The Ecology and Politics of Large Dams.* London: Zed Books.

Merleau-Ponty, M. 1945. *Phénoménologie de la perception.* Paris: Gallimard.

Mintz, S. 1974. *Caribbean Transformations.* Baltimore: Johns Hopkins University Press.

———. 1997. "The Localization of Anthropological Practice: From Area Studies to Transnationalism." *Critique of Anthropology* 18 (2): 117–33.

National Center for Health Statistics. 1998. *Health, United States, 1998, with Socioeconomic Status and Health Chartbook.* Hyattsville, Md.: National Center for Health Statistics.

———. 2000. *Health, United States, 2000, with Adolescent Health Chartbook.*

Navarro, V. 1990. "Race or Class Versus Race and Class: Mortality Differentials in the United States." *Lancet* 336 (8725): 1238–40.

Nelson-Pallmeyer, J. 1992. *Brave New World Order: Must We Pledge Allegiance?* Maryknoll, N.Y.: Orbis Books.

Neptune-Anglade, M. 1986. *L'autre moitié du développement: À propos du travail des femmes en Haiti*. Pétion-Ville, Haiti: Éditions des Alizés.

Nightingale, E., K. Hannibal, J. Geiger, et al. 1990. "Apartheid Medicine: Health and Human Rights in South Africa." *Journal of the American Medical Association* 264 (16): 2097–102.

O'Neill, W. 1993. "The Roots of Human Rights Violations in Haiti." *Georgetown Immigration Law Journal* 7 (1): 87–117.

Packard, R. 1989. *White Plague, Black Labor: Tuberculosis and the Political Economy of Health and Disease in South Africa*. Berkeley: University of California Press.

Pan American Health Organization. 2001. Haiti: Country Health Profiles. Available at *http://www.paho.org/English/SHA/prflHAI.htm*.

Pollak, M. 1988. *Les homosexuels et le SIDA: Sociologie d'une epidémie*. Paris: A. M. Matailie.

Racine, M. M. B. 1999. *Like the Dew That Waters the Grass: Words from Haitian Women*. Washington, D.C.: EPICA.

Rey, T. 1999. "Junta, Rape, and Religion in Haiti, 1993–1994." *Journal of Feminist Studies in Religion* 15 (2): 73–100.

Ridgeway, J., ed. 1994. *The Haiti Files: Decoding the Crisis*. Washington, D.C.: Essential Books.

Rosaldo, M., and L. Lamphere, eds. 1974. *Women, Culture, and Society*. Stanford: Stanford University Press.

Roy, A. 1999. *Cost of Living*. London: Flamingo.

Sen, A. 1992. "Missing Women." *British Medical Journal* 304 (6827): 587–88.

———. 1998. "Mortality as an Indicator of Economic Success and Failure." (Text of the Innocenti Lecture of UNICEF, delivered in Florence, March 1995.) *Economic Journal* 108 (446): 1–25.

———. 1999. *Development as Freedom*. New York: Knopf.

Simpson, C. 1993. *The Splendid Blond Beast: Money, Law, and Genocide in the Twentieth Century*. New York: Grove Press.

"Symposium: The Haitian Refugee Crisis: A Closer Look." 1993. *Georgetown Immigration Law Journal* 7 (1): 1–147.

Tjaden, P., and N. Thoennes. 1998. *Prevalence, Incidence, and Consequences of Violence Against Women: Findings from the National Violence Against Women Survey*. Washington, D.C.: U.S. Department of Justice, National Institute of Justice/CDC Research in Brief.

Trouillot, M-R. 1990. *Haiti, State Against Nation: The Origins and Legacy of Duvalierism*. New York: Monthly Review Press.

UNAIDS/World Health Organization. 2000. Haiti: Epidemiological Fact Sheets on HIV/AIDS and Sexually Transmitted Infections, 2000 Update. Available at *http://www.who.int/emc-hiv/fact_sheets/pdfs/haiti_en.pdf*.

United Nations Development Programme. 1990. *Human Development Report, 1990*. New York: Oxford University Press for UNDP.

———. 2001. *Human Development Report, 2001*. New York: Oxford University Press for UNDP.

United Nations Human Rights Commission. 1995. *Situation of Human Rights in Haiti*. Geneva: United Nations Economic and Social Council.

U.S. Central Intelligence Agency. 2000. *The World Factbook 2000*. Available at *http://www.umsl.edu/services/govdocs/wofact2000/*.

———. 2001. *The World Factbook 2001*; entry for "Haiti." Avaialble at *http://www.cia.gov/cia/publications/factbook/*.

Wali, A. 1989. *Kilowatts and Crisis: Hydroelectric Power and Social Dislocation in Eastern Panama*. Boulder: Westview Press.

Wallerstein, I. 1974. *The Modern World-System: Capitalist Agriculture and the Origins of the European World-Economy in the Sixteenth Century*. San Diego: Academic Press.

———. 1987. "World-Systems Analysis." In *Social Theory Today*, edited by A. Giddens and J. Turner, pp. 309–24. Stanford: Stanford University Press.

Ward, M. 1993. "A Different Disease: HIV/AIDS and Health Care for Women in Poverty." *Culture, Medicine, and Psychiatry* 17 (4): 413–30.

Weise, J. 1971. "The Interaction of Western and Indigenous Medicine in Haiti in Regard to Tuberculosis." Ph.D. diss., Department of Anthropology, University of North Carolina at Chapel Hill.

Wilson, W. J. 1980. *The Declining Significance of Race: Blacks and Changing American Institutions*. Chicago: University of Chicago Press.

World Bank. 1994. *Social Indicators of Development*. Baltimore: Johns Hopkins University Press.

World Health Organization. 1985. "Maternal Mortality: Helping Women Off the Road to Death." *WHO Chronicle* 40: 175–83.

———. 1995. *Bridging the Gaps*. Geneva: World Health Organization.

———. 2000. *World Health Report 2000. Health Systems: Improving Performance*. Geneva: World Health Organization.

World Health Organization, United Nations Children's Fund, United Nations Population Fund. 2001. *Maternal Mortality in 1995: Estimates Developed by WHO, UNICEF, UNFPA*. Geneva: World Health Organization.

Testimony by FannyAnn Eddy at the U.N. Commission on Human Rights

—Human Rights Watch

FannyAnn Eddy founded the Sierra Leone Lesbian and Gay Association and was known as a lesbian rights activist throughout Africa. The following is testimony she gave at the 60th Session of the U.N. Commission on Human Rights. On September 29, 2004, Eddy, mother of a 10-year-old son, was found dead on the floor of the Sierra Leone Lesbian and Gay Association, where she had been working alone the previous night. She had been raped repeatedly and stabbed, and her neck was broken.

Item 14—60th Session, U.N. Commission on Human Rights

Distinguished members of the Commission, my name is FannyAnn Eddy and I am representing MADRE. I am also a member of the Sierra Leone Lesbian and Gay Association.

I would like to use this opportunity to bring to your attention the dangers vulnerable groups and individuals face not only in my beloved country, Sierra Leone, but throughout Africa.

My focus of interest is the lesbian, gay, bisexual and transgender community, which most African leaders do not like to address. In fact, many African leaders do not want to even acknowledge that we exist. Their denial has many disastrous results for our community.

We do exist. But because of the denial of our existence, we live in constant fear: fear of the police and officials with the power to arrest and detain us simply because of our sexual orientation. For instance, recently a young gay man was arrested in Freetown for being dressed as a woman. He was held in detention for a full week without any charge being brought. Though I personally was able to argue with the authorities to release him, most people like him would have been held indefinitely because there are very few of us who are able to speak up.

Testimony by FannyAnn Eddy at the U.N. Commission on Human Rights on behalf of the Sierra Leone Lesbian and Gay Association.

We live in fear that our families will disown us, as it is not unusual for lesbian, gay, bisexual, and transgender people to be forced out of their family homes when their identity becomes known. Many people who are forced from their homes because of their sexual orientation or gender identity are young with nowhere else to go, and thus become homeless, have no food, and resort to sex work in order to survive.

We live in fear within our communities, where we face constant harassment and violence from neighbors and others. Their homophobic attacks go unpunished by authorities, further encouraging their discriminatory and violent treatment of lesbian, gay, bisexual and transgender people.

When African leaders use culture, tradition, religion and societal norms to deny our existence they send a message that tolerates discrimination, violence and overall indignity.

This denial has especially disastrous results in the context of HIV/AIDS. According to a recent research study published in December 2003 by the Sierra Leone Lesbian and Gay Association in collaboration with Health Way Sierra Leone, 90% of men who have sex with men also have sex with women, either their wives or girlfriends. Of that group, 85% said that they do not use condoms. Clearly the message of sexual education and transmission of HIV is not delivered to these men in Sierra Leone. It is clear that many men get married not because that is what their inner being desires, but because that is what society demands—because they live in a society which forces them to fear for their freedom or their lives because of their sexual orientation. The silence surrounding them—the refusal to acknowledge their existence or address their health care needs—endangers not only them but their wives and girlfriends.

Yet, despite all of the difficulties we face, I have faith that the acknowledgement by the Commission of the inherent dignity and respect due to lesbian, gay people can lead to greater respect for our human rights. As evidenced by the liberation struggle in South Africa, where the constitution bars discrimination based on sexual orientation, respect for human rights can transform society. It can lead people to understand that in the end, we are all human and all entitled to respect and dignity.

Silence creates vulnerability. You, members of the Commission on Human Rights, can break the silence. You can acknowledge that we exist, throughout Africa and on every continent, and that human rights violations based on sexual orientation or gender identity are committed every day. You can help us combat those violations and achieve our full rights and freedoms, in every society, including my beloved Sierra Leone.

Facts on Child Labour

–International Labour Organization

The International Labour Organization is the United Nations specialized agency that seeks the promotion of social justice and internationally recognized human and labour rights. It sponsors a World Day Against Child Labour each year. The Fact Sheet reprinted here was prepared for World Day Against Child Labour in June 2004. For more information visit their website at www.ilo.org/childlabour.

One out of six children in the world today is involved in child labour, doing work that is damaging to his or her mental, physical and emotional development.

These children work in a variety of industries, and in many parts of the world. The vast majority are in the agricultural sector, where they may be exposed to dangerous chemicals and equipment. Others are street children, peddling or running errands to earn a living. Some are domestic workers, prostitutes, or factory workers. All are children who have no fair chance of a real childhood, an education, or a better life.

Children work because their survival and that of their families depend on it. Child labour persists even where it has been declared illegal, and is frequently surrounded by a wall of silence, indifference, and apathy.

But that wall is beginning to crumble. While the total elimination of child labour is a long-term goal in many countries, certain forms of child labour must be confronted immediately. An ILO study has shown for the first time that the economic benefits of eliminating child labour will be nearly seven times greater than the costs. This does not include the incalculable social and human benefits of eliminating the practice: nearly three-quarters of working children are engaged in what the world recognizes as the worst forms of child labour, including trafficking, armed conflict, slavery, sexual exploitation and hazardous work. The effective abolition of child labour is one of the most urgent challenges of our time.

Child domestic labour refers to situations where children are engaged to perform domestic tasks in the home of a third party or employer that are exploitative. Whenever such exploitation is extreme—and includes trafficking, slavery-like situations, or work that is hazardous and harmful to a child's physical or mental health—it is considered one of the worst forms of child labour.

Reprinted by permission of the International Labour Organization.

Almost without exception, children who are in domestic labour are victims of exploitation. They often leave their own family at a very early age to work in the houses of others and are considered almost as 'possessions' of the household. They are exploited economically: forced to work long hours with no time off and low or no wages. They generally have no social or legal protection.

Child domestic workers are deprived of the rights due to them as children in international law, including the right to play, visits with their family and friends, and decent accommodation. They are denied an education, jeopardizing their chances of a better future. Both girls and boys face physical or mental abuse, with the possibility of sexual abuse being particularly high for girls. Despite this, more girls under 16 are in domestic labour than in any other category of work.

Key Statistics

- 246 million children are child labourers.
- 73 million working children are less than 10 years old.
- No country is immune: There are 2.5 million working children in the developed economies, and another 2.5 million in transition economies.
- Every year, 22,000 children die in work-related accidents.
- The largest number of working children—127 million—age 14 and under are in the Asia-Pacific region.
- Sub-Saharan Africa has the largest proportion of working children: nearly one-third of children age 14 and under (48 million children).
- Most children work in the informal sector, without legal or regulatory protection:
    - 70% in agriculture, commercial hunting and fishing or forestry;
    - 8% in manufacturing;
    - 8% in wholesale and retail trade, restaurants and hotels;
    - 7% in community, social and personal service, such as domestic work.
- 8.4 million children are trapped in slavery, trafficking, debt bondage, prostitution, pornography and other illicit activities.
    - 1.2 million of these children have been trafficked.

10

World Poverty and Hunger Fact Sheet

–UN Bulletin on the Eradication of Poverty

The World Poverty and Hunger Fact Sheet reproduced below was included in the U.N. Bulletin on the Eradication of Poverty for 2003. The Bulletin is published annually. For more information go to www.un.org/esa/socdev/poverty/documents

Background

- 1.2 billion people live on less than $1 a day, the absolute poverty level.[1]
- 24,000 persons die each day due to hunger, 16,000 of whom are children under five years of age.[2]
- 800 million people, or one in every six, are malnourished, 200 million of whom are children.
- The average life expectancy of people living in areas with chronic hunger is 38 years. People living in wealthy nations have an average life expectancy of 70 years.[3]
- Access to food is a basic human right that is no different from the right to life.

Poverty and hunger are closely linked—those who live in poverty are likely to suffer from hunger or malnutrition. Poverty and hunger are often caused by lack of education, employment and healthcare.

Regional Manifestations

- Nearly one half of the world's hungry are in South Asia and one third are in sub-Saharan Africa.[4]
- South Asia is home to about one third of the world's malnourished; about one out of every five persons in the region is chronically undernourished.
- In Latin America and the Caribbean, about 55 million people have suffered from some degree of malnutrition in the past decade.

Reprinted by permission of the International Labour Organization.

- Undernourished populations in India (233 million), South Asia, China (119 million) and sub-Saharan Africa (196 million) represented roughly 9 per cent of the world's population in 2000.[5]

Global Action

The United Nations, FAO, and the World Bank have made concerted efforts to tackle poverty and hunger simultaneously. The Millennium Development Goal target to halve poverty and hunger by 2015 is proving to be a strong motivating force that is driving the efforts of governments and organizations worldwide to urgently address poverty and hunger reduction.

Economic growth and more equitable access to resources and markets in the context of sustainable development are essential for poverty reduction and food security worldwide. These are challenges that require broad multilateral cooperation among governments, civil society and the private sector.

NOTES

1. See report of the Secretary-General on the implementation of the United Nations Millennium Declaration (A/58/323), para. 52

2. http://www.wfp.org/country_brief/hunger_map/facts.html

3. FAO "The State of Food Insecurity in the World, 2002", http://www.fao.org/docrep/005/y7352e/y7352e00.htm#TopOfPage

4. http://www.thp.org/

5. http://www.fao.org/worldfoodsummit/english/newsroom/focus/focus2.htm

eleven

Women and the Poor: The Challenge of Global Justice

–Nawal El Saadawi

Nawal El Saadawi is a novelist, physician, writer, and activist who champions women's rights. She is founder and president of the Arab Women's Solidarity Association and has lectured and taught at colleges and universities around the world. The article that follows, "Women and the Poor: The Challenge of Global Justice," appears in her 1997 book, The Nawal El Saadawi Reader, *which was published by Zed books.*

Why do we have inequality and poverty in the world? I notice that some people still use the phrase 'Third World' to name us, that is to name the people who live in Africa, Asia and South America. This term is no longer used by many people, including myself, because we live in one world (not three) and we are dominated or governed by one global system which is now called the New World Order. However, we know that in fact it is an old world order which uses new methods of exploitation and domination, both economic and intellectual. Language and the media have become more efficient at obscuring the real aims of those international institutions or groups that speak about peace, development, justice, equality, human rights, and democracy, but whose agreements and decisions lead to the opposite, that is, to war, poverty, inequality and dictatorship.

While I was writing this, I came across a recent issue of the magazine *International Viewpoint*. On its back cover I read a letter written by the Secretary General of Oxfam in Belgium in which he explains why he resigned from the NGO World Bank Group.[1]

> The remedies provided by the World Bank for development are poisoned remedies that accelerate the process [of poverty, hunger and unemployment]. For my soul and conscience I am obliged to tell you 'enough'. You have stolen the correct discourse of the NGOs [nongovernmental organizations] on development, eco-development, poverty, and people's participation. At the same time your policies of structural adjustment and your actions accelerate social dumping in the South by obliging it to enter defenseless into the World Market. . . . Africa is dying, but the World Bank is enriching itself. Asia and Eastern Europe are being robbed of all

"Women and the Poor: The Challenge of Global Justice" from *The Nawal El Saadawi Reader* by Nawal El Saadawi. Copyright 1997. Reprinted by permission of Zed Books.

their riches, and the World Bank supports the initiatives of the IMF, and GATT, that authorize this pillage, which is both intellectual and material. Latin America, like other continents, watches in horror as its children serve as a reserve army of labor and, worse, a reserve of organs for the new transplantation market in North America.

These are the words of an expert who worked very close to the international institutions that speak about development, peace, social justice, democracy, human rights . . . and decide what should be done. These international institutions are often considered to be economic or social only. In fact, they are political as well and the international military machine supports them.

We all know that the United States of America is the most powerful country in military terms in the world. In 1993 the financial editor of the *Chicago Tribune* proposed that the USA should become a mercenary state using its monopoly power in the 'security market' to maintain its control over the world economic system, selling 'protection' to other wealthy powers who would pay a 'war premium'.

How can we speak about real developments in Africa, Asia, or South America without knowing the real reasons for poverty and maldevelopment, and for the increasing gap between the rich and the poor not only at the international and regional levels but also within each country, at the national level? We have to make a correct diagnosis of the problem if we wish to have the right remedies. We cannot speak about global injustice without speaking about inequality between countries, inequality between classes in each country, and inequalities between the sexes. All these different levels of inequality are linked together in the patriarchal capitalist system that governs the world today.

What Is Development?

Countries in our region and in the South generally are subjected to what is called 'development'. Development is not something we choose. It is dictated to us through local governments dominated by the international institutions such as the World Bank, the International Monetary Fund (IMF) and the General Agreement on Tariffs and Trade (GATT). The result of development carried out in line with the policies of these institutions continues to be increasing poverty, and an increasing flow of money and riches from South to North. From 1984 to 1990 the application of structural adjustment policies (SAPs) in the South led to the transfer of $178 billion from the South to the commercial banks in the North.

'Development' is just another word for neocolonialism. We need to be very careful when we use the word 'development'. The word 'aid' is just as deceiving: we know that money and riches flow from the South to the North, not in the opposite direction. A very small portion of what was taken from us comes back to us under the name 'aid'. This creates the false idea that we receive aid from the North.

In this way, we are robbed not only of our material resources, but also of our human dignity. Human dignity is based on being independent and self-reliant, on producing what we eat rather than living on aid coming from the exterior. 'Aid' is a myth that should be demystified. Many countries in the South have started to raise the slogan 'Fair trade not aid'. What the South needs in order to fight against poverty is a *new international economic order* based on justice, and on fair trade laws between countries, not 'aid' or charity. Charity and injustice are two faces of the same coin. If we have real equality between people and between countries, there will be nothing called 'charity' or 'aid'.

Countries in the South plead for justice, equality and democracy in the global society; their plea is for a *new world order based on justice*. The title New World Order has been taken from the South by the powerful military machine in the North to continue the now undivided rule of the neocolonial order following the end of the Cold War. This New World Order was inaugurated by launching the Gulf War. The media and the international information order concealed the real economic reasons behind the Gulf War (oil) behind a false morality built on phrases such as 'human rights', 'democracy', 'liberation of Kuwait', et cetera.

This was repeated with the war in Somalia. All wars in human history have been concealed behind humane, or religious camouflage. If we reread the Old Testament we discover how the war to invade the land of Canaan was considered a holy war ordered by Jehovah (God).

Today we live in a world dominated by a unipolar power, by one superpower which is the USA. The USA dominates the United Nations (UN), the World Bank, the IMF, GATT and SAPs et cetera. Through these international agreements and institutions the North is strengthening its grip on the world economy. The USA and powerful European countries in the North have become a *de facto* board of management for the world economy, protecting their interests and imposing their will on the South.

The problems facing the South are rooted in the North, problems like increasing poverty, low commodity prices, the huge debt burden, unequal trade agreements. The trend to privatization and deregulation forced on the South has coincided with huge and rapid increase in the profits of transnational corporations (TNCs). It is known that 90 per cent of TNCs are based in the North. They control 70 per cent of world trade. Five hundred of these corporations have almost complete control of the world economy. The South is forced to open up the agricultural sector to the TNCs, endangering its ability to feed itself.

Many fertile agricultural countries in the South, such as Egypt, where the valley of the Nile is cultivated with three crops a year, are unable to feed themselves. In Egypt we import 90 per cent of our food.[2] The export of cotton from Egypt has diminished to one tenth of what it was in 1984, and the import of cotton has tripled.

The average monthly wage of the Egyptian worker in 1994 is 300 Egyptian pounds, whereas his foreign colleague in Egypt is paid 4,000 pounds per month. Some 40 per cent of the population in Egypt live below the poverty line. That is, their annual income is less than $386. The World Bank and the IMF help the TNCs to relocate their units of production to the countries of the South where social costs are low. Here labour laws are not applied or do not exist, social and health insurance is lacking, labour unions are weak and dominated by their governments, collective agreements between trade unions or workers and their employers often do not exist, and legislation is enacted to favour the employers. Governments are dominated by TNCs, women and children can be used as labour at lower wages especially in the informal sector, and the pollution of the environment is uncontrolled since the technologies used are under almost no constraints.

What Is a Good Government in the South?

The result of this international economic and international information order is constant pressure on economies to be more competitive. The aim is more and more profit with lower and lower costs. The aim cannot be achieved except through growing pressure on governments in the South to cut spending and diminish social costs—especially those related to subsidies that reduce the prices of essential foods, and to health and educational services, energy, et cetera. In 1977 there were widespread demonstrations in Egypt, mainly composed of the poor, women and youths. These demonstrations erupted as a result of the government's decision to raise the prices of most essential foods. The decision came after continuous pressure from the World Bank.

A good government is now defined as the government that accepts the conditions of the World Bank and submits the nation's economy to the interests of TNCs and other international groups. A good government is a government that accepts what is called 'aid' in order to achieve what is called 'development'.

In Egypt two words, 'aid' and 'development' have resulted in increased poverty and increased deprivation. Between 1975 (when American aid began) and 1986, Egypt imported commodities and services from the USA to a total of $30 billion. During the same period, Egypt exported to the USA total commodities worth only $5 billion.[3] This shows the real aim of this 'aid', namely to enrich the capitalist US economy and not to help Egypt advance on the road to development.

Religion, the Poor, and Women

In this world economic order, the indispensable sacrifices of structural adjustment are required for the globalization of the economy and of markets. They are the indispensable 'desert crossing' *en route* to the Eden of development (to use the words of the World Bank). This fatalistic, almost metaphysical conception of necessity, has recourse to religion. Religion is the ideology used by the rich to exploit the poor in the South. The majority of the poor in the world are women, youth, and children. These days a new term, 'the feminization of poverty', is often mentioned. It means that more women are becoming poor. According to UN figures, the number of rural women living in absolute poverty rose over the 1970s and 1980s by about 50 per cent (from an estimated 370 million to 565 million), and women (who are half the world's population) work two thirds of the total labour hours worked, earn one tenth of total world income, and own one hundredth of world possessions.

Gender, or women's, oppression is inseparable from class, race, and religious oppression. The patriarchal class system propagates the idea that the oppression of women and the poor is a divine law and is not man-made:

The rich man in his castle
the poor man at his gate.
God made them high or lowly,
and ordained their estate.

We all know that in all religions women have an inferior position relative to men. This is especially true for the monotheistic religions. Adam is superior to Eve, and in almost all religions women should be governed by men. In human history, to exploit women and the poor was not possible without the use of religion. Slavery was considered to be a divine law by prominent philosophers in the past and even in our own days.

Now we are faced by a resurgence of religious so-called fundamentalism. Some people think it is only Islamic. This is not true. Religious fundamentalism is an international phenomenon. The international patriarchal class system is encouraging the revival of religion all over the world. Christian fundamentalism was encouraged in the USA by Reagan and Bush. They also used, and often encouraged, Islamic fundamentalism in our region, the so-called Middle East, in order to fight against the Soviet Union and communism. In Egypt it was Sadat who encouraged religious fundamentalism to neutralize the socialist, the progressive liberal, and the Nasserite political currents in the country. In Algeria, it was the state (under Chadli) that encouraged the religious groups to grow in power.

The term often used to describe this phenomenon is 'state fundamentalism'. State political power and religious political power are two faces of the same coin. They feed each other. Sometimes they clash and fight each other in their struggle to dominate the state. This is what is now happening under Mubarak. In fact, they are old friends and new enemies. Sadat was killed by the fundamentalists after he had encouraged them to grow. The son killed the father. This is an oft-repeated story with which we are familiar in history. Wherever there is a religious survival, women are among the first victims. All fundamentalist groups, whether Christian, Jewish, or Islamic, are antagonistic to women's liberation and women's rights. The backlash against women's rights is thus also a universal phenomenon, and is not restricted to our region.

Women and Population Control

The capitalist patriarchal system (reframed as the New World Order) has developed population control policies to facilitate more exploitation of the poor and women in the so-called Third World. It is no surprise that population control institutions (such as the Population Council, the UN International Planned Parent-hood Federation [IPPF], the multinational pharmaceutical corporations, US Aid) work in collaboration with the neocolonial global institutions such as the World Bank and the IMF. Population control policies are a new biological war against women and the poor whose aim is to keep the economic and intellectual resources of the world under the control of minority power structures in the North and their collaborators in the South.

To hide their anti-women, anti-poor policies, population controllers have stolen the language of the women's liberation movements. Phrases such as 'women's needs', 'free choice', 'reproductive rights', 'empowerment of women' and 'family planning' are used to elaborate strategies against women and the poor. In the North, 20 per cent of the world's people consume 80 per cent of global resources. Instead of working towards global justice or a more egalitarian distribution of wealth and power, the multinational corporations work to eliminate the poor people in the so-called Third World. Women are pushed to consume unsafe contraceptive methods such as the injectable contraceptive Depo Provera, and the contraceptive implant Norplant. The basic needs of women—such as food, education, health, employment, social, economic and political participation, and a life free of violence (whether inflicted from inside the family or by the state)—are neglected.

Population control programmes started in the 1950s under the banner of 'poverty eradication'. The results have been the eradication of the poor, not poverty. Poverty is increasing year after year. More and more people in our countries are killed by hunger, more than those killed by war. Population control programmes nowadays are working under new titles, such as 'to curb environmental destruction', 'to ensure sustainable growth', et cetera. But nothing of all this is happening. The reality is that women in the South are subjected to a range of coercive technologies and drugs, which have often destroyed their health and lives. People in the South are not looked upon as people but as demographic variables or population indices.

Yet people in the South are not really poor. Our continents are rich but our riches are robbed by continuous pillage by colonial and neocolonial powers.

The New Economic World Order and the media have consistently equated poverty in the South with population growth. This is another myth which hides the real causes of economic and political crises in our countries. After the oil crises, credit-based development was forced on the South. It resulted in the debt crisis and increasing poverty and unemployment.

Commodification and trafficking in women (in the South and in the North as well) are increasing. Women are looked upon as bodies to be exploited and used to produce more profit. They must be veiled, covered physically according to the religious fundamentalists, but should be undressed according to the postmodern capitalists, or made to buy makeup and body conditioners. Sex is a commodity, a thriving industry. Sex shops and pornography, the commerce of sex, spread like fire.

Veiling of the Mind

The mass media and the international information order are working together with the international economic order to veil the minds of billions of people living on our planet. The new technology of communications transmits lies and myths all over the world in a matter of minutes or seconds.

The new international order is working to foster *globalization* or *global multinational capitalism* (the postmodern stage of capitalist development). The globalization of the economy requires the globalization of information, mass media and culture. This requires the breaking down of national and regional barriers to permit the free flow of capital, commodities, labour and information. Global capitalism requires global flexibility to ensure the so-called free market (freedom of the powerful to dominate the weak). Despite the competitive struggles between the different powerful groups in the North and between the TNCs, a global market requires the establishment of a market of consumers who develop similar needs, similar interests, similar desires, and similar habits of living in a certain way: that is, similar patterns of consumption. These patterns of consumption are constituted by a similar outlook on life, similar values and ideas. This is a postmodern culture which is similar in many ways across the globe, irrespective of regional or national location.

The beauty mentality and its material products such as makeup, perfumes, earrings, fashion, et cetera are sold globally by global media (TV, radio, newspaper, magazines, movies, videos, songs, music). The aim is to create a conception of beauty that becomes part of the culture and has its set of values, feelings and desires which are absorbed by the conscious and the subconscious mind. The cultural unconscious and the political unconscious are not separate from the conscious. The relation between culture, politics and economics is very important; this is true not only of the economic and political processes within which the cultural takes form, but also of the psychological processes that engage in its production and reception. I remember a French woman who came to me in 1993 and criticized Muslim women for wearing veils. This French woman had a thick coating of makeup on her face, but she was completely unaware that this also was a veil. The French woman's veil was considered by the global media as modern and beautiful, but the other veil was considered backward and ugly; yet the two veils were almost the same since they both hid the real face of the woman.

Unveiling of the Mind

When we started the Arab Women's Solidarity Association in 1982 we had two major objectives: the unveiling of the mind, and political power through unity and solidarity. We faced strong opposition from local Arab governments (who work with the international capitalist powers) and from fanatical religious groups and from a variety of political parties. But we continued to resist. We had to fight at different levels and on different fronts, to link the psychological with the economic, the political with the historical, the cultural with the religious, the sexual with the social.

To unveil the mind necessitated exposing the contradictions of the New World Order (both economic and cultural). This order encourages globalization and unification when these serve its economic interests, but fights against globalization or unification between people if they resist its policies. To unveil the mind we had to expose the link between religion and politics, between capitalism and religious fundamentalism.

The globalization needed by the international capitalist system leads people in different countries or cultures to resist homogenization resulting from the global culture, or so-called universal values. It is a self-defence mechanism. It is an attempt to hold on to an authentic identity, or authentic culture or heritage, and these are some of the factors in the growth of religious fundamentalism, racism, and ethnic struggles. It is a protest movement (especially among the youth), but very often takes on reactionary, retrograde, anti-women, and anti-progressive characteristics thus leading to division and discord; it thus serves the purpose of capitalist globalization because it divides the people who are resisting it.

How to Empower the Resistance

We need unity and solidarity between men and women who resist this global injustice at the local level as well as at the international level. But we need a movement that is progressive, not backward, which seeks unity in diversity, by breaking down barriers built on discrimination (by gender, class, race, religion, et cetera), and by discovering what we have in common as human beings with common interests that may express themselves differently. People can unite and cooperate if they struggle for greater equality and against all forms of discrimination. This requires establishing a network step by step from the local up to the global level to face the international capitalist network. We can use modern technology such as videos, cassettes, public radio, TV, et cetera, and begin with local, grassroots networks to create our own mass media. For example, we all know the role the cassette played in the Iranian Revolution. Many of the religious fundamentalist groups in Algeria, Egypt and other parts of the world are using the cassette, transmitters, cellular telephones, et cetera, to reach masses of people.

Women and the poor in the South have to cooperate with the progressive forces in the North who are fighting the same battle, but resistance starts at home. We can only change the international order by each one of us, step by step, changing the system in which we live.

Without genuine democracy this movement cannot succeed. Democracy as practised in the North under the patriarchal class system is just a set of institutions such as a parliament or a congress. It is a limited, formal and false democracy which excludes the majority of women and the poor from elections and other means of expression. We need real democracy. This real democracy starts at the personal level, at home, in the family. If we have men or husbands who are dictators in the family how can we have democracy in the state, since it is based on the family unit? Democracy is day-to-day practice and should be rooted in child-hood, in the psyche, in beliefs, ethics, attitudes, and private life as well as public life.

It is necessary to undo the separation between the private and the public be-cause in this separation lies the oppression of women and the poor. We need a new family, a new educational system at home and at the primary, secondary, and university levels. We have to work together at home and locally, nationally, region-ally, and globally to restore our dignity, to satisfy our physical and mental needs, to achieve self-reliance and the right to choose our own way towards economic and intellectual progress.

NOTES

Keynote address to the Global '94 Congress, Tampere, Finland, 3–7 July 1994.
1.   Pierre Galland, 'World Bank: "Criminal"', *International Viewpoint*, April 1994.
2.   *Al-Arabi* (Cairo); 4 April 1994, p. 4.
3.   Interview with Mahmoud Wahba, president of Egypt American Businessmen, *El-Shaab*, Cairo, Egypt, 26 April 1994, p. 4.

Questions for Thinking, Writing, and Discussion

1. Based on your reading, describe several ways to measure a society's "progress" or "well-being" and discuss what you take to be their strengths and their weaknesses. If you were asked to make such an evaluation, what measure (or measures) would you employ?

2. What are the challenges that face anyone who seeks to calculate the number of people living below the poverty line or going hungry in the world today? Describe them in some detail. Do you think it is possible to arrive at a reasonably accurate accounting? Why? Why not?

3. How does Michael Yates support his claim that inequality of income and wealth is a necessary contradiction of capitalism? How successfully does he defend this claim?

4. The articles in this section provide a lot of statistical information. Identify the statistics you find most surprising or disturbing or implausible, and then use the Internet to update or elaborate on them. Based on your research, write an essay in which you discuss your findings and the questions they raise or the conclusions to which they lead.

5. What statistics are missing from this section? Is there information that you think would have been useful and important to have in order to discuss poverty, inequality, and suffering? Use the Internet and other resources to find those statistics and then discuss how they impact on the picture that the articles in this section paint of their subject.

6. What does Paul Farmer mean by "structural violence"? Why does he use this term? Do you think this is a useful concept?

7. What, according to FannyAnn Eddy, are the consequences of the failure of the government of Sierra Leone and of other African nations to acknowledge the existence of the lesbian, gay, bisexual, and transgender community in Africa?

8. According to the International Labour Organization, one out of six children in the world today is involved in child labor. Choose one or more of the key statistics cited in Facts on Child Labour, Article 9, and, using Paul Farmer's approach, try to imagine and tell the story of some child or children whose reality is reflected in these statistics.

Suggestions for Further Reading

Bales, Kevin. *Disposable People: New Slavery in the Global Economy.* Berkeley: University of California Press, 2000.

Beneria, Lourdes. *Gender Development and Globalization: Economics as if People Mattered.* New York: Routledge, 2003.

Black, Jan Knippers. *Inequality in the Global Village Recycles Rhetoric and Disposable People.* West Hartford, Connecticut: Kumarin Press, 1999.

Chomsky, Noam. *Profit Over People: Neoliberalism and Global Order.* New York: Seven Stories Press, 1999.

Farmer, Paul. *Pathologies of Power: Health, Human Rights, and the New War on the Poor.* Berkeley: University of California Press, 2003, Chap. 1, 29–50.

Farmer, Paul, et al. *Women, Poverty and AIDS: Sex, Drugs, and Structural Violence.* Monroe, Maine: Common Courage Press, 1996.

Friedman, Thomas. *The Lexus and the Olive Tree.* New York: Farrar, Straus & Giroux, 1999.

Reddy, Sanjay G., and Thomas Pooge. "How Not to Count the Poor." www.socialanalysis.org

Seabrook, Jeremy. *Children of Other Worlds: Exploitation in the Global Market.* London and Sterling, Virginia: Pluto Press, 2001.

Seeger, Joni. *The Penguin Atlas of Women in the World.* New York and London: Penguin Books, 2003.

Silvers, Jonathon. "Child Labor in Pakistan," *Atlantic Monthly* 277 (February 1996), 79–92.

Yates, Michael D. *Naming the System: Inequality and Work in the Global Economy,* New York: Monthly Review Press, 2003.

Young Kim, Jim, et al. *Dying for Growth: Global Inequality and the Health of the Poor.* Monroe, Maine: Common Courage Press, 2000.

Transnational Institutions
and the Global Economy

What is called globalization is really another name for the dominant role
of the United States.

Henry Kissinger, former U.S. Secretary of State

Welcome to the Age of Globalization. If we were to choose a name that properly characterizes the period in which we are living, "The Age of Globalization" would probably win hands down, and years from now it will undoubtedly appear as a chapter heading in history texts, along with "The Age of Exploration," "The Age of Conquest," and immediately following "The Nation State." Until recently, nation states, loosely defined, were the most powerful entities on the international scene. They made war, negotiated treaties, and regulated trade. Some would say that the nation state never exercised its power or responsibilities in a neutral manner. Nation states evolved in relation to the rise of industrialization and from the start represented the interests of capitalism as an economic system and acted as its representative on behalf of the merchant or business class. It is this equation of corporate interests with the interests of the state that is reflected in the much quoted slogan "What's good for General Motors is good for the country."

With the growth of transnational and multinational corporations, nations alone often lack the capability and the resources to carry out many of their former economic regulatory responsibilities. For example, of the world's 100 largest economic entities, 51 are now corporations and only 49 are countries. Further, combined sales of the top 200 corporations are larger than the combined economies of all countries minus the largest 10.[1] For this reason, many of the economic functions of the nation state have been taken over or transferred to multinational entities such as OPEC, the Organization of Petroleum Exporting Countries; ASEAN, the Association of South East Asian Nations; and the EU, the European Union, and to transnational institutions such as the World Bank; the IMF, the International Monetary Fund; and the WTO, the World Trade Organization.

Both the IMF and the World Bank were created at the Bretton Woods conference in 1944 and were designed to stabilize the postwar economies of Europe and to prevent worldwide economic crises in the future. The IMF ostensibly defends the international monetary system by making sure that its members are able to fulfill their economic responsibilities to each other and to this end lends money to poor nations that are experiencing economic difficulty. The World Bank functions as a development agency by investing in programs that will promote growth and progress in developing nations. Both the IMF and the World Bank make their loans contingent on economic reform. The economic reforms that they impose usually require severe cuts in social services to free up money to pay off the loans and they tend to be strongly market oriented. They are tied to opening up the economies of the debtor nations to market forces and usually result in depressed wages and working conditions, which are justified as being necessary to attract corporate investment.

The World Trade Organization has primary responsibility for dealing with the global rules of trade among nations. Created in 1995, the WTO supplanted the General Agreement on Tariffs and Trade (GATT), a series of postwar trade treaties intended to remove international trade barriers. These multilateral trade agreements were then adopted by the WTO and provide its members with special trade rights. The WTO also includes intellectual property agreements, which provide for trade and investment in ideas and creativity or, as they are specified here, "intellectual property." Crucial to the operation of the WTO is the Dispute Settlement Understanding, which settles disputes between countries.

While aspects of globalized economic integration can be found throughout much of history, for example, the transnational slave trade, the age of globalization begins to take shape during the later part of the twentieth century when we see an unprecedented integration of the world's economies.[2] By the end of the twentieth century, plants were closing in the United States and moving to other countries in search of cheaper resources and "cheap" labor. Capital, money that is used for investment rather than spent on consumption, followed. Developing nations sought to attract investment by offering tax breaks and ever cheaper natural resources and so-called cheap labor, in what has been called "the race to the bottom."

A useful definition of globalization for our purposes is offered by the authors of Article 2 in this section. They define it this way: "globalization refers to the process in which goods and services, including capital, move more freely within and among nations." As, in their words, "national boundaries become more and more porous, and to some extent, less and less relevant," transnational agencies have acquired more policymaking and regulatory power. While this is not necessarily bad in itself and might, under certain conditions, even be seen as a positive step toward creating a genuinely global community of shared wealth and resources, critics argue that the major transnational institutions consistently represent the interest of the wealthiest corporations, individuals, and countries, and that their policies exacerbate the extremely unequal distribution of wealth that exists in the world today. The authors of the 1999 United Nations Human Development Report have this to say:

> Intergovernmental policy-making in today's global economy is in the hands of the major industrial powers and the international institutions they control—the World Bank, The International Monetary Fund, the Bank for International Settlements. Their rule-making may create a secure environment for open markets, but there are no countervailing rules to protect human rights and promote human development. And developing countries, with 80% of the world's people but less than a fifth of the global GDP, have little influence.[3]

Article 1 of this section is by Joseph Stiglitz, a former executive of the World Bank. In it Stiglitz, who is not unsympathetic to globalization, takes a hard look at how World Bank and IMF policies have impacted on the developing world. Like the authors of the U.N. report quoted above, Stiglitz acknowledges that it is "the West that has driven the globalization agenda, ensuring that it garners a disproportionate share of the benefit, at the expense of the developing world." He deplores the growing divide between rich and poor in the world and the destruction of the environment that has all too often been a consequence of globalization policies. He is also concerned about the general problem of governance of the IMF and other international economic institutions. In his estimation, they are too vulnerable to pressure from the wealthiest industrial nations and their most powerful business interests.

Nonetheless, Stiglitz believes that people everywhere have reaped some benefits from the new global integration and he seems hopeful about the ability of globalization to bring further improvements. He traces globalization's failures to its narrowly defined economic aspects and to the reliance on free market ideology that has characterized the policies of both the IMF and the World Bank. Originally created to intervene in the global markets to both encourage expansionary economic policies and stabilize those markets, both institutions now adopt a laissez-faire, capitalist model that assumes that both the powerful and the powerless are equally well positioned to take advantage of market forces and benefit from them. They insist as a condition of loaning money to poor countries that those countries adopt policies that have a devastating impact on the poor. These policies require developing nations to cut deficits, usually by cutting social services like schools and health care, and raise taxes. Originally called "structural adjustment policies," they have been widely decried by activists in every nation in the world and were recently renamed, in what many would consider an Orwellian irony, "poverty reduction and growth programs." In Stiglitz's own words, "the result [of these policies] for many people has been poverty and for many countries social and political chaos."

In Article 2, "Race, Poverty, and Globalization," john a. powell and S. P. Udayakumar focus our attention on the changes in technology and policy that have created a global market markedly different from that which came before. Unlike the recent past when trade was all about commodities, or things produced expressly for the market (rather than immediate consumption), information and capital are the major things being traded in today's world. The process of trading information and capital is itself more mobile than the production process that produces and trades commodities such as cooking pots, winter coats, and TV sets. All of this has tipped the balance so that, unlike in the past where one of the roles of government was to protect working people from the irrationality and unpredictability of the market, today the U.S. government along with transnational institutions makes its first priority the protection of capital and ensuring its unimpeded flow. But according to the authors of this article, this need not be an inevitable consequence of globalization. They point to Japan and many nations in Europe that have aggressively pushed for globalization while at the same time continuing to offer protection to labor and the environment within their own borders. It is the United States, which has emerged as *the* predominant world power, that, according to powell and Udayakumar, shows little concern for protecting either labor, the environment, or its own social welfare system. That means that at home and abroad, people of color and women bear the brunt of globalization's negative impact, as social services on which families depend are slashed and jobs are sent around the world in search of ever "cheaper" labor and ever more inhuman working conditions. According to the authors, in the end, globalization is transforming both the role of government and the meaning of citizenship in the United States as it elevates concern with the freedom of the market over commitment to the traditional freedoms once at the heart of U.S. democracy.

The disproportionate impact of structural adjustment programs on women, especially women of color, and the ways in which globalization has transformed women's work is further explored in Article 3, "On the Backs of Women and Children," by Jan Jindy Pettman. According to Pettman, the overall effect of globalization is what some have called "the feminization of poverty," namely the impoverishment of women and children worldwide. However, Pettman is also careful to remind us that in this regard, as in all other areas, differences in class, nationality, race/ethnicity and culture, age, etc. affect the ways in which globalization impacts on the lives of individual women.

Drive along many highways in the United States today and you will find signs spaced at regular intervals telling you which corporations or what private individual has assumed responsibility for keeping that stretch of highway clean. Drive around some suburban areas and you are equally likely to find signs announcing which corporation or civic group has assumed responsibility for the flowerbeds and other plantings that beautify the community. These are examples of privatization in its most benign form. Functions previously assumed by state, federal, and local government are now increasingly assumed by the private sector. The push to privatize what were previously governmental responsibilities and social services provided for the common good is the focus of the next two articles.

In Article 4 William Tabb looks at the impact of privatization on our cities, New York City in particular, and challenges its underlying assumption: that what is good for real estate and other business interests will serve the interests of the people who live there. In response to those who assure us that economic growth will eventually be beneficial for one and all, Tabb points out that it was the unregulated operation of the market in the first place that created urban problems and prompted government intervention. And he observes that it was the tax breaks demanded by business as the price of avoiding their flight that starved the city coffers in the first place and created government's inability to fund social services adequately. When private interests step up and step in, they use, in effect, the same dollars they would have paid in taxes, but now retain control over them. That means that under privatization it is business, not government as a representative of the people, that decides how the funds are spent and what aspects of public life and public space will be improved.

Perhaps the most interesting point in Tabb's article is the parallel he draws between the fiscal crises of the cities and the economic crises in parts of the developing world, both of which create the conditions for private or foreign investors to come in and dictate the terms of their participation. What were previously national assets providing government services like water, electricity, phone service, and garbage removal are now commodities to be purchased on the open market, their cost to be determined by market forces. In this way, according to Tabb, the poor are further impoverished because they now have to pay for a commodity, whereas before they received a service. What they can expect from their tax dollars declines, as does their ability to exercise power over the shrinking area of political life and the definition of what constitutes the public interest. The rich receive multiple benefits from the new system. They no longer have to pay taxes to provide services to poor and working people and they can pay only for what they require. This both lowers the cost to them and raises the quality of what they get at the expense of the majority. And their power to shape both the role of government and nature of public space increases enormously.

Article 5, "Plunder and Profit" by David Moberg, examines the roles of the IMF, the World Bank, and the World Trade Organization in the privatization of public assets and public services by focusing on the privatization of water in Cochabamba, the third largest city in Bolivia. In his article, Moberg tells the story of how the Bolivian government, under pressure from the World Bank and the IMF, came to agree to sell the municipal water system in Cochabamba to Aguas del Tunari, a company largely owned by the U.S. construction giant Bechtel. This case is important because it provides a classic example of how international financial institutions promote the interest of multinational corporations and the particular role the WTO plays in such transactions. The World Trade Organization has the power and responsibility to negotiate and oversee trade rules for the international community, but unlike other transnational institutions, the WTO has the power to enforce its decisions by leveling sanctions against those nations found to be in violation. When, two months after privatization, the new water company roughly tripled local water rates (meaning that in many cases families would be required to pay as much as one-fourth of their income for water), there were huge protests and in response the contract was finally cancelled. But under the rules of the WTO and the World Bank, powerful companies frustrated in their efforts to profit from such transactions can sue for damages when the transactions are aborted. To do so, Bechtel availed itself of international trade agreements that blatantly elevate the corporate interests of globalization over the interests of poor nations and their people. A few months after signing the original contract with the Bolivian government, Bechtel quietly added new investors and reincorporated its subsidiary in the Netherlands, thus making the contract subject to a previously existing international trade agreement between Bolivia and the Netherlands. Although Bechtel, through its subsidiary, had invested less than a million dollars, under this agreement, it was entitled to sue for damages of *at least 25 million* to compensate for the loss of profits it might have made.

Article 6, "The WTO and Globalization" by Michael Parenti, provides a more detailed account of the operation of the WTO and an examination of its use of the doctrine of "free trade" in the interests of multinational corporations. Parenti reports that in the name of promoting "freedom" by eliminating trade barriers, the WTO has forced many member nations to eliminate laws designed to protect the consumer and the environment. For example, the Japanese have been forced to accept greater pesticide residues in imported food, marine life and endangered-species protection laws have been reversed, and a ban on the import of hormone-ridden U.S. beef by the European Union was overturned as an "illegal restraint of trade." In the area of intellectual property rights, GATT favored multinational agribusiness over individuals and communities. For example, the WTO ruled that a U.S. corporation, Rice Tec, holds the patents to many of the varieties of basmati rice that India's farmers have grown for decades. In these decisions and others like them the WTO uses the rhetoric of free trade to create monopoly corporate control.

In Article 7 Michel Chossudovsky provides a sweeping overview of the relationship between the evolving policies of the transnational financial institutions and the extremely unequal distribution of wealth that we considered in Part Five. He contends that the structural adjustment programs of the World Bank and IMF, renamed "poverty alleviation," actually create the conditions that lead to the "globalization of poverty" and undermine civil society throughout large parts of the world. The severe cuts demanded under structural adjustment produce feelings of desperation and hopelessness in poor nations that in turn lead to social unrest. In anticipation of public protests and in order to protect the privileges of its national elites, many governments in developing nations move to strengthen their internal security forces and the military. In short, economic repression entails political repression. Recent popular uprisings in Caracas, Tunis, Nigeria, Morocco, Mexico, Russia, and Ecuador, many of which were brutally suppressed, are enumerated here by Chossudovsky.

Chossudovsky goes on to suggest that the new form of economic and political domination that we have been considering actually constitutes a new form of colonialism, whereby "people and governments are subordinated through the seemingly 'neutral' interplay of market forces." According to him, this "market colonialism" brings with it a form of economic genocide that is imposed on developing nations by the manipulation of market forces by transnational financial institutions in the interests of the north. Here the World Trade Organization, with its ability to negotiate and enforce trade agreements that promote the interests of multinational corporations, plays a critical role. The deregulation of trade under the WTO rules allows multinational corporations to extend their control of local markets and over virtually every aspect of local economics in the developing world. The resulting "market colonialism," which is rationalized by a rhetoric that extols the "freedom" of the market, is more difficult to identify but every bit as brutal as the colonial exploitation of the earlier period. This new colonial expropriation is carried out under the TRIP agreements that make possible the biopiracy deplored by Vandana Shiva in her article in Part Two and the patenting of human life forms, including plants, animals, microorganisms, genetic material, and genetic manipulation by large corporations like Monsanto. Under the WTO's intellectual property agreements, we are witnessing the wholesale expropriation of indigenous peoples' knowledge by corporate interests. According to this view, when taken together, the policies, rules, and agreements implemented by the World Bank, the IMF, and the WTO lead to the recolonization of national economies.

Article 8, the concluding essay in this section, is by Arundhati Roy, who asks "Shall We Leave It to the Experts?" In this piece, which provides a smooth transition to the accounts of how globalization operates in everyday life presented in Part Seven and Part Eight, Roy invites us to examine globalization by looking at what its impact will be on India, a country of vast social and economic inequalities. Is globalization, she asks, about eliminating world poverty or is it simply the old colonialism repackaged in modern dress? According to Roy, "creating a good climate for investment" becomes the new euphemism for Third World repression.

Roy focuses much of her attention on a contract to privatize power between the Houston-based and now much discredited natural gas company Enron and the Indian government. The story of this on-again, off-again, on-again deal as told by Roy is a story of bribery, corruption, and undue U.S. interference. In the end, the project, which Indian experts call "the most massive fraud" in India's history, guarantees Enron a more than 30% return on equity or more than double what Indian law permits. As predicted before it was built, the power produced by the Enron plant is extremely expensive, so expensive in fact that the government of Maharashtra, the Indian state in which the plant is located, decided that it would be cheaper to pay the mandatory fixed charges for maintenance and administration of the plant, charges required under the contract, and then simply purchase its power elsewhere. When in 2001 the Maharashtra government announced it was unable to pay Enron's bills, Enron announced it would invoke a counter guarantee clause in the contract that would allow it to auction off government properties held as collateral. The U.S. government weighed in behind Enron, cautioning India against undermining the investment climate. Roy's article concludes that leaving it to the experts may work well for a small group of national and international elites whose interests they represent but that globalization and the new expertise it has called forth will not serve the interests of the Indian people.

NOTES

1. "The Rise of Corporate Global Power," by Sarah Anderson and John Cavanagh, The Institute for Policy Research, 2000. For the full report go to www.ips-dc.org.

2. Leith Mullings, "Notes on Globalization," *TransAfrica Forum Globalization Monitor,* Vol. 1, No. 1 (October 2000), p. 1.

3. United Nations Human Development Report 1999.

one

Globalization and Its Discontents: The Promise of Global Institutions

—Joseph Stiglitz

Joseph E. Stiglitz is university professor at Columbia University in New York. He received his Ph.D. from the Massachusetts Institute of Technology in 1967 and has taught at Princeton, Stanford, the Massachusetts Institute of Technology, and All Souls College, Oxford. He served on the Council of Economic Advisors from 1993 to 1995 during the Clinton administration and then became Chief Economist and Senior Vice-President of the World Bank from 1997 to 2000. In 2001 he was awarded the Nobel Prize in Economics. The selection that follows is taken from the first chapter of his 2002 book Globalization and Its Discontents: The Promise of Global Institutions, *which was published by W.W. Norton.*

International bureaucrats—the faceless symbols of the world economic order—are under attack everywhere. Formerly uneventful meetings of obscure technocrats discussing mundane subjects such as concessional loans and trade quotas has now become the scene of raging street battles and huge demonstrations. The protests at the Seattle meeting of the World Trade Organization in 1999 were a shock. Since then, the movement has grown stronger and the fury has spread. Virtually every major meeting of the International Monetary Fund, the World Bank, and the World Trade Organization is now the scene of conflict and turmoil. The death of a protestor in Genoa in 2001 was just the beginning of what may be many more casualties in the war against globalization.

Riots and protests against the policies of and actions by institutions of globalization are hardly new. For decades, people in the developing world have rioted when the austerity programs imposed on their countries proved to be too harsh, but their protests were largely unheard in the West. What is new is the wave of protests in the developed countries. . . .

Why has globalization—a force that has brought so much good—become so controversial? Opening up to international trade has helped many countries grow far more quickly than they would otherwise have done. International trade helps economic development when a country's exports drive its economic growth.

"The Promise of Global Institutions" from *Globalization and Its Discontents* by Joseph E. Stiglitz. Copyright © 2002 by Joseph E. Stiglitz. Used by permission of W. W. Norton & Company.

Export-led growth was the centerpiece of the industrial policy that enriched much of Asia and left millions of people there far better off. Because of globalization many people in the world now live longer than before and their standard of living is far better. People in the West may regard low-paying jobs at Nike as exploitation, but for many people in the developing world, working in a factory is a far better option than staying down on the farm and growing rice.

Globalization has reduced the sense of isolation felt in much of the developing world and has given many people in the developing countries access to knowledge well beyond the reach of even the wealthiest in any country a century ago. The antiglobalization protests themselves are a result of this connectedness. Links between activists in different parts of the world, particularly those links forged through Internet communication, brought about the pressure that resulted in the international landmines treaty—despite the opposition of many powerful governments. Signed by 121 countries as of 1997, it reduces the likelihood that children and other innocent victims will be maimed by mines. Similar, well-orchestrated public pressure forced the international community to forgive the debts of some of the poorest countries. Even when there are negative sides to globalization, there are often benefits. Opening up the Jamaican milk market to U.S. imports in 1992 may have hurt local dairy farmers but it also meant poor children could get milk more cheaply. New foreign firms may hurt protected state-owned enterprises but they can also lead to the introduction of new technologies, access to new markets, and the creation of new industries.

Foreign aid, another aspect of the globalized world, for all its faults still has brought benefits to millions, often in ways that have almost gone unnoticed: guerrillas in the Philippines were provided jobs by a World Bank–financed project as they laid down their arms; irrigation projects have more than doubled the incomes of farmers lucky enough to get water; education projects have brought literacy to the rural areas; in a few countries AIDS projects have helped contain the spread of this deadly disease.

Those who vilify globalization too often overlook its benefits. But the proponents of globalization have been, if anything, even more unbalanced. To them, globalization (which typically is associated with accepting triumphant capitalism, American style) *is* progress; developing countries must accept it, if they are to grow and to fight poverty effectively. But to many in the developing world, globalization has not brought the promised economic benefits.

A growing divide between the haves and the have-nots has left increasing numbers in the Third World in dire poverty, living on less than a dollar a day. Despite repeated promises of poverty reduction made over the last decade of the twentieth century, the actual number of people living in poverty has actually increased by almost 100 million.[1] This occurred at the same time that total world income actually increased by an average of 2.5 percent annually.

In Africa, the high aspirations following colonial independence have been largely unfulfilled. Instead, the continent plunges deeper into misery, as incomes fall and standards of living decline. The hard-won improvements in life expectancy gained in the past few decades have begun to reverse. While the scourge of AIDS is at the center of this decline, poverty is also a killer. Even countries that have abandoned African socialism, managed to install reasonably honest governments, balanced their budgets, and kept inflation down find that they simply cannot attract private investors. Without this investment, they cannot have sustainable growth.

If globalization has not succeeded in reducing poverty, neither has it succeeded in ensuring stability. Crises in Asia and in Latin America have threatened the economies and the stability of all developing countries. There are fears of financial contagion spreading around the world, that the collapse of one emerging market currency will mean that others fall as well. For a while, in 1997 and 1998, the Asian crisis appeared to pose a threat to the entire world economy.

Globalization and the introduction of a market economy has not produced the promised results in Russia and most of the other economies making the transition from communism to the market. These countries were told by the West that the new economic system would bring them unprecedented prosperity. Instead, it brought unprecedented poverty: in many respects, for most of the people, the market economy proved even worse than their Communist leaders had predicted. The contrast between Russia's transition, as engineered by the international economic institutions, and that of China, designed by itself, could not be greater: While in 1990 China's gross domestic product (GDP) was 60 percent that of Russia, by the end of the decade the numbers had been reversed. While Russia saw an unprecedented increase in poverty, China saw an unprecedented decrease.

The critics of globalization accuse Western countries of hypocrisy, and the critics are right. The Western countries have pushed poor countries to eliminate trade barriers, but kept up their own barriers, preventing developing countries from exporting their agricultural products and so depriving them of desperately needed export income. The United States was, of course, one of the prime culprits, and this was an issue about which I felt intensely. When I was chairman of the Council of Economic Advisers, I fought hard against this hypocrisy. It not only hurt the developing countries; it also cost Americans, both as consumers, in the higher prices they paid, and as taxpayers, to finance the huge subsidies, billions of dollars. My struggles were, all too often, unsuccessful. Special commercial and financial interests prevailed—and when I moved over to the World Bank, I saw the consequences to the developing countries all too clearly.

But even when not guilty of hypocrisy, the West has driven the globalization agenda, ensuring that it garners a disproportionate share of the benefits, at the expense of the developing world. It was not just that the more advanced industrial countries declined to open up their markets to the goods of the developing countries—for instance, keeping their quotas on a multitude of goods from textiles to sugar—while insisting that those countries open up their markets to the goods of the wealthier countries; it was not just that the more advanced industrial countries continued to subsidize agriculture, making it difficult for the developing countries to compete, while insisting that the developing countries eliminate their subsidies on industrial goods. Looking at the "terms of trade"—the prices which developed and less developed countries get for the products they produce—after the last trade agreement in 1995 (the eighth), the *net* effect was to lower the prices some of the poorest countries in the world received relative to what they paid for their imports.* The result was that some of the poorest countries in the world were actually made worse off.

Western banks benefited from the loosening of capital market controls in Latin America and Asia, but those regions suffered when inflows of speculative hot money (money that comes into and out of a country, often overnight, often little more than betting on whether a currency is going to appreciate or depreciate) that had poured into countries suddenly reversed. The abrupt outflow of money left behind collapsed currencies and weakened banking systems. The Uruguay Round also strengthened intellectual property rights. American and other Western drug companies could now stop drug companies in India and Brazil from "stealing" their intellectual property. But these drug companies in the developing world were making these life-saving drugs available to their citizens at a fraction of the price at which the drugs were sold by the Western drug companies. There were thus two sides to the decisions made in the Uruguay Round. Profits of the Western drug companies would go up. Advocates said this would provide them more incentive to innovate; but the increased profits from sales in the developing world were small, since few could afford the drugs, and hence the incentive effect, at best, might be limited. The other side was that thousands were effectively condemned to death, because governments and individuals in developing countries could no longer pay the high prices demanded. In the case of AIDS, the international outrage was so great that drug companies had to back down, eventually agreeing to lower their prices, to sell the drugs at cost in late 2001. But the underlying problems—the fact that the intellectual property regime established under the Uruguay Round was not balanced, that it overwhelmingly reflected the interests and perspectives of the producers, as opposed to the users, whether in developed or developing countries—remain.

Not only in trade liberalization but in every other aspect of globalization even seemingly well-intentioned efforts have often backfired. When projects, whether agriculture or infrastructure, recommended by the West, designed with the advice of Western advisers, and financed by the World Bank or others have failed, unless there is some form of debt forgiveness, the poor people in the developing world still must repay the loans.

---

*This eighth agreement was the result of negotiations called the *Uruguay Round* because the negotiations began in 1986 in Punta del Este, Uruguay. The round was concluded in Marrakech on December 15, 1993, when 117 countries joined in this trade liberalization agreement. The agreement was finally signed for the United States by President Clinton on December 8, 1994. The World Trade Organization came into formal effect on January 1, 1995, and over 100 nations had signed on by July. One provision of the agreement entailed converting the GATT into the WTO.

If, in too many instances, the benefits of globalization have been less than its advocates claim, the price paid has been greater, as the environment has been destroyed, as political processes have been corrupted, and as the rapid pace of change has not allowed countries time for cultural adaptation. The crises that have brought in their wake massive unemployment have, in turn, been followed by longer-term problems of social dissolution—from urban violence in Latin America to ethnic conflicts in other parts of the world, such as Indonesia.

These problems are hardly new—but the increasingly vehement worldwide reaction against the policies that drive globalization is a significant change. For decades, the cries of the poor in Africa and in developing countries in other parts of the world have been largely unheard in the West. Those who labored in the developing countries knew something was wrong when they saw financial crises becoming more commonplace and the numbers of poor increasing. But they had no way to change the rules or to influence the international financial institutions that wrote them. Those who valued democratic processes saw how "conditionality"— the conditions that international lenders imposed in return for their assistance— undermined national sovereignty. But until the protestors came along there was little hope for change and no outlets for complaint. *Some* of the protestors went to excesses; *some* of the protestors were arguing for higher protectionist barriers against the developing countries, which would have made their plight even worse. But despite these problems, it is the trade unionists, students, environmentalists— ordinary citizens—marching in the streets of Prague, Seattle, Washington, and Genoa who have put the need for reform on the agenda of the developed world.

Protestors see globalization in a very different light than the treasury secretary of the United States, or the finance and trade ministers of most of the advanced industrial countries. The differences in views are so great that one wonders, are the protestors and the policy makers talking about the same phenomena? Are they looking at the same data? Are the visions of those in power so clouded by special and particular interests?

What is this phenomenon of globalization that has been subject, at the same time, to such vilification and such praise? Fundamentally, it is the closer integration of the countries and peoples of the world which has been brought about by the enormous reduction of costs of transportation and communication, and the breaking down of artificial barriers to the flows of goods, services, capital, knowledge, and (to a lesser extent) people across borders. Globalization has been accompanied by the creation of new institutions that have joined with existing ones to work across borders. In the arena of international civil society, new groups, like the Jubilee movement pushing for debt reduction for the poorest countries, have joined long-established organizations like the International Red Cross. Globalization is powerfully driven by international corporations, which move not only capital and goods across borders but also technology. Globalization has also led to renewed attraction to long-established international *intergovernmental* institutions: the United Nations, which attempts to maintain peace; the International Labor

Organization (ILO), originally created in 1919, which promotes its agenda around the world under its slogan "decent work"; and the World Health Organization (WHO), which has been especially concerned with improving health conditions in the developing world.

Many, perhaps most, of these aspects of globalization have been welcomed everywhere. No one wants to see their child die, when knowledge and medicines are available somewhere else in the world. It is the more narrowly defined *economic* aspects of globalization that have been the subject of controversy, and the international institutions that have written the rules, which mandate or push things like liberalization of capital markets (the elimination of the rules and regulations in many developing countries that are designed to stabilize the flows of volatile money into and out of the country).

To understand what went wrong, it's important to look at the three main institutions that govern globalization: the IMF, the World Bank, and the WTO. There are, in addition, a host of other institutions that play a role in the international economic system—a number of regional banks, smaller and younger sisters to the World Bank, and a large number of UN organizations, such as the UN Development Program or the UN Conference on Trade and Development (UNCTAD). These organizations often have views that are markedly different from the IMF and the World Bank. The ILO, for example, worries that the IMF pays too little attention to workers' rights, while the Asian Development Bank argues for "competitive pluralism," whereby developing countries will be provided with alternative views of development strategies, including the "Asian model"—in which governments, while relying on markets, have taken an active role in creating, shaping, and guiding markets, including promoting new technologies, and in which firms take considerable responsibility for the social welfare of their employees—which the Asian Development Bank sees as distinctly different from the American model pushed by the Washington-based institutions. . . .

The IMF and the World Bank both originated in World War II as a result of the UN Monetary and Financial Conference at Bretton Woods, New Hampshire, in July 1944, part of a concerted effort to finance the rebuilding of Europe after the devastation of World War II and to save the world from future economic depressions. The proper name of the World Bank—the International Bank for Reconstruction and Development—reflects its original mission; the last part, "Development," was added almost as an afterthought. At the time, most of the countries in the developing world were still colonies, and what meager economic development efforts could or would be undertaken were considered the responsibility of their European masters.

The more difficult task of ensuring global economic stability was assigned to the IMF. Those who convened at Bretton Woods had the global depression of the 1930s very much on their minds. Almost three quarters of a century ago, capitalism faced its most severe crisis to date. The Great Depression enveloped the whole world and led to unprecedented increases in unemployment. At the worst point, a quarter of America's workforce was unemployed. The British economist John

Maynard Keynes, who would later be a key participant at Bretton Woods, put forward a simple explanation, and a correspondingly simple set of prescriptions: lack of sufficient aggregate demand explained economic downturns; government policies could help stimulate aggregate demand. In cases where monetary policy is ineffective, governments could rely on fiscal policies, either by increasing expenditures or cutting taxes. While the models underlying Keynes's analysis have subsequently been criticized and refined, bringing a deeper understanding of why market forces do not work quickly to adjust the economy to full employment, the basic lessons remain valid.

The International Monetary Fund was charged with preventing another global depression. It would do this by putting international pressure on countries that were not doing their fair share to maintain global aggregate demand, by allowing their own economies to go into a slump. When necessary it would also provide liquidity in the form of loans to those countries facing an economic downturn and unable to stimulate aggregate demand with their own resources.

In its original conception, then, the IMF was based on a recognition that markets often did not work well—that they could result in massive unemployment and might fail to make needed funds available to countries to help them restore their economies. The IMF was founded on the belief that there was a need for *collective action at the global level* for economic stability, just as the United Nations had been founded on the belief that there was a need for collective action at the global level for political stability. The IMF is a *public* institution, established with money provided by taxpayers around the world. This is important to remember because it does not report directly to either the citizens who finance it or those whose lives it affects. Rather, it reports to the ministries of finance and the central banks of the governments of the world. They assert their control through a complicated voting arrangement based largely on the economic power of the countries at the end of World War II. There have been some minor adjustments since, but the major developed countries run the show, with only one country, the United States, having effective veto. (In this sense, it is similar to the UN, where a historical anachronism determines who holds the veto—the victorious powers of World War II—but at least there the veto power is shared among five countries.)

Over the years since its inception, the IMF has changed markedly. Founded on the belief that markets often worked badly, it now champions market supremacy with ideological fervor. Founded on the belief that there is a need for international pressure on countries to have more expansionary economic policies—such as increasing expenditures, reducing taxes, or lowering interest rates to stimulate the economy—today the IMF typically provides funds only if countries engage in policies like cutting deficits, raising taxes, or raising interest rates that lead to a contraction of the economy. Keynes would be rolling over in his grave were he to see what has happened to his child.

The most dramatic change in these institutions occurred in the 1980s, the era when Ronald Reagan and Margaret Thatcher preached free market ideology in the United States and the United Kingdom. The IMF and the World Bank became the new missionary institutions, through which these ideas were pushed on the reluctant poor countries that often badly needed their loans and grants. The ministries of finance in poor countries were willing to become converts, if necessary, to obtain the funds, though the vast majority of government officials, and, more to the point, people in these countries often remained skeptical. In the early 1980s, a purge occurred inside the World Bank, in its research department, which guided the Bank's thinking and direction. Hollis Chenery, one of America's most distinguished development economists, a professor at Harvard who had made fundamental contributions to research in the economics of development and other areas as well, had been Robert McNamara's confidant and adviser. McNamara had been appointed president of the World Bank in 1968. Touched by the poverty that he saw throughout the Third World, McNamara had redirected the Bank's effort as its elimination, and Chenery assembled a first-class group of economists from around the world to work with him. But with the changing of the guard came a new president in 1981, William Clausen, and a new chief economist, Ann Krueger, an international trade specialist, best known for her work on "rent seeking"—how special interests use tariffs and other protectionist measures to increase their incomes at the expense of others. While Chenery and his team had focused on how markets failed in developing countries and what governments could do to improve markets and reduce poverty, Krueger saw government as the problem. Free markets were the solution to the problems of developing countries. In the new ideological fervor, many of the first-rate economists that Chenery had assembled left.

Although the missions of the two institutions remained distinct, it was at this time that their activities became increasingly intertwined. In the 1980s, the Bank went beyond just lending for projects (like roads and dams) to providing broad-based support, in the form of *structural adjustment loans*; but it did this only when the IMF gave its approval—and with that approval came IMF-imposed conditions on the country. The IMF was supposed to focus on crises; but developing countries were always in need of help, so the IMF became a permanent part of life in most of the developing world.

The fall of the Berlin Wall provided a new arena for the IMF: managing the transition to a market economy in the former Soviet Union and the Communist bloc countries in Europe. More recently, as the crises have gotten bigger, and even the deep coffers of the IMF seemed insufficient, the World Bank was called in to provide tens of billions of dollars of emergency support, but strictly as a junior partner, with the guidelines of the programs dictated by the IMF. In principle, there was a division of labor. The IMF was supposed to limit itself to matters of *macroeconomics* in dealing with a country, to the government's budget deficit, its monetary policy, its inflation, its trade deficit, its borrowing from abroad; and the World Bank was supposed to be in charge of *structural issues*—what the country's government spent money on, the country's financial institutions, its labor markets, its trade policies. But the IMF took a rather imperialistic view of the matter: since almost any structural issue could affect the overall performance of the economy, and hence the government's budget or the trade deficit, it viewed almost everything as falling within its domain. It often got impatient with the World Bank, where even in the years when free market ideology reigned supreme there were frequent controversies about what policies would best suit the conditions of the country. The IMF had the answers (basically, the same ones for every country), didn't see the need for all this discussion, and, while the World Bank debated what should be done, saw itself as stepping into the vacuum to provide the answers.

The two institutions could have provided countries with alternative perspectives on some of the challenges of development and transition, and in doing so they might have strengthened democratic processes. But they were both driven by the collective will of the G-7 (the governments of the seven most important advanced industrial countries),* and especially their finance ministers and treasury secretaries, and too often, the last thing they wanted was a lively democratic debate about alternative strategies.

A half century after its founding, it is clear that the IMF has failed in its mission. It has not done what it was supposed to do—provide funds for countries facing an economic downturn, to enable the country to restore itself to close to full employment. In spite of the fact that our understanding of economic processes has increased enormously during the last fifty years, and in spite of IMF's efforts during the past quarter century, crises around the world have been more frequent and (with the exception of the Great Depression) deeper. By some reckonings, close to a hundred countries have faced crises.[2] Worse, many of the policies that the IMF pushed, in particular, premature capital market liberalization, have contributed to global instability. And once a country was in crisis, IMF funds and programs not only failed to stabilize the situation but in many cases actually made matters worse, especially for the poor. The IMF failed in its original mission of promoting global stability; it has also been no more successful in the new missions that it has undertaken, such as guiding the transition of countries from communism to a market economy.

The Bretton Woods agreement had called for a third international economic organization—a World Trade Organization to govern international trade relations, a job similar to the IMF's governing of international financial relations. Beggarthy-neighbor trade policies, in which countries raised tariffs to maintain their own economies but at the expense of their neighbors, were largely blamed for the spread of the depression and its depth. An international organization was required not just to prevent a recurrence but to encourage the free flow of goods and services. Although the General Agreement on Tariffs and Trade (GATT) did succeed in lowering tariffs enormously, it was difficult to reach the final accord; it was not until 1995, a half century after the end of the war and two thirds of a century after the Great Depression, that the World Trade Organization came into being. But

*These are the United States, Japan, Germany, Canada, Italy, France, and the UK. Today, the G-7 typically meets together with Russia (the G-8). The seven countries are no longer the seven largest economies in the world. Membership in the G-7, like permanent membership in the UN Security Council, is partly a matter of historical accident.

the WTO is markedly different from the other two organizations. It does not set rules itself; rather, it provides a forum in which trade negotiations go on and it ensures that its agreements are lived up to.

The ideas and intentions behind the creation of the international economic institutions were good ones, yet they gradually evolved over the years to become something very different. The Keynesian orientation of the IMF, which emphasized market failures and the role for government in job creation, was replaced by the free market mantra of the 1980s, part of a new "Washington Consensus"—a consensus between the IMF, the World Bank, and the U.S. Treasury about the "right" policies for developing countries—that signaled a radically different approach to economic development and stabilization.

Many of the ideas incorporated in the consensus were developed in response to the problems in Latin America, where governments had let budgets get out of control while loose monetary policies had led to rampant inflation. A burst of growth in some of that region's countries in the decades immediately after World War II had not been sustained, allegedly because of excessive state intervention in the economy. The ideas that were developed to cope with problems arguably specific to Latin American countries have subsequently been deemed applicable to countries around the world. Capital market liberalization has been pushed despite the fact that there is no evidence showing it spurs economic growth. In other cases, the economic policies that evolved into the Washington Consensus and were introduced into developing countries were not appropriate for countries in the early stages of development or early stages of transition.

To take just a few examples, most of the advanced industrial countries— including the United States and Japan—had built up their economies by wisely and selectively protecting some of their industries until they were strong enough to compete with foreign companies. While blanket protectionism has often not worked for countries that have tried it, neither has rapid trade liberalization. Forcing a developing country to open itself up to imported products that would compete with those produced by certain of its industries, industries that were dangerously vulnerable to competition from much stronger counterpart industries in other countries, can have disastrous consequences—socially and economically. Jobs have systematically been destroyed—poor farmers in developing countries simply couldn't compete with the highly subsidized goods from Europe and America—before the countries' industrial and agricultural sectors were able to grow strong and create new jobs. Even worse, the IMF's insistence on developing countries maintaining tight monetary policies has led to interest rates that would make job creation impossible even in the best of circumstances. And because trade liberalization occurred before safety nets were put into place, those who lost their jobs were forced into poverty. Liberalization has thus, too often, not been followed by the promised growth, but by increased misery. And even those who have not lost their jobs have been hit by a heightened sense of insecurity.

Capital controls are another example: European countries banned the free flow of capital until the seventies. Some might say it's not fair to insist that developing countries with a barely functioning bank system risk opening their markets. But putting aside such notions of fairness, it's bad economics; the influx of hot money into and out of the country that so frequently follows after capital market liberalization leaves havoc in its wake. Small developing countries are like small boats. Rapid capital market liberalization, in the manner pushed by the IMF, amounted to setting them off on a voyage on a rough sea, before the holes in their hulls have been repaired, before the captain has received training, before life vests have been put on board. Even in the best of circumstances, there was a high likelihood that they would be overturned when they were hit broadside by a big wave.

The application of mistaken economic theories would not be such a problem if the end of first colonialism and then communism had not given the IMF and the World Bank the opportunity to greatly expand their respective original mandates, to vastly extend their reach. Today these institutions have become dominant players in the world economy. Not only countries seeking their help but also those seeking their "seal of approval" so that they can better access international capital markets must follow their economic prescriptions, prescriptions which reflect their free market ideologies and theories.

The result for many people has been poverty and for many countries social and political chaos. The IMF has made mistakes in all the areas it has been involved in: development, crisis management, and in countries making the transition from communism to capitalism. Structural adjustment programs did not bring sustained growth even to those, like Bolivia, that adhered to its strictures; in many countries, excessive austerity stifled growth; successful economic programs require extreme care in *sequencing*—the order in which reforms occur—and pacing. If, for instance, markets are opened up for competition too rapidly, before strong financial institutions are established, then jobs will be destroyed faster than new jobs are created. In many countries, mistakes in sequencing and pacing led to rising unemployment and increased poverty.[3] After the 1997 Asian crisis, IMF policies exacerbated the crises in Indonesia and Thailand. Free market reforms in Latin America have had one or two successes—Chile is repeatedly cited—but much of the rest of the continent has still to make up for the lost decade of growth following the so-called successful IMF bailouts of the early 1980s, and many today have persistently high rates of unemployment—in Argentina, for instance, at double-digit levels since 1995—even as inflation has been brought down. The collapse in Argentina in 2001 is one of the most recent of a series of failures over the past few years. Given the high unemployment rate for almost seven years, the wonder is not that the citizens eventually rioted, but that they suffered quietly so much for so long. Even those countries that have experienced some limited growth have seen the benefits accrue to the well-off, and especially the *very* well-off—the top 10 percent—while poverty has remained high, and in some cases the income of those at the bottom has even fallen.

Underlying the problems of the IMF and the other international economic institutions is the problem of governance: who decides what they do. The institutions are dominated not just by the wealthiest industrial countries but by commercial and financial interests in those countries, and the policies of the institutions naturally reflect this. The choice of heads for these institutions symbolizes the institutions' problem, and too often has contributed to their dysfunction. While almost all of the activities of the IMF and the World Bank today are in the developing world (certainly, all of their lending), they are led by representatives from the industrialized nations. (By custom or tacit agreement the head of the IMF is always a European, that of the World Bank an American.) They are chosen behind closed doors, and it has never even been viewed as a prerequisite that the head should have any experience in the developing world. The institutions are not representative of the nations they serve.

The problems also arise from who *speaks* for the country. At the IMF, it is the finance ministers and the central bank governors. At the WTO, it is the trade ministers. Each of these ministers is closely aligned with particular constituencies *within* their countries. The trade ministries reflect the concerns of the business community—both exporters who want to see new markets opened up for their products and producers of goods which compete with new imports. These constituencies, of course, want to maintain as many barriers to trade as they can and keep whatever subsidies they can persuade Congress (or their parliament) to give them. The fact that the trade barriers raise the prices consumers pay or that the subsidies impose burdens on taxpayers is of less concern than the profits of the producers—and environmental and labor issues are of even less concern, other than as obstacles that have to be overcome. The finance ministers and central bank governors typically are closely tied to the financial community; they come from financial firms, and after their period of government service, that is where they return. Robert Rubin, the treasury secretary during much of the period described in this book, came from the largest investment bank, Goldman Sachs, and returned to the firm, Citigroup, that controlled the largest commercial bank, Citibank. The number-two person at the IMF during this period, Stan Fischer, went straight from the IMF to Citigroup. These individuals naturally see the world through the eyes of the financial community. The decisions of any institution naturally reflect the perspectives and interests of those who make the decisions; not surprisingly, as we shall see repeatedly in the following chapters, the policies of the international economic institutions are all too often closely aligned with the commercial and financial interests of those in the advanced industrial countries.

For the peasants in developing countries who toil to pay off their countries' IMF debts or the businessmen who suffer from higher value-added taxes upon the insistence of the IMF, the current system run by the IMF is one of taxation without representation. Disillusion with the international system of globalization under the aegis of the IMF grows as the poor in Indonesia, Morocco, or Papua New Guinea have fuel and food subsidies cut, as those in Thailand see AIDS increase as a result of IMF-forced cutbacks in health expenditures, and as families in many developing countries, having to pay for their children's education under so-called cost recovery programs, make the painful choice not to send their daughters to school.

Left with no alternatives, no way to express their concern, to press for change, people riot. The streets, of course, are not the place where issues are discussed, policies formulated, or compromises forged. But the protests have made government officials and economists around the world think about alternatives to these Washington Consensus policies as the one and true way for growth and development. It has become increasingly clear not to just ordinary citizens but to policy makers as well, and not just those in the developing countries but those in the developed countries as well, that globalization as it has been practiced has not lived up to what its advocates promised it would accomplish—or to what it can and should do. In some cases it has not even resulted in growth, but when it has, it has not brought benefits to all; the net effect of the policies set by the Washington Consensus has all too often been to benefit the few at the expense of the many, the well-off at the expense of the poor. In many cases commercial interests and values have superseded concern for the environment, democracy, human rights, and social justice.

Globalization itself is neither good nor bad. It has the *power* to do enormous good, and for the countries of East Asia, who have embraced globalization *under their own terms*, at their own pace, it has been an enormous benefit, in spite of the setback of the 1997 crisis. But in much of the world it has not brought comparable benefits. For many, it seems closer to an unmitigated disaster.

NOTES

1. In 1990, 2.718 billion people were living on less than $2 a day. In 1998, the number of poor living on less than $2 a day is estimated at 2.801 billion—World Bank, *Global Economic Prospects and the Developing Countries 2000* (Washington, DC: World Bank, 2000), p. 29. For additional data, see *World Development Report* and *World Economic Indicators*, annual publications of the World Bank. Health data can be found in UNAIDS/WHO, *Report on the HIV/AIDS Epidemic 1998.*

2. See Gerard Caprio, Jr., et al., eds., *Preventing Bank Crises: Lesons from Recent Global Bank Failures. Proceedings of a Conference Co-Sponsored by the Federal Reserve Bank of Chicago and the Economic Development Institute of the World Bank.* EDI Development Studies (Washington, DC: World Ban, 1998).

3. While there have been a host of critiques of the structural adjustment program, even the IMF's review of the program noted its many faults. This review includes three parts: internal review by the IMF staff (IMF Staff, *The ESAF at Ten Years: Economic Adjustment and Reform in Low-Income Countries.* Occasional Papers #156, February 12, 1998); external review by an independent reviewer (K. Botchwey, et al., *Report by a Group of Independent Experts Review: External Evaluation of the ESAF* [Washington, DC: IMF, 1998]); and a report from IMF staff to the Board of Directors of the IMF, distilling the lessons from the two reviews (IMF Staff, *Distilling the Lessons from the ESAF Reviews* [Washington, DC: IMF, July 1998]).

Race, Poverty, and Globalization
–john a. powell and S.P. Udayakumar

john powell directs the Kirwan Institute on Race and Ethnicity at Ohio State University, where he also teaches law. S. P. Udayakumar runs the South Asian Community Center for Education and Research at Nagercoil, Tamil Nadu, India. Their article "Race, Poverty and Globalization" appeared originally in Poverty and Race *(May/June 2000).*

The world economy is in a state of what is commonly viewed as unprecedented growth. But with this growth has come dangerous and destructive economic disparity. On the one hand, we see the "impressive" economy in the Northern Hemisphere, particularly in the United States, where Silicon Valley, a region of 2.3 million people, has produced tens of thousands of millionaires, with 64 new ones every day. There are regular U.S. reports of historically low unemployment rates, labor shortages and booming economy.

On the other hand, many people of color, particularly those in the Southern Hemisphere, do not have enough food to eat, resulting in malnutrition and disease. They face growing inflation while their governments, which used to subsidize some aspects of their marginal living, are urged to stop subsidies for food and adopt a more market-oriented economics. Many workers in these economies are trapped in poor working conditions with low pay. Women are often expected to do backbreaking farm and domestic work, with few rights or benefits. Yet many of the fiscal policies pushed onto developing countries and adopted in northern countries exacerbate the problem of the most marginal while celebrating the wealth of the rich.

In the North as well, people of color often find themselves being left farther and farther behind. Even as states in the U.S. and the nation as a whole report budget surpluses, we seem unable or unwilling to provide adequate housing for the growing number of working-class and homeless families, to repair the physical structure of schools that house low-income students of color, or to provide social services or medical attention for those most in need.

"Race, Poverty, and Globalization" by john a. powell and S. P. Udayakumar, *Poverty and Race*, May/June 2000. Copyright 2000. Reprinted by permission of the Poverty & Race Research Action Council.

Sweatshops that employ people of color working as virtual slave laborers are tolerated—even encouraged—as part of the new world trade. The public space people of color and marginal groups are most dependent on—whether it is public hospitals, schools, parks, or a social welfare system—is constantly attacked as inconsistent with the needs of capital and the market. Indeed, we are encouraged to remake public space to mimic private space with a market, anti-democratic orientation where we are consumers, not citizens.

How are these disparate conditions related to globalism, and why are people of color under the most severe threat from this process? Certainly, other people are also under a threat from this globalization process, and some would assert that democracy and capitalism itself may be undone by this process if it is not checked. To answer the above question and to understand why minorities and other marginal populations are most at risk, it is first necessary to better understand what globalism is, particularly the type of globalism that dominates today's markets.

What Is Globalism?

In the most general sense, globalism refers to the process in which goods and services, including capital, move more freely within and among nations. As globalism advances, national boundaries become more and more porous, and to some extent, less and less relevant.

Since many of our early industries, such as steel, were location-sensitive, there was a natural limitation to globalization. To be sure, some things remain location-sensitive, but mobility is the trend. It is assumed that liberalizing laws and structures, so that goods and services can become more globally focused, will produce more wealth, and indeed this seems to be true. Using this general understanding of globalism and globalization, it would be accurate to say this process has been developing and growing for well over a hundred years.

But there have been many changes in the globalization process in the last two decades that makes it distinct from earlier incarnations. The major thing being traded in today's global market is information and capital itself, rather than commodities or other products. Technological change allows capital to move almost instantaneously. Changes in monetary policies, as well as in what is being traded and the importance of capital, have created a global market distinctively different from previous eras. Earlier products and capital were more rooted to a place. Today, many of the things traded and produced in the global market, such as knowledge and computer technology, are extremely mobile or rootless.

The United States has emerged as the only world superpower. This has allowed the U.S. tremendous influence in setting the terms for global trade. The style of globalism pushed by the United States has favored the free movement and protection of capital, while being at best indifferent and at worst hostile to the more place-dependent labor. It is the dual relationship of mobile capital and fixed, unorganized and unprotected labor that has created the conditions for capital to dominate. This has been greatly enhanced by the U.S. position toward organized labor and capital. While the U.S. has been aggressive in protecting capital both at home and abroad, it has encouraged both the weakening of organized labor and removing protections for workers.

While both Japan and Europe have aggressively pushed for globalism, each has been more willing to protect labor, the environment and certain markets—at least within their own borders. It is the United States that has consistently been the most radical on liberalizing capital and protecting it as it moves across boundaries, and the most hostile to protecting labor and fragile markets. Protecting labor expresses itself not only in strong unions and workers' benefits but also in a strong social welfare system. The United States has purposefully moved toward weaker labor unions, as well as an anemic social welfare system. It has used the globalism it advocates as justification for keeping workers' jobs insecure, pay and benefits relatively low. Workers are told that pushing hard for benefits will cause capital to leave to another location in the country or the world where workers are willing to work for less with fewer benefits.

The United States and the international organizations over which it has substantial influence, such as the International Monetary Fund, have demanded protection of capital and encouraged or tolerated the suppression of labor and the environment in the weaker southern countries. Capital is actively being directed to markets with low wages, where workers are sometimes abused and labor organizations suppressed. The wealth this globalism is creating is being forcefully subsidized by vulnerable workers and the environment, especially in the Southern Hemisphere. This logic is then used to weaken the position of labor in the North, as we are required to compete with unorganized, suppressed labor in the South.

While sweatshops and slave labor may attract capital investments, what about the futures of black welfare mothers in Detroit or the Aborigines in Australia, who need government assistance to take advantage of, say, the educational system? How or why does U.S.-style globalism affect their needs? U.S.-style globalism not only attempts to suppress labor, but also seeks to suppress social welfare systems and support for public expenditures that do not directly benefit the expansion of capital. The social welfare system and other public services, such as schools, social services in the North and food subsidies in the South, are supported through taxes, and taxes reduce short-term benefits to capital.

In the North, it is women and minorities who are most dependent on the public sector. These racial and gender correlations make it all the easier to attack the legitimacy of taxation for this purpose. Taxes are seen as undesirable because they reduce profits and interfere with the market. But the public space, including the welfare system, can only be supported by the public in the form of taxes. Whether we are talking about education or other public services, we are encouraged to believe that they should be as limited as possible and made to mimic the market. Those who cannot thrive in the market environment without help, especially if they are people of color, are seen as free-loaders and illegitimate. In many ways, much of the public space in the United States becomes associated with people of color.

Goodbye, Democratic Vision?

Public purposes and civic goods—to the extent they are even recognized—are no longer to be achieved through public institutions but are to be privatized. The democratic vision associated with public functions is to be abandoned or seriously curtailed in favor of the ideal of efficiency. There is an abiding belief that democracy must be limited because it interferes with the private decisions of market experts, thereby reducing wealth and capital. And anything that is perceived as interfering with the growth of capitalism—be it the social welfare system, labor unions, civil rights or government programs—is being curtailed, while government policies and structures that protect capital, including the military, are enhanced.

Although proponents of this style of globalism purport to support democracy, it is only in a role subservient to capital. In the United States, we are softly encouraged to vote, while being constantly reminded that in these global matters that shape our everyday life, we have no say. We are told that no city, state or nation can or should try to influence this powerful but uncontrollable process. We are reminded that one can regulate capital, and any attempt to do so will hurt the economy.

The deregulation of capital is made to appear both good and natural. Our attention is drawn away from the fact that there are powerful organizations supported by the U.S. government's leadership that protect and facilitate the flow of capital. These institutions include the World Bank, International Development Association, International Finance Corporation, International Monetary Fund, World Trade Organization, etc.

Unfortunately, there are no organizations of equal stature to protect the interests of workers, racial minorities, the environment, or women and children. There are, of course, several treaties and international instruments dealing with some of these issues, such as the Convention on International Trade in Endangered Species, Convention on the Elimination of All Forms of Discrimination Against Women, Declaration on the Rights of Persons Belonging to National or Ethnic, Religious or Linguistic Minorities, and so forth.

However, they are nearly impotent, compared with the institutions with far-reaching and substantial goals of protecting capital. When citizens try to raise such issues, it is simply asserted that making working conditions or the environment part of trade agreements would unduly interfere with free trade. American-style globalism has not just transformed the flow of capital, it has transformed the role of government and the meaning of citizenship.

People are now brought together as consumers but kept apart as citizens. The transformed role of government is not to protect citizens or the precious safety net of public space but to protect and facilitate the flow of capital. So today we speak of free markets but not of free labor. We speak of an expanding global market, but a diminishing public space, and we hardly speak at all of citizen participation and justice. This is an authoritarian vision where armies police people and nations, so capital might be free.

It is very doubtful that capital, despite advances in technology, would be nearly as mobile as it is without the nationally brokered agreements that have the force of law and the coercive power of the state behind them. But while capital relies on the government to do its bidding, we enjoy freedom as individuals without the power that only comes from the collective action of informed citizens. While it might be true that cities and states, and certainly private individuals, can do little to influence globalism, it is clearly false that nations, especially the United States, are powerless in the face of globalism.

Undermining Social Movements

During the last part of the 20th century, the Civil Rights Movement, the women's movement and the environmental movement advanced their claims for inclusion and justice. An attack on the public role of the state is a powerful strategy to limit the aspirations of these groups. They are made impotent in a forum where wealth, not votes, dictates policies. These groups are marginalized in an economic arena that transforms the market, with decisions made behind closed doors, and not in public and civic spaces.

Destruction of the public space also results in a decline of the public voice. In the United States, this decline in the role and scope of democracy in the relationship to the market occurred just when the Civil Rights Movement began to make significant gains in securing for blacks and other minorities real access to the political process.

This article, then, is not an attack on globalism per se but on the excess and undemocratic nature of the U.S.-style globalism popular now, which is particularly hostile to people of color and other marginal groups. This style of globalism disempowers average Americans in every way, except as consumers. Globalization has been happening for over a century and will continue. It must be re-envisioned to appropriately protect capital, but also to protect labor, the environment and people of color. These concerns must be seen as interrelated, not as separate. Furthermore, we must create the necessary international structures with transparency and accountability in order to make this vision a reality and to develop suitable remedies for the plight of marginalized peoples. These steps should not be seen as hostile to business, but as an appropriate cost of doing business in a justice-oriented and sustainable global economy.

Despite the rhetoric about the unmitigated good that can come from U.S.-style globalism, there is an increasing call to look more closely at the process as it relates to people and the environment throughout the world. Some assert that U.S.-style globalism threatens democracy. Others argue that this style of globalism threatens capitalism itself. We think that both claims may be right.

We believe it is critical to look more closely at what globalism means for people in general and people of color in particular. Given its more recent history of developing a social compact that includes all people, the United States should not be championing a style of globalism that is blind to the needs of some sectors. If this process continues, we are likely to permanently re-inscribe a subordinated, life-threatening status for people of color all over the globe and rationalize it with an invisible hand. We can change this by working to make the invisible visible.

On the Backs of Women and Children

–Jan Jindy Pettman

Jan Jindy Pettman lectures on political science at the Australian National University. "On the Backs of Women and Children" is an excerpt from her book Worlding Women, *published by Routledge in 1996.*

On the Backs of Women and Children

Structural adjustment and conditionality (the conditions imposed by financial institutions such as the World Bank in return for loans) amount to a transfer of wealth from poor to rich states. They also effect a transfer of many social costs from public to private sectors, from state to household, and from paid to unpaid labour. These transfers are especially damaging to women.

State employment policies affect women differently, because public-sector employment is a major source of women's employment, especially in education, health and social-security areas. Cuts in these areas directly reduce women's employment. Global restructuring is presently being carried out at the expense of women and children. Structural adjustment policies that reduce social-security expenditure and abolish food subsidies force women, especially poor women, to make an 'invisible readjustment' (UNICEF, 1995) to compensate for the reduction of often already inadequate support. They create a crisis in reproduction that

Excerpts from *Worlding Women* by J. Pettman. Reprinted by permission of Taylor & Francis.

terrorises poorer women and children (Afshar and Dennis, 1992; Imam, 1994). States' attempts to promote export-orientated growth disorganise and feminise the labourforce, removing any protection from casual workers, who become super-exploitable and expendable labour.

One overall effect is the feminisation of poverty, or the global impoverishing of women and their children, though it affects many poorer men, too. Facing state cuts, falling wages, increasing unemployment and growing poverty, household survival strategies include more informal economic activity, taking in lodgers, selling homemade goods or food and providing services on the side, including prostitution (Smith and Wallerstein, 1992). It is difficult to gather and assess information here because of different notions of what 'work' is, and the privatised nature of informal and outwork, which is so often women's work.

Women's experiences of work are also mediated by age and lifecycle changes. The term 'women' is often revealed on closer inspection to include many young women and children of both sexes. The cheap labour of the global assembly line is mainly very young women, 'illeducated teenagers' (Standing, 1992: 368). Child labour is a massive part of the IPE [International Political Economy] globally, and especially in poorer states, where children as young as six or seven toil in agriculture, factories and sweatshops, in domestic labour and sex work (Fyfe, 1989; Myers, 1991). Within their families, too, girls do considerable house- and child-care work, often compromising any opportunities for schooling. Young children of both sexes contribute essential labour on family farms, plots of land, in seasonal work and household-based production (Kanbargi, 1991; Bonnett, 1993). Often it is children's labour in small factories and businesses that provides the only, though minute, family income. There is much illicit trade in children, for factory and housework, and for sex work. Recruitment procedures include buying children from impoverished parents or those unable to meet debt repayments, making children bonded labourers who are supposed to work to pay off the 'debt'; a trade in bodies with pain for both children and the relinquishing parents. In these circumstances, the conditions under which they work justify the description of child slavery (Lee-Wright, 1990).

Many children and young women are migrant workers, moving from rural areas to towns, cities, factories, EPZs [export-processing zones], the streets, bars and brothels. Many more young women are part of the trade in women's bodies across state borders or to oil-rich Middle East or rich western and East Asian states as workers, including as sex workers or mail-order brides. This traffic in women reflects the hierarchy of states and wealth in the IPE. It reflects, too, the growing feminisation of the changing international division of labour, and is part of an emerging international political economy of sex.

Women's working outside the home and especially travelling away for work disrupts family forms and roles. As many younger women move away, older women acquire more work, including at times responsibility for the care and upbringing of children of their daughters or nieces. Many female-headed households are now headed by grandmothers. This is especially so where AIDS has devastated those of young and early middle years, as in some parts of Central and East Africa (G. Seidel, 1993).

Not all women in paid employment are super-exploited, though very few anywhere earn the income or have the opportunities of their equivalent men. But class is a crucial dimension of women's lives. Elite and middle-class women everywhere live in conditions of material security that set them apart dramatically from poor women, though in neotraditional families the cost may be heightened surveillance and control. And in many states, some women's freedom to take paid work depends on their employing other women to share their domestic labour and childcare responsibilities. Class, alongside racialised and nationalised differences, are fundamental axes of power and subordination, within as well as between states.

We cannot make sense of productive relations, of the growth and nature of EPZs, of TNCs [transnational corporations] and the impact of current economic crises if we do not gender our account. We cannot simply add women, for the sexual division of labour is constitutive of the international division of labour. As well, we cannot make sense of different women's lives, their work or their status, if we do not locate those women within the international political economy, and assess the impact on women of the growing crises in much of the world in terms of trade dependency, dependent development and debt dependency (Sen and Grown, 1987). These impacts are not limited to the third world, or to the dramatically restructuring transition states, but shape state labour markets, the welfare state and corporatist labour politics in first-world states as well. Women's different but related location within a global political economy both links and divides women of the world.

* * *

A fundamental split in current development debates is over whether the struggle is to incorporate women more equally into development planning and programs, or whether it is 'development' that needs problematising and challenging. This latter is especially so for those who critique development within patterns of global domination and subordination; and those who argue that understanding the relations between women and development means listening to and learning from women in different places and different struggles. The problem is not how to bring women into development. Development is already dependent on women's work as cheap labour, in informal and subsistence sectors, in household work and community care.

BIBLIOGRAPHY

Afshar, Haleh and Dennis, Carolyne eds 1992, *Women and Structural Adjustment Policies in the Third World*, Macmillan, London.

Bonnet, Michel 1993, 'Child Labour in Africa', *International Labour Review*, vol. 132, no. 3, pp. 371–90.

Fyfe, Alex 1989, *Child Labour*, Polity Press, Cambridge.

Imam, Ayesha 1994, 'SAP is really sapping us', *New Internationalist*, July, pp. 12–13.

Kanbargi, Ramesh ed. 1991, *Child Labour in the Indian Sub-continent: Dimensions and Implications*, Sage, New Delhi.

Lee-Wright, Peter 1990, *Child Slaves*, Earthscan, London.

Myers, William ed. 1991, *Protecting Working Children*, Zed Books/UNICEF, London.

Seidel, Gill 1993, 'Women at Risk: Gender and AIDS in Africa', *Disasters*, vol. 17, no. 2, pp. 133–42.

Sen, Gita and Grown, Caren 1987, *Development, Crises and Alternative Visions: Third World Women's Perspectives*, Monthly Review Press, New York.

Smith, Joan and Wallerstein, Immanuel 1992, *Creating and Transforming Households in the World Economy*, Cambridge University Press, Cambridge and New York.

Standing, Guy 1992, 'Global Feminization through Flexible Labour' in *The Political Economy of Development and Underdevelopment*, eds C. Wilber and K. Jameson, McGraw Hill, New York.

UNICEF 1995, *The State of the World's Children*, Oxford University Press, Oxford.

Privatization and Urban Issues: A Global Perspective

–William K. Tabb

William K. Tabb is professor of economics at Queens College, CUNY. He received his Ph.D. from the University of Wisconsin in 1968. "Privatization and Urban Issues: A Global Perspective" appeared originally in Monthly Review *in February 2001.*

In my remarks today, I want to situate privatization generally, and its manifestations in the urban context specifically, in a global perspective. I am employing the phrase "global perspective" not in its common usage (to mean a comparison of national patterns of privatization) but rather in order to consider the phenomenon that has come to be known as globalization and the impact of this capacious

"Privatization and Urban Issues: A Global Perspective" by William K. Tabb. Copyright 2001 Monthly Review Press. Reprinted by permission of Monthly Review Foundation.

analytic category on urban policy and governance issues—one of the most central of which is privatization.

I know you have been visiting urban revitalization projects—especially that cutting-edge American contribution, the business improvement district (BID), of which many city officials and real-estate people are so proud. For those of you who knew or knew of New York in the bad old days of filthy streets and street people, the current reduced numbers of visible homeless and reduced amounts of crime and litter are likely to be impressive. The city looks good, quite good indeed. For the more affluent, the city is a fine place and if one believes in trickle-down social policy, privatization has been a remarkable success.

Let me be clear that as a matter of personal consumption, I enjoy many of the fruits of privatization. I have occasion to visit Wall Street, where the studio of our local community radio station is oddly located. I do last-minute preparations for my show in J. P. Morgan's atrium, where I sit in resplendent surroundings resembling a European cathedral, complete with vaulted ceilings, at a table by an indoor fountain and sip my cappuccino at a table provided by the management and subsidized by generous tax concessions by taxpayers. I work extensively at the research facilities of the New York Public Library, the one with the lions in front, which has recently been given a facelift by corporate sponsors, its shabby facilities refurbished handsomely. The park behind the library—once a haven for derelicts and drug dealers—has been transformed. It has a large staff picking up trash and rearranging the outdoor chairs and is policed in a low-key but effective way. The gardening staff is first-rate and the beautiful park attracts thousands of office workers from surrounding buildings where, on a sunny day, we all enjoy the lawn as we eat our lunches—perhaps purchased from one of the booths in the park. The surrounding buildings support the cost of maintaining the park. I suspect the higher rents they now receive make this a pretty good investment. For those with serious money there is a gorgeous restaurant in the park. In nice weather, its outdoor bar attracts a youthful crowd wearing clothes that cost more than most New Yorkers earn in a month or even in a year.

It is good for the city's economy that business improvement districts have gentrified a city in which the local government was unable to provide such services. The same corporations that demanded the lower taxes that starved the public sector have found a privatized way of paying for the services they want while avoiding paying for public schools, emergency rooms at the hospitals, shelters for the homeless, or subsidized housing for the working class.

I want to introduce some of these distributional issues by first looking at the globalization process and its impacts and then making a comparison to the restructuring that has accompanied globalization writ large with the transformation of urban spaces.

Globalization is often seen as the growing, and in some versions unprecedented, international integration of economic life. It is typically described in terms of the dramatic increase in trade and foreign direct investment relative to production, the surge in international financial transactions, and growth of global economic institutions such as multinational corporations and international organizations. There is general awareness that globalization is characterized by very different levels of global mobility, according to which elements of the economy are being referred to. That mobility is greater the more abstract and less human is the potential engine. Finance is the most global part of the world economy, while workers are the least.

There is, of course, this economic base to globalization, driven as it is by market forces and a new type of scale economies, which come from Internet access to arm's-length suppliers and customers, and to wider contracting alliances. The corresponding governance discussion has been about the norms and standards appropriate under the new circumstances, and the policies and institutions suitable to the more open political economy. However, when we raise a social justice perspective on the unfairness of such outcomes we are told that the market is just too efficient or simply just too powerful and therefore must dominate social and political outcomes. The point is really that the opportunities, costs, and benefits of globalization reflect capitalist relations.

Globalization has a material basis in technological change and is manifest in increased trade, investment, and financial flows but centrally it reflects enhanced corporate power and an accompanying ideological shift in favor of free markets, and the imposition of *laissez-faire* policies. The ideological shift that accompanies globalization, which is captured in the word neoliberalism, needs to be centrally understood in terms of the power shift in favor of corporate dominance. The discussion is not about what people deserve from their governments but about the transfer of power to private actors. In fact, an unexpectedly close synonym to contemporary globalization is *privatization*. It is this privatization that is being celebrated by the officials and urban entrepreneurs you are meeting with and that you have been brought together to learn to implement.

It would be surprising if the same sort of downsizing of government and privatization that are at the heart of globalization as the expansion of capitalist social relations were not occurring at the level of our cities. Indeed, at the urban level something of the same conversation is going on. Making cities work better is discussed in a context of asserting that government cannot do the job, that markets can and that privatizing as much as possible is the answer. Omitted from such conversations are the incidence of benefits and the costs to working-class citizens in terms of the services they can expect for their tax dollars and the decreased power they have over public decisions on wages and working conditions. The public sector has not always done the job many of us would like but at least through the political process, social justice issues are a legitimate concern. In the market, it is one dollar, one vote. In societies with very unequal distributions of income and wealth, power accumulates in the hands of the relative few. Without a progressive role for government and public policy, the concerns of the few take precedence over the needs of the many. This is as true at the local level as at the global one.

In the new urban policy-making of privatization, it is assumed that what is good for real-estate and other business interests will be best for the rest of the city's residents. After all, protecting and enhancing the tax base and promoting job creation is the key to wider prosperity and an ability to pay for social programs. This is the same rationale that was offered for globalization's restructurings. Economic growth and greater efficiency will eventually be good for everyone and there is no alternative in any case. This conventional wisdom further suggests that efforts to help the poor and provide social services to the working class are simply too expensive and better done through privatization and the market. Government failure is prominent and the market can do better.

There is little awareness in such conversations that it was the market which created urban problems and government intervention came about as a result. This is the case not only in the sense that profits are privatized and social costs externalized onto the state but also in the sense that as capitalism grows and changes it transforms the built environment. The deterioration of our central cities was part of a long postindustrial transformation, just as their revitalization is a result of their new economic base in services—banking and communications, tourism and health services, legal and accounting, advertising and other business services. The detritus of the old industrial base and the abandoned victims of age, alcoholism, and drugs have been removed—out of sight now and so out of mind, no longer a concern for policy makers who, as in earlier eras of slum clearance and urban renewal, celebrate the physical revitalization of urban space.

The city's strategy had been to deny services for the poor by making it more and more difficult to obtain those services and redefining entitlements out of existence (except where forced by court challenges to begrudgingly, and to as limited an extent as they could get away with, restore benefits). In New York, this has consisted of forcing people who want to apply for entitlements to suffer long lines, endure repeated visits, and produce obscure documentation. The city even denies people food stamps, a federal program to feed the malnourished that is funded by the Federal government. By criminalizing poverty, closing public spaces, removing benches that people might sleep on, the city discouraged and harassed the poor.

It is not too much of a stretch to say that the fiscal crisis of the cities has been used in a manner similar to the leverage gained on debtor states experiencing financial crisis and balance of payments problems. The rescue is predicated on accepting the entry of foreign investors on favorable terms. National assets are privatized; local telephone and electric companies, for example, which lose money are sold to private investors. This raises money for the governments from the sale price and from the cessation of state subsidies. The new owners may improve service. They almost always raise prices, which forces the working class to reduce its consumption. The improved service which may result is distributed through the market to those who can afford to pay. The public sector does not make a profit because it is charged with delivering services to those who need them. The increased reliance on the private sector makes ability to pay the criteria for service. Cost savings can occur through private companies hiring lower-waged workers who do not receive the same benefit packages as public-sector workers.

If previously taxation was based on ability to pay, the poor are further impoverished. They must now buy a commodity where before they received a service, even if admittedly sometimes an unsatisfactory one, while the rich save because they no longer have to pay taxes to support the provision of public services for the masses. They buy only for their own requirements, thus allowing higher quality at lower cost since they pay only for their own consumption after privatization. This is why the affluent always oppose public provision of goods and services, preferring (for example) to pay to have their own garbage removed and offering the same option to the residents of low-income communities, which had received public services out of general tax revenues and now go without services they cannot afford. The reason garbage collection and fire protection were made public services is because disease and fire can spread to wealthy neighborhoods and so it was in the interests of everyone that service delivery was high enough to prevent contagion. Providing subsidized mass transit came to be a public function because private companies were caught in a cycle of rising costs, which was met by raising fares but which led to loss of ridership and bankruptcy. Employers gained from transportation subsidies that allowed them to pay lower wages to workers who must commute.

Because globalization has increased the bargaining power of capital, the most mobile factor of production, labor—not so mobile—has been forced to bear more of the tax burden. Attracting and retaining mobile capital has required greater subsidies to business at the expense of labor. When advocates of privatization say that "BIDs work," they mean that when local governments grant the power to tax to wealthy subunits of a city, the organizations created can target provision of quality public service to the immediate area—services such as the removal of litter, the staffing of local guides to direct visitors, and provision of public amenities and their maintenance—at lower cost than if the corporate beneficiaries from such tightly targeted benefits had to contribute their share of taxes to provide amenities to all neighborhoods in the city.

Is the resurgence of the downtowns of global cities a bad thing? Not necessarily. But let us understand that local elites prefer privatization for these reasons, and let us not confuse their class-based criteria for those that would prevail in a democratic society premised on inclusion and equity. Privatization, BIDs in particular, allow a reoccupation of public space by affluent users. While, in the better instances, some social services have been provided, there has been little or no monitoring and we simply do not know where the poor have gone. Poverty, drug addiction, and homelessness are unlikely to have disappeared but they are largely invisible in the downtown areas. The longest economic expansion in our economy's history has been the major factor in the change. It remains to be seen what will happen when a downturn comes.

In the best of times, the United States does not address unmet needs for housing, education, and healthcare. It accepts city government's efforts, such as BIDs, to help the corporate sector secede from the local communities in which it does business. What will happen when the business cycle turns? We will surely be told then that because of the fiscal crisis it is not the time to address social justice concerns. Yet now, in the supposed best of times, those who raise these issues (even if merely to win some working class votes in an election) are accused of waging class warfare.

If public services are inefficient, we should ask why this is the case and what can be done. But this is not an excuse for expecting redistributionally-based services to the less affluent to pay for themselves. The market test is an inappropriate one. Where privatization has occurred, regulation needs to accompany grants of monopoly privilege to for-profit providers and workers and the public must be protected. Progressive city planners forced to work within a framework of privatization can raise questions about what taxpayers get in return for subsidies. They can insist on recapturing subsidies when promises of job creation and public amenities do not materialize. They can insist that cities comply with agreements made and that cities not give away the store. The magnitude of real costs and benefits and their incidence need to be carefully studied.

There is work for progressive urbanists in making these relationships clear and in advocating for those who resist the depredations of capital in urban space. The defense of the social and a renewed focus on the needs of people over profit are always central tasks. The bottom line however, in the phrase so overused by the privatizers, is that we should be talking not about greater market efficiency in an irrational system, but a different system. Not one in which the people are always on the defense—trying to protect themselves from further inroads of the profit logic, upward redistributions in land use, and appropriation of public resources by the powerful—but the creation of a society in which people's needs come first and the hold of class oppression is broken. But that very necessary discussion is not on the agenda of those who have financed this gathering, so you will have to excuse me for mentioning it.

Plunder and Profit

–David Moberg

David Moberg is a senior editor of In These Times. *Before joining the publication, he completed his work for a Ph.D. in anthropology at the University of Chicago and worked for* Newsweek. *He has received fellowships from both the John D. and Catherine T. MacArthur Foundation and the Nation Institute for research on the new global economy. His article "Plunder and Profit" appeared in* In These Times, *March 29, 2004.*

In September 1999, Bolivian officials signed a 40-year contract with a private company named Aguas del Tunari to take over the municipal water system of Cochabamba, the country's third largest city. The company, largely owned by U.S. construction giant Bechtel, was the sole bidder for the contract, which guaranteed 15 percent annual profit in inflation-indexed dollars.

With the encouragement of the International Monetary Fund (IMF) and the World Bank, since 1985 Bolivian governments have sold national public assets to foreign investors and opened their markets to global trade. Despite the promise of development by following the "Washington consensus" of economic liberalization, it remained the poorest country in Latin America. But World Bank officials still insisted that Bolivia privatize Cochabamba's water utility and that residents, no matter how poor, pay full cost of the service without subsidy.

Two months after Bechtel's subsidiary took over, it roughly tripled local water rates, telling the poor they could pay one-fourth of their income for water or have the spigot shut off. There were massive protests for several months until the contract was cancelled.

But a few months after signing the contract, Bechtel surreptitiously added new investors and reincorporated its subsidiary in the Netherlands. When it lost the contract, Bechtel sued Bolivia—under terms of a bilateral investment treaty between Bolivia and Netherlands—for damages of at least $25 million for loss of profits it might have made, even though it had invested less than $1 million. Last month, the Bolivian government argued in secret hearings before an investment tribunal affiliated with the World Bank that the treaty doesn't apply, partly because Dutch nationals never controlled Aguas del Tunari.

"Plunder and Profit" by David Moberg from *In These Times*, March 29, 2004. Copyright © 2004. Reprinted by permission.

Cochabamba remains a celebrated battleground in the intensifying worldwide dispute over the privatization of public services, from water and electrical utilities to education, healthcare and pensions. Its ongoing legal struggle reflects the ways in which poor countries often are pressured to privatize a wide range of public assets and services, and then locked into failed policies by international trade agreements.

Free Market Faith

Rich countries—working through international institutions like the World Bank—rarely help poor countries modernize and strengthen public services. But they often push them to privatize and commercialize public services, a move that they themselves would never make. Leading the tide of globalization, international financial institutions are aggressively and undemocratically promoting an ideological agenda of privatization and commercialization.

"The IMF, the World Bank and the World Trade Organization care about dismantling the state," says Nancy Alexander, director of the Citizens' Network on Essential Services (CNES), a research and advocacy group. "They're faith-based organizations. They don't care who dismantles the state."

International financial institutions claim that such reforms help reduce poverty, but they often simply are promoting the interests of multinational corporations in water, energy, telecommunications and other industries. Multinational corporate investment in privatization peaked in the late '90s, and many firms have since pulled back in response to protests or financial difficulties. So the World Bank, IMF and related institutions are increasingly offering financial aid, subsidies and guarantees to private multinationals to induce them to privatize.

"In the end, it's not an argument about economics. That's not the bottom line," says Doug Hellinger, executive director of the Development Group on Alternative Policies, which is critical of the IMF and World Bank. "It's ideological, but it's also about giving access to companies on terrific terms. It's really about the IMF representing its northern countries and their corporations."

The World Bank theoretically acknowledges a role for the public sector, but in practice it has pushed privatization since the mid-'80s. This year's budget for water privatization, for example, is triple last year's, and over the past decade the portion of the bank's lending for water projects tied to privatization soared. In 2002 it adopted a strategy that emphasized development led by private corporations, and it works closely with the WTO to impose on poor countries the kinds of pro-corporate policies richer countries have the freedom to negotiate.

Indirect Pressure

When countries suffer from financial crises or crippling debt, the IMF and World Bank often insist on privatization of state-owned enterprises, utilities and social services as a condition for financial help. But sometimes, Alexander explains, they push privatization indirectly. For example, they typically require cuts in government budgets, public services and aid to localities. They press for decentralization of public services, dismantling of utilities into smaller units, assessment of market prices for services and elimination of cross-subsidies that may reduce costs for the poor. Financially squeezed by these policies, municipalities may be tempted to privatize the decentralized services. The multinationals then cherry pick the most profitable pieces serving more affluent urban areas, leaving the government responsible for poor and unprofitable rural areas or urban shantytowns.

While some public services in developing countries work well, others are deeply flawed. But as CNES economist Tim Kessler argues, the World Bank acts as if the only alternative is privatization, not improving public services with outside financial and technical aid and with greater citizen accountability. In any case, privatized utilities need strong public regulation, which is difficult and expensive to do well. Paradoxically, weak and corrupt governments, whose public services could most benefit from reform, are least able to regulate privatized systems. Often they sell public goods on the cheap to cronies and patrons, making privatization really "briberization," says former World Bank chief economist Joseph Stiglitz.

Management Matters

Advocates argue that privatization increases efficiency and investment, fosters competition, shrinks deficits and improves services. There are many instances, such as in Chile, where privatized public enterprises increased efficiency and improved service. But in developed countries public utilities generally are as efficient as or better than private.

In developing countries, there also are countless horror stories of price gouging, poor service, meager investment and discrimination against the poor from every continent and in every arena of privatization. For example, Suez, one of two multinationals controlling at least 70 percent of the world's private water contracts, recently lost or abandoned water operations in Argentina, Philippines and Puerto Rico once hailed as model successes. A newly released study by a network of citizens groups that collaborated with the World Bank, "Structural Adjustment: The SAPRI Report," concluded that privatization did not accelerate growth and the form of ownership did not determine efficiency of services as much as management policy.

Despite the failures of privatization, the World Bank and IMF have not shifted their focus to strengthening and democratizing public services. Instead, they are increasing funding to subsidize, to commercially guarantee and to promote privatization (as head of an expert panel on water infrastructure sponsored by the World Bank and multinational water companies). Former IMF managing director Michel Camdessus who recommended last year that there should be more subsidies and guarantees for water privatizers and that the bank should deal more with state and local governments (which typically are less savvy in negotiating with giant multinationals than national governments).

At the WTO, the richer countries want to include more services under the General Agreement on Trade in Services (GATS), potentially opening historically public functions to competition that would benefit multinational service corporations and would indirectly privatize. Once a service is opened under GATS, countries cannot reverse course—for example, make healthcare an exclusively public service—without paying every country that claims it lost a trade opportunity. GATS rules also would severely restrict domestic regulation of service industries.

If the rich countries, along with the World Bank, IMF and WTO, persist in their current privatizing strategies, Cochabamba may turn out to have been an early skirmish in a much wider war.

The WTO and Globalization

–Michael Parenti

Author and lecturer Michael Parenti received his Ph.D. in political science from Yale University and has taught at a number of colleges and universities in the United States and abroad. He is the author of 18 books and some 250 articles. The discussion of the WTO that follows is taken from his widely used college text Democracy for the Few *(seventh ed.), published by Thompson Wadsworth.*

The goal of the transnational corporation is to become truly transnational, poised above the sovereign power of any particular nation, while being serviced by the sovereign powers of all nations. Cyril Siewert, chief financial officer of Colgate Palmolive Company, could have been speaking for all transnationals when he remarked, "The United States doesn't have an automatic call on our [corporation's] resources. There is no mindset that puts this country first."[1]

"The WTO and Globalization," Michael Parenti, from *Democracy for the Few* (7th ed.), Thompson Wadsworth, 2002, pp. 171–175.

With NAFTA [North American Free Trade Agreement] and GATT [General Agreement on Tariffs and Trade], this becomes quite evident. The giant transnationals have been elevated above the sovereign powers of nation-states. The GATT agreements created the WTO [World Trade Organization], an international association of over 120 signatory nations. The WTO has the authority to prevent, overrule, or dilute any laws of any nation deemed to burden the investment and market prerogatives of transnational corporations. It sets up three-member panels composed of "trade specialists" who act as judges over economic issues, placing themselves above the national sovereignty and popular control of any nation, thereby insuring the supremacy of international finance capital, a process called "globalization," and treated as an inevitable natural development beneficial to all.

Elected by no one and drawn from the corporate world, these panelists meet in secret and can have investment stakes in the very issues they adjudicate, being limited by no conflict-of-interest provisions. Their function is to allow the transnational companies to do whatever they like without any restraints or regulations placed on them by any country. Not one of GATT's five hundred pages of rules and restrictions are directed against private business; all are against governments. Signatory governments must lower tariffs, end farm subsidies, treat foreign companies the same as domestic ones, honor all corporate patent claims, and obey the rulings of a permanent elite bureaucracy, the WTO. Should a country refuse to change its laws when a WTO panel so dictates, the WTO can impose fines or international trade sanctions, depriving the resistant country of needed markets and materials.[2]

Acting as the supreme global adjudicator, the WTO has ruled against laws deemed "barriers to free trade." It has forced Japan to accept greater pesticide residues in imported food. It has kept Guatemala from outlawing deceptive advertising on baby food. It has eliminated the ban in various countries on asbestos, fuel-economy, and emission standards for cars. And it has ruled against marine-life protection laws and the ban on endangered-species products. The European Union's prohibition on the import of hormone-ridden U.S. beef had overwhelming popular support throughout Europe, but a three-member WTO panel decided the ban was an illegal restraint on trade. The decision on beef put in jeopardy a host of other food-import regulations based on health concerns. The WTO overturned a portion of the U.S. Clean Air Act banning certain additives in gasoline because it interfered with imports from foreign refineries. And the WTO overturned that portion of the U.S. Endangered Species Act forbidding the import of shrimp caught with nets that failed to protect sea turtles.[3]

"Free" trade is not fair trade; it benefits strong nations at the expense of weaker ones, and rich interests at the expense of the rest of us, circumventing what little democratic sovereignty we have been able to achieve.[4] "Globalization" means turning the clock back on many twentieth-century reforms: no freedom to boycott products, no prohibitions against child labor, no guaranteed living wage or benefits, no public services that might conceivably compete with private profit-making, no health and safety protections that might cost the corporations any money.

GATT allows multinationals to impose monopoly property rights on indigenous and communal agriculture. In this way agribusiness can better penetrate locally self-sufficient communities and monopolize their resources. Ralph Nader gives the example of the neem tree, whose extracts contain naturally pesticidal and medicinal properties. Cultivated for centuries in India, the tree has attracted the attention of various pharmaceutical companies, who filed monopoly patents, causing mass protests by Indian farmers. As dictated by the WTO, the pharmaceuticals now have exclusive control over the marketing of neem tree products, a ruling that is being reluctantly enforced in India. Tens of thousands of erstwhile independent farmers must now work for the powerful pharmaceuticals on terms set by them.

In a similar vein, the WTO ruled that the U.S. corporation RiceTec has the patent rights to the many varieties of basmati rice grown for centuries by India's farmers. It also ruled that a Japanese corporation had exclusive rights in the world to produce curry powder. In these instances, "free trade" means monopoly corporate control. Such developments caused Malaysian prime minister Mahathir Mohamad to observe:

> We now have a situation where theft of genetic resources by western biotech TNCs [transnational corporations] enables them to make huge profits by producing patented genetic mutations of these same materials. What depths have we sunk to in the global marketplace when nature's gifts to the poor may not be protected but their modifications by the rich become exclusive property?
>
> If the current behavior of the rich countries is anything to go by, globalization simply means the breaking down of the borders of countries so that those with the capital and the goods will be free to dominate the markets.[5]

Under the free-trade agreements, all public services are now at risk. A public service can be charged with causing "lost market opportunities" for business, or creating an unfair subsidy. To offer one instance: the single-payer automobile insurance program proposed by the province of Ontario, Canada, was declared "unfair competition." Ontario could have its public auto insurance only if it paid U.S. insurance companies what they estimated would be their present and *future* losses in Ontario auto insurance sales, a prohibitive cost for the province. Thus the citizens of Ontario were not allowed to exercise their democratic sovereign power to institute an alternative not-for-profit auto insurance system.

Education is a trillion-dollar industry, and private corporations want a big piece of it. If the issue is ever brought before the WTO or whatever trade council, public education and protests against corporate-run schools could be seen as a barrier to free-market investments and lost market earnings for corporations involved in privatizing schools. It is probably only the fear of a heated public outcry that keeps the forces of privatization from moving more precipitously into the "education market."

International "free trade" agreements like GATT and NAFTA have hastened the corporate acquisition of local markets, squeezing out smaller businesses and worker collectives. Under NAFTA, better-paying U.S. jobs were lost as firms closed shop and contracted out to the cheaper Mexican labor market. At the same time thousands of Mexican small companies were forced out of business. Mexico was flooded with cheap, high-tech, mass-produced corn and dairy products from giant

U.S. agribusiness firms (themselves heavily subsidized by the U.S. government), driving small Mexican farmers and distributors into bankruptcy, displacing large numbers of poor peasants. The newly arrived U.S. companies in Mexico have offered extremely low-paying jobs, and highly unsafe and unhealthy work conditions.

Under NAFTA, the U.S.-based Ethyl Corporation sued the Canadian government for $250 million in "lost business opportunities" and "interference with trade" because Canada banned MMT, an Ethyl-produced gasoline additive considered carcinogenic by Canadian officials. Fearing they would lose the case, Canadian officials caved in, agreeing to lift the ban on MMT, pay Ethyl $10 million in compensation, and issue a public statement calling MMT "safe." California also banned the unhealthy additive; this time a Canadian-based Ethyl company sued California under NAFTA for placing an unfair burden on free trade.[6]

We are told that to remain competitive under GATT, we will have to increase our output while reducing our labor and production costs, in other words, work harder for less. We will have to spend less on social services and introduce more wage concessions, more restructuring, deregulation, and privatization. Only then might we cope with the impersonal forces of globalization that are sweeping us along. In fact, there is nothing impersonal about these forces. "Free trade" agreements, including new ones that have not yet been submitted to Congress, have been consciously planned by big business and its governmental minions over a period of years in pursuit of a deregulated world economy that undermines all democratic checks upon business practices, and leaves all the world's population in the merciless embrace of a global free market. The people of any one province, state, or nation are now finding it increasingly difficult to get their governments to impose protective regulations or develop new forms of public-sector production out of fear of being overruled by the WTO or some other international trade panel.[7]

NOTES

1. Quoted in *New York Times*, May 21, 1989.

2. See Lori Wallach and Michelle Sforza, *The WTO* (New York: Seven Stories, 2000); and John R. MacArthur, *The Selling of "Free Trade": NAFTA, Washington, and the Subversion of American Democracy* (New York: Hill & Wang, 2000).

3. *New York Times*, April 30, 1996, and May 9, 1997; *Washington Post*, October 13, 1998.

4. From a report by the United Nations Development Program, *New York Times*, July 13, 1999.

5. Quoted in *People's Weekly World*, December 7, 1996.

6. MacArthur, *The Selling of "Free Trade"*; John Ross, "Tortilla Wars," *Progressive*, June 1999; and Sarah Anderson and John Cavanagh, "Nafta's Unhappy Anniversary," *New York Times*, February 7, 1995.

7. For a concise but thorough treatment, see Steven Shrybman, *A Citizen's Guide to the World Trade Organization* (Ottawa and Toronto: Canadian Center for Policy Alternatives and James Lorimer, 1999).

The Globalization of Poverty
–Michel Chossudovsky

Michel Chossudovsky is professor of economics at the University of Ottowa in Canada. He has taught as visiting professor at academic institutions in Western Europe, Latin America, and Southeast Asia; has acted as economic adviser to governments of developing countries; and has worked as a consultant for a number of international organizations. The selection that follows is from his 2003 book The Globalization of Poverty and the New World Order, *published by Global Outlook.*

Since the early 1980s, the "macro-economic stabilization" and structural adjustment programs imposed by the IMF and the World Bank on developing countries (as a condition for the renegotiation of their external debt) have led to the impoverishment of hundreds of millions of people. Contrary to the spirit of the Bretton Woods agreement, which was predicated on "economic reconstruction", and the stability of major exchange rates, the structural adjustment program has contributed largely to destabilizing national currencies and ruining the economies of developing countries.

Internal purchasing power has collapsed, famines have erupted, health clinics and schools have been closed down and hundreds of millions of children have been denied the right to primary education. In several regions of the developing world, the reforms have been conducive to a resurgence of infectious diseases including tuberculosis, malaria and cholera. While the World Bank's mandate consists of "combating poverty" and protecting the environment, its support for large-scale hydroelectric and agro-industrial projects has also speeded up the process of deforestation and the destruction of the natural environment, leading to the forced displacement and eviction of several million people.

Global Geopolitics

In the wake of the Cold War, macro-economic restructuring has supported global geopolitical interests including US foreign policy. Structural adjustment has been used to undermine the economies of the former Soviet Bloc and dismantle its system of state enterprises. Since the late 1980s, the IMF-World Bank "economic medicine" has been imposed on Eastern Europe, Yugoslavia and the former Soviet Union with devastating economic and social consequences.

"The Globalization of Poverty" by Michel Chossudovsky is reprinted by permission of the author.

While the mechanism of enforcement is distinct, the structural adjustment program has, since the 1990s, been applied also in the developed countries. Whereas the macro-economic therapies (under the jurisdiction of national governments) tend to be less brutal than those imposed on the South and the East, the theoretical and ideological underpinnings are broadly similar. The same global financial interests are served. Monetarism is applied on a world scale and the process of global economic restructuring strikes also at the very heart of the rich countries. The consequences are unemployment, low wages and the marginalization of large sectors of the population. Social expenditures are curtailed and many of the achievements of the welfare state are repealed. State policies have encouraged the destruction of small and medium-sized enterprises. Low levels of food consumption and malnutrition are also hitting the urban poor in the rich countries. According to a recent study, 30 million people in the United States are classified as "hungry".[1]

The impacts of structural adjustment, including the derogation of the social rights of women and the detrimental environmental consequences of economic reform, have been amply documented. While the Bretton Woods institutions have acknowledged "the social impact of adjustment", no shift in policy direction is in sight. In fact, since the early 1990s, coinciding with the collapse of the Eastern bloc, the IMF-World Bank policy prescriptions (now imposed in the name of "poverty alleviation") have become increasingly harsh and unyielding.

Social Polarization and the Concentration of Wealth

In the South, the East and the North, a privileged social minority has accumulated vast amounts of wealth at the expense of the large majority of the population. This new international financial order feeds on human poverty and the destruction of the natural environment. It generates social apartheid, encourages racism and ethnic strife, undermines the rights of women and often precipitates countries into destructive confrontations between nationalities. Moreover, these reforms—when applied simultaneously in more than 150 countries—are conducive to a "globalization of poverty", a process which undermines human livelihood and destroys civil society in the South, East and the North.

IMF Economic Medicine

Under IMF jurisdiction, the same "menu" of budgetary austerity, devaluation, trade liberalization and privatization is applied simultaneously in more than 150 indebted countries. Debtor nations forego economic sovereignty and control over fiscal and monetary policy, the Central Bank and the Ministry of Finance are reorganized (often with the complicity of the local bureaucracies), state institutions are undone and an "economic tutelage" is installed. A "parallel government", which bypasses civil society, is established by the international financial institutions (IFIs). Countries which do not conform to the IMF's "performance targets" are blacklisted.

While adopted in the name of "democracy" and so-called "good governance", the structural adjustment program requires the strengthening of the internal security apparatus and the military intelligence apparatus: political repression—with the collusion of the Third World élites—supports a parallel process of "economic repression".

"Good governance" and the holding of multi-party elections are added conditions imposed by donors and creditors, yet the very nature of the economic reforms precludes a genuine democratization—i.e. their implementation invariably requires (contrary to the "spirit of Anglo-Saxon liberalism") the backing of the military and the authoritarian state. Structural adjustment promotes bogus institutions and a fake parliamentary democracy which, in turn, supports the process of economic restructuring.

Throughout the Third World, the situation is one of social desperation and the hopelessness of a population impoverished by the interplay of market forces. Anti-SAP riots and popular uprisings are brutally repressed: **Caracas, 1989**: President Carlos Andres Perez, after having rhetorically denounced the IMF of practicing "an economic totalitarianism which kills not with bullets but with famine", declares a state of emergency and sends regular units of the infantry and the marines into the slum areas (*barrios de ranchos*) on the hills overlooking the capital. The Caracas anti-IMF riots had been sparked off as a result of a 200 percent increase in the price of bread. Men, women and children were fired upon indiscriminately. "The Caracas morgue was reported to have up to 200 bodies of people killed in the first three days (. . .) and warned that it was running out of coffins."[2] Unofficially, more than a thousand people were killed; **Tunis, January 1984**: the bread riots instigated largely by unemployed youth protesting the rise of food prices; **Nigeria, 1989**: the anti-SAP student riots leading to the closing of six of the country's universities by the Armed Forces Ruling Council; **Morocco, 1990**: a general strike and a popular uprising against the government's IMF-sponsored reforms; **Mexico, 1993**: the insurrection of the Zapatista Liberation Army in the Chiapas region of southern Mexico; protest movements against the IMF reforms in the Russian Federation and the storming of the Russian parliament in 1993; mass protest movement of the people of Ecuador against the adoption of the US dollar as their national currency in January 2000 leading to the resignation of the President; **Cochabamba, Bolivia, April 2000**: thousands of peasants protest against the privatization of the country's water resources and the imposition of user fees.

The list is long.

Economic Genocide

Structural adjustment is conducive to a form of "economic genocide" which is carried out through the conscious and deliberate manipulation of market forces. When compared to previous periods of colonial history (e.g. forced labor and slavery), its social impact is devastating. Structural adjustment programs affect directly the livelihood of more than four billion people. The application of the structural adjustment program in a large number of individual debtor countries favors the internationalization of macroeconomic policy under the direct control of the IMF and the World Bank acting on behalf of powerful financial and political interests (e.g. the Paris and London Clubs, the G7). This new form of economic and political domination—a form of "market colonialism"—subordinates people and governments through the seemingly "neutral" interplay of market forces. The Washington-based international bureaucracy has been entrusted by international creditors and multinational corporations with the execution of a global economic design, which affects the livelihood of more than 80 percent of the world's population. At no time in history has the "free" market—operating in the world through the instruments of macro-economics—played such an important role in shaping the destiny of sovereign nations.

Destroying the National Economy

The restructuring of the world economy, under the guidance of the Washington-based financial institutions, increasingly denies individual developing countries the possibility of building a national economy: the internationalization of macro-economic policy transforms countries into open economic territories and national economies into "reserves" of cheap labor and natural resources. The application of the IMF's "economic medicine" tends to further depress world commodity prices because it forces individual countries to simultaneously gear their national economies towards a shrinking world market.

At the heart of the global economic system lies an unequal structure of trade, production and credit which defines the role and position of developing countries in the global economy. What is the nature of this unfolding world economic system; on what structure of global poverty and income inequality is it based? By the turn of the century, the world population will be over six billion, of which five billion will be living in poor countries. While the rich countries (with some 15 percent of the world population) control close to 80 percent of total world income, approximately 60 percent of the world population representing the group of "low-income countries" (including India and China)—with a population in excess of 3.5 billion people—receives 6.3 percent of total world income (less than the GDP of France and its overseas territories). With a population of more than 600 million people, the gross domestic product of the entire sub-Saharan African region is approximately half that of the state of Texas.[3] Together, the lower and middle-income countries (including the former "socialist" countries and the former Soviet Union), representing some 85 percent of world population, receive approximately 20 percent of total world income. (See Table 1.)

In many indebted Third World countries, real salaried earnings in the modern sector had, by the early 1990s, already declined by more than 60 percent. The situation of the informal sector and the unemployed was even more critical. In Nigeria, under the military government of General Ibrahim Babangida, for instance, the minimum wage declined by 85 percent in the course of the 1980s. Wages in Vietnam were below US$ 10 a month, while the domestic price of rice had risen

Table 1 The Distribution of World Population and Income (1998)

	Population (Millions)	Share of World Population (%)	Per Capita Income (in US$)	Total Income (US$ billions)	Share of World Income (%)
Low Income Countries	3 515	59.6	520	1 828	6.3
Middle Income Countries	1 496	25.4	2 950	4 413	15.3
Total Poor Countries	5 011	85.0	1 250	6 264	21.7
Sub-Saharan Africa	628	10.6	480	301	1.0
South Asia	1 305	22.1	430	561	1.9
China	1 239	21.0	750	929	3.2
Former USSR & Eastern Europe	395	6.7	1 965	776	2.7
Total Third World	4 616	78.3	1 180	5 447	18.9
Total Rich Countries*	885	15.0	25 510	22 576	78.3
OECD**	932	15.8	20 853	19 435	67.4
World Total	5 897	100.0	4 890	28 836	100.0

Source: Estimated from World Bank data in *World Development Report*, 1999/2000, Washington DC, 2000, pp. 230–231
*Rich countries are high income countries.
**Turkey and Mexico are included.
Technical Note: Total poor countries is the sum of low income countries and middle income countries.
Total third world countries is total poor countries less former USSR & Eastern Europe.

to the world level as a result of the IMF program carried out by the Hanoi government: a Hanoi secondary school teacher, for instance, with a university degree, received in 1991 a monthly salary of less than US$ 15.[4] In Peru—in the aftermath of the IMF-World Bank sponsored Fujishock implemented by President Alberto *Fujimori* in August 1990—fuel prices increased 31 times overnight, whereas the price of bread increased 12 times. The real minimum wage had declined by more than 90 percent (in relation to its level in the mid-1970s).

The Dollarization of Prices

While there are sizeable variations in the cost of living between developing and developed countries, devaluation, combined with trade liberalization and the deregulation of domestic commodity markets (under the structural adjustment program), is conducive to the "dollarization" of domestic prices. Increasingly, the domestic prices of basic food staples are brought up to their world market levels. This New World Economic Order, while based on the internationalization of commodity prices and a fully integrated world commodity market, functions increasingly in terms of a watertight separation between two distinct labor markets. This global market system is characterized by a duality in the structure of wages and labor costs between rich and poor countries. Whereas prices are unified and brought up to world levels, wages (and labor costs) in the Third World and Eastern Europe are as much as 70 times lower than in the OECD countries. Income disparities between nations are superimposed on extremely wide income disparities between social-income groups within nations. In many Third World countries, more than 60 percent of national income accrues to the upper 20 percent of the population. In many low and middle-income developing countries, 70 percent of rural households have a per capita income between 10 and 20 percent of the national average. These vast disparities in income between and within countries are the consequence of the structure of commodity trade and the unequal international division of labor which imparts to the Third World and, more recently, to the countries of the former Soviet bloc, a subordinate status in the global economic system. The disparities have widened in the course of the 1990s as a result of the remolding of national economies under the structural adjustment programme [see Note 3].

The "Thirdworldization" of the Former Eastern Bloc

The end of the Cold War has had a profound impact on the global distribution of income. Until the early 1990s, Eastern Europe and the Soviet Union were considered as part of the developed "North"—i.e. with levels of material consumption, education, health, scientific development, etc. broadly comparable to those prevailing in the OECD countries. Whereas average incomes were on the whole lower, Western scholars, nonetheless, acknowledged the achievements of the Eastern Bloc countries, particularly in the areas of health and education.

Impoverished as a result of the IMF-sponsored reforms, the countries of the former socialist Bloc are now categorized by the World Bank as "developing economies", alongside the "low" and "middle-income countries" of the Third World. The Central Asian republics of Kazakhstan and Turkmenistan appear next to Syria, Jordan and Tunisia in the "lower middle-income" category, whereas the Russian Federation is next to Brazil with a per capita income of the order of US$ 3,000. This shift in categories reflects the outcome of the Cold War and the underlying process of "thirdworldization" of Eastern Europe and the former Soviet Union.

The Role of Global Institutions

The inauguration of the World Trade Organization (WTO) in 1995 marked a new phase in the evolution of the post war economic system. A new triangular division of authority among the IMF, the World Bank and the WTO has unfolded. The IMF had called for more effective "surveillance" of developing countries' economic policies and increased coordination between the three international bodies signifying a further infringement on the sovereignty of national governments.

Under the new trade order (which emerged from the completion of the Uruguay Round at Marrakech in 1994), the relationship of the Washington based institutions to national governments is to be redefined. Enforcement of IMF-World Bank policy prescriptions will no longer hinge upon ad hoc country-level loan agreements (which are not legally binding documents). Henceforth, many of the mainstays of the structural adjustment program (e.g. trade liberalization, privatization and the foreign investment regime) have been permanently entrenched in the articles of agreement of the new WTO. These articles set the foundations for policing countries (and enforcing "conditionalities") according to international law.

The deregulation of trade under WTO rules, combined with new clauses pertaining to intellectual property rights, enable multinational corporations to penetrate local markets and extend their control over virtually all areas of national manufacturing, agriculture and the service economy.

Entrenched Rights for Banks and Multinational Corporations

In this new economic environment, international agreements negotiated by bureaucrats under intergovernmental auspices have come to play a crucial role in the remoulding of national economies. The Articles of Agreement of the WTO provide what some observers have entitled a *"charter of rights for multinational corporations"* derogating the ability of national societies to regulate their national economies threatening national level social programs, job creation policies, affirmative action and community based initiatives. The WTO articles threaten to lead to the disempowerment of national societies as it hands over extensive powers to global corporations.

The WTO was put in place following the signing of a "technical agreement" negotiated behind closed doors by bureaucrats. Even the heads of country-level delegations to Marrakech in 1994 were not informed regarding the statutes of the

WTO, which were drafted in separate closed sessions by technocrats. The WTO framework ensures a "single undertaking approach" to the results of the Uruguay Round—thus, "membership in the WTO entails accepting all the results of the Round without exception."[5]

Following the Marrakech meeting, the 550-page Agreement (plus its numerous appendices) was either rubber-stamped in a hurry, or never formally ratified by national parliaments. The articles of agreement of the WTO resulting from this "technical agreement"—including Dispute Settlement procedures—were casually entrenched in international law. The 1994 Marrakech Agreement—which instates the WTO as a multilateral body—bypasses the democratic process in each of the member countries. It blatantly derogates national laws and constitutions, while providing extensive powers to global banks and multinational corporations. These powers have, in fact, become entrenched in the articles of agreement of the WTO.

The process of actual creation of the WTO following the Final Act of Uruguay Round is blatantly illegal. Namely, a totalitarian intergovernmental body has been casually installed in Geneva, empowered under international law with the mandate to police country-level economic and social policies, derogating the sovereign rights of national governments. Similarly, the WTO almost neutralizes "with the stroke of a pen" the authority and activities of several agencies of the United Nations including the United Nations Conference on Trade and Development (UNCTAD) and the International Labor Organization (ILO). The articles of the WTO are not only in contradiction with pre-existing national and international laws; they are also at variance with "The Universal Declaration of Human Rights". Acceptance of the WTO as a legitimate organization is tantamount to an "indefinite moratorium" or repeal of the Universal Declaration of Human Rights.

In addition to the blatant violation of international law, WTO rules provide legitimacy to trade practices which border on criminality, including: "intellectual piracy" by multinational corporations; the derogation of plant breeders rights—not to mention genetic manipulation by the biotechnology giants, and the patenting of life forms including plants, animals, micro-organisms, genetic material and human life forms under the TRIPs agreement.

In the sphere of financial services, the provisions of the General Agreement on Trade and Services (GATS) provide legitimacy to large-scale financial and speculative manipulations directed against developing countries, which are often conducive to the demise of country-level monetary policy.

Under WTO rules, the banks and multinational corporations (MNCs) can legitimately manipulate market forces to their advantage leading to the outright re-colonization of national economies. The WTO articles provide legitimacy to global banks and MNCs in their quest to destabilize institutions, drive national producers into bankruptcy and ultimately take control of entire countries.

NOTES

1. According to the Tufts University Centre on Hunger, Poverty and Nutrition Policy.
2. *Financial Times*, 3 March 1989.

3. It is worth noting that the share of the Third World in total world income has declined steadily since the onslaught of the debt crisis. Whereas the group of low-income countries increased its share of world population by more than 2 percent in the three-year period between 1988 and 1991, its share of world income declined from 5.4 to 4.9 percent. Similarly, sub-Saharan Africa's share of world income declined in the same period from 0.9 to 0.7 percent. In 1993, the World Bank redefined the basis of measuring and comparing per capita income. The figures contained in Table 1 are based on a new World Bank methodology which indicates a higher share for the low income countries than during the 1980s.

4. Interviews conducted by author in Hanoi and Ho Chi Minh City in January 1991.

5. For details see the text of *The Final Act Establishing the World Trade Organization* at the WTO webpage at http://www.wto.org/

Shall We Leave It to the Experts?
–Arundhati Roy

Prize-winning novelist and peace activist Arundhati Roy was born in 1961 in Bengal, India, and grew up in Kerala. She studied architecture at the Delhi School of Architecture but went on to work in films and write screenplays and essays. Her article "Shall We Leave It to the Experts?" appeared in The Nation *in February 2002 and has been widely reprinted.*

India lives in several centuries at the same time. Somehow we manage to progress and regress simultaneously.

As a nation we age by pushing outward from the middle—adding a few centuries on either end of the extraordinary CV. We greaten like the maturing head of a hammerhead shark with eyes looking in diametrically opposite directions.

I don't mean to put a simplistic value judgment on this peculiar form of "progress" by suggesting that Modern is Good and Traditional is Bad—or vice versa. What's hard to reconcile oneself to, both personally and politically, is the

"Shall We Leave It to the Experts?" by Arundhati Roy. Copyright © 2001 by Arundhati Roy. Reprinted by permission of the author. First published in *The Nation* magazine, January 18, 2002 and printed in Arundhati Roy, *Power Politics*, 2nd ed. (Cambridge: South End Press, 2002).

schizophrenic nature of it. That applies not just to the ancient/modern conundrum but to the utter illogic of what appears to be the current national enterprise. In the lane behind my house, every night I walk past road gangs of emaciated laborers digging a trench to lay fiber-optic cables to speed up our digital revolution. In the bitter winter cold, they work by the light of a few candles.

It's as though the people of India have been rounded up and loaded onto two convoys of trucks (a huge big one and a tiny little one) that have set off resolutely in opposite directions. The tiny convoy is on its way to a glittering destination somewhere near the top of the world. The other convoy just melts into the darkness and disappears. A cursory survey that tallies the caste, class and religion of who gets to be on which convoy would make a good Lazy Person's concise *Guide to the History of India.* For some of us, life in India is like being suspended between two of the trucks, one leg in each convoy, and being neatly dismembered as they move apart, not bodily, but emotionally and intellectually.

Fifty years after independence, India is still struggling with the legacy of colonialism, still flinching from the "cultural insult." As citizens we're still caught up in the business of "disproving" the white world's definition of us. Intellectually and emotionally, we have just begun to grapple with communal and caste politics that threaten to tear our society apart. But meanwhile, something new looms on our horizon. On the face of it, it's just ordinary, day-to-day business. It lacks the drama, the large-format, epic magnificence of war or genocide or famine. It's dull in comparison. It makes bad TV. It has to do with boring things like jobs, money, water supply, electricity, irrigation. But it also has to do with a process of barbaric dispossession on a scale that has few parallels in history. You may have guessed by now that I'm talking about the modern version of globalization.

What is globalization? Who is it for? What is it going to do to a country like India, in which social inequality has been institutionalized in the caste system for centuries? A country in which 700 million people live in rural areas. In which 80 percent of the landholdings are small farms. In which 300 million people are illiterate. Is the corporatization and globalization of agriculture, water supply, electricity and essential commodities going to pull India out of the stagnant morass of poverty, illiteracy and religious bigotry? Is the dismantling and auctioning off of elaborate public sector infrastructure, developed with public money over the past fifty years, really the way forward? Is globalization going to close the gap between the privileged and the underprivileged, between the upper castes and the lower castes, between the educated and the illiterate? Or is it going to give those who already have a centuries-old head start a friendly helping hand?

Is globalization about "eradication of world poverty," or is it a mutant variety of colonialism, remote-controlled and digitally operated? These are huge, contentious questions. The answers vary depending on whether they come from the villages and fields of rural India, from the slums and shantytowns of urban India, from the living rooms of the burgeoning middle class or from the boardrooms of the big business houses. Today India produces more milk, more sugar and more food grain than ever before. And yet, in March 2000, just before President

Clinton's visit to India, the Indian government lifted import restrictions on 1,400 commodities, including milk, grain, sugar, cotton, tea, coffee and palm oil. This despite the fact that there was a glut of these products on the market.

As of April 1—April Fool's Day—2001, according to the terms of its agreement with the World Trade Organization, the Indian government had to drop its quantitative import restrictions. The Indian market is already flooded with cheap imports. Though India is technically free to export its agricultural produce, in practice most of it cannot be exported because it doesn't meet the First World's "environmental standards." (You don't eat bruised mangoes or bananas with mosquito bites or rice with a few weevils in it, whereas we don't mind the odd mosquito and the occasional weevil.)

Developed countries like the United States, whose hugely subsidized farm industry engages only 2 to 3 percent of its total population, are using the WTO to pressure countries like India to drop agricultural subsidies in order to make the market "competitive." Huge, mechanized corporate enterprises working thousands of acres of farmland want to compete with impoverished subsistence farmers who own a couple of acres.

In effect, India's rural economy, which supports 700 million people, is being garroted. Farmers who produce too much are in distress, farmers who produce too little are in distress and landless agricultural laborers are out of work as big estates and farms lay off their workers. They're all flocking to the cities in search of employment.

"Trade Not Aid" is the rallying cry of the head men of the new Global Village, headquartered in the shining offices of the WTO. Our British colonizers stepped onto our shores a few centuries ago disguised as traders. We all remember the East India Company. This time around, the colonizer doesn't even need a token white presence in the colonies. The CEOs and their men don't need to go to the trouble of tramping through the tropics, risking malaria, diarrhea, sunstroke and an early death. They don't have to maintain an army or a police force, or worry about insurrections and mutinies. They can have their colonies and an easy conscience. "Creating a good investment climate" is the new euphemism for Third World repression. Besides, the responsibility for implementation rests with the local administration.

Enron in India

The fishbowl of the drive to privatize power, its truly star turn, is the story of Enron, the Houston-based natural gas company. The Enron project was the first private power project in India. The Power Purchase Agreement between Enron and the Congress Party–ruled state government of Maharashtra for a 740-megawatt power plant was signed in 1993. The opposition parties, the Hindu nationalist Bharatiya Janata Party (BJP) and the Shiv Sena, set up a howl of *swadeshi* (nationalist) protest and filed legal proceedings against Enron and the state government. They alleged malfeasance and corruption at the highest level. A year later, when state elections were announced, it was the only campaign issue of the BJP–Shiv Sena alliance.

In February 1995 this combine won the elections. True to their word, they "scrapped" the project. In a savage, fiery statement, the opposition leader L.K. Advani attacked the phenomenon he called "loot through liberalization." He more or less directly accused the Congress Party government of having taken a $13 million bribe from Enron. Enron had made no secret of the fact that in order to secure the deal, it paid out millions of dollars to "educate" the politicians and bureaucrats involved in the deal.

Following annulment of the contract, the US government began to pressure the Maharashtra government. US Ambassador Frank Wisner made several statements deploring the cancellation. (Soon after he completed his term as ambassador, he joined Enron as a director.) In November 1995 the BJP–Shiv Sena government in Maharashtra announced a "renegotiation" committee. In May 1996 a minority federal government headed by the BJP was sworn in at New Delhi. It lasted for exactly thirteen days and then resigned before facing a no-confidence vote in Parliament. On its last day in office, even as the motion of no confidence was in progress, the Cabinet met for a hurried "lunch" and reratified the national government's counterguarantee (which had become void because of the earlier "canceled" contract with Enron). In August 1996 the government of Maharashtra signed a fresh contract with Enron on terms that would astound the most hard-boiled cynic.

The impugned contract had involved annual payments to Enron of $430 million for Phase I of the project (740 megawatts), with Phase II (1,624 megawatts) being optional. The "renegotiated" power purchase agreement makes Phase II of the project mandatory and legally binds the Maharashtra State Electricity Board (MSEB) to pay Enron the sum of $30 billion! It constitutes the largest contract ever signed in the history of India.

Indian experts who have studied the project have called it the most massive fraud in the country's history. The project's gross profits work out to between $12 billion and $14 billion. The official return on equity is more than 30 percent. That's almost double what Indian law and statutes permit in power projects. In effect, for an 18 percent increase in installed capacity, the MSEB has to set aside 70 percent of its revenue to pay Enron. There is, of course, no record of what mathematical formula was used to "re-educate" the new government. Nor any trace of how much trickled up or down or sideways or to whom.

But there's more: In one of the most extraordinary decisions in its not entirely pristine history, in May 1997 the Supreme Court of India refused to entertain an appeal against Enron.

Today, everything that critics of the project predicted has come true with an eerie vengeance. The power that the Enron plant produces is twice as expensive as its nearest competitor and seven times as expensive as the cheapest electricity available in Maharashtra. In May 2000 the Maharashtra Electricity Regulatory Committee (MERC) ruled that temporarily, until as long as was absolutely necessary, no power should be bought from Enron. This was based on a calculation that it would be cheaper to just pay Enron the mandatory fixed charges for the maintenance and administration of the plant that it is contractually obliged to pay than to actually buy any of its exorbitant power. The fixed charges alone work out to around $220 million a year for Phase I of the project. Phase II will be nearly twice the amount.

Two hundred and twenty million dollars a year for the next twenty years. Meanwhile, industrialists in Maharashtra have begun to generate their own power at a much cheaper rate, with private generators. The demand for power from the industrial sector has begun to decline rapidly. The MSEB, strapped for cash, with Enron hanging like an albatross around its neck, will now have no choice but to make private generators illegal. That's the only way that industrialists can be coerced into buying Enron's exorbitantly priced electricity.

In January 2001 the Maharashtra government (the Congress Party is back in power with a new chief minister) announced that it did not have the money to pay Enron's bills. On January 31, only five days after an earthquake in the neighboring state of Gujarat, at a time when the country was still reeling from the disaster, the newspapers announced that Enron had decided to invoke the counterguarantee and that if the government did not come up with the cash, it would have to auction the government properties named as collateral security in the contract.

But Enron had friends in high places. It was one of the biggest corporate contributors to President George W. Bush's election campaign. US government officials warned India about vitiating the "investment climate" and running the risk of frightening away future investors. In other words: Allow us to rob you blind, or else we'll go away.

Last June the MSEB announced that it was ending its agreement with the Dabhol Power Corporation, a joint venture of Enron—which has the largest stake—General Electric and Bechtel. DPC ceased operations soon afterward, and is pressuring the government to cover its debts. Royal Dutch/Shell, the Anglo-Dutch petroleum group, TotalFinaElf and Gaz de France are currently bidding to take over Enron, Bechtel and GE's collective stake in the plant in a "distress sale."

Globalizing Dissent

Recently, globalization has come in for some criticism. The protests in Seattle and Prague will go down in history. Each time the WTO or the World Economic Forum wants to have a meeting, ministers have to barricade themselves with thousands of heavily armed police. Still, all its admirers, from Bill Clinton, Kofi Annan and A.B. Vajpayee (the Indian Prime Minister) to the cheering brokers in the stalls, continue to say the same lofty things: If we have the right institutions of governance in place—effective courts, good laws, honest politicians, participatory democracy, a transparent administration that respects human rights and gives people a say in decisions that affect their lives—then the globalization project will work for the poor as well. They call this "globalization with a human face."

The point is, if all this were in place, almost anything would succeed: socialism, capitalism, you name it. Everything works in Paradise, a Communist State as well as a Military Dictatorship. But in an imperfect world, is it globalization that's going to bring us all this bounty? Is that what's happening in India now that it's on the fast track to the free market? Does any one thing on that lofty list apply to life in India today? Are state institutions transparent? Have people had a say—have they even been informed, let alone consulted—about decisions that vitally affect their lives? And are Clinton (or now Bush) and Prime Minister Vajpayee doing everything in their power to see that the "right institutions of governance" are in place? Or are they involved in exactly the opposite enterprise? Do they mean something else altogether when they talk of the "right institutions of governance"?

The fact is that what's happening in India today is not a "problem," and the issues that some of us are raising are not "causes." They are huge political and social upheavals that are convulsing the nation. One is not involved by virtue of being a writer or activist. One is involved because one is a human being.

If you're one of the lucky people with a berth booked on the small convoy, then Leaving It to the Experts is, or can be, a mutually beneficial proposition for both the expert and yourself. It's a convenient way of shrugging off your own role in the circuitry. And it creates a huge professional market for all kinds of "expertise." There's a whole ugly universe waiting to be explored there. This is not at all to suggest that all consultants are racketeers or that expertise is unnecessary, but you've heard the saying: There's a lot of money in poverty. There are plenty of ethical questions to be asked of those who make a professional living off their expertise in poverty and despair.

For instance, at what point does a scholar stop being a scholar and become a parasite who feeds off despair and dispossession? Does the source of your funding compromise your scholarship? We know, after all that World Bank studies are among the most quoted studies in the world. Is the World Bank a dispassionate observer of the global situation? Are the studies it funds entirely devoid of self-interest?

Take, for example, the international dam industry. It's worth $32–$46 billion a year. It's bursting with experts and consultants. Given the number of studies, reports, books, PhDs, grants, loans, consultancies, environmental impact assessments—it's odd, wouldn't you say, that there is no really reliable estimate of how many people have been displaced by big dams in India? That there is no estimate for exactly what the contribution of big dams has been to overall food production in India? That there hasn't been an official audit, a comprehensive, honest, thoughtful, postproject evaluation, of a single big dam to see whether or not it has achieved what it set out to achieve? Whether or not the costs were justified, or even what the costs actually were?

Cynics say that real life is a choice between the failed revolution and the shabby deal. I don't know . . . maybe they're right. But even they should know that there's no limit to just how shabby that shabby deal can be. What we need to search for and find, what we need to hone and perfect into a magnificent, shining thing, is a new kind of politics. Not the politics of governance, but the politics of resistance. The politics of opposition. The politics of forcing accountability. The politics of slowing things down. The politics of joining hands across the world and preventing certain destruction. In the present circumstances, I'd say that the only thing worth globalizing is dissent. It's India's best export.

Questions for Thinking, Writing, and Discussion

1. Dictionaries often offer definitions that are only one or two sentences long, but academics often write entire essays seeking to define a particular term. Your job is to write an essay in which you draw on the articles in this section to arrive at a definition of globalization.

2. What, according to Joseph Stiglitz, are the best and the worst consequences of globalization?

3. What, according to Joseph Stiglitz, is the reason that globalization as carried out by the World Bank and the IMF has had such a devastating effect on much of the developing world?

4. What features or aspects of globalization that received little attention in the Stiglitz article are discussed in Article 2 by john a. powell and S. P. Udayakumar? How do they enhance your understanding?

5. powell and Udayakumar and Jan Jindy Pettman argue that the harsh costs of globalization are borne disproportionately by people of color and white women. How do they support this conclusion? Have they made a good case for it?

6. Both Articles 4 and 5 discuss privatization. What exactly is privatization? Whose interests does it serve? What is the connection between privatization and globalization?

7. In his article, William Tabb talks about some of the ways in which he personally has benefited from privatization. If this is the case, why is he so critical of it?

8. In what ways does the privatization of water in Cochabamba, Bolivia either illustrate or challenge—or both—the critique of globalization that Stiglitz offers in Article 1?

9. In Article 7, Michel Chossudovsky draws a connection between IMF and World Bank policies and an increase in political repression and militarization in the developing world. How does he portray the connection? Is such a connection inevitable?

10. Using the articles by Michel Chossudovsky and Michael Parenti, explain how the WTO works and describe its relationship to the World Bank and the IMF.

11. As you know from your readings in Part One, the language we use to describe something plays an important role in how it is seen. In this context, discuss the use of the terms "free trade" and "free trade agreements" by the transnational economic institutions we have been studying and discuss the political implications of this choice of language.

12. Several articles in this section discuss the operation of "structural adjustment programs" in the developing world. In Part Five, Paul Farmer discusses "structural violence." Do you think he used this term with the programs and policies of the World Bank and the IMF in mind? Why or why not?

13. In her essay "Shall We Leave it to the Experts?" Arundhati Roy describes a contract between U.S.-based Enron and the state of Maharashtra in India that created the first private power project in that country. Compare and contrast this project with the project to privatize water in Cochabamba described in Article 5. How do these projects illustrate the role of the WTO in enforcing World Bank and IMF policies?

14. How does the way Arundhati Roy frames the problems associated with globalization differ from the way some other thinkers in this volume have portrayed them?

Suggestions for Further Reading

Amin, Samir. *Capitalism in the Age of Globalization. The Management of Contemporary Society*. London: Zed Books, 1997.

Fair Globalization: Making It Happen, Report of the World Commission on the Social Dimension of Globalization. International Labour Organization of the United Nations, 2004.

Friedman, Thomas L., and Ignacio Ramone. "Dueling Globalizations: A Debate Between Thomas L. Friedman and Ignacio Ramone." *Foreign Policy*, Fall 1999.

Garson, Barbara. *Money Makes the World Go Round: One Investor Tracks Her Cash Through the Global Economy*. New York and London: Penguin Books, 2002.

Gladwin, Christina H. *Structural Adjustment and African Women Farmers*. Gainesville: University of Florida Press, 1991.

Herman, Edward S. The Threat of Globalization. www.globalpolicy.org/glabaliz/define/hermantk.htm

Hinton, William. *The Great Reversal: The Privitization of China 1978–1989*. New York: Monthly Review Press, 1990.

Katz, Claudio. "Free Trade Area of the Americas: NAFTA Marches South." *NACLA Report on the Americas*, Vol. XXXV, No. 4, January/February 2003, 27–31.

Khor, Martin. *Rethinking Globalization, Critical Issues and Policy Choices*. London: Zed Books, 2001.

Kim, Samuel S. *East Asia and Globalization*. Rowman & Littlefield, 2000.

Kremer, Michael, and Seema Jayachandran. "Odious Debt." *The Brookings Institution Policy Brief 103*, July, 2002.

Madeley, John. *Hungry for Trade? How the Poor Pay for Free Trade*. London: Zed Books, 2000.

Mullings, Leith. "Notes on Globalization." *TransAfrica Forum Globalization Monitor*, Volume I, Issue 1, October 2002, 3–4.

Nussbaum, Martha C. *Women and Human Development*. Cambridge University Press, 2001.

Opara, Ifeoma. "Trade Related Aspects of Intellectual Property Rights and HIV/AIDS Medicines." *Transafrica Forum Globalization Monitor,* Volume I, Issue 3, Spring 2004, 2–4.

Rivero, Oswaldo De. *The Myth of Development, the Non-viable Economies of the 21st Century.* London: Zed Books, 2001.

Sassen, Saskia. "Countergeographies of Globalization: The Feminization of Survival." www.transsssssformaties.org/bibliotheek/sassgender.htm

Sen, Amartya. *Development As Freedom.* New York: Anchor Books, 2000.

Soros, George. *George Soros on Globalization.* New York: Public Affairs, 2002.

United Nations Human Development Report 1999. *Globalization with a Human Face.* New York: Oxford University Press, 1999.

www.50years.org (50 Years Is Enough: U.S. Network for Global Economic Justice)

www.corpwatch.org (Corporate Watch)

www.globalpolicy.org (Global Policy Forum)

www.imf.org (International Monetary Fund)

www.worldbank.org (The World Bank)

www.wto.org (World Trade Organization)

Globalization in Everyday Life

The market is being made the organizing principle for the provisioning
of food, water, health, education and other basic needs, it is being made
the organizing principle of governance, it is being made the measure
of our humanity.

–Vandana Shiva

Early in this book (Part Five), Paul Farmer reminds us that statistics alone cannot convey the realities of peoples' lives, so his article "Suffering and Structural Violence" moves quickly from considering poverty and health *data* to examining the lives of actual human beings trying to live in the world that these statistics describe. In this part of the book, we make a similar move. We follow Arundhati Roy's lead offered in the concluding essay of Part Six and look at globalization as it impacts on the lives of people and communities all over the world.

To the CEO, the globalization expert, the government official, globalization is all about growth: about opening up markets, removing "barriers" to trade by increasing the unfettered movement of goods, services, people, and capital across borders; eliminating protectionist laws; and creating conditions favorable to capital throughout the world. But one question that has been asked by many authors and articles throughout this book is whether growth always means progress. Is growth in itself an unambiguous good? Or does growth come at a price? And if so, who pays the piper? Is it possible to grow the economy but starve the people and destroy the environment?

The articles in this section take a closer look at how the policies of the World Bank, the IMF, and the WTO operate in the real world. What does happen when we allow the needs of capital to dictate economic and social policy? What are the consequences of pursuing growth without factoring in human need and human cost? The articles you are about to read respond to these questions by painting a picture of life in the global village as it is shaped by these policies. Many of the authors acknowledge and deplore the existing great divide between rich and poor within nations and around the globe and, not surprisingly, many attribute the unremitting poverty experienced by so many to the structural adjustment policies prescribed by the World Bank and the IMF—in particular, the huge burden imposed on these economies by debt repayment. According to one World Bank statistic, the developing world spends approximately $13 on debt repayment for every $1 it receives in grants.[1]

In Article 1, "The Human Face of Economics in Argentina," authors Ann Scholl and Facundo Arrizabalaga report that "so much capital leaves the South for the North in debt repayment, that one former executive director of the World Bank claimed that the current decapitalization of Latin America is comparable to the plunder during the colonial conquest." And they quote author/activist Susan George, who compares the effects of debt to the effects of war saying that, like war, debt allows you to get control of other people's resources. In this and other respects, globalization is said by many to function as a kind of second conquest or second colonization, displacing native peoples from their lands and transferring control of natural resources to wealthy and powerful interests in the North. (See, for example, Article 6, "Latin American Indigenous Movements in the Context of Globalization," and Article 3, "Plan Puebla Panama".) A number of these articles point out that the unequal distribution of wealth and privilege that creates a small group of elites enjoying a high standard of living in contrast to the masses of people living in want is mirrored by a corresponding gap between the privileges enjoyed by whites at the expense of people of color both within countries and around the world, and the inequality that is reflected in the privileged position men enjoy in relation to women. The authors of Article 11 use the term "global apartheid" to describe conditions around the world that they contend amount to a global version of white minority rule.

The ways in which globalization is changing women's roles in the global economy are the subject of a number of articles in this section. In Article 14 Barbara Ehrenreich and Arlie Russell Hochschild trace the movement of women, many of whom are women of color, from the South to the North in search of employment, where they often end up serving as nannies, maids, and sex workers. This migration needs to be understood in the context of the global inequalities that structure the wage scale. For example, the authors tell us that the wages that a Filipina woman working as a domestic would earn in Hong Kong are about fifteen times what she would make back home teaching school. Other ways in which globalization impacts on women's work, gender roles, and the family are also discussed in Article 13, "Squeezed by Debt and Time, Mothers Ship Babies to China," Article 2, "The Maquila in Guatemala: Facts and Trends," and Article 9, "The Impact of Water Privitization on South African Women." The latter examines the specific ways in which the privitization of water (in this case in South Africa) impacts on women because of the responsibilities traditionally ascribed to them. No wonder then that sociologist Saskia Sassen has coined the phrase "the feminization of survival" to describe an important dynamic of the new economy.[2]

Trapped in a vicious cycle of debt, many developing nations are forced to restructure their economies to favor debt repayment. (See, for example, Article 8 "Debt, Reforms, and Social Services in Africa," and Article 5, "Ground Down in the Fields: Coffee and State Authority in Colombia.") This means, for example, that agriculture is directed away from much needed production of food for local consumption and toward exporting a few cash crops that can earn the foreign exchange needed for debt payments but which have devastating long-term effects on a country's agriculture and its economy at large. Agriculture in the developing world is also impacted upon by farm subsidies granted by the U.S. government and the European Union to a small portion of their own farmers. The consequences of these subsidies for countries like Mali and Burkina Faso are described in Article 17, written jointly by the Presidents of those countries. (See also Article 18, "How Europe Sows Misery in Africa.") Taken together, the combination of such subsidies granted by rich countries to some of their own agriculture interests and the transnational policies that remove trade barriers and thereby open the economies of developing nations to products from around the world make it almost impossible for Third World nations to make significant strides in addressing pressing social and economic needs at home. (See, for example, Article 20, "The Crisis of Potato Growers in U.P.," and Article 19, "India's Poor Starve as Wheat Rots.")

Several of the articles in this section discuss the rise in militarism and the decline in civic participation that often accompanies globalization, a topic already introduced in Part Six by Michel Chossudovsky. These authors also raise disturbing questions about U.S. support for military dictatorships in various parts of the developing world and the relationship between this support and the logic of globalization. The self-serving rule of corrupt dictators, regimes often installed and maintained with the help of the U.S. government and supported by the World Bank, have only served to increase the hardships of those already paying the cost of globalization and have been an important contributing factor to the economic problems of many countries in the developing world.[3] The preponderance of authoritarian regimes in the Third World constitute yet another legacy of colonialism.[4]

Other articles elaborate further on the concern for the environment, which previous authors have touched upon, in light of globalization's commitment to growth at any cost. (See Article 16, "The Globalized Village," Article 6, "Latin American Indigenous Movements in the Context of Globalization," Article 12, "The Chad-Cameroon Pipeline," Article 15, "Exporting Harm: The High-Tech Trashing of Asia," and Article 22, "The World Bank and the 'Next Green Revolution'.") For example, projects supported by the World Bank have resulted in deforestation, hydroelectric projects, and oil drilling in the Amazon rainforest, and have had a devastating effect on agriculture throughout the developing world. Another serious concern are the intellectual property rights issues raised by the World Trade Organization's rulings. What are the long-term consequences of allowing large multinational corporations to take out patents on life forms? What will be the long-term consequences of granting large pharmaceutical companies in the North monopoly control over production of certain medicines? What does this monopoly control mean in a world where millions of children in the Third World are deprived of access to simple vitamins and where two million people in Africa die needlessly each year from malaria because they cannot afford to pay the $1.50 it costs to purchase the newest malaria drug (ACT), a drug that is capable of eliminating symptoms within three days?

Finally, several articles (see Article 7, "Globalization and the Caribbean," and Article 21, "Study Finds TV Trims Fiji Girls' Body Image and Eating Habits") introduce a topic that has not received very much attention so far in this volume—the ways in which globalization is exporting U.S. culture and values to the far reaches of the planet. Daily papers throughout the United States are filled with stories about Wal-Mart's incursions into other countries, most notably the furor raised by the company's decision to build a superstore half a mile from the sacred Teotihuacan pyramids outside of Mexico City and the opening of a McDonald's franchise near the ancient *zocolo* in Oaxaca. McDonald's opened its first store in Mexico in 1985 and by 2004 the number had increased to 292. McDonald's was quickly followed by Burger King, Pizza Hut, KFC, and other foreign fast food chains. In Article 7, Orville Taylor examines the effects of American culture on the Caribbean by looking at the fast food industry. He tells us that American products are so expensive relative to local foods that when they become available they eat up a large chunk of local incomes. For example, we are told that in Jamaica it takes one-tenth of the Jamaican weekly minimum wage to purchase a Whopper combo. In addition, the licenses and franchise fees required to open these stores means that a significant portion of the profits they make return directly to the United States instead of contributing to the Jamaican economy. Article 21 reports on the effect that the introduction of U.S. television programming is having on women and girls in a province of Fiji's main island, Viti Levu. The single television channel available provides a steady diet of U.S., British, and Australian sitcoms including "Beverley Hills 90210," "Melrose Place," "Seinfeld," and "Xena, Warrior Princess." As a result, in this culture, which traditionally valued a robust and rounded body in both women and men, eating disorders that were previously unheard of are on the rise. It appears that eating disorders like bulimia and anorexia, which are more prevalent in industrialized countries, are just another one of the costs of "progress."

NOTES

1. From "Global Development Finance, World Bank 1999," reported on http://www.globalissues.org/TradeRelated/Facts.asp?p=1

2. Saskia Sassen, "Countergeographies of Globalization: The Feminization of Survival," http://www.transformaties.org/bibliotheek/sassgender.htm

3. For a discussion of the U.S. role in propping up such dictators, see Stephen Rosskamm Shalom, *Imperial Alibis,* Boston: South End Press, 1993.

4. See, for example, Clive Thomas, *The Rise of the Authoritarian State in Peripheral Societies,* Monthly Review Press, 1984.

The Human Face of Economics in Argentina

–Ann Scholl and Facundo Arrizabalaga

Ann Scholl is a social anthropologist and freelance journalist. Facundo Arrizabalaga is a lawyer and freelance journalist. They both live in Argentina. "The Human Face of Economics in Argentina," by Ann Scholl and Facundo Arrizabalaga, appeared on ZNet on February 27, 2004.

Returning to Argentina last year was like coming back to a different country. Everything was worn, tattered, older, poorer. Buses, paving stones, paint on school buildings, people's faces, the taste of ice-cream. Now Argentina had become a 'proper' Third World country. It is no longer the envy of the rest of Latin America. It can no longer be compared to Spain or Italy. It now fits its place on the map. And the human cost of a crisis called 'economic' is laid bare. Economic: An indescript word to describe a crisis that means people's lives, futures, dreams. Like inequality, hunger or unemployment. Words, now so familiar and overused their significance has become alien. Words that have become clinical; so antiseptic they are almost soothing.

The journey from Buenos Aires' Parisian centre—where the elite still enjoy a high standard of living—to the villas miseria which ring the city is like moving between two worlds. Here, generations now, continue to be unemployed and live in an environment without opportunities, excluded from society and subsist on a meagre 150 pesos (around $50) state Jefes y Jefas de Hogar subsidy per month. The streets are unpaved, homes are humble 4-wall constructions, running tap water is scarce and the nearest hospital is a two hour walk away. Inequality, hunger and unemployment are an everyday reality here.

In the barrio of Matanza fifty neighbours have joined together to form one of the numerous Movimientos de Trabajadores Desocupados (MTD)—unemployed worker's movements—that have arisen throughout Argentina. They use a former school building as a community centre. Here they run a bakery, a vegetable garden, have some sewing machines, a t-shirt workshop and are planning to set up an

"The Human Face of Economics" by Ann Scholl and Facundo Arrizabalaga, ZNet, February 27, 2004. Copyright 2004. Reprinted by permission of the authors.

477

alternative educational programme. They are different from other MTDs as they refuse to accept the Jefes y Jefas de Hogar subsidy. "The state has taken absolutely everything away from us, even our identity," says Toty Flores, one of the founding members. He expresses his humiliation at being offered 150 pesos per month by the government, which is not even enough for a family to subsist on for one week.

The group believes that the state subsidy generates a culture of survival and destroys the struggle to reclaim work and self-respect. They are seeking to recover this lost dignity through their autonomous self-help project and generate their own employment in a new environment different from the economic system that represses them. They take all their decisions in asambleas—communal meetings—and work around a philosophy of equal opportunities and free choice. When the peso currency was devalued and the price of flour went up—from 18 pesos for 50 kilos to 53 pesos—they agonized over how to produce at the bakery without raising the cost of bread. They wanted to continue solidarity with the neighbours, maintain the current employees, and still provide themselves with a subsistence wage. In the end they decided to produce and sell double to maintain margins.

The gulf between the sensitive and caring decision making and economic principles based on solidarity and community participation carried out by the MTD in Matanza contrasts starkly with the autocratic decisions taken by the international financial institutions in their offices from Buenos Aires to Davos, where the fate of billions of people's lives is surgically determined.

The World Bank loaned $600 million to Argentina in order to fund the Jefes de Hogar program. Argentina is caught up in a vicious circle of debt which continues to maim the country's people, natural resources and sovereignty. It was during the Washington backed dictatorship that Argentina's debt was largely incurred. The regime accumulated around $36 billion between 1976 and 1983. Henry Kissinger gave his approval for the brutal regime to rule by terror: 30 000 students, activists, social workers, or anyone slightly related to a 'communist' cause were imprisoned, tortured and 'disappeared' during these years. Martinez de Hoz, the then minister of the economy, directed the loaned money to corporations and military tyranny. This is why there is a strong legal position that claims a large proportion of Argentina's foreign debt is illegal, or odious, as Alexander Sacks explains: "If a despotic power incurs a debt not for the needs or in the interest of the State, but to strengthen its despotic regime, to repress the population that fights against it, etc., this debt is odious for the population of all the State. This debt is not an obligation for the nation; it is a regime's debt, a personal debt of the power that has incurred it, consequently it falls with the fall of this power." In 1981 the debt acquired by the military was nationalized. This act signified that the argentine people, who never even gave their consent to borrow these loans, were assigned the responsibility to pay them back. They have been suffering the consequences ever since.

When Argentina failed to pay portions of $132 billion to its creditors in December 2001—the largest sovereign default on record—the biggest 'economic' crisis in its history began. This means that children are malnourished in a country that once fed Europe. Argentina's creditors, policed by the IMF, require the government to structure the economy to favour debt repayment.

An export based economy, which earns foreign exchange, is demanded. In Argentina's case genetically modified soya is exported. A country overwhelmingly rich in natural resources that once produced high quality wheat and meat has been transformed into a 'soya republic,' producing animal forage for cattle in Europe. Deforestation, floods and pesticide contamination are only a few of the, often irreversible, environmental costs. An agriculture orientated towards exporting a few cash crops causes farmers to neglect food production for local consumption. Therefore staple foods become more expensive and hunger and malnutrition occur. As indebted countries compete to export to the north prices for these crops go down. Susan George, writer and long time campaigner on debt eloquently explains: "I really believe that there is a war going on. Debt is war because you can do everything with debt that you can with classical warfare except to occupy territory. In classical war you get hold of other people's resources, and that's what we're doing with debt. We're getting the cheapest raw materials we've had in sixty years."

The IMF's structural adjustment requirements create more poverty as the government is directed to fund the debt and interest incurred and cut down on health, education and social welfare. The IMF requires the government to privatise state owned enterprises, devalue the local currency in order to enhance competitiveness for export and of course adopt "free trade." Embracing 'import liberalisation,' as part of the free trade package has disastrous consequences. In Concordia, a major orange producing region in Argentina's Mesopotamia, oranges imported from Israel rather than local oranges were sold in the fruit and vegetable shops, as, within the logic and 'free' competition of 'free' trade they were cheaper. Oranges rotted on the trees in local orchards and unemployment rose dramatically while oranges were flown in from the other side of the world. The direct consequences of these 'economic' measures are paid for with human lives: Generations now have lived without opportunities as the state serves its creditors rather than the population.

Debt is used as a method of socio-economic control. Structural Adjustment policies limit state participation in the economy. This is why President Kirchner's meetings with IMF officials precede any national political news in the argentine newspapers. As Chomsky clarifies: "For about half the world's population right now, national economic policy is effectively run by bureaucrats in Washington": So much capital leaves the south for the north in debt repayment, that one former executive director of the World Bank claimed the current decapitalization of Latin America is comparable to the plunder during the colonial conquest. By 1990 Latin America's debt had risen from $200 billion to $433 billion. Between 1982 and 1996 a staggering $740 billion left the region for repayment. Debt accounts for less than 6% of the bank's outstanding portfolio, but its use as a political tool is invaluable: It maintains the subordination of the Third World in the absence of official colonies. The U.S.'s urgent request to cancel 90% of Iraq's debt, under the 'odious debt' argument that the Iraqi people should not have to pay back money contracted under Saddam's dictatorship, exemplifies just how strategic debt repayment is. Concern for human rights and welfare are yet again relative, when corporations such as Halliburton and U.S. supremacy are at stake.

Currently over half the population live below the poverty line in Argentina. However, the victims of debt are not only confined to indebted 3rd World countries. Northern governments give their banks tax concessions using taxpayer's money and therefore it is the working population who assume the risks of lending for the banks. In addition, when corporations transfer jobs to the South under the 'advantages' (cheap labour, slack labour laws etc.) of 'free' trade this causes unemployment in the North.

Most importantly, international financial institutions such as the IMF and the World Bank and numerous private banks and governments, who knowingly lent billions of dollars, not only to the dictatorship in Argentina, but to Suharto in Indonesia, the dictatorships in Guatemala and El Salvador, Saddam Hussein in Iraq, Duvalier in Haiti, Pinochet in Chile, Somoza in Nicaragua, Noriega in Panama, and who continue to support the 'drug war' in Colombia, the illegal occupation of Iraq, Karimov in Uzbekistan and the apartheid in Israel, have not only contributed and continue to contribute to wars, massacres and despots, but were and are active accomplices. It is now their duty to recognize these debts as odious, instead of creating more hunger, more deaths and more 'economic' terror.

The Maquila in Guatemala: Facts and Trends

–Corey Mattson, Marie Ayer, and Daniela Mijal Gerson

"The Maquila in Guatemala: Facts and Trends" was written by Corey Mattson, Marie Ayer, and Daniela Mijal Gerson and appears on the STITCH Website. STITCH is a network of women unionists, organizers, and activists that builds connections between Central American and U.S. women organizing for economic justice. For more information visit www.stitchonline.org

What Is a Maquila?

The use of the word maquila in Central America originates from the Arabic word makila, which referred to the amount of flour retained by the miller in compensation for grinding a farmer's corn in colonial times. Retaining some of its original meaning, today the word is associated with another kind of processing—the assembly of components for export, usually from imported parts. Although of distinct origins, the term maquila is often times used interchangeably with the word sweatshops. According to Sweatshop Watch, "Historically, the word 'sweatshop' originated in the Industrial Revolution to describe a subcontracting system in which the middleman earned profits from the margin between the amount they received for a contract and the amount they paid to the workers. The margin was said to be 'sweated' from the workers because they received minimal wages for excessive hours worked under unsanitary conditions."[1]

The maquilas of Guatemala and other developing countries are one consequence of economic globalization—the integration of the world's markets for goods and services, as well as production and finance. Products of the globalization of production, maquilas are fueled by an abundant supply of international labor, capital mobility and free trade. Since the end of WWII, the level of international economic integration has risen steadily. Policy barriers to integration (e.g. tariffs and capital controls) have been removed and economic flows have increased—creating an attractive environment for transnational corporations (TNCs) to outsource at every level of production. Accordingly, garment industry TNCs

"The Maquila in Guatemala: Facts and Trends" by Corey Mattson, Marie Ayer, and Daniela Mijal Gerson (2004 version). Copyright 2004. Reprinted by permission of STITCH.

distribute their production across the globe, making their clothing in countries with the lowest labor cost and weakest regulations.

As garment industry giants move from country to country seeking the lowest labor costs and the highest profits, they exploit workers the world over. Indeed, "The very structure of the garment industry encourages the creation of sweatshops. Retailers sit at the top of the apparel pyramid, placing orders with brand-name manufacturers, who in turn use sewing contractors to assemble the garments. Contractors recruit, hire and pay the workers, who occupy the bottom level of the pyramid."[2]

A Short History of the Maquila in Guatemala

Although the first piece of legislation to promote export-oriented business was passed in the mid-1960's, the maquila sector did not become firmly established in Guatemala until the 1980's—arriving relatively late compared to other countries in Central America and the Caribbean Basin. The early attempts by the Guatemalan government to attract maquila investment (namely passing three laws between 1966 and 1982) failed to calm the fear of potential investors who were scared away by the political insecurity caused by the guerilla insurgency in the countryside and the military's counter insurgency war. Even the millions of dollars spent by the U.S. Agency for International Development (U.S.AID) to foster maquila development throughout the 1970's produced miniscule results. Due to Guatemala's deplorable human rights record, U.S.AID funding was suspended under President Carter.

With the revival of U.S. foreign assistance in 1986 the maquila industry finally took off. Specifically, the U.S.AID maquila promotion program (reinstated following the election of a civilian president) set Guatemala upon a course that AID promoters and entrepreneurs describe as "maquila led industrialization." The primary goal of the program was to cultivate a new class of maquila entrepreneurs that would eventually lead and manage the "neoliberal" revolution in the country. By 1989, general U.S. official assistance totaled more than $800 million dollars, doubling the U.S. assistance given to Guatemala in the preceding 40 years. The United States played a key role in promoting non-traditional exports as an engine for growth and industrial development and establishing the Nontraditional Products Exporters Association (AGEXPRONT) in 1982. Since then, AGEXPRONT has been promoting and assisting companies to export non-traditional products, like raspberries, flowers and clothing. The organization of this trade association has increased the strength of both domestic entrepreneurs as well as U.S. corporate interests, helping to further facilitate maquila expansion in Guatemala. USAID has continuously provided critical financial and technical assistance to the organization; in 1990, they funded over four-fifths of the organization's budget.[3]

The next few years witnessed the establishment of important legislation creating a favorable economic and legal framework for the fledgling maquila industry, gains won by U.S. AID and the newly organized entrepreneurs. Four specific laws were passed by the Guatemalan government guaranteeing certain benefits to maquila entrepreneurs: Decree 21-84 (1984); Decree 29-89 (1989—Law of Promotion and Development of Export Activities and Drawback); Decree 65-89 (1989—Free Trade Zone law); Decree 9-98 (1998—Investment Law). Together these decrees bestowed to maquila entrepreneurs a ten-year tax holiday, low customs duties, and streamlined bureaucratic procedures.

The U.S. AID program was coupled with trade benefits for Guatemala and the region under the Caribbean Basin Initiative (CBI),[4] designed by the Reagan Administration to curb political instability and Communist insurgency in the region. Under CBI, duty (or import tax) would be charged only on the "value added" to products assembled from U.S. materials. Although this duty applied to apparel imported from the region, quotas were liberalized, meaning that companies were allowed to ship more goods to the U.S. Thus, the Caribbean basin and Central America offered cheap access to the coveted U.S. market. Seeking this market access and fleeing strong labor movements and rising labor costs in their own countries, many East Asian investors set up shop in Central America. In Guatemala, the Korean Embassy facilitated a veritable boom of Korean investment in the late 1980s. Guatemala continues to have one of the highest concentrations of Korean-owned apparel plants outside of Korea. In Guatemala, almost 60% of maquilas are Korean-owned. In contrast, U.S. investment accounts for only 7% of the maquila industry in Guatemala.

This massive organizational and financial assistance, a legal framework, beneficial trade rules for accessing the U.S. market, and expectations of a future peace signing between the government and Guatemala National Revolutionary Unity (URNG), all helped to create a favorable environment for the development of the maquila industry. According to the United States Department of Commerce, the value of Guatemalan apparel imports to the United States rose from $6.4 million in 1983 to $349.6 million in 1991 to $395 billion in the year 2000. The growth of the maquila industry reinforced Guatemala's reliance on trade with the United States. The U.S. remains the country's largest and most important trading partner, supplying 34.3% of Guatemala's imports and receiving 59% of its exports in 2004.[5]

The Social and Economic Impact of the Maquila

The impact of increased maquila activity is visible throughout peripheral areas of Guatemala City, where large, new factories dot the rugged landscape and shantytowns of tin and cardboard amble up precariously steep hills. Despite the tremendous growth of maquilas in Guatemala, they have not provided the country with a sensible and humane path to industrial development. As the industry has functioned thus far, the maquila sector operates as a foreign enclave within Guatemala, an export platform for multinational corporations without significant connections to other branches of the Guatemalan economy. Maquila owners (both foreign and Guatemalan) take advantage of the low cost of labor within the country, as well as the incentives offered by the Guatemalan government and international trade rules, to cheaply and conveniently access the gigantic United States apparel market. Also, much of the increased growth of maquilas does not greatly benefit local economies through increased overall investment. Assembling imported inputs into low value goods contributes very little value to the country's economy. In fact, most of the maquila profits are repatriated to the United States or Asia. Like the small amount of corn paid to the miller for his or her service, the meager wages paid to workers are the main economic benefit to the country.

The maquila has been the birth of a new working class in Guatemala, comprised of tens of thousands of workers, many of whom have left their landless poverty in the countryside to seek their fortune in the city. According to the Apparel & Textile Exporters Commission of Guatemala (VESTEX), the Guatemalan apparel industry is comprised of 230 factories, with 73,746 sewing machines (installed capacity) and directly generates more than 116,246 jobs.[6] Approximately 80% of maquila workers are women, a significant fact given that men have historically constituted the vast majority of manufacturing workers. (As a result of the current economic crisis in the country, the number of men working in the maquilas is on the rise, as is their inclusion in work traditionally done only by women in the maquila such as sewing and cleaning. What impact this change will have on female workers remains to be seen.) More women are now working outside the home in the formal economy than ever before, but for low pay and for long hours. Presently, women maquila workers are organizing against great odds to fight the oppressive working conditions in the maquilas.

Working Conditions in the Maquilas of Guatemala

The working conditions inside maquilas are often appalling. Unventilated workrooms, unsafe workshops, verbal abuse, sexual harassment and abuse, firings for pregnancy, arbitrary dismissals and forced overtime are just some of the issues workers face in Guatemalan maquilas. Given this grim reality and the fact that conditions vary from factory to factory, most maquila workers do not work in the same plant for very long. In fact, somewhere between 10% and 30% of the maquila workforce resigns or is fired every month. Most maquila workers move from job to job, seeking the best rate for their time. Many work only long enough to save money to start their treacherous trek to the U.S.

The minimum wage as of August 2004 is Q1,190 per month (U.S. $4.95 per day)[7], which is less than the cost of the Basic Food Basket[8]—the minimum food expenses for an average family (5.38 members), calculated to be Q1,362 per month. The minimum living expenses for a family, or the Basket of Goods and Services[9] is calculated to be Q2,486.18 per month. According to the UN Mission for Guatemala, the majority of Guatemalan workers would need a 140% salary increase to reach a decent standard of living.

In addition to the stress of supporting a family on a maquila wage, many workers incur health problems due to factory conditions. Bathroom access is restricted causing kidney infections. Permission to see a doctor is often denied, allowing illness to reach a critical stage before it is treated. Respiratory problems are common due to poor ventilation. Although the legal workweek is 44 hours long, it is not uncommon to work 70 to 80 hour weeks in the maquila. This increases the number of industrial accidents and causes repetitive motion injuries. As a result, many workers do not work more than a few years in the maquila before health problems force them back into the informal economy.

Worker Solidarity

In an effort to change these conditions, maquila workers have repeatedly attempted to organize unions in Guatemala. However, this has proved to be extremely difficult. Although both the Guatemalan Constitution and Labor Code guarantee workers' freedom of association hardly any of these laws are enforced. This leaves workers extremely vulnerable to employer attacks. Unionization campaigns by workers are routinely met with retaliatory firings, psychological intimidation, the relocation of factories, and even attempted murder. The history of the union campaign at the Camisas Modernas plant, owned by Phillips Van Heusen (PVH), illustrates the obstacles to union organizing in Guatemala.

After six years of struggle, in 1997 the workers at Camisas Modernas won what was the only collective bargaining agreement in Guatemala's maquila sector at the time, helping turn the plant into a model factory where workers were paid a decent wage, received all legally-mandated benefits, and could work a normal work week of 44 hours. Unfortunately, PVH abruptly closed the factory right before Christmas, 1998 and shifted production to five different non-union plants in the area.[10]

Currently, there are only three independent maquila unions in Guatemala: SITRACHOI, SITRACIMA, and the workers at the Nobland International (NB) apparel factory, SITRANB. Both SITRACHOI and SITRACIMA formed in 2001, facing violent physical attacks for their union activity. These two unions attained collective bargaining agreements in 2003 as a result of the international pressure placed on the Guatemalan government for its failure to investigate the attacks, yet the unions remain weakened and internally divided. In the most recent organizing effort, workers at Nobland received legal recognition for their union in December, 2003. SITRANB is currently in the process of negotiating a collective bargaining agreement (August, 2004). Workers in this union have also faced intimidation, harassment, and death threats, and several international organizations are working to support their struggle and put pressure on the brands that purchase from the factory.

The Future

On December 21, 2004, all textile and apparel quotas are scheduled to be eliminated for the 148 countries of the World Trade Organization (WTO), bringing near complete free trade of textiles and apparel. In other words, "As of 2005, Central

America and Caribbean basin countries will no longer have privileged access to U.S. markets, as textile quotas across the world come to an end, trade preferences disappear, and tax incentives are abolished."[11] With the phase out of the Multi-Fiber Agreement in 2005, "China will become fully integrated into the world market, unleashing on to the market a huge productive capacity for both high and low value products, and approximately 1 billion extremely poorly paid workers."[12] With these changes in international trade rules in store, the maquila in Guatemala will be facing serious restructuring.

The changes in trading rules will somewhat alter the comparative advantage of producing countries, and competitiveness will be based on a more complex set of factors. "Apparel manufacturing will most likely be concentrated in those countries offering the lowest labor costs, most efficient production, and most developed transportation and telecommunications infrastructure. Apparel firms are also looking for countries that can produce both the raw materials, i.e., textiles, and finished garments. Countries that provide 'full-package' services—from textiles production to cutting, sewing and packaging—will be the most competitive."[13] Subsequently, Central America's traditional comparative advantage (low salaries, preferential access to the US market, and special tax incentives) will no longer sufficiently serve to attract maquila investors. Central American and Caribbean countries' biggest asset is their proximity to the U.S. market, which would allow them to specialize in high value fashion-sensitive products that are subject to change every four to six weeks in accordance with consumer trends. Perhaps Guatemala, more than any other Central American country, is well positioned to do just that. The Guatemalan business sector has been promoting "full package production" in its maquila sector, meaning that the contracting firm is supplying the client with a completely finished good, rather than simply assembling imported pieces into low value goods. Maquilas in Guatemala are creating a new comparative advantage as they are beginning to design, source, cut, sew, assemble, label, package, and ship their products. The future of the maquila sector in Guatemala depends on the success of embracing the full-package production model—catering to high value fashion sensitive clients.[14]

In order to survive, the Guatemalan maquila must continue developing the "full package production" outfit so that it is both highly flexible and capable of rapid response. Yet for workers this means even less employment stability, more forced overtime requirements, and increased intensity of work. Furthermore, many fear that even if the changes in 2005 do not actually result in massive job loss, it will cause working conditions and labor relations to spiral downwards as China and other Asian countries redefine the race to the bottom.

NOTES

1. Sweatshop Watch. http://www.sweatshopwatch.org/swatch/industry/
2. Ibid.
3. Human Rights Watch.

4. Formerly known as the Caribbean Basin Economic Recovery Act of 1984 and later amplified as the Caribbean Basin Trade Partnership Act of 2000.

5. CIA world factbook. http://www.cia.gov/cia/publications/factbook/geos/gt.html#Econ. Last updated May 11, 2004.

6. VESTEX, http://www.vestex.com.gt/htmltonuke.php?filnavn=perfilindustria_en.htm

7. El Periódico, July 30, 2004; and *Guatemala in Context*, A CEDEPCA Publication, 18th edition—June, 2004.

8. A Basic Food Basket is the measure of the cost of a family's basic dietary requirements.

9. A Basket of Goods and Services is the measure of the cost of food, health, housing, clothing, education, transportation and leisure activities.

10. US/LEAP, People of Faith Network, United Students against Sweatshops, *An Investigative Report into the Closing of a Model Maquiladora Factory in Guatemala*, June 1999. http://www.usleap.org/Maquilas/PVHCampaign/PVHreport.html

11. Clewer, Lorraine, *Big Fish, Little Fish: The World Trade Organisation and Central American Maquila Workers*, January 2002.

12. Ibid.

13. Lora Jo Foo and Nikki Fortunate Bas, Sweatshop Watch, *Free Trade's Looming Threat to the World's Garment Workers*, October 30, 2003.

14. Clewer, 2002.

BIBLIOGRAPHY

Asociación Para El Avance De Las Ciencias Sociales En Guatemala (AVANCSO). "El significado de la maquila en Guatemala". Cuaderno de Investigación No. 10, Guatemala, February 1994.

Clewer, Lorraine. January 2002. "Big Fish, Little Fish: The World Trade Organisation and Central American Maquila Workers". maquila@guaweb.net

———. January 2001. "Concept Paper: The Maquila Project in Context". maquila@guaweb.net

Lora, Jo Foo, and Nikki Fortunate Bas. *Free Trade's Looming Threat to the World's Garment Workers*. Sweatshop Watch, October 30, 2003.

Paz Antolin, Maria José. January 2002. *Desvistiendo la maquila: Interrogantes sobre el desarrollo de la Maquila en Guatemala—una aproximación a los conceptos de valor agregado y paquete completo.* Serie: Hacia estrategias sindicales frente a la maquila, No. 2. Impreso en Editorial Serviprensa S. A., Ciudad de Guatemala: Guatemala.

Petersen, Kurt. *The Maquiladora Revolution in Guatemala*. Yale University Press, 1992.

Prensa Libre, June 7, 2000. Guatemala City.

Prensa Libre, February 19, 2001. Guatemala City.

Quiroa Cuellar, Elizabeth. November 2001. *Jóvenes mujeres Mayas trabajadoras de la maquila; Impacto socio-laboral: Un reto para el movimiento sindical.* Serie: Hacia estrategias sindicales frente a la maquila, No. 1. Impreso en Editorial Serviprensa S.A., Ciudad de Guatemala: Guatemala.

Sweatshop Watch. http://www.sweatshopwatch.org/swatch/industry/

Trejo, Alba. "Ocho maquiladoras de ropa abandonan el país". *El Periódico*. May 15, 2002.

US/LEAP, People of Faith Network, United Students against Sweatshops. *An Investigative Report into the Closing of a Model Maquiladora Factory in Guatemala.* June 1999. http://www.usleap.org/Maquilas/PVHCampaign/PVHreport.html

Plan Puebla Panama

–Global Exchange

This brief summary of Plan Puebla Panama appears on the Global Exchange Website. Global Exchange is an international human rights organization dedicated to promoting environmental, political, and social justice. It was founded in 1988. For more information visit www.globalexchange.org

Plan Puebla Panama (PPP) is a mega project which seeks to open up the southern half of Mexico and Central America to private foreign investment and establishing the foundation for the Free Trade Area of the Americas (FTAA). The plan depends upon multi-lateral development bank support and private investment to create infrastructure that will attract industry and expand natural resource extraction. With the Inter-American Development Bank as the head of the PPP's financial structure and major credit and technical assistance coming from the International Monetary Fund and World Bank, among others, controversial projects have already begun.

This is the first step in the latest push to globalize the Americas with the end goal of incorporating all of the Western Hemisphere (except Cuba) under the FTAA. Essentially the PPP will create development corridors from the 9 southern Mexican states of Puebla, Veracruz, Oaxaca, Chiapas, Tabasco, Campeche, Yucatan, and Quintana Roo, through the most southern Central American country of Panama. The PPP will create an elaborate infrastructure of ports, highways, airports, and railways aimed to connect the development of the petroleum, energy, maquiladora, and agricultural industries. While the PPP's proponents assert that its main objective is to improve the quality of life for area inhabitants, critics of the Plan see it as an attempt to exploit the abundant, cheap labor force and precious natural resources in order to attract foreign investment eager to reap the benefits of an area stricken with poverty and rich in biodiversity.

Maquiladoras, factories in which low paid workers assemble import component parts for re-export, will be strategically placed throughout the region to attract the 50% of the population in the nine states that make less than the regular hourly wage of $1.90/hr (1999). Since Southern Mexico is home to 714 of the nations' 850 poorest municipalities (National Council of Population (CONAPO)), the Fox administration hopes to use this comparative advantage to compete with the

Reprinted by permission of Global Exchange.

maquiladora industry in Asia. In fact, this year alone has seen the creation of 92 maquiladoras in the region where employers can count on wages that are 30%–40% lower than those in the northern half of the country. Labor activists contend that the PPP hopes to create mass migration to areas concentrated with maquiladoras where transnationals have historically paid unlivable wages. International trade law and unilateral corporate agreements include loopholes that exempt transnational corporations from national labor and environmental laws. Critics conclude that the lack of environmental and labor regulations, coupled with unlivable wages, will guarantee that transnational corporations reap the benefit while the social and cultural fabric of small communities is dismantled.

Environmental activists fear that the exploitation of primary materials (minerals, timber, petroleum, biodiversity, and water) will lead to environmental degradation for exportation without profit being dispersed to local communities. Mexico currently ranks 2nd in the world in rate of deforestation (National Forest Inventory 2000) and 73rd in environmental sustainability among 122 nations (La Jornada, 7/23/01). The PPP, many organizations have warned, will lead to further environmental degradation due to the planned deforestation, overexploitation of natural resources, inefficient laws, and extreme poverty.

The elimination of the ejido system, or communal land holdings, as guaranteed under Article 27 of the Mexican constitution, in order to further foreign investment under NAFTA, catalyzed the corporate consolidation of land in northern Mexico. The modification of Article 27 represented a significant impact to the indigenous and peasant communities. By allowing the sale, purchase or rent of ejido land and the elimination of the redistribution petition, large agribusinesses and landowners have the ability to increase land acquisition while leaving many landless without any social provision to ensure land security and sustainability for the poor communities. Also, the use of land as collateral risks farm foreclosure, the loss of land rights, and provokes the concentration of natural resources. As a result of its elimination, transnational corporations under the PPP will continue to have access to hundreds of hectares of primary resources, while installing unsustainable land practices, like monocultures of African Palm and the Eucalyptus plantations.

The Mesoamerican Biological Corridor (MBC), a central component of the PPP, states that its focus is to create innovative ways to manage biodiversity. But critics assert that it will facilitate the exploitation and privatization of biodiversity and its accompanying traditional knowledge. The exemplification of this process is a practice known as biopiracy which indigenous groups in Chiapas and Oaxaca have already spoken out against, describing them as "a robbery of our traditional indigenous knowledge and resources." Mesoamerica is one of the most biologically rich and diverse regions on the planet and the survival of indigenous cultures and unique ecosystems make Mesoamerica a region rich in "green gold." Mesoamerica is now subject to mass privatization of genetic resources, as well as whole ecosystems, especially water. This, coupled with unsustainable primary resource exploitation, converts Mesoamerica to an attractive region for extraction by multinational corporations.

In the end, critics conclude that the PPP will lead to massive displacement of campesino and indigenous communities, further environmental degradation, and development with the end goal of exportation for profit rather than eliminating poverty. As a result, in less than a year since the announcement of the PPP, hundreds of organizations and communities have formed campaigns of resistance in order to pressure global powers to support alternative economic development models.

These principles guide our work to stop the Plan Puebla Panama. To join the NoPPP e-mail: acerca@sover.net or visit http://www.asej.org/ACERCA/ppp/ppp.html#noppp

GE Goes South

–JoAnn Wypijewski

JoAnn Wypijewski, former managing editor of The Nation, writes about labor and politics for CounterPunch. The following piece is an excerpt from an article entitled "GE Brings Bad Things to Life," which was published in The Nation, February 12, 2001.

There are loftier monuments to human progress in Bloomington, Indiana—the Kinsey Institute, the alma mater of one-half the DNA discovery team of Watson and Crick, the site of the original Dog and Pony Show—but nothing so exuberantly represents the excess of American household convenience as the General Electric side-by-side refrigerator-freezer, manufactured exclusively in the city since 1967 in the biggest such factory in the world. This "Cadillac of refrigerators" (up to $2,449 retail) has been rolling off Bloomington assembly lines under the label GE or Hotpoint or the redoubtable Kenmore at a rate of 230 an hour, 4,700 a day, 1.6 million a year. But the mood at the plant is far changed from what it was thirty

"GE Brings Bad Things to Life" (Excerpt) by JoAnn Wypijewski. Reprinted with permission from the February 12, 2001 issue of *The Nation*. For subscription information call 1-800-333-8536. Portions of each week's *Nation* magazine can be accessed at http://www.thenation.com

years ago, when the Bloomington *Herald-Telephone* ran boosterish photographs of bright-faced GE workers rewarded with checks in the thousands of dollars for their cost-saving suggestions.

In 1999 plant management announced that profitability was falling, that $65 million in cost savings was needed, and it was the job of members of International Brotherhood of Electrical Workers Local 2249 to come up with the money. When they did, the company said it wasn't good enough. Half the production would have to be moved to Celaya, Mexico, where instead of $24 an hour in wages and benefits, labor can be bought for $2 an hour. This past December, 733 GE workers in Bloomington were cast off; in the next few months hundreds more will be out of a job and hard put to match their income and benefits anyplace else in town. When it's all over, 1,400 of the plant's 3,200 jobs will be gone.

GE is the largest manufacturer in Bloomington, but in times of "prosperity," stories like this one don't tear through a town the way they did in the 1980s. Bloomington's official unemployment rate is 1.1 percent. Hoosier basketball coach Bobby Knight lost his, but jobs are in greater number than ever. The city's biggest employer, Indiana University, is expanding; its newest offering, a School of Informatics for the techno age. Real estate is moving at a rapid clip, and the signposts of development are everywhere as this "Crossroads of America" town increasingly becomes a destination for tourists, well-off retirees and small high-tech companies. But there's a bitter wind blowing through the boom. Over the past two years 3,665 well-paid factory jobs have left Bloomington. In Indiana as a whole, since 1994, 15,000 workers a year on average have lost their jobs. The most passionate political dispute in town involves what environmentalists, rural preservationists and others call "the NAFTA highway," a proposed Interstate extension that would put Bloomington on a high-speed freight route from Canada to Mexico. The United Way's Josh Cazares, who also coordinates the local Jobs With Justice, tells of full-time workers taking supplemental part-time gigs, making regular visits to food pantries. "There's a lot of insecurity," Cazares says.

. . . Over the past two decades GE has transformed itself into the biggest non-bank financial corporation in the world, the biggest owner of planes and vehicles and credit-card debt. Between 1982 and 1997 (a time when American household debt reached previously unimagined heights), GE increased the value of its shares 1,155 percent. It did this while expanding its financial services department and discarding about half its US manufacturing work force. It has moved production offshore, also engineering, and lately gave an ultimatum to its US suppliers, companies that sell everything from screws to heavy machinery: Move operations to Mexico or lose GE's business. It is a master of mergers and acquisitions, making 125 such deals in 1999 alone and capping 2000 with the $45 billion acquisition of Honeywell, where heads will roll to keep stock prices up. Nor are white-collar and service workers in the GE empire any more secure. With the sinking of Montgomery Ward, 28,000 people lost their jobs; 600 are to be cut at NBC; and though GE's profits were up 19 percent, Wall Street analysts are saying 80,000 of its workers could be jobless before 2001 is over. . . .

The Bloomington plant, more than a million square feet, sprawls along the city's industrial strip, Curry Pike. Its warehouse can accommodate whole cargo trains, its workers forklifting through a maze of mighty refrigerators stacked eight high. Inside, refrigerator doors and inner linings and cases as large as thirty cubic feet dangle overhead, pulled along on chains from one floor to another and onto the lines. Almost everything is made by hand or simple machine. At the plant's easternmost edge is Profile Drive, a token of the town's debt to the popular refrigerator.

GE's mass layoff is not the first in Bloomington in recent years, only the largest. Bill Abbott, who works the night shift in the warehouse, drives to work each day following a trail of bad omens. There's the old Wetterau site, a distribution center for IGA supermarkets that closed in 1997, taking down 114 Teamsters with it. One of Bill's workmates had made $17 an hour there; its nonunion successor, a division of Sara Lee, pays $8. Across the street a We're Hiring! sign advertises a temp agency. Catty-corner, the parking lot is padlocked and sprouting weeds at what had been Westinghouse, then ABB tool and die, both union, first one then the other slowly drained of thousands of jobs; the site was finally abandoned in 1999, another 175 workers down. Just past GE is Cook medical supplies, exemplar of the new breed of companies, fiercely antiunion, hiring at just above minimum wage; and Otis Elevator—union, $15.41 an hour, once employing over 1,000, now down to 527 and counting. Along the strip are a dozen firms with smaller parking lots and smaller wages. One of them, Griner Engineering, is exploring possibilities for producing machine parts in Mexico to meet the price demands of its big industrial customers.

Ground Down in the Fields: Coffee and State Authority in Colombia

–Joshua Frank

Joshua Frank is an independent journalist and writer. An earlier version of his article "Ground Down in the Fields: Coffee and the State Authority in Colombia," which follows, appeared on Znet.

The global coffee industry has endured colossal changes over the past fifty years. Production of beans has shifted from country to country. Profiteering from the product has increased almost exponentially through huge sales at retail outlets such as Starbucks and Seattle's Best. But not all involved in the coffee market have benefited equally. Small coffee farmers have suffered tremendous losses. Environmental degradation has also increased as ancient forests have been cleared in hopes that the bare land can be transformed into fertile ground, worthy of growing cash crops. Countries have lost entire export industries as multinational corporations race to purchase the cheapest beans they can find. And no country has felt the pain of these transformations more than Colombia.

In the mid-1970s, coffee in Colombia accounted for 50% of their legal exports. During the global craze of the 1990s, as retail shops opened up on street corners throughout the industrialized world, Colombia's coffee industry bottomed out. By 1995, the country's coffee industry had suffered tremendously. Coffee dropped from 50 to 7% of Colombia's legal exports. Thousands of farmers fled the country; many more traded coffee for more lucrative crops such as coca and opium. And oil has now replaced coffee as the number one legal export, even though coffee farmers continue to employ more workers than any industry in the country.

Coffee prices in South America peaked during the late 1960s to 1970s; a pound of coffee from the fields of Colombia sold at an average of $3. But by October 2001, the price of coffee per pound had dropped to $0.62. The Colombian market at the time was regulated by the Colombia Coffee Federation (FNC), a quasi labor union that represented coffee producers and helped protect the coffee industry, which at the time accounted for 50% of Colombia's legal exports.

"Coffee and State Authority in Colombia" by Joshua Frank is reprinted by permission of the author.

The organization was founded in 1928, and quickly became the political voice for rural farmers, who had little clout and minimal access to policy makers. Almost all coffee farmers were benefiting during those lucrative years. Agriculture was the business to be in if you wanted to make a safe living in Colombia. However, these boom years didn't last long.

The FNC since the 1970s has lost its once formidable power. The FNC failed to ride the wave of free-market expansion as other countries began producing cheap beans. They did not recognize or protect the farmers as production costs increased, while world consumption declined. In fact, the FNC was unable or unwilling to respond to the influence of world financial institutions that were increasing their presence and therefore control in the region. Consequently, production costs increased to offset the negative effects of global demand, which were dictated by elite institutions.

In *The Economics and Politics of Transition to an Open Market Economy: Colombia*, Sebastian Edwards writes, "In Colombia, as in most developing countries during the late 1980s and early 1990s, policy discussions were also affected by the views of multinational institutions. Possibly the most important 'external' actor was the World Bank which . . . had a fruitful, long-term relationship with Colombia."

Edwards continues, "Although Colombia did not suspend payments to foreign creditors during the 1980s, the international financial community drastically reduced its Colombian exposure after 1982. In Jose Antonio Ocampo's words, Colombia was the victim of a 'neighborhood effect'—it suffered the consequences of being a Latin American nation—and experienced a severe decline of net resources transfers from the rest of the world. Moreover, during the early 1980s Colombia faced a significantly negative terms of trade shock, as the price of coffee—the country's main export—declined significantly in the world economy."

The decisions of how to deal with the World Bank, for example, were not the FNC's to make but nevertheless had negative consequences for their authority to dictate the Colombian market. Indeed, the State's role was more influential in dictating and allowing for influence from such institutions. Global demands and stresses inflicted by such elites inevitably fractured the coffee community in Colombia through multiple trade factors, often referred to as the neoliberal model. This economic model draws on the old meaning of the word "liberal." It includes endorsing the free-market system, deregulation of sectors, privatization, and an overall disregard for government oversight and taxation.

As the FNC failed to halt Colombia's rush into this system, they did not see what lay on the road ahead regarding Colombia's coffee industry. The neoliberal model is now known to many in the U.S. as Clinton economics, after President Clinton and his former Treasury Secretary Robert Rubin muscled through neoliberal trade legislation including Fast Track and the North American Free Trade Agreement while fully endorsing the World Trade Organization and the World Bank.

As more and more farmers began producing coffee beans (estimates ranged from 750,000 to 900,000 farms in 1972), prices began to steadily decline. Well over 200,000 farms were lost by the mid-1990s as the oversupply of coffee in Colombia reached record highs. Colombia was not alone in its overproduction of beans. In late 2001 it was reported that 60 countries produced 132 million pound bags of coffee, but world markets consumed only 108 million bags.

Free markets ruled the international coffee trade during the 1980s. Major multinational buyers like Nestle, Philip Morris, and Proctor and Gamble raced to the bottom of the price chain, as they looked to profit by buying the most inexpensive beans they could find. Colombia was sure to lose, as its beans were traditionally known for high quality and gourmet flavor. No niche was to be found in a climate dominated by additive flavors and cheap beans. Production costs were also relatively high for a third-world country. The power of the FNC traditionally had raised the standard of living for the estimated 500,000 coffee farms in Colombia. Any drop in their per-pound production costs would greatly impact these farmers' standard of living. And, in fact, did.

Nevertheless, neoliberalism dictated the next winner in the world of coffee. Following the 1973 Paris Peace Accords, Vietnam quickly came into focus as a potential mass producer of cheap beans, because agricultural wages in Vietnam have always been rock-bottom; in 1980 the average farm worker there made a mere $0.09 a day.

The climate in Vietnam was also ideal for producing beans, and the global capitalists were more than ready to capitalize on these prime conditions. Free-market economists would argue that this is standard supply and demand economics. The world's demand was flourishing, so it was only right for buyers to seek out the cheapest means of production. However, what this model fails to recognize is the harsh effects such policies have on small farmers in rural areas throughout the world. The numbers show this neoliberal failure with a sobering jolt.

By 1999 Vietnam nudged its way into the top three global producers of coffee. They tied with Colombia as the second largest producer, at 12 million bags per year, trailing the goliath of coffee production, Brazil, which produced 46.85 million bags of coffee in 2002. One decade before, Vietnam was a virtual no-name on the world coffee circuit, and now they hope to one day take the top spot as the world's largest coffee producer. The state's role in Vietnam mattered little, because it was and is the multinationals that have chosen their plush fields for cultivation.

While the neoliberal model created some winners, it has also produced many more losers. Transnational corporations and gourmet coffee dealers have posted record profits, as the price per pound has dramatically slumped. The largest victors in this market have been the retail chain Starbucks and the largest multinational coffee buyer, Nestle. As these corporations' bottom lines fatten, rural poverty in the countries they harvest in is growing almost exponentially.

International coffee prices have now reached a 35-year low. The last 3 years have been the hardest on the global market, decreasing its value more than 50%. Taking into account inflation, the prices are now at historic lows.

Currently, Colombia has $34 billion dollars in external debt. Because of this, the International Monetary Fund and the World Bank dictate how best Colombia can pay back these dues. The debt has forced the country to expand production of exports to generate hard currency in order to pay back the loans. This macro-expansion has contributed to the overproduction of coffee beans and a weakening of real wages for farmers. And the global demand for coffee has deteriorated since the 1980s, so the increase in production has yielded a massive oversupply of coffee beans. Unlike the subsidized agriculture in the U.S.—Colombia is not able to dump their goods on other countries—the beans, and it seems the farmers, simply go to waste.

Under the guise of neoliberalism, restrictions on supply are nonexistent. No regulatory measures are in place to halt the overproduction of coffee in Colombia. The impact has been horrific; as export revenues for multinational corporations have grown, real wage earnings for farmers have stagnated.

As the Colombian government fully endorsed these trade measures, their culpability in the debacle goes without question. However, industrialized countries, policy institutions like the IMF, and multinationals like Starbucks have in effect spearheaded the pace of globalization in Colombia; it has not been the Colombian government alone.

Coffee beans have been primarily an export commodity since the early 1900s. And reliance on free markets to dictate the flow of coffee has been the famous mantra Colombians use when discussing supply and demand strategies. The FNC has historically monitored Colombian coffee markets, with their eyes toward the industrialized future. As the FNC allowed multinationals to dictate production, they lost control of the coffee trade. This was a result not only of demand, but because large multinationals took over as the primary trade regulators for the industry. In the past, the coffee industry in Colombia relied on the FNC for regulatory measures more than they relied on the State government. So it can be said that the FNC has acted as a puppeteer for thousands of coffee farmers in Colombia since its inception early last century. And that puppeteer handed over the strings to the likes of the IMF, the World Bank, and other multinationals.

Oxfam's 2003 coffee report gives an example of the multinationals' power: The big four coffee producers are Kraft, Nestle, Proctor and Gamble, and Sara Lee. Each markets and sells coffee brands worth $1 billion or more in annual sales. Together with German titian Tchibo they buy almost half the world's coffee beans each year. Profit margins are very high, as Nestle has made an estimated 26% profit margin with their instant coffee product. Sara Lee's coffee profits are estimated to be nearly 17%, a very high figure compared with other food and drink brands. Colombian farmers, for example, are getting a price that is below the costs of production while these companies make bundles selling their coffee products. In 2003 alone, Kraft increased their net profits by 80% from the previous year, while Nestle increased theirs by 18% (maketradefair.com).

Third-world markets are now managed more by transnational corporations and policy institutions than by State entities. The development of economic transactions across borders, particularly international borders, undermines State autonomy. This in effect marginalizes the State and the FNC as an economic player in the global community. And in Colombia the loser has been the small farmer.

The neoliberal economy encourages private entities to dictate the flow of goods and capital. Therefore, wealth and power have been transferred into the hands of private actors from the clutches of the FNC and the State. Such private actors overpowered the FNC and the State, and decided for themselves who was included and excluded in global production networks. In the case of Colombia, as the FNC and the State allowed private players to manage the flow of coffee, they also became more and more irrelevant in countering the strong race-to-the-bottom market forces. The negative effects have been felt tremendously by Colombia's poor agricultural communities.

As statelessness embodies these sectors, it becomes clearer and clearer that no governing organization is wholly representing these poor Colombian farmers. Left to the devices of neoliberalism alone, it is unlikely that coffee production in Colombia will again make up 50% of its legal exports. It is also unlikely that the transfer of coffee production to coca and opium will decrease any time soon. Farmers simply want and need to make a living. Collectively, the strength of the new market is embodied in multinational corporations and private players, not State and local authorities—sovereignty has seemingly knelt to the neoliberal capitalist model.

Colombia's coffee problem provides a clear indication that free-market economics is powerful enough to benefit a few, as well as strong enough to crush others.

Latin American Indigenous Movements in the Context of Globalization

–Juan Houghton and Beverly Bell

Juan Houghton is an anthropologist, writer, and organizer from Colombia. Beverly Bell is Director of the Center for Economic Justice. The article that follows is excerpted from a report published by the Interhemispheric Resource Center and available on the Global Policy Forum's Website. The Global Policy Forum's mission is to monitor policymaking at the United Nations, promote accountability of global decisions, educate and mobilize for global citizen participation, and advocate on vital issues of international peace and justice.

Globalization has increased, in previously unsuspected ways, the risks for indigenous peoples living on lands that contain strategic resources for market exploitation: water, oil, gas, forests, minerals, biodiversity. Increased foreign investment and increased profit depend upon the exploitation of natural resources, and these natural resources are predominantly found on indigenous lands. As the Chilean political scientist Sandra Huenchuán Navarro says, "Though indigenous people don't know it, the most powerful determining factor of their destiny is the New York Stock Exchange or transnational companies' logic of global investment."[1]

Throughout the Americas, indigenous peoples are losing economic and social ground. Their fragile control over their lands, waters, and other natural resources is loosening. Both academic researchers and indigenous organizations show that market-driven global processes are increasing environmental deterioration and poverty in indigenous communities, blocking the viability of sustainable indigenous communities and societies.[2] In response, indigenous peoples are mounting new forms of resistance and organizing. While concentrating on consolidating their autonomy, the political and economic conjuncture brought on by globalization has also forced indigenous peoples to engage in new fights.

From "Latin American Indigenous Movements in the Context of Globalization" by Juan Houghton and Beverly Bell, October 11, 2004, Interhemispheric Resource Center. Reprinted by permission.

A Second Conquest

Indigenous peoples' experience of the nation-state and dominant society is one of systematic exclusion and dispossession. Globalization has greatly worsened this condition, based on agreements between nation-states, corporations, and financial institutions forged without the input or consent of civil society groups. National governments are taking it upon themselves to negotiate natural resources on the international market with little concern about whether these resources are on indigenous, black, or peasant lands. These projects are often negotiated behind the backs of indigenous peoples, in open violation of Convention 169 of the ILO that states that indigenous peoples have the right to be consulted before decisions that affect their territories or natural resources are made.

In this context, many indigenous people perceive "globalization" as a euphemism for a second colonization. The following statement from the "Abya Yala Indigenous Peoples' Mandate," from a continental congress of indigenous peoples in Quito in 2002, is typical of dozens more emanating from indigenous federations and gatherings in recent years. This one, directed to the ministers for economic issues in the Americas, states: It has come to our attention that, representing various countries, you are meeting to design a project for Latin American integration. However, we who were the first inhabitants of these lands, and therefore the hosts, have not been notified, much less consulted. Because of this, we consider your presence to be suspect and unwelcome.[3]

In one of countless similar examples, the National Indigenous Organization of Colombia (ONIC) called free trade pacts "a new crusade to re-colonize our territories, our cultures, our consciences, and nature itself."[4] The "Declaration of Chilpancingo," produced at the National Gathering of Indigenous Mexican Peoples and Organizations in Mexico in 2002, talked about trade pacts "which turn over our sovereignty to large national and transnational capital, turn their backs on the interests of the majority, and seek to maintain a homogeneous nation, rejecting the plurality and diversity of our peoples."[5]

Opposition to Free Trade Agreements

Among trade pacts, the FTAA has been the main focus of attention and opposition. The "Abya Yala Indigenous Peoples' Mandate" also speaks for much of the opposition to the FTAA:

The FTAA will lead to greater destruction of the environment [which will cause us] to be evicted from our own territories. We will be led down the path of submitting to the privatization of water and the generalized use of genetically modified foods. Labor rights and working conditions will deteriorate. The living conditions and health of our peoples will worsen as the privatization of social services is accepted and implemented. Many small- and medium-sized businesses that are still surviving will go bankrupt. Democratic rights in society will be further limited. Severe poverty, inequality, and inequity will increase. The ancestral cultures and ethical values we still have will be destroyed. They will even end up dismantling nation-states and turning them into incorporated colonies. What kind of integration are you trying to tell us about when, as your plans are carried out, we are being disintegrated and eliminated? What kind of integration are you proposing if the basis of your proposal is competition, the desire to accumulate and obtain profits at any cost, inequity, disrespect for peoples and cultures, and the desire to make us all part of the market, part of rampant consumerism? What kind of integration are you proclaiming if the first and foremost relationship of human beings is to mother earth, and you do not have such a relationship?"[6]

Similar statements have been made by: the National Encounter of Mexican Indigenous Peoples and Organizations,[7] the Confederation of Indigenous Nations of Ecuador (CONAIE),[8] the Interethnic Association of Development of the Peruvian Jungle (AIDESEP), the National Indigenous Organization of Colombia (ONIC) in the Congress of the Indigenous Peoples of Colombia (November 2001) and in the International Seminar Against Neoliberalism,[9] the National Indian Council of Venezuela (CONIVE), Coordination of Indigenous Organizations of the Cuenca Amazonia (COICA), the Civic Council of Popular and Indigenous Organizations of Honduras (COPINH), the General Kuna Congress of Panamá, various Chilean and Bolivian organizations, and the Pan Amazonian Social Forum.[10]

The Battle for Control Over Natural Resources

In most countries of Latin America, structural adjustment has meant moving economies back to reliance on raw materials, through the extraction of natural resources by multinational companies, sometimes in association with local business, and with the willing help of governments.[11] This renewed "raw materialization" of global Southern economies has meant aggressive takeover of indigenous land and resources. Green markets, carbon dioxide sinks, genetic information, oil, gas, and water are all subject to rapid privatization processes led by national governments and to sale on the stock market.

In the Amazon, wood, pharmaceutical, and oil extraction is increasing. The Plan Puebla-Panama promotes the construction of highways and railroads, the development of oil and electricity industries, and the creation of a huge free trade zone in an area throughout Mesoamerica—an area rich in resources and biodiversity.[12] The highlands and eastern area of Bolivia are being affected by gas and water projects. Two million hectares of the Ecuadorian Amazon have been ceded to oil companies, and 50% of the Colombian Amazon is considered by oil companies available for direct contracting.[13]

In Nicaragua, the Korean transnational Kumkyung has a 30-year concession on the forest resources of the Awas Tingni indigenous people. In Madre de Dios in Peru, in the Colombia Pacific, in the southern region of Chile, at the Amazonian borders of Brazil, and in Guyana—all indigenous territories—forest plantations are growing. The increase in tree plantings is intended to maintain a stock of exploitable trees to keep world paper prices low and to continue lowering the price of vegetable oils used by transnational food companies. This, in turn, has turned entire indigenous regions previously dedicated to agriculture, as in the case of Mapuche lands in Chile, or to sustainable forest harvesting, in places like Chajerado and Embera lands in Colombia, into areas used only for short-term and intensive forest extraction.

Multinational and local companies mining for gold, copper, ferro-nickel, and other minerals, have transformed indigenous lands in Venezuela, Brazil, Colombia, and Panama. There is a permanent war being waged by gold miners and illegal armed groups against indigenous communities residing on these and other lands, including the Yanomami, Curripaco, Baniva, and Kuna.[14] The indigenous peoples are often forced to pay taxes even as they play the role of private guards for these transnational businesses.

One result is a new round of displacement of peoples from their resource-rich lands. A recent study on the impact of globalization on indigenous territories by Chilean political scientist Huenchuán emphasizes that over the past centuries many indigenous peoples were forced off of their lands and took refuge in "places that were often considered hostile ecosystems but are areas of high biological diversity and have an ecological importance far beyond their immediate boundaries." Now that many of these lands have been targeted by multinationals for resource extraction, indigenous communities are again being forcibly removed en masse.[15]

Plans for Displacement

The neoliberal model in Latin America has another new face that is even more painful for the indigenous: the Andean Region Initiative, also known as Plan Colombia, and Plan Dignity in Bolivia, with their exorbitant price tags. These initiatives involve wars against the opposition and a chemical war against the mostly indigenous people who grow coca and poppies for survival and, in the case of coca, for sacred purposes as well. In addition to disrespecting the cultures whose cosmologies are based on the coca leaf, the aerial spraying of Round-Up damages environmental and human health. The spraying occurs in selective areas where the governments wish to control insurgent movements as well as indigenous lands and resources. In Colombia, for example, there has been no direct fumigation of land controlled by the death squads run by the Colombian military.

There is also a notable militarization of the entire continent with the installation of dozens of new national and U.S. army military bases on indigenous lands. Indigenous and campesino peoples and movements experience repression in the areas affected, as well as increased poverty. The so-called drug wars have been effective in accelerating displacement of indigenous peoples and campesinos from resource-rich lands. This has occurred as much through direct military action against communities as through aerial fumigation of the food base of communities whom the military wishes to push out.

Moreover, these measures secure U.S. corporate investment in the region, as U.S. initiatives provide weapons and financial resources to countries that accept a growing U.S. military presence and adopt a policy of protecting U.S. investments.[16] In Bolivia, for example, Plan Dignity has been effective not as a challenge to drugs, but as a challenge to popular opposition to privatization of state-owned natural resources. The militarization of these and other countries in Latin America has paved the way for expansion of neoliberal globalization.

Reshaping Autonomy Struggles

Under the current terms of economic integration, national sovereignty itself has become virtually expendable, its power often trumped by laws of international trade pacts and the demands of international financial institutions (IFIs). The weakening of roles and positions of nation-states accentuates the internal economic crises of individual countries and the social and political instability of the whole region.

This creates a new context for self-determination for indigenous peoples. States' unwillingness to "represent" the interests of their civil societies—in this case indigenous peoples—has decreased their legitimacy and strengthened throughout the continent the idea of autonomy that indigenous peoples have been defending for centuries. As the states' inability to respond to society as a whole provokes increasing crises in their claims of representation, and ability to govern, indigenous peoples have begun an inverse process. They are relying on their history and social structure, on recent political developments, and on the clarity with which they have promoted the consolidation of indigenous governments and jurisdictions. Indigenous governments have gained legitimacy in spite of the difficulties, and laws are often enforced in autonomously run areas more effectively than where standard governmental legislation exists. Where neither federal governments nor laws protect or represent people and their lands, indigenous peoples, campesino communities, and peoples of African descent are bursting onto the scene to take on local, regional, and national power.

Indigenous peoples have historically had to build their political entities inside nation-states, which mediated and still mediate many of their relationships with the world. While a decade ago, they took their concerns only to the state, now they must also go to the international arena. At one level, the margins of their political power are expanded as they deal directly with multilateral organizations like the World Bank, the InterAmerican Development Bank (IDB), the Ibero-American Fund for the Development of Indigenous Peoples (a multilateral organization created by the Ibero-American heads of state, also known as the Indigenous Fund), and the Andean Community of Nations, which approach them looking for consent on projects and consensus around political operations.[17] They also have to deal with corporations who negotiate local investment and resource exploitation projects directly with local indigenous leaders.

Yet, because of the asymmetrical power at work, indigenous peoples find themselves subordinated to new forms of governance. Gains in autonomy are in danger of being quickly lost to the World Bank, IDB, and other multinational institutions that are now able to impose policies and initiatives directly on indigenous communities, organizations, and lands. The legal changes imposed by the trade and investment organizations are coupled with the coercive power that comes along with loans and development aid. Structural adjustment-driven decentralization has opened the door for the direct incorporation and absorption of some indigenous communities into the scenario of dependence, indebtedness, and business associations that are all increasingly threatening indigenous communities. Indigenous peoples' desire to govern their own territories, combined with their poverty and isolation, render them vulnerable to these programs, which operate on the same policy imperatives that are heavily pushed by the region's governments, and often with even more socially and economically devastating impacts.

NOTES

1. Huenchu án Navarro, Sandra. "Territorial Impacts of Economic Globalization in Latin American and Caribbean Indigenous Territories." Statement presented in the XXII Latin American Congress of Sociology of the Latin American Sociology Association (ALAS). University of Concepción, Concepción, Chile, 1999.

2. See the Declaration of the Indigenous Caucus of the UN Indigenous Peoples' Working Group in Geneva, July 25, 2003.

3. The "Abya Yala Indigenous Peoples' Mandate," from the Continental Congress to prepare the Second Summit of Indigenous Peoples' of the Americas, Quito, October 30, 2002.

4. "Indigenous Peoples of the Americas and the FTAA," National Indigenous Organization of Colombia (ONIC), in Memorias, International Seminar, "The Peoples of South America Building Alternatives to Neoliberalism," Bogotá, September, 2002.

5. "Declaration of Chilpancingo," National Encounter of Indigenous Peoples and Organizations, September 12 and 13, 2002, Chilpancingo in ALAI, Latin America in Movement, September 13, 2002. Forty-eight indigenous organizations participated in this gathering, including one of the most representative groups in Mexico (ANIPA) and the most influential regional groups.

6. The "Abya Yala Indigenous Peoples' Mandate," Op. Cit. The summit where the statement was released took place in the context of the Continental Days of Struggle Against the FTAA on the same date. CONAIE of Ecuador, CONAMAC from Bolivia, COICA and CSUTCB from Bolivia, the Kuna Youth Movement of Panamá, ONIC from Colombia, and sectoral and regional organizations from Mexico and Chile were present at the summit.

7. National Encounter of Indigenous Peoples and Organizations, "Chilpancingo Declaration," September 12–13, 2002, Chilpancingo, in Latin America in Movement (ALAI) Sept 9, 2002. Forty-eight indigenous organizations participated in this gathering including the most representative organization in the country (ANIPA) and the most influential regional organizations.

8. See Boletín ICCI-ARY Rimay, No. 30–50.

9. National Indigenous Organization of Colombia, "Indigenous Peoples of the Americas and the FTAA," in Summary of Events, International Seminar, "South American Peoples Building Alternatives to Neoliberalism," Bogotá, September 2002, and "Life and Dignity for Indigenous Peoples and Colombians," Summary of Events, Congress of the Indigenous Peoples of Colombia, 2001.

10. A good register of statements from indigenous organizations on this topic can be found on the websites of the Latin American Information Agency, ALAI (http://alainet.org), of Adital (www.adital.org.br), of the International Agency of Indigenous Press, AIPIN (www.redindigena.net/noticias/boletines), and of COICA (www.coica.org).

11. Structural adjustment refers to the series of economic reforms which are imposed by the IFIs in exchange for loans and aid.

12. For more information, see Center for Economic Research and Communitarian Participation and Action (CIEPAC), http://www.ciepac.org/ppp.htm.

13. Colombian Oil Company (ECOPETROL) Land Map, Bogota, February 2003.

14. For example, garimpeiros, the Brazilian term for gold miners who do semi-industrial dredging of the river beds of the Amazon and the Orinoco, were responsible for the deaths of hundreds of Yanomami indigenous people in 1993.

15. Huenchu án Navarro. Op. Cit. ONIC made a similar statement at the U' wa Por La Vida hearing in Cubará, 1997.

16. See bulletins of the International Agency of Indigenous Press (AIPIN).

17. IFIs, which have traditionally focused on lending to national governments, are increasing their involvement with NGOs, as well as with state- and provincial-level governments. The World Bank and IDB, especially, are developing direct relations with indigenous organizations, through such initiatives as the World Bank's consultations on political operations. Via institutions like the Ibero-American Fund for the Development of Indigenous Peoples, the World Bank and the IDB are also giving grants and training "experts" in indigenous organizations.

7
seven

Globalization and the Caribbean
–Orville W. Taylor

Orville W. Taylor is a lecturer in sociology at the University of the West Indies in Ja-maica. His discussion of globalization in the Caribbean appeared in the Summer 2003 issue of the TransAfrica Forum's Globalization Monitor. *TransAfrica Forum is a non-profit organization dedicated to educating the general public—particularly African Americans—on the economic, political, and moral ramifications of U.S. foreign policy as it affects Africa and the Diaspora in the Caribbean and Latin America.*

The recent popularity of the term globalization is somewhat misleading because it implies that it is a process that has begun relatively recently. While it has taken on a new significance since 1995, characterized by the formation and subsequent dominance of the World Trade Organization (WTO), it is in reality the latest version of the historical spread of capitalism, which led to the creation of the entire African Diaspora, including in the Caribbean.

Nevertheless, it is the phenomenal spread of American culture and the in-creased exposure of smaller nation-states to the rigours of the world political econ-omy that mainly characterize this new strand of globalization. Many Caribbean nationals have historically had a deep affinity for America and things American, and while the interpretation of this article may be critical, it is not anti-American.

McDonaldization

For my purposes, there are two aspects of the issue which are of concern. First, there is what George Ritzer calls 'McDonaldization,' an attraction to the 'modern' American way of life. The second is the increasing fragility of Caribbean states to the dictates of a hostile world political economy. Epitomized by the fast-food in-dustry, American culture has interpenetrated the Caribbean (though not com-pletely). It affects local ideologies and identities, and significantly influences consumption patterns. The net effect of adopting North American tastes is that there is significant expatriation of profits to pay licences and franchise fees. Ameri-can products eat up a sizeable portion of local incomes. For example, it takes 1/10th of the Jamaican weekly minimum wage to consume a Whopper combo.

"Globalization and the Caribbean" by Orville W. Taylor, *TransAfrica Forum*, Vol. 1, Issue II, Summer, 2003. © 2003 by TransAfrica Forum Globalization Monitor.

Even more problematic is that American corporations in the Caribbean tend to be vertically-integrated structures with limited forward and backward linkages in the local economy. In the end, the employment effect is less than desirable and the foreign trade balance is exacerbated.

Apart from the direct economic and cultural outcomes, much of the Mc-Donaldized lifestyle is inimical to good health. Notwithstanding this, as outlined in an earlier work, some local branches of international fast food corporations sell far more than any of their North American counterparts. Thus, the irony is that there is a higher demand for stuff which is not only expensive, but also unwholesome. *We love you, but do you love us?*

Yet, this effect of globalization is not new. The asymmetry of international trade between 'core' and 'periphery' countries is itself as old as colonialism. What is new, however, is a new variation on the theme of international inequality since the WTO has risen to the heights of the world economy. The WTO presides over a regime which advocates free trade and the supposed removal of all sort of artificial boundaries and barriers. No country must have preferential treatment in accessing any international market. In this regard, the organization has the power to impose sanctions on countries which breach its guidelines.

On the other hand, while there are rules and standards applicable to trade, there are no enforceable standards regarding the conditions under which production takes place. The result is that the English-speaking Caribbean, with just about the highest labour standards among developing countries, is forced to compete in a world where their less democratic competitors, often with U.S. investment, operate with lower labour costs. This puts them at a disadvantage for being democratic.

As a signal case, in 1997 President Clinton, acting on behalf of Chiquita Banana, brought the European Union before the WTO because of its preferential treatment to West Indian bananas. The inequity and injustice of the situation is obvious when one realizes that Chiquita, along with its counterparts Dole and Del Monte, control more than 60 percent of the world banana market—yet were fighting for the 3 percent produced by the Caribbean.

As a result of this intervention the Caribbean banana industry was devastated, resulting in the closure of several plantations and the loss of livelihood of large chunks of the Black Caribbean populace. The tiny island nations of St. Lucia, St. Vincent, and Dominica suffered great losses. In these three nations, the banana industry engaged between 30 and 50 percent of the labour force and contributed between 40 and 80 percent of foreign exchange earnings. Dominica, the most dependent on the industry, has been particularly hard hit. Apart from the massive loss of jobs Dominica is now in a crisis to the extent that it cannot meet its fiscal obligations.

Ironically, St. Lucia, with a number of Caribbean politicians in tow, welcomed Clinton with much fanfare on the weekend of January 19, 2003. His visit cost in excess of $20,000 and the bearer of the cost was not disclosed, but suspected of being local. Not only did it seem that the memories were short but like much of the rest of the world, the Caribbean flies like a moth to the flames.

Debt, Reforms, and Social Services in Africa

–Mandisi Majavu

Mandisi Majavu is a freelance journalist and a student at the University of South Africa. His article "Debts, Reforms, and Social Services in Africa" appeared on ZNet on September 19, 2004.

A study conducted by the UN estimates that 3,900 children die each day because of dirty water or poor hygiene. In sub-Saharan Africa, it is believed that only 58 percent of the 684 million people have clean water, compared with an average of 79 percent for the entire developing world.

According to the report, at least 30 percent of the region's water systems are inoperable because of age or disrepair. The UN goal of providing three-quarters of the population with safe drinking water by 2015 seems a bit ambitious.

The research report attributes Africa's slow progress to conflict, political instability, population growth and the low priority that is given to water and sanitation.

One would have thought that factors like water privatisation and the $360 billion debt burden on a continent where most people live on less than $1 per day would have been high up on the list of factors that prevent Africans from having access to clean water.

Each year, African countries spend about $15 billion repaying debts to the IMF and World and other creditors. Needless to say, servicing these debts diverts money from spending on things like health care, providing citizens with clean water, and education. It is estimated that African countries pay $1.51 in debt service for every $1 they receive in aid.

In June, this year, the G-8 countries agreed to provide around $31 billion in debt relief to 41 Heavily Indebted Poor Countries (HIPC), 34 of which are in Africa. Obviously, $31 billion does not in any way reduce the debts of African countries to sustainable levels. In fact, for a very long time activists have pointed it out that the Heavily Indebted Poor Countries Initiative only serves the interests of creditors by continuing to extract the maximum possible in debt repayments from the world's poorest countries.

"Debt Reform and Social Services" by Mandisi Majavu. ZNet, September 20, 2004. Copyright 2004. Reprinted by permission of the author.

Another goal that seems like a pipe-dream is the Millennium Development Goal (MDG). Drawn up in 1990, the MDG aim was to reduce poverty and boost trade. However, 14 years later very little trade has been cultivated. As for poverty? It has increased.

Africa's exports have dropped from 10 percent of the world's market 50 years ago to 2.7 percent today. Also, economic growth fell from 36 percent between 1960 and 1980 (when countries exercised more control over their economies) to minus 15 percent between 1980 and 1998.

Furthermore, the fact that western trade is heavily subsidized by $1 billion a day further depresses the economic situation.

And so, despite a wealth of natural resources, the continent is struggling to lift its economic growth rate. African economies expanded by an estimated 3.2 percent last year, less than half of China's rate of between 8 percent and 9 percent; while India's economy grows at between 7 percent and 8 percent. Africa accounts for only 1.5 percent of global gross domestic product while its share of the global population is about 13 percent. And its share of global world trade is only 2.1 percent.

Africa's economy, which is about $600 billion, has also seen foreign investment drop over the last year to $6 billion from $14 billion. The IMF's and the World Bank's solution to the investment question is that in order for the continent to achieve the foreign investment it needs, it would have to accelerate reforms — meaning a further liberalization of African economies.

It is the same reforms that have facilitated the increase of poverty levels on the continent by 43 percent over the last decade. As things stand, it is estimated that about 300 million Africans live in poverty, and by 2015 that number is expected to increase by 45 million.

Diseases are also starting to take their toll in terms of human resources. About 6,500 Africans die each day from HIV/AIDS related illnesses, and about 2 million people die every year from malaria.

Since the 1980s, deaths from malaria have steadily risen in Africa, as the disease has become resistant to the most popular treatment. Malaria alone is the third biggest killer in the Horn of Africa and claims around 250 lives a day; while Zimbabwe, which is situated within the Southern Africa, records an average of between 1,000 and 1,500 deaths per year.

The aid agency, Medecins Sans Frontieres, believes the reason for such high numbers of deaths is simply because the majority of Africans cannot afford to pay the US$1.50 required for the Artemisinin Combination Therapy (ACT), and most African governments cannot afford to subsidize the drugs. The ACT is a new, more effective drug, which eradicates symptoms of malaria within three days.

Simply put, the ACT drugs, which were endorsed by the World Health Organisation in 2002, cost double that of other medicines and therefore are not widely available.

MSF estimates that it would cost between US$100 million and US$200 million to introduce ACT treatments throughout Africa.

What the African continent really needs is not private investment and economic reforms, rather, African countries need to start using the resources they have to improve health care, education, provide clean water to Africans and feed their young children. And not spend about $15 billion each year on repaying wealthy and powerful institutions like the IMF and the World Bank.

The Impact of Water Privatization on South African Women

–Meredith Throop

Meredith Throop, a student intern with TransAfrica Forum, researched and wrote the following account of the impact of water privatization on South African women. It appeared in TransAfrica Forum's Globalization Monitor *in the Fall 2004 issue.*

Water privatization, an increasingly momentous issue in the arenas of conservation, development and poverty reduction, may become the most controversial global phenomena of this century. Governments at all levels have determined goals and means by which to reduce poverty, diseases, and gender inequities. Yet many argue that the foundation on which these social injustices are based only grows stronger as control of basic goods and services is transferred to the private sector.

In South Africa, the hope for the health and prosperity of the poor is dependent upon water availability and accessibility. One of the most conflict-ridden developments in post-apartheid South Africa has been this ceding of ownership, operation, distribution, and management of water and water services from the public into

"Water and the African World," *TransAfrica Forum*, Volume II, Issue 1, Fall 2004. © 2004 by TransAfrica Forum Globalization Monitor.

private hands. Today in South Africa there are roughly 16 million people, or 40% of the population, that do not have an adequate supply of safe drinking water because of recent private sector, cost-cutting initiatives. There is a growing concern that the livelihoods, health, dignity and survival of South African women living in poverty are at risk.

I have just returned from an academic trip to South Africa where we examined an array of development issues and conducted independent research. This article will summarize my observations of the impact of water privatization on impoverished South African women.

Brief History: From Apartheid to Privatization

South Africa's history of apartheid, a system of racial domination based on segregation through legislation (1948–1994), engendered a legacy of inequality where white South Africa and black South Africa received drastically different water service and delivery. In 1994, the African National Congress (ANC) party was elected into power, marking an end to the apartheid regime in South Africa. Although the ANC government emerged from the apartheid era with an enormous debt burden and need for social restructuring, the conviction that the political conversion would rapidly cultivate a social and economic transformation filled millions of impoverished South African women with hope. Because of the government's desire to enhance competitiveness and reduce public spending, however, the ANC has been attempting to satisfy the most basic needs for all of its citizens through a commitment to the capitalist, free-market economic model. Water privatization has become a fundamental government policy for the ANC, and there is more than doubt that the private sector, which acts primarily on economic incentives, will ameliorate the potent inequities that continue to thrive today.

In 1996, the ANC party, led by Nelson Mandela, wrote a new constitution with the promise of "a better life for all". Today, however, the availability of drinking water and consequently the right to life (safety, food, health, dignity, economic opportunity, and education) are denied to thousands of poor black South African women who cannot afford the heightened price tag on water. While both men and women living in poverty have been adversely affected by the government's decision to privatize public water services, women have, through their traditional roles in the home, workplace and society, been disproportionately impacted.

Every day women and girls walk long distances to fetch water for their families, often at the expense of education, income-generating activities, cultural and political involvement, and rest and recreation. Women primarily bear the sole responsibility for the management and transport of water, as well as cooking, washing, gardening, cleaning, and providing drinking water for their families. As accessibility to water deteriorates, poor women's livelihoods and thus the livelihoods of entire families become increasingly vulnerable.

Poverty in South Africa runs thick among the historically disadvantaged black African populations and is overwhelmingly concentrated among women. Poverty has manifested itself in poor infrastructure and sub-standard and unreliable basic services, as well as in widespread unemployment. Black urban communities surrounding predominantly white areas have been underserved for decades due to lack of economic resources and political power and representation. Privatization can potentially worsen this neglect of "un-official" communities which are not as capable of paying as much for water as residents from wealthier communities. Furthermore, profit-based water delivery services find little incentive to deliver clean water to the millions of people living in informal settlements. The local South African governments that work most closely with the people are required to provide basic services to all communities to help alleviate poverty. According to the *Municipal Service Partnerships White Paper* (*Gazettes* 21126, Notice 1689, 26 April 2000, Department of Provincial and Local Government), the local, national and provincial governments have the task of eradicating poverty, boosting local economic development, creating jobs and carrying out the process of reconstruction and development.

Pressurize to Privatize

The same year that the South African Constitution was established, the ANC firmly committed itself to a neo-liberal, macroeconomic strategy known as GEAR (Growth, Employment and Redistribution), released in June of 1996. One of the economic reforms within GEAR is the privatization of state assets such as water. Although the ANC government claims to be acting independently on their decision to privatize water services, it is undeniable that pressure to do so is swiftly escalating from powerful Inter-Governmental Organizations (IGOs) such as the World Trade Organization (WTO), the International Monetary Fund (IMF) and the World Bank. The IMF and the World Bank have aggressively pursued the privatization of water, arguing that private corporate management will be more cost effective and efficient for South Africa. With its tremendous debt and extreme restructuring needs, the ANC government is left with little option other than to obtain loans from the IMF and World Bank.

Multinational corporations such as Suez and Biwater have been extremely influential in the decision to privatize South Africa's water. Biwater, a multinational British water company, was awarded a 30-year concession in Nelspruit, South Africa in 1999. That community has complained of service fees that have since nearly tripled, and of cut-offs for those who have not been able to pay the steep prices for water. Biwater officials have reported that access to water for the poor is being prevented by a lack of credit and income.

Impoverished women living in rural areas and informal settlements are the most neglected under such a model. The informal settlements, where poverty and unemployment run rampant, are home to more than 8 million South Africans.

During my visit to the informal settlement of Crossroads, Mandy, an impoverished African mother of several children, expressed her helplessness. She said, "My children are always dirty and smelly. I have to leave while it is still dark if I want to reach the water before the line is too long. If I don't leave until it is light out I get home so late. When we must have water there is no time for anything else."

Innovative Cost-Recovery: Pre-Paid Water Consumption

South African townships have been experiencing rapid price hikes in areas where drinking water used to be free. In the city of Nelspruit, for example, water fees have nearly tripled since the transfer of water service to Biwater, and the company has been quick to cut off service for those who cannot afford to pay. One of the methods by which Biwater, Suez, and other water companies ensure cost recovery is through a recently implemented technology, the prepaid water meter system. This device requires customers to pay for water before consumption. Pre-paid water meters allow the water to flow from the tap only when a charged card is put into the system. Water service is terminated if the card's balance is depleted, and is restored only when the consumer can pay again. The service is rapidly spreading throughout South African townships and has already been installed in many black South African municipalities with habitually poor payment records.

As Thidi Tshiguuho, a young Zulu woman from the Limpopo province explained in an interview, "The people don't understand why they should have to pay for the water. It has always been a service that has come to these areas [townships and impoverished rural communities] for free. And they really don't have the extra money to begin buying their water right now. So people got angry of course, and they tore all of the meters down."

Water-Borne Disease: The Case of Empangening

On a global scale, the World Health Organization estimates that 2.3 billion people suffer from water-borne diseases each year. Privatization has exacerbated the prevalence of water-borne sickness in South Africa. The increased incidence of cholera (five-fold more than the past twenty years combined) is a direct result of the use of various cost-recovery techniques; the most deleterious change is the removal of free communal standpipes and their replacement with pre-paid water meters. What happens when women are not able to generate hard cash to put on their water cards? Children go dirty and hungry, the sick deteriorate, families suffer and employment projects are forced to close.

During August of 2000, shortly after pre-paid water meters were installed in the Ngwelezane township at Empangeni, Suez began cutting off households that fell behind on their payments. As cut-offs spread, sending South African women to polluted rivers, streams, and open pits to draw water, so did cholera. Cholera-causing bacteria infect the intestines causing diarrhea, vomiting, leg cramps, and the rapid loss of body fluids, leading to severe dehydration, shock and possible death. After the installation of prepaid meters in the KwaZulu-Natal province, public hospitals reported nearly 114,000 cases of cholera, more than five times as many cases as had been reported over the previous 20 years! The disease was so rampant that hospitals opened 14 hydration centers around Empangeni where medics worked 24-hour shifts. The city ran short of ambulances, and the national South African defense forces came in to shuttle patients to hospitals and medical tents. The military was needed for six months while those who didn't have money to pay for water continued to fall deathly ill by the thousands.

Inadequate water and sanitation service exacerbates the condition of people suffering from immune deficiencies such as HIV/AIDS. Because women bear the main burden of caring for ill family members and friends, they are disproportionately handicapped when clean water is not accessible for their bedridden friends and family members. It is imperative that victims of HIV/AIDS remain adequately hydrated; when women cannot afford to use clean water there is little to no alternative to contaminated water. In Orangefarm, Suez requires residents to physically unclog the city pipes with their own hands when they are blocked; this has lent to the rapid spread of water-borne diseases to which susceptible HIV/AIDS victims are fatally prone.

Furthermore, transfer of water services to the private sector, where the public good is not the top priority, may weaken protection of water quality. Private corporations have few economic incentives to address the long-term health problems associated with water pollutants. Some corporations have a long-standing history of understating or misrepresenting the health impacts of water-quality problems that do occur.

Undermining Dignity

Many women feel humiliated because of problems in accessing water. Women are forced to beg for water from neighbors when they have no money. From an early age, damaging stigma weighs on their children as they go for weeks with spoiled, pungent clothing. For most impoverished women living in informal settlements throughout South Africa, there is simply not enough water to lead a dignified life.

Pre-paid water meters are taking a toll on social cohesion in impoverished neighborhoods and communities. A faulty tap near one's own house was not a problem when neighbors could share water, but since the installation of pre-paid water meters, the survival and dignity of women depend on the depth of their pocket books. When water goes dry and women are forced to choose between feeding their children and buying water, some opt to pilfer a neighbor's water during the night. Animosity and tension begin to break up neighbors who once held a common bond. Violence over water is resulting in divisions among communities living in poverty. Rich or poor, humans must have access to clean drinking water in order to survive.

South Africa is barely beginning to recover from an era of extreme inequalities in terms of political and economic opportunities. Social problems stemming from privatizing water could undermine other necessary development in South Africa. Clean water must be made available in regions where basic human water needs are not being met. Water must continue to be treated as a public resource while other economic improvements and projects are being implemented. Efforts to privatize must be accompanied by formal agreements to provide for basic human needs and to ensure equitable access to impoverished and historically neglected populations. In a country where six hundred thousand white farmers consume over sixty percent of the country's water supply for irrigation, while fifteen million black South Africans do not yet have direct access to clean water, there is still much to be done.

Mandy is surrounded by thousands of shacks like hers, all built atop a trash field that extends as far as the eye can see. The afternoon is ripe with the smell of human waste penetrating all of our senses. When asked how she manages without ready access to water, Mandy replied, pointing off into the horizon, " . . . sometimes I beg from the people over there. They have government houses and they get water. But it is bad begging for water, you know. Awful. But the worst is when you can't help your children or wash their clothes. And they smell so bad and everyone knows it." And does she hope that someday water will come to the Crossroads? "They are all liars. Liars. They say you will have water and your children will have school. It is not true. They haven't done anything. At night we have no toilets. We must cross the railroad and crouch over in the bushes with the snakes. Men are waiting for us over there. It is dangerous but we have no water here so we have no choice."

10 ten

Water Privatization Charts

–Ifeoma Opara

Ifeoma Opara, who prepared the water privatization charts reprinted below, was the 2003–2004 Phillipe Wamba Research Fellow at the Institute for International Public Policy, TransAfrica Forum. They appeared in the Forum's Globalization Monitor in the Fall Issue, 2004.

Major International Water Companies

Africa	Latin America/Caribbean	North America
ONDEO	ONDEO	Vivendi
Vivendi	American Water	Azurix
SAUR	Vivendi	United Water
Thames Water	Agbar	ONDEO
	Severn Trent/WIMPEY	

Percentage of Water & Sanitation Services Privatized/Project Value of Market

Region	Percentage Privatized, 1997 (%)	Percentage Privatized, 2010 (%)	Value of Privatized Market, 2010 (US$, billions)
Western Europe*	20	35	10
Central and Eastern Europe	4	20	4+
North America	5	15	9
Latin America	4	60	9+
Africa	3	33	3
Asia	1	20	10

*Excluding France and UK, Source: Vivendi (1999).
Source: http://www.thewaterpage.com/int_companies1.htm
        www.psiru.org

"Water Privatization Charts," Ifeoma Opera, *TransAfrica Forum*, Vol. II, Issue 1, Fall 2004. © 2004 by TransAfrica Forum Globalization Monitor.

Types of Public-Private Partnership Water Privatization Contracts

Contract Type	Description	Examples
Cooperatives	They can position themselves to be the service providers for certain (often poorer, informal) areas of a city and manage facilities in these areas. Often used in rural areas, in conjunction with NGO's.	Port-au-Prince, Haiti; Orangi, Pakistan
Service Contracts	Public authority retains overall responsibility for the operation and maintenance (O&M) of the system, and contracts out specific components. Service contracts last 1–3 years and include services such as meter reading, billing and maintenance.	Mexico City; Santiago, Chile; Madras, India
Management Contracts	Public authority transfers responsibility for the management of a full range of activities within a specific field, such as O&M. Remuneration is based on key performance indicators. Public authority typically finances working and investment capital and determines cost recovery policy. Usually contracts last between three and five years.	Cartagena, Colombia; Gdansk, Poland; Mali; Johannesburg, South Africa
Lease contracts	Private operator rents the facilities from a public authority and is responsible for O&M of the complete system and tariff collection. Lesser effectively buys the right to the revenue stream and thus shares significant commercial risks. Usually contracts last between five to fifteen years.	Cote d'Ivoire; Guinea; Czech Republic
BOT (Build, Operate, Transfer)	Usually need to procure large discreet items of infrastructure e.g. water treatment plants that require significant finance. The private operator is required to finance, construct, O&M the facility for a specific period of time (usually more than 20 years) before transferring the facility back to the public authority. Variations: BOOT (Build, Own, Operate, Transfer) and BOO (Build, Own, Operate).	Mendoza, Argentina; Izmit, Turkey
Concessions	Private operator takes responsibility for O&M and investment; ownership of assets still rests with the public authority. Concessions are substantial in scope (usually a whole city or region) and tenders are usually bid on the tariff 25–30 years.	Buenos Aires, Argentina; Manilla, Philippines; Cancun, Mexico
Divestiture	Full private ownership and responsibility under a regulatory regime.	England and Wales

Information collected from Webster & Sansom, 1999.
Available @ http://www.thewaterpage.com/ppp_new_main.htm

eleven

Global Apartheid:
AIDS and Murder by Patent
–Salih Booker and William Minter

Salih Booker is executive director of Africa Action, the oldest Africa advocacy organiza-
tion in the United States. He is a board member of the Interhemispheric Resource Cen-
ter (IRC) and Foreign Policy in Focus analyst and Advisory Committee member.
William Minter is editor of AfricaFocus Bulletin. He studied at the University of
Ibadan in Nigeria and has taught in Tanzania and Mozambique at the secondary
school of the Mozambique Liberation Front (FRELIMO). He holds a Ph.D. in sociol-
ogy and a certificate in African studies from the University of Wisconsin at Madison.
The article that follows was published in the July 9, 2001 issue of The Nation.

In mid-April, worldwide protests forced an international cartel of pharmaceutical
giants to withdraw a lawsuit against the South African government. The suit—an
effort by "Big Pharma" to protect its enormous profit—sought to block implementation of a 1997 South African law that would make it easier to acquire lifesaving
medicines for more than 4 million South Africans living with HIV/AIDS. Like the
proponents of apartheid before them, these companies acted to maintain the rules
of a system that denies the value of black lives in favor of minority privilege. The
result in Africa has been murder by patent.

The global pattern of AIDS deaths—2.4 million in sub-Saharan Africa last
year, out of 3 million worldwide; only 20,000 in North America but most in minority communities—also evokes the racial order of the old South Africa. To date, access to lifesaving medicines and care for people living with HIV and AIDS have
been largely determined by race, class, gender and geography. AIDS thus points to
more fundamental global inequalities than those involving a single disease, illumi-
nating centuries-old patterns of injustice. Indeed, today's international political
economy—in which undemocratic institutions systematically generate economic
inequality—should be described as "global apartheid."

Global apartheid, stated briefly, is an international system of minority rule
whose attributes include: differential access to basic human rights; wealth and

"Global Apartheid" by Salih Booker and William Minter. Reprinted with permission from the July 9,
2001 issue of *The Nation*. For subscription information call 1-800-333-8536. Portions of each week's
Nation magazine can be accessed at http://www.thenation.com.

power structured by race and place; structural racism, embedded in global economic processes, political institutions and cultural assumptions; and the international practice of double standards that assume inferior rights to be appropriate for certain "others," defined by location, origin, race or gender.

Global apartheid thus defined, we believe, is more than a metaphor. The concept captures fundamental characteristics of the current world order missed by such labels as "neoliberalism," "globalization" or even "corporate globalization." Most important, it clearly defines what is fundamentally unacceptable about the current system, strips it of the aura of inevitability and puts global justice and democracy on the agenda as the requirements for its transformation. . . .

Perhaps more than any other manifestation of global apartheid, the AIDS pandemic exposes the fact that the distribution of current suffering associated with global inequality, as in the past five centuries, is clearly linked to the place and race. According to the World Health Organization (WHO), forty-four of the fifty-two countries with life expectancies of less than fifty years are in Africa (with life expectancies still declining due to AIDS). The glacial pace of the international response to AIDS reflects an entrenched double standard characteristic of the apartheid system. As Dr. Peter Piot of UNAIDS remarked just before the World AIDS conference in South Africa last year, "If this had happened with white people, the reaction would have been different."

Health is one of the fundamental human rights embodied in the 1946 constitution of the WHO and the 1948 Universal Declaration of Human Rights. Specifically, the WHO constitution says, "The enjoyment of the highest attainable standard of health is one of the fundamental rights of every human being without distinction of race, religion, political belief, economic or social condition." Article 25 of the Universal Declaration states that "Everyone has the right to a standard of living adequate for the health and well-being of himself and his family, including food, clothing, housing and medical care and necessary social services." As even mainstream economists increasingly recognize, health is one of the fundamental prerequisites for development. Along with education and income, it is one of the three components of the UN's Human Development Index, which has gained wide acceptance in theory, if not in practice, as a better benchmark than purely economic indicators like per capita income. In fact, health is the human right that in practice most visibly marks distinction of race, or of economic or social condition.

Whether governments and international organizations actually have an obligation to enforce this right is hotly disputed. The Bush Administration, following in the steps of its predecessors, stressed in its March 30 response to the UN's draft declaration on AIDS that "for legal and constitutional reasons, the United States cannot accept a 'rights based approach' to HIV/AIDS—any more than it can accept a rights based approach to food, shelter or hunger." At the UN High Commission on Human Rights in April, the United States alone abstained on an otherwise unanimously supported Brazilian resolution recognizing "that access to medication in the context of pandemics such as HIV/AIDS is one fundamental element . . . of the right . . . to health."

The scale of the AIDS pandemic is unprecedented. But AIDS is like other widespread diseases in that it is fueled not only by unequal access to medical care but also by social and economic conditions. Poverty and gender inequality fuel the pandemic in Africa. Malnutrition reduces resistance to disease. Migrant labor patterns (well entrenched in Africa from colonialism and apartheid) raise the risk of infection. The proximate cause of the spread of AIDS is HIV, but vulnerability to infection is linked not only to behavior but especially to unequal power relations between women and men, and to poverty and living conditions. Poverty, in turn, is linked to race and to the structural position of communities within countries and of countries within the world economy.

Thus debating what is to be done about AIDS keeps leading back to broader issues. Unless women have the freedom to negotiate the terms of sex, increased awareness and availability of condoms will have only limited impact. Health services deprived of basic resources will be unable to meet the need for treatment or prevention of AIDS. Meeting in Abuja, Nigeria, in April, African leaders agreed on a target of spending at least 15 percent of their national budgets on health, two or three times the current levels. But their chances of meeting this target are slim if they are forced to give priority to paying illegitimate foreign debts over making investments in public health (or if they choose to divert resources to war or personal gain).

Some cite such factors as excuses for inaction. Even as prices of antiretroviral drugs drop in response to protest and generic competition, the lack of health infrastructure and the inability of governments to pay even the reduced prices become new rationales for denying antiretroviral treatment to Africans. As one unidentified international health official told the *Washington Post* on April 23, while deploring the political stance of activists, "We may have to sit by and just see these millions of people die."

The alternate response is to address the reasons for lack of infrastructure and inability to pay. That leads back to policies imposed by international financial institutions in the 1980s and 1990s and, in a longer view, to harsh historical legacies that policy-makers still refuse to confront. Granted, corruption and policy mistakes by African leaders also play a role. But in Africa and in other developing regions, unsustainable debt and weakened health systems result in large part from economic policy conditions imposed by international creditors during the past two decades. The imposition of "user fees" for primary healthcare, for example, drove large numbers away from public health services, contributing to increased rates of sexually transmitted diseases. More generally, cutbacks in the public sector helped send health professionals to the private sector or abroad and reduced investments in healthcare delivery systems. Creditors representing a collective economic colonialism managed by the World Bank and IMF increasingly dictated public health and other policies of poor countries. Debt provided the leverage to enforce the economic *diktat* of global apartheid by the rich upon the poor.

The capacity of postindependence African countries to chart their own course was heavily affected by the fact that neither political nor economic structures had yet broken free of the colonial legacies of authoritarian governance and economic dependence on export of primary commodities. Despite victories by prodemocracy forces in Africa over the past decade, including the demise of formal apartheid in South Africa, and despite modest recoveries in economic growth rates in recent years, AIDS struck a continent that was extraordinarily vulnerable.

Today's inequalities build on a foundation of the old inequalities of slavery and colonialism, plus the destructive aftermath of cold war crusades. Like apartheid in South Africa, global apartheid entrenches great disparities in wealth, living conditions, life expectancy and access to government institutions with effective power. It relies on the assumption that it is "natural" for different population groups to have different expectations of life. In apartheid South Africa, that was the rationale for differentiating everything according to race, from materials for housing to standards of education and healthcare. Globally it is now the rationalization used to defend the differential between Europe and Africa in funding for everything from peacekeeping to humanitarian assistance ($1.23 a day for European refugees, 11 cents a day for African refugees). As one relief worker said, "You must give European refugees used to cappuccino and CNN a higher standard of living to maintain the refugees' sense of dignity and stability."

Gradations of privilege according to group are closely linked to the possibility of crossing barriers from the "homelands" to the more privileged geographical areas. Like apartheid's influx control, the immigration barriers of developed countries do not succeed in stopping the flow despite raising the costs of enforcement. Moreover, the global governance regime that is assigned responsibility for maintaining the current economic order—as was the case with apartheid in its heyday—allocates key decisions to institutions resistant to democratic control: a global version of "white minority rule."

We are not the first to note the striking parallels between the world system and the old South Africa. Canada-based international relations scholar Gernot Kohler wrote a monograph on global apartheid in 1978 noting multiple parallels: "a white minority is dominant in the system, has a vastly higher standard of living than the multiracial majority, and is privileged in several other dimensions." British political scientist Titus Alexander elaborated the concept in his book *Unraveling Global Apartheid* in 1996, noting that "The G7 countries have 12 per cent of the world's population, but they use over 70 per cent of its resources in cash terms and dominate all major decision-making bodies."

Like these commentators, we do not suggest that the mechanisms of South African apartheid are precisely duplicated at the global level. But we do argue that the parallels are more than a casual turn of phrase.

To those who say that the current global political and economic orders have to do with more than race, we respond that while that is true, in fact the old apartheid was also not just "about race." It was also an extreme mode of controlling labor by managing differential access to territorial movement and political rights. Racial oppression makes exploitation easier to manage, while exploitation continues within as well as between racial groups. Others have noted that there is no single government or system of international governance that rules the global system as the former apartheid regime did South Africa. True, today's global institutions—from the WTO to the World Bank to various UN agencies—do fall short of a world government. And no racial distinctions appear in their constitutions. But their power over national governments in the global South is in many cases overwhelming. And representation and leadership within these bodies—particularly in the international financial institutions with the most power—do show a strong de facto correlation with race.

At the global level, control of the movement of labor by immigration laws, representation within global institutions and allocation of public investment are of course far more complex and differentiated than the apartheid system in South Africa (though it was also more complex than generally recognized). The resulting global inequality, however, is even starker than that within any country, including apartheid South Africa. A 1999 World Bank income inequality study by B. Milanovic estimates that the richest 1 percent of people in the world receive as much income as the poorest 57 percent. The study also estimates that more than three-quarters of the difference is accounted for by differences between countries, while the remainder is from inequalities within countries. Given such differences, the resemblance between apartheid's influx control and current efforts to stop the "illegal" flow of immigrants from South (and East) to North should be no surprise.

Finally, many have cautioned against a framework that blames the "external" West for everything, thereby relieving African and other local tyrants of their responsibilities for this state of affairs. We maintain that there are integral interrelationships between the global context and the lack of accountability of governments to their peoples. The system works differently from the periods of colonialism or cold war patronage, but the common element is that the structure builds in rewards for elites that respond to external pressures more than to the demands of their own people.

Global apartheid is not only an appropriate description of the current world order; it can also help in efforts to transform it. Protests in the "Seattle" series have most commonly been framed in race-neutral terms that obscure the differential impact of global inequality. We maintain that it is only by understanding globalization in terms of race as well as markets that we can accurately probe the foundations on which the current global system is built and develop a transnational culture of solidarity against a clearly defined enemy.

Our success should be measured by the extent to which we can compel the governments of rich countries, as well as multilateral institutions, to reduce the hemorrhaging of resources from South to North; dramatically increase investment in global public goods to redress current inequalities; and accept that realizing fundamental human rights for all is an obligation—not an optional charitable response. Some priority steps are clear and immediate: Address the AIDS pandemic through adequate funding for treatment and prevention, cancel the illegitimate debt, stop imposing catastrophic economic policies on poor countries and stop trade rules that value corporate profit over human life. And, as both an indispensable means and an end in itself, democratize the institutions that make such decisions and eliminate their policies and practices of discrimination by race, gender and HIV status. The US Congress should reserve 5 percent of the anticipated budget surplus each year to fight the AIDS pandemic and to support related global health needs. In addition, Washington can require the full cancellation of the debts owed by African countries to the World Bank and the IMF as a condition for future US appropriations to those institutions. And finally, the Administration should uphold the rights of African nations to insure access to lifesaving medications—including generically manufactured drugs—at the lowest cost for their citizens and should drop the US pressure against Brazil at the WTO, as it forms part of a strategy seeking to undermine those rights.

Our language, moreover, should make it clear that we hold global institutions and those who run them responsible. Allowing the defenders of privilege to monopolize the term "globalization" for their own vision too easily allows them to portray themselves as agents of an impersonal process and to paint advocates of global justice as narrow nationalists or naïve opponents of technological progress. If we do not intend to surrender the globe to them, then we should not surrender the term globalization. Thus, it should not be necessary to explain that "antiglobalization" protesters are not against the "widening of worldwide interconnectedness," trade with other countries or advances in science but rather against "corporate globalization" or "neoliberal globalization." It is also not enough to counter with proposals for "people's globalization" or "globalization from below."

Rather, we should make it clear that genuine globalization requires that global democracy replace global apartheid. Despite the apparent diversity of issues, this is precisely what the emerging movement for global justice demands. We look not to some imagined past of national autonomy but to a future in which growing interconnectedness means justice and diversity rather than continued inequality and discrimination. Moreover, the last few years show a potential for greater impact that is just beginning to be felt—in protests from Seattle to Johannesburg to Quebec, in passage of the international landmine treaty and in shifting the debate on poor-country debt from "forgiveness" to "cancellation" to "reparations."

AIDS makes it plain. The fight against global apartheid is a matter of life and death for much of humankind and for the very concept of our common humanity.

12
twelve

The Chad-Cameroon Pipeline
–Adrienne Frazier

Adrienne Frazier, who wrote the following article about the Chad-Cameroon Pipeline, works for TransAfrica Forum. It appeared in the Forum's Globalization Monitor, Vol. I, *Issue II, Summer 2003.*

The Chad-Cameroon Pipeline runs 663 miles from an oil field in the south of Chad to a marine export facility on the Atlantic in Kribi, Cameroon, roughly the distance between downtown Washington, D.C. and Chicago, IL[1]. The pipeline which began pumping in July 2003 is through environmentally and socially sensitive areas, which have traditionally been difficult to access. The path runs through waterways, rainforests and near the habitat of the Bakola people, the oldest inhabitants of the region. The pipeline route is also within miles of Yaoundé, the capital of Cameroon and Doba, Chad's largest city.

Oil Companies and the World Bank

The World Bank is financing the pipeline by using private sources for 81% of its projected cost. The sponsors are ExxonMobil and Chevron of the U.S., and Petronas of Malaysia. The companies are financing 40%, 30%, and 25% of the project respectively. The corporate lead on the project is ExxonMobil, the same company responsible for the largest oil spill in U.S. history. The Exxon Valdez leaked 260,000 barrels of oil in Prince William Sound, Alaska in March 1989 when it ran aground on a reef. Though censured and publicly vilified for that spill, there is little accountability on the oil companies' part should a disaster strike along the pipeline in Africa. Citizens in Chad and Cameroon have been largely ignored, as have environmental and human rights groups.

Though originally projected to be finished near the end of 2003, the pipeline began pumping oil six months early. At peak, the field's 300 wells will produce up to 250,000 barrels of oil per day. The amount of oil being exported from the region could one day be greater if, as projected, other oil companies begin construction of more oil fields to take advantage of the pipeline to the coast. At present, Africa

"The Chad-Cameroon Pipe Line" by Adrienne Frazier, *TransAfrica Forum*, Vol. 1, Issue II, Summer, 2003. © 2003 by TransAfrica Forum Globalization Monitor.

accounts for 14% of U.S. oil imports; by 2015, that figure is expected to have grown to 25%.

From the start, the pipeline has been marred in controversy. ExxonMobil and its partners in the project were reluctant to finance the project without insurance that their investment would be protected in the politically volatile and geographically isolated region. In the early 1990s, some of the richest companies in the world approached the World Bank seeking to insure their investment before beginning construction. The oil companies' move to seek Bank support was strategic. Chad and Cameroon, as developing countries, cannot afford to provoke the ire of the World Bank for fear of risking current and future World Bank grants, loans, and projects in the region. In addition to the royalties and promised payments, the governments face losing future investments from the Bank as well as corporate interest if the pipeline project falls apart.

Popular Input

Additionally, should President Idriss Deby of Chad or President Paul Biya of Cameroon misuse or steal the funds while in office, it is the citizens of Chad and Cameroon that will be left to foot the loans for the project. Should the project fail, they will have a much more difficult time in accessing foreign aid though they may very well have never reaped the rewards of the oil. In many ways, Chad and Cameroon are more heavily invested in the project than the pipeline's financiers. Environmentalists, religious groups, human rights organizations, and others active in the region, have pointed to the well-documented corruption and human rights violations of President Deby's government. Though no one denies the need for funds for either of the desperately poor countries, these groups called for a moratorium on the project early in its discussion because the regions lacked agencies to research and/or handle the effects of the pipeline's unintended consequences, including a change in human migration patterns or environmental damage. It is widely feared that the people of Chad and Cameroon will never see the profits from the project.

In answer to those concerns, the World Bank created an unprecedented independent review group to monitor the project's completion. The International Advisory Group (IAG) was created as a model for future Bank projects. The IAG is the only official group where individuals affected by a Bank project can go to have their concerns heard and possibly addressed. However, at best, the IAG has operated with mixed success. Many of the concerns that the IAG raised regarding the project's environmental effects, the way the projected funds will be spent, and the social consequences of the project have since been dismissed by those in senior management positions at the Bank.

It is hoped that the Revenue Management Law, passed in 1998, will prevent mismanagement or theft of the profits from the pipeline. The law dictates how the profits from the pipeline are allocated. Twenty percent of the project's profits are to go to a savings account, and the remaining 80% is to be spent on priority social sectors defined as education, health and social services, infrastructure, and water management among others. The law is the first of its kind and therefore untested. However, critics note that there is little government transparency and a high degree of corruption. Fueling the concerns of Chadian citizens and activist organizations on the ground, in December 2001, President Deby used $4.5 million of a $25 million signing bonus to purchase weapons.

Because the pipeline, the largest currently funded venture on the continent, runs through a region far-removed from existing roads and railroads, the project entailed construction of new roads to reach the pipeline's construction sites. However, locals have complained that most of the construction jobs go to foreigners brought in for the pipeline project. Of those jobs available to locals, most are for low-skilled workers and are of short duration.

The project also raises environmental and health concerns. With the new roads comes an ease of access to largely untouched rainforests for timber companies and animal hunters. Cameroon already has one of the world's highest deforestation rates, which is likely to increase with the new access via roadway. Public health officials worry that waves of people looking for work on the construction crew or looking to profit from the construction have fueled a population boom along the route, for which the region is unprepared. There is not adequate housing or sanitation. There has also been a boom to prostitution in these areas, and it is feared that HIV/AIDS could increase dramatically in the regions as well.

In sum, Chad and Cameroon are not adequately prepared for a project of this size and scope. The countries lack the infrastructure to manage environmental damage or unforeseen consequences. Meanwhile, the potential for disaster is great; the pipeline runs through environmentally sensitive areas and, at times, runs near large human populations as well. Further, the degree of government corruption is matched by the relative lack of transparency on the part of the World Bank and the oil companies. The oil companies received investment protection through the World Bank for the project, but Chad and Cameroon citizens have no such guarantees. If it fails or if profits are misspent by officials, funding for the countries could dry up for years, leaving them with only hefty loans.

NOTE

1. The distance between Washington, D.C. and Chicago, IL is approximately 698 miles.

13
thirteen

Squeezed by Debt and Time, Mothers Ship Babies to China

–Somini Sengupta

Somini Sengupta serves as the New Delhi bureau chief for the New York Times, *the first South Asian American to hold that position. She was born in Calcutta, raised mostly in southern California, and received a B.A. in English and Development Studies from UC Berkeley in 1988. The article that follows appeared in the* New York Times *in September of 1999.*

She spent her days at home with her newborn son, knowing that every day she did not work was another day without money to pay back her $20,000 smugglers' debt. She spent her nights awake, hushing the baby so he would not disturb her husband or the three other restaurant workers who shared their three-room apartment in northern Manhattan.

She named the boy Henry, and for four precious months, she nursed him, even after friends warned that she would soon have to let him go.

On the second Thursday in July, the woman, Xiu, finally did. Wrapping a tiny gold bracelet around his wrist, she placed her son in the arms of a friend, who, for $1,000, agreed to take him to China.

Xiu's mother is raising him there now, along with the 10-year-old daughter left behind last year when Xiu joined her husband in New York. She plans to bring Henry back when he reaches school age. But until then, she remains here, waiting to be a mother to her child. For weeks after Henry was shipped off, she would hear him cry at night.

"It seemed like she just gave up the baby to a complete stranger," said Sara Lee, a social worker at the Chinatown clinic of St. Vincent's Hospital and Medical Center, interpreting for Xiu one recent morning. "It's really killing her. She said no words can express her sadness."

Xiu's story has become increasingly common among the city's newest Chinese immigrants. Working long hours in garment factories for paltry pay, lacking affordable child care and the safety net of an extended family, growing numbers of Chinese

Somini Sengupta, "Squeezed by Debt and Time, Mothers Ship Babies to China," *New York Times*, September 14, 1999. Copyright 1999 New York Times Co. Reprinted by permission.

immigrant women—a great many of whom, like Xiu, are here illegally—are sending their infants to China, according to doctors, nurses, social workers and labor organizers.

It is impossible to determine just how widespread the practice is, but it appears to involve hundreds of babies a year in New York, if not more. At the Chinatown Health Center, 10 to 20 percent of the 1,500 babies delivered last year were sent away, according to Celia Ng, the nursing coordinator there. And at the St. Vincent's Hospital Chinatown clinic, according to Ms. Lee, one-third to one-half of the women who seek prenatal care say they plan to send their babies to China.

Most of the mothers are married. Some of their pregnancies, though not all, are planned. And many give birth knowing that soon, they, too, may end up sending their babies away.

The children, American citizens by birth, are usually raised by grandparents. The expectation, though hardly a guarantee, is that the children will be summoned back when they are old enough to begin school. It is a reunion that often comes at considerable emotional cost to parents and children, in the opinion of doctors and social workers.

Their story is another example of the way families have been and continue to be fractured by immigration. Men and women from all over the world come to the United States, leaving children with relatives back home until they gain a foothold. And some immigrant parents send their American children, particularly teen-agers, to the old country, to save them from troubled city streets.

Sending infants to the old country is not unique to the Chinese. But social service agencies working in other immigrant communities say that while it is not unheard of, the practice is still uncommon, usually limited to cases of extreme hardship. Among Dominicans, for instance, it is usually young, single mothers who send their children to the homeland, social workers say.

It is the combination of the large debts owed to their smugglers and the long hours they must work that has made this practice increasingly common among Chinese immigrants. There is an additional cruel dilemma: having left China and its rigid one-child policy, they are finally able to have larger families without fear of penalties or recrimination. But as poor, illegal immigrants here, they say, they are hard pressed to take care of their young.

That more of these mothers are sending their babies to China, people who work with them say, reflects the tougher working and living conditions facing Chinese immigrants today. With the threat of factories' moving abroad driving down wages, and a steady supply of cheap, illegal immigrant labor, mostly from Fujian Province in southern China, a new generation of garment sweatshops has blossomed across the city in recent years, according to garment workers' advocates and those who study Chinese immigration. Wages have fallen, and it is increasingly common for garment shops to require employees to work weekends.

"A lot of people simply have no time for their children," said Joanne Lum of the Chinese Staff and Workers Association, who works with garment workers in Chinatown and the Sunset Park section of Brooklyn.

Since her son was sent home, Xiu has returned to work. She sews women's pants six days a week and sends home $200 each month. At least every other week, she calls home. Every time, her daughter, Kei Wan, asks her to return home.

Kei Wan's chances of coming here any time soon are slim at best, her mother said, since she would have to be smuggled in at great expense.

This was not the picture Xiu had in mind when her husband summoned her here. They had been apart for eight years, she raising their little girl in a small town in southern China, he working as a cook at a Chinese restaurant in Manhattan. When Xiu finally arrived, she brought with her little more than nervous dreams: to work hard, save money, and raise a bigger, more prosperous family than she could imagine doing in China.

In a matter of months, Xiu became pregnant. And that is when she learned of this unforeseen tangle in the immigrant life. "It's not easy," she said, fingering the pictures of her children she keeps in a plastic picture album, "to be a mother here."

It is not illegal to send these American-born children to China. They are American citizens and can travel on American passports. Their couriers are legal residents and so are allowed to travel back and forth.

But while social workers and others say the practice is well known and widespread among New York's Chinese immigrants, that is not to say that the mothers are eager to discuss it. Workers at clinics across the city said they knew of many cases, but only a few mothers agreed to speak to a reporter, and would give their first names only. None agreed to be photographed.

Certainly, most Chinese immigrants do not send their babies away. They manage by staying home, imploring an elderly relative to baby-sit or paying for child care. Day care costs at least $20 a day in Chinatown, a large sum for a garment worker like Xiu, who, in a six-day workweek, takes home less than $300.

A couple of years ago, Ms. Lee saw a flier in the clinic bathroom. For a fee—the going rate is $1,000, plus air fare—someone was offering to take babies to China. Around that time, she noticed an increase in the number of women who sent their babies to China. So she made it a part of her practice to ask all her prenatal patients what they planned to do after giving birth.

Today, she tells each one how painful it can be for a mother to send an infant away. It is hard on fathers as well, though they are more likely to have been separated from their children for many years. She explains how difficult it can be when the child finally comes back, but as a stranger.

"I can't imagine being separated from my kids," said Ms. Lee, whose own children are 1 and 3. "But they have a problem, no matter what."

Zhu, a single woman from Guangdong Province, says that sending her child home is the only way she can imagine surviving in this country. Just before her first child, Thomas, was born last month, Zhu, 36, gave up her job as a home health aide in Brooklyn. Since then, she has lived on her savings, but they will soon be exhausted. So when the Lunar New Year rolls around in February, Zhu, unmarried and alone in New York, plans to take Thomas to China, where her own mother will raise him for a few years, until she can afford to have him by her side once more.

Fortunately for Zhu, she is a legal immigrant. She can take Thomas to China herself. When she can afford it, she can even visit.

That good fortune is beyond Xiu's reach. The other day, the two mothers sat next to each other at the Chinatown clinic run by St. Vincent's Hospital, Xiu keeping her eyes on baby Thomas sleeping against his mother's belly, Zhu admiring the pictures of Xiu's children.

They were talking of the choices they had made, and Xiu was wiping away irrepressible tears.

How hard it was, she said, to walk into the clinic that morning and see babies in their mothers' arms. How hard it was, she said, when the woman who took Henry home called to say that he had cried incessantly on the one-and-a-half-day journey. At least, she said, she had nursed him for the first four months of his life. She would feel so guilty otherwise.

Would it have been easier, she wondered aloud, if she had been younger? A quick rebuttal came from Angel, 33, an immigrant from Guangdong. Five years ago, when she was 28, her husband sent their daughter back home. It wasn't any easier, she said.

At the time, Angel said, she had no choice. She had a good job at a photography shop in Chinatown, and her boss had agreed to let her take a month off after the birth. There was no one to watch the baby all day, nor money for a sitter. Barely 4 weeks old, the baby was sent away.

Three years later, when Angel brought her back to New York, the little girl seemed as miserable as her mother had been when she sent her away. She sat on the sofa in the living room of their apartment in Woodside, Queens, and cried quietly.

A small, sprightly woman who looks half her age, Angel still cries at the memory. It has brought her one lesson. She says she is not planning on any more children.

Nannies, Maids, and Sex Workers in the New Economy

–Barbara Ehrenreich and Arlie Russell Hochschild

Barbara Ehrenreich is a social critic and political activist. She attended Reed College and received a Ph.D. in biology from The Rockefeller University. She writes for The Progressive *as well as many other magazines and was a regular columnist for* Time *from 1991 to 1997. Arlie Russell Hochschild is professor of sociology at University of California Berkeley, where she received her Ph.D. in 1969. Since 1998 she has been director of the Center for Working Families. The essay that follows is taken from the introduction to their anthology* Global Woman: Nannies, Maids, and Sex Workers in the New Economy, *published by Henry Holt and Company in 2003.*

"Whose baby are you?" Josephine Perera, a nanny from Sri Lanka, asks Isadora, her pudgy two-year-old charge in Athens, Greece.

Thoughtful for a moment, the child glances toward the closed door of the next room, in which her mother is working, as if to say, "That's my mother in there."

"No, you're *my* baby," Josephine teases, tickling Isadora lightly. Then, to settle the issue, Isadora answers, "Together!" She has two mommies—her mother and Josephine. And surely a child loved by many adults is richly blessed.

In some ways, Josephine's story—which unfolds in an extraordinary documentary film, *When Mother Comes Home for Christmas*, directed by Nilita Vachani—describes an unparalleled success. Josephine has ventured around the world, achieving a degree of independence her mother could not have imagined, and amply supporting her three children with no help from her ex-husband, their father. Each month she mails a remittance check from Athens to Hatton, Sri Lanka, to pay the children's living expenses and school fees. On her Christmas visit home, she bears gifts of pots, pans, and dishes. While she makes payments on a new bus that Suresh, her oldest son, now drives for a living, she is also saving for a modest dowry for her daughter, Norma. She dreams of buying a new house in which the

Introduction by Barbara Ehrenreich and Arlie Russell Hochschild from *Global Woman: Nannies, Maids, and Sex Workers in the New Economy*, edited by Barbara Ehrenreich and Arlie Russell Hochschild. © 2002 by Barbara Ehrenreich and Arlie Russell Hochschild. Reprinted by permission of Henry Holt and Company LLC.

whole family can live. In the meantime, her work as a nanny enables Isadora's parents to devote themselves to their careers and avocations.

But Josephine's story is also one of wrenching global inequality. While Isadora enjoys the attention of three adults, Josephine's three children in Sri Lanka have been far less lucky. According to Vachani, Josephine's youngest child, Suminda, was two—Isadora's age—when his mother first left home to work in Saudi Arabia. Her middle child, Norma, was nine; her oldest son, Suresh, thirteen. From Saudi Arabia, Josephine found her way first to Kuwait, then to Greece. Except for one two-month trip home, she has lived apart from her children for ten years. She writes them weekly letters, seeking news of relatives, asking about school, and complaining that Norma doesn't write back.

Although Josephine left the children under her sister's supervision, the two youngest have shown signs of real distress. Norma has attempted suicide three times. Suminda, who was twelve when the film was made, boards in a grim, Dickensian orphanage that forbids talk during meals and showers. He visits his aunt on holidays. Although the oldest, Suresh, seems to be on good terms with his mother, Norma is tearful and sullen, and Suminda does poorly in school, picks quarrels, and otherwise seems withdrawn from the world. Still, at the end of the film, we see Josephine once again leave her three children in Sri Lanka to return to Isadora in Athens. For Josephine can either live with her children in desperate poverty or make money by living apart from them. Unlike her affluent First World employers, she cannot both live with her family and support it.

Thanks to the process we loosely call "globalization," women are on the move as never before in history. In images familiar to the West from television commercials for credit cards, cell phones, and airlines, female executives jet about the world, phoning home from luxury hotels and reuniting with eager children in airports. But we hear much less about a far more prodigious flow of female labor and energy: the increasing migration of millions of women from poor countries to rich ones, where they serve as nannies, maids, and sometimes sex workers. In the absence of help from male partners, many women have succeeded in tough "male world" careers only by turning over the care of their children, elderly parents, and homes to women from the Third World. This is the female underside of globalization, whereby millions of Josephines from poor countries in the south migrate to do the "women's work" of the north—work that affluent women are no longer able or willing to do. These migrant workers often leave their own children in the care of grandmothers, sisters, and sisters-in-law. Sometimes a young daughter is drawn out of school to care for her younger siblings.

This pattern of female migration reflects what could be called a worldwide gender revolution. In both rich and poor countries, fewer families can rely solely on a male breadwinner. In the United States, the earning power of most men has declined since 1970, and many women have gone out to "make up the difference." By one recent estimate, women were the sole, primary, or coequal earners in more than half of American families.[1] So the question arises: Who will take care of the children, the sick, the elderly? Who will make dinner and clean house?

While the European or American woman commutes to work an average twenty-eight minutes a day, many nannies from the Philippines, Sri Lanka, and India cross the globe to get to their jobs. Some female migrants from the Third World do find something like "liberation," or at least the chance to become independent breadwinners and to improve their children's material lives. Other, less fortunate migrant women end up in the control of criminal employers—their passports stolen, their mobility blocked, forced to work without pay in brothels or to provide sex along with cleaning and child-care services in affluent homes. But even in more typical cases, where benign employers pay wages on time, Third World migrant women achieve their success only by assuming the cast-off domestic roles of middle- and high-income women in the First World—roles that have been previously rejected, of course, by men. And their "commute" entails a cost we have yet to fully comprehend.

The migration of women from the Third World to do "women's work" in affluent countries has so far received little scholarly or media attention—for reasons that are easy enough to guess. First, many, though by no means all, of the new female migrant workers are women of color, and therefore subject to the racial "discounting" routinely experienced by, say, Algerians in France, Mexicans in the United States, and Asians in the United Kingdom. Add to racism the private "indoor" nature of so much of the new migrants' work. Unlike factory workers, who congregate in large numbers, or taxi drivers, who are visible on the street, nannies and maids are often hidden away, one or two at a time, behind closed doors in private homes. Because of the illegal nature of their work, most sex workers are even further concealed from public view.

At least in the case of nannies and maids, another factor contributes to the invisibility of migrant women and their work—one that, for their affluent employers, touches closer to home. The Western culture of individualism, which finds extreme expression in the United States, militates against acknowledging help or human interdependency of nearly any kind. Thus, in the time-pressed upper middle class, servants are no longer displayed as status symbols, decked out in white caps and aprons, but often remain in the background, or disappear when company comes. Furthermore, affluent careerwomen increasingly earn their status not through leisure, as they might have a century ago, but by apparently "doing it all"—producing a full-time career, thriving children, a contented spouse, and a well-managed home. In order to preserve this illusion, domestic workers and nannies make the house hotel-room perfect, feed and bathe the children, cook and clean up—and then magically fade from sight.

The lifestyles of the First World are made possible by a global transfer of the services associated with a wife's traditional role—child care, homemaking, and sex—from poor countries to rich ones. To generalize and perhaps oversimplify: in an earlier phase of imperialism, northern countries extracted natural resources and agricultural products—rubber, metals, and sugar, for example—from lands they conquered and colonized. Today, while still relying on Third World countries for agricultural and industrial labor, the wealthy countries also seek to extract something harder to measure and quantify something that can look very much like love. Nannies like Josephine bring the distant families that employ them real maternal affection, no doubt enhanced by the heartbreaking absence of their own children in the poor countries they leave behind. Similarly, women who migrate from country to country to work as maids bring not only their muscle power but an attentiveness to detail and to the human relationships in the household that might otherwise have been invested in their own families. Sex workers offer the simulation of sexual and romantic love, or at least transient sexual companionship. It is as if the wealthy parts of the world are running short on precious emotional and sexual resources and have had to turn to poorer regions for fresh supplies.

There are plenty of historical precedents for this globalization of traditional female services. In the ancient Middle East, the women of populations defeated in war were routinely enslaved and hauled off to serve as household workers and concubines for the victors. Among the Africans brought to North America as slaves in the sixteenth through nineteenth centuries, about a third were women and children, and many of those women were pressed to be concubines, domestic servants, or both. Nineteenth-century Irishwomen—along with many rural Englishwomen—migrated to English towns and cities to work as domestics in the homes of the growing upper middle class. Services thought to be innately feminine—child care, housework, and sex—often win little recognition or pay. But they have always been sufficiently in demand to transport over long distances if necessary. What is new today is the sheer number of female migrants and the very long distances they travel. Immigration statistics show huge numbers of women in motion, typically from poor countries to rich. Although the gross statistics give little clue as to the jobs women eventually take, there are reasons to infer that much of their work is "caring work," performed either in private homes or in institutional settings such as hospitals, hospices, child-care centers, and nursing homes.

The statistics are, in many ways, frustrating. We have information on legal migrants but not on illegal migrants, who, experts tell us, travel in equal if not greater numbers. Furthermore, many Third World countries lack data for past years, which makes it hard to trace trends over time; or they use varying methods of gathering information, which makes it hard to compare one country with another. Nevertheless, the trend is clear enough for some scholars to speak of a "feminization of migration."[2] From 1950 to 1970, for example, men predominated in labor migration to northern Europe from Turkey, Greece, and North Africa. Since then, women have been replacing men. In 1946, women were fewer than 3 percent of the Algerians and Moroccans living in France; by 1990, they were more than 40 percent.[3] Overall, half of the world's 120 million legal and illegal migrants are now believed to be women.

Patterns of international migration vary from region to region, but women migrants from a surprising number of sending countries actually outnumber men, sometimes by a wide margin. For example, in the 1990s, women make up over half of Filipino migrants to all countries and 84 percent of Sri Lankan migrants to the Middle East.[4] Indeed, by 1993 statistics, Sri Lankan women such as Josephine vastly outnumbered Sri Lankan men as migrant workers who'd left for Saudi Arabia, Kuwait, Lebanon, Oman, Bahrain, Jordan, and Qatar, as well as to all countries of the Far East, Africa, and Asia.[5] About half of the migrants leaving Mexico, India, Korea, Malaysia, Cyprus, and Swaziland to work elsewhere are also women. Throughout the 1990s women outnumbered men among migrants to the United States, Canada, Sweden, the United Kingdom, Argentina, and Israel.[6]

Most women, like men, migrate from the south to the north and from poor countries to rich ones. Typically, migrants go to the nearest comparatively rich country, preferably one whose language they speak or whose religion and culture they share. There are also local migratory flows: from northern to southern Thailand, for instance, or from East Germany to West. But of the regional or cross-regional flows, four stand out. One goes from Southeast Asia to the oil-rich Middle and Far East—from Bangladesh, Indonesia, the Philippines, and Sri Lanka to Bahrain, Oman, Kuwait, Saudi Arabia, Hong Kong, Malaysia, and Singapore. Another stream of migration goes from the former Soviet bloc to western Europe—from Russia, Romania, Bulgaria, and Albania to Scandinavia, Germany, France, Spain, Portugal, and England. A third goes from south to north in the Americas, including the stream from Mexico to the United States, which scholars say is the longest-running labor migration in the world. A fourth stream moves from Africa to various parts of Europe. France receives many female migrants from Morocco, Tunisia, and Algeria. Italy receives female workers from Ethiopia, Eritrea, and Cape Verde.

Female migrants overwhelmingly take up work as maids or domestics. As women have become an ever greater proportion of migrant workers, receiving countries reflect a dramatic influx of foreign-born domestics. In the United States, African-American women, who accounted for 60 percent of domestics in the 1940s, have been largely replaced by Latinas, many of them recent migrants from Mexico and Central America. In England, Asian migrant women have displaced the Irish and Portuguese domestics of the past. In French cities, North African women have replaced rural French girls. In western Germany, Turks and women from the former East Germany have replaced rural native-born women. Foreign females from countries outside the European Union made up only 6 percent of all domestic workers in 1984. By 1987, the percentage had jumped to 52, with most coming from the Philippines, Sri Lanka, Thailand, Argentina, Colombia, Brazil, El Salvador, and Peru.[7]

The governments of some sending countries actively encourage women to migrate in search of domestic jobs, reasoning that migrant women are more likely than their male counterparts to send their hard-earned wages to their families rather than spending the money on themselves. In general, women send home anywhere from half to nearly all of what they earn. These remittances have a significant impact on the lives of children, parents, siblings, and wider networks of kin—as well as on cash-strapped Third World governments. Thus, before Josephine left for Athens, a program sponsored by the Sri Lankan government taught her how to use a microwave oven, a vacuum cleaner, and an electric mixer.

As she awaited her flight, a song piped into the airport departure lounge extolled the opportunity to earn money abroad. The songwriter was in the pay of the Sri Lanka Bureau of Foreign Employment, an office devised to encourage women to migrate. The lyrics say:

> After much hardship, such difficult times
> How lucky I am to work in a foreign land.
> As the gold gathers so do many greedy flies.
> But our good government protects us from them.
> After much hardship, such difficult times,
> How lucky I am to work in a foreign land.
> I promise to return home with treasures for everyone.

Why this transfer of women's traditional services from poor to rich parts of the world? The reasons are, in a crude way, easy to guess. Women in Western countries have increasingly taken on paid work, and hence need other—paid domestics and caretakers for children and elderly people—to replace them.[8] For their part, women in poor countries have an obvious incentive to migrate: relative and absolute poverty. The "care deficit" that has emerged in the wealthier countries as women enter the workforce *pulls* migrants from the Third World and postcommunist nations; poverty *pushes* them.

In broad outline, this explanation holds true. Throughout western Europe, Taiwan, and Japan, but above all in the United States, England, and Sweden, women's employment has increased dramatically since the 1970s. In the United States, for example, the proportion of women in paid work rose from 15 percent of mothers of children six and under in 1950 to 65 percent today. Women now make up 46 percent of the U.S. labor force. Three-quarters of mothers of children eighteen and under and nearly two-thirds of mothers of children age one and younger now work for pay. Furthermore, according to a recent International Labor Organization study, working Americans averaged longer hours at work in the late 1990s than they did in the 1970s. By some measures, the number of hours spent at work have increased more for women than for men, and especially for women in managerial and professional jobs.

Meanwhile, over the last thirty years, as the rich countries have grown much richer, the poor countries have become—in both absolute and relative terms—poorer. Global inequalities in wages are particularly striking. In Hong Kong, for instance, the wages of a Filipina domestic are about fifteen times the amount she could make as a schoolteacher back in the Philippines. In addition, poor countries turning to the IMF or World Bank for loans are often forced to undertake measures of so-called structural adjustment, with disastrous results for the poor and especially for poor women and children. To qualify for loans, governments are usually required to devalue their currencies, which turns the hard currencies of rich countries into gold and the soft currencies of poor countries into straw. Structural adjustment programs also call for cuts in support for "noncompetitive industries," and for the reduction of public services such as health care and food subsidies for the poor. Citizens of poor countries, women as well as men, thus have a strong incentive to seek work in more fortunate parts of the world.

But it would be a mistake to attribute the globalization of women's work to a simple synergy of needs among women—one group, in the affluent countries, needing help and the other, in poor countries, needing jobs. For one thing, this formulation fails to account for the marked failure of First World governments to meet the needs created by its women's entry into the workforce. The downsized American—and to a lesser degree, western European—welfare state has become a "deadbeat dad." Unlike the rest of the industrialized world, the United States does not offer public child care for working mothers, nor does it ensure paid family and medical leave. Moreover, a series of state tax revolts in the 1980s reduced the number of hours public libraries were open and slashed school-enrichment and after-school programs. Europe did not experience anything comparable. Still, tens of millions of western European women are in the workforce who were not before—and there has been no proportionate expansion in public services.

Secondly, any view of the globalization of domestic work as simply an arrangement among women completely omits the role of men. Numerous studies, including some of our own, have shown that as American women took on paid employment, the men in their families did little to increase their contribution to the work of the home. For example, only one out of every five men among the working couples whom Hochschild interviewed for *The Second Shift* in the 1980s shared the work at home, and later studies suggest that while working mothers are doing somewhat less housework than their counterparts twenty years ago, most men are doing only a little more.[9] With divorce, men frequently abdicate their child-care responsibilities to their ex-wives. In most cultures of the First World outside the United States, powerful traditions even more firmly discourage husbands from doing "women's work." So, strictly speaking, the presence of immigrant nannies does not enable affluent women to enter the workforce; it enables affluent *men* to continue avoiding the second shift.

The men in wealthier countries are also, of course, directly responsible for the demand for immigrant sex workers—as well as for the sexual abuse of many migrant women who work as domestics. Why, we wondered, is there a particular demand for "imported" sexual partners? Part of the answer may lie in the fact that new immigrants often take up the least desirable work, and, thanks to the AIDS epidemic, prostitution has become a job that ever fewer women deliberately choose. But perhaps some of this demand on sex tourism grows out of the erotic lure of the "exotic." Immigrant women may seem desirable sexual partners for the same reason that First World employers believe them to be especially gifted as caregivers: they are thought to embody the traditional feminine qualities of nurturance, docility, and eagerness to please. Some men feel nostalgic for these qualities, which they associate with a bygone way of life. Even as many wage-earning Western women assimilate to the competitive culture of "male" work and ask respect for making it in a man's world, some men seek in the "exotic Orient" or "hot-blooded tropics" a woman from the imagined past.

Of course, not all sex workers migrate voluntarily. An alarming number of women and girls are trafficked by smugglers and sold into bondage. Because trafficking is illegal and secret, the numbers are hard to know with any certainty. Kevin Bales estimates that in Thailand alone, a country of 60 million, half a million to a million women are prostitutes, and one out of every twenty of these is enslaved.[10] Many of these women are daughters whom northern hill-tribe families have sold to brothels in the cities of the south. Believing the promises of jobs and money, some begin the voyage willingly, only to discover days later that the "arrangers" are traffickers who steal their passports, define them as debtors, and enslave them as prostitutes. Other women and girls are kidnapped, or sold by their impoverished families, and then trafficked to brothels. Even worse fates befall women from neighboring Laos and Burma, who flee crushing poverty and repression at home only to fall into the hands of Thai slave traders.

If the factors that pull migrant women workers to affluent countries are not as simple as they at first appear, neither are the factors that push them. Certainly relative poverty plays a major role, but, interestingly, migrant women often do not come from the poorest classes of their societies.[11] In fact, they are typically more affluent and better educated then male migrants. Many female migrants from the Philippines and Mexico, for example, have high school or college diplomas and have held middle-class—albeit low-paid—jobs back home. One study of Mexican migrants suggests that the trend is toward increasingly better-educated female migrants. Thirty years ago, most Mexican-born maids in the United States had been poorly educated maids in Mexico. Now a majority have high school degrees and have held clerical, retail, or professional jobs before leaving for the United States.[12] Such women are likely to be enterprising and adventurous enough to resist the social pressures to stay home and accept their lot in life.

Noneconomic factors—or at least factors that are not immediately and directly economic—also influence a woman's decision to emigrate. By migrating, a woman may escape the expectation that she care for elderly family members, relinquish her paycheck to a husband or father, or defer to an abusive husband. Migration may also be a practical response to a failed marriage and the need to provide for children without male help. In the Philippines, migration is sometimes called a "Philippine divorce." And there are forces at work that may be making the men of poor countries less desirable as husbands. Male unemployment runs high in the countries that supply female domestics to the First World. Unable to make a living, these men often grow demoralized and cease contributing to their families in other ways. Many female migrants tell of unemployed husbands who drink or gamble their remittances away. Notes one study of Sri Lankan women working as maids in the Persian Gulf: "It is not unusual . . . for the women to find upon their return that their Gulf wages by and large have been squandered on alcohol, gambling and other dubious undertakings while they were away."[13]

To an extent then, the globalization of child care and housework brings the ambitious and independent women of the world together: the career-oriented upper-middle-class woman of an affluent nation and the striving woman from a crumbling Third World or postcommunist economy. Only it does not bring them together in the way that second-wave feminists in affluent countries once liked to imagine—as sisters and allies struggling to achieve common goals. Instead, they come together as mistress and maid, employer and employee, across a great divide of privilege and opportunity.

This trend toward global redivision of women's traditional work throws new light on the entire process of globalization. Conventionally, it is the poorer countries that are thought to be dependent on the richer ones—a dependency symbolized by the huge debt they owe to global financial institutions. However, dependency also works in the other direction, and it is a dependency of a particularly intimate kind. Increasingly often, as affluent and middle-class families in the First World come to depend on migrants from poorer regions to provide child care, homemaking, and sexual services, a global relationship arises that in some ways mirrors the traditional relationship between the sexes. The First World takes on a role like that of the old-fashioned male in the family—pampered, entitled, unable to cook, clean, or find his socks. Poor countries take on a role like that of the traditional woman within the family—patient, nurturing, and self-denying. A division of labor feminists critiqued when it was "local" has now, metaphorically speaking, gone global.

To press this metaphor a bit further, the resulting relationship is by no means a "marriage," in the sense of being openly acknowledged. In fact, it is striking how invisible the globalization of women's work remains, how little it is noted or discussed in the First World. Trend spotters have had almost nothing to say about the fact that increasing numbers of affluent First World children and elderly persons are tended by immigrant care workers or live in homes cleaned by immigrant maids. Even the political groups we might expect to be concerned about this trend—antiglobalization and feminist activists—often seem to have noticed only the most extravagant abuses, such as trafficking and female enslavement. So if a metaphorically gendered relationship has developed between rich and poor countries, it is less like a marriage and more like a secret affair.

NOTES

1. See Ellen Galinsky and Dana Friedman, *Women: The New Providers*, Whirlpool Foundation Study, Part 1 (New York: Families and Work Institute, 1995), p. 37.

2. In addition to material directly cited, this introduction draws from the following works: Kathleen M. Adams and Sara Dickey, eds., *Home and Hegemony: Domestic Service and Identity Politics in South and Southeast Asia* (Ann Arbor: University of Michigan Press, 2000); Floya Anthias and Gabriella Lazaridis, eds., *Gender and Migration in Southern Europe: Women on the Move* (Oxford and New York: Berg, 2000); Stephen Castles and Mark J. Miller, *The Age of Migration: International Population Movements in the Modern World* (New York and London: The Guilford Press, 1998); Noeleen Heyzer, Geertje Lycklama à Nijehold, and Nedra Weerakoon, eds., *The Trade in Domestic Workers: Causes, Mechanisms, and Consequences of International Migration* (London: Zed Books, 1994); Eleanore

Kofman, Annie Phizacklea, Parvati Raghuram, and Rosemary Sales, *Gender and International Migration in Europe: Employment, Welfare, and Politics* (New York and London: Routledge, 2000); Douglas S. Massey, Joaquin Arango, Graeme Hugo, Ali Kouaouci, Adela Pellegrino, and J. Edward Taylor, *Worlds in Motion: Understanding International Migration at the End of the Millennium* (Oxford: Clarendon Press, 1999); Janet Henshall Momsen, ed., *Gender, Migration, and Domestic Service* (London: Routledge, 1999); Katie Willis and Brenda Yoeh, eds., *Gender and Immigration* (London: Edward Elgar Publishers, 2000).

3. Illegal migrants are said to make up anywhere from 60 percent (as in Sri Lanka) to 87 percent (as in Indonesia) of all migrants. In Singapore in 1994, 95 percent of Filipino overseas contract workers lacked work permits from the Philippine government. The official figures based on legal migration therefore severely underestimate the number of migrants. See Momsen, 1999, p. 7.

4. Momsen, 1999, p. 9.

5. Sri Lanka Bureau of Foreign Employment, 1994, as cited in G. Gunatilleke, *The Economic, Demographic, Sociocultural and Political Setting for Emigration from Sri Lanka International Migration*, vol. 23 (3/4), 1995, pp. 667–98.

6. Anthias and Lazaridis, 2000; Heyzer, Nijehold, and Weerakoon, 1994, pp. 4–27; Momsen, 1999, p. 21; "Wistat: Women's Indicators and Statistics Database," version 3, CD-ROM (United Nations, Department for Economic and Social Information and Policy Analysis, Statistical Division, 1994).

7. Geovanna Campani, "Labor Markets and Family Networks: Filipino Women in Italy," in Hedwig Rudolph and Mirjana Morokvasic, eds., *Bridging States and Markets: International Migration in the Early 1990s* (Berlin: Edition Sigma, 1993), p. 206.

8. This "new" source of the Western demand for nannies, maids, child-care, and elder-care workers does not, of course, account for the more status-oriented demand in the Persian Gulf states, where most affluent women don't work outside the home.

9. For information on male work at home during the 1990s, see Arlie Russell Hochschild and Anne Machung, *The Second Shift: Working Parents and the Revolution at Home* (New York: Avon, 1997), p. 277.

10. Kevin Bales, *Disposable People: New Slavery in the Global Economy* (Berkeley: University of California Press, 1999), p. 43.

11. Andrea Tyree and Katharine M. Donato, "A Demographic Overview of the International Migration of Women," in *International Migration: The Female Experience*, ed. Rita Simon and Caroline Bretell (Totowa, N.J: Rowman & Allanheld, 1986), p. 29. Indeed, many immigrant maids and nannies are more educated than the people they work for.

12. Momsen, 1999, pp. 10, 73.

13. Grete Brochmann, *Middle East Avenue: Female Migration from Sri Lanka to the Gulf* (Boulder, Colo.: Westview Press, 1993), pp. 179, 215.

Exporting Harm:
The High-Tech Trashing of Asia
–The Basel Action Network

The following is a brief excerpt from the Executive Summary of a report entitled Exporting Harm: The High-Tech Trashing of Asia. *The report was prepared by The Basal Action Network (BAN) and Silicon Valley Toxics Coalition (SVTC) with contributions by Toxic Links India, SCOPE (Pakistan), and Greenpeace (China). It was published by BAN in February 2002. The complete text of the report is available on the Internet at www.ban.org*

Electronic waste or E-waste is the most rapidly growing waste problem in the world. It is a crisis not only of quantity but also a crisis born from toxic ingredients—such as the lead, beryllium, mercury, cadmium, and brominated-flame retardants that pose both an occupational and environmental health threat. But to date, industry, government and consumers have only taken small steps to deal with this looming problem.

This report reveals one of the primary reasons why action to date in the United States has been woefully inadequate. Rather than having to face the problem squarely, the United States and other rich economies that use most of the world's electronic products and generate most of the E-Waste, have made use of a convenient, and until now, hidden escape valve—exporting the E-waste crisis to the developing countries of Asia.

Yet trade in E-waste is an export of real harm to the poor communities of Asia. The open burning, acid baths and toxic dumping pour pollution into the land, air and water and exposes the men, women and children of Asia's poorer peoples to poison. The health and economic costs of this trade are vast and, due to export, are not born by the western consumers nor the waste brokers who benefit from the trade.

The export of E-waste remains a dirty little secret of the high-tech revolution. Scrutiny has been studiously avoided by the electronics industry, by government officials, and by some involved in E-waste recycling. This often willful denial has been aided by the cynical labeling of this trade with the ever-green word "recycling".

Reprinted by permission of The Basel Action Network.

The current U.S. system begins its path of failure before the electronics ever enter the marketplace. First, manufacturers refuse to eliminate hazardous materials or design for disassembly. Second, government policies fail to hold manufacturers responsible for end-of-life management of their products. Thus, finally, consumers, are the unwitting recipients of a toxic product abandoned by those with the greatest ability to prevent problems. Left with few choices, consumers readily will turn to recycling. But it appears that too often, this apparent solution simply results in more problems, particularly when the wastes are toxic.

Few of us realize that the obsolete computer we pay someone to take, in hopes it would be recycled, might end up in China or some other far-off Asian destination. Although it has been a secret well-kept from most consumers, the export "solution" has been a common practice for many years. But until now, nobody, not even many recyclers, seemed to know the Asian fate of these "Made-in-USA" wastes, or what "recycling" in Asia really looks like.

As detailed and illustrated in this report, the field investigation revealed extremely hazardous and dangerous E-waste "recycling" operations that pollute the air, water, and soil of Asian countries. These operations are very likely to be seriously harming human health. Vast amounts of E-waste material, both hazardous and simply trash, is burned or dumped in the rice fields, irrigation canals and along waterways.

E-waste exports to Asia are motivated entirely by brute global economics. Market forces, if left unregulated, dictate that toxic waste will always run "downhill" on an economic path of least resistance. If left unchecked, the toxic effluent of the affluent will flood towards the world's poorest countries where labor is cheap, and occupational and environmental protections are inadequate. A free trade in hazardous wastes leaves the poorer peoples of the world with an untenable choice between poverty and poison—a choice that nobody should have to make.

sixteen

The Globalized Village

–L. Rajiva

L. Rajiva was born in Velloe in the southern part of India and holds a Master's degree in international relations and political theory from Johns Hopkins University. The essay that follows appeared on AlterNet on October 21, 2003.

The road from Madras to my hometown Vellore in the southern part of India makes for a bumpy ride, regardless of one's choice of transportation—be it a sturdy socialist-era Ambassador car or a newer lightweight import, a crowded dirty bus or an air-conditioned taxi. There are no lanes and the traffic moves erratically and at will, as the black tar fades indistinguishably into the neighboring sand and thorn bushes.

One side of the road has been dug up as part of the preliminary work for the Golden Quadrilateral. Hundred-year-old trees have been cut down to make way for this ambitious national highway that is expected to span the length and breadth of the country. My mother claims that this summer feels a lot hotter thanks to the ceaseless construction. But to what avail this additional three degrees of boiling heat in July when the monsoon fails? Nobody pays attention to the two lanes we have now; why should they care about getting four more?

Another sign of "progress" along the way is the Hyundai factory. It is one of the many gleaming new buildings—including medical colleges catering to non-resident Indians (Indians who have emigrated outside their country)—dotting the road in this part of the country. Globalization is alive and well in the villages of India.

The meals on the trains used to be served in moistened banana leaves that were plucked in front of you and thrown away after; today they are wrapped in tin foil or come in plastic or cardboard containers like the cheerfully colored juice packs. The Suzuki-owned Marutis have been joined by a wide array of foreign makes. I read of high-flying elite and their Porsches and Mercedes Benz—although why anyone would risk taking them out on an Indian road is hard to imagine. I see the plastic knives and forks and cloth napkins in a small town restaurant, internet access in little shops and booths everywhere you go, a small but well

"The Globalized Village" by L. Rajiva, *Alternet* October 21, 2003. Copyright 2003. Reprinted by permission of www.alternet.org

stocked air-conditioned supermarket with shopping carts, bored store girls and wide empty aisles.

For a foreign-returned Indian, these symbols of "progress" soothe one's guilt for leaving behind the millions who live an attenuated existence in these paddy fields, huts and impoverished villages. It makes us feel that, finally, the world is getting better thanks to technology and capitalism. The campesino and the conglomerate are working hand in hand as the free market triumphs again.

But the gaudy veneer of liberalization is wafer-thin. Lurking beneath is a darker picture, easily visible to anyone who truly wants to see.

Let's take the Hyundai factory as an example. Ever since it opened for business, water has been in short supply for miles around. The locals don't have the water to drink, cook or bathe. In the scorching heat, this shortage is not an inconvenience but a death sentence. This past year, the death toll from an unexpectedly hot dry summer reached the thousands.

How does globalization feel when you have to walk a mile to the well with a squalling infant tugging at your sari and nothing to cover your head from the ferocious sun except a thin piece of old cotton? The Hyundai factory guzzles water, electricity and land. But it's good to have something more than the trundling old Ambassadors to drive around. People tell me it's a fine place to work. And won't it be splendid to see the Hyundais zip up and down the Golden Quadrilateral when it's completed.

Jobs, transportation and industry are what globalization brings with it for some, but who stands by to measure the immense fallout borne by everyone else? The collateral damage of multinational companies cannot compete with the devastation inflicted by war. Cancun can't compete with Iraq for the media's attention. But is death from dehydration any less painful than being killed by a bullet?

In the state of Karnataka, small farmers like the campesinos at Cancun have committed ritual suicide to express their outrage at the destruction of their lives by multinationals. They are the immediate and dramatic victims of globalization but the damage is far more widespread if less visible. Some indigenous medicines and herbs used for centuries are now in the danger of becoming the exclusive property of corporations eager to patent them.

A recent case involved turmeric, the yellow spice used to color rice and other foods in India. In 1995, two expatriate Indians at the University of Mississippi Medical Center, Suman Das and HariHar Cohly, applied for a patent for the use of turmeric as a salve for wounds—an age-old Indian remedy. The Indian Council for Scientific and Industrial Research promptly challenged the patent, even producing an article written in 1953 in the Journal of the Indian Medical Association that quoted ancient Sanskrit texts that referred to such use. The patent was eventually withdrawn. But nine other such patents on turmeric have since been filed. Patents have also been granted for specific uses of other indigenous products like basmati rice and neem leaves.

Intellectual property rights are at the core of the World Trade Organization debate between the developed and underdeveloped countries. American trade lawyers argue that since patent laws are not frequently used in poorer countries, their governments do not understand them. They claim that only new applications of traditional foods and herbs are being patented, not pre-existing practices. They argue that without patent protection, drug companies have little incentive to undertake long-term and expensive research.

Hidden behind the rhetoric of the free market is a demand for the state to protect the corporation and grant it monopoly rights. And contrary to the rhetoric of the competitive market, it is the biggest companies—such as the pharmaceutical megacorporations with their wealthy executives and fat profit margins—that will profit most from this type of state protection. Meanwhile, millions of children are deprived of the simple vitamins that could save them from disease and death. If the market really worked as it should, freely, the campesinos would win much more frequently than they do now.

But to frame the debate as one between campesino and conglomerate, between the countryside and commerce is to have already lost the war. For capital-G Globalization—like Modernity, Science, Progress, or any other capitalized abstraction—casts itself as irresistible and irreversible. Only Luddites, medievalists, agrarian romantics and the Birkenstock brigade are foolish enough to stand in its way. These are the straw men created by corporate apologists in order to dismiss the anti-globalization movement as irrational or adolescent.

We need new ways of speaking. Modernity is not the enemy. It is the relentless nature of a certain type of economic production, which is propagandized and supported by the state. Without agricultural subsidies, the big farmers would be out of business, beaten out by the small farmers. The conglomerates would be routed by the campesinos.

The resistance to multinationals is not a resistance to globalization. It is a demand to retain the perspective of the village, the perspective of all that is human. What we need today are activists *for* globalization—but a humane globalization, not an inhuman one.

seventeen

Your Farm Subsidies Are Strangling Us

–Amadou Toumani Toure and Blaise Compaore

Jointly written by Amadou Toumani Toure, the President of Mali, and Blaise Compaore, the President of Burkina Faso, the article that follows appeared on the OpEd page of the New York Times *on July 11, 2003.*

After too many years of Africa's being pushed to the global background, it's heartening to see the world's attention being focused on our continent. International support—both financial and otherwise—is certainly needed to help combat the severe poverty and disease gripping our nations. But first and foremost, African needs to be allowed to take its destiny into its own hands. Only self-reliance and economic growth and development will allow Africa to become a full member of the world community.

With the creation of the New Economic Partnership for African Development in 2001, African leaders have committed themselves to following the principles of good governance and a market economy. Nothing is more central to this goal than participating in world trade. As the presidents of two of Africa's least developed countries—Burkina Faso and Mali—we are eager to participate in the multilateral trading system and to take on its rights and obligations.

Cotton is our ticket into the world market. Its production is crucial to economic development in West and Central Africa, as well as to the livelihoods of millions of people there. Cotton accounts for up to 40 percent of export revenues and 10 percent of gross domestic product in our two countries, as well as in Benin and Chad. More than that, cotton is of paramount importance to the social infrastructure of Africa, as well as to the maintenance of it rural areas.

This vital economic sector in our countries is seriously threatened by agricultural subsidies granted by rich countries to their cotton producers. According to the International Cotton Advisory Committee, cotton subsidies amounted to about $5.8 billion in the production year of 2001 to 2002, nearly equal the amount of cotton trade for this same period. Such subsidies lead to worldwide overproduction

Reprinted by permission of His Excellency Amadou Toumani.

and distort cotton prices, depriving poor African countries of their only comparative advantage in international trade.

Not only is cotton crucial to our economies, it is the sole agricultural product for our countries to trade. Although African cotton is of the highest quality, our production costs are about 50 percent lower than in developed countries even though we rely on manual labor. In wealthier countries, by contrast, lower-quality cotton is produced on large mechanized farms, generating little employment and having a questionable impact on the environment. Cotton there could be replaced by other, more valuable crops.

In the period from 2001 to 2002, America's 25,000 cotton farmers received more in subsidies—some $3 billion—than the entire economic output of Burkina Faso, where two million people depend on cotton. Further, United States subsidies are concentrated on just 10 percent of its cotton farmers. Thus, the payments to about 2,500 relatively well-off farmers has the unintended but nevertheless real effect of impoverishing some 10 million rural poor people in West and Central Africa.

Something has to be done. Along with the countries of Benin and Chad, we have submitted a proposal to the World Trade Organization—which is meeting in Cancun, Mexico, in September to discuss agricultural issues—that calls for an end to unfair subsidies granted by developed countries to their cotton producers. As an interim measure, we have also proposed that least-developed countries be granted financial compensation for lost export revenues that are due to those subsidies.

Our demand is simple: apply free trade rules not only to those products that are of interest to the rich and powerful, but also to those products where poor countries have a proven comparative advantage. We know that the world will not ignore our plea for a fair playing field. The World Trade Organization has said it is committed to addressing the problems of developing countries. The United States has convinced us that a free market economy provides the best opportunities for all members of the world community. Let us translate these principles into deeds at Cancun.

How Europe Sows Misery in Africa
–Kevin A. Hassett and Robert Shapiro

Kevin A. Hassett is the director of economic policy studies at the American Enterprise Institute. A former senior economist at the Federal Reserve Board, Hassett was also Senator McCain's chief economic adviser during the senator's 2000 presidential campaign. Robert Shapiro was an undersecretary of commerce in the Clinton administration and is currently a fellow of the Brookings Institution. Their article "How Europe Sows Misery in Africa" was published in the Washington Post *on July 22, 2004.*

The average person in sub-Saharan Africa earns less than $1 a day. The average cow in Europe—thanks to government subsidies—earns about $2 a day. And therein lies a tale of the power of European farm interests, and the weakness of African economies.

A burgeoning volume of economics literature argues that the largest factors stunting African economic development include not only disease, drought, warfare and mismanagement, but also the European Union's "Common Agricultural Policy," or CAP. Why? Because the EU's policy has spawned subsidies and tariffs that have richly rewarded European farms and swollen European food output, while depressing world food prices and undercutting African exports.

Yet the economic evidence of harm in Africa has elicited nary a peep, squawk or moo from the EU. Over the past two weeks, European agriculture ministers have been haggling over changes in the CAP, which now consumes some 40 billion euros, roughly half of the EU budget. The EU farm commissioner has proposed trimming subsidies, but France rejected the deal with Germany's support, and the proposal was shelved.

This deadlock in Europe spells misery in Africa. Take Malawi, for example. Its economy is in shambles: CAP tariffs and quotas keep its chief exports, corn and sorghum, out of European markets; CAP export subsidies help European producers crowd out Malawi sales in third-country markets; and CAP price supports drive down the prices that Malawi crops can fetch abroad by driving up European production.

"How Europe Sows Misery in Africa" by Kevin A. Hassett and Robert Shapiro, *Washington Post*, June 22, 2003. Copyright © 2003. Reprinted by permission of the authors.

President Bush has blamed Europe's policies barring imports of genetically modified food for prolonging famine in Africa by discouraging Africa's use of such food varieties. But the suffering in Africa goes on and on because of a more conventional chain of distortions caused by the CAP. Economic development stalls without investment; investment usually won't expand unless demand rises first; and demand won't expand in sub-Saharan Africa, where more than 60 percent of the labor force works in agriculture, unless agricultural income grows. By preventing much of Africa from developing its agricultural resources, the CAP hurts the continent's ability to attract the financial, technological and human capital to drive economic and social progress.

Africa is particularly vulnerable to EU farm subsidies because proximity and decades of colonial and post-colonial relations make Europe and Africa efficient trading partners, in the same way the United States naturally dominates trade with Latin America. While the U.S. government can also be faulted for subsidizing farm products, EU farm subsidies dwarf our own in most areas. The result is that while once-poor Asians and Latin Americans grow more prosperous, more than 659 million people in sub-Saharan Africa (excluding South Africa) are stuck with annual incomes averaging $320, life expectancies of less than 50 years, and little prospect of ever doing much better.

Driving this dynamic is a tawdry system of large agribusinesses thriving on government largess at the expense of the world's most vulnerable people. This injustice is sustained because politicians receive their share of the profits. It is a perfect money machine. The CAP sets price guarantees far higher than world prices or production costs. So agribusinesses produce as much as they can and dump whatever is left over on markets in developing countries. To be certain that low-cost countries don't undercut them abroad, European producers also receive hefty export subsidies to add to their fat domestic profits. To close the circle, politicians seeking reelection know whom to call for financial support.

The dairy market is one of the starkest examples of EU excess. Thanks to CAP subsidies for cows, milk production dominates Europe's agricultural sector and European milk products flood many developing markets. A French or German agribusiness produces a ton of butter and, under CAP price guarantees, receives more than 3,250 euros (currently about $3,800) while the wholesale price of a ton of butter in America today is less than $1,400. The 3,250 euros belong to those agribusinesses regardless of market prices or conditions, so it's no surprise that European dairy production far outstrips European demand.

CAP subsidies also guarantee that butter from dairy-producing African nations such as Botswana or Gabon can't compete with Europe's high-priced spreads. Europe's "butter mountains" weigh heavily on international markets. As a result of the CAP, which places a 153 percent tariff on foreign-produced butter, Botswanan and Gabonese dairy producers never get more than a small slice of the EU market.

Even though population density, weather, and the cost of capital and labor all make the EU a naturally inefficient dairy producer—EU dairy production costs are, on average, twice as high as international prices—Europe accounts for 40 percent of world exports of whole milk powder and more than one-third of world cheese exports. European voters may believe that these policies defend quaint dairy farms dotting the French or Dutch countryside, but the truth is that most of the subsidies go directly to the bottom line of multinational agribusinesses such as Aria Foods and Nestle.

Subsidies for EU sugar producers are even larger and more damaging to rival producers. Sugar should be the ideal product of the tropics, where sugar cane grows. Sugar cane farmers can produce more than twice as much per acre as rivals in cooler climates who grow sugar beet. Moreover, land prices, wages and other production costs in tropical countries are a small fraction of what they are in any European country.

Yet the EU, with the world's highest sugar-production costs, is the world's biggest sugar exporter. European farmers receive guaranteed prices for sugar beet, even if they sell their product abroad at lower prices. At home, European processors sell their sugar at high prices; to keep the business within the family, CAP tariffs of 140 percent keep foreign sugar out of the EU market. While EU politicians insist all these sugar subsidies help the little guy, single large firms account for the entire domestic sugar market—both sales and production—in at least eight European countries. Meanwhile, price guarantees and export subsidies enable EU producers, some from as far north as Finland, to claim a significant share of the sugar market even in tropical Africa.

And Joseph Dual, the chairman of the EU parliament's agriculture and rural development committee, which must approve any sugar subsidy reform, is himself a major French sugar beet farmer.

Most African nations have few assets to support economic development apart from cheap, fertile land and low-priced labor. Given the hurdles erected by Europe, their only response can be to grow products that the EU doesn't subsidize, such as coffee, which cannot be produced in the temperate or chilly zones of Europe.

When African farmers have crops that might gain a foothold in EU markets, other defenses kick in. For instance, EU guidelines for crops containing alfatoxins, a mold byproduct associated with some liver cancers, are unnecessarily restrictive. A World Bank study found that these rules disproportionately harm African farmers. Even the absence of an EU standard can be an obstacle. One Mauritanian enterprise found a German firm interested in marketing cheese made with camel's milk. But the EU halted the deal because there were no regulations covering camel cheese. The African producer has been in limbo for years waiting for Brussels to write the regulations.

A recent study from the Institute of Economic Affairs in Britain estimates that EU agriculture policies have reduced African exports of milk products by more than 90 percent, livestock by nearly 70 percent, meat by almost 60 percent, nongrain crops by 50 percent and grains by more than 40 percent. If we assume from this that the CAP reduces Africa's total potential agricultural exports by half, it suggests that without the CAP, the current $10.9 billion in annual food-related exports from sub-Saharan Africa (excluding South Africa) could grow to nearly $22 billion. Moreover, the International Food Policy Research Institute, a Washington-based group that focuses on food needs in developing countries, has found that in sub-Saharan nations, every $1 in agricultural income produces an additional $1.42 increase in GDP. So, the end of the CAP could raise sub-Saharan GDP by nearly $26.4 billion per year—enough to increase the annual income of every person in these countries by nearly 13 percent. If these benefits flowed to rural Africans, it could save hundreds of thousands of lives and improve the lots of millions more.

The United States is not an innocent bystander. U.S. cotton, sugar, dairy and corn subsidies exacerbate Africa's problems and impede our ability to press for fundamental multinational reforms. (James D. Wolfensohn, the president of the World Bank, has estimated that wealthy nations spend more than $300 billion on agriculture subsidies, as much as sub-Saharan Africa's entire economic output.)

Most Americans, like most Europeans, seem unaware of the devastating impact of these policies. And once people do know, it's easy for them to despair of ever changing the policies. So when the World Trade Organization meets in Cancun, Mexico, this fall, it won't be enough to say that we stand with the world's neediest countries. We should express our outrage, use our influence to bring about deeper cuts in subsidies and make fundamental reform a centerpiece of our foreign policy for the developing world.

India's Poor Starve as Wheat Rots

–Amy Waldman

Formerly a contributing editor of the Washington Monthly, *Amy Waldman is a reporter for the* New York Times. *Her article "India's Poor Starve as Wheat Rots" appeared in the* New York Times *in December of 2000.*

KHANNA, India   Surplus from this year's wheat harvest, bought by the government from farmers, sits moldering in muddy fields here in Punjab State. Some of the previous year's wheat surplus sits untouched, too, and the year's before that, and the year's before that.

To the south, in the neighboring state of Rajasthan, villagers ate boiled leaves or discs of bread made from grass seeds in late summer and autumn because they could not afford to buy wheat. One by one, children and adults —as many as 47 in all—wilted away from hunger-related causes, often clutching pained stomachs.

"Sometimes, we ate half a bread," said Phoolchand, a laborer whose 2-year-old daughter died during that period. "Sometimes, a whole bread."

More than two decades after a "green" revolution made India, the world's second-most-populous country, self-sufficient in grain production, half of India's children are malnourished. About 350 million Indians go to bed hungry every night. Pockets of starvation deaths, like those in the Baran district of Rajasthan, have surfaced regularly in recent years.

Yet the government is sitting on wheat surpluses—now at about 53 million metric tons—that would stretch to the moon and back at least twice if all the bags were lined up. Persistent scarcity surrounded by such bounty has become a source of shame for a nation that has taken pride in feeding itself.

Advocates for the poor and those pushing for economic reforms ask how a country can justify hoarding so much excess when so many of its people regularly go hungry.

"It's scandalous," said Jean Drèze, an economist who has been helping to document starvation deaths for a Supreme Court case brought by the People's Union for Civil Liberties, an advocacy group, to compel the government to use the surplus to relieve hunger.

Amy Waldman, "India's Poor Starve as Wheat Rots," *New York Times*, December 2, 2002. Copyright 2002 New York Times Co. Reprinted by permission.

The reason, experts and officials agree, is the economics—and particularly the politics—of food in India, a country that has modernized on many fronts but that remains desperately poor.

Critics say the central government, led for the last four years by the Hindu nationalist Bharatiya Janata Party, has catered to political allies and powerful farm lobbies in a few key states by buying more and more grain from farmers at higher and higher prices. At the same time, it has been responding to pressure from international lenders by curbing food subsidies to consumers.

One result has been huge stockpiles going to waste, while higher prices for food and inefficient distribution leave basic items like bread, a staple of the rural poor diet, out of reach for many. Even though the surplus is supposed to be distributed to the poor, politics and corruption often limit their access.

"It's not an economic issue anymore—it's a straightforward political issue," said Jairam Ramesh, the senior economic adviser to the Congress Party, the country's main opposition party.

Answering such criticism, Asok Kumar Mohapatra, who was until recently a joint secretary with the Department of Food and Public Distribution, said any system trying to feed a billion people was apt to have inefficiencies. "It's easy to find fault with this kind of organization," he said. But he, too, acknowledged the politics involved. "The simple thing is they have lobbies," he said of the farmers, "and lobbies work everywhere."

Both the glut in Punjab and the deprivation in Rajasthan reflect a government in transition between a quasi-socialist past and a free-market future, and one that at the local level especially seems deeply ambivalent about its obligations to its poorest citizens.

After a devastating famine in 1943 that killed three million people and humbling food scarcities in the 1960's, Indian central governments have been determined to ensure that the country could feed itself.

A nationwide system was set up to distribute subsidized food via a network of "ration shops" that today number 454,000. At the same time, India made great advances in increasing its productivity, by developing high-yield seeds and investing in infrastructure, like irrigation.

The green agricultural revolution quadrupled staple food production, from 50 million metric tons in 1950 to 209 million metric tons by 2000.

The fruits of those efforts can be witnessed nowhere more vividly than in Punjab. Today it is India's only state (along, perhaps, with neighboring Haryana, which was carved from Punjab), that derives more than 40 percent of its income from agriculture; until recently it had the highest per capita income in India. It has some of the country's best roads and, with only 2 percent of the country's land, grows 55 percent of its food.

While farmers in poorer states have either no grain surplus or no mechanism by which to sell it to the government, Punjab has 1,600 wholesale grain markets, including the one here in Khanna, the largest in Asia.

But the same system that has built up Punjab has also run into trouble on almost every front, and even the farmers here know it cannot last.

Over the past four years, even as advisory committees recommended stabilizing or lowering the support prices paid to farmers, prices instead went up, and up—to about $129 a metric ton, 2,200 pounds, for wheat this year from about $99 in 1997.

Punjab farmers, eager to cash in, are farming so much rice and wheat that they are depleting the state's water and soil, creating a long-term threat to the country's agricultural self-sufficiency.

"We know every year we take the water level down," said Bachittar Singh, 67, a farmer with 125 acres near here. "But what alternative do we have?"

Then there is the effect of such policies on the price of grain itself. The high prices paid to farmers by the government have inflated consumer prices, making it harder for the poor to buy grain. In some cases, the government, wanting to keep market prices in India high, has exported grain at lower prices than it was selling it to its citizens.

By the mid-1990s, India was spending close to 1 percent of its gross domestic product on food subsidies, with much of that lost to waste and theft. Under strong pressure from the World Bank and other international lenders to curb spending, the government decided in 1997 that only those below the poverty line would be able to buy heavily subsidized food. Everyone else would have to buy it only slightly below market price.

But with politics, indifference and corruption conspiring to limit the number of those identified as poor, the amount of food being bought from ration shops dropped significantly and stockpiles soared. The problem is compounded by the fact that even many of those classified as poor are unable to buy the subsidized grain because of inaccessible ration shops or dealers who steal the grain for sale on the black market.

Today the government has run out of warehouse space and has taken to storing the grain in fields rented from farmers. A recent report found that it was spending more on storage than on agriculture, rural development, irrigation and flood control combined.

Some of the wheat, often protected only by porous jute bags and black plastic tarpaulins, is rotten; even official estimates concede that 200,000 tons are "damaged," with the real total probably far higher. Inspectors have found worm-infested wheat at schools where the state is supposed to provide free lunch.

It is about 400 miles from the abundance here to the barren, scrubby landscape of Baran, in the southeast corner of Rajasthan. This year was the third year of drought, and the most brutal, with rainfall down by 70 percent.

In the village of Swaans, isolated by jolting dirt roads and dry riverbeds, one man, Gobrilal, lost an 8-year-old son to hunger this fall. He sat recently beneath the shade of a thatched shelter, surrounded by children who were all rib cages and swollen bellies, and recounted two months of agony.

On good days they ate once a day, but many days they ate nothing. Gobrilal's son began vomiting, even while asking for food, and died two days later. "If we had money," his father said listlessly, "we would have bought him wheat so he wouldn't have died."

20
twenty

The Crisis of Potato Growers in U.P.

–Vandana Shiva

Vandana Shiva is a physicist, ecologist, activist, and editor. She directs the Research Foundation for Science, Technology and Natural Resource Policy in India, where she has established Navdanya, *a movement for biodiversity conservation and farmers' rights. "The Crisis of Potato Growers" appeared on ZNet on April 24, 2003.*

The Harvest of Trade Liberalisation Policies

Following Andhra Pradesh and Punjab, agricultural debts and farmers' suicides are now knocking on the doors of U.P., especially for potato growers. While the farmers are spending Rs. 255/quintal on production, potatoes are being sold for Rs. 40/quintal, leaving farmers at a loss of Rs. 200 for every quintal produced. Per hectare the costs of production are between Rs. 55,000/ha to Rs. 65,000/ha, of which Rs. 40,000 is the cost of seed alone.*

That the independent farmer is struggling to survive against immeasurably difficult odds is borne out by the number of suicides by farmers throughout the country. By 2000, more than 20,000 farmers from all over the country had fallen victim to the high costs of production, spurious seed, crop loss, falling farm prices, and rising debt.

The crisis for potato growers, like the crisis for producers of tomatoes, cotton and oil seeds, and other crops is directly related to World Bank and WTO driven trade liberalisation policies, of which the new Agricultural policies is a direct outcome.

The policies of globalisation and trade liberalisation have created the farm crisis in general and the potato crisis in particular at 3 levels.

1. A shift from "food first" to "trade first" and "farmer first" to "corporation first" policies.
2. A shift from diversity and multifunctionality of agriculture to monocultures and standardisation, chemical and capital intensification of production, and

"The Crisis of Potato Growers in U.P." by Vandana Shiva, ZNet *Commentary*, April 24, 2003. © 2003 by Vandana Shiva. Reprinted by permission of the author.
*U.P. is the Indian province of Uttar Pradesh; Rs. stands for rupees; quintal, crore, and lakh are terms of measurement.

deregulation of the input sector, especially seeds, leading to rising costs of production.
3. Deregulation of markets and withdrawal of the state from effective price regulation, leading to collapse in prices of farm commodities.

1. From Farmer First to Corporation First

The new agriculture policies are based on withdrawing support to farmers, and creating new subsidies for agro-processing industry and agribusiness. In a debate on the potato crisis, the U.P. Agriculture Minister referred to subsidies given for cold storage and transport. These subsidies do not go to farmers and producers. They go to traders and corporations. Pepsico's entry into Punjab was the first example of this trade first policy.

When the market rate for tomatoes was Rs. 2.00 per kg, Pepsico was paying farmers only Rs. 0.80 to 0.50 per kg, but collecting ten times that amount as a transport subsidy from government. Cold storage owners in U.P. have received Rs. 50 crore in subsidies, but this is not a subsidy to farmers. A farmer pays the cold storage owner Rs. 120/sack for storage. Cold storage owners are hiking charges to exploit the crisis. With 1 crore 3 lakh metric tonnes of potato production in U.P., this is a massive drain of financial resources from indebted farmers to traders, from producers to business and industry.

The annual budgets since liberalization have been adding to the subsidies for the corporate sector—tax holidays for building silos and cold storages, incentives for exporting, subsidized transportation to the ports of the trader's choice. The recently announced 5-year export policy of the government has allocated Rs. 100 crores towards aided corporations to transport grain from FIC to the ports. In addition, public money is used to take land away from farmers to build transportation facilities for agri-business to help them transport the grain even faster.

The experience of the 2001 wheat export exposes the government's lack of commitment to its people. Against an economic cost of Rs. 8300 per tonne to the FCI and an open market price of Rs. 7,000 per tonne, India was offered a price of Rs. 4,300 per tonne in the international open market in May 2001.

Over and above selling the wheat at the BPL rates, the government agreed to bear the freight charge from Rajpura to Jamnagar port in Guarat and pay a commission to Cargill. Thus, wheat whose cost to the government included the MSP (Rs. 580 of 2000) as well as the commission, market charges, levies and cess paid by FCI, increasing the real cost by another Rs. 70 a quintal, was sold at less than Rs. 420 a quintal, giving the corporation a subsidy of Rs. 130 a quintal.

In fact, since 2000, Cargill has emerged as the biggest buyer of subsidised Indian wheat for exports.

2. Monocultures and Standardisation

The impact of the new agriculture policy has been to promote a shift from food grains to vegetables and perishable commodities. While grains can be stored and consumed locally, potatoes and tomatoes must be sold immediately. A vegetable centred policy thus decreases food security and increases farmers' vulnerability to the market. While this promotes monocultures of perishable commodities, the word used for these monocultures is "diversification" in typical globalisation doublespeak.

Further, the State Minister for Agriculture, Hukam Singh deo Yadav, and the U.P. Agriculture Minister, Hukum Singh, both cited the variability of size and the standardisation of the agro-processing industry as a reason for not procuring potatoes from farmers in spite of the distress. Size does not matter for the Indian kitchen. Our "Aaloo ki sabzi" and "Aaloo paratha" do not need the Russet Burbank that McDonald needs for its French fries (renamed "Freedom Fries" during the Iraq war because of France's non-cooperation with the U.S.).

The McDonald corporation needed the Russet Burbank because of its size. For example, 40% of all McDonald fries must be two to three inches long, another 40% must be over three inches; and the remaining 20% can be under two inches—and the Russet Burbank fits perfectly. The economic forces of food processing push cultivation to a single crop yielding uniformity, threatening the ecological stability of agriculture more than it has been in the past.

Seed monopolies and genetic uniformity go hand in hand. Potatoes for processing are being introduced in the name of 'diversification'—but given the experience of potato cultivation in the U.S., from where Pepsico technology is being transferred, it will lead to genetic uniformity and high vulnerability. Today in the U.S. only 12 varieties of the 2,000 species of potato are cultivated. 40% of all potato cultivation is of a single variety—the Russet Burbank. In 1970, only 28% of America's total potato acreage was planted with this variety. Acres and acres of the same kind of potato are ecologically very vulnerable, as the Irish potato famine reminds us.

The introduction of uniformity is justified as a trade-off for raising yields of horticultural crops miraculously. Pepsi's promotion literature stated that 'yields of horticultural produce in India are substantially lower than international standards.' The project proposal for Pepsi Food argued that 'in Mexico, Pepsi's subsidiary Sabritas launched a seed programme that increased potato yields by 58%—from 19 to 30 tonnes per hectare in three years.'

In India, comparable yields have been achieved by farmers and agricultural scientists. Potato yields of more than 40 tonnes per hectare have been realised during field trials in Jalandhar by the Central Potato Research Institute. Yields averaging about 50–60 tonnes per hectare are also achieved by Gujarat farmers, who grow their potatoes on river beds in Banaskantha district. Just as in the first Green Revolution, the existence of indigenous high yielding varieties of rice was denied to justify the introduction of high response varieties, costly potato seeds are being introduced under "crop diversification," locking farmers into dependency and debt.

This link of monocultures and monopolies over seed explains the high cost of production under trade led agriculture policies.

3. Price Regulation

While the government does keep going through the gimmicks of announcing procurement prices and procurement centres, government intervention in price regulation and procurement has all but disappeared under globalization. The government announced Rs. 195/quintal as the procurement price of potatoes, and the opening of 8 centres for procurement.

However, no government procurement is being done to support farmers and ensure a fair price. Prices have therefore fallen to Rs. 40–100/quintal, a bonanza for the agro-processing industry which makes even more profits from chips, but a disaster for the grower who is being pushed to suicide in despair. With potatoes at Rs. 0.40 a kg, the agro-processing industry is paying less than Rs. 0.08 to farmers for chips they sell at Rs. 10.00 for 200 gms. For 1,31,00,000 metric tonnes of potatoes this amounts to a transfer of Rs. 20 billion from impoverished peasants of U.P. to global MNCs such as Pepsi and McDonald.

And the plight of potato farmers in Punjab is no different. As the *Tribune* reports,

> Forced to grow potato in the past few years under crop diversification agriculture programme, the farmers have been finding it difficult to earn enough by selling the produce to meet the cost of inputs.
>
> After incurring heavy losses for growing potato, hundreds of farmers have decided to sell their holdings to meet liabilities of loans of banks and commission agents.
>
> Mr. Chotta Singh (Name changed) of Gill Kalan village of this district said, "I grew potato in 20 acres, 10 acres owned by me and 10 acres taken on lease. I spent Rs. 12,000 an acre on potato cultivation and today if I sell my entire produce at the prevailing price of Rs. 100 a quintal, I will incur loss of Rs. 1 lakh." He added that to meet part of his loan liability of Rs. 11 lakh, he had disposed of one acre.
>
> Mr. Shawinder Singh, another farmer, pointed out that he took to potato farming hoping that he would repay his entire loan of Rs. 3 lakh in two to three years, as potato was considered a "paying crop." But now he found that his debt had reached Rs. 5 lakh because he failed to fetch a remunerative price and he had to sell it at a throw-away price to get cash to meet routine liabilities. ("Traders syndicate exploits farmers," *Chander Prakash, Tribune*, 3 Apr 03.)

And the plight of potato farmers in U.P. is the same as the plight of wheat and rice farmers in Punjab and Haryana and soya farmers in M.P., and cotton and groundnut farmers in A.P.

In October 2000, almost half the 10 lakh tonnes of paddy [potato] that arrived at Haryana mandis was sold to private traders because of declining state procurement. Of this, 47% was sold at almost 14% below MSP rates of Rs. 510 for common paddy. There were also reports of rice being sold to millers and private procurers at Rs. 400.

In Punjab, farmers, who had already sold their jewelry and livestock to raise money for paddy inputs, were borrowing from commission agents and other moneylenders in order to meet their basic food and shelter needs while waiting for their paddy to be sold at rates far below the MSP. By October 11, the first suicide story came in; Avtar Singh of Kakra village in Samana District committed suicide when he could not sell his paddy at a low of Rs. 400 for more than a week.

In March 2001, Punjab became the first state to admit the fact that farmers, unable to clear their debts, have started committing suicide.

The dysfunctionality of agriculture under globalisation is leading to farmers paying with their very lives. However, this dysfunctionality is beneficial to agribusiness, which is harvesting the artificially accumulated stocks and artificially manipulated collapse of domestic markets to make super profits.

This policy of "trade first" is suicidal not just for farmers, but for the food security of the country as a whole.

Study Finds TV Trims Fiji Girls' Body Image and Eating Habits

—Erica Goode

Erica Goode has been a writer for the New York Times since 1998. Before that she served as an assistant managing editor at U.S. News and World Report. She graduated from the University of Michigan in 1974 and received a Master of Science in social psychology from the University of California, Santa Cruz, in 1978. The article that follows appeared in the New York Times on May 20, 1999.

"You've gained weight" is a traditional compliment in Fiji, anthropologists say.

In accordance with traditional culture in the South Pacific nation, dinner guests are expected to eat as much as possible. A robust, nicely rounded body is the norm for men and women. "Skinny legs" is a major insult. And "going thin," the Fijian term for losing a noticeable amount of weight, is considered a worrisome condition.

Erica Goode, "Study Finds TV Trims Fiji Girls' Body Image and Eating Habits," *New York Times*, May 20, 1999. Copyright 1999 New York Times Co. Reprinted by permission.

But all that may be changing, now that Heather Locklear has arrived.

Just a few years after the introduction of television to a province of Fiji's main island, Viti Levu, eating disorders—once virtually unheard of there—are on the rise among girls, according to a study presented yesterday at the American Psychiatric Association meetings in Washington. Young girls dream of looking not like their mothers and aunts, but like the wasp-waisted stars of "Melrose Place" and "Beverly Hills, 90210."

"I'm very heavy," one Fijian adolescent lamented during an interview with researchers led by Dr. Anne E. Becker, director of research at the Harvard Eating Disorders Center of Harvard Medical School, who investigated shifts in body image and eating practices in Fiji over a three-year period.

The Fijian girl said her friends also tell her that she is too fat, "and sometimes I'm depressed because I always want to lose weight."

Epidemiological studies have shown that eating disorders are more prevalent in industrialized countries, suggesting that cultural factors play a role in setting off the conditions. But few studies have examined the effects of long-term cultural shifts on disordered eating in traditional societies.

Dr. Becker and her colleagues surveyed a group of 63 Fijian secondary school girls, whose average age was 17. The work began in 1995, one month after satellites began beaming television signals to the region. In 1998, the researchers surveyed another group of 65 girls from the same schools, who were matched in age, weight and other characteristics with the subjects in the earlier group.

Fifteen percent of the female students in the 1998 survey reported that they had induced vomiting to control their weight, the researchers said, in comparison with 3 percent in the 1995 survey. And 29 percent of the students scored highly on a test of eating-disorder risk compared with 13 percent three years before.

Girls who said they watched television three or more nights a week in the 1998 survey were 50 percent more likely to describe themselves as "too big or fat" and 30 percent more likely to diet than girls who watched television less frequently, the researchers found.

Before 1995, Dr. Becker said, there was little talk of dieting in Fiji. "The idea of calories was very foreign to them." But in the 1998 survey, 69 percent of the girls said they had been on a diet at some point in their lives. In fact, preliminary data suggest more teen-age girls in Fiji diet than their American counterparts.

The results of the study have not been published, but were reviewed by the psychiatric association's scientific program committee before being accepted for presentation at the meetings.

Several of the students told Dr. Becker and her colleagues that they wanted to look like the Western women they saw on television shows like "Beverly Hills 90210." One girl said that her friends "change their mood, their hairstyles, so that they can be like those characters." "So in order to be like them, I have to work on myself, exercising and my eating habits should change," she said.

But Dr. Marshall Sahlins, Charles F. Grey professor emeritus of Anthropology at the University of Chicago, said that he doubts that television was the only factor in the changes. "I think that television is a kind of metaphor of something more profound," he said.

In contrast to the solitary couch-potato viewing style displayed by many Americans, watching television is a communal activity in Fiji, Dr. Becker said. Fijians often gather in households with television sets, and sit together, drinking kava and talking about their day's activities, the TV on in the background.

"What we noticed in 1995 is that people had a sort of curiosity, but it was a dismissive curiosity, like watching something that seemed ridiculous," Dr. Becker said. "But over the years they have come to accept it as a form of entertainment."

Fiji residents have access to only one television channel, she said, which broadcasts a selection of programs from the United States, Britain and Australia. Among the most popular are "Seinfeld," "Melrose Place," which features Ms. Locklear, "E.R.," "Xena, Warrior Princess," and "Beverly Hills 90210."

Dr. Becker said that the increase in eating disorders like bulimia may be a signal that the culture is changing so quickly that Fijians are having difficulty keeping up. Island teenagers, she said, "are acutely aware that the traditional culture doesn't equip them well to negotiate the kinds of conflicts" presented by a 1990's global economy.

In other Pacific societies, Dr. Becker said, similar cultural shifts have been accompanied by an increase in psychological problems among adolescents. Researchers speculated, for example, that rapid social change played a role in a rash of adolescent suicides in Micronesia in the 1980's.

22
twenty-two

The World Bank and the "Next Green Revolution"
Devastating IMF/World Bank Sponsored Environmental Projects in the Name of Progress

—Brian Tokar

Brian Tokar has been an activist, author, and a voice for ecological radicalism since the 1970s. He is a faculty member and Biotechnology Project Director at Vermont's Institute for Social Engineering. His article "The World Bank and the 'Next Green Revolution'" appeared in Z-Mag Online in April 2004.

"Sustainable Development"

The World Bank has underwritten some of the most environmentally devastating projects ever undertaken in the name of progress and "development." The Bank has supported deforestation, hydroelectric projects, and oil drilling in the Amazon rainforest; huge dams and oil and gas pipeline construction in Africa; and massive water diversion schemes such as India's notorious Narmada Valley dam complex.

In the past decade, Bank officials have adopted the language of "sustainable development" and withdrawn funds from a few of the most notorious projects in their portfolio. But few advocates for the environment or the rights of indigenous peoples have any illusions that the institution's priorities ever substantively shifted along with its rhetoric.

The idea of "sustainable development" emerged from policy discussions at the United Nations throughout the 1980s and was popularized in the lead-up to the UN's high-profile environment and development summit in Rio de Janeiro in 1992. Merging the language of long-term sustainability from the environmental movement with the "development" discourse of neocolonialism, sustainable development became a rationale for advocating the continued expansion of capitalist

"The World Bank and the 'Next Green Revolution'" by Brian Tokar. Reprinted by permission of Brian Tokar. This article is excerpted from Brian Tokar's latest book, *Gene Traders: Biotechnology, World Trade and the Globalization of Hunger*, published in 2004 by Toward Freedom. Brian Tokar is the director of the Biotechnology Project at the Institute for Social Engineering in Plainfield, VT, and is also the author of *Earth for Sale* (South End Press, 1997) and *Redesigning Life?* (Zed Books, 2001).

market economies in the global South, while paying lip service to the needs of the environment and the poor.

The notion of environmental sustainability as an alternative to limitless economic growth was transformed into a rhetorical justification for economic growth in defiance of environmental and social limits. Almost imperceptibly, the discussion shifted from how to stem environmental destruction to finding new ways to sustain economic growth. Since the mid-1990s, virtually every activity of the Bank, however controversial, has been justified as aiding both "poverty reduction" and "sustainable development."

In the agricultural sector, the Bank's strategy has helped displace people engaged in subsistence and local market-oriented production, in favor of commercial production for global markets. In virtually every corner of the so-called "developing world," the Bank has underwritten policies that divert once independent farmers toward the chemical-intensive production of cash crops. Bank officials say their goal is to "broaden farmers' rights and opportunities, and to help them create livelihoods of their own choice," beyond the "single option" of subsistence.

For marginalized farmers throughout the world, this has brought an increasing dependence on unstable world crop prices, rising indebtedness for costly equipment and chemical inputs, and, often, the forced removal of people from traditional lands that have sustained their communities for countless generations. Rather than helping alleviate poverty, this kind of "development," in the words of Japanese economist and political analyst Ichiyo Muto, "has so far only transformed undeveloped poverty into developed poverty, traditional poverty into modernized poverty designed to function smoothly in the world economic system."

The Bank's policy of shifting developing countries toward cash crop production began in the 1950s, with an initial focus on specialty crops such as cocoa, rubber, and palm oil. With the development of the so-called "high yielding varieties" of wheat and rice in the 1960s, Bank lending was often limited to governments that promoted the use of the new seeds and accepted their dependence on mechanization and costly chemical inputs. Seeds were often given away and enterprising farmers were offered attractive loan packages subsidized by the Bank. These policies came to define the so-called "Green Revolution" of the 1960s and 1970s.

While these new crops brought significant short-term increases in agricultural productivity, their use lowered water tables and severely threatened crop diversity. The dwarf characteristics of these non-indigenous crop varieties deprived farmers of important agricultural byproducts, including sufficient straw to feed livestock. The virtually endless need for new equipment and inputs buried farm families in unsustainable long-term indebtedness.

World Bank lending for agricultural projects declined from 30 percent of the Bank's portfolio in the 1980s to only 10 percent during the 1990s, but still amounts to nearly $3 billion per year, the largest source of agricultural development funds in the world. Close to half of the Bank's portfolio is in structural adjustment loans tied to specific changes mandated for the host country's economic policy; these are essentially identical in scope to the Structural Adjustment Programs (SAPs) imposed by the Bank's sister institution, the International Monetary Fund (IMF). Structural adjustment compels countries to reorient their economies toward the repayment of international debts, including IMF and World Bank loans, usually at the expense of public services, environmental protection, and local production for local needs.

In the case of agricultural lending, the Bank mandates debtor nations to shift agricultural production toward cash crops for export, liberalize agricultural trade, and remove public subsidies for staple food production, while replacing fixed prices for staple goods with market-determined ones. Producers are shifted from subsistence food crops toward fruits, vegetables, and flowers grown for export. Under SAPs, credit is offered to individual producers and denied to traditional communal activities, destabilizing rural societies and encouraging unprecedented concentrations of individual land ownership. Loans are often tied to specific production methods, including the increased use of hazardous pesticides and other costly inputs.

The Bank and Biotechnology

The Bank's current support for biotechnology in agriculture has two aspects. The first includes technical assistance and "capacity building" for governments, aimed at facilitating the introduction of new biotechnologies and establishing biotech-friendly regulatory regimes. The second is direct support for biotech research. The Bank's capacity building agenda has five main areas of activity:

- Evaluating the potential of biotechnology to address local problems, especially through the use of cost/benefit and risk analysis
- Promoting partnerships between corporations, private funding sources, and public agencies
- Designing and implementing regulatory systems
- "Educating" farmers and consumers
- Promoting international cooperation in regulatory policy, financing, and technology transfer

The Bank also offers technical training, policy and management advice, analysis of countries' regulatory systems, and consultations with representatives from various social sectors to discuss proposed policies and their likely impacts. The underlying assumption is often that biotechnology is the wave of the future and that rational public policy can only serve to facilitate its development.

The Bank has provided some $2.3 billion in direct loans for research, of which $50 million is for biotechnology. This includes some less controversial techniques, such as tissue culture and the use of DNA markers to assist plant breeders, but also genome mapping and transgenics. Less controversial pursuits are often viewed as "stepping stones" to more "advanced" applications, such as the development of new genetically modified crops. Over 80 percent of research funding is committed to six key countries: India, Kenya, Brazil, Indonesia, Peru, and Ethiopia. Some

$20 million—40 percent of the total—is for projects in India, where the Bank supports development of insecticide-producing Bt rice, as well as genetically engineered (GE) varieties of cotton, pigeon peas, chickpeas, and various horticultural crops.

Also in India, the Bank has provided assistance for a controversial project in which genes from high protein amaranth seeds have been spliced into the DNA of potatoes to increase the potatoes' protein content. This project was announced with great fanfare in 2003. While the protein content of the potatoes reportedly increased by nearly half, they contained a small fraction of the amount found in whole amaranth or even wheat and rice. The peas, lentils, and other legumes that are an important part of traditional Indian diets—but have been marginalized in cash crop-oriented agricultural development projects—provide even more protein. As with the $100 million effort to develop a GE "golden" rice containing increased beta carotene (a Vitamin A precursor), biotechnologists are promising a high-tech "cure" to hunger, while ignoring far more realistic and readily available solutions.

In Kenya, the Bank has provided support for a project largely financed by the U.S. Agency for International Development (USAID), along with Monsanto and a number of other private donors. The stated aim is to offer GE varieties of sweet potatoes, a staple crop in rural areas that rarely attracts the interest of corporate researchers. After 11 years of research, which created a very high public profile for the Monsanto and USAID sponsored Kenyan researcher Dr. Florence Wambugu, only one local sweet potato variety has been genetically modified, imparting resistance to a virus that farmers routinely fend off by far less invasive means. Under field conditions, the potato failed to demonstrate any significant virus resistance. Indeed, more than 20 years of Bank agricultural projects in Kenya have failed to meaningfully assist poor farmers, according to the Bank's own analysts. In most other countries, Bank-funded biotechnology research is largely directed toward technological capacity building, genetic analysis, and research support for the regulatory sector.

The "Next Green Revolution"

The World Bank's interest in biotechnology emerged in the 1980s, just as corporations such as Monsato were beginning to shift their research priorities toward developing new transgenic crops. It began funding agricultural projects with distinct biotechnology components in 1982 and commissioned a study in 1988 to "assess the contribution that biotechnology might make to agricultural productivity, and to identify the socioeconomic, policy and management issues that might impede its successful application." The study culminated in an international seminar in Canberra, Australia, in 1989, as well as a report published in 1991.

In many ways, this report defined the Bank's biotechnology agenda for the next decade and beyond. The focus then, as now, was on facilitating the adoption of biotech methods in the so-called "developing world," with an emphasis on tissue culture and advanced diagnostics, but also on genetic engineering and gene mapping. The report predicted that biotechnology would bring "modest but continued increases in productivity of the major crops," and help small farmers survive in an economic climate that favors the concentration of farmland ownership.

Not only has genetic engineering failed to produce long-promised yield improvements, the Bank's lending policies continue to further concentrate land ownership. Nonetheless, the Bank seeks to minimize the social and economic costs of adopting biotech methods, aid in the development of Intellectual Property Rights (IPRs; i.e., patents and licensing) regimes for seeds and plants, offer expertise in risk assessment and biosafety procedures, promote and support research on non-commercial staple food crops, help integrate biotechnology into existing national research programs, and promote public-private partnerships to advance biotechnology.

The implementation of these strategies came into sharper focus following the publication of a 1997 report and a subsequent series of international meetings, which crystallized the earlier discussions into the development of a focused biotechnology strategy. The latter report offered a far more measured and realistic assessment of the state of biotechnology research, balancing this with a broad overview of the known environmental consequences of GE crops. It proposed a substantially broader agenda, aimed at developing scientific and regulatory expertise to assess and identify potential problems, as well as research on new crop varieties through the existing Bank-supported agricultural research centers in various countries. Numerous consultations and international seminars that followed the report's publication proposed an even broader pro-biotech focus, including the protection of IPRs and the development of public-private partnerships promoting biotechnology.

During the same period, the Bank was increasing its collaboration with the agrochemical industry, even while promoting concepts such as sustainability and Integrated Pest Management (IPM). The Pesticide Action Network (PAN) reviewed Bank documents describing over 100 agricultural projects approved between 1997 and 2000, and found a persistent focus on intensifying production and increasing farmers' access to agrochemicals, despite a 1998 policy emphasizing IPM-based alternatives.

PAN also uncovered an ongoing Staff Exchange Program, through which the Bank had entered into business partnerships with nearly all the leading pesticide companies, including biotech giants Aventis, Novartis, and Dow. "For public monies to support the placement of World Bank staff at these companies," argued Marcia Ishii-Eiteman, coordinator of PAN North America's World Bank Accountability Project, "constitutes a gross violation of the Bank's pest management policy and its business partnership guidelines. It is also antithetical to the Bank's commitment to sustainable development and a misuse of public funds."

The Staff Exchange Program involves 189 corporations, governments, universities, and international agencies, including leading transnational companies involved in agribusiness, pharmaceuticals, petroleum, mining, timber, and banking. The Bank trades staff members with various partner institutions for periods of up to two years, with a provision for adding additional years, and assignments are targeted toward mutual institutional needs. Exchanges with agribusiness/biotech companies were most active during the late 1990s and the beginning of this century.

For example, an Aventis (now Bayer CropScience) marketing analyst spent nearly four years helping the International Bank for Reconstruction and Development, the largest and most visible Bank division, to develop its position on agricultural biotechnology, as well as strategies for leveraging financing from the private sector through the Bank's International Finance Corporation. A Dow sales officer worked on projects in Africa and Mexico, and served on teams studying agricultural inputs and biotechnology. Novartis' (now Syngenta's) head of public affairs spent a year working on outreach and communications strategies for the Bank's rural development unit. Meanwhile, Bank officials stationed at Novartis and Rhone Poulenc Agro (now part of Bayer) in the late 1990s worked on biotechnology regulatory issues and rural development partnerships. Through these exchanges, the Bank adjusted its biotechnology strategies to better satisfy the leading biotech seed developers, and corporations gained access to influence public policies in the global South.

Biosafety in India: A Model Project

In 1996, the annual Conference of Parties to the UN's Convention on Biological Diversity (a product of the 1992 Rio "Earth Summit") launched negotiations toward an international protocol on the safe handling and transport of genetically modified organisms (GMOs). African nations, along with others concerned about how future imports of GMOs might threaten the integrity of indigenous plant and animal species, forged an international consensus requiring countries seeking to export intact, viable GMOs—such as live plants, seeds, and microorganisms—to obtain the consent of the importing country. Despite numerous obstacles imposed by the major GMO-producing countries—particularly the U.S., Canada, and Argentina—a full text was developed in Cartagena, Colombia, in 1999 and approved in Montreal in January 2000. The Pacific Island nation of Palau became the 50th country to ratify the Cartagena Protocol on Biosafety in June 2003, bringing it into effect following a 90-day waiting period. As of February 2004, 87 countries had ratified the protocol.

The Biosafety Protocol requires that countries seeking to export living modified organisms (LMOs) obtain "prior informed consent" from the importing country. Where organisms are intended for introduction into the environment (e.g., seeds), detailed information on their identity, traits, and characteristics needs to be communicated, and the receiving country may invoke the Precautionary Principle in deciding whether to allow the import. In the case of organisms intended for contained use, such as in laboratories, the exporter only needs to label the LMOs and specify rules for their safe handling and use.

GMOs intended for food, feed, or processing are largely exempt, but must carry the label, "May contain living modified organisms," as well as a certification that they are not intended for environmental release. Pharmaceutical products regulated by the World Health Organization are exempted entirely. Countries that have not ratified this protocol—including the U.S., which hasn't signed the Biodiversity Convention and, therefore, is not eligible to do so— are expected to trade with so-called Party states in a manner that is consistent with the document's objectives, though there are no means to enforce this.

In March 2003, the Bank approved detailed plans for a 3-year, $3 million dollar project designed to help India fulfill its obligations under the Biosafety Protocol. The project is designed to enhance the capacity of various government agencies and research centers to implement the agreement's provisions. In partnership with India's Ministry of Environment and Forests, the Bank will help build "technical capacity for risk assessment, management and monitoring"; establish the required database system and clearinghouse mechanisms for GMO imports; support the development of infrastructure for research, risk assessment, and monitoring; and strengthen laws, regulatory frameworks, and "communication strategies." Some 1,600 individuals will participate in a series of risk evaluation courses, with primary support for four existing biotech research centers in India.

The Bank's Project Brief reviews in some detail the agencies and facilities that are currently engaged in biotechnology regulation and research in India and addresses ways to significantly expand the capacity of these institutions. The Bank assumes that, having ratified the Cartagena Protocol, India will inevitably see an "increased movement" of GMOs into and within the country. The proposal postulates an ever-growing need for researchers to identify and monitor laboratory research as well as field trials; ensure safe handling of GMOs; evaluate environmental risks and monitor and regulate commerce in engineered organisms.

An ever-expanding array of scientists and public officials will engage in the detection, tracking, and evaluation of GMOs. While some researchers may shift their priorities from the development of new GE organisms to the evaluation of their safety, this project entails a significant expansion in the capacity of Indian researchers to work with GMOs and promote their "societal acceptance."

Greenwashing Corporate Agendas

Despite these clear institutional biases at the Bank and its numerous affiliated agencies, many analysts still assert that the Bank represents an alternative to the aggressive, commercially driven promotion of biotech products that is characteristic of the leading biotech transnationals. The more overt promotion of GE and other controversial biotechnologies is left to another organization, directly supported by the biotech companies, which maintains close institutional ties to the Bank. This is the International Service for the Acquisition of Agri-biotech Applications (ISAAA).

Long-time Bank advisor Gabrielle Persley, formerly biotechnology manager of the Bank's Agriculture and Rural Development Department, serves as the director of programs on ISAAA's board. While some Bank officials have disavowed any direct link to the ISAAA, the history of institutional ties between the two organizations is quite compelling. The ISAAA is directly supported by Monsanto, Syngenta, Bayer, Pioneer, Cargill, and other corporate biotech leaders, along with the Rockefeller, McKnight, and Hitachi Foundations, among others. Its stated goal is "to bring together institutions from national programs in the South, and from the private sector in the North, into partnerships to transfer biotechnology applications."

The ISAAA boasts programs in Africa (Kenya, South Africa, Tanzania, and Uganda) and Asia (Indonesia, Malaysia, the Philippines, Thailand, and Vietnam), has initiated projects in Latin America (Argentina, Brazil, Costa Rica, and Mexico), and offers fellowships to scientists engaged in technology transfer activities. Researchers at the Barcelona-based Genetic Resources Action International (GRAIN) describe the ISAAA fellows as an emerging "advocacy elite," often maintaining a strong and lasting identification with their corporate benefactors. Recent projects include manipulation of virus resistance genes in potatoes and papayas, development of diagnostics for maize diseases, genetic engineering of cassava and sweet potatoes, cell culture techniques for the propagation of commercial tree species, and the assessment of Bt corn technologies for Asia.

In Asia, the ISAAA's history began with a 1996 meeting of its board at the International Rice Research Institute headquarters in the Philippines. Ongoing research and technology transfer projects in Asia, and around the world, follow the general pattern of Bank-funded efforts but are much more heavily tilted toward the development of new transgenic crop varieties. These include efforts to develop GE virus resistant potatoes in Mexico, tomatoes in Indonesia, and papayas in Malaysia.

As with similar Bank-supported efforts, these research priorities reflect little regard for local crop diversity or actual agronomic problems. Large sums are committed to the development of GE varieties that aim to do what local farmers can often accomplish by far less invasive means, while introducing new problems more serious than those they are purported to solve. The ISAAA also seeks to help developing countries circumvent the biotech industry's maze of IPR rules by facilitating licensing arrangements that give researchers easier access to new, proprietary technologies. While Monsanto spends $10 million a year suing and harassing U.S. farmers to strictly obey their "technology agreements" and other IPR rules, the goal in the global South is clearly to promote the rapid acceptance of new GE crops at all costs.

The main vehicle for direct links between the World Bank and the private sector is the Bank's International Finance Corporation (IFC), with an explicit role of leveraging financing from the private sector for international development projects. In the late 1990s, the IFC developed a $30 million Biodiversity Enterprise Fund for Latin America, which aimed to encourage "sustainable uses" of that region's biodiversity. The Fund encouraged investment in questionable activities including bioprospecting, elite forms of ecotourism, and establishing tree plantations as "carbon sinks" to relieve the climate burden of methane production from cattle ranches.

Today, more than 15 Biodiversity Enterprise Funds exist worldwide under the umbrella of the Conservation Finance Alliance (CFA). Two World Bank officials serve on the steering committee of this organization, along with staff from the Nature Conservancy, Worldwide Fund for Nature (WWF), Conservation International, and other organizations dedicated to "free market" approaches to environmental problems.

These Funds pledge to provide needed capital to mostly small, locally based enterprises in regions of high biodiversity, while offering investors opportunities to simultaneously satisfy financial, social, and environmental goals. The CFA's examples of "proven sustainable finance mechanisms" include user fees for tourism, payments for bioprospecting, debt-for-nature swaps (trading small portions of a country's debt for reallocation of particular lands for conservation), conservation trust funds, and "carbon investment projects." Many of these measures have indeed reaped financial rewards for investors—and public relations points for cooperative NGOs—at the expense of indigenous peoples and the ecosystems upon which they have traditionally relied. The CFA's online guidebook cites some seemingly admirable projects: encouraging small farmers in Central America to grow organic cocoa, for example. But it also promises returns on investments of up to 30 percent, a goal that appears quite incompatible with the mission of supporting human-scaled, ecologically sustainable practices in rainforests and other fragile ecosystems.

As corporations and the largest NGOs collaborate in ever-more elaborate schemes to sustain the myth that extracting profits and sustaining the environment can be made compatible, it is clear that the World Bank will continue to play a key role in advancing and legitimizing this dubious agenda, at the behest of global agribusiness and other extractive industries.

Questions for Thinking, Writing, and Discussion

1. Pick an example of the impact of World Bank and IMF policies on a developing nation that you find particularly interesting. Explain the case you have chosen in some detail and discuss what about it interests you and what conclusions you are prepared to draw from it.

2. Explain the purpose and likely consequences of implementing Plan Puebla Panama.

3. Many articles in this section discuss the impact of the World Bank's structural adjustment policies on agriculture in the developing world. How has World Bank policy changed agriculture and what are the implications of those changes for eradicating poverty?

4. How has globalization impacted on indigenous peoples in Latin America? How and why do the values of indigenous people and the values of globalization come into conflict?

5. How has globalization impacted specifically on women and gender roles? How has women's place in the economy changed as a result of globalization?

6. In their essay, Barbara Ehrenreich and Arlie Hochschild talk about the globalization of traditional female services. Explain what they are referring to. Do you think they have made a good case for their claim that this phenomenon is a result of globalization?

7. Several articles in this part and elsewhere in the text discuss the privatization of water. Write a short essay in which you discuss the origins and consequences of this problem and use it to discuss the pros and cons of globalization.

8. A number of authors in this part and elsewhere in the text compare globalization to a second colonization. What do they mean by this? What evidence do they offer in support of this claim? Do you agree or disagree? Why?

9. What do authors Salih Booker and William Minter mean by the term "Global Apartheid"? How do they explain and illustrate this concept?

10. What is the relationship between globalization and the rise of militarism in the developing world?

11. In his article, Brian Toker contends that the World Bank has written some of the most devastating projects undertaken in the name of progress and "development." What kind of examples does he offer in support of his claim?

12. How has globalization resulted in the spread of U.S. culture and U.S. values to other parts of the world? What examples do the articles in this part offer of this phenomena? Can you think of other examples? How about examples of globalization bringing aspects of other cultures and other cultural values to the United States? Can you think of any examples? Is this culture sharing a positive or a negative offshoot of globalization?

Suggestions for Further Reading

Ahn, Christine. *Free Trade and America's Working Poor.* Food First, 2003.

Ault, Amber, and Eve Sandberg, "Our Policies, Their Consequences: Zambian Women's Lives under Structural Adjustment," *Feminist Frontiers V*, Laurel Ricgardson, Verta Taylor, and Nancy Whittier, eds. New York, McGraw-Hill, 2000, 503–6.

Basel Action Network (BAN) and Silicon Valley Toxics Coalition (SVTC) with contributions by Toxics Link India, SCOPE (Pakistan), Greenpeace China. *Exporting Harm: The High-Tech Trashing of Asia*, February 25, 2002.

Bond, Patrick. *Unsustainable South Africa: Environment, Development and Social Protest.* London: Merling Press and Pietermaritzburg, University of Natal Press, 2002.

Bond, Patrick. "From Racial to Class Apartheid: South Africa's Frustrating Decade of Freedom," *Monthly Review*, March 2004, 43–53.

Barlow, Maude, and Tony Clark. "Water Privatization: The World Bank's Latest Market Fantasy," http://www.globalpolicy.org/socecon/bwi-wto/wbank/2004/01waterpriv.htm.

Kahn, Joseph. "Making Trinkets in China, and a Deadly Dust," *New York Times*, June 15, 2003.

Lee, Sherry. "Ghosts in the Machines." *South China Morning Post Magazine*, May 12, 2002.

Longwe, Sara Hilupekile. "Gender Implications of Bank Privitization in Developing Countries," www.50years.org/cms/ejn/story/76

McDonald, David A. *Environmental Justice in South Africa.* Ohio University Press, 2002.

Muller, Anders Riel, and Raj Patel. "Shining India? Economic Liberalization and Rural Poverty in the 1990s," Food First/Institute for Food and Development Policy, May 2004. www.foodfirst.org/pubs/policy/pb10.html

Shiva, Vandana, "Globalization and Its Fall Out," www.zmag.org/Sustainers/Content/2003-04/02shiva.cfm

Spenser, Michael. "The Leshotho Highlands Water Project," *TransAfrica Forum Globalization Monitor*, Vol. I, Issue II, Summer 2003.

Toward a More Equitable Future: Grassroots Movements for Social Change

It is not that we should simply seek new and better ways for managing
society, the economy, and the world. The point is that we should
fundamentally change how we behave.
—*Vaclav Havel, 1992*

In this concluding section of the book we take a brief look at some examples of how people are responding to globalization at the local level. The idea that a small community of indigenous people could block their government's plans to use part of their land to build a large international airport initially seems incredible, but this is just what the people of Atenco, a small rural village outside of Mexico City, have successfully done. I had the privilege of visiting Atenco in May of 2003 and heard first-hand how the community came together to protect their land, livelihood, and culture. In Article I Claudio Albertini tells the story of their struggle and improbable victory. He also reports on efforts by a community group in Oaxaca to prevent McDonald's from erecting a store near the central plaza of that ancient city and an effort on the part of a group in Cuernavaca to block CostCo's efforts to build a large hypermarket at an important cultural site on the edge of town. As it turns out, the CostCo construction project would have required the destruction of 5 hectares of ancient woods. Albertini tells the story of how local residents with the support of the local Greenpeace unit have mounted their campaign against this corporate giant.

In Article 2 Vandana Shiva takes us to Plachimada, a small hamlet in southern India where local residents successfully shut down a Coca-Cola plant in an effort to protect the water supply.* In the light of worldwide efforts to privitize water and the devastating impact this privitization is having on poor people everywhere, the campaign to stop Coke in Plachimada takes on special importance. Another equally improbable victory, that of village women in Nigeria over multinational corporate giant ChevronTexaco Oil, is the subject of Article 3. A group of 150 unarmed women stormed the company's Escravos pipeline terminal and temporarily shut down operations throughout Nigeria. Their demand—jobs for their sons and help in improving living conditions in the local villages, including providing them with electricity. After 30 years of growing rich on Nigeria's oil, it was time, the women believed, for the corporation to give back something to the community.

The late 1990s and the early years of the twenty-first century saw a rise in campus student activism as college students across the United States organized against the use of sweatshop labor in the production of university logo clothing. Liza Featherstone's article describes the United Students Against Sweatshops campaigns directed at persuading college administrators and board members to nullify contracts with corporations that produce their clothing under sweatshop conditions. This campaign has since expanded to include student boycotts of Taco Bell on behalf of migrant farm workers and of Coca-Cola to protest human rights violations by that corporate giant in its plants in other parts of the world. For an update on student activism since Featherstone's article was published in 2000, you can visit the United Students Against Sweatshop Website: http://www.studentsagainstsweatshops.org/press/press.php.

The efforts of waste-pickers and their supporters to increase government support for recycling and improve living conditions for thousands of scavengers who live and scavenge at the Payatas dumpsite outside of Manila in the Philippines is the focus of Article 5. This article describes the efforts of a local people's organization, *Lupang Pangako* Urban Poor Association, along with the Payatas Scavenger's Association, to exert pressure on the Philippine government to improve the roads leading to the dump and to provide utilities like water and electricity to the residents of the dump's shanty town. As the authors point out, these efforts have the long-term possibility of advancing environmental protection and poverty reduction at the same time.

Challenging the assumption made by the traditional banking community that loans could only be made to people who are able to provide collateral to secure them, an impossibility for the poorest of the poor, Professor Muhammad Yunus, founder of the Grameen Bank, provides microcredit to poor people in rural Bangladesh. The bank extends banking facilities to poor men and women and makes loans, primarily to poor women, in order to create opportunities for self-employment. Article 6 tells the exciting success story of one man's efforts to have an impact on rural poverty by going against the most basic practices of the banking community.

This section also includes a list of NGOs and other organizations working all over the world on many of the issues that we have considered in this book. From indigenous people's rights to women's rights, to development programs, to environmental issues, and a host of other concerns, these organizations are making a difference and responding to globalization by trying to create development strategies that improve the lives of people, protect the environment, and eradicate poverty at the same time. The Websites of the organizations are provided so that you can visit them and get an even broader picture of how people around the world are responding to globalization and working together to put human needs first. It is neither possible nor desirable to turn back the clock, but it is both possible and desirable to make conscious decisions about the kind of globalization we are prepared to support and the kind of world we want to live in and hand over to those who come after us.

NOTE

*The struggle at Plachimada is on-going. Watch for news reports or visit indiaresource.org for updates.

one

Small Is Beautiful
Airports, McDonald's, and Hypermarkets in Mexico
–Claudio Albertini

Claudio Albertini teaches contemporary history at the Universidad Autónoma de la Ciudad de México (UACM) in Mexico City. He has written extensively about Indian struggles in Guatemala and Chiapas for independent Guatemalan, Mexican, Italian, and French publications. His article "Small is Beautiful: Airports, McDonald's, and Hypermarkets in Mexico," appeared on ZNet in September 2003.

Mexico, as we all know, is a land of contradictions and paradoxes. The historian John Womack opens his famous book on Emiliano Zapata saying theirs is "a history of peasants who did not want to change, and thus started a revolution".

Today, at the beginning of the Third Millennium, and in direct contrast to neoliberal homogenization, a large number of widely diverse social, political, economic and cultural activities remain present. Native peoples continue to strongly defend their right to determine their own means of livelihood, communal spaces and lifestyles, which are in clear contrast to prevailing values. Their resistance fuels a permanent social war—at times covert, at times apparent—which, among other things, plays on the imagination. This war sometimes affects city dwellers, producing interesting feedback effects. As an example of this, let us consider three recent grassroots movements that have had significant nationwide repercussions.

The first is the movement against the construction of a new airport near Atenco, a rural village a few kilometers east of Mexico City. In October 2001 President Vicente Fox, offering ridiculously low compensations, decreed the expropriation of the village's communal land for reasons of public interest. Atenco, deprived of its main economic resources, was thus doomed to disappear. Fearlessly, its inhabitants organized periodic demonstrations in Mexico City. Marching in closed ranks, they would invade the city center waving their machetes—"not weapons, but work tools", they explained—making them resound rhythmically against the asphalt of the urban jungle. When the government started surveying and demolishing, Atenco's inhabitants put up barricades without hesitation.

"Small Is Beautiful: Airports, McDonald's, and Hypermarkets in Mexico" by Claudio Albertini," *ZNet Commentary*, September 17, 2002. Copyright 2002. Reprinted by permission of the author.

Mainstream newspapers and television, strongly supporting the project, accused them of being lunatics opposing progress—or dangerous subversives. Nonetheless, the movement was increasingly attracting support. At the end of July the crowds were becoming restless. A demonstration degenerated and the police beat a demonstrator to death. In the face of a massive wave of solidarity, the government was forced to back down and revoke the expropriation decree. It was later revealed that the project concealed a massive fraud and that it would have been five times more expensive than enlarging the existing airport. Now the *Atencos* (as they are popularly known) are considering the possibility of breaking with the state and establishing an autonomous municipality like the Zapatistas.

Another interesting case is that of Oaxaca, a beautiful provincial city recently declared World Heritage. Thanks to Pro-Oax, a civil society organization promoted by the painter Francisco Toledo, the old city center has been restored in the last few years and cultural institutions of a high standard have flourished. The old Dominican monastery has been converted into a high class museum of indigenous culture, and the arts institute can boast an art history library among the best in Latin America.

The city has been in a state of ferment since the beginning of the summer, as the mayor has given McDonald's the authorization to open a new shop on the main square, the *Zocalo*. Here, in the shade of hundred-year-old trees and historical buildings, traditional restaurants offer local specialties—the same spicy cuisine that attracted Italo Calvino's attention in his novel *Sapore sapere*. A new movement was immediately born, promoted by Pro-Oax, to protest against the infamous multinational, well known for underpaying its employees, serving low-quality meat, causing deforestation and using genetically modified ingredients.

As in Atenco, the secret weapon was local imagination. Sunday August 18 Pro-Oax organized a large open-air party at the Zocalo, giving away 4,000 tamales— the famous corn roulades that are the pride of the local cuisine—and hundreds of liters of fruit shakes. One of several banners, all ironic and good-humored, read *No to McZocalo*. Within a couple of hours, Pro-Oax activists, wearing McDonald's-style hats, had collected more than 5,000 signatures asking for the revocation of McDonald's license and the holding of a referendum.

On August 27 the Grand Commission of the Local Parliament officially declared that it shared the concern of preserving the historical old city center. McDonald's was caught on the hop—although it is too early to tell, it is hard to believe that the multinational will decide to expose itself to new protests, which may have devastating effects on its already tarnished image.

The third movement is based in the city of Cuernavaca, capital of the small state of Morelos, sixty kilometers south of Mexico City. Here the multinational CostCo expects to build a hypermarket inside the wonderful state owned park where the *Casinò de la Selva* hotel used to be.

Malcolm Lowry readers will surely remember that the initial scene of *Under the Volcano* is set exactly in that building: "palatial, a certain air of desolate splendor pervades it." In its sumptuous gardens, with a marvelous view, the consul and his brother Hugh, a veteran from the Spanish war, had passionate discussions about communism, fascism and human destiny.

Setting aside such literary recollections, it is still true that the hotel, now partially demolished, has been one of the most important centers of cultural life in Cuernavaca for decades.

In June 2001, with the complicity of the local government, CostCo bought the land for a paltry sum, which didn't take into account many works of art including some important murals, all of which are public property. It then obtained permission to destroy five hectares of woods, thus arousing the ecologists' anger after having enraged painters.

The *Frente Cívico por la defensa del Casinò de la Selva* was established in September of the same year. The Frente, supported by the local Greenpeace unit, organized an awareness campaign mainly aimed at the preservation of the hundred-years-old trees.

Popular response was quite weak at the beginning. On Wednesday August 21, however, the police made a big mistake—they violently repressed a peaceful demonstration of the *Frente*, arresting 32 people (including Pietro Ameglio, an Italian-born naturalized Mexican citizen), beating and jailing them.

These events triggered the "Atenco effect"—what started as a hesitant movement of intellectuals ended up involving not only wide sectors of the urban population, but also peasants from nearby villages. Among these is Tepoztlán, a community that a few years ago was the center of a large movement against the creation of a golf course.

Given these circumstances, and also due to pressure from Greenpeace and Amnesty International, the Morelos government was forced to hastily release the prisoners. On Tuesday August 27, 15,000 demonstrators invaded the conservative town of Cuernavaca—noticeably, among them, a group from Atenco with their unfailing machetes. "Better a naturalized Mexican than a degenerate Mexican", a banner read, alluding to the xenophobic campaign promoted by the local press against Ameglio and a couple of other foreign activists.

Now the *Frente* is asking for a referendum which it has a good chance of winning. In the meanwhile it has called for a "cart war" against CostCo, which comprises several supermarket chains, including the well known Comercial Mexicana. This form of boycott had already been exercised during the Vietnam War—shoppers fill their carts and leave the supermarket without making any purchases.

The moral of the story? Machetes and corn can have the upper hand over financial maneuvers.

PS   What about the Zapatistas? A lot has been said—often a lot of nonsense—about the *comandancia's* prolonged silence. It's not worth spending any time here on the absurd speculations made on this topic. One thing is certain. Marcos, after often saying too much, is now keeping quiet, but the communities putting up resistance are making themselves heard. And they do it in several ways, for example by strengthening the structures of the autonomous municipalities, by increasingly denouncing the "dirty war" (three killings in the past few weeks) and by keeping up the meetings with the Mexican and international civil society. Over the past few weeks even a new free radio has appeared, transmitting rebellious messages on 102.9 FM from an unidentified mountain in South-East Mexico . . .

Building Water Democracy
People's Victory Against Coca-Cola in Plachimada
–Vandana Shiva

Vandana Shiva is a physicist, ecologist, activist, and editor. She directs the Research Foundation for Science, Technology and Natural Resource Policy in India, where she has established Navdanya, a movement for biodiversity conservation and farmers' rights. "Building Water Democracy: People's Victory Against Coca-Cola in Plachimada" (India), by Vandana Shiva, appeared on ZNet on May 12, 2004.

Two years ago, adivasi women in a small hamlet, Plachimada, in Palghat, Kerala, started a movement against Coca-Cola. Today, the Coca-Cola plant in Plachimada has been shut down. The victory of the Plachimada movement is a major step in reversing corporate hijacking of our precious water resources. It provides both inspiration and lessons for building water democracy in other parts of India and in the rest of the world.

The Coca-Cola plant in Plachimada was commissioned in March 2000 to produce 1,224,000 bottles of Coca-Cola, Fanta, Sprite, Limca, Thums Up, Kinley Soda, and Maaza. The Panchayat was issued a conditional license for installing a motor for drawing water. However, the company started to illegally extract millions of litres of clean water from more than 6 bore wells installed by it using electric pumps in order to manufacture millions of bottles of soft drink.

"Building Water Democracy: People's Victory Against Coca-Cola in Plachimada" by Vandana Shiva. *ZNet Commentary*, May 13, 2004. © 2004 by Vandana Shiva. Reprinted by permission of the author.

According to the local people, Coca-Cola was extracting 1.5 million litres per day. The water level started to fall, going from 150 feet to 500 feet. Not only did Coca-Cola "steal" the water of the local community, it also polluted what was left. The company is also pumping wastewater into dry bore wells within the company premises for disposing of solid waste.

Earlier it was depositing the waste material outside the company premises, and during the rainy season it spread into paddy fields, canals, and wells, causing serious health hazards.

As a result of this, 260 bore wells which were provided by public authorities for drinking water and agriculture facilities have become dry. Complaints were also being received from tribals and farmers that storage of water and sources of water were being adversely affected by indiscriminate installation of bore wells for tapping ground water, leading to serious consequences for crop cultivation in the area on which residents of the Panchayat depend for their living: e.g., maintenance of traditional drinking water sources, preservation of ponds and water tanks, maintenance of waterways and canals, and shortage of drinking water. When the Panchayat asked for details, the company failed to comply.

The Panchayat therefore served a show cause notice and cancelled the license. Coca-Cola tried to bribe the Panchayat President A. Krishnan with Rs.300 million, but he refused to be corrupted and coopted. In 2003, the district medical officer informed the people of Plachimada their water was unfit for drinking.

The women already knew their water was toxic. Instead of drawing water from the wells in their homes they had to walk miles. Coca-Cola had created a water scarcity in a water abundant region. And the women of Plachimada were not going to allow this "hydropiracy". They started a "dharna" (sit-in) at the gates of Coca-Cola. On Earth Day 2003, they invited me to celebrate one year of their agitation.

On 21st September, 2003 a huge rally was organized to give an ultimatum to Coca-Cola. On 21st and 22nd of January, 2004 a World Water Conference brought global activists like Jose Bove and Maude Barlow to Plachimada to support the local activists.

A movement started by local adivasi women had unleashed a national and global wave of people's energy in their support. On 17th February, 2004 the Kerala Chief Minister, under pressure of the growing movement and the aggravation of the water crisis because of a drought, ordered closure of the Coke plant. The victory of the movement in Plachimada was the result of creating broad alliances and using multiple strategies.

The rainbow alliances, beginning with the local women and activists like Veloor Swaminthan, Convenor of the anti Coca-Cola task force in Plachimada, grew to include the local Gram Panchayat and its members Girija Devi, Geetha Mohandas, Sheeba Radhakrishnan, Aruchamy K, Sivakam, Subbayyan, MK Arumugham, K Varathara, A Krishnan, President, K Parthan, Presitha Mohandas, M Shanmugham, G Ponnukkuttam, N Chellankutty, C Murughan.

The local Panchayat used its constitutional rights to serve notice to Coca-Cola. The Perumatty Panchayat also filed a public interest litigation in the Kerala High Court against Coca-Cola.

The courts support the women's demands. In an order given on 16th December 2003, Justice Balakrishnana Nair ordered Coca-Cola to stop pirating Plachimada's water. As the Honorable Justice stated:

> The Public Trust Doctrine primarily rests on the principle that certain resources like air, sea waters and the forests have such a great importance to the people as a whole that it would be wholly unjustified to make them a subject of private ownership. The said resources being a gift of nature, they should be made freely available to everyone irrespective of the status in life. The doctrine enjoins upon the government to protect the resources for the enjoyment of the general public rather than to permit their use for private ownership or commercial purpose. . . .
>
> Our legal system—based on English common law—includes the public trust doctrine as part of its jurisprudence. The State is the trustee of all natural resources, which are by nature meant for public use and enjoyment. Public at large is the beneficiary of the seashore, running waters, airs, forests and ecologically fragile lands. The State as a trustee is under a legal duty to protect the natural resources. These resources meant for public use cannot be converted into private ownership. . . .
>
> In view of the above authoritative statement of the Honourable Supreme Court, it can be safely concluded that underground water belongs to the public. The State and its instrumentalities should act as trustees of this great wealth. The State has got a duty to protect ground water against excessive exploitation and the inaction of the State in this regard is tantamount to infringement of the right to life of the people, guaranteed under Article 21 of the Constitution of India.
>
> The Apex Court has repeatedly held that the right to clean air and unpolluted water forms part of the right to life under Article 21 of the Constitution. So, even in the absence of any law governing ground water, I am of the view that the Panchayat and the State are bound to protect ground water from excessive exploitation. In other words, the ground water, under the land of the 2nd respondent, does not belong to it.
>
> Even assuming the experts' opinion that the present level of consumption by the 2nd respondent is harmless, the same should not be permitted for the following reasons:
>
> The underground water belongs to the general public and the 2nd respondent has no right to claim a huge share of it and the Government have no power to allow a private party to extract such a huge quantity of ground water, which is a property, held by it in trust.
>
> If the 2nd respondent is permitted to draw such a huge quantity of ground water, then similar claims of the other landowners will also have to be allowed. The same will result in drying up of the underground aqua-reservoirs.
>
> Accordingly, the following directions are issued:
>
> The 2nd respondent shall stop ground water for its use after one month from today.
>
> The Panchayat and the State shall ensure that the 2nd respondent does not extract any ground water after the said time limit. This time is granted to enable the 2nd respondent to find out alternative sources of water.

The alliance grew to include people like Veerandra Kumar of Mathrubhumi and me. And we mobilized our networks to offer our full support to the local movement. The January conference was co-organised with the local Panchayat. It brought on one platform every political party, and the leader of the opposition V.S. Achuthanandan who kept up the pressure in the Kerala Assembly to translate the Court decision into Executive action.

The literary movement provided leadership through Dr. Sukumar Azhikode. And global support came in the presence of Jose Bove, Maude Barlow, European Parliamentarians and activists from across the world. The women's protest, the heart and soul of the movement, got support through legal action, parliamentary action and scientific research. This pluralism and diversity in support of local action was the secret of the victory of people against Coke in Plachimada.

This is the strength of our multiplicities and complementarities; we have to mobilize in other parts of India where Coke and Pepsi are mining and stealing people's water resources. The Plachimada Declaration issued at the World Water conference of 21st–23rd January, 2004 states:

Plachimada Declaration

Water is the basis of life; it is the gift of nature; it belongs to all living beings on earth.

Water is not a private property. It is a common resource for the sustenance of all.

Water is the fundamental right of man. It has to be conserved. Protected and managed. It is our fundamental obligation to prevent water scarcity and pollution and to preserve it for generations.

Water is not a commodity. We should resist all criminal attempts to marketise, privatize and corporatise water. Only through these means we can ensure the fundamental and inalienable right to water for the people all over the world.

The Water Policy should be formulated on the basis of this outlook.

The right to conserve, use and manage water is fully vested with the local community. This is the very basis of water democracy. Any attempt to reduce or deny this right is a crime.

The production and marketing of the poisonous products of the Coca-Cola, Pepsi Cola corporates lead to total destruction and pollution and it also endangers the very existence of local communities.

The resistance that has come up in Plachimada, Pududdery and in various parts of the world is the symbol of our valiant struggle against the devilish corporate gangs who pirate our water.

We, who are in the battlefield in full solidarity with the Adivasis who have put up resistance against the tortures of the horrid commercial forces in Plachimada, exhort the people all over the world to boycott the products of Coca-Cola and Pepsi Cola.

Coca-Cola—Pepsi Cola: "Quit India".

Nigerian Women Win Out Against Oil Giants

—New Pittsburgh Courier

The following account of a successful 10-day peaceful protest by hundreds of women in Nigeria against ChevronTexaco appeared in The New Pittsburgh Courier *on May 27, 2002.*

NIGERIA   Hundreds of women carrying straw mats and thermoses abandoned ChevronTexaco's main oil terminal, ending a peaceful 10-day protest that crippled the oil giant's Nigerian operations and won an unprecedented company pledge to build modern towns out of poor villages.

"I give one piece of advice to all women in all countries: they should not let any company cheat them," said Anunu Uwawah, a leader of the protest at the southeastern Nigerian Escravos terminal.

Uwawah and her comrades were ferried back to their villages in Chevron-Texaco boats this week, along the way passing hundreds of oil workers returning to the facility.

The last of the protesters were expected to leave July 26, said company spokesman Wole Agunbiade.

He said operations were quickly returning to normal at the company's southeastern Escravos terminal, which accounts for close to half a million barrels a day, the bulk of the company's Nigeria exports.

"Chevron has shown a lot of restraint, commitment to good neighborliness, peace and dialogue," Agunbiade said. "I would like to believe this is the hallmark of Chevron negotiations, and will continue to be."

The women had trapped about 700 American, British, Canadian and Nigerian workers inside the terminal. Two hundred employees were allowed to leave on Sunday and hundreds more two days later, leaving just a few dozen inside.

"Women Win Out Against Oil Giants." Reprinted by permission of GRM Associates, Inc. Agents for The New Pittsburgh Courier from the issue of July 27, 2002. Copyright © 2002 by *The New Pittsburgh Courier*.

The women kept their hold on the terminal by threatening to take off their clothes—a powerful traditional shaming gesture—in a last-ditch gesture to humiliate the company.

The peaceful, all-woman protest was a departure for the oil-rich Niger Delta, where armed men frequently use kidnapping and sabotage to pressure oil multinationals into giving them jobs, protection, money or compensation for alleged environmental damage. Hostages generally are released unharmed.

The New Student Movement
–Liza Featherstone

Liza Featherstone is a New York–based journalist who has written for the New York Times, *the* Los Angeles Times, Newsday, Rolling Stone, *and the* Washington Post, *among other publications. Her article "The New Student Movement" appeared in* The Nation *in May 2000.*

"We have the university by the balls," said Nati Passow, a University of Pennsylvania junior, in a meeting with his fellow antisweatshop protestors. "Whatever way we twist them is going to hurt." Passow was one of thirteen Penn students—the group later grew to include forty—occupying the university president's office around the clock in early February to protest the sweatshop conditions under which clothing bearing the U-Penn logo is made. The Penn students, along with hundreds of other members of United States Against Sweatshops nationwide, were demanding that their university withdraw from the Fair Labor Association (FLA), an industry-backed monitoring group, and instead join the Worker Rights Consortium (WRC), an organization independent of industry influence, founded by

"The New Student Movement" by Liza Featherstone. Reprinted with permission from the May 15, 2000 issue of *The Nation*. For subscription information call 1-800-333-8536. Portions of each week's *Nation* magazine can be accessed at http://www.thenation.com.

students in close cooperation with scholars, activists and workers'-rights organizations in the global South.

At first the administration met the students with barely polite condescension. In one meeting, President Judith Rodin was accompanied by U-Penn professor Larry Gross, an earring-wearing baby boomer well-known on campus for his left-wing views, who urged the protesters to have more faith in the administration and mocked the sit-in strategy, claiming he'd "been there, done that." President Rodin assured them that a task force would review the problem by February 29, and there was no way she could speed up its decision. She admonished them to "respect the process."

Watching the Penn students negotiate with their university's president, it was clear they didn't believe any of her assurances. They knew there was no reason to trust that the administration would meet one more arbitrary deadline after missing so many others—so they stayed in the office. After eight days of torture by folk-singing, acoustic guitar, recorders, tambourines and ringing cell phones, as well as a flurry of international news coverage, Judith Rodin met the protesters halfway by withdrawing from the FLA. (To students' frustration, the task force decided in early April to postpone a decision about WRC membership until later this spring.)

The most remarkable thing about the Penn students' action was that it wasn't an isolated or spontaneous burst of idealism. Penn's was just the first antisweatshop sit-in of the year; by mid-April students at the universities of Michigan, Wisconsin, Oregon, Iowa and Kentucky, as well as SUNY-Albany, Tulane, Purdue and Macalester, had followed suit. And the sit-in wasn't the protesters' only tactic: Purdue students held an eleven-day hunger strike. Other students chose less somber gestures of dissent. In late February the University of North Carolina's antisweatshop group, Students for Economic Justice, held a nude-optional party titled "I'd Rather Go Naked Than Wear Sweatshop Clothes." In late March, in an exuberant expression of the same principle, twelve Syracuse students biked across campus nude. The protests were a coordinated effort; members of United Students Against Sweatshops (USAS), which was founded three years ago and now has chapters at more than 200 schools, work closely with one another, a process made easier by the many listservs and websites that the students use to publicize actions, distribute information and help fuel turnout.

Though the largest, most successful—and before Seattle, the most visible—thread of the movement has focused on improving work conditions in the $2.5 billion collegiate apparel industry, university licensing policies have not been the only targets of recent anticorporate agitation on campus. This year, from UC-Davis to the University of Vermont, students have held globalization teach-ins, planned civil disobedience for the April IMF/World Bank meetings, protested labor policies at the Gap and launched vigorous campaigns to drive Starbucks out of university dining services. In snowy January, at the conservative Virginia Commonwealth University, twenty students slept outside the vice president's office for two nights to protest the university's contract with McDonald's (the school promised the fast-food behemoth a twenty-year monopoly over the Student Commons). Students at Johns Hopkins and at Wesleyan held sit-ins demanding better wages for university workers. And at the end of March hundreds of students, many bearing hideously deformed papier-mâché puppets to illustrate the potential horrors of biotechnology, joined Boston's carnivalesque protest against genetic engineering.

With a *joie de vivre* that the American economic left has probably lacked since before WWI, college students are increasingly engaged in well-organized, thoughtful and morally outraged resistance to corporate power. These activists, more than any student radicals in years, passionately denounce the wealth gap, globally and in the United States, as well as the lack of democratic accountability in a world dominated by corporations. While some attend traditionally political schools like Evergreen, Michigan and Wisconsin, this movement does not revolve around usual suspects; some of this winter's most dramatic actions took place at campuses that have always been conservative, like the University of Pennsylvania, Virginia Commonwealth and Johns Hopkins. At this article's writing in late April, students were staging several significant anticorporate protests every week. It is neither too soon, nor too naïvely optimistic, to call it a movement. . . .

Much of the struggle concerns the corporatization of higher education. Universities are run increasingly like private firms, and have ever-more intimate relations with private industry [see David L. Kirp, "The New U," April 17]. During one antisweat occupation in mid-April, for example, student activists at the University of Oregon led a campus tour of sites that illustrated the institution's numerous ties to corporations (one stop was the Phil Knight Library, named after Nike's president and CEO). A nationwide student group called 180/Movement for Democracy and Education, based at the University of Wisconsin, articulates this problem, and its connection to other issues, more consistently than any other group, even leading teach-ins on how World Trade Organization policies affect higher education. But almost all of the current student struggles—whether over tuition increases, apparel licenses, socially responsible investing, McDonald's in the student union, the rights of university laundry workers, a dining-hall contractor's investment in private prisons or solidarity with the striking students in Mexico—focus on the reality of the university as corporate actor.

Battle lines are now being drawn on a number of campuses, including Penn and Wisconsin, over whether universities will give in to student demands and agree to join the Worker Rights Consortium. WRC members require their apparel licensees to comply with a strict code of conduct—guaranteeing workers a living wage and the right to organize unions—and mandate full public disclosure of wages, factory locations and working conditions. By denying industry any role in its governance and giving power instead to a board composed of administrators, students and human rights scholars and activists, the WRC provides a nascent model for the kind of university decision-making the students would like to see: a process free of corporate influence. It is also a model in which, so far, student activists have set the terms of discussion. No wonder so many university administrators, many of whom now like to be called "CEOs," have resisted it so savagely, even, in several cases, permitting quite forceful police treatment of peaceful protesters.

Yet many universities that once rebuffed the students' entreaties have since backed down, a testament to the skill and energy of the student organizers. The wave of sit-ins this spring was deliberately timed to precede the WRC's early April founding conference. Before the Penn sit-in, only a handful of institutions, none of which had substantial apparel-licensing contracts, belonged to the new organization; now forty-seven institutions belong, and the WRC founding meeting was attended by students or administrators from forty schools. The night before the meeting, the entire ten-school University of California system joined the organization and sent a representative to New York for the event. Some institutions joined without any building takeovers, choosing to avert bad publicity through graceful capitulation. "A lot of them joined without a sit-in because they thought there would be a sit-in the next day," says Maria Roeper, an antisweat activist taking a semester off from Haverford to coordinate the WRC.

Indeed, student activists have managed to put administrators on the defensive. On April 7 student antisweat protesters wearing duct tape over their mouths—to protest the fact that students have no say in campus decisions—met the University of Oregon president at the airport, frightening him so badly he left the baggage claim and hid in the bathroom. Even more striking, that same day, was the sight of dozens of suited university administrators at the WRC conference scurrying to "organize" among themselves. Many were pressured into WRC membership and worry that they won't have as much influence as they want over the new monitoring organization. Administrators were supposed to elect their representatives to the governing board at the founding meeting, but instead they asked for more time; they are now expected to do so later this spring, after holding their own meeting in Chicago. "It's only natural that they should want to do that," says Roeper. "The student group [USAS] did have a lot of power."

Industry, too, is getting nervous. Top officials of the Fair Labor Association, founded in 1996 by the Clinton Administration along with business representatives and some human rights groups, have been touring campuses, trying to convince students of their organization's good intentions. (Unlike the WRC, the FLA allows industry to choose its own monitors and doesn't include provisions for a living wage.) A week before the consortium's founding conference, Nike, which supports the FLA, canceled its contract with Brown University, objecting to the university's WRC membership. Nike has repeatedly denounced the WRC, calling it a "gotcha" monitoring system. "Nike is using Brown to threaten other schools," said Brown antisweat activist Nicholas Reville at the conference. More recently, Nike's Phil Knight, who had pledged $30 million to the University of Oregon for its sports stadium, indignantly withdrew the offer after the school announced its membership in the WRC.

In the recent history of student activism, the new emphasis on economics represents quite a shift. Ten years ago, there was plenty of student organizing, but it was fragmentary and sporadic, and most of it focused on what some, mostly its detractors, liked to call "identity politics," fighting the oppression of racial and sexual minorities, and of women. Admirable as they were—and effective in improving social relations on many campuses—there was little sense of solidarity among these groups, and they often seemed insular, bearing little relation to life outside the university.

That political moment is over, partly because in the larger world, organized feminism is in a lull and the mainstream gay movement now focuses on issues like inclusion in the military, gay marriage and hate-crimes legislation—moderate goals that don't speak to student idealism. By contrast, the economic left—especially the labor movement, and the burgeoning resistance to global capital—is enjoying a resurgence, both in numbers and in vision. The new student anticorporatists are building strong relationships with unions, which are, in turn, showing remarkable dedication to the new generation. During February's Penn sit-in, a different union local brought the students dinner almost every night. "Seattle helped the unions see that the students were serious," explains Simon Greer, Jobs With Justice's Workers' Rights board director. When the University of Wisconsin sent in the cops to drag away fifty-four peaceful antisweat protesters, George Becker, president of the United Steelworkers, issued a statement denouncing the administration's "oppressive actions."

The early-nineties struggles haven't vanished without a trace; indeed, it sometimes seems as if, through the anticorporate movement, they have returned to their early-seventies roots as movements for radical liberation. Many of the leaders are women, and feminist analysis informs the movement's focus; the antisweat activists, for instance, frequently point out that most sweatshop workers are women. And although the struggle against homophobia has largely disappeared from the student progressive agenda, the tactics—militant, theatrical and often campy direct action—of early-nineties groups like ACT UP and Queer Nation have clearly influenced the new crew of student activists.

Anticorporatism also has the potential to be a movement for racial justice. Farah Mongeau, a University of Michigan law student and member of U-M's Students of Color Coalition (SCC), points out, "[Sweatshop labor] obviously affects people of color. People of color are the ones who work in the sweatshops." Yet, although many core organizers are South Asian, the antisweatshop movement is mostly white. Organizing by students of color is on the upswing, but its relationship to the anticorporate groups can be uneasy. Some students of color say this is partly because white activists receive better treatment from those in power. At Michigan in February, SCC members protesting a racist secret society held a sit-in at the same time as the antisweat organization and resented the fact that while they were ignored for weeks, the predominantly white group got a meeting with the president immediately. Likewise, Justin Higgins, sophomore class president at North Carolina Central University, a historically black and working-class college, who in February had just joined the regional student anti-WTO/IMF coalition, said he wasn't planning to go to Washington, DC, and wasn't sorry to have missed Seattle. "If there had been black students [in Seattle]," Higgins said, "there would have been real bullets, not rubber bullets."

On the other hand, some less visible economic-justice campaigns on campus have been more racially mixed: those fighting university tuition hikes, for instance. And the student movement's relationship with labor may help break down its whiteness. In its early stages, very few black students were involved in the Johns Hopkins action demanding higher wages for university workers, for example, though the low-wage workers at the school are predominantly people of color. But when local unions got involved in the sit-in, they were able to recruit members of the black student group. On other campuses, multiracial alliances between anti-corporate and prison activists are beginning to emerge. In early April students at ten campuses launched a boycott campaign against Sodexho-Marriott, which operates more than 500 campus dining halls, is the largest investor in US private prisons and is also currently facing censure from the National Labor Relations Board. In an April sit-in at SUNY-Albany, activists, in addition to sweatshop-related demands, insisted that the university drop Sodexho-Marriott if the company did not divest from private prisons and improve its labor practices.

Filipino Dump Activists Turn Waste into Wealth
–Eugenio Gonzales and Liz Stanton

Eugenio Gonzales has been working with NGOs and grant-making foundations in the Philippines for many years. Currently he is an independent consultant of the International Labour Organization. Liz Stanton is the editorial director of the National Assets Project and teaches economics at the University of Massachusetts-Amherst. The article that follows appeared originally in Dollars & Sense, November/December 2004.

To visitors from outside, the Payatas dumpsite outside Manila is at best an eyesore and at worst a vision of hell on Earth. For the thousands of families who earn their livelihoods by recycling materials in Payatas, though, garbage is a form of wealth. "In good times, we can earn more than twice the minimum wage of factory workers just by picking through the garbage," says Zaldy Arevan, an officer of the Payatas Scavengers Association.

Metro Manila is the Philippines' largest urban center, with a growing population of over 10 million. In recent years, four dumpsites—Smokey Mountain, Carmona, Payatas, and San Mateo—have served the metropolis. One by one these sites have been closed, mainly because they were filled beyond their capacity. In early 2001, the last one, the San Mateo landfill, was closed following protests from nearby residents. They had had enough of the stench of the garbage and the daily rumbling of heavy garbage trucks that polluted the air and damaged their roads.

Mountains of garbage piled up on city streets as the 16 Metro Manila municipalities were left to fend for themselves. Illegal dumpsites sprang up in rural areas, endangering the water supply and the health of both rural and urban communities. The re-opening of the Payatas dumpsite and the opening of a new landfill in Rodriguez Town outside of Metro Manila have eased the situation, at least temporarily.

The Ecological Solid Waste Management Act, signed into law in early 2001 at the urging of activists, NGOs, and sympathetic government officials, has encouraged

Eugenio Gonzales and Liz Stanton, "Filipino Dump Activists Turn Waste into Wealth," *Dollars & Sense*, November/December 2004. Copyright 2004. Reprinted by permission of *Dollars & Sense*, a progressive economic magazine ⟨www.dollarsandsense.org⟩

recycling as one response to the landfill crisis. Of the 5,350 metric tons of waste generated daily in Metro Manila in the late 1990s, only 6% was being recycled. Thanks to the new law, the recycling rate now may have reached 15%, according to estimates by the Washington, D.C.-based Earth Day Network.

The Payatas Dump

Payatas, the country's largest open dumpsite, occupies 50 acres in Quezon City, the largest city in Metro Manila. Despite its lack of required liners and piping systems, it receives around 1,200 tons of trash per day. Since the mid-1970s when Payatas starting operating, hundreds and later thousands of waste-pickers migrated to work and to live in the dump. They stayed in shacks—usually made from recycled wood, roofing materials, and cardboard—with no access to roads, water, or electricity. In exchange for votes, politicians slowly gave the waste-pickers access to basic utilities, but even today very few have title to their homes.

Roughly 6,000 waste-pickers make or supplement their livings by combing through this mountain of garbage. Families living on the margins of the dump sort out plastics, bottles, metal, and other materials to sell to junk shops that consolidate the recyclables and deliver them to factories for reprocessing. "They work in unsanitary and dangerous conditions but they have no other alternative livelihood," says Celia Tuason of the Vincentian Missionaries Social Development Foundation, an NGO that has worked in Payatas for more than 10 years.

When garbage trucks arrive at the dumpsite entrance, young boys jump onto the back of each truck to pick quickly through the load. These boys, called "jumpers," are hired by junk shop owners to do this work. Inside the entrance, hundreds of waste-pickers wait. They are called "*mangangalahig*," after the pointed tool called a *kalahig* that they use to pick through the garbage. They assemble behind the truck and immediately sift through the garbage as it falls off. They have mastered the art of avoiding being buried by the garbage or run over by the truck, but accidents sometimes happen.

Women and elderly scavengers who lack the physical abilities of the jumpers and the *mangangalahigs* are forced to rely on more tedious but less competitive ways to pick through the waste. They go to areas of the dump that are being leveled by bulldozers, in hope that plastics or metals will be unearthed that may still be of value. There are fewer waste-pickers, and consequently less competition, in these locations, but these workers—called "*suros*," a local term for dredging—face the added risk of being run over by the bulldozers.

The final stage of waste picking is performed by the "*sala*," literally, "to sift through." They go to the areas of the dump that have already been burned or are still burning. Using tongs, the workers sift through the ash looking for metal and other items of value. Others extract clumps of burnt garbage and use nearby waterways to remove the ash, hoping to find useful items. This least rewarding job in the dumpsite is also the riskiest: their chances of recovering items of much value are slim, and the *sala* are constantly subjected to smoke and flames.

On July 10, 2000, more than 200 waste-pickers lost their lives when a huge section of the garbage mountain collapsed after strong rains. Most of those who died were *salas* buried under smoldering garbage. After the accident, the government promptly closed the site. A few months later, however, the dump was re-opened at the request of the waste-pickers themselves, although the collapsed section has been permanently closed. The tragedy attracted more NGOs and government agencies to provide health care and other kinds of assistance to the Payatas scavengers, but their lives remain difficult, and the future of the site is still in question.

The Promised Land

In 1993, the Vincentian Missionaries Social Development Foundation started a savings and credit program for the scavengers of the Payatas dumpsite. The foundation's program catered mainly to women, using a modified Grameen Bank microloan approach that emphasized savings rather than outside funding as a source of capital. Borrowers founded a people's organization, the *Lupang Pangako* (or "Promised Land") Urban Poor Association, Inc. (LUPAI).

From initial seed capital of $2,000 in government funds, LUPAI now manages around $300,000 in savings accounts for its 7,000 members. Today, many LUPAI members engage in micro-enterprises such as small stores, junk shops, and metalworking, which provide goods and services to the scavengers and other local residents. In addition to the revolving credit program, LUPAI has piloted a community mortgage program through which some of its members have acquired ownership of the land where their houses stand. The program has also provided funds for improving streets and water systems. "I have seen how much they have improved their lot in spite of the difficulties and the little help that we could give them. This inspires me to carry on with my work," says Celia Tuason of the Vincentians.

In addition, LUPAI works with other organizations, like the Payatas Scavengers' Association, to improve the living conditions around the dumpsite. As a result of their advocacy, roads leading up to and inside the dump have been improved, and utilities like water and electricity have been provided to the scavengers' homes.

As the Payatas case shows, waste recycling can contribute to poverty reduction. A 1996 survey of waste-picker households in Payatas found that families earned an average of $175 per month, or 20% more than the legislated minimum wage. In addition to cash income, the dump provides some free household goods, such as building materials, furniture, and clothes. The scavengers lack secure rights to access the waste stream, though: they could be "evicted" from the dumpsite at any time because they have no title to the land. In addition, the scavengers' income has fallen as upstream recycling has increased with government regulation and incentives. Whereas in previous years a scavenger typically earned $8 per day, now he or she is lucky to earn $3 per day. Some scavengers, seeing an opportunity, have already banded together to collect garbage upstream, before it arrives at the dump.

For a fee, they collect garbage from homes, offices, and malls. This provides additional income to their sorting and recycling activities.

Still, the financial cost of handling solid waste in Metro Manila is estimated to be around $56 per ton. The scavengers, therefore, provide a vital environmental and cost-saving service by removing an estimated 65 tons of recyclables per day from the waste stream. If they were paid by the government for the savings they provide, they could earn roughly $3,600 per day, or $1.3 million a year. This would be equivalent to 30% of the average yearly income of all the waste pickers in Payatas—a significant boost to families barely eking out a living at the site.

By treating trash as an asset, the scavengers of Payatas not only secure livelihoods, but also help the Philippines to solve its garbage crisis. If the control and eventual closure of municipal dumpsites like Payatas leads to the proliferation of illegal dumpsites across the country, both the environment and public welfare will suffer. If, instead, creative strategies are adopted by groups like LUPAI, and the government, the crisis could be turned into an opportunity to advance the twin goals of environmental protection and poverty reduction.

The Grameen Bank

The following account of the origins, mission, and operation of The Grameen Bank was taken from the bank's website. For more information visit www.grameen-info.org

Grameen Bank (GB) has reversed conventional banking practice by removing the need for collateral and created a banking system based on mutual trust, accountability, participation and creativity. GB provides credit to the poorest of the poor in rural Bangladesh, without any collateral. At GB, credit is a cost effective weapon to fight poverty and it serves as a catalyst in the overall development of socio-

© The Grameen Bank, www.grameen-info.org

economic conditions of the poor who have been kept outside the banking orbit on the grounds that they are poor and hence not bankable. Professor Muhammad Yunus, the founder of "Grameen Bank" and its Managing Director, reasoned that if financial resources can be made available to the poor people on terms and conditions that are appropriate and reasonable, "these millions of small people with their millions of small pursuits can add up to create the biggest development wonder."

As of July, 2004, it has 3.7 million borrowers, 96 percent of whom are women. With 1267 branches, GB provides services in 46,000 villages, covering more than 68 percent of the total villages in Bangladesh.

Grameen Bank's positive impact on its poor and formerly poor borrowers has been documented in many independent studies carried out by external agencies including the World Bank, the International Food Policy Research Institute (IFPRI) and the Bangladesh Institute of Development Studies (BIDS).

A Short History of Grameen Bank

The origin of Grameen Bank can be traced back to 1976 when Professor Muhammad Yunus, Head of the Rural Economics Program at the University of Chittagong, launched an action research project to examine the possibility of designing a credit delivery system to provide banking services targeted at the rural poor. The Grameen Bank Project (Grameen means "rural" or "village" in Bangla language) came into operation with the following objectives:

- extend banking facilities to poor men and women;
- eliminate the exploitation of the poor by money lenders;
- create opportunities for self-employment for the vast multitude of unemployed people in rural Bangladesh;
- bring the disadvantaged, mostly the women from the poorest households, within the fold of an organizational format which they can understand and manage by themselves; and
- reverse the age-old vicious circle of "low income, low saving & low investment", into a virtuous circle of "low income, injection of credit, investment, more income, more savings, more investment, more income".

The action research demonstrated its strength in Jobra (a village adjacent to Chittagong University) and some of the neighboring villages during 1976–1979. With the sponsorship of the central bank of the country and support of the nationalized commercial banks, the project was extended to Tangail district (a district north of Dhaka, the capital city of Bangladesh) in 1979. With the success in Tangail, the project was extended to several other districts in the country. In October 1983, the Grameen Bank Project was transformed into an independent bank by government legislation. Today Grameen Bank is owned by the rural poor whom it serves. Borrowers of the Bank own 90% of its shares, while the remaining 10% is owned by the government.

Breaking the Vicious Cycle of Poverty Through Microcredit

The Grameen Bank is based on the voluntary formation of small groups of five people to provide mutual, morally binding group guarantees in lieu of the collateral required by conventional banks. At first only two members of a group are allowed to apply for a loan. Depending on their performance in repayment the next two borrowers can then apply and, subsequently, the fifth member as well.

The assumption is that if individual borrowers are given access to credit, they will be able to identify and engage in viable income-generating activities—simple processing such as paddy husking, lime-making, manufacturing such as pottery, weaving, and garment sewing, storage and marketing and transport services. Women were initially given equal access to the schemes, and proved not only reliable borrowers but astute entrepreneurs. As a result, they have raised their status, lessened their dependency on their husbands and improved their homes and the nutritional standards of their children. Today over 90 percent of borrowers are women.

Intensive discipline, supervision, and servicing characterize the operations of the Grameen Bank, which are carried out by "Bicycle bankers" in branch units with considerable delegated authority. The rigorous selection of borrowers and their projects by these bank workers, the powerful peer pressure exerted on these individuals by the groups, and the repayment scheme based on 50 weekly installments, contribute to operational viability to the rural banking system designed for the poor. Savings have also been encouraged. Under the scheme, there is provision for 5 percent of loans to be credited to a group fund and Tk 5 is credited every week to the fund.

The success of this approach shows that a number of objections to lending to the poor can be overcome if careful supervision and management are provided. For example, it had earlier been thought that the poor would not be able to find remunerative occupations. In fact, Grameen borrowers have successfully done so. It was thought that the poor would not be able to repay; in fact, repayment rates reached 97 percent. It was thought that poor rural women in particular were not bankable; in fact, they accounted for 94 percent of borrowers in early 1992. It was also thought that the poor cannot save; in fact, group savings have proven as successful as group lending. It was thought that rural power structures would make sure that such a bank failed; but the Grameen Bank has been able to expand rapidly. Indeed, from fewer than 15,000 borrowers in 1980, the membership had grown to nearly 100,000 by mid-1984. By the end of 1998, the number of branches in operation was 1128, with 2.34 million members (2.24 million of them women) in 38,957 villages. There are 66,581 centres of groups, of which 33,126 are women. Group savings have reached 7,853 million taka (approximately USD 162 million), out of which 7300 million taka (approximately USD 152 million) are saved by women.

It is estimated that the average household income of Grameen Bank members is about 50 percent higher than the target group in the control village, and 25 percent higher than the target group non-members in Grameen Bank villages. The landless have benefited most, followed by marginal landowners. This has resulted in a sharp reduction in the number of Grameen Bank members living below the poverty line, 20 percent compared to 56 percent for comparable non-Grameen Bank members. There has also been a shift from agricultural wage labour (considered to be socially inferior) to self-employment in petty trading. Such a shift in occupational patterns has an indirect positive effect on the employment and wages of other agricultural waged labourers. What started as an innovative local initiative, "a small bubble of hope", has thus grown to the point where it has made an impact on poverty alleviation at the national level".

A Sampling of NGOs Working for Social Change

The following is a sampling of some of the NGOs (nongovernmental agencies) around the world that are working to solve the problems identified in this book. In each case a brief description of the organization taken from its Website is provided, along with the Web address, so that you can go directly to the site and learn more. Please note that this list provides only a sampling of such groups, and remember that one of the criteria employed in preparing this list, namely that the group have its own Website, necessarily limits the groups that can be included.

Arab Women's Solidarity Association
⟨www.awsa.net⟩ is a progressive organization founded in Egypt in 1982 by Nawal El Saadawi. It was established by a group of 120 women who agreed that the struggle for the liberation of Arab people and freedom from economic, cultural, and media domination cannot be separated from the liberation of Arab women. As an international organization, AWSA promotes Arab women's active participation in social, economic, cultural, and political life.

Basel Action Network (BAN)
⟨www.ban.org⟩ is an international network of activists seeking to prevent the globalization of the toxic chemical crisis. BAN is based in Seattle, Washington (USA) and conducts both domestic (U.S.) and international programs to halt *toxic trade*—an ugly form of trade in toxic wastes, toxic products, and toxic technologies that are exported from rich to poorer countries. At the same time, they work proactively in both the United States and around the world to ensure national self-sufficiency in waste management through clean production and toxic-use reductions and in support of the principle of global environmental justice—where no peoples or environments are disproportionately poisoned and polluted due to the dictates of unbridled market forces and trade.

The Coalition Against Trafficking in Women (CATW)
⟨catwinternational.org⟩ is a nongovernmental organization that promotes women's human rights. It works internationally to combat sexual exploitation in all its

forms, especially prostitution and trafficking in women and children, in particular, girls.

50 Years Is Enough: U.S. Network for Global Economic Justice

⟨www.50years.org⟩ is a coalition of over 200 U.S. grassroots, women's, solidarity, faith-based, policy, social- and economic-justice, youth, labor, and development organizations dedicated to the profound transformation of the World Bank and the International Monetary Fund (IMF). The Network works in solidarity with over 185 international partner organizations in more than 65 countries. Through education and action, the Network is committed to transforming the international financial institutions' policies and practices, to ending the outside imposition of neoliberal economic programs, and to making the development process democratic and accountable.

Global Exchange

⟨globalexchange.org⟩ is an international human rights organization dedicated to promoting political, social, and environmental justice globally. Since its founding in 1988 it has been working to increase global awareness among the U.S. public while building partnerships around the world.

Global Policy Forum

⟨www.globalpolicy.org⟩ monitors policymaking at the United Nations, promotes accountability of global decisions, educates and mobilizes for global citizen participation, and advocates on vital issues of international peace and justice. GPF works with partners around the world to strengthen international law and create a more equitable and sustainable global society. GPF uses a holistic approach, linking peace and security with economic justice and human development, and places a heavy emphasis on networking to build broad coalitions for research, action, and advocacy.

Greenpeace

⟨www.greenpeace.org⟩ is a nonprofit organization with a presence in 40 countries across Europe, the Americas, Asia, and the Pacific. As a global organization, Greenpeace focuses on the most crucial worldwide threats to our planet's biodiversity and environment.

India Resource Center

⟨www.IndiaResource.org⟩ works to support movements against corporate globalization in India. They provide timely information on transnational corporations to Indian movements and educate and mobilize key constituencies in the U.S. and other countries to take action in support of campaigns in India. India Resource Center is a project of Global Resistance. Global Resistance works to strengthen the movement against corporate globalization by supporting and linking local, grassroots struggles against globalization around the world. Their goal is to ensure that those most impacted by globalization are engaged in and at the forefront of the movement against corporate globalization.

Indigenous Environmental Network (IEN)
⟨ienearth.org⟩ is a network of Indigenous Peoples empowering indigenous nations and communities toward sustainable livelihoods, demanding environmental justice, and maintaining the Sacred Fire of our traditions.

International Lesbian and Gay Association (ILGA)
⟨ilga.org⟩ is a worldwide network of national and local groups dedicated to achieving equal rights for lesbian, gay, bisexual, and transgendered (LGBT) people everywhere. Established in 1978, it is to this day the only international nonprofit and nongovernmental community-based federation focused on presenting discrimination on grounds of sexual orientation as a global issue.

MADRE: Demanding Human Rights for Women and Families Around the World
⟨www.madre.org⟩ is an international women's human rights organization that works in partnership with women's community-based groups in conflict areas worldwide. Our programs address issues of armed conflict and forced displacement; women's health and reproductive rights; economic justice and community development; indigenous peoples' rights and resources, food security, and sustainable development; human rights advocacy; youth; and U.S. foreign policy. MADRE provides resources and training to enable its sister organizations to meet immediate needs in their communities and develop long-term solutions to the crises they face.

Médecins Sans Frontières (also known as Doctors Without Borders or MSF)
⟨doctorswithoutborders.org⟩ delivers emergency aid to victims of armed conflict, epidemics, and natural and man-made disasters, and to others who lack health care due to social or geographical isolation. MSF was founded in 1971 by a small group of French doctors who believed that all people have the right to medical care regardless of race, religion, creed, or political affiliation, and that the needs of these people supersede respect for national borders. It was the first nongovernmental organization to both provide emergency medical assistance and publicly bear witness to the plight of the populations it served.

Navdanya Seeds.of.Freedom
⟨navdanya.org⟩ Since 1987, Navdanya has been saving seeds, promoting chemical-free organic agriculture, creating awareness of the hazards of genetic engineering, defending people's knowledge from biopiracy, and defending people's food rights and food sovereignty in the face of globalization. Through grassroots conservation efforts, awareness campaigns, and cultural festivals, Navdanya works to protect the rich biodiversity that is the basis of cultural and material sustenance of our people.

Public Services International (PSI)
⟨world-psi.org⟩ is a global union federation made up of more than 600 trade unions. It represents more than 20 million workers who deliver public services in 160 countries around the world. PSI and its affiliates are committed to building

quality public services that meet the needs of workers and communities. Priorities include global campaigns for water, energy, and health services. PSI promotes gender equality, worker rights, trade union capacity building, equity, and diversity.

RAWA, the Revolutionary Association of the Women of Afghanistan

⟨www.rawa.org⟩ was established in Kabul, Afghanistan, in 1977 as an independent political/social organization of Afghan women fighting for human rights and for social justice in Afghanistan. RAWA's objective was to involve an increasing number of Afghan women in social and political activities aimed at acquiring women's human rights and contributing to the struggle for the establishment of a government based on democratic and secular values in Afghanistan. Despite the suffocating political atmosphere, RAWA very soon became involved in widespread activities in different socio-political arenas including education, health, and income generation, as well as political agitation.

Refugee Women in Development (RefWID), Inc.

⟨www.refwid.org⟩ is the only international women-in-development institution focusing on refugee, displaced, and returnee women in the United States and overseas. RefWID advocates to heighten awareness of human rights abuses against uprooted women, and seeks to support the civil and democratic institutional development capacities of women who have experienced mass human rights abuses, domestic violence, rape trauma, war, and civil strife. RefWID builds capacity in developing countries that seeks to empower women so they can advocate on their own behalf and assume leadership positions in civil and democratic institution-building. RefWID operates from a unique perspective that seeks to integrate the knowledge and experience of marginalized women into appropriate and sustainable development initiatives.

Trickle Up

⟨trickleup.org⟩ Founded in 1979, the Trickle Up program's mission is to help the lowest income people worldwide take the first step up out of poverty, by providing conditional seed capital and business training essential to the launch of a microenterprise. This proven social and economic empowerment model is implemented in partnership with local agencies.

Visions in Action Volunteers in International Development

⟨www.visionsinaction.org⟩ is an international nonprofit organization committed to achieving social and economic justice in the developing world through the participation of communities of self-reliant, grassroots volunteers.

The World Development Movement (WDM)

⟨wdm.org.uk⟩ tackles the underlying causes of poverty. It lobbies decisionmakers to change the policies that keep people poor. It researches and promotes positive alternatives and works alongside people in the developing world who are standing up to injustice.

Questions for Thinking, Writing, and Discussion

1. Use the Internet to find out what is happening now in the Mexican village of Atenco. What consequences have resulted from their efforts to block the international airport? Is the fight against the airport over?

2. Although people living in Plachimada have won a temporary victory over Coca-Cola as this book goes to press, the struggle there is not over. Use the Internet to write a piece in which you update the account of this struggle.

3. Use the Internet to find out what current initiatives have captured the attention and energy of college students today and write an account of where and how college students are using their clout to fight for social justice.

4. Article 5 describes one grassroots movement directed toward fighting poverty and protecting the environment. Use the Internet to identify other such initiatives and do a write-up of those that interest you most.

5. Professor Muhammad Yunus, founder of the Grameen Bank, came up with the idea of microcredit. Use the Internet to identify other NGOs that extend microcredit and write a paper in which you explain the concept and discuss its successes and failures.

6. Use the list of NGOs provided in this part to see what kinds of activities NGOs around the world are engaging in and write a paper in which you discuss those that interest you the most.

7. If you had unlimited energy, resources, and support, what kind of NGO would you create to press for a more humane globalization and why do you think it would be effective?

8. Identify an NGO that is not included on the list provided in this part and do a write-up in which you describe and evaluate its mission and program.

Afterword
The Costs of American Privilege

–Michael Schwalbe

Michael Schwalbe teaches sociology at the University of North Carolina, Chapel Hill. His article first appeared in Counterpunch, October 2002.

When it comes to knowledge of the U.S. government, foreign students often put American students to shame. Many of the American students in my classes don't know how Congress is organized, what cabinet members do, or how governmental powers are divided among the executive, judicial, and legislative branches. The foreign students who have shown up in my classrooms over the years tend to know about these matters and more.

The gap is even wider with regard to knowledge of U.S. behavior around the globe. When foreign students refer to exploitive U.S. trade policies, military interventions abroad, and support for repressive dictatorships—as if any educated person would of course know about such things—American students are often stunned. Foreign students are equally amazed when their remarks are greeted with blank stares.

But this level of ignorance is not so amazing, really. It's a predictable consequence of privilege. Like white privilege and male privilege in our society, American privilege brings with it the luxury of obliviousness.

Privilege comes from membership in a dominant group and is typically invisible to those who have it. Many whites do not see themselves as enjoying "white privilege," yet as Peggy McIntosh has pointed out, there are dozens of ways that whites are privileged in U.S. society.

For example, whites can live anywhere they can afford to, without being limited by racial segregation; whites can assume that race won't be used to decide whether they will fit in at work; whites who complain usually end up speaking to the white person in charge; whites can choose to ignore their racial identity and think of themselves as human beings; and, in most situations, whites can expect to be treated as individuals, not as members of a category.

"The Costs of American Privilege" by Michael Schwalbe. *Counterpunch*, October 4, 2002. Copyright 2002. Reprinted by permission of the author.

Men likewise enjoy privileges as members of the dominant gender group. For example, men can walk the streets without being sexually harassed; men can make mistakes without those mistakes being attributed to their gender; men can count on their gender to enhance their credibility; men can expect to find powerful sponsors with whom they can bond as men; and, even in female-dominated occupations, men benefit from being seen as better suited to higher-paying, administrative jobs.

Whites and men tend not to see these privileges because they are taken to be normal, unremarkable entitlements. This is how things appear to members of a dominant group. What's missing is an awareness that life is different for others. Not having to think about the experiences of people in subordinate groups is another form of privilege.

In contrast, women and people of color usually see that those above them in the social hierarchy receive unearned benefits. At the least, they must, for their own protection, pay attention to what members of more powerful groups think and do. This is why women often know more about men than men know about themselves, and why blacks know more about whites than whites know about themselves.

It is no surprise, then, that foreign students, especially those from Third World countries, often know more about the U.S. than most American students do. People in those countries must, as a matter of survival, pay attention to what the U.S. does. There is no equally compelling need for Americans to study what happens in the provinces. And so again the irony: people in Third World countries often know more about the U.S. than many Americans do.

We can thus put these at the top of the list of American privileges: not having to bother, unless one chooses, to learn about other countries; and not having to bother, unless one chooses, to learn about how U.S. foreign policy affects people in other countries. A corollary privilege is to imagine that if people in other countries study us, it's merely out of admiration for our way of life.

The list of American privileges can be extended. For example, Americans can buy cheap goods made by superexploited workers in Third World countries; Americans can take a glib attitude toward war, since it's likely to be a high-tech affair affecting distant strangers; and Americans can enjoy freedom at home, because U.S. capitalists are able to wring extraordinary profits out of Third World workers and therefore don't need to repress U.S. workers as harshly.

But privileges are not without costs. Most obviously there is the cost of ignorance about others. This carries with it the cost of ignorance about ourselves.

One thing we don't learn, when we refuse to learn about or from others, is how they see us. We then lose a mirror with which to view ourselves. Combined with power, the result can be worse than innocent ignorance. It can be smug self-delusion, belief in the myth of one's own superiority, and a presumed right to dictate morality to others.

We also bear the cost of limiting our own humanity. To be human is to be able to extend compassion to others, to empathize with them, and to reflect honestly on how they are affected by our actions. Privilege keeps us from doing these things and thereby stunts our growth as human beings.

The ignorance that stems from privilege makes Americans easy to mislead when it comes to war. Being told that they are "fighting for freedom," and knowing no better, thousands of American sons and daughters will dutifully kill and die. The ugly truth that they are fighting for the freedom of U.S. capitalists to exploit the natural resources and labor of weaker countries is rarely perceived through the vacuum of knowledge created by American privilege.

But of course it is the people in those weaker countries who bear the greatest costs of American privilege. In war, they will suffer and die in far greater numbers. In peace, or times of less-violent exploitation, their suffering will continue and once again become invisible to citizens living at the core of the empire.

There are positive aspects of American privilege, and from these we can take hope. Most of us enjoy freedom from repression in our daily lives, and we value our rights to associate and to speak out. Perhaps, then, we can appreciate the anger created when U.S. foreign policy denies other people these same rights. Perhaps, too, we can use our freedoms to more fully fight such injustices. If so, then our privileges as Americans will be put to noble and humane use.

If Americans are often afflicted with ignorance and moral blindness when it comes to the rest of the world, this is not a failing of individuals. These problems result from a system of domination that confers privilege. And so we can't make things right simply by declining privilege. In the long run, we have to dismantle the system that gives it to us.

Index

607